Connecticut Researcher's Handbook

GALE GENEALOGY AND LOCAL HISTORY SERIES

Series Editor: J. Carlyle Parker, Head of Public Services and Assistant Library Director, California State College, Stanislaus; and Founder and Librarian Volunteer, Modesto California Branch Genealogical Library of the Genealogical Department of the Church of Jesus Christ of Latter-day Saints, Salt Lake City, Utah

Also in this series:

BLACK GENESIS—*Edited by James M. Rose and Alice Eichholz*

BLACK ROOTS IN SOUTHEASTERN CONNECTICUT, 1650-1900—*Edited by Barbara W. Brown and James M. Rose*

CITY, COUNTY, TOWN, AND TOWNSHIP INDEX TO THE 1850 FEDERAL CENSUS SCHEDULES—*Edited by J. Carlyle Parker*

FREE BLACK HEADS OF HOUSEHOLDS IN THE NEW YORK STATE FEDERAL CENSUS, 1790-1830—*Edited by Alice Eichholz and James M. Rose*

GENEALOGICAL HISTORICAL GUIDE TO LATIN AMERICA—*Edited by Lyman De Platt*

GENEALOGICAL RESEARCH FOR CZECH AND SLOVAK AMERICANS—*Edited by Olga K. Miller*

AN INDEX TO GENEALOGICAL PERIODICAL LITERATURE, 1960-1977—*Edited by Kip Sperry*

AN INDEX TO THE BIOGRAPHEES IN 19TH-CENTURY CALIFORNIA COUNTY HISTORIES—*Edited by J. Carlyle Parker*

LIBRARY SERVICE FOR GENEALOGISTS—*Edited by J. Carlyle Parker*

MONTANA'S GENEALOGICAL AND LOCAL HISTORY RECORDS—*Edited by Dennis Lee Richards*

A PERSONAL NAME INDEX TO ORTON'S "RECORDS OF CALIFORNIA MEN IN THE WAR OF THE REBELLION, 1861 TO 1867"—*Edited by J. Carlyle Parker*

PERSONAL NAME INDEX TO THE 1856 CITY DIRECTORIES OF CALIFORNIA—*Edited by Nathan C. Parker*

PERSONAL NAME INDEX TO THE 1856 CITY DIRECTORIES OF IOWA—*Edited by Elsie L. Sopp*

A SURVEY OF AMERICAN GENEALOGICAL PERIODICALS AND PERIODICAL INDEXES—*Edited by Kip Sperry*

General Editor: Paul Wasserman, Professor and former Dean, School of Library and Information Services, University of Maryland

Managing Editor: Denise Allard Adzigian, Gale Research Company

Connecticut Researcher's Handbook

Volume 12 in the Gale Genealogy and Local History Series

Thomas Jay Kemp

Head
Turn of River Library
Stamford, Connecticut

Gale Research Company
Book Tower, Detroit, Michigan 48226

Library of Congress Cataloging in Publication Data

Kemp, Thomas Jay.
    Connecticut researcher's handbook.

    (Genealogy and local history series ; v. 12)
      1. Connecticut—Genealogy—Bibliography. 2. Connecti-
cut—History, Local—Sources—Bibliography. 3. Connecticut—Genealogy—Societies, etc.—Directories.
4. Connecticut—History, Local—Societies, etc.—Directories. 5. Connecticut—Genealogy—Library resources.
6. Connecticut—History, Local—Library resources.
I. Title. II. Series.
Z1265.K45   [F93]   974.6'0025   81-6339
ISBN 0-8103-1488-6

Copyright © 1981 by
Thomas Jay Kemp

To my parents,
Mr. and Mrs. Willard Henry and Eleanor Frances Huse Kemp, Jr.
and to the late
Miss Grace Hope Walmsley

VITA

Thomas Jay Kemp is the head of the Turn of River Library, a branch of the Ferguson Library in Stamford, Connecticut. Formerly he was the head of the Weed Memorial Library in Stamford, and for eight years he was responsible for the Genealogy and Local History Collection of the Ferguson Library. He has lectured widely and is the author of numerous books and articles.

Mr. Kemp serves as a member of the American Library Association's Reference and Adult Services Division, History Section, Genealogy Committee; and as vice-chair of the Connecticut Library Association's Local History and Genealogy Section. He is a member of the Association for the Bibliography of History, Society of American Archivists, and other professional, genealogical, and hereditary societies.

He received his B.A. in history and M.L.S. from Brigham Young University and has had further training at Harvard University, Rochester Institute of Technology, and Columbia University.

TABLE OF CONTENTS AND GENERAL INDEX

Contents and General Index

Contents and General Index

Contents and General Index

Contents and General Index

ACKNOWLEDGMENTS

In compiling this guide I have been grateful to the staffs of many libraries who have built up excellent collections and made their libraries attractive to use.

In particular, I am grateful for the use of the collections and the helpfulness of the staffs of the following institutions: the American Antiquarian Society, Worcester, Mass.; Blount Library, Mystic, Conn.; Bridgeport (Conn.) Public Library; Connecticut Historical Society, Hartford, Conn.; Connecticut State Library, Hartford, Conn.; Eckert College, William Luther Cobb Library, St. Petersburg, Fla.; Fairfield (Conn.) University, Nyselius Library; Ferguson Library, Stamford, Conn.; Genealogical Department of The Church of Jesus Christ of Latter-day Saints, Salt Lake City, Utah; Godfrey Memorial Library, Middletown, Conn.; Greenwich (Conn.) Library; Harvard University Libraries, Cambridge, Mass.; Library of Congress, Washington, D.C.; New Canaan (Conn.) Historical Society; New England Historic Genealogical Society, Boston, Mass.; New Haven (Conn.) Colony Historical Society; New York Public Library; Newbury Library, Chicago, Ill.; Pequot Library, Southport, Conn.; Southern Connecticut State College, Hilton C. Buley Library, New Haven, Conn.; University of Bridgeport, (Conn.), Magnus Wahlstrom Library; and Wesleyan University, Olin Memorial Library, Middletown, Conn.

I also acknowledge the inspiration of four of Connecticut's outstanding men: Lucius Barnes Barbour, George S. Goddard, Charles R. Hale and Donald Lines Jacobus. They were archivists, librarians, historians and genealogists who have set a record of accomplishment and excellence that knows no equal in any other state in collecting, indexing, perserving and interpreting our past. All Connecticut local historians and genealogists owe them a debt of gratitude.

I have always noted with amusement the authors who profoundly acknowledged the help of their typist. But now as I close five years of work, I, too, am profoundly grateful to the work of my typist, Mrs. JoAnne Cordone, without whose help, patience, perseverance and clairvoyance this book would never have been completed.

And to my family and friends, my thanks for their support and encouragement and for their bearing with me and without me these last years.

INTRODUCTION

This guide has been compiled to assist the local historian and genealogist in researching Connecticut's past. It is not a "how to," but a "where to," listing the name, address, and telephone number of every cemetery, genealogical society, historical society, library, newspaper, probate court, and town clerk in the state. It also brings together the largest and most complete bibliography of articles, books, dissertations, microfilmed records, and original records held in archives and libraries ever prepared for Connecticut.

The scope was designed to include all materials published up to and including 1980. The author personally reviewed almost every article and book cited. The only materials specifically excluded were family genealogies published as books or articles. However, if a family genealogy contained significant local history material not duplicated elsewhere, as James P. Boughman's THE MALLORYS OF MYSTIC: SIX GENERATIONS IN AMERICAN MARITIME ENTERPRISE (Middletown, Conn.: Wesleyan University Press, 1972. 496 p.), it was included.

The editor felt that to compile an inclusive bibliography of Connecticut genealogies would be an overwhelming task, as virtually every genealogy would have some Connecticut link. The multivolumed work GENEALOGIES IN THE LIBRARY OF CONGRESS: A BIBLIOGRAPHY and the single-volume A COMPLEMENT TO GENEALOGIES IN THE LIBRARY OF CONGRESS: A BIBLIOGRAPHY, both edited and compiled by Marion Kaminkow, and the GENEALOGICAL PERIODICAL ANNUAL INDEX are useful to assist the researcher in finding materials.

This book is arranged by topic in two parts. The first part contains all works about Connecticut of a general nature arranged under the following headings:

Adoption Records	Census Records
Art and Music	Church Records
Associations	City Directories
Bible Records	Connecticut State Archives
Bibliography	Counties
Biography	Court and Legal Records
Buildings	Divorce Records
Business, Industry and	Ethnic Groups
Science	Genealogical Research

Introduction

Cemetery Records	Genealogical Societies
General	Migration Records
Historical Societies	Military Records
Land Records	Naturalization Records
Libraries	Newspapers
Loyalists	Taxation
Maps, Gazetteers and	Vital Records
Related Materials	Witchcraft

Part 2 contains all works that specifically pertain to a Connecticut county or town. Material that covers several towns or counties is listed more than once.

The following is a list of the subject headings used in part 2 and the scope of any special information given under each heading. Works that pertain to a specific topic, as "Census Records," "Military Records," etc., are listed under the appropriate headings. All other works and general items are listed under "Published Works and Other Records."

CEMETERIES AND CEMETERY RECORDS

Includes the name, address and telephone number of every cemetery in the state. Cemeteries included in the Hale Index also give their Hale Number and citation. Charles R. Hale directed the transcription of the tombstones in over 2,000 Connecticut cemeteries as a government project for the WPA. These transcripts, on file at the Connecticut State Library, comprise some 59 typed volumes and several hundred card file drawers. It serves as a general index to tens of thousands of individuals buried in Connecticut. These records have been microfilmed by the Genealogical Department of The Church of Jesus Christ of Latter-day Saints.

CENSUS RECORDS

Includes bibliographic references to all published census materials, articles, indexes and similar works.

CHURCH RECORDS

Includes references to all church records that have been microfilmed and church records deposited in an institution separate from the original church. As the records on deposit at the Connecticut State Library are so extensive, only microfilmed church records at the State Library were included. For a complete list of their holdings see: LIST OF CHURCH RECORDS IN THE CONNECTICUT STATE LIBRARY (Hartford: Conn. State Library, 1976. 35 p.).

GENEALOGICAL SOCIETY

Includes the name, address and telephone number of any local genealogical society. Bibliographic reference is also made to any periodical of the society.

LAND RECORDS

Includes references to all land records deposited outside the jurisdiction of the local town clerk and to all published or microfilmed land records.

LIBRARY

Includes the name, address and telephone number of all public, academic, and special libraries of interest to genealogists and local historians.

MILITARY RECORDS

Includes bibliographic reference to all published, microfilmed, and original military records and histories.

NEWSPAPERS

Includes the name, address, telephone number and frequence of publication of currently published newspapers. Newspapers indexed in the CHARLES R. HALE INDEX TO DEATH AND MARRIAGE NOTICES or indexed by any library or other similar agency, are referenced by name with the inclusive dates of the indexing given. Reference is also given to the number of newspaper titles published in each town as given in A PRELIMINARY CHECKLIST OF CONNECTICUT NEWSPAPERS 1755-1975. This two-volume work was compiled by Don Gustafson and published by the Connecticut State Library in 1978. This useful work is a union list of the newspapers of Connecticut and gives details of institutional holdings of original and microfilmed copies of newspapers.

PROBATE RECORDS

Includes the name, address and telephone number of each probate court, its date of creation, the names of its parent probate courts, any courts formed from its jurisdiction, and the names of all the towns included in the probate district. Reference is also made to probate records on deposit at the State Library, State Archives and other similar institutions. All microfilmed probate records are also listed.

SCHOOL RECORDS

Includes references to all original, published, and microfilmed school records found in libraries and similar institutions, but not the active records of a local school board.

TAX RECORDS

Includes references to all original, published, and microfilmed tax records found in libraries and similar institutions, but not the active records of local tax offices.

VITAL RECORDS

Includes the address and telephone number of local town clerks. If the town was included in the BARBOUR INDEX TO CONNECTICUT VITAL RECORDS the inclusive dates and nature of the records indexed are given.

Introduction

The BARBOUR INDEX was compiled under the direction of Lucius Barnes Barbour. It is a general index to vital records but includes other entries as well. It is arranged in two parts. One is alphabetically arranged by town and the other is a general alphabetical list for the state. The time period varies for each town. The details as to what records were indexed and for what time periods are given in the entry for each town. It is a common misconception that the BARBOUR INDEX only comes up to the year 1850. This is not true. The time period of the records indexed varied from town to town. Many towns have records indexed in the 1860s. Bozrah has some of its records indexed up to 1871.

Reference is also made to all original and microfilmed copies of vital records held by libraries and similar institutions.

VOTER RECORDS

Includes references to all original, published, and microfilmed voter records found at libraries and similar institutions, but not the active records of local Registrars of Voters.

PUBLISHED WORKS AND OTHER RECORDS

Includes references to all other books, articles, dissertations, microfilmed records and original records deposited in archives and libraries that pertain to each town but do not fall under the previous subject headings.

The CONNECTICUT RESEARCHER'S HANDBOOK has taken five years to compile. It began as an article and grew to its present size. Bringing together all of this information was like trying to record everything you could see in the extensive Carlsbad Caverns. After recording everything in one chamber, the path would lead on to the next room full of more objects and natural wonders even more impressive than the first, then on to the next, and then on to another. Likewise, each repository opened up new records, books and articles that led to the next "cavern" opening up even more information leading on to the next. Each time it seemed that the book was complete there was one more library to visit or periodical to index that pointed to still more areas to explore. No handbook or bibliography is ever complete, but it is the editor's desire to have made this as complete as possible to assist local historians and genealogists in their research.

Thomas J. Kemp
Stamford, Connecticut

ABBREVIATIONS

American Hist. Soc. - American Historical Society

ASCH - Association for the Study of Connecticut History

Assn. - Association

Bailey - Bailey, Frederick W. EARLY CONNECTICUT MARRIAGES AS FOUND ON ANCIENT CHURCH RECORDS PRIOR TO 1800. 7 vols. New Haven: Author, 1896-1906.

Barbour Index - Index to Connecticut Vital Records compiled by Lucius Barnes Barbour.

CA - CONNECTICUT ANCESTRY

CANTIQUARIAN - CONNECTICUT ANTIQUARIAN

CHS - Connecticut Historical Society

CHSB - CONNECTICUT HISTORICAL SOCIETY BULLETIN

CM - CONNECTICUT MAGAZINE

CN - CONNECTICUT NUTMEGGER

CQ - CONNECTICUT QUARTERLY

CR - CONNECTICUT REVIEW

Co. - County

Conn. - Connecticut

CSL - Connecticut State Library

DAR - Daughters of the American Revolution

Flint Gen. Soc. Q. - FLINT (MICHIGAN) GENEALOGICAL SOCIETY QUARTERLY

GPO - U.S. Government Printing Office

Historical Soc. of Penn. - Historical Society of Pennsylvania

LDS - Genealogical Department of The Church of Jesus Christ of Latter-day Saints

Abbreviations

Mass. - Massachusetts

NEHGR - NEW ENGLAND HISTORIC GENEALOGICAL SOCIETY REGISTER

NEQ - NEW ENGLAND QUARTERLY

NGSQ - NATIONAL GENEALOGICAL SOCIETY QUARTERLY

NHCHS - New Haven Colony Historical Society

NYGBR - NEW YORK GENEALOGICAL AND BIOGRAPHICAL SOCIETY RECORD

NYGBS - New York Genealogical and Biographical Society

Preliminary Checklist - Gustafson, Don. A PRELIMINARY CHECKLIST OF CONNECTICUT NEWSPAPERS 1755-1975. 2 vols. Hartford: Conn. State Library, 1978.

R.I. - Rhode Island

TAG - THE AMERICAN GENEALOGIST

UCONN - University of Connecticut

WPA - Works Progress Administration

Part 1

CONNECTICUT GENERAL SUBJECTS

CONNECTICUT GENERAL SUBJECTS

ADOPTION RECORDS

Associations

Open Door Society of Connecticut, Inc., P.O. Box 478, Hartford, Conn., 06101.

Books and Articles

ADOPTION POLICIES AND PRACTICES OF PUBLIC AND PRIVATE AGENCIES IN CONNECTICUT. Hartford: Open Door Society of Conn., 1976. 23 p.

Heiss, Willard. "Adoptions." GENEALOGY 42 (January 1979): 1-3.

"Sherry H. v. Probate Court." CONNECTICUT LAW JOURNAL 40, no. 38 (March 20, 1979): 11-15.

ART AND MUSIC

Adams, John Coleman. "Gibson, the Artist-Naturalist of Connecticut." CM 7 (1902): 340-55.

Allen, N.H. "Old Time Music and Musicians." CQ 1 (1895): 274-79, 368-73; 2 (1896): 54-58, 153-57; 3 (1897): 66-76, 286-93; 4 (1898): 319-28.

Bartlett, Ellen Strong. "A Patriarch of American Portrait Painters--Nathaniel Jocelyn." CM 7 (1903): 589-601.

Broaddus, Margaret. "Thomas P. Rossiter: In Pursuit of Diversity." AMERICAN ART AND ANTIQUES 2 (1979): 106-13.

Cogan, Lillian Blankley. "Art as Expressed in the Domestic Utensils of Early American Life in Connecticut." CANTIQUARIAN 17 (1965): 11-15.

CONNECTICUT AND AMERICAN IMPRESSIONISM. Storrs: University of Connecticut, William Benton Museum of Art, 1980. 184 p.

De Voe, Shirley Spaulding. "Painted Household Furniture and Accessories in Connecticut 1800-1850." CANTIQUARIAN 21 (1969): 4-7.

French, Henry Willard. ART AND ARTISTS IN CONNECTICUT. Boston, Mass.: Lee and Shepard, 1879. 176 p.

Little, Nina Fletcher. "European Landscapes on Connecticut Overmantels." CANTIQUARIAN 16 (1964): 3-8.

_____. "Little Known Connecticut Artists, 1790-1810." CHSB 22 (1957): 97-128.

_____. "Little Known Connecticut Limners, 1790-1810." ART IN AMERICA 45 (Winter 1957): 74-77.

_____. "Some Eighteenth Century Connecticut Landscapes." ART IN AMERICA 37 (October 1949): 202-11.

Mattatuck Historical Society. THE CONNECTICUT ARTISTS COLLECTION. Waterbury, Conn.: Author, 1968. 84 p.

_____. A TENTATIVE LIST OF CONNECTICUT ARTISTS. Waterbury, Conn.: Author, 1964. 47 p.

Monroe, Myra E. Dowd. "Connecticut Artists and Their Work: Gilbert Munger." CM 8 (1904): 775-84.

Randall, Alice Sawtelle. "Connecticut Artists and Their Work." CM 9 (1905): 139-43.

Randall, Herbert. "Achievements of a Connecticut Sculptor, Paul Weyland Bartlett." CM 9 (1905): 389-94.

_____. "Connecticut Artists and Their Work: Exhibition at the Atheneum in Hartford and the Canvases of Several Contemporary Painters." CM 8 (1903): 108-13.

Whitmore, Harriet E.G. "Miniature Painting in the Colonial Days." CM 7 (1902-03): 356-61, 542-48.

ASSOCIATIONS

ANTIQUARIAN & LANDMARKS SOCIETY, INC. OF CONNECTICUT

Antiquarian & Landmarks Society, Inc., of Connecticut. 394 Main Street, Hartford, 06103. (203) 247-8996.

CONNECTICUT ANTIQUARIAN, Vol. 1, June 1949--Semiannual. Index Vol. 1-30, (1949-1978).

CHILDREN OF THE AMERICAN REVOLUTION

"Children of the American Revolution." CQ 2 (1896): 297-301; 3 (1897): 120; 4 (1898): 341.

COLONIAL DAMES OF AMERICA, CONNECTICUT SOCIETY

Hartford, CSL. Record Group 143. Papers of the Society 1900-1942.

"Colonial Dames." CQ 3 (1897): 120, 247.

"Colonial Dames' Loan Exhibition, Hartford." CQ 2 (1896): 302-4.

"Colonial Dames' Loan Exhibition, New Haven." CQ 2 (1896): 301.

CONNECTICUT COMMANDERY OF THE MILITARY ORDER OF FOREIGN WARS.

"Order of Foreign Wars." CQ 2 (1896): 187, 297; 3 (1897): 121.

CONNECTICUT FORESTRY ASSOCIATION

Winslow, Mary. "The Connecticut Forestry Association." CQ 4 (1898): 341-42.

CONNECTICUT SOCIETY OF THE SONS OF THE AMERICAN REVOLUTION

"Connecticut Society of the Sons of the American Revolution." CQ 1 (1895): 95, 213, 311-12; 2 (1896): 186-87, 292; 3 (1897): 120, 247; 4 (1898): 111, 231-32. CM 5 (1899): 392-496.

DAUGHTERS OF THE AMERICAN REVOLUTION

CONNECTICUT DAUGHTERS OF THE AMERICAN REVOLUTION. Yearbook.

"The Daughters of the American Revolution." CQ 2 (1896): 101, 187-92, 292-92; 3 (1897): 119-20, 247-49, 367-68; 4 (1898): 101-2, 232-33, 338-40; 5 (1899): 122-23, 392.

Hartford, CSL. Record Group 123. Papers of the Ruth Wyllys Chapter. 1892–1970.

Monat, Emilie M. CONNECTICUT STATE OF THE DAUGHTERS OF THE AMERICAN REVOLUTION. Hartford: Finlay Brothers, 1929. 220 p.

"New London Loan Exhibition." CQ 2 (1896): 304–5.

Root, Mary Philtheta. CHAPTER SKETCHES, CONNECTICUT DAUGHTERS OF THE AMERICAN REVOLUTION. New Haven: Conn. Chapters, DAR, 1901. 531 p.

_____. CHAPTER SKETCHES, CONNECTICUT DAUGHTERS OF THE AMERICAN REVOLUTION, PATRIOTS' DAUGHTERS. New Haven: Conn. Chapters, DAR, 1904. 390 p.

THE LOYAL LEGION

"The Loyal Legion." CQ 1 (1895): 312.

MASONS

Case, James R. DAVID WOOSTER, FATHER OF FREEMASONRY IN CONNECTICUT. N.p.: Philosophic Lodge of Research, A.F. and A.M. of Connecticut, 1970. 10 p.

_____. FREEMASONRY IN CONNECTICUT: CONNECTICUT MASONS IN THE AMERICAN REVOLUTION. N.p.: Grand Lodge A.F. and A.M. of Connecticut, 1974. 60 p.

Lipson, Dorothy Ann. "Freemasonry in Connecticut 1789–1835." Ph.D. dissertation, University of Connecticut, 1974. 516 p.

_____. FREEMASONRY IN FEDERAL CONNECTICUT. Princeton, N.J.: Princeton University Press, 1977. 380 p. Index.

NATIONAL SOCIETY OF UNITED STATES DAUGHTERS OF 1812

Hartford, CSL. Record Group 120. Papers, Scrapbooks, etc. 1905–1963.

ORDER OF FOUNDERS AND PATRIOTS OF AMERICA, CONNECTICUT SOCIETY

"Founders and Patriots." CQ 2 (1896): 291.

Hall, Newman A. "The Order of Founders and Patriots of America." LEAGUE BULLETIN 31 (March 1979): 17–18.

Hartford, CSL. Record Group 130. Papers of the Order from 1896–1914.

SOCIETY OF COLONIAL WARS

PAPERS AND ADDRESSES OF THE SOCIETY OF COLONIAL WARS IN THE STATE OF CONNECTICUT. 2 vols. N.p., n.d.

"Society of Colonial Wars in the State of Connecticut." CQ 1 (1895): 96, 312, 407; CM 5 (1899): 392.

SOCIETY OF COLONIAL WARS IN THE STATE OF CONNECTICUT. REGISTER OF PEDIGREES AND SERVICES OF ANCESTORS. Hartford: Case, Lockwood and Brainard Co., 1941. 1,394 p.

SOCIETY OF MAYFLOWER DESCENDANTS IN THE STATE OF CONNECTICUT

THE SOCIETY OF MAYFLOWER DESCENDANTS IN THE STATE OF CONNECTICUT 1980. Orange, Conn.: Mrs. Robert J. Galwey, 1980. 95 p.

"Mayflower Descendants." CQ 4 (1898): 112.

"New England Society of Mayflower Descendants." CQ 2 (1896): 296-97; 3 (1897): 121.

SOCIETY OF THE CINCINNATI

Davies, Wallace Evan. "The Society of the Cincinnati in New England 1783-1800." WILLIAM AND MARY QUARTERLY 5 (1961): 3-35.

Hume, Edgar E. "Early Opposition to the Cincinnati." AMERICANA 30 (1936): 597-638.

Lewis, A.N. "The Venerable and Illustrious Order of the Cincinnati. 1783-1900. History of the Connecticut State Society." CM 6 (1900): 416-27.

PAPERS OF THE CONNECTICUT STATE SOCIETY OF THE CINCINNATI 1783-1807. Hartford: Connecticut Historical Society, 1946.

RECORDS OF THE CONNECTICUT STATE SOCIETY OF THE CINCINNATI 1783-1804. Hartford: Connecticut Historical Society, 1916.

SOCIETY OF THE DAUGHTERS OF THE REVOLUTION IN CONNECTICUT

"Society of the Daughters of the Revolution in Connecticut." CQ 1 (1895): 96-97, 214, 407-8.

SOCIETY OF THE WAR FOR THE UNION

"The Society of the War for the Union." CQ 1 (1895): 408.

SONS OF THE REVOLUTION

"Sons of the Revolution." CQ 2 (1896): 186.

BIBLE RECORDS

BIBLE RECORDS FROM CONNECTICUT. INDEX CARDS. (CSL, LDS 1449 pt. 1-9).

Connecticut Chapter of the National Society Daughters of Founders and Patriots of America, Inc. FAMILY RECORDS. New Haven: Tuttle, Morehouse and Taylor, 1935. 305 p. Index.

The Connecticut State Library has made a concentrated effort to collect copies of family records recorded in Bibles. The CSL has twenty-six volumes of compiled family Bible records which have been indexed. It also has hundreds of family Bible records kept alphabetically by surname in file cabinets.

Family Bible records are published regularly in CONNECTICUT ANCESTRY and in the CONNECTICUT NUTMEGGER (See Genealogical Societies).

BIBLIOGRAPHY

Bassett, Thomas Day Seymour. "A Bibliography of New England Bibliographies." NEW ENGLAND QUARTERLY MAGAZINE 44 (1971): 278-300.

Bates, Albert Carlos. "Check List of Connecticut Almanacs, 1709-1850." American Antiquarian Society PROCEEDINGS 24 (1914): 93-215.

_____. A LIST OF OFFICIAL PUBLICATIONS OF CONNECTICUT, 1774-1788 AS SHOWN BY THE BILLS FOR PRINTING. Hartford, Conn.: Hartford Printing Co., 1917. 54 p.

_____. SECOND SUPPLEMENTARY LIST OF BOOKS PRINTED IN CONNECTICUT, 1709-1800. Hartford, Conn.: Acorn Club of Connecticut, 1947. 11 p.

Kemp, Thomas Jay. "Basic Connecticut Reference Books for the Genealogist's Home Library." CA 23 (1980): 72-73.

Mead, Nelson Prentiss. PUBLIC ARCHIVES OF CONNECTICUT, COUNTY, PROBATE AND LOCAL RECORDS. Washington, D.C.: American Historical Association Annual Report, 1908. 127 p.

Magnesi, John. "Masters' Theses on Connecticut: A Bibliography." CHSB 42 (1977): 40-61, 75-93.

Schnare, Robert E. LOCAL HISTORICAL RESOURCES IN CONNECTICUT: A GUIDE TO THEIR USE. Darien: Conn. League of Historical Societies, 1976. 28 p.

Sperry, Kip. CONNECTICUT SOURCES FOR FAMILY HISTORIANS AND GENEALOGISTS. Logan, Utah: Everton Publishers, 1980. 112 p. Index.

Stark, Bruce Purinton. "Checklist of Recent Dissertations on Connecticut History." ASCH NEWSLETTER, Spring 1979, pp. 2-5.

_____. "A Guide to Connecticut History Bibliography." CONNECTICUT HISTORY 20 (1979): 27-36.

Van Dusen, Albert Edward. "Connecticut History to 1763: A Selective Bibliography." CONNECTICUT HISTORY 15 (1975): 49-57.

BIOGRAPHY

ASSEMBLY BOOK AND CONNECTICUT PUBLIC REGISTER. BIOGRAPHICAL SKETCHES OF THE STATE OFFICERS, REPRESENTATIVES IN CONGRESS, GOVERNOR'S STAFF, AND SENATORS AND MEMBERS OF THE GENERAL ASSEMBLY OF THE STATE OF CONNECTICUT. Hartford: Evening Post Assn., 1895.

Bohan, Peter J., and Philip H. Hammerslaugh. EARLY CONNECTICUT SILVER, 1700-1840. Middletown: Wesleyan Univ. Press, 1970. 288 p.

Carlevale, Joseph William. WHO'S WHO AMONG ITALIAN DESCENT IN CONNECTICUT. New Haven: Carlevale Pub. Co., 1942. 281 p.

CONNECTICUT PIONEERS IN AVIATION. Hartford: Conn. Aeronautical Historical Assn., 1963.

Curtis, George Munson. EARLY SILVER OF CONNECTICUT AND ITS MAKERS. Meriden, Conn.: International Silver Co., 1913. 115 p.

DeVoe, Shirley Spaulding. THE TINSMITHS OF CONNECTICUT. Middletown: Wesleyan Univ. Press, 1968. 200 p.

Duffy, Ward E. WHO'S WHO IN CONNECTICUT. New York: Lewis Historical Pub. Co., 1933. 302 p.

ENCYCLOPEDIA OF CONNECTICUT BIOGRAPHY, GENEALOGICAL MEMORIAL. 5 vols. New York: American Historical Society, 1911.

Everest, Charles William. POETS OF CONNECTICUT; WITH BIOGRAPHICAL SKETCHES. 1843. Reprint. Freeport, N.Y.: Books for Libraries Press, 1973. 468 p.

French, Henry Willard. ART AND ARTISTS IN CONNECTICUT. 1879. Reprint. New York: Kennedy Graphics Inc., 1970. 176 p.

GENEALOGICAL AND BIOGRAPHICAL RECORDS OF AMERICAN CITIZENS: CONNECTICUT. 26 vols. Hartford: n.p., 1929-49.

GENEALOGICAL AND FAMILY HISTORY OF THE STATE OF CONNECTICUT. 4 vols. New York: Lewis Historical Pub. Co., 1911.

Grannis, Lewis Carlisle. CONNECTICUT COMPOSERS. New Haven: Conn. State Federation of Music Clubs, 1935. 125 p.

Hart, Samuel. REPRESENTATIVE CITIZENS OF CONNECTICUT: BIOGRAPHI-CAL MEMORIAL. New York: American Hist. Soc., 1916. 473 p.

Hoopes, Penrose Robinson. CONNECTICUT CLOCKMAKERS OF THE EIGHTEENTH CENTURY. New York: Dover Publications, 1974. 182 p.

King, Susanne D. CONNECTICUT'S TWENTIETH CENTURY PILGRIMS. Hartford: American Revolution Bicentennial Commission of Conn., 1977. 198 p.

Little, Nina Fletcher. "Little-Known Connecticut Limners, 1790-1810." ART IN AMERICA 45 (Winter): 74-77.

Loomis, Dwight, and Calhoun, Joseph Gilbert. THE JUDICIAL AND CIVIL HISTORY OF CONNECTICUT. Boston: Boston History Co., 1895. 639 p.

Nash, Elizabeth Todd. FIFTY PURITAN ANCESTORS 1628-1660: GENEALOGI-CAL NOTES 1560-1900. New Haven: Tuttle, Morehouse and Taylor, 1902. 182 p.

Nash, Frederick H. YE NAMES & AGES OF ALL YE OLD FOLKS IN EVERY HAMLET, CITY AND TOWN IN YE STATE OF CONNECTICUT, NOW LIVING, WITH YE SKETCHES OF TWENTY LIVING CENTENARIANS. New Haven: Price, Lee and Co., 1884. 52 p. (LDS 1486).

Osborn, Norris Galpin. MEM OF MARK IN CONNECTICUT. 5 vols. Hartford, Conn.: Goodspeed, 1904-10.

Perry, Charles E. FOUNDERS AND LEADERS OF CONNECTICUT 1633-1783. 1934. Reprint. Freeport, N.Y.: Books for Libraries Press, 1971. 319 p.

Sheldrick, Helen M., ed. PIONEER WOMEN TEACHERS OF CONNECTICUT 1767-1970. Winsted, Conn.: Dowd Printing Co., 1971. 149 p.

Spaulding, J.A. ILLUSTRATED POPULAR BIOGRAPHY OF CONNECTICUT. Hartford: Case, Lockwood and Brainard Co., 1871. 375 p.

WHO'S WHO OF FAIRFIELD COUNTY EXECUTIVES 1979. Greenwich: Greenwich Way, 1979. 169 p.

BUILDINGS

Allen, Richard Saunders. "Covered Bridges in Connecticut." CANTIQUARIAN 2 (November 1950): 11-19.

_____. "Footnotes to 'Covered Bridges in Connecticut.'" CANTIQUARIAN 3 (June 1951): 24-25.

"Beautiful Homes of Connecticut." CM 7 (1902): 387-94.

Brainard, Newton Cass. THE HARTFORD STATE HOUSE OF 1796. Hartford, Conn.: Connecticut Historical Society, 1964. 68 p.

"Capitol Observes 100 Years." LEAGUE BULLETIN 31 (June 1979): 5-7, 18.

Connecticut. State Librarian. "Connecticut Houses." REPORT OF THE STATE LIBRARIAN. 1922, pp. 64-86; 1930, pp. 77-115.

Delaney, Barbara S. "A Preservation Trust for Connecticut." CANTIQUARIAN 27 (July 1975): 28-30.

Faude, Wilson H. "Old State House, Hartford, Connecticut." ANTIQUES 117 (1980): 626-33.

Felch, W. Farrard. "Historic Homes." CQ 1 (1895): 3-13, 123-33, 288-97.

Fisher, Thomas R. "Technical Preservation in Connecticut." LEAGUE BULLETIN 32 (September 1980): 17-18.

Friedland, Edward P. "Historic Preservation in Action." CANTIQUARIAN 26 (December 1974): 23-25.

Garvan, Anthony N.B. ARCHITECTURE AND TOWN PLANNING IN COLONIAL CONNECTICUT. New Haven: Yale University Press, 1951. 166 p.

Griswold, Harlan H. "Historic Preservation in Connecticut . . . Why?" CANTIQUARIAN 24 (December 1972): 21-28.

Isham, Norman Morrison. EARLY CONNECTICUT HOUSES. New York: Dover Publications, 1965. 303 p.

Keith, Elmer Davenport. SOME NOTES ON EARLY CONNECTICUT ARCHI-
TECTURE. Hartford: Antiquarian and Landmarks Society of Connecticut, 1974.
48 p.

Kelly, John Frederick. ARCHITECTURAL GUIDE FOR CONNECTICUT. New
Haven, Conn.: Yale University Press, 1935. 44 p.

_____. CONNECTICUT'S OLD HOUSES, A HANDBOOK AND GUIDE.
Stonington, Conn.: Pequot Press, 1963. 73 p.

_____. EARLY CONNECTICUT ARCHITECTURE. 2 vols. New York:
W. Helburn, 1931.

_____. EARLY DOMESTIC ARCHITECTURE OF CONNECTICUT. New Haven,
Conn.: Yale University Press, 1933. 30 p.

_____. EARLY DOMESTIC ARCHITECTURE OF CONNECTICUT. New Haven,
Conn.: Yale University Press, 1924. Reprint. New York: Dover Publications,
1963. 210 p.

_____. "A Seventeenth-Century Connecticut Log House." OLD TIME NEW
ENGLAND 31 (October 1940): 29-40.

_____. "Three Early Connecticut Weather-Vanes." OLD TIME NEW ENGLAND
31 (April 1940): 96-99.

"The Late Frederick C. Palmer's Last Completed Commission." CANTIQUARIAN
24 (June 1972): 18-19.

Leibundguth, Arthur W. "History of Historic Preservation in Connecticut."
CANTIQUARIAN 27 (July 1975): 10-28.

Litchfield Associates. A GUIDE TO HISTORIC SITES IN CONNECTICUT.
Middletown: Wesleyan University Press, 1963.

Little, Nina Fletcher. "Early Connecticut Wall Painting." CANTIQUARIAN
5 (December 1953): 23-26.

Mason, H.F. Randolph. HISTORIC HOUSES OF CONNECTICUT, OPEN TO
THE PUBLIC. Chester, Conn.: Pequot Press, 1973. 72 p.

"Modern Science as Exemplified in Highland Court." CM 8 (1903): 385-94.

Palmer, Frederic. "The Nomenclature of Rooms in the 17th and 18th Century Connecticut House." CANTIQUARIAN 15 (July 1963): 18-20, 25.

Ransom, David F. GEO. KEELER, ARCHITECT. Hartford, Conn.: Stowe Day Foundation, 1978. 218 p. Index.

_____. "James G. Batterson and the New State House." CHSB 45 (January 1980): 1-15.

_____. "Upjohn's Other Works." CHSB 45 (July 1980): 65-74.

Rolleston, Sara Emerson. HERITAGE HOUSES: THE AMERICAN TRADITIONS IN CONNECTICUT 1660-1900. New York: Viking Press, 1979. 176 p.

_____. HISTORIC HOUSES AND INTERIORS IN SOUTHERN CONNECTICUT. New York: Hastings House, 1976. 208 p. Index.

Sinnott, Edmund Ware. "Old Connecticut Meeting--Houses." CANTIQUARIAN 6 (November 1954): 11-19.

Taylor, William Harrison. "The Connecticut Capitol." CM 5 (1899): 202-14.

Terry, Mrs. Alfred Howe. "More Old Connecticut Houses." CANTIQUARIAN 2 (July 1950): 9-14; 4 (June 1952): 23-28.

Tomlinson, Juliette. "Asher Benjamin--Connecticut Architect." CANTIQUARIAN 6 (November 1954): 26-29.

Warren, William Lamson. CONNECTICUT ART AND ARCHITECTURE: LOOK-ING BACKWARDS TWO HUNDRED YEARS. Hartford: American Revolution Bicentennial Commission of Connecticut, 1976. 64 p.

Warren, William Lamson, and Sprats, William. "Master Joiner: Connecticut's Federalist Architect." CANTIQUARIAN 9 (December 1957): 11-21.

BUSINESS, INDUSTRY, AND SCIENCE

Abbe, Nellie Grace. "Traffic on the Connecticut River Half a Century Ago." CQ 3 (1897): 266-74.

Akagi, Roy Hidemichi. THE TOWN PROPRIETORS OF THE NEW ENGLAND COLONIES. A STUDY OF THEIR DEVELOPMENT, ORGANIZATION, ACTIVITIES AND CONTROVERSIES, 1620-1770. Philadelphia: University of

Pennsylvania Press, 1924. Reprint. Glouster, Mass.: Peter Smith, 1963. 348 p.

Bailyn, Bernard. THE NEW ENGLAND MERCHANTS IN THE SEVENTEENTH CENTURY. Cambridge, Mass.: Harvard, 1955. 249 p.

Baker, George Pierce. THE FORMATION OF THE NEW ENGLAND RAILROAD SYSTEMS: A STUDY OF RAILROAD COMBINATION IN THE NINETEENTH CENTURY. Cambridge, Mass.: Harvard, 1937. 283 p. Index.

Barbour, Frederick K. "Connecticut Furniture: The Story of a Project." CANTIQUARIAN 14 (December 1962): 18-25.

_____. "Some Connecticut Case Furniture." ANTIQUES 883 (April 1963): 434-37.

Barr, Lockwood. "Connecticut Tower Clocks by Eli and Samuel Terry." ANTIQUES 71 (February 1957): 164-65.

Barroll, Henry H. "Connecticut's High Industry Under the Sea." CM 7 (1902): 252-56.

Bates, Albert Carlos. "Connecticut's Engraved Bills of Credit, 1709-1946." American Antiquarian Society PROCEEDINGS 46 (1937): 219-42.

Betts, Frederick Augustus. "The Origin and Development of Connecticut Insurance." CM 7 (1901): 2-44, 109-16.

Betts, Wyllis. COUNTERFEIT HALF PENCE CURRENT IN THE AMERICAN COLONIES, AND THEIR ISSUE FROM THE MINTS OF CONNECTICUT AND VERMONT. New York: American Numismatic and Archaeological Society, 1886. 17 p.

Bohan, Peter, and Hammerslough, Philip. EARLY CONNECTICUT SILVER, 1700-1840. Middletown, Conn.: Wesleyan University Press, 1970. 288 p.

Bronson, Henry A. "Historical Account of Connecticut Currency, Continental Money, and the Finances of the Revolution." NHCHS PAPERS 1 (1865): 1-192.

Bulkeley, Houghton. CONTRIBUTIONS TO CONNECTICUT CABINET MAKING. Hartford: CHS, 1967. 97 p.

Bullock, C. Seymour. "Anniversary of American Commerce." CM 11 (1907): 361-98.

_____. "The Development of Steam Navigation." CM 9 (1905): 440-55, 765-74; 10 (1906): 97-108, 298-318.

_____. "First Steamships to Cross the Atlantic Ocean." CM 11 (1907): 49-64.

_____. "Perilous Journeys of Some of the First Steamboats in American Waters." CM 10 (1906): 695-714.

Burr, Nelson Rollin. THE EARLY LABOR MOVEMENT IN CONNECTICUT, 1790-1860. West Hartford, Conn.: Author, 1972. 26 p.

Chase, Ada R. "Amos D. Allen, Connecticut Cabinetmaker." ANTIQUES 70 (August 1956): 146-47.

_____. "Two Eighteenth Century Clockmakers." ANTIQUES 38 (September 1940): 116-18.

Clapp, Jonathan T. "Northwestern Connecticut's Iron Hill Heritage." CANTIQUARIAN 29 (December 1977): 17-27.

Comstock, Helen. "Aaron Roberts and Southeastern Connecticut Cabinetmaking." ANTIQUES 86 (October 1964): 437-41.

"Connecticut Cabinetmakers." CHSB 32, no. 4 (October 1967); 33, no. 1 (January 1968).

"Connecticut's Engraved Bills of Credit, 1709-1746." AMERICAN ANTIQUARIAN SOCIETY PROCEEDINGS 46 (1946): 219-42.

Countryman, William A. "Connecticut's Position in the Manufacturing World." CM 7 (1902): 323-27, 627-46.

Daniels, Bruce Collin. "Money-Value Definitions of Economic Classes in Colonial Connecticut, 1700-1776." HISTOIRE SOCIALE-SOCIAL HISTORY 7 (November 1974): 346-52.

Davis, Andrew McFarland. "A Connecticut Land Bank." TRANSACTIONS: Publications of the Colonial Society of Massachusetts 5 (1897-98): 96-111; 6 (1899-1900): 6-11.

Deyrup, Felicia Johnson. ARMS MAKERS OF THE CONNECTICUT VALLEY, A REGIONAL STUDY OF THE ECONOMIC DEVELOPMENT OF THE SMALL ARMS INDUSTRY, 1798-1870. Northampton, Mass.: Smith College, 1948. 290 p.

Edwards, Frances M. "Tobacco." CANTIQUARIAN 9 (July 1957): 15-19.

Emerick, Brian J. "Eastern Connecticut's Textile Heritage." CANTIQUARIAN 29 (June 1977): 4-22.

Fox, Betsy Pratt. "A Survey of Lighting Devices in the Society's Collections." CANTIQUARIAN 32 (December 1980): 15-22.

Fuller, Grace Pierpont. AN INTRODUCTION TO THE HISTORY OF CON-NECTICUT AS A MANUFACTURING STATE. Northampton, Mass.: Smith College, 1915. 64 p.

Gardner, Charles R. "Connecticut Glass." ANTIQUES 28: 101-3.

_____. "Connecticut Glass." CANTIQUARIAN 22 (June 1970): 9-11.

Goldsborough, Jennifer Faulds. "Connecticut Silver." CANTIQUARIAN 22 (December 1970): 18-27.

Grant, Ellsworth Strong. YANKEES DREAMERS AND DOERS. Chester, Conn.: Pequot Press, 1974. 269 p. Index.

Grant, Marion Hepburn. THE INFERNAL MACHINES OF SAYBROOK'S DAVID BUSHNELL: PATRIOT INVENTOR OF THE AMERICAN REVOLUTION. Old Saybrook, Conn.: Bicentennial Committee, 1976. 66 p.

Griswold, Roger M. "First Sailing Vessels and Merchant Marines on the Connecticut River." CM 10 (1906): 463-73.

Hammerslough, Philip H. "The Silver of Early Connecticut." CANTIQUARIAN 6 (June 1954): 12-16.

Harlow, Thompson Ritner. "Connecticut Engravers 1774-1820." CHSB 36 (1971): 97-136.

Haynes, Williams. "Horseshoe Nails to Squeeze Bottles: A New Look at Connecticut History." CANTIQUARIAN 9 (July 1957): 5-14.

Hendrickson, Clarence I. HISTORY OF TOBACCO PRODUCTION IN NEW ENGLAND STATES. Storrs, Conn.: Storrs Agricultural Experiment Station, 1930.

Hooker, Roland Mather. THE COLONIAL TRADE OF CONNECTICUT. Tercentenary Publication, no. 50. New Haven: Yale University Press, 1936. 42 p.

Hoopes, Penrose Robinson. CONNECTICUT CLOCKMAKERS OF THE EIGHTEENTH CENTURY. New York: N.p., 1974. 182 p.

_____. CONNECTICUT'S CONTRIBUTION TO THE DEVELOPMENT OF THE STEAMBOAT. New Haven, Conn.: Yale University Press, 1936. 31 p.

_____. EARLY CLOCKMAKING IN CONNECTICUT. Tercentenary Publication, no. 23. New Haven: Yale University Press, 1934. 26 p.

_____. SHOP RECORDS OF DANIEL BURNAP, CLOCKMAKER. Hartford: Connecticut Historical Society, 1958. 188 p.

_____. "Some Minor Connecticut Clockmakers." ANTIQUES 28 (September 1935): 104-5.

Howell, Kenneth T., and Carlson, Einar W. EMPIRE OVER THE DAM: THE STORY OF WATERPOWERED INDUSTRY, LONG SINCE PASSED FROM THE SCENE. Chester, Conn.: Pequot Press, 1974. 269 p.

_____. MEN OF IRON, FORBES AND ADAM. Lakeville, Conn.: Pocketknife Press, 1980. 159 p.

Hulbert, E.M. "Cooper Mining in Connecticut." CQ 3 (1897): 23-32.

Ingrahm, Edward. "Clockmaking in Connecticut." CANTIQUARIAN 3 (June 1951): 10-16.

"The Individuality of Connecticut Furniture." ANTIQUES 28 (1938): 110-13.

Jerome, Chauncey. HISTORY OF THE AMERICAN CLOCK BUSINESS FOR THE PAST SIXTY YEARS AND LIFE OF CHAUNCEY JEROME. New Haven, Conn.: F.C. Dayton, Jr., 1860. 144 p.

Judd, Sylvester. "The Fur Trade on the Connecticut River in the Seventeenth Century." NEHGR 11 (1857): 217-29.

Kearney, Paul W. "Yankee Clockmakers." AMERICAN HOROLOGIST AND JEWELER 17 (1950): 69-76.

Kingsbury, Frederick J. "The First Apothecary Shops in Connecticut." CM 8 (1904): 738-41.

Kuslan, Louis I. CONNECTICUT SCIENCE, TECHNOLOGY AND MEDICINE IN THE ERA OF THE AMERICAN REVOLUTION. Conn. Bicentennial Series, no. 27. Hartford: American Revolution Bicentennial Commission of Conn., 1978. 65 p. Index.

"Lambert Hitchcock of Hitchcocks-Ville, Connecticut: America's Most Famous Chairmaker and the Story of His Original Manufacturing." CANTIQUARIAN 18 (July 1966): 9-16.

Lathrop, William Gilbert. THE BRASS INDUSTRY IN THE UNITED STATES: A STUDY OF THE ORIGINS AND DEVELOPMENT OF THE BRASS INDUSTRY IN THE NAUGATUCK VALLEY AND ITS SUBSEQUENT EXTENSION OVER THE NATION. 1926. Reprint. New York: Arno Press, 1972. 174 p.

_____. THE DEVELOPMENT OF THE BRASS INDUSTRY IN CONNECTICUT. New Haven, Conn.: Yale University Press, 1936. 31 p.

Leavitt, John F. "The New England Coastwise Trade." CANTIQUARIAN 22 (June 1970): 4-8.

Luther, Clair Franklin. THE HADLEY CHEST. Hartford, Conn.: Case, Lockwood and Brainard, 1935. 144 p.

_____. "A Newly Discovered Connecticut Chest." ANTIQUES 19 (January 1931): 20-22.

McKnight, Everett James. "Peter Morton--An Early American Merchant and Importer." CM 10 (1906): 350-581.

Magruder, T.L. "General Custer and the Spencer Carbine or Custer would not have Died for our Sins with the Connecticut Rifle." CHSB 45 (January 1980): 16-21.

Markham, F.G. "Early Coinage of Money in America." CM 7 (1902): 381-86.

Martin, Margaret Elizabeth. MERCHANTS AND TRADE OF THE CONNECTICUT RIVER VALLEY, 1750-1820. Northampton, Mass.: Smith College, 1939. 284 p.

Mayer, J.R. "Medad Hills, Connecticut Gunsmith." ANTIQUES 44 (July 1943): 18-19.

Mead, Nelson Prentiss. CONNECTICUT AS A CORPORATE COLONY. Lancaster, Pa.: New Era Printing Co., 1906. 119 p.

Nettels, Curtis P. "The Beginnings of Money in Connecticut." TRANSACTIONS, WISCONSIN ACADEMY OF SCIENCES, ARTS AND LETTERS 13 (1911): 1-28.

New Haven Colony Historical Society. AN EXHIBITION OF CONNECTICUT PEWTER. New Haven, Conn.: New Haven Colony Historical Society, 1969. 72 p.

Osterweis, Rollin Gustav. "The Sesquecentennial History of the Arts and Sciences, New Haven." CONNECTICUT ACADEMY OF ARTS AND SCIENCE TRANSACTIONS 38 (1949): 103-49.

Owens, Hans C. "John Cheney, Connecticut Engraver; with Checklist of Lithographs and Engravings." ANTIQUES 25 (May 1934): 172-75.

Palmer, Frederic. "The Amasa Day Chest of Drawers." CANTIQUARIAN 20 (December 1968): 20-24.

Parsons, Francis. "Brainard--A Poet of Hartford's Early Literati." CM 7 (1902): 371-80.

Partridge, Albert L. "Wood Clocks: Connecticut Carries On." ANTIQUES 50 (August 1946): 100-101, 110-16.

_____. "Wood Clocks, Connecticut Enters the Eight-Day Field." ANTIQUES 41 (June 1952): 526-29.

Phipps, Frances. "Makers of Connecticut Clocks." CANTIQUARIAN 22 (June 1970): 16-20.

Pollak, Oliver B. "Keeping Time in Connecticut." CANTIQUARIAN 32 (December 1980): 23-24.

Pynchon, W.H.C. "Iron Mining in Connecticut." CM 5 (1899): 20-26, 232-38, 277-85.

Ramsey, Elizabeth. HISTORY OF TOBACCO PRODUCTION IN THE CONNECTICUT VALLEY. Northampton, Mass.: Smith College, 1930. 206 p.

Richardson, John M. "Varieties of Connecticut Cents." NUMISMATIC REVIEW 3 (1946): 5-9.

Robinson, Everett N. "Connecticut's Heritage from Tinsmith and Tin Peddling." ANTIQUARIAN 3 (November 1951): 22-30.

Saladino, Gaspare John. "The Economic Revolution in Late Eighteenth-Century Connecticut." Ph.D. dissertation, University of Wisconsin, 1964. 453 p.

Schmitt, Dale Joseph. "Labor in Early Connecticut." CONNECTICUT REVIEW 7 (April 1974): 16-24.

Scott, Kenneth. "Caesar Trick: Colonial Counterfeiter." CANTIQUARIAN 7 (July 1955): 14-17.

_____. "Counterfeiting in Colonial Connecticut." NUMISMATIC NOTES AND MONOGRAPHS, no. 140 (1957): 243 p.

Soltow, Lee. "Watches and Clocks in Connecticut, 1800, A Symbol of Socio-economic Status." CHSB 45 (1980): 115-22.

Speck, Robert M. "The Connecticut Water Machine Verses the Royal Novy." AMERICAN HERITAGE 32 (December 1980): 32-38.

Straight, Stephen M. "We had Mass Transit Years Ago in the Trolleys throughout Connecticut." CANTIQUARIAN 26 (December 1974): 15-20.

Swan, Aaron M. "The Chapins and Connecticut Valley Chippendale." ANTIQUARIAN 16 (April 1931): 21-24.

Sweet, Gordon. "Oyster Conservation in Connecticut: Past and Present." GEOGRAPHICAL REVIEW 31 (1946): 591-608.

Truxes, Thomas M. "Connecticut in the Irish-American Flaxseed Trade, 1750-1775." EIRE-IRELAND 12 (1977): 34-62.

_____. "Connecticut in the Irish-American Trade, 1750-1775." Master's Thesis, Trinity College, 1975. 166 p.

Turner, F.E. "Simeon North and the American Flintlock." ANTIQUARIAN 17 (July 1931): 24-25.

Van Dusen, Albert C. "Colonial Connecticuts' Trade With the West Indies."

NEW ENGLAND SOCIAL STUDIES BULLETIN 13 (March 1956): 11-19.

Walker, Gladys. "From Turtle to Trident: A 200-Year Odyssey." CON-NECTICUT 36 (June 1973): 34-40.

Walradt, Henry Freeman. THE FINANCIAL HISTORY OF CONNECTICUT FROM 1789 TO 1861. New Haven: Connecticut Academy of Arts and Sciences, 1912. 139 p.

Walsh, James P. CONNECTICUT INDUSTRY AND THE REVOLUTION. Conn. Bicentennial Series, no. 29. Hartford: American Revolution Bicentennial Commission of Conn., 1978. 82 p. Index.

Warren, H.C. "Thoroughfares in the Early Republic Controlled by Corporations." CM 8 (1904): 721-29.

Warren, William Lamson. "Some Remarks on Connecticut Chests." CANTI-QUARIAN 16 (June 1964): 14-18.

Watkins, Laura Woodside. "A Checklist of New England Stoneware Potters." ANTIQUES 42 (August 1942): 80-83.

Weaver, Glen. "Industry in an Agrarian Economy, Early Eighteenth Century Connecticut." CHSB 19 (1954): 82-92.

_____. JONATHAN TRUMBULL, CONNECTICUT'S MERCHANT MAGISTRATE, 1710-1785. Hartford: Connecticut Historical Society, 1956. 182 p.

Weller, John L. THE NEW HAVEN RAILROAD: ITS RISE AND FALL. New York: Hastings House, 1969. 248 p. Index.

Withington, Sidney. THE FIRST TWENTY YEARS OF RAILROADS IN CON-NECTICUT. Tercentenary Publication, no. 45. New Haven: Yale University Press, 1935. 32 p.

_____. Standard Time Began in Connecticut." CANTIQUARIAN 2 (November 1950): 20-21.

Woodward, Patrick Henry. INSURANCE IN CONNECTICUT. Boston: D.H. Hurd, 1897. 126 p.

CEMETERY RECORDS

Benes, Peter. "Lt. John Hartshorn: Gravestone Maker of Haverhill and Norwich." ESSEX INSTITUTE HISTORICAL COLLECTIONS 109 (1973): 152-64.

Caulfield, Ernest. "Connecticut Gravestones." CHSB 16 (1951): 1-5, 25-31; 17 (1952): 1-6; 18 (1953): 25-32; 19 (1954): 105-8; 21 (1956): 1-21; 23 (1958): 33-39; 25 (1960): 1-6; 27 (1962): 76-84; 28 (1963): 22-29; 30 (1965): 11-17; 31 (1966): 24-29; 32 (1967): 65-79; 40 (1975): 33-45; 41 (1976): 33-56.

Davis, Norman C., Jr. "Index by Family Names Cited to Gravestones of Westchester County, New York and Fairfield County, Conn., Recorded in 1870-1892, with Additions and Corrections Through 1896." CA 18 (1975): 13-15, 45-48.

Eardeley, William Applebie Daniel. CONNECTICUT CEMETERIES, 1673-1910. 8 vols. Brooklyn, N.Y.: Author, 1914-17.

Hayward, Kendall Payne. "List of Connecticut Stonecutters or Engravers & Sculptors." CHSB 15 (1950): 1-5.

Kull, Andrew. NEW ENGLAND CEMETERIES: A COLLECTOR'S GUIDE. Brattleboro, Vt.: Stephen Greene Press, 1975. 253 p. Index.

Slater, James A., and Caulfield, Ernest. "The Colonial Gravestone Carvings of Obidiah Wheeler." PROCEEDINGS OF THE AMERICAN ANTIQUARIAN SOCIETY 84: 73-104.

Weatherby, Una F. "Early Connecticut Gravestone Design." CANTIQUARIAN 4 (June 1952): 15-21.

CENSUS RECORDS

The Federal Census for Connecticut is available to the public for the years 1790-1880 and 1900-1910. The 1790-1850 censuses have been indexed by the Connecticut State Library. A computerized index for these same years is also available from Accelerated Indexing Systems (see Jackson, below). A Soundex Index exists for those families with children ten years old or younger for the 1880 census and for all individuals in the 1900 census.

Bickford, Christopher P. "The Lost Connecticut Census of 1762 Found." CHS 44 (April 1979): 33-43.

Greene, Evarts B., and Harrington, Virginia D. AMERICAN POPULATION

BEFORE THE FEDERAL CENSUS OF 1790. Gloucester, Mass.: Peter Smith, 1966. 228 p. Index.

HEADS OF FAMILIES AT THE FIRST CENSUS OF THE UNITED STATES TAKEN IN THE YEAR 1790: CONNECTICUT. Washington, D.C.: Government Printing Office, 1908. 227 p.

Holbrook, Jay Mack. CONNECTICUT 1670 CENSUS. Oxford, Mass.: Holbrook Research Institute, 1977. 74 p.

"Index to Connecticut Census 1790-1850." CN 4 (1971-72): 247-52, 388-93, 527-31; 5: 58-64, 227-32, 369-76, 514-21; 6 (1973): 305-11; 10 (1977-78): 355-59, 421-26, 598-603; 11 (1978): 35-40, 228-33.

Jackson, Ronald Vern, et al. CONNECTICUT 1800 CENSUS INDEX. Bountiful, Utah: Accelerated Indexing Systems, 1974. 157 p.

_____. CONNECTICUT 1810 CENSUS INDEX. Bountiful, Utah: Accelerated Indexing Systems, 1976. 109 p.

_____. CONNECTICUT 1820 CENSUS INDEX. Bountiful, Utah: Accelerated Indexing Systems, 1977. 124 p.

_____. CONNECTICUT 1830 CENSUS INDEX. Bountiful, Utah: Accelerated Indexing Systems, 1977. 138 p.

_____. CONNECTICUT 1840 CENSUS INDEX. Bountiful, Utah: Accelerated Indexing Systems, 1978. 150 p.

_____. CONNECTICUT 1850 CENSUS INDEX. Bountiful, Utah: Accelerated Indexing Systems, 1978. 339 p.

_____. EARLY CONNECTICUT VOLUME 1, 1600-1789, 1791-1799. Bountiful, Utah: Accelerated Indexing Systems, Inc., 1980. 79 p.

Jacobus, Donald Lines. "Errors in the Census of 1790 (Connecticut)." NEHGR 77 (1923): 80-81.

Kemp, Thomas Jay. "The Connecticut State Military Census of 1917." CA 22 (February 1980): 117-22.

"A Lost Connecticut Census Found!" NOTES & NEWS CHS 3 (3) (1976): 1.

State Military Census, 1917. Including lists of manpower, automobiles, nurses, enemy aliens, farmers, radio operators, etc. (CSL Archives RG 29).

CHURCH RECORDS

General

Baldwin, Alice Mary. CLERGY OF CONNECTICUT IN REVOLUTIONARY DAYS. Tercentenary Publication, no. 56. New Haven: Yale University Press, 1936. 31 p.

Connecticut State Library Index to Connecticut Church Records on Deposit. (CSL, LDS 1447 pt. 1-33, 1448 pt. 1-36).

Coons, Paul Wakeman. THE ACHIEVEMENT OF RELIGIOUS LIBERTY IN CONNECTICUT. Tercentenary Publication, no. 60. New Haven: Yale University Press, 1936. 32 p.

Delp, Robert W. "A Spiritualist in Connecticut: Andrew Jackson Davis, The Hartford Years, 1850-1854." NEQ 53 (1980): 345-62.

Emerson, Everett H. "Thomas Hooker and the Reformed Theology: The Relationship of Hooker's Conversion Reaching to Its Background." CHURCH HISTORY 24 (1955): 369-70.

Fowler, William Chauncey. THE MINISTERS OF CONNECTICUT IN THE REVOLUTION. Hartford, Conn.: Case, Lockwood and Brainard, Co., 1877. 144 p.

Greene, Maria Louise. DEVELOPMENT OF RELIGIOUS LIBERTY IN CONNECTICUT. Boston: Houghton Mifflin Co., 1905. Reprint. New York: Da Capu Press, 1970. 555 p.

Jarvis, Lucy Cushing. SKETCHES OF CHURCH LIFE IN COLONIAL CONNECTICUT. New Haven: Tuttle, Morehouse and Taylor, 1902. 188 p.

Keller, Charles Roy. THE SECOND GREAT AWAKENING IN CONNECTICUT. Hamden, Conn.: Archon Books, 1968. 275 p.

Kelly, John Frederick. EARLY CONNECTICUT MEETINGHOUSES BEING AN ACCOUNT OF THE CHURCH EDIFICES BUILT BEFORE 1830 BASED CHIEFLY UPON TOWN AND PARISH RECORDS. 2 vols. New York: Columbia University Press, 1948.

LIST OF CHURCH RECORDS IN THE CONNECTICUT STATE LIBRARY. Hartford: CSL, 1976. 35 p.

Lucas, Paul R. VALLEY OF DISCORD: CHURCH AND SOCIETY ALONG THE CONNECTICUT RIVER: 1636-1725. Hanover, N.H.: University Press of New England, 1976. 275 p. Index.

Mitchell, Mary Hewett. THE GREAT AWAKENING AND OTHER REVIVALS IN THE RELIGIOUS LIFE OF CONNECTICUT. New Haven, Conn.: Yale University Press, 1934. 59 p.

Moran, Gerald Francis. "The Puritan Saint: Religious Experience, Church Membership, and Piety in Connecticut, 1636-1776." Ph.D. dissertation, Rutgers University, 1973. 456 p.

Pitkin, Mrs. Albert Hastings. "Our Neighborhood Churches During the American Revolution." CQ 3 (1897): 430-40.

Reardon, John Joseph. "Religious and Other Factors in the Defeat of the 'Standing Order' in Connecticut, 1800-1818." HISTORICAL MAGAZINE OF THE PROTESTANT EPISCOPAL CHURCH 30 (1961): 93-110.

Schmidt, Dale Joseph. "Preparation for the Great Awakening in Connecticut." RELIGION IN LIFE 47 (1978): 430-40.

Shiels, Richard Douglas. "Connecticut Clergy in the Second Great Awakening." Ph.D. dissertation, Boston University, 1976. 456 p.

Smith, Martin H. "Ordination Service of a Century Ago." CM 9 (1905): 403-5.

Stewart, George. A HISTORY OF RELIGIOUS EDUCATION IN CONNECTICUT TO THE MIDDLE OF THE NINETEENTH CENTURY. New Haven: Yale University Press, 1924. 402 p.

WPA Historical Records Survey. CHURCH RECORDS SURVEY. (CSL Archives RG 33, Boxes 271-89).

WPA Historical Records Survey. GUIDE TO VITAL STATISTICS IN THE CHURCH RECORDS CF CONNECTICUT. New Haven: Connecticut Historical Records Survey, U.S. WPA, 1942. 190 p.

Baptist

Backus, Isaac. HISTORY OF NEW ENGLAND WITH PARTICULAR REFERENCE TO THE DENOMINATION OF CHRISTIANS CALLED BAPTISTS. 2 vols. Newton, Mass.: Backus Historical Society, 1871.

Evans, Philip Saffery. HISTORY OF CONNECTICUT BAPTIST STATE CON-
VENTION, 1823-1907. Hartford: Smith-Linsley Co., 1909. 297 p.

Hartford. CSL. Record Group 33, Box 273-77. CHURCH RECORDS SUR-
VEY. Card files containing notes on source materials, summaries of church
histories and descriptions of their records. There is an index by county for
Baptist churches.

Record of Marriages Performed by Rev. Greenleaf S. Webb. (Baptist) 1816-
1821. (Rutgers University, LDS 888, 819)

Congregational

United Church of Christ. Connecticut Conference. 125 Sherman Street,
Hartford, 06105. (203) 233-5564.

Bacon, Leonard, et al. CONTRIBUTIONS TO THE ECCLESIASTICAL HISTORY
OF CONNECTICUT. New Haven: W.L. Kinsley, 1861. 562 p.

Bates, Albert Carlos. LIST OF CONGREGATIONAL ECCLESIASTICAL SOCI-
ETIES ESTABLISHED IN CONNECTICUT BEFORE OCTOBER 1818, WITH THEIR
CHANGES. Hartford, Conn.: Historical Society, 1913. 35 p.

Beaskey, James R. "Emerging Republicanism and the Standing Order: The
Appropriation Act Controversy in Connecticut 1793 to 1795." WILLIAM AND
MARY QUARTERLY 29 (1972): 587-610.

Blake, Silas Leroy. THE SEPARATES OR STRICT CONGREGATIONALISTS OF
NEW ENGLAND. Boston: Pilgrim Press, 1902. 211 p.

Bliss, Robert M. "A Secular Revival: Puritanism in Connecticut, 1675, 1708."
JOURNAL OF AMERICAN STUDIES 6 (1972): 129-52.

Cohen, Sheldon Samuel. "The Connecticut Colony Government and the Policy
of the Congregational Churches, 1708-1760." Ph.D. dissertation, New York
University, 1963. 300 p.

CONTRIBUTIONS TO THE ECCLESIASTICAL HISTORY OF CONNECTICUT.
2 vols. N.p.: Conn. Conference of the United Church of Christ, 1861, 1967.

East, Robert Abraham. "Puritanism and New Settlement." NEQ 17 (1944):
255-64.

Fowler, William Chauncey. THE MINISTERS OF CONNECTICUT IN THE

REVOLUTION. Hartford, Conn.: Case, Lockwood and Brainard, 1877. 144 p.

Goen, C.C. REVIVALISM AND SEPARATISM IN NEW ENGLAND, 1740-1800: STRICT CONGREGATIONALISTS AND SEPARATE BAPTISTS IN THE GREAT AWAKENING. New Haven: Yale University Press, 1962. 370 p.

Hartford. CSL Record Group 33. Box 278. CHURCH RECORDS SURVEY. Card file notes on source materials, summaries of church histories and description of their records. There is an index by town for Congregational churches.

Jones, Mary Jeanne Anderson. CONGREGATIONAL COMMONWEALTH CONNECTICUT, 1636-1662. Middletown: Wesleyan University Press, 1968. 233 p. Index.

LIST OF CONGREGATIONAL ECCLESIASTICAL SOCIETIES ESTABLISHED IN CONNECTICUT BEFORE OCTOBER 1818 WITH THEIR CHANGES. Hartford: CHS, 1913. 35 p.

Meyer, Frank W. CONNECTICUT CONGREGATIONALISM IN THE REVOLUTIONARY ERA. Hartford: American Revolution Bicentennial Commission in Conn., 1977. 75 p. Index.

Moran, Gerald Francis. "The Puritan Saint: Religious Experience, Church Membership, and Piety in Connecticut, 1636-1776." Ph.D. dissertation, Rutgers University, 1974. 456 p.

Parker, Edwin Pond. "The Congregationalist Separates of the Eighteenth Century in Connecticut." NHCHS Papers 8 (1914): 151-61.

Rankin, Samuel Harrison. "Conservatism and the Problem of Change in the Congregational Churches of Connecticut, 1660-1760." Ph.D. dissertation, Kent State University, 1971. 358 p.

Thornburg, John F. GOD SENT REVIVAL: THE STORY OF ASAHEL NETTLETON AND THE SECOND GREAT AWAKENING. Grand Rapids, Mich.: Evangelical Press, 1977. 238 p. Index.

Weaver, Glenn. "Anglican-Congregationalist Tensions in Pre-Revolutionary Connecticut." HISTORICAL MAGAZINE OF THE PROTESTANT EPISCOPAL CHURCH 26 (1957): 269-85.

Episcopal

Episcopal Diocese of Connecticut. Archives. 1335 Asylum Avenue; Hartford, Conn. 06105. (203) 233-4481.

Publishes: HISTORIOGRAPHER OF THE EPISCOPAL DIOCESE OF CONNECTI-CUT. Quarterly.

Beardsley, Ebsen Edwards. HISTORY OF THE EPISCOPAL CHURCH IN CON-NECTICUT, FROM THE SETTLEMENT OF THE COLONY TO THE DEATH OF BISHOP SEABURY. 2 vols. New York: Hurd and Houghton, 1869.

Burr, Nelson Rollin. FIRST AMERICAN DIOCESE: CONNECTICUT, ITS ORIGIN, ITS GROWTH, ITS WORK. Hartford, Conn.: Church Missions Publishing Co., 1970. 48 p.

_____. THE STORY OF THE DIOCESE OF CONNECTICUT: A NEW BRANCH OF THE VINE. Hartford: Church Missions Pub. Co., 1962. 568 p.

Cameron, Kenneth Walter. ANGLICANISM IN EARLY CONNECTICUT AND NEW ENGLAND: A SELECTIVE BIBLIOGRAPHY. Hartford, Conn.: Transcendental Books, 1977. 92 p.

_____. HISTORICAL RESOURCES OF THE EPISCOPAL DIOCESE OF CON-NECTICUT. Hartford: Transcendental Books, 1966. 316 p.

Ellis, Joseph J., III. "Anglicans in Connecticut, 1725-1750: The Conversion of the Missionaries." NEW ENGLAND QUARTERLY 44 (1971): 66-81.

Hart, Samuel. BISHOP SEABURY AND CONNECTICUT CHURCHMANSHIP. New Haven, Conn.: Convention of the Diocese of Connecticut, 1896. 32 p.

_____. BISHOP SEABURY'S COMMUNION OFFICE. New York: Whittaker, 1883. 73 p.

_____. "John Williams, D.D., LL.D. Fourth Bishop of Connecticut." CM 5 (1899): 239-41.

Hawks, Francis Lister, and Perry, William Stevens. DOCUMENTARY HISTORY OF THE PROTESTANT CHURCH IN CONNECTICUT, 1701-1789. 2 vols. Hartford, Conn.: Historiographer, 1959.

_____. DOCUMENTARY HISTORY OF THE PROTESTANT EPISCOPAL CHURCH IN THE UNITED STATES OF AMERICA CONTAINING NUMEROUS HITHERTO UNPUBLISHED DOCUMENTS CONCERNING THE CHURCH IN CONNECTICUT. 2 vols. New York: J. Pott, 1863-1864. Reprint. Hartford, Conn.: Historiographer, 1952.

Jarvis, Lucy Cushing. SKETCHES OF CHURCH LIFE IN COLONIAL CON-

NECTICUT BEING THE STORY OF THE TRANSPLANTING OF THE CHURCH OF ENGLAND INTO FORTY-TWO PARISHES OF CONNECTICUT, WITH THE ASSISTANCE OF THE SOCIETY FOR THE PROPAGATION OF THE GOSPEL WRITTEN BY MEMBERS OF THE PARISHES IN CELEBRATION OF THE 200TH ANNIVERSARY OF THE SOCIETY. New Haven: Tuttle, Morehouse and Taylor, 1902. 188 p.

"Journal of the Official Acts (Protestant Episcopal) 1851-1899. Vols. 1-5 of Bishop John Williams Bishop of Connecticut." Handwritten. (CSL, LDS 1461).

Kinloch, Hector G. "Anglican Clergy in Connecticut, 1701-1785." Ph.D. dissertation, Yale University, 1959.

Mappen, Marc A. "Anglican Heresy in Eighteenth Century Connecticut: The Disciplining of John Beach." HISTORICAL MAGAZINE OF THE PROTESTANT EPISCOPAL CHURCH 48 (December 1979): 465-72.

O'Neil, Maud. "A Struggle for Religious Liberty: An Analysis of the Work of the S.P.G. in Connecticut." HISTORICAL MAGAZINE OF THE PROTESTANT EPISCOPAL CHURCH 20 (1951): 173-89.

Seymour, Origen Storrs. THE BEGINNINGS OF THE EPISCOPAL CHURCH IN CONNECTICUT. Tercentenary Commission Publication, no. 30. New Haven: Yale University Press, 1934. 32 p.

_____. "The Establishment of the Episcopacy in Connecticut." DAR MAGA-ZINE 2 (1892): 284-88.

Shepard, James. THE EPISCOPAL CHURCH AND EARLY ECCLESIASTICAL LAWS OF CONNECTICUT. 1908. Reprint. Hartford, Conn.: Transcendental Books, 1974. 65 p.

Steiner, Bruce E. "Anglican Officeholding in Pre-Revolutionary Connecticut: The Parameters of New England Community." WILLIAM AND MARY QUARTERLY 31 (1974): 369-406.

_____. SAMUEL SEABURY, 1729-1796; A STUDY IN THE HIGH CHURCH TRADITION. Athens, Ohio: Ohio University Press, 1971. 508 p.

_____. CONNECTICUT ANGLICANS IN THE REVOLUTIONARY ERA: A STUDY IN COMMUNAL TENSIONS. Conn. Bicentennial Series, no. 28. Hartford: American Revolution Bicentennial Commission of Conn., 1978. 111 p. Index.

Weaver, Glenn. "Anglican-Congregationalist Tensions in Pre-Revolutionary

Connecticut." HISTORICAL MAGAZINE OF THE PROTESTANT EPISCOPAL CHURCHES 26 (1957): 269-85.

WPA Historical Records Survey. INVENTORY OF THE CHURCH ARCHIVES OF CONNECTICUT. NO. 1 PROTESTANT EPISCOPAL. New Haven: Connecticut Historical Records Survey, Division of Professional and Service Projects, WPA, 1940. 309 p.

Jewish

Jewish Historical Society of Greater Hartford. 335 Bloomfield Avenue, 06117. (203) 236-4571, ext. 35.

Jewish Historical Society of New Haven. 119 Davenport Avenue, 06519. (203) 787-3183.

Goldberg, Arthur. "The Jew in Norwich, Connecticut: A Century of Jewish Life." RHODE ISLAND JEWISH HISTORICAL NOTES 7 (November 1975): 79-103.

Gordon, Morton L. "The History of the Jewish Farmer in Eastern Connecticut." Ph.D. dissertation, Yeshiva University, 1974. 236 p.

THE JEW IN NORWICH: A CENTURY OF JEWISH LIFE. Norwich: Norwich Jewish Tercentenary Committee, 1956. 57 p.

Koenig, Samuel. AN AMERICAN JEWISH COMMUNITY: THE STORY OF THE JEWS IN STAMFORD, CONNECTICUT. WPA Typescript, 1940. 187 p. (CSL Archives RG 33 Box 102).

_____. "The Social Aspects of the Jewish Mutual Benefit Societies." SOCIAL FORCES 18 (1939): 268-74.

Marcus, Jacob Rader. "Light on Early Connecticut Jewry." AMERICAN JEWISH ARCHIVES 1 (1948): 3-52.

Mittelstein, Rachel. "Mutual Aid Societies." WPA Typescript, 1939. (CSL Archives RG 33 Box 85).

Silverman, Morris. HARTFORD JEWS 1659-1970. Hartford: CHS, 1970. 449 p.

Lutheran

Scaer, David P. "The Centennial Celebration of Lutheranism in Connecticut."

CONCORDIA HISTORICAL INSTITUTE QUARTERLY 38 (1965): 95-101.

WPA Historical Records Survey. INVENTORY OF THE CHURCH ARCHIVES OF CONNECTICUT, NO. 2. LUTHERAN. New Haven: Connecticut Historical Records Survey, Division of Professional and Service Projects, WPA, 1941. 188 p. (LDS 924, 002)

Methodist

Commission on Archives and History, Southern New England Conference, United Methodist Church. 745 Commonwealth Avenue, Boston, Mass., 02215. (617) 353-3034.

Moravian

Reichel, William Cornelius. A MEMORIAL OF THE DEDICATION OF MONU-MENTS ERECTED BY THE MORAVIAN HISTORICAL SOCIETY TO MARK THE SITES OF ANCIENT MISSIONARY STATIONS IN NEW YORK AND CON-NECTICUT. New York: C.B. Richardson, 1860. 154 p.

Presbyterian

Lucas, Paul R. "Presbyterianism Comes to Connecticut: the Toleration Act of 1669." JOURNAL OF PRESBYTERIAN HISTORY 50 (1972): 129-47.

WPA Historical Records Survey. INVENTORY OF THE CHURCH ARCHIVES OF CONNECTICUT PRESBYTERIANS. New Haven: Connecticut Historical Records Survey, Division of Professional and Service Projects, WPA, 194- (LDS 854,483)

Quakers

Burr, Nelson Rollin. "The Quakers in Connecticut: A Neglected Phase of History." FRIENDS HISTORICAL ASSOCIATION BULLETIN 31 (Spring 1942): 11-26.

Rogerenes

Bolles, John Rogers. "The Rogerenes." NEQ 16 (1943): 3-19.

_____. THE ROGERENES; SOME HITHERTO UNPUBLISHED ANNALS BE-LONGING TO THE COLONIAL HISTORY OF CONNECTICUT. Boston: Stanhope Press, 1904. 396 p. Index.

Brinton, Ellen Starr. "Books By and About the Rogerenes." BULLETIN OF THE NEW YORK PUBLIC LIBRARY 49 (1945): 627-48.

Roman Catholic

Byrne, William. HISTORY OF THE CATHOLIC CHURCH IN THE NEW ENGLAND STATES. 2 vols. Boston: Hurd and Everts, Co., 1899.

Cullen, Thomas Francis. "William Barber Tyler (1806-1849) First Bishop of Hartford, Conn." CATHOLIC HISTORICAL REVIEW 23 (1937): 17-30.

Duggan, Thomas Stephen. CATHOLIC CHURCH IN CONNECTICUT. New York: States History Co., 1930. 622 p. Index.

Ellis, John Tracy. CATHOLICS IN COLONIAL AMERICA. Baltimore: Helicon Press, 1965. 486 p.

Lapomarda, Vincent A. THE JESUIT HERITAGE IN NEW ENGLAND. Worcester, Mass.: College of the Holy Cross, 1977. 321 p.

Munich, Austin Francis. THE BEGINNINGS OF ROMAN CATHOLICISM IN CONNECTICUT. Tercentenary Publication, no. 41. New Haven: Yale University Press, 1935. 32 p.

Riley, Arthur J. CATHOLICISM IN NEW ENGLAND TO 1788. Washington, D.C.: Catholic University of America Press, 1936. 479 p.

Rooney, James A. "Early Times in the Diocese of Hartford." CATHOLIC HISTORICAL REVIEW 1 (1915): 148.

Wolkovich-Valkavicius, William. LITHUANIAN PIONEER PRIEST OF NEW ENGLAND, THE LIFE, STRUGGLES AND TRAGIC DEATH OF REV. JOSEPH ZEBRIS, 1860-1915. Brooklyn: Franciscan Press, 1980. 214 p. Index.

Shakers

Brainard, Jessie Miriam. "Mother Ann's Children in Connecticut. The Enfield Shakers." CQ 3 (1897): 460-74.

Williams, Emily. "Spirituality as Expressed in Song." CM 9 (1905): 745-51.

Universalist

WPA Historical Records Survey. INVENTORY OF THE CHURCH ARCHIVES OF CONNECTICUT. NO. 6. UNIVERSALISM. New Haven: Conn. Historical Records Survey, Division of Professional and Service Projects, WPA, n.d. 82 p.

CITY DIRECTORIES

McCain, Diana Ross. "An Annotated Bibliography of Connecticut City, County and Business Directories, 1861-1910, in the Connecticut Historical Society, Supplemented by a Checklist of Additional Directories Located at the Connecticut State Library and at Selected Connecticut Public Libraries." Master's thesis, Southern Connecticut State College, 1979. 238 p.

CONNECTICUT STATE ARCHIVES

Connecticut State Library, 231 Capitol Avenue, Hartford, 06115. (203) 566-4301.

Claus, Robert. GUIDE TO ARCHIVES IN THE CONNECTICUT STATE LIBRARY. 2d ed. Hartford: Conn. State Library, 1978. 18 p.

Turner, Sylvie. "The Connecticut Archives." CHSB 33 (1968): 81-89.

COUNTIES

Levinson, Rosaline. COUNTY GOVERNMENT IN CONNECTICUT: ITS HISTORY AND DEMISE. Storrs: Institute of Public Service, Conn., 1966. 237 p.

See also individual counties in part 2: FAIRFIELD COUNTY, HARTFORD COUNTY, LITCHFIELD COUNTY, MIDDLESEX COUNTY, NEW HAVEN COUNTY, NEW LONDON COUNTY, TOLLAND COUNTY and WINDHAM COUNTY.

COURT AND LEGAL RECORDS

Andrews, Charles McLean. THE CONNECTICUT INTESTACY LAW. Tercentenary Publication, no. 2. New Haven: Yale University Press, 1933. 32 p.

Atwater, Ellen Bessie. "In the Courts of the Kings?" CM 8 (1903): 33-48, 289-96, 475-82.

Bates, Albert Carlos. "Early Connecticut Laws." PAPERS BIBLIOGRAPHICAL SOCIETY OF AMERICA 40 (1946): 151-58.

Capen, Edward Warren. THE HISTORICAL DEVELOPMENT OF THE POOR LAW IN CONNECTICUT. New York: Columbia University Press, 1905. Reprint. New York: AMS Press, 1968. 520 p.

Case, Bert Francis. "Trials in Early Justice Courts in Connecticut." CM 11 (1907): 43-47.

CHECKLIST OF PROBATE RECORDS IN THE CONNECTICUT STATE LIBRARY. Hartford: Conn. State Library, 1976. 19 p.

Connecticut. Judicial Department. HISTORY, ORGANIZATION, OPERATIONS. JUDICIAL DEPARTMENT, STATE OF CONNECTICUT. Hartford, Conn.: 1979. 9 p.

Davis, Ridgway I. "Connecticut Probate Courts Are Slow to Change." NATIONAL CIVIL REVIEW 60 (1971): 204-10.

Eno, Joel Nelson. "First Court Trials in Connecticut." CM 11 (1907): 577-82.

Farrell, John Thomas. THE SUPERIOR COURT DIARY OF WILLIAM SAMUEL JOHNSON 1772-1773 WITH APPROPRIATE RECORDS AND FILE PAPERS OF THE SUPERIOR COURT OF THE COLONY OF CONNECTICUT FOR THE TERMS, DECEMBER 1772, THROUGH MARCH 1773. Washington, D.C.: American Historical Association, 1942. 293 p. Index.

Flaherty, David H. "A Select Guide to the Manuscript Court Records of Colonial New England." AMERICAN JOURNAL OF LEGAL HISTORY 11 (1967): 107-26.

Foote, William Clift. "Portraiture of the Justices of the Supreme Court of Connecticut." CM 12 (1908): 321-23.

Fowler, William Chauncey. LOCAL LAW IN MASSACHUSETTS AND CON-NECTICUT, HISTORICALLY CONSIDERED. Albany, N.Y.: J. Munsell, 1872. Freeport, N.Y.: Books for Libraries Press, 1971. 171 p.

Holdsworth, William K. "LAW AND SOCIETY IN COLONIAL CONNECTICUT, 1636-1672." Ph.D. dissertation, Claremont Graduate School, 1974. 739 p.

Jacobus, Donald Lines. "Connecticut Superior Court Records." TAG 28 (1952): 104-6.

Kirby, Ephraim. REPORTS OF CASES ADJUDGED IN THE SUPERIOR COURT

OF THE STATE OF CONNECTICUT. FROM THE YEAR 1785 TO JANUARY 1789; WITH SOME DETERMINATIONS IN THE SUPREME COURT OF ERRORS. 1898. Reprint. Waterbury, Conn.: Dennis and Co., 1952. 53 p.

Loomis, Dwight and Calhoun, Joseph Gilbert. JUDICIAL AND CIVIL HISTORY OF CONNECTICUT. Boston: Boston History Co., 1895. 639 p.

Maltbie, William M. "Judicial Administration in Connecticut Colony Before the Charter of 1662." CONNECTICUT BAR JOURNAL 23 (1949): 147-58, 228-47.

"Oldest Wills Extant in America." CM 10 (1906): 474.

Prager, Herta, and Price, William W. "A Bibliography on the History of the Courts of the Thirteen Original Colonies, Maine, Ohio and Vermont." AMERICAN JOURNAL OF LEGAL HISTORY 1 (1957): 336-62; 2 (1958): 35-52, 148-54.

RECORDS OF THE JUDICIAL DEPARTMENT (PART A): COURT RECORDS IN THE CONNECTICUT STATE LIBRARY, 1636-1945. Hartford: Conn. State Library, 1977. 39 p.

"Records of the Particular Court of Connecticut 1639-1663." CHS COLLECTIONS 22 (1928): 1-302. (LDS 897, 077).

RECORDS OF THE PARTICULAR COURT OF THE COLONY OF CONNECTI-CUT: ADMINISTRATION OF SIR EDMOND ANDROS: ROYAL GOVERNOR 1687-1688. N.p., 1935. 43 p.

REPORT OF THE SECRETARY OF STATE AND STATE LIBRARIAN TO THE GENERAL ASSEMBLY ON ANCIENT COURT RECORDS. Hartford: Case, Lockwood and Brainard Co., 1889. 38 p.

Ridgway, Davis I. "Connecticut's Court Reorganization: A Move Toward Integration." NATIONAL CIVIC REVIEW 66 (1977): 547-52.

Stevenson, Noel C. "Connecticut Court Reports." TAG 28 (1952): 26-28; 29 (1953): 38-41.

Tomlinson, Richard G. "Probate Records." CN 7 (1974): 334-37.

DIVORCE RECORDS

See also entries under each county in part 2.

Cohn, Henry S. "Connecticut's Divorce Mechanism, 1636-1969." AMERICAN JOURNAL OF LEGAL HISTORY 14 (1970): 35-54.

Divorce and Land Records 1755-1789. (CSL, LDS 1466).

Hartford. CSL, Record Group 16. Box 5. Divorce Records.

ETHNIC GROUPS

General

Hartford. CSL, Record Group 33. WPA ETHNIC GROUPS SURVEY.

Steahr, Thomas E. ETHNIC ATLAS OF CONNECTICUT, 1970. Hartford: American Revolution Bicentennial Commission of Connecticut, 1976. 117 p.

Blacks

Libraries: Prudence Crandall Memorial Museum, Canterbury Green, Canterbury, 06331. (203) 566-3005.

Connecticut Afro-American Historical Society, Inc., 444 Orchard Street, New Haven, 06511 (203) 776-4907. Publishes: DRUM TALK, 1978-- . Bimonthly.

Bingham, Alfred M. "Squatter Settlements of Freed Slaves in New England." CHSB 41 (1976): 65-80.

Brown, Barbara W., and Rose, James M., eds. BLACK ROOTS IN SOUTH-EASTERN CONNECTICUT, 1650-1900. Gale Genealogy and Local History Series, vol. 8. Detroit: Gale Research Co., 1980. 722 p. Index.

Brown, J.E. BLACKS IN CONNECTICUT, A HISTORIC PROFILE. New Haven: Conn. Afro-American Historical Society, 1979.

Buechler, John. "Brace, Bran, and other St. Albans." NEW ENGLAND GALAXY 20 (1978): 35-41.

Buffalo, John, and Clay, Carl. "Black Hartford 1843-1860." Paper for University of Hartford Summer Session, 1972. 39 p.

Comstock, Eliza. "The Bill of Sale of a Negro Slave in 1721." CM 10 (1906): 692.

_____. "The Will of a Negro Slave in 1773." CM 10 (1906): 693.

Donnan, Elizabeth. "The New England Slave Trade After the Revolution." NEQ 3 (1930): 251-78.

Fowler, William Chauncey. THE HISTORICAL STATUS OF THE NEGRO IN CONNECTICUT. Charleston, S.C.: Walker, Evans and Cogswell, 1901. 81 p.

Greene, Lorenzo Johnston. THE NEGRO IN COLONIAL NEW ENGLAND, 1620-1776. New York: Columbia University Press, 1942. 404 p.

_____. "Slave-Holding New England and Its Awakening." JOURNAL OF NEGRO HISTORY 13 (1928): 492-533.

Hill, Isaac J. A SKETCH OF THE 29TH REGIMENT OF CONNECTICUT COLORED TROOPS, GIVING A FULL ACCOUNT OF ITS FORMATION, OF ALL THE BATTLES THROUGH WHICH IT PASSED, AND ITS FINAL DISBAND-MENT. Baltimore: Dougherty, Maquire and Co., 1867. 42 p.

Logan, Gwendolyn Evans. "The Slave in Connecticut During the American Revolution." CHSB 30 (1965): 73-80.

McCarron, Anna T. "Trial of Prudence Crandall for Crime of Educating Negroes in Connecticut." CM 12 (1908): 225-32.

Marcus, Ronald. SERVICE RECORD OF STAMFORD, CONNECTICUT BLACK SOLDIERS DURING THE CIVIL WAR. Stamford: Stamford Historical Society, 1972.

Mitchell, Mary Hewitt. "Slavery in Connecticut and Especially in New Haven." NHCHS PAPERS 10 (1951): 286-312.

Motley, Constance B. "A Letter Taken from Oyster River Quarter Records 1666-1775: Wills of Margaret Willis and George Willard (Both Dated 1780)." JOUR-NAL OF NEGRO HISTORY 61 (1976): 309, 312.

Newton, Alexander Herritage. OUT OF THE BRIARS, AN AUTOBIOGRAPHY AND SKETCH OF THE TWENTY-NINTH REGIMENT, CONNECTICUT VOLUN-TEERS. Philadelphia: African Methodist Episcopal Book Concern, 1910. Re-print. Miami, Fla.: Mnemosyne Publishing Co., 1969. 269 p.

Norton, Frederick Calvin. "Negro Slavery in Connecticut." CM 5 (1899): 320-28.

Platt, Orville H. "Negro Governors." NHCHS Papers 6 (1900): 315-35.

"Prudence Crandall." CM 5 (1899): 386–88.

Rasmussen, James A. "Norwalk, Connecticut, Manumissions." TAG 53 (1977): 9–11.

Rogers, John E. INNER CITY BICENTENNIAL BOOKLET 1776–1976. Hartford: University of Hartford, 1975. 64 p.

Rose, James, and Eichholz, Alice, eds. BLACK GENESIS. Gale Genealogy and Local History Series, vol. 1. Detroit: Gale Research Co., 1978. 200 p. Index.

Rose, James M., and Brown, Barbara. "The Carter Family of Colchester–A Black Genealogical Tapestry." CONNECTICUT ANCESTRY 20 (September 1977): 32–43.

_____. "Genealogical Records of Blacks in Connecticut." CONNECTICUT ANCESTRY 19 (May 1977): 159–64.

_____. TAPESTRY: A LIVING HISTORY OF THE BLACK FAMILY IN SOUTH-EASTERN CONNECTICUT. New London, Conn.: New London Historical Society, 1979. 163 p.

Saunders, Ernest. THE AUTOBIOGRAPHY OF A DUAL AMERICAN: THE LIFE STORY OF A BLACK AMERICAN IN A WHITE SOCIETY. New Haven, Conn.: Connecticut Afro-American Historical Society, 1979. 80 p.

_____. BLACKS IN THE CONNECTICUT NATIONAL GUARD: A PICTORIAL AND CHRONOLOGICAL HISTORY 1870 TO 1919. New Haven: Conn. Afro-American Historical Society, 1977. 96 p.

Small, Edwin W., and Small, Miriam Rossiter. "Prudence Crandall, Champion of Negro Education." NEW ENGLAND QUARTERLY 17 (1944): 506–29.

Smith, Martin H. "Reminiscences of Old Negro Slavery Days." CM 9 (1905): 145–53, 753–63; 10 (1906): 113–28, 319–31.

Stark, Bruce. "Slavery in Connecticut: A Re-Examination." CONNECTICUT REVIEW 9 (November 1975): 75–81.

Steiner, Bernard Christian. HISTORY OF SLAVERY IN CONNECTICUT. Baltimore: Johns Hopkins Press, 1893. 84 p.

Warner, Robert Austin. NEW HAVEN NEGROES, A SOCIAL HISTORY. New Haven: Yale University Press. 309 p.

Weed, Ralph Foster. SLAVERY IN CONNECTICUT. Tercentenery Publication, no. 37. New Haven: Yale University Press, 1935. 32 p.

White, David Oliver. CONNECTICUT'S BLACK SOLDIERS 1775-1783. Connecticut Bicentennial Series, no. 4. Chester: Pequot Press, 1973. 71 p.

_____. "Hartford's African Schools, 1830-1868." CHSB 39 (1974): 47-53.

French

French Guidebook Committee. FRENCH IN CONNECTICUT: A CULTURE AND HISTORICAL GUIDE. Norwalk: American Association of Teachers of French, Connecticut Chapter, 1979. 88 p.

Gingras, Raymond. QUELQUES FRANCOS AU CONNECTICUT: NOTES, REFERENCES ET INDEX DES NECROLOGIES DANS DES JOURNCEUX DE 1963 A 1975. Quebec: N.p., 1976. 189 p.

Ledoux, Albert H. THE FRANCO-AMERICANS OF CONNECTICUT, 1880. N.p.: 1977. 257 p. Index.

Indians

American Indian Archaeological Institute, P.O. Box 260, Washington, D.C., 06793. (203) 868-0518. Publishes ARTIFACTS. Quarterly.

Conn. Archives. Records concerning Connecticut Indians. 2 vols. 1647-1789. (CSL Archives, LDS 48305).

Conn. Archives. Records concerning Connecticut Indians. 2d Series. 2 vols. 1666-1800. (CSL Archives, LDS 48305).

Connecticut Indian Affairs Council. AMERICAN INDIANS IN CONNECTICUT: A REPORT OF A STATEWIDE CENSUS. Hartford: Connecticut Indian Affairs Council, Department of Environmental Protection, 1977. 24 p.

Cook, Sherbourne Friend. THE INDIAN POPULATION OF NEW ENGLAND IN THE SEVENTEENTH CENTURY. Berkeley: University of California Press, 1976. 91 p.

DeForest, John William. HISTORY OF THE INDIANS OF CONNECTICUT FROM THE EARLIEST KNOWN PERIOD TO 1850. Hartford: Hamersley, 1851. 509 p. Index.

Gay, Julius. THE TUNXIS INDIANS. Hartford, Conn.: Case, Lockwood and Brainard, 1901. 21 p.

Guillette, Mary E. AMERICAN INDIANS IN CONNECTICUT: PAST TO PRESENT. Hartford: Connecticut Indian Affairs Council, 1979. 130 p.

Ingersoll, Elinor Houghton Bulkeley. CONNECTICUT CIRCA 1625, ITS INDIANS TRAILS, VILLAGES AND SACHEMDOMS. Wethersfield: Connecticut Society of the Colonial Dames, 1934. 26 p.

Johnson, Philip A. "Land of the Uncas." CANTIQUARIAN 21 (December 1969): 19-23.

Martin, Stanley. "Indian Derivatives in Connecticut Place Names." NEQ 12 (1939): 364-69.

Nelson, Ralph L. "Among the Last of the Mohegans." CONNECTICUT 35 (March 1972): 42-44.

Orcutt, Samuel. INDIANS OF THE HOUSATONIC AND NAUGATUCK VALLEYS. 1882. Reprint. Hartford, Conn.: J.E. Edwards, 1972. 220 p.

Phyfe, R. Eston. "Indians Legends in Connecticut." CM 12 (1908): 63-72.

Rainey, Froelich Gladstone. "A Compilation of Historical Data Contributing to the Ethnography of Connecticut and Southern New England Indians." BULLETIN OF THE ARCHAEOLOGICAL SOCIETY OF CONNECTICUT, April 1936, pp. 3-49.

Smith, Jane T. Hills. LAST OF THE NEHANTICS. East Lyme, Conn.: East Lyme Historical Society, n.d. 17 p.

Spier, John. "A Vindication of the American Aboriginal." CM 11 (1907): 145-49.

Spiess, Mathias. THE INDIANS OF CONNECTICUT. New Haven: Yale University Press, 1933. 33 p.

_____. "Podunck Indian Sites." BULLETIN OF THE ARCHAEOLOGICAL SOCIETY OF CONNECTICUT, December 1936; April 1937; March 1938.

Swigart, Edmund. THE PREHISTORY OF THE INDIANS OF WESTERN CONNECTICUT. Washington, Conn.: American Indian Archaeological Institute, 1974. 49 p.

Vaughan, Alden T. NEW ENGLAND FRONTIER PURITANS AND INDIANS 1620-1675. Boston: Little, Brown and Co., 1965. 430 p. Index.

Williams, Frederick H. "Prehistoric Remains of the Tunxis Valley." CQ 3 (1897): 150-66, 403-23.

Irish

Stone, Frank Andrews. THE IRISH--IN THEIR HOMELAND, IN AMERICA, IN CONNECTICUT. Peoples of Connecticut Multicultural Ethnic Heritage Project, no. 1. Storrs, Conn.: UCONN, 1975. 113 p.

Italian

Carlevale, Joseph William. WHO'S WHO AMONG AMERICANS OF ITALIAN DESCENT IN CONNECTICUT. New Haven, Conn.: Carlevale Pub. Co., 1942. 416 p.

Polish

Slominski, Lynda, and Blejwas, Stanislaus A. THE POLES: IN THEIR HOME-LAND, IN AMERICA, IN CONNECTICUT. Peoples of Connecticut Multicultural Ethnic Heritage Studies Series, no. 6. Storrs: World Education Project, 1980. 222 p.

Scotch-Irish

Stone, Frank Andrews. SCOTS & SCOTCH IRISH IN CONNECTICUT, A HISTORY. Peoples of Connecticut Multicultural Ethnic Heritage Project, no. 5. Storrs, Conn.: UCONN, 1978. 69 p.

GENEALOGICAL RESEARCH

Abbe, Elizabeth. "Connecticut Genealogical Research: Sources and Suggestions." NEHGR 134 (1980): 3-26.

Barlow, Claude W. NEW ENGLAND GENEALOGY: A RESEARCH GUIDE WITH SPECIAL EMPHASIS ON MASSACHUSETTS AND CONNECTICUT. Cleveland: Western Reserve Historical Society, Genealogical Committee, 1976. 28 p.

_____. SOURCES FOR GENEALOGICAL SEARCHING IN CONNECTICUT AND MASSACHUSETTS. Syracuse, N.Y.: Central New York Genealogical Society, 1973. 23 p.

Brush, Clarke. SOURCES OF INFORMATION IN CONNECTICUT. Genealogical Publication, no. 2. Washington, D.C.: National Genealogical Society, 1933. 21 p. Index. (LDS 844, 973).

Case, Margery. "Connecticut Resources for Genealogical Research." NGSQ 36 (1948): 2-4.

"Genealogical Department Index to Notes and Queries." CQ 3 (1897): 503-13; 4 (1898): 426-32; CM 5 (1899): iv-vi; 9 (1905): vi-ix.

Hayward, Kendall. "Know Your Area and Your Working Tools." CONNECTICUT NUTMEGGER 6 (September 1973): 192-95.

Kemp, Thomas Jay. "Basic Connecticut Reference Books for the Genealogist's Home Library." CA 23 (November 1980): 72-73.

Peck, Brainerd T. "Some Connecticut Sources." CN 13 (1980): 187-91.

Roberts, Gary Boyd. "Some Reflections on Modern Connecticut Genealogical Scholarship." CN 12 (1979): 371-85.

Wright, Norman Edgar. GENEALOGY IN AMERICA. Volume 1. MASSACHUSETTS, CONNECTICUT AND MAINE. Salt Lake City, Utah: Deseret Book Co., 1968. 299 p. Index.

GENEALOGICAL SOCIETIES

CONNECTICUT SOCIETY OF GENEALOGISTS, P.O. Box 435, Glastonbury, 06033. (203) 633-4203.

Publishes: CONNECTICUT NUTMEGGER. 1968-- . Quarterly.

Hartford. CSL, Record Group 117. Records of the Society.

Ricker, Jacquelyn L. "Editorial." CN 13 (1980): 2-3.

STAMFORD GENEALOGICAL SOCIETY, P.O. Box 249, Stamford, 06904.

(See STAMFORD--Genealogical Society).

GENERAL

Adams, Arlon Taylor. "The First Written Constitution Known to History." CM 8 (1903): 273-78.

Anderson, Ruth O.M. FROM YANKEE TO AMERICAN: CONNECTICUT 1865-1714. Chester: Pequot Press, 1975. 96 p.

Andrews, Charles McLean. CONNECTICUT AND THE BRITISH GOVERNMENT. New Haven, Conn.: Yale University Press, 1933. 31 p.

_____. CONNECTICUT'S PLACE IN COLONIAL HISTORY. New Haven: Yale University Press, 1924. 49 p.

_____. "On Some Aspects of Connecticut History." NEQ 17 (1944): 3-24.

Atwood, Barbara P. "Connecticut's Lady Historians." NEQ 12 (1970): 32-41.

Babbidge, Homer D., Jr. "The Sorry State of History." ASCH NEWSLETTER, Winter 1980, pp. 1-5.

Bacon, Edwin Munroe. THE CONNECTICUT RIVER AND THE VALLEY OF THE CONNECTICUT. New York: G.P. Putnam's Sons, 1906. Reprint. New York: Johnson Reprint Co., 1970. 487 p.

Bacon, Leonard Woolsey. A DISCOURSE ON THE EARLY CONSTITUTIONAL HISTORY OF CONNECTICUT. Hartford: Case, Tiffany and Burnham, 1843. 24 p.

_____. "Old Times in Connecticut." NEW ENGLANDER 144: 1-31.

Baldwin, Simeon Eben. "The Early History of the Ballot in Connecticut." PAPERS OF THE AMERICAN HISTORICAL ASSOCIATION 4 (1888): 407-22.

Bartlett, Charles J. "Medical Licensure in Connecticut." CONNECTICUT MEDICAL JOURNAL 6 (1942): 182-90.

Bates, Albert Carlos. THE CHARTER OF CONNECTICUT; A STUDY. Hartford: Connecticut Historical Society, 1932. 72 p.

_____. "Connecticut Almanacs of Last Century." CQ 4 (1898): 408-16.

_____. "Expedition of Sir Edmund Andros to Connecticut in 1687." AMERI-CAN ANTIQUARIAN SOCIETY PROCEEDINGS 48 (1939): 276-99.

Beasley, James R. "Emerging Republicanism and the Standing Order: The Appropriation Act Controversy in Connecticut, 1793-1795." WILLIAM AND MARY QUARTERLY 29 (1972): 587-610.

Birdsall, Richard Davenport. "A Federalist View of the Lyon-Griswold Fracas." CANTIQUARIAN 20 (1968): 19-21.

Blakeslee, Philip C. LINES WEST: A BRIEF HISTORY. New Haven: CAMM Associates, 1974. 32 p.

Bomhoff, Carl. "Connecticut, 1817-1850." CONNECTICUT REVIEW 1 (April 1968): 72-84.

Browning, Amos A. "The Mayorality in Connecticut." CM 5 (1899): 27-33.

Buenker, John D. "The Politics of Resistance: The Rural-Based Yankee Republican Machines of Connecticut and Rhode Island." NEQ 47 (1947): 212-37.

Bushman, Richard L. FROM PURITAN TO YANKEE: CHARACTER AND SOCIAL ORDER IN CONNECTICUT, 1690-1765. Cambridge, Mass.: Harvard, 1967. 343 p. Index.

Carlton, William R. "Overland to Connecticut in 1645: A Travel Diary of John Winthrop, Jr." NEQ 13 (1940): 494-510.

Carpenter, William Henry, and Arthur, Timothy Shay. THE HISTORY OF CONNECTICUT, FROM ITS EARLIEST SETTLEMENT TO THE PRESENT TIME. Philadelphia: Lippincott, Grambo and Co., 1854. 287 p.

Casey, Marcus A. "A Typographical Galaxy." CQ 2 (1896): 25-42.

CIVIL OFFICERS RECORDS, 1669-1756, WITH INDEX. (CSL, LDS 1467).

Clark, George Larkin. HISTORY OF CONNECTICUT, ITS PEOPLE AND INSTITUTIONS. New York: Putnam Co., 1914. 609 p.

Clemens, Virginia. "Sarah Knight's Rugged Ride on the Old Post Road." CONNECTICUT 36 (April 1973): 34-35, 64-65.

Cohen, Sheldon S. "Connecticut's Eccentric Historian." NEW ENGLAND GALAXY 13 (1971): 3-14.

Coleman, Roy V. A NOTE CONCERNING THE FORMULATION OF THE FUNDAMENTAL ORDERS UNITING THE THREE RIVER TOWNS OF CONNECTI-CUT, 1639. Westport: Author, 1934. 13 p.

_____. THE OLD PATENT OF CONNECTICUT. Westport: Author, 1936. 56 p.

Collier, Bonnie B. "The Ohio Western Reserve: Its Influence on Political Parties in Connecticut in the Late Eighteenth Century." CONNECTICUT RE-VIEW 9 (November 1975): 50-61.

Connecticut Development Commission. GOVERNMENT ORGANIZATION; AN ANALYSIS OF THE HISTORY AND STRUCTURE OF GOVERNMENT IN CON-NECTICUT. Hartford: Author, 1964. 63 p.

Connecticut State Librarian. "Return of the Trumbull Papers." REPORT OF THE STATE LIBRARIAN, 1922, pp. 14-20.

Crofut, Florence S. Marcy. GUIDE TO THE HISTORY AND HISTORIC SITES OF CONNECTICUT. 2 vols. New Haven: Yale University Press, 1937.

Cutler, William Richard. GENEALOGICAL AND FAMILY HISTORY OF THE STATE OF CONN. 4 vols. New York: Lewis Historical Pub. Co., 1911.

Daniel, Elizabeth Gertrude. "Connecticut at the Paris Exposition." CM 6 (1900): 363-64, 431-37.

Daniels, Bruce Colin. THE CONNECTICUT TOWN: GROWTH AND DEVELOP-MENT, 1635-1790. Middletown: Wesleyan University Press, 1979. 288 p.

_____. "Connecticut's Villages Become Mature Towns: The Complexity of Local Institutions, 1676 to 1776." WILLIAM AND MARY QUARTERLY 34 (1977): 83-103.

_____. "Democracy and Oligarchy in Connecticut Towns: General Assembly Officeholding, 1701-1790." SOCIAL SCIENCE QUARTERLY 56 (1975): 460-76.

_____. "Family Dynasties in Connecticut's Largest Towns, 1700-1760." CANADIAN JOURNAL OF HISTORY 8 (1973): 99-110.

_____. "Large Town Officeholding in Eighteenth-Century Connecticut: The Growth of Oligarchy." JOURNAL OF AMERICAN STUDIES 9 (1975): 1-2.

_____. "Town Government in Connecticut, 1636-1675: The Founding of Institutions." CONNECTICUT REVIEW 9 (November 1975): 39-49.

Delaney, Edmund T. THE CONNECTICUT SHORE. Barre, Mass.: Author, 1969. 120 p.

Deming, Dorothy, and Andrews, Charles McLean. THE SETTLEMENT OF CONNECTICUT TOWNS. New Haven, Conn.: Yale University Press, 1933. 75 p.

Dewey, Melvil. "The Expenses of a Congressman in 1777." CM 10 (1906): 28-32.

DeVito, Michael C. CONNECTICUT'S OLD TIMBERED CROSSINGS. Warehouse Point, Conn.: DeVito Enterprises, 1964. 71 p.

Dexter, Franklin Bowditch. "The History of Connecticut, As Illustrated by the Names of Her Towns." American Antiquarian Society PROCEEDINGS 3 (1885): 421-48.

Dinkin, Robert J. "The Nomination of Governors and Assistants in Colonial Connecticut." CHSB 36 (1971): 92-96.

Dunn, Richard S. "John Winthrop Jr., Connecticut Expansionist: The Failure of His Designs on Long Island 1663-1675." NEQ 29 (1956): 3-26.

Dwight, Theodore. THE HISTORY OF CONNECTICUT FROM THE FIRST SETTLEMENT TO THE PRESENT TIME. New York: Harper, 1841. 450 p.

Emerson, Everett H. "Thomas Hooker and the Reformed Theology: The Relationship of Hooker's Conversion Reaching to Its Background." CHURCH HISTORY 24 (1955): 369-70.

Eno, Joel Nelson. "The Conquest for Land--Connecticut's Changes and Exchanges of Territory." CM 10 (1906): 475-82.

Everest, Charles William. THE POETS OF CONNECTICUT. Hartford: Case, Tiffany and Burnham, 1843. Reprint. Freeport, N.Y.: Books for Libraries, 1973. 468 p.

FAMILY RECORDS (HERETOFORE UNPUBLISHED). Hartford, Conn.: Chapter of the National Society Daughters of Founders and Patriots of America, 1935. 305 p.

Fanshaw, William. "First Impressions or Memoranda on the Road During a Short Trip from New York to Montreal, and Returning, from August 14 to 27, 1840." CANTIQUARIAN 25 (1973): 12-23.

"The Fitch Papers." Thomas Fitch, Governor 1754-1766. CHS COLLECTIONS, vols. 17 and 18. (LDS 897, 074- 897, 075).

Fowler, David H. "Connecticut's Freemen: The First Forty Years." WILLIAM AND MARY QUARTERLY 15 (1958): 312-33.

Fox, Douglas M. "Reorganizing Connecticut State Government." STATE GOVERNMENT 52, no. 2 (1979): 80-84.

Freer, W.D. "Golf Clubs in Connecticut." CM 6 (1900): 254-84.

Frost, Jerry William. CONNECTICUT EDUCATION IN THE REVOLUTIONARY ERA. Chester: Pequot Press, 1974. 59 p.

Gilman, Daniel Coit. THE CHARITIES AND REFORMATORIES OF CONNECTI-CUT. New Haven, Conn.: Tuttle, Morehouse and Taylor, 1870. 40 p.

Gocher, William Henry. WADSWORTH ON THE CHARTER OAK. Hartford: W.H. Gocher, 1904. 399 p.

Gold, T.S. "Notes on Forestry in Connecticut." CQ 4 (1898): 372-75.

Goodwin, Nathaniel. GENEALOGICAL NOTES; OR CONTRIBUTIONS TO THE FAMILY HISTORY OF SOME OF THE FIRST SETTLERS OF CONNECTICUT AND MASSACHUSETTS. Baltimore: Genealogical Pub. Co., 1969. 362 p.

Griswold, Harlan H. "The Care and Feeding of Connecticut History." ASCH NEWSLETTER, Winter 1980, pp. 5-11.

Haffenden, Philip S. "The Crown and the Colonial Charters, 1675-1688." WILLIAM AND MARY QUARTERLY 15 (1958): 297-311, 452-66.

Hale, Edward Everett. "Edward Everett Hale's Memoirs of Connecticut." CM 10 (1906): 413-21.

HANDBOOK FOR CONNECTICUT TOWN CLERKS. Storrs: Institute of Public Service, Conn., 1979. 104 p.

Hard, Walter F. THE CONNECTICUT RIVER. New York: Rinehart, 1947. 310 p.

Harder, Peter J. "Politics, Efficiency and Rural Schools in Connecticut, 1866-1919." CHS 44 (1979): 52-60.

Hawes, Austin F. "The Forests of Connecticut." CM 10 (1906): 260-70.

Haynes, Williams. "Connecticut's Own Major." CANTIQUARIAN 7 (1955): 8-19.

Heath, Frederick Morrison. "Change and Response in Connecticut: 1800-1850." CANTIQUARIAN 19 (1967): 20-27.

_____. "Politics and Steady Habits: Issues and Elections in Connecticut, 1894-1914." Ph.D. dissertation, Columbia University, 1965. 329 p.

Hickey, Donald R. "New England's Defense Problem and the Genesis of the Hartford Convention." NEQ 50 (1977): 587-604.

Hildebrandt, Bary, and Hildebrandt, Susan H. COASTAL CONNECTICUT, EASTERN REGION. Old Saybrook, Conn.: Peregrine Press, 1979. 114 p. Index.

Hill, Evan, et al. THE CONNECTICUT RIVER. Middletown: Wesleyan University Press, 1972. 142 p.

Hill, G. Albert. "Colonial Milestones Along Connecticut Highways." CANTIQUARIAN 2 (1950): 15-19.

Hinman, Royal Ralph. A CATALOGUE OF THE EARLY PURITAN SETTLERS OF THE COLONY OF CONNECTICUT. Hartford: Case, Tiffany and Co., 1852. Reprint. Baltimore, Md.: Genealogical Publishing Co., 1968. 336 p.

_____. LETTERS FROM THE ENGLISH KINGS AND QUEENS; CHARLES II, JAMES II, WILLIAM AND MARY, ANNE, GEORGE II, ETC. TO THE GOVERNORS OF THE COLONY OF CONNECTICUT, TOGETHER WITH THE ANSWERS THERETO, FROM 1635 TO 1749. Hartford, Conn.: J.B. Eldredge, 1836. 372 p.

Hoadley, Charles Jeremy. PUBLIC RECORDS OF THE COLONY OF CON-
NECTICUT 1689-1776. 15 vols. Hartford: Case, Lockwood and Brainard,
1868-1890. (LDS 908, 423-908, 426).

_____. PUBLIC RECORDS OF THE STATE OF CONNECTICUT, 1776-1803.
11 vols. Hartford: Case, Lockwood and Brainard, Co., 1894. (LDS 844,
827-44, 828).

_____. THE THREE CONSTITUTIONS OF CONNECTICUT, 1638-9, 1662,
1818. WITH NOTES ON TOWN REPRESENTATION. Hartford, Conn.: Case,
Lockwood and Brainard, Co., 1901. 128 p.

Holcombe, Harold G. "Stone Walls in Eastern Connecticut." CANTIQUARIAN
2 (1950): 24-31.

Hollister, Gideon Hiram. HISTORY OF CONNECTICUT, FROM THE FIRST
SETTLEMENT OF THE COLONY TO THE ADOPTION OF THE PRESENT CON-
STITUTION. 2 vols. New Haven: Durrie and Reck, 1855. (LDS 599,297).

Holman, Mabel Cassine. "Along the Connecticut River." CM 11 (1907):
561-67.

Hooper, Marion. LIFE ALONG THE CONNECTICUT RIVER. Brattleboro, Vt.:
Stephen Daye Press, 1939. 120 p.

Ives, Joel S. "The Foreigner in New England." CM 9 (1905): 244-56.

Janick, Herbert F., Jr. A DIVERSE PEOPLE: CONNECTICUT 1914 TO THE
PRESENT. Chester: Pequot Press, 1975. 124 p. Index.

_____. "Government for the People: The Leadership of the Progressive Party
in Connecticut." Ph.D. dissertation, Fordham University, 1968. 330 p.

Jefferies, John W. TESTING THE ROOSEVELT COALITION: CONNECTICUT
SOCIETY AND POLITICS IN THE ERA OF WORLD WAR II. Knoxville: University of Tennessee Press, 1979. 312 p. Index.

Jenkins, E.H. "The Growing of Tobacco in Connecticut." CM 9 (1905):
336-48.

Jodziewicz, Thomas. "Dual Localism in Seventeenth-Century Connecticut:
Relations Between the General Court and the Towns, 1636-1691." Ph.D.
dissertation, College of William and Mary, 1974. 365 p.

"John Cotton Smith Papers. Lt. Governor, Acting Governor and Governor of Conn." CHS COLLECTIONS, vol. 25. (LDS 897, 077).

Johnston, Alexander. CONNECTICUT: A STUDY OF A COMMONWEALTH DEMOCRACY. Boston: Houghton Mifflin, 1887. 409 p.

_____. THE GENESIS OF A NEW ENGLAND STATE. Baltimore: Johns Hopkins University, 1882. 29 p.

Jones, Edward Payson. THREE HUNDRED EARLY FAMILIES OF CONNECTICUT. Typescript. Winsted: N.p., n.d. (LDS 1456).

Jones, Mary Jeanne Anderson. CONGREGATIONAL COMMONWEALTH CONNECTICUT, 1636-1662. Middletown: Wesleyan University Press, 1968. 233 p. Index.

Jordan, Philip H., Jr. "Connecticut Politics During the Revolution and Confederation." Ph.D. dissertation, Yale University, 1962.

Kellogg, Joseph M. SOME CONNECTICUT FAMILIES. 12 vols. Hartford: Conn. State Library. (LDS 002, 997-002,998).

Kihn, Phylis. "The Value Family in Connecticut." CHSB 34 (1969): 79-93.

Klein, Woody. "335 Years of Town Meetings." CONNECTICUT 36 (July 1973): 22-24, 60.

Lane, Jarlath Robert. "A Political History of Connecticut During the Civil War." Ph.D. dissertation, Catholic University of America, 1941. 321 p.

"The Law Papers. Governor Jonathan Law 1741-1750." CHS COLLECTIONS, vols. 11, 13, 15. (LDS 897, 071-899,073).

Lawrence, Henry W. "Connecticut's Rotten Burroughs." YANKEE 2 (July 1936): 31-33.

Lee, William Storrs. THE YANKEES OF CONNECTICUT. New York: Holt and Co., 1957. 301 p.

Lewis, Thomas Reed, Jr. "From Suffield to Saybrook: An Historical Geography of the Connecticut River Valley in Connecticut Before 1800." Ph.D. dissertation, Rutgers University, 1978. 255 p.

Lucas, Paul R. VALLEY OF DISCORD: CHURCH AND SOCIETY ALONG THE CONNECTICUT RIVER: 1636-1725. Hanover, N.H.: University Press of New England, 1976. 275 p. Index.

Main, Jackson Turner. CONNECTICUT SOCIETY IN THE ERA OF THE AMERICAN REVOLUTION. Conn. Bicentennial Series, vol. 21. Hartford: American Revolution Bicentennial Commission of Conn., 1977. 83 p. Index.

Mann, Bruce Hartling. "Parishes, Law, and Community in Connecticut, 1700-1760." Ph.D. dissertation, Yale University, 1977. 224 p.

Miller, Perry Gilbert. "Thomas Hooker and the Democracy of Early Connecticut." NEQ 4 (1941): 663-712.

Mills, Lewis Sprague. THE STORY OF CONNECTICUT. West Rindge, N.H.: R.R. Smith, 1958. 497 p.

Mills, William Stowell. THE STORY OF THE WESTERN RESERVE OF CONNECTICUT. New York: Brown and Wilson, 1900. 141 p.

Mitchell, Isabel Stewart. ROADS AND ROAD-MAKING IN COLONIAL CONNECTICUT. Tercentenary Publication, no. 14. New Haven: Yale University Press, 1933. 32 p.

Markham, Francis G. "Volcanic and Seismic Disturbances in Southern Connecticut." CM 9 (1905): 68-74.

Morgan, Edmund S. THE PURITAN DILEMMA: THE STORY OF JOHN WINTHROP. Boston: Little, Brown and Co., 1958. 224 p. Index.

Morgan, Forest. CONNECTICUT AS A COLONY AND AS A STATE. 4 vols. Hartford: Publishing Society of Conn., 1904.

Morse, Jarvis Means. A NEGLECTED PERIOD OF CONNECTICUT'S HISTORY 1818-1850. New Haven: Yale University Press, 1933. Reprint. New York: Octagon Books, 1970. 359 p.

_____. THE RISE OF LIBERALISM IN CONNECTICUT, 1828-1850. New Haven, Conn.: Yale University Press, 1933. 45 p.

_____. UNDER THE CONSTITUTION OF 1818. THE FIRST DECADE. New Haven, Conn.: Yale University Press, 1933. 20 p.

Murray, Mary. "Connecticut's Depression Governor: Wilbur L. Cross." CONNECTICUT HISTORY 16 (August 1975): 44-64.

Niles, John Milton. THE CONNECTICUT CIVIL OFFICER. Hartford: Huntington and Savage, 1847. 368 p.

Noonan, Carroll John. "Nativism in Connecticut, 1829-1860." Ph.D. dissertation, Catholic University of America, 1935. 351 p.

Norton, Frederick Calvin. THE GOVERNORS OF CONNECTICUT. Hartford: Conn. Magazine, 1905. 385 p.

Nutting, Parker Bradley. "Charter and Crown: Relations of Connecticut with the British Government, 1662-1776." Ph.D. dissertation, University of North Carolina, 1972. 522 p.

Osborn, Norris Galpin. HISTORY OF CONNECTICUT IN MONOGRAPHIC FORM. 5 vols. New York: States History Co., 1925.

Peck, Ellen Brainerd. "Early Text Books in Connecticut." CM 4 (1898): 61-72.

Peirce, Neal R. THE NEW ENGLAND STATES: PEOPLE, POLITICS AND POWER IN THE SIX NEW ENGLAND STATES. New York: W.W. Norton, 1976. 447 p. Index.

Perry, Charles Edward. FOUNDATIONS FOR EDUCATIONAL LEADERSHIP: CONNECTICUT DEVELOPS A PUBLIC SCHOOL SYSTEM 1636-1876. Hartford: Association of Retired Teachers of Connecticut, 1976. 84 p. Index.

_____. HISTORY OF THE ASSOCIATION OF RETIRED TEACHERS OF CONNECTICUT, 1946-1976. Manchester: Association of Retired Teachers of Connecticut, 1976. 40 p.

Peters, Samuel. GENERAL HISTORY OF CONNECTICUT, FROM ITS FIRST SETTLEMENT UNDER GEORGE FENWICK TO ITS LATEST PERIOD OF AMITY WITH GREAT BRITAIN PRIOR TO THE REVOLUTION. Freeport, N.Y.: Books for Libraries, 1969. 285 p.

Pettit, Norman. "Hooker's Doctrine of Assurance: A Critical Phase in New England Spiritual Thought." NEQ 47 (1974): 518-34.

"Pitkin Papers. William Pitkins, Governor." CHS COLLECTIONS, vol. 19, 1921. (LDS 897,075).

Porter, Noah. "Memoir of the Honorable William H. Buckingham, LLD." NEHGR 30 (1876): 9-15.

Poteet, James Mark. "Preserving the Old Ways: Connecticut, 1690-1770." Master's thesis, University of Virginia, 1973. 465 p.

_____. "Unrest in the Land of Steady Habits, The Hartford Riot of 1722." PROCEEDINGS OF THE AMERICAN PHILOSOPHICAL SOCIETY 119 (1975): 223-32.

Purcell, Richard Joseph. CONNECTICUT IN TRANSITION, 1775-1818. Washington, D.C.: American Historical Association, 1918. 471 p. Index.

Pynchon, W.H.C. "The Ancient Lavas of Connecticut." CQ 2 (1896): 309-19.

_____. "Some Common Evidences of Glacial Action in Connecticut." CQ 4 (1898): 294-303.

Rathbun, Julius G. "The 'Wide Awakes,' The Great Political Organization of 1860." CQ 1 (1895): 327-35.

Rossiter, Clinton. "Thomas Hooker." NEQ 25 (1952): 459-88.

Roth, David Morris, and Meyer, Freeman. FROM REVOLUTION TO CONSTITUTION: CONNECTICUT 1763 TO 1818. Chester: Pequot Press, 1975. 111 p. Index.

Sanford, Elias Benjamin. A HISTORY OF CONNECTICUT. Hartford: S.S. Scranton, 1922. 450 p.

Schmitt, Dale Joseph. "The Response to Social Problems in Seventeenth Century Connecticut." Master's thesis, University of Kansas, 1970. 306 p.

Schneck, Elizabeth Hubbell. "The Duty of a Politician in Early America." CM 11 (1907): 601-7.

Seymour, Jack M. SHIPS, SAILORS AND SAMARITANS: THE WOMEN'S SEAMEN'S FRIEND SOCIETY OF CONNECTICUT, 1859-1976. New Haven: Eastern Press, 1976. 157 p. Index.

Shepard, Odell. CONNECTICUT, PAST AND PRESENT. New York: Knopf, 1939. 316 p. Reprint. St. Clair Shores, Mich.: Scholarly Press, 1973.

Skauen, Deborah W. "Connecticut-Massachusetts Political Relations, 1635-1662." Masters thesis, Tufts University, 1969.

Sprunger, Keith L. "The Dutch Career of Thomas Hooker." NEQ 46 (1973): 17-44.

Squire, Walter Thomas. CHARITIES AND CORRECTIONS IN CONNECTICUT. Conn. Tercentenary Pub., no. 57. New Haven: Yale University Press, 1936. 29 p.

Steiner, Bernard Christian. "Connecticut's Ratification of the Federal Constitution." American Antiquarian Society PROCEEDINGS 25 (1915): 1-60.

_____. THE HISTORY OF EDUCATION IN CONNECTICUT. Washington, D.C.: GPO, 1893. 300 p.

Stone, George M. "Work for the Blind in Connecticut." CM 5 (1899): 171-82.

Sutherland, John, and Tenzer, Morton. "Oral History in Connecticut: The State of the Art." CONNECTICUT HISTORY 15 (1975): 9-18.

"The Talcott Papers. Joseph Talcott, Governor 1724-1741." CHS COLLECTIONS, vols. 4 and 5. (LDS 897,069).

Taylor, Robert Joseph. COLONIAL CONNECTICUT: A HISTORY. Millwood, N.Y.: KTD Press, 1979. 285 p. Index.

THIS WAS CONNECTICUT. Boston: Little, Brown, 1977. 222 p.

Thomas, Edmund B. "Politics in the Land of Steady Habits: Connecticut's First Political Party System." Ph.D. dissertation, Clark University, 1972. 330 p.

Todd, Charles Burr. IN OLDE CONNECTICUT; BEING A RECORD OF QUAINT CURIOUS AND ROMANTIC HAPPENINGS THERE IN COLONIE [SIC] TIMES AND LATER. New York: Grafton Press, 1906. Reprint. Detroit, Mich.: Singing Tree Press, 1968. 244 p.

Trecker, Janice Law. PREACHERS, REBELS AND TRADERS: CONNECTICUT 1818-1865. Chester: Pequot Press, 1975. 95 p. Index.

Trumbull, Benjamin. A COMPLETE HISTORY OF CONNECTICUT, CIVIL AND ECCLESIASTICAL, FROM THE EMIGRATION OF ITS FIRST PLANTERS, FROM ENGLAND, IN THE YEAR 1630, TO THE YEAR 1764: AND TO THE CLOSE OF THE INDIAN WARS. WITH APPENDIX CONTAINING THE PATENT OF NEW ENGLAND. 2 vols. New London: H.D. Utley, 1898. (LDS 873,944).

Tucker, Louis Leonard. PURITAN PROTAGONIST: PRESIDENT THOMAS CLAP OF YALE COLLEGE. Chapel Hill: University of North Carolina Press, 1962. 283 p.

Tuttle, Sam. SAM TUTTLE'S PICTURE BOOK OF OLD CONNECTICUT. Scotia, N.Y.: Americana Review, 1979. 133 p. Index.

Vail, J.H. "Connecticut at the Atlanta Exposition." CQ 2 (1896): 342-58.

Van Dusen, Albert Edward. CONNECTICUT. New York: Random House, 1961. 470 p. Index.

_____. "John Winthrop, Jr.: Connecticut's Most Versatile Colonial Leader." CANTIQUARIAN 15 (1963): 7-17.

_____. PURITANS AGAINST THE WILDERNESS: CONNECTICUT HISTORY TO 1763. Chester: Pequot Press, 1975. 150 p. Index.

Vaughan, Alden T. NEW ENGLAND FRONTIER PURITANS AND INDIANS 1620-1675. Boston: Little, Brown and Co., 1965. 430 p. Index.

Wallerstein, Mrs. Henry. "Woman's Education in Connecticut." CM 5 (1899): 97-98.

Warner, George H. "The Connecticut Children's Aid Society." CM 6 (1900): 514-21.

Weaver, Glenn. JONATHAN TRUMBULL: CONNECTICUT'S MERCHANT MAGISTRATE, 1710-1785. Hartford: CHS, 1956. 182 p.

Welles, Edwin Stanley. "Times for Holding the Annual Town Meeting of Election in Connecticut." CM 7 (1901): 146-49.

Welles, Roger. "Constitutional History of Connecticut." CM 5 (1899): 86-93, 159-62.

Welling, James Clark. CONNECTICUT FEDERALISM OR ARISTOCRATIC POLITICS IN A SOCIAL DEMOCRACY. New York: New York Historical Society, 1890. 43 p.

Whiton, L.E. "Aristocracy Versus Democracy; The Struggle for Supremacy." CM 9 (1905): 33-48.

"Wolcott Papers. Roger Wolcott, Governor 1750-1754." CHS COLLECTIONS, vol. 16.

Woodbridge, Robert L. "Wilbur Cross: New Deal Ambassador to a Yankee Culture." NEQ 41 (1968): 323-40.

Zeichner, Oscar. CONNECTICUT'S YEARS OF CONTROVERSY, 1750-1776. Williamsburg, Va.: University of North Carolina Press, 1949. Reprint. Hamden, Conn.: Archon Books, 1970. 404 p.

HISTORICAL SOCIETIES

ANTIQUARIAN AND LANDMARKS SOCIETY INC. OF CONNECTICUT, 394 Main Street, Hartford, 06103. (203) 247-8996.

Publishes: THE CONNECTICUT ANTIQUARIAN. 1949-- . Semiannual. Cumulative Index for Vols. 1-20.

ASSOCIATION FOR THE STUDY OF CONNECTICUT HISTORY. Patricia Bodak, Membership Chairman. Yale University Library, Box 1603A, Yale Station, New Haven, 06520.

Publishes: ASCH NEWSLETTER. October 1977-- . Frequency varies.

CONNECTICUT HISTORY. 1967-- . Frequency varies; now issued annually.

CONNECTICUT HISTORICAL COMMISSION. 59 South Prospect Street, Hartford, 06106. (203) 506-3005.

> Morris, William J. "The Grants-in-Aid Program of the Connecticut Historical Commission." CANTIQUARIAN 20 (June 1968): 17-18.
>
> Roth, Matt. "Connecticut Historical Commission." LEAGUE BULLETIN 31 (June 1979): 8, 18.

CONNECTICUT HISTORICAL SOCIETY. 1 Elizabeth Street, Hartford, 06105. (203) 236-5621.

> Publishes: CHS ANNUAL REPORT. 1890-- . Annual.
>
> CHS BULLETIN. 1934-- . Quarterly.
>
> CHS COLLECTIONS. 1860-1932.
>
> HISTORICAL NOTICES OF CONNECTICUT. 1842. Papers and Reports. Vol. 1-- . 1909-- .
>
> Barnard, Henry. "An Account of the Society." AMERICAN QUARTERLY REGISTER 13 (1841): 284-92.
>
> "List of Bound Newspapers in the Connecticut Historical Society." CHS PAPERS AND REPORTS (1893): 30-34.

CONNECTICUT LEAGUE OF HISTORICAL SOCIETIES. P.O. Box 906, Darien, 06820.

> Publishes: CONNECTICUT LEAGUE OF HISTORICAL SOCIETIES BULLE-
> TIN. 1949-- . Quarterly. (Name changed to LEAGUE BULLETIN, Vol.
> 10, No. 1, January 1958).

> Wood, Ella F. "The Connecticut League of Historical Societies."
> HISTORY NEWS 20 (1965): 221-23.

CONNECTICUT TRUST FOR HISTORIC PRESERVATION. 152 Temple Street,
New Haven, Conn. 06510. (203) 562-6312.

Publishes: CONNECTICUT PRESERVATION. 3/year. July 1978-- .

LAND RECORDS

COLONIAL LAND RECORDS 1640-1846. (CSL, LDS 1480).

Humason, H. Monroe. "The Story of the Ownership of Land." NEW CANAAN
HISTORICAL SOCIETY ANNUAL, 1949, pp. 46-61.

LAND LOTTERIES AND DIVORCES, 1755-1789. (CSL, LDS 1466).

Mead, Nelson Prentiss. "Land System of Connecticut Towns." POLITICAL
SCIENCE QUARTERLY 21 (1906): 59-76.

Rosenberg, John S. "Preserving Farmland." BLAIR & KETCHUM'S COUNTY
JOURNAL 6, no. 2 (1979): 68-76.

LIBRARIES

THE CHURCH OF JESUS CHRIST OF LATTER-DAY SAINTS--BRANCH GENEA-
LOGICAL LIBRARIES.

> MANCHESTER. Hartford Stake. 30 Woodside Avenue, Manchester, 06040.
> (203) 649-6547.

> NEW CANAAN. New Canaan Ward. South Avenue, New Canaan, 06820.
> (203) 966-1305.

CONNECTICUT STATE LIBRARY. 231 Capitol Avenue, Hartford, 06115. (203)
566-3056.

> CHECKLIST OF PROBATE RECORDS IN THE CONNECTICUT STATE
> LIBRARY. Hartford: Conn. State Library, 1976. 19 p.

Claus, Robert. GUIDE TO ARCHIVES IN THE CONNECTICUT STATE LIBRARY. 2d ed. Hartford: Conn. State Library, 1978. 18 p.

LAYING OF THE CORNER-STONE OF THE CONNECTICUT STATE LIBRARY AND SUPREME COURT BUILDING AT HARTFORD, MAY 25, 1909. Hartford, Conn.: The State, 1909. 39 p.

LIST OF CHURCH RECORDS IN THE CONNECTICUT STATE LIBRARY. Hartford: Conn. State Library, 1976. 35 p.

RECORDS OF THE JUDICIAL DEPARTMENT (PART A): COURT RECORDS IN THE CONNECTICUT STATE LIBRARY, 1936-1945. Hartford: Conn. State Library, 1977. 39 p.

Woods, Barry. GUIDE TO PICTORIAL ARCHIVES IN THE CONNECTICUT STATE LIBRARY. Hartford: Connecticut State Library, 1977. 31 p. Index.

Connecticut Library Association. CONNECTICUT LIBRARY ATLAS. Hartford: Conn. Library Assn., 1976. 126 p. Index.

"Cozy Corners in Public Libraries." CM 9 (1905): 386-88.

Hewins, Caroline M. "The Development of the Public Library in Connecticut and the Work of the Connecticut Public Library Committee." CM 9 (1905): 161-84.

LOYALISTS

Bates, Walter. KINGSTON AND THE LOYALISTS OF THE "SPRING FLEET" OF 1783 WITH REMINISCENCES OF EARLY DAYS IN CONNECTICUT. 1889. Reprint. Fredericton, N.B.: Non-Entity Press, 1980. 32 p.

Cohen, Sheldon S. CONNECTICUT'S LOYALISTS GADFLY: THE REVEREND SAMUEL ANDREW PETERS. Conn. Revolutionary Series, vol. 17. Chester: Pequot Press, 1976. 66 p.

East, Robert Abraham. CONNECTICUT'S LOYALISTS. Conn. Bicentennial Series, no. 6. Chester: Pequot Press, 1974. 54 p.

Farnham, Thomas J. "Mercantilism and the Rehabilitation of the Loyalists." CR 2 (April 1969): 76-83.

Gipson, Lawrence Henry. JARED INGERSOLL; A STUDY OF AMERICAN LOYALISM IN RELATION TO THE BRITISH COLONIAL GOVERNMENT. New York: Russell and Russell, 1969. 432 p.

Gilbert, George A. "Connecticut Loyalists." AMERICAN HISTORICAL RE-
VIEW 4 (1899): 273-91.

Hogan, Neil. "A Loyalist Execution." NEW ENGLAND GALAXY 20 (1978):
52-60.

Jarvis, Charles M. "An America's Experience in the British Army, Manuscript
of Colonel Stephen Jarvis, Born in 1756 in Danbury, Connecticut." CM 11
(1907): 191-215, 477-90.

Larned, Ellen D. "A Revolutionary Boycott (July 16, 1774)." CQ 1 (1895):
153-54.

Lawson, Harvey M. "My Country is Wrong--Tragedy of Colonel Joshua Chandler."
CM 10 (1906): 287-92.

"A Letter from a Repentant Royalist. London, April 13, 1784." CQ 1 (1895):
271-73.

Manners, William. "Tory or Rebel?" FAIRFIELD COUNTY 5 (December
1975): 62-63, 126-31.

Mather, Frederick Gregory. REFUGEES OF 1776 FROM LONG ISLAND TO CON-
NECTICUT. Albany, N.Y.: J.B. Lyon, 1913. 1,204 p. (LDS 164, 690).

Olson, Virginia H. "Notes and Sources: Connecticut Loyalists Who Went to
Canada." CA 17 (1974): 18-25, 51-59.

Peck, Epaphroditus. "Loyal to the Crown Moses Dunbar, Tory and His Fidelity
to Church and King--Executed for Treason." CM 8 (1903): 129-36, 297-300.

_____. LOYALISTS OF CONNECTICUT. Conn. Tercentenary Publication,
no. 31. New Haven: Yale University Press, 1934. 32 p.

Shepard, James. "Tories of Connecticut." CQ 4 (1898): 139-51, 257-63.

Siebert, Wilbur Henry. "The Refugee Loyalists of Connecticut." ROYAL
SOCIETY OF CANADA: TRANSACTIONS Series 3, 10 (1916): 75-92.

Tebbenhoff, Edward H. "The Associated Loyalists: An Aspect of Militant
Loyalism." NEW YORK HISTORICAL SOCIETY QUARTERLY 63 (1979): 115-44.

Tyler, John W. CONNECTICUT LOYALISTS: AN ANALYSIS OF LOYALIST
LAND CONFISCATIONS IN GREENWICH, STAMFORD AND NORWALK. New
Orleans: Polyanthos Press, 1977. 135 p.

Villers, David Henry. "Loyalism in Connecticut, 1763-1783." Ph.D. dissertation, University of Conn., 1976. 489 p.

Welton, X. Alansen. "The First Political Disturbances in Connecticut--The Tory Agitation." CM 12 (1908): 113-21.

Zeichner, Oscar. "The Rehabilitation of Loyalists in Connecticut." NEQ 11 (1938): 308-30.

MAPS, GAZETTEERS, AND RELATED MATERIALS

Allen, Morse S. "Connecticut Places Names." CANTIQUARIAN 15 (December 1963): 20-24.

Allen, Morse S., and Hughes, Arthur H. "More on Connecticut Place Names." CANTIQUARIAN 21 (December 1969): 13-18.

"Connecticut Villes." CHSB 35 (1970): 33-64.

Dexter, Franklin Bowditch. "The History of Connecticut, as Illustrated by the Names of her Towns." American Antiquarian Society PROCEEDINGS 3 (1885): 421-98.

Eno, Joel Nelson. "Ancient Place-Names in Connecticut." CM 12 (1908): 93-96.

_____. "The Nomenclature of Connecticut Towns." CM 8 (1903): 330-35; CN 13 (1980): 198-203.

Friis, Herman R. "A Series of Population Maps of the Colonies and the United States, 1625-1790." GEOGRAPHICAL REVIEW 30 (1945): 463-70.

Gannett, Henry. A GEOGRAPHIC DICTIONARY OF CONNECTICUT AND RHODE ISLAND. Baltimore: Genealogical Publishing Co., 1978. 98 p.

Hawley, Charles W. "Old Names of Connecticut Towns." BULLETIN OF THE STAMFORD GENEALOGICAL SOCIETY 3 (1961): 61-63.

Hooker, Roland Mather. BOUNDARIES OF CONNECTICUT. Conn. Tercentenary Commission Publication, no. 11. New Haven: Yale University Press, 1933. 38 p.

Hughes, Arthur H., and Allen, Morse S. CONNECTICUT PLACE NAMES. Hartford: CHS, 1976. 907 p.

LAND OWNERSHIP MAPS: A CHECKLIST OF NINETEENTH CENTURY UNITED STATES COUNTY MAPS IN THE LIBRARY OF CONGRESS. Washington, D.C.: Library of Congress, 1967. 86 p. Index.

Martin, Stanley. "Indian Derivatives in Connecticut Place-Names." NEQ 12 (June 1939): 364-69.

Montgomery, Marshall H. "The Oblong." NEW CANAAN HISTORICAL SOCIETY ANNUAL, 1951, pp. 24-32.

Pease, John Chauncey, and Niles, John Milton. A GAZETTEER OF THE STATES OF CONNECTICUT AND RHODE ISLAND. Hartford: William S. Marsh, 1819. 389 p.

Sellers, Helen Earle. CONNECTICUT TOWN ORIGINS: THEIR NAMES, BOUNDARIES, EARLY HISTORIES AND FIRST FAMILIES. Chester: Pequot Press, 1973. 96 p.

Smith, Allen. CONNECTICUT: A THEMATIC ATLAS. Berlin: Atlas Pub., 1974. 90 p.

Speck, Frank Goldsmith, ed. "Geographical Names and Legends at Mohegan." In U.S. BUREAU OF AMERICAN ETHNOLOGY. ANNUAL REPORT, 1925-26, pp. 253-59.

STORY OF ONE CORNER OF CONNECTICUT IN SIXTEEN MAPS. Mystic: Mystic River Historical Society and the Groton Bicentennial Committee, 1976. 16 p.

Thompson, Edmund Burke. MAPS OF CONNECTICUT BEFORE THE YEAR 1800. Windham: Hawthorn House, 1940. 66 p.

_____. MAPS OF CONNECTICUT FOR THE YEARS OF THE INDUSTRIAL REVOLUTION 1801-1860. Windham: Hawthorn House, 1942. 111 p.

Trumbull, James Hammond. INDIAN NAMES OF PLACES, ETC. IN AND ON THE BORDERS OF CONNECTICUT: WITH INTERPRETATIONS OF SOME OF THEM. Hartford: Case, Lockwood and Brainard Co., 1881. 93 p.

Tyler, Clarice E. "Topographical Terms in the Seventeenth Century Records of Connecticut and Rhode Island." NEQ 2 (1929): 382-401.

Victor, Alexander O. "Some Connecticut Maps." CANTIQUARIAN 5 (December 1953): 16-22.

Wright, Henry Andrew. "Some Vagaries in Connecticut Valley Indian Place Names." NEQ 12 (1939): 535-44.

MIGRATION RECORDS

Baldwin, Simeon Eben. "Connecticut in Pennsylvania." NEW HAVEN COLONY HISTORICAL SOCIETY PAPERS 8 (1914): 1-19.

_____. THE SECESSION OF SPRINGFIELD FROM CONNECTICUT. Cambridge, Mass.: John Wilson and Son, 1908. 82 p.

Boyd, Julian Parks. "Connecticut's Experiment in Expansion: The Susquehannah Company, 1753-1803." JOURNAL OF ECONOMICS AND BUSINESS HISTORY 4 (November 1931): 38-69.

Boyd, Julian Parks, and Taylor, Robert Joseph. THE SUSQUEHANNAH COMPANY PAPERS. 11 vols. Ithaca, N.Y.: Cornell University Press, 1962-70.

Brady, James Edward. "Wyoming: A Study of John Franklin and the Connecticut Settlement into Pennsylvania." Ph.D. dissertation, Syracuse University, 1973. 329 p.

Coddington, John Isley. "The Migrations Into and Out of Connecticut During the Colonial Period." CA 15 (1973): 91-97, 125-27.

Collier, Bonne B. "The Ohio Western Reserve: Its Influence on Political Parties in Connecticut in the Late Eighteenth Century." CR 9 (November 1975): 50-61.

"Connecticut Born Residents of New Mexico, 1870." NEW MEXICO GENE-ALOGIST 2 (October 1963): 4, 55-56.

Crouse, Nellis Maynard. "Causes of the Great Migration, 1630-1640." NEQ 5 (1936): 3-36.

Dunn, Richards. "John Winthrop, Jr., Connecticut Expansionist: The Failure of His Designs on Long Island, 1663-1675." NEQ 29 (1956): 3-26.

Gallaher, Ruth A. "From Connecticut to Iowa." PALIMPSET 22 (1941): 65-78.

Goodrich, John Ellsworth. "Immigration to Vermont, 1760-1790." VERMONT HISTORICAL SOCIETY PROCEEDINGS, 1908-09, pp. 65-87.

Granger, James N. "Connecticut and Virginia a Century Ago." CQ 3 (1897): 100-105, 190-98.

Hamilton, Frank Lorenzo. "The 'Henry Lee' Argonauts of 1849." CQ 1 (1895): 229-32.

Hawes, Frank Mortimer. "New Englanders in the Florida Census of 1850: Persons Born in Connecticut." NEHGR 76 (1922): 52-54.

Hoxie, Frances Alida. "Connecticut's Forty-Niners." WESTERN HISTORICAL QUARTERLY 5 (1974): 17-28.

Huey, Paul R., and Phillips, Ralph D. "The Migration of a Connecticut Family to Eastern New York in the Eighteenth Century." CN 13 (1980): 390-93.

Koenig, Samuel. IMMIGRANT SETTLEMENTS IN CONNECTICUT: THEIR GROWTH AND CHARACTERISTICS. Hartford: Conn. State Dept. of Education, 1938. 67 p.

Krumbhlaar, Anna Conyngham Stevens. "Colonel Zebulon Butler and Wyoming Valley." CM 6 (1900): 143-52.

Larned, Ellen D. "New Connecticut or Western Reserve." CQ 2 (1896): 386-95; 3 (1897): 88-99.

_____. "Notes by an Ohio Pioneer--1788-'89." CQ 2 (1896): 244-46.

McCracken, George E. "The Connecticut Pennsylvanians." TAG 55 (1979): 72-82.

Mather, Frederic Gregory. REFUGEES OF 1776 FROM LONG ISLAND TO CONNECTICUT. Albany, N.Y.: J.B. Lyon, 1913. 1,204 p. (LDS 164, 690).

Mills, William Stowell. HISTORY OF THE WESTERN RESERVE OF CONNECTICUT. New York: Brown and Wilson, 1900. 141 p.

Morrow, Rising Lake. CONNECTICUT INFLUENCES IN WESTERN MASSACHUSETTS AND VERMONT. Conn. Tercentenary Publication, no. 58. New Haven: Yale University Press, 1936. 24 p.

Ohler, Clara Paine. "Connecticut and the Building of the Empire of the Old Northwest." CM 12 (1908): 47-62.

Olson, Albert Laverne. AGRICULTURAL ECONOMY AND THE POPULATION IN EIGHTEENTH-CENTURY CONNECTICUT. Connecticut Tercentenary Publication, no. 40. New Haven: Yale University Press, 1935. 31 p.

Olson, Virginia H. "Notes and Sources: Connecticut Loyalists Who Went to Canada." CA 17 (1974): 18-25, 51-59.

Pantle, Alberta. "The Connecticut Kansas Colony, Letters of Charles B. Lines to The NEW HAVEN (CONN.) DAILY PALLADIUM." KANSAS HISTORICAL QUARTERLY 22 (1956): 1-50, 138-88.

Peck, Mrs. Lou E. "Connecticut Yankees in Alabama 1850." BULLETIN OF THE STAMFORD GENEALOGICAL SOCIETY 11 (1965): 65-68, 103-5; 12 (1969-70): 34-35, 117-18; 13 (1970): 23-25, 36; 16 (1973-74): 18-22, 58-63, 129-34.

"Persons Born in Connecticut, 1850 Oregon Census." CN 13 (1980): 210-11.

Phillips, Josephine E. "Ohio's Deep Roots in Connecticut." OHIO STATE ARCHAEOLOGICAL AND HISTORICAL QUARTERLY 48 (1934): 74-82.

Rindler, Edward Paul. "The Migration from the New Haven Colony to Newark, East New Jersey: A Study of Puritan Values and Behavior, 1630-1720." Ph.D. dissertation, University of Pennsylvania, 1977. 448 p.

Rosenberry, Lois Kimball Matthews. THE EXPANSION OF NEW ENGLAND. Boston: Houghton Mifflin Co., 1909. 303 p. Index.

_____. MIGRATIONS FROM CONNECTICUT AFTER 1800. Conn. Tercentenary Publication, no. 54. New Haven: Yale University Press, 1936. 29 p.

_____. MIGRATIONS FROM CONNECTICUT PRIOR TO 1800. Conn. Tercentenary Publication, no. 28. New Haven: Yale University Press, 1934. 36 p.

Sachse, William Lewis. "The Migration of New Englanders to England, 1640-1660." AMERICAN HISTORICAL REVIEW 43 (1937): 251-78.

Smith, Mrs. Mabel Woods. "Connecticut Born Persons Listed in the 1855-1865-1875 New York State Census Records for the Town of Lenox, Madison County, New York." BULLETIN OF THE STAMFORD GENEALOGICAL SOCIETY 10 (1967): 6-7.

Stephenson, Jean. "The Connecticut Settlement of Nova Scotia Prior to the Revolution." NGSQ 42 (1954): 53-60.

Warfle, Richard Thomas. "Connecticut's Critical Period: The Response to the Susquehannah Affair 1769-1774." Ph.D. dissertation, University of Conn., 1972. 211 p.

_____. CONNECTICUT'S WESTERN COLONY: THE SUSQUEHANNAH AFFAIR. Connecticut Bicentennial Series, vol. 32. Chester: Pequot Press, 1979. 60 p.

MILITARY RECORDS

General

Burpee, Charles W. "Connecticut's Soldiery." CQ 3 (1897): 254-65.

Cohen, Sheldon S. "Captain Robert Niles, Connecticut State Navy." AMERICAN NEPTUNE 39 (1979): 190-208.

Connecticut Archives. Militia Records. (Selected Papers). Series 1-3, 1678-1820. Typescript. Index. (LDS 1465).

"Connecticut Coast Guards (list)." NGSQ 26 (1938): 54.

DAR NATIONAL SOCIETY. THE TWENTY-FIRST REPORT (1917-1918). Washington, D.C.: GPO, 1919.

Gates, Stewart Lewis. "Disorder and Social Organization: The Militia in Connecticut Public Life, 1660-1860." Ph.D. dissertation, University of Conn., 1975. 289 p.

Goddard, George S. "The Connecticut Military Census." In REPORT OF THE STATE LIBRARIAN TO THE GOVERNOR: 1818, pp. 24-26. Hartford, Conn.: State, 1919.

_____. "Department of War Records." REPORT OF THE STATE LIBRARIAN TO THE GOVERNOR. Hartford, Conn.: State of Connecticut, 1922. Pp. 88-93; 1930, pp. 30-32.

Jenson, Carl D., and Burton, Edward W. FLYING YANKEES: A HISTORY OF THE FIRST FIFTY YEARS OF THE CONNECTICUT AIR NATIONAL GUARD. N.p., 1973. 111 p.

Militia Records of Connecticut. Miscellaneous. 1786-1931. (CSL Archives, LDS 1472).

Neeser, Robert Wilden. "The Ships of the United States Navy . . . 1776-1915-Connecticut." U.S. NAVAL INSTITUTE PROCEEDINGS 42 (1916): 522 ff.

O'Dea, Eamon. "When Connecticut Put the Cavalry on Bicycles." YANKEE 43 (August 1979): 68-71.

REPORT OF THE ADJUTANT GENERAL TO THE GOVERNOR. Hartford: Office of the Adjutant General, 1849-- .

Saunders, Ernest. BLACKS IN THE CONNECTICUT NATIONAL GUARD: A PICTORIAL AND CHRONOLOGICAL HISTORY 1870 TO 1919. New Haven: Afro-American Historical Society, 1977. 96 p.

Starr, Harris E. SECOND COMPANY GOVERNOR'S FOOT GUARD, 1775-1965. North Haven, Conn.: William J. Mack, 1950. 189 p.

Strickland, Daniel W. CONNECTICUT FIGHTS: THE STORY OF THE 102ND REGIMENT. New Haven: Quinnipiack Press, 1930. 404 p.

"War Service Records." FAMILIES OF ANCIENT NEW HAVEN 1 (1923): 238-53; 2 (1924): 485-503.

Colonial

Andrews, Frank DeWitte. CONNECTICUT SOLDIERS IN THE FRENCH AND INDIAN WAR. Vineland, N.J.: Author, 1925. 41 p.

Bradstreet, Howard. THE STORY OF THE PEQUOT WAR OF 1637. Hartford: Polygon Press, 1930. 46 p.

_____. THE STORY OF THE WAR WITH THE PEQUOTS RE-TOLD. New Haven, Conn.: Yale University Press, 1933. 32 p.

Clark, David Sanders. "Journals and Orderly Books Kept by Connecticut Soldiers During the French and Indian War 1755-1762." NEHGR 94 (1940): 225-30; 95 (1941): 18-20.

Colonial Wars 1615-1775. (Selected Papers). Typescript. Index. (Archives, LDS 1463).

Detzer, David W. "The Causes of the Pequot War." CR 1 (October 1970): 85-88.

Egleston, Thomas. THE STORY OF THE PEQUOT PRESS. New York: Order of the Founders and Patriots of America, 1905. 33 p.

French and Indian War. (Miscellaneous) 1757-1826. (CSL Archives, LDS 1471).

Gardiner, Lion. A HISTORY OF THE PEQUOT WAR. Cincinnati: J. Harpel, 1860. 36 p.

Hart, Francis Russell. "Struggle for Control of America: Connecticut Soldiers in Caribbean Wars." CM 12 (1908): 254-64.

Marcus, Richard Henry. "The Militia of Colonial Connecticut 1639-1775: An Institutional Study." Ph.D. dissertation, University of Colorado, 1965. 381 p.

"A Muster Roll of Capt. Thomas Hobby's Company, 1761." CQ 3 (1897): 106-8.

ROLL AND JOURNAL OF CONNECTICUT SERVICE IN QUEEN ANNE'S WAR 1710-1711. Hartford: Acorn Club of Conn., 1916. 62 p.

"Rolls of Connecticut Men in the French and Indian War, 1755-1762." CHS COLLECTIONS, vols. 9 and 10 (LDS 897,070-897,071).

Shepard, James. CONNECTICUT SOLDIERS IN THE PEQUOT WAR OF 1637. Meriden: Journal Pub. Co., 1913. 32 p. (LDS 438,342).

Soule, Sherwood. "A Connecticut Soldier in the French and Indian War, Life of Gideon Hotchkiss, Born 1716 at Cheshire, Connecticut." CM 11 (1907): 409-16.

Trumbull, Benjamin. A COMPENDIUM OF THE INDIAN WARS IN NEW ENGLAND MORE PARTICULARLY SUCH AS THE COLONY OF CONNECTICUT HAVE BEEN CONCERNED AND ACTIVE IN NEW HAVEN, AUGUST 25TH ANNO 1767. Hartford: Edwin Valentine Mitchell, 1926. 62 p.

Vaughan, Alden T. "Pequots and Puritans: The Causes of the War of 1637." WILLIAM AND MARY QUARTERLY 21 (1964): 256-69.

Revolutionary War and War of 1812

Adams, Benjamin Pettengill. "The Last Years of Connecticut Under the British Crown." CM 10 (1906): 223-34.

Barrow, Thomas C. CONNECTICUT JOINS THE REVOLUTION. Chester: Pequot Press, 1973. 45 p.

Bill, Ledyard. "Roll of Capt. Nathaniel Webb's Co., in the Fourth Connecticut Regiment Revolutionary War, Col. John Durkee, Commanding." NEHGR 22 (1868): 281-82.

Blake, Francis Everett. "Wagon Master's Returns, 1782-1783." NEHGR 51 (1897): 39-42.

Burr, William Hanford. "The Invasion of Connecticut by the British." CM 10 (1906): 139-52.

Callahan, North. CONNECTICUT'S REVOLUTIONARY WAR LEADERS. Conn. Bicentennial Series, vol. 3. Chester: Pequot Press, 1973. 52 p.

Casagrande, Gordon. "The Revolutionary Soldier." FAIRFIELD COUNTY 5 (December 1975): 64-67, 134-41.

Clark, George L. SILAS DEANE, A CONNECTICUT LEADER IN THE AMERICAN REVOLUTION. New York: G.P. Putnam's Sons, 1913. 287 p.

Clark, Henry Austin. "A Connecticut Revolutionary Roll." NEHGR 60 (1906): 331.

Clarke, A.H. A COMPLETE ROSTER OF COLONEL DAVID WATERBURY JR.'S REGIMENT OF CONNECTICUT VOLUNTEERS. New York: A.S. Clark, 1897. 20 p.

Collier, Christopher. CONNECTICUT IN THE CONTINENTAL CONGRESS. Conn. Bicentennial Series, vol. 2. Chester: Pequot Press, 1973. 78 p.

_____. ROGER SHERMAN'S CONNECTICUT: YANKEE POLITICS AND THE AMERICAN REVOLUTION. Middletown: Wesleyan University, 1971. 409 p.

Collier, Thomas S. "Revolutionary Privateers of Connecticut, With Accounts of State Cruisers." In RECORDS AND PAPERS OF THE NEW LONDON COUNTY HISTORICAL SOCIETY, vol. 1, pt. 4, 1890.

Connecticut. Adjutant General. RECORD OF SERVICE OF CONNECTICUT MEN IN THE I.--WAR OF THE REVOLUTION, II.--WAR OF 1812, III.--MEXICAN WAR. Hartford: Case, Lockwood and Brainard, 1889. 180 p.

"Connecticut Militia 1781-83. Commissioned Officers, May 1782, Connecticut." DAR MAGAZINE 97 (1963): 445-46, 472.

CONNECTICUT PENSION ROLL 1834. N.p., n.d. 160 p.

"Connecticut Troops in 1775. List of Names Appearing on the Payroll of the 9th Company in the 8th Regiment of Connecticut Troops, Abraham Tyler Capt., for the Service of 1775." NEHGR 26 (1872): 333.

Crankshaw, Mrs. Charles William. AN INDEX OF VETERANS OF CONNECTICUT DURING THE YEARS 1812, 1813, 1814, 1815, 1816, WAR OF 1812. 2 vols. N.p.: 1964.

Cutler, Charles L. CONNECTICUT'S REVOLUTIONARY PRESS. Conn. Bicentennial Series, vol. 19. Chester: Pequot Press, 1975. 61 p.

Daniels, Bruce Collins. CONNECTICUT'S FIRST FAMILY: WILLIAM PITKIN AND HIS CONNECTIONS. Conn. Bicentennial Series, vol. 11. Chester: Pequot Press, 1975. 64 p.

Destler, Chester McArthur. "A Bibliography of Connecticut During the American Revolution." CONNECTICUT HISTORY 16 (1975): 7-36.

_____. CONNECTICUT: THE PROVISIONS STATE. Conn. Bicentennial Series, vol. 5. Chester: Pequot Press, 1973. 58 p.

Draper, Mrs. Amos G. "Pension Records of the Revolutionary Soldiers from Connecticut." DAR REPORT 21 (1911): 131-299.

Esker, Katie Prince Ward. "Certain Revolutionary Soldiers and Patriots of Connecticut With Proof of Service Found in Pension Records of Other Soldiers." NGSQ 35 (1947): 108-11.

Extracts from Meetings Held to Determine Procedure of Conn. Towns in Revolutionary War 1774-1784. (CSL Archives, LDS 1478).

Fales, Edward, Jr. ARSENAL OF THE REVOLUTION: THE FIRST OF "THE 14TH COLONY." Lakeville, Conn.: Lakeville Journal, 1976. 96 p.

Fennelly, Catherine. CONNECTICUT WOMEN IN THE REVOLUTIONARY ERA. Conn. Bicentennial Series, vol. 15. Chester: Pequot Press, 1975. 60 p.

Furlong, Patrick J. "A Sermon for the Mutinous Troops of the Connecticut Line, 1782." NEQ 43 (1970): 621-31.

Gerlach, Larry R. CONNECTICUT CONGRESSMAN: SAMUEL HUNTINGTON, 1731-1796. Conn. Bicentennial Series, vol. 20. Hartford: American Revolution Bicentennial Commission, 1976. 142 p.

Goodyear, Edward B. "Revolutionary War Pay Roll, 1777." NGSQ 9 (1920): 45.

Grant, Marion Hepburn. THE INFERNAL MACHINES OF SAYBROOK'S DAVID BUSHNELL: PATRIOT INVENTOR OF THE AMERICAN REVOLUTION. Old Saybrook, Conn.: Bicentennial Committee, 1976. 66 p.

Hagelin, Wladimir, and Brown, Ralph A. "Connecticut Farmers at the Battle of Bunker Hill: The Diary of Colonel Experience Storrs." NEQ 28 (1955): 72-93.

Hartford. CSL, Record Group 1. Revolutionary War material.

Hayes, Joseph Thomas. "Connecticut Light Horse, 1776-1783." THE MILITARY COLLECTOR AND HISTORIAN 22 (1970): 109-12.

Hayes, John Thomas. CONNECTICUT'S REVOLUTIONARY CAVALRY: SHELDON'S HORSE. Conn. Bicentennial Series, vol. 13. Chester: Pequot Press, 1975. 93 p.

Hewitt, Grace D. "Reminiscences of the War of 1812." CM 12 (1908): 122-23.

Hinman, Royal Ralph. A HISTORICAL COLLECTION, FROM OFFICIAL RECORDS, FILES ETC. OF THE PART SUSTAINED BY CONNECTICUT, DURING THE WAR OF THE REVOLUTION. Hartford, Conn.: E. Gleason, 1842. 643 p.

Howard, George P. "Patriot Hunting? Look Also in Other States." (Conn. Naval Records in the Revolution) TAG 51 (1975): 217-22.

Howard, James L. THE ORIGIN AND FORTUNE OF TROOP B 1788 GOVERNOR'S INDEPENDENT TROOP OF HOUSE GUARDS 1911 TROOP B CALVARY CONNECTICUT NATIONAL GUARD 1917. Hartford: Case, Lockwood and Brainard Co., 1921. 261 p.

Ifkovic, John William. CONNECTICUT'S NATIONALIST REVOLUTIONARY: JONATHAN TRUMBULL, JUNIOR. Hartford: American Bicentennial Commission in Conn., 1977. 103 p. Index.

Jacobus, Donald Lines. "Revolutionary War Records." HISTORY AND GENEALOGY OF THE FAMILIES OF OLD FAIRFIELD, vol. 3. Fairfield: The Eunice Dennie Burr Chapter, D.A.R., n.d. 533 p.

Kennelly, Eleanor. "The Connecticut Revolution of 1766--Connecticut's Reaction to the Stamp Act." CHSB 45 (1980): 45-61.

Kuslan, Louis I. CONNECTICUT SCIENCE, TECHNOLOGY, AND MEDICINE IN THE ERA OF THE AMERICAN REVOLUTION. Conn. Bicentennial Series, no. 27. Hartford: American Revolution Bicentennial Commission of Conn., 1978. 65 p. Index.

Larned, Ellen D. "A Teamster Boy in the Revolution." CQ 2 (1896): 50-51.

"The Last of our Revolutionary Widows." CQ 2 (1896): 98.

Lettierri, Ronald John. CONNECTICUT'S YOUNG MAN OF THE REVOLUTION: OLIVER ELLSWORTH. Conn. Bicentennial Series, no. 30. Hartford: American Revolution Bicentennial Commission of Conn.,1978. 106 p.

_____. "Young Man of the Revolution: An Examination of the Public Career of Oliver Ellsworth, 1773-1788." Master's thesis, Indiana State University, 1974. 208 p.

"Lists and Returns of Connecticut Men in the Revolution 1775-1783." CHS COLLECTIONS, vol. 12, 1909.

McCusker, Honor. "The Connecticut Troops in the Siege of Boston." MORE BOOKS 11 (1933): 377-80.

McDevitt, Robert F. CONNECTICUT ATTACKED: A BRITISH VIEWPOINT, TRYON'S RAID ON DANBURY. Conn. Bicentennial Series, no. 10. Chester: Pequot Press, 1974. 76 p.

Main, Jackson Turner. CONNECTICUT SOCIETY IN THE ERA OF THE AMERICAN REVOLUTION. Hartford: American Revolution Bicentennial Commission in Conn., 1977. 83 p. Index.

Mather, Frederick Gregory. THE REFUGEES OF 1776 FROM LONG ISLAND TO CONNECTICUT. Albany, N.Y.: J.B. Lyon, 1913. 1,204 p. (LDS 164,690).

Middlebrook, Louis Frank. HISTORY OF MARITIME CONNECTICUT DURING THE AMERICAN REVOLUTION 1775-1783. 2 vols. Salem, Mass.: Essex Institute, 1925.

Murphy, William Gordon. "Connecticut's Contribution to the Cause of American Liberty." CM 10 (1906): 495-509.

Niven, John. CONNECTICUT HERO: ISRAEL PUTNAM. Hartford: American Revolution Bicentennial Commission in Conn., 1977. 101 p. Index.

O'Brien, Michael J. "The Connecticut Irish in the Revolution: Numerous Celtic Names Listed in the Muster Rolls." AMERICAN IRISH HISTORICAL SOCIETY JOURNAL 22 (1919): 196–214.

"Orderly Books and Journals Kept by Connecticut Men While Taking Part in the American Revolution 1775–1778." CHS COLLECTIONS, vol. 7, 1899. (LDS 897, 070). 385 p.

Paullin, Charles Oscar. "Connecticut Navy of the American Revolution." NEQ 35 (1907): 714–25.

Pitkin, Albert Hastings. "Our Neighborhood Churches During the American Revolution." CQ 3 (1897): 430–40.

Powell, William S. "A Connecticut Soldier Under Washington: Elisha Bostwick's Memoirs of the First Years of the Revolution." WILLIAM AND MARY QUARTERLY 6 (1962): 94–107.

Reichenbach, Karl H. "The Connecticut Clergy and the Stamp Act." UNIVERSITY OF MICHIGAN HISTORICAL ESSAYS 11 (1921): 141–58.

Revolutionary War. (Selected Papers). 1763–1820. (CSL Archives, LDS 1462).

Revolutionary War. Orderly Books of Regiments and Companies of Conn. (CSL Archives, LDS 1474).

Revolutionary War Papers. Private Collections. (CSL Archives, LDS 1475).

Revolutionary War Rolls, 1775–1783. Conn. Service Jackets. Indexed. (NARS, LDS 830,280 to 830,307. Index reel is LDS 830,280).

"Roll of Capt. Nathaniel Webb's Co., in the Fourth Connecticut Regiment." NEHGR 22 (1868): 281–82.

"Rolls and Lists of Connecticut Men in the Revolution 1775–1783." CHS COLLECTIONS, vol. 8 (1901); 12 (1909). (LDS 897,070).

Rommell, John G. CONNECTICUT'S YANKEE PATRIOT: ROGER SHERMAN. Conn. Bicentennial Series, no. 34. Hartford: American Revolution Bicentennial Commission, 1980. 71 p.

Roth, David Morris. "Connecticut and the Coming of the Revolution." CR 7 (October 1973): 49–65.

_____. CONNECTICUT'S WAR GOVERNOR: JONATHAN TRUMBULL. Conn. Bicentennial Series, no. 9. Chester: Pequot Press, 1974. 99 p.

Rubicam, Milton. "Revolutionary War Rolls of Connecticut Units in the National Archives." TAG 26 (1950): 79-83.

_____. "Connecticut in the American Revolution." CR 9 (November 1975): 10-20.

Stark, Bruce Purinton. CONNECTICUT SIGNER: WILLIAM WILLIAMS. Conn. Bicentennial Series, no. 12. Chester: Pequot Press, 1975. 87 p.

Stevens, Mary K. "The Convention Troops in Connecticut." CQ 3 (1897): 144-49.

Thompson, Marvin Gardner. CONNECTICUT ENTREPRENEUR: CHRISTOPHER LEFFINGWELL. Conn. Bicentennial Series, no. 33. Hartford: American Revolution Bicentennial Commission, 1980. 50 p.

Trumbull, John. "Letter to Governor Jonathan Trumbull of Connecticut, Ticonderoga: July 12, 1776." FORT TICONDEROGA MUSEUM BULLETIN 6 (1932): 144-45.

U.S. National Archives and Record Service. INDEX TO COMPILED SERVICE RECORDS OF REVOLUTIONARY WAR SOLDIERS WHO SERVED WITH THE AMERICAN ARMY IN CONNECTICUT MILITARY ORGANIZATIONS. Microfilm Publication Pamphlet, M920. Washington, D.C.: 1977. 7 p.

Van Dusen, Albert Edward. "The Trade of Revolutionary Connecticut." Ph.D. dissertation, University of Pennsylvania, 1948. 419 p.

Wallace, Willard Mosher. CONNECTICUT'S DARK STAR OF THE REVOLUTION: GENERAL BENEDICT ARNOLD. Hartford: American Revolution Bicentennial Commission of Conn., 1978. 74 p. Index.

Walsh, James P. CONNECTICUT INDUSTRY AND THE REVOLUTION. Conn. Bicentennial Series, no. 29. Chester: Pequot Press, 1978. 82 p.

War of 1812. (Selected Papers). 1812-1819. Typescript. Index (CSL Archives, LDS 1464).

Welles, Edwin Stanley. INSPECTION RETURNS ON THE 5TH COMPANY, 6TH REGIMENT OF CONNECTICUT MILITIA FOR THE YEARS 1813 AND 1814. Hartford: Case, Lockwood and Brainard, 1933.

Welles, Roger. THE REVOLUTIONARY WAR LETTERS OF CAPTAIN ROGER WELLES OF WETHERSFIELD AND NEWINGTON, CONNECTICUT, WITH FOUR SUCH LETTERS FROM THREE NEWINGTON SOLDIERS. Hartford, Conn.: 1932. 40 p.

White, Davis D. CONNECTICUT'S BLACK SOLDIERS 1775-1783. Conn. Bicentennial Series, no. 4. Chester: Pequot Press, 1973. 71 p.

Willingham, William F. CONNECTICUT REVOLUTIONARY: ELIPHALET DYER. Conn. Bicentennial Series, no. 19. Chester: Pequot Press, 1976. 56 p.

Wilson, Ruth Mack, and Keller, Kate Van Winkle. CONNECTICUT'S MUSIC IN THE REVOLUTIONARY ERA. Conn. Bicentennial Series, no. 31. Hartford, Conn.: American Revolution Bicentennial Commission, 1979. 142 p.

Civil War

Beecher, Herbert W. HISTORY OF THE FIRST LIGHT BATTERY CONNECTICUT VOLUNTEERS 1861-1865. PERSONAL RECORDS AND REMINISCENCES. 2 vols. New York: A.T. De La Mare Printing and Pub. Co., Ltd., 1901.

Bennett, Edgar B. FIRST CONNECTICUT HEAVY ARTILLERY; HISTORICAL SKETCH AND PRESENT ADDRESSES OF MEMBERS. Hartford: Star Printing Co., 1889. 53 p.

Blakeslee, Bernard F. HISTORY OF THE SIXTEENTH CONNECTICUT VOLUN-TEERS. Hartford: Case, Lockwood and Brainard Co., 1875. 116 p.

Brownell, Henry Howard. "The Battle of the Hartford and Tennessee." CQ 3 (1897): 454-59.

Buckingham, Samuel Giles. THE WAR GOVERNOR OF CONNECTICUT. Springfield: W.F. Adams, 1894. 537 p.

Caldwell, Charles R. THE OLD SIXTH REGIMENT, ITS WAR RECORD, 1861-5. New Haven: Tuttle, Morehouse and Taylor, 1875. 227 p.

Connecticut. Adjutant-General. CATALOGUE OF CONNECTICUT VOL-UNTEER ORGANIZATIONS, (INFANTRY, CAVALRY AND ARTILLERY,) AD-DITIONAL ENLISTMENTS, CASUALTIES, ETC. Hartford: Brown and Gross, 1869. 937 p.

_____. CATALOGUE OF CONNECTICUT VOLUNTEER ORGANIZATIONS,

WITH ADDITIONAL ENLISTMENTS AND CASUALTIES TO JULY 1, 1864. Hartford: Case, Lockwood and Co., 1864. 847 p.

_____. RECORD OF SERVICE OF CONNECTICUT MEN IN THE ARMY AND NAVY OF THE UNITED STATES DURING THE WAR OF THE REBELLION. Hartford: Case, Lockwood and Brainard Co., 1889. 1,071 p.

"Connecticut Officers at Louisburg." CHS COLLECTIONS, vol. 13, 1911, pp. 66-67.

CONNECTICUT WAR RECORD. Vol. 1, No. 1. 1863-1865. (Newspaper) New Haven: Peck and Peck, 1863-65.

Croffut, William Augustus, and Morris, John M. MILITARY AND CIVIL HISTORY OF CONNECTICUT DURING THE WAR OF 1861-65 COMPRISING A DETAILED ACCOUNT OF THE VARIOUS REGIMENTS AND BATTERIES. . . . New York: Ledyard Bill, 1868. 891 p.

Emmett, L.D. "Connecticut and the Battlefield of Antietam." CM 11 (1907): 614-16.

Finian, William J. MAJOR GENERAL ALFRED HOWE TERRY (1827-1890) HERO OF FORT FISHER. Hartford: Conn. Civil War Centennial Commission, 1965. 52 p.

Finn, William J. "The Mountain County Regiment." THE LURE OF THE LITCHFIELD HILLS 14 (1942): 6-7, 27-28.

THE FIRST REGIMENT CONNECTICUT VOLUNTEER HEAVY ARTILLERY IN THE WAR OF THE REBELLION 1861-1865. Hartford: Case, Lockwood and Brainard Co., 1889. 57 p.

Griswold, Mary Hoadley. "Connecticut Heroism in the Civil War." CM 12 (1908): 330-32.

Hartford. CSL, Record Group 13. Bounty Claim Papers. 1866-1877. List of Connecticut Men in Regiments of Other States. Regimental Records and Histories. Requests for Certificates Attesting to Civil War Service 1868-1871.

Hill, Isaac J. A SKETCH OF THE 29TH REGIMENT OF CONNECTICUT COLORED TROOPS, GIVING A FULL ACCOUNT OF ITS FORMATION, OF ALL THE BATTLES THROUGH WHICH IT PASSED, AND ITS FINAL DISBAND-MENT. Baltimore: Daugherty, Magazine and Co., 1867. 42 p.

HISTORY OF THE FIRST CONNECTICUT ARTILLERY AND OF THE SIEGE TRAINS OF THE ARMIES OPERATING AGAINST RICHMOND 1862-1865. Hartford: Case, Lockwood and Brainard Co., 1893. 272 p.

HISTORY OF THE TWENTY-SECOND REGIMENT CONNECTICUT VOLUNTEER INFANTRY, 1862-3. Hartford: Hartford Printing Co., 1896. 16 p.

Jurgen, Robert J., and Keller, Allan. MAJOR GENERAL JOHN SEDGWICK U.S. VOLUNTEERS (1813-64). Hartford: Conn. Civil War Centennial Commission, 1964. 31 p.

Keller, Allan. ANDREW HULL FOOTE GUNBOAT COMMODORE (1806-1863). Hartford: Conn. Civil War Centennial Commission, 1964. 48 p.

Kellogg, Robert H., et al. DEDICATION OF THE MONUMENT AT ANDERSONVILLE GEORGIA OCTOBER 23, 1907. IN MEMORY OF THE MEN OF CONNECTICUT WHO SUFFERED IN SOUTHERN MILITARY PRISONS 1861-1865. Hartford: Case, Lockwood and Brainard, Co., 1908. 73 p.

Lane, Jarlath Robert. A POLITICAL HISTORY OF CONNECTICUT DURING THE CIVIL WAR. Washington, D.C.: Catholic University of America, 1941. 321 p.

Marvin, Edwin E. OFFICIAL RECORD OF THE SERVICE OF THE MEN OF THE FIFTH REGIMENT, CONNECTICUT INFANTRY IN THE WAR OF 1861. Hartford: Wiley, Waterman and Eaton, 1889. 394 p.

Murray, Thomas Hamilton. HISTORY OF THE NINTH REGIMENT, CONNECTICUT VOLUNTEER INFANTRY, "THE IRISH REGIMENT," IN THE WAR OF THE REBELLION, 1861-65. New Haven: Price, Lee and Adkins Co., 1903. 440 p.

"Muster Rolls." CHS COLLECTIONS 15 (1914): 111-60.

"Nathan Whitings List of Soldiers Commissary Book." CHS COLLECTIONS 13 (1911): 68-83.

Newton, Alexander Heritage. OUT OF THE BRIARS, AN AUTOBIOGRAPHY AND SKETCH OF THE TWENTY-NINTH REGIMENT, CONNECTICUT VOLUNTEERS. Philadelphia: African Methodist Episcopal Book Concern, 1910. 269 p.

Niven, John. CONNECTICUT FOR THE UNION: THE ROLE OF THE STATE IN THE CIVIL WAR. New Haven: Yale University Press, 1965. 493 p. Index.

Page, Charles D. HISTORY OF THE FOURTEENTH REGIMENT, CONNECTICUT VOL. INFANTRY. Meriden: Horton, 1906. 509 p.

ROSTER, MUSTER ROLL AND CHRONOLOGICAL RECORD OF THE TWENTY-SIXTH REGIMENT, CONNECTICUT VOLUNTEERS, AND MEMORANDA OF THE ASSOCIATION OF THE TWENTY-SIXTH REGIMENT, CONNECTICUT VOLUNTEERS. Norwich: Frank Utley Print, 1888. 56 p.

ROSTER OF THE THIRD REGIMENT, CONNECTICUT VOLUNTEERS. Hartford: Calhoun Printing Co., 1861. 12 p.

ROSTER OF THE TWENTY-EIGHTH REGIMENT, CONNECTICUT VOLUNTEERS, 1862-1897. Winsted: Dowd Printing Co., 1897. 31 p.

Roth, David Morris. CONNECTICUT'S WAR GOVERNOR: JONATHAN TRUMBULL. Chester: Pequot Press, 1974. 99 p.

Scofield, Loomis. HISTORY OF THE TWENTY-EIGHTH REGIMENT CONNECTICUT VOLUNTEERS. New Canaan, Conn.: New Canaan Advertiser, 1915. 24 p.

Sheldon, Withrop Dudley. THE TWENTY-SEVENTH, A REGIMENTAL HISTORY. New Haven: Morris and Benham, 1866. 144 p. (LDS 896, 829).

"The Sixth Militia Company. Connecticut." CHSB 25 (1960): 61-64.

Sprague, Homer Baxter. HISTORY OF THE 13TH INFANTRY REGIMENT OF CONNECTICUT VOLUNTEERS, DURING THE GREAT REBELLION. Hartford: Case, Lockwood and Co., 1867. 353 p.

Storrs, John W. THE "TWENTIETH CONNECTICUT" A REGIMENTAL HISTORY. Ansonia: Naugatuck Valley Sentimental, 1886. 306 p.

THE STORY OF THE TWENTY-FIRST REGIMENT, CONNECTICUT VOLUNTEER INFANTRY, DURING THE CIVIL WAR 1861-1865. Middletown: Stewart Printing Co., 1900. 498 p.

Talmadge, John E. "A Peace Movement in Civil War Connecticut." NEQ 37 (1968): 306-21.

Taylor, John C., and Hatfield, Samuel P. HISTORY OF THE FIRST CONNETICUT ARTILLERY AND OF THE SEIGE TRAINS OF THE ARMIES OPERATING AGAINST RICHMOND, 1862-1865. Hartford: Case, Lockwood and Brainard, 1893. 270 p.

Thorpe, Sheldon Brainerd. THE HISTORY OF THE FIFTEENTH CONNECTICUT VOLUNTEERS IN THE WAR FOR THE DEFENSE OF THE UNION 1861-1865. New Haven: Price, Lee and Adkins Co., 1893. 362 p.

Tourtellotte, Jerome. A HISTORY OF COMPANY K OF THE SEVENTH CON-NETICUT VOLUNTEER INFANTRY IN THE CIVIL WAR, COMPILED BY A MEMBER WHO WAS SECOND IN RANK IN THE COMPANY WHEN THE REGIMENT LEFT THE STATE FOR THE FRONT AND SECOND IN RANK IN THE REGIMENT WHEN IT RETURNED TO THE STATE FOR FINAL DISCHARGE. N.p., 1910. 217 p.

Tyler, Elnathen B. "WOODEN NUTMEGS" AT BULL RUN. Hartford: G.L. Coburn, 1872. 86 p.

U.S. National Archives and Record Service. INDEX TO COMPILED SERVICE RECORDS OF VOLUNTEERS UNION SOLDIERS WHO SERVED IN ORGANIZA-TIONS FROM THE STATE OF CONNECTICUT. Microfilm publication, no. 535. Washington, D.C.: 1964. 4 p.

Vaill, Dudley Landon. THE COUNTY REGIMENT, A SKETCH OF THE SECOND REGIMENT OF CONNECTICUT VOLUNTEER HEAVY ARTILLERY, ORGINALLY THE NINETEENTH VOLUNTEER INFANTRY, IN THE CIVIL WAR. Litchfield: Litchfield County University Club, 1908. 108 p.

Vaill, Theodore Frelinghuysen. HISTORY OF THE SECOND CONNECTICUT VOLUNTEER HEAVY ARTILLERY, ORIGINALLY THE NINETEENTH CONNECTI-CUT VOLUNTEERS. Winsted: Winsted Printing Co., 1868. 366 p.

Walker, William Carey. HISTORY OF THE EIGHTEENTH REGIMENT CONN. VOLUNTEERS IN THE WAR FOR THE UNION. Norwich: The Committee, 1885. 444 p.

Walkley, Stephen. HISTORY OF THE SEVENTH CONNECTICUT VOLUNTEER INFANTRY HAWLEY'S BRIGADE, TERRY'S DIVISION TENTH ARMY CORPS, 1861-1865. Hartford, Conn.: 1905. 326 p.

Weld, Stanley Buckingham. CONNECTICUT PHYSICIANS IN THE CIVIL WAR. Hartford: Conn. Civil War Centennial Commission, 1963. 61 p.

Spanish-American War

Connecticut. Adjutant-General. RECORD OF SERVICE OF CONNECTICUT MEN IN THE ARMY, NAVY AND MARINE CORPS OF THE UNITED STATES IN THE SPANISH-AMERICAN WAR, PHILIP-PINE INSURRECTION AND CHINA RELIEF EXPEDITION FROM APRIL 21, 1898 TO JULY 4, 1904. Hartford: Case, Lockwood and Brainard, 1919. 222 p.

_____. ROSTER OF CONNECTICUT VOLUNTEERS WHO SERVED IN THE WAR BETWEEN THE UNITED STATES AND SPAIN 1898-1899. Hartford: Case, Lockwood and Brainard, Co., 1899. 42 p.

Hale, Charles E. LIST OF SPANISH-AMERICAN WAR VETERANS WHO DO NOT BELONG TO THE SPANISH WAR VETERANS ORGANIZATION. N.p.: Author, n.d. 10 p. (LDS 1473).

World War I

Breen, William J. "Mobilization and Cooperative Federalism: The Connecticut State Council of Defense, 1917-1919." HISTORIAN 42(1979): 58-84.

Connecticut. Office of the Adjutant General. SERVICE RECORDS CONNECTICUT MEN AND WOMEN IN THE ARMED FORCES OF THE UNITED STATES DURING WORLD WAR 1917-1920. 3 vols. New Haven: United Printing Services, n.d.

Hills, Ratcliffe M. THE WAR HISTORY OF THE 102 D REGIMENT UNITED STATES INFANTRY. Hartford, Conn.: 1924. 38 p.

McCarthy, Robert J. A HISTORY OF TROOP A CAVALRY, CONNECTICUT NATIONAL GUARD AND ITS SERVICE IN THE GREAT WAR AS CO. D, 102D MACHINE GUN BATTALION. New Haven, Conn.: Tuttle, Morehouse and Taylor, 1919. 93 p.

NATURALIZATION RECORDS

The Connecticut State Library maintains naturalization records received from the Superior Court and County Courts by county and thereafter alphabetically by applicant dating from 1700 to 1900. The CSL is completing a name index to these records.

There are no naturalization records for Fairfield County on file at the CSL.

These records are in the Archives Record Group 3 Main 2, Boxes 585-602.

NEWSPAPERS

Brigham, Clarence Saunders. "Connecticut Bibliography of American Newspapers 1690-1820." AMERICAN ANTIQUARIAN SOCIETY PROCEEDINGS 23 (1902): 254-330.

THE CONNECTICUT MEDIA DIRECTORY. Framingham, Mass.: New England Newselip Agency, 1979. 68 p.

"Early Newspaper Genealogical Gleanings--Connecticut Courant August 25, 1788." IDAHO GENEALOGICAL SOCIETY QUARTERLY 10 (December 1967) and 11 (January 1968): 7-9.

"Extracts from the Connecticut Journal, 1776." TAG 35 (1959): 155-57.

Gustafson, Don. A PRELIMINARY CHECKLIST OF CONNECTICUT NEWS-PAPERS 1755-1975. 2 vols. Hartford: CSL, 1978.

"List of Bound Newspapers in the Connecticut Historical Society." CHS PAPERS AND REPORTS, 1893, pp. 30-34.

Macom, Benjamin. "Connecticut Journalism in 1705." CQ 2 (1896): 99.

McNulty, John Bard. OLDER THAN THE NATION: THE STORY OF THE HARTFORD COURANT. Stonington: Pequot Press, 1964. 231 p.

Morse, Jarvis Means. CONNECTICUT NEWSPAPERS IN THE EIGHTEENTH CENTURY. Tercentenary Publication, no. 36. New Haven: Yale University Press, 1935.

New England Library Association. Bibliography Committee. A GUIDE TO NEWSPAPER INDEXES IN NEW ENGLAND. Holden, Mass.: 1978. 91 p.

Spaulding, E. Wilder. "The CONNECTICUT COURANT, A Representative Newspaper in the Eighteenth Century." NEQ 3 (1930): 443-63.

Williams, Bill. "The Newspaper Chase." CONNECTICUT 42 (November 1979): 64-66, 112-15, 118-19.

TAXATION

Gipson, Lawrence Henry. "Connecticut Taxation and Parliamentary Aid Preceding the Revolutionary War." AMERICAN HISTORICAL REVIEW 36 (1931): 721-39.

_____. CONNECTICUT TAXATION, 1750-1775. Conn. Tercentenary Commission Publication, no. 10. New Haven: Yale University Press, 1931. 44 p.

_____. "Studies in Colonial Connecticut Taxation: 1. The Taxation of the Connecticut Towns, 1750-1775. 2. Connecticut Taxation and Parliamentary Aid Preceding the Revolutionary War." Circular no. 65, pp. 284-98, 721-39. Bethlehem, Pa.: Lehigh University, Institute of Research, 1931.

Jones, Frederick Robertson. HISTORY OF TAXATION IN CONNECTICUT, 1636-1776. Baltimore, Md.: Johns Hopkins Press, 1896. 70 p.

U.S. National Archives and Records Service. CARD INDEX TO "OLD LOAN" LEDGERS OF THE BUREAU OF THE PUBLIC DEBT, 1790-1836. Washington, D.C.: 1965. 4 p.

_____. INTERNAL REVENUE ASSESSMENT LISTS FOR CONNECTICUT, 1862-1866. Washington, D.C.: 1969. 7 p.

_____. RECORDS OF THE CONNECTICUT, NEW HAMPSHIRE AND RHODE ISLAND CONTINENTAL LOAN OFFICES, 1777-1789. Washington, D.C.: 1976. 8 p.

VITAL RECORDS

Bailey, Frederick William. EARLY CONNECTICUT MARRIAGES AS FOUND ON ANCIENT CHURCH RECORDS PRIOR TO 1800. 7 vols. Reprint. Baltimore: Genealogical Publishing Co., 1968. (LDS 2805).

Banks, Charles Edward. "Genealogical Items from the Medical Journal of John E. Winthrop." TAG 23 (1946-47): 62-64, 124-28, 231-34; 24 (1948): 41-47, 108-15.

Barbour Index. (CSL, LDS 1452. Name index, 2,887-2,966 and town index, 2,967-2,983).

Bowman Vital Records Index from Newspapers in Connecticut and Massachusetts. (CSL, LDS 1450 pt. 1-2).

Cook, Levis D. "Register of the Rev. John Sharpe, Chaplain to the Queen's Forces in New York, 1707-1712." TAG 35 (1959): 184-85.

Goddard, George S. "Barbour Collection of Connecticut Vital Records." In REPORT OF THE STATE LIBRARIAN TO THE GOVERNOR. Hartford: State of Connecticut, 1922, pp. 23-25.

HANDBOOK FOR CONNECTICUT TOWN CLERKS. Storrs: Institute of Public Service, Conn., 1979. 104 p.

Meeker, Mrs. William. "Marriage Notices." CN 6 (1974): 622-30.

Mortality Records 1850-1880. (CSL, LDS 30,729 pt. 1-2).

Sawyer, Ray C. MARRIAGES AND DEATHS OF CONNECTICUT PEOPLE PUBLISHED IN THE CHRISTIAN INTELLIGENCER OF THE REFORMED DUTCH

CHURCH FROM 1830 TO 1874. Hartford: CSL, 1939. 60 p. Index.

Shepard, Willard O. "Marriage in Connecticut." YANKEE 3 (May 1937): 26-27.

"The State's Vital Statistics." CM 5 (1899): 129.

WPA Historical Records Survey. GUIDE TO VITAL STATISTICS IN THE CHURCH RECORDS OF CONNECTICUT. New Haven: Conn. Historical Records Survey, WPA, 1942. 190 p. (LDS 924,002).

WITCHCRAFT

Child, Frank Samuel. A COLONIAL WITCH: BEING A STUDY OF THE BLACK ART IN THE COLONY OF CONNECTICUT. New York: Baker and Taylor, 1897. 307 p.

Hoadly, Charles J. "A Case of Witchcraft in Hartford." CM 5 (1899): 557-61.

Holdsworth, William K. "Adultery or Witchcraft? A New Note on an Old Case in Connecticut." NEQ 48 (September 1975): 394-409.

Jacobus, Donald Lines. "Connecticut Witches." NEW HAVEN GENEALOGI-CAL MAGAZINE 4 (1927): 951-58.

Keeney, Steven H. "Witchcraft in Colonial Connecticut and Massachusetts: An Annotated Bibliography." BULLETIN OF BIBLIOGRAPHY AND MAGAZINE NOTES 33 (1976): 61-72.

Langdon, Carolyn S. "Connecticut Witchcraft--What Was it?" CHSB 38 (1973): 23-29.

Levermore, Charles Herbert. "Witchcraft in Connecticut." NEW ENGLAND MAGAZINE 6 (1933): 636-44.

_____. "Witchcraft in Connecticut." NEW ENGLANDER 184: 788-817.

_____. "Witchcraft in Connecticut, 1647-1697." NEW ENGLANDER AND YALE REVIEW 8 (1885): 788-817.

Morgan, Forrest. "Witchcraft in Connecticut." AMERICAN HISTORICAL MAGAZINE 1 (1906): 216-38.

Taylor, John Metcalf. THE WITCHCRAFT DELUSION IN COLONIAL CON-
NECTICUT, 1647-1697. New York: Grafton Press, 1908. Reprint. Williams-
town, Mass.: Corner House Publishers, 1974. 172 p.

Tomlinson, Richard G. "Connecticut Witches." CN 5 (1972): 4-8.

_____. WITCHCRAFT TRIALS OF CONNECTICUT. Glastonbury: Conn.
Society of Genealogists, 1978. 80 p.

Part 2

CONNECTICUT COUNTIES

CONNECTICUT CITIES AND TOWNS

CONNECTICUT COUNTIES

FAIRFIELD COUNTY

Organized as an original county in 1666. Counties organized from Fairfield County include Litchfield County.

TOWNS AND CITIES IN FAIRFIELD COUNTY

Bethel, Bridgeport, Brookfield, Danbury, Darien, Easton, Fairfield, Greenwich, Monroe, New Canaan, New Fairfield, Newtown, Norwalk, Redding, Ridgefield, Shelton, Sherman, Stamford, Stratford, Trumbull, Weston, Westport, Wilton.

PUBLISHED WORKS AND OTHER RECORDS

Birth Records of D. Jerome Sands, M.D. of Port Chester, N.Y., 1840-1952. In DAR NEW YORK UNPUBLISHED RECORDS, vol. 378, pp. 19-38. (LDS 913,005).

"Blackened Chimneys on the Coast." FAIRFIELD COUNTY 5 (December 1975): 57, 104-5.

"Border Country: No-one in Horseneck, Stamford or Middlesex was Safe from British Raiders." FAIRFIELD COUNTY 5 (December 1975): 60-61, 122-24.

Card, Lester. MARRIAGES AND DEATHS IN FAIRFIELD COUNTY 1790-1855. Norwalk, Conn.: n.d. Index. 372 p. (LDS 1680).

COMMEMORATIVE BIOGRAPHICAL RECORD OF FAIRFIELD COUNTY, CON-NECTICUT, CONTAINING BIOGRAPHICAL SKETCHES OF PROMINENT AND REPRESENTATIVE CITIZENS, AND OF MANY OF THE EARLY SETTLED FAMI-LIES. Chicago: J.H. Beers and Co., 1899. 1348 p.

Danenberg, Elsie Nicholas. NAVAL HISTORY OF FAIRFIELD COUNTY MEN IN THE REVOLUTION: A TALE UNTOLD. Fairfield: Fairfield Historical Society, 1977. 200 p.

Fairfield County Historical Society. REPORTS AND PAPERS. 9 vols. Bridgeport, Conn.: 1882-1896-97.

"The Fairfield County Historical Society." CQ 2 (1896): 184.

"Fairfield County in '76: The Part it Played in the Revolution." FAIRFIELD COUNTY 5 (December 1975): 47-51.

Hartford. CSL, Record Group 3. Vault 14. Divorce Records, Superior Court. 1711-1798.

Hartford. CSL, Record Group 3, Main 2. Boxes 245-249. Papers on Confiscated Estates, County Court.

Hartford. CSL, Record Group 3. Vault 14. Papers on Confiscated Estates and Loyalists, Superior Court.

Hartford. CSL, Record Group 29. Box 11. State Military Census of 1917. List of Fairfield County Male Residents 16-20 without Dependents, 1917.

Hartford. CSL, Record Group 29. Box 12. State Military Census of 1917. List of Fairfield County Men Eligible for Military Service (i.e., 19 or 20 Years Old by June 1918).

Hartford. CSL, Record Group 33. Boxes 139-140. Materials for a History of Fairfield County. Typescript. WPA Writers' Project.

Hawley, Charles W. "Old Names of Connecticut Towns." BULLETIN OF THE STAMFORD GENEALOGICAL SOCIETY 3 (1961): 61-63.

Heireth, Mrs. Russell. "Methodist Church Marriage Register. Vista, and East Woods, N.Y. Circuit (Several Lower Fairfield County Entries.)" CA 15 (1972): 80-83.

Hurd, Duane Hamilton. HISTORY OF FAIRFIELD COUNTY, CONNECTICUT, WITH ILLUSTRATIONS AND BIOGRAPHICAL SKETCHES OF ITS PROMINENT MEN AND PIONEERS. Philadelphia: J.W. Lewis and Co., 1881. 878 p.

Jacobus, Donald Lines. "Fairfield County, Conn., County Court Records." TAG 34 (1958): 255-56.

_____. HISTORY AND GENEALOGY OF THE FAMILIES OF OLD FAIRFIELD. 6 vols. Fairfield: Eunice Dennie Burr Chapter, DAR, 1929. (LDS 599,305-599,307).

Jarman, Rufus. "Our Own Witches." FAIRFIELD COUNTY 5 (October 1975): 50-57.

McLean, Louise H. "The Eighteenth Century Tourist in Fairfield County." DARIEN HISTORICAL SOCIETY ANNUAL, 1967, pp. 4-13.

Mead, Spencer Percival. WILLS OF FAIRFIELD COUNTY 1648-1757. 2 vols. Greenwich, Conn.: 1929, 1939. Index (LDS 1680).

Pearce, Arthur. "Fairfield County Newspapers." FAIRFIELD COUNTY 4 (July 1974): 38-51.

Stokes, Charles J. HISTORIC CHURCHES OF FAIRFIELD COUNTY. Westport: Mark Publications, 1969. 95 p.

Street, Ona Cates. "Browsing Through History: A Country Gravestone-Robber Glimpses the Past." FAIRFIELD COUNTY 3 (November 1973): 33-35, 44-45.

Volkel, Lowell M. AN INDEX TO THE 1800 CENSUS OF FAIRFIELD AND HARTFORD COUNTIES, STATE OF CONNECTICUT. Danville, Ill.: Author, 1968. 89 p.

Wall, Patricia Q. "Index to Fairfield County Maritime Records, 1777-1789." N.p.: 1974.

WHO'S WHO OF FAIRFIELD COUNTY EXECUTIVES 1979. Greenwich, Ct.: Greenwich Way, 1979. 169 p.

Wilson, Lynn Winfield. HISTORY OF FAIRFIELD COUNTY, CONNECTICUT 1639-1928. 3 vols. Chicago, Ill.: S.J. Clarke Publishing Co., 1929.

HARTFORD COUNTY

Organized as an original county in 1666. Counties organized from Hartford County include Litchfield, Middlesex and Windham Counties.

TOWNS AND CITIES IN HARTFORD COUNTY

Avon, Berlin, Bloomfield, Bristol, Burlington, Canton, East Granby, East Hartford, East Windsor, Enfield, Farmington, Glastonbury, Granby, Hartford, Manchester, Marlborough, New Britain, Newington, Plainville, Rocky Hill, Simsbury, Southington, South Windsor, Suffield, West Hartford, Wethersfield, Windsor, and Windsor Locks.

PUBLISHED WORKS AND OTHER RECORDS

Burpee, Charles Winslow. HISTORY OF HARTFORD COUNTY, CONNECTICUT 1633-1928. 3 vols. Hartford: S.J. Clarke Pub. Co., 1928.

COMMEMORATIVE BIOGRAPHICAL RECORD OF HARTFORD COUNTY, CONNECTICUT, CONTAINING BIOGRAPHICAL SKETCHES OF PROMINENT AND REPRESENTATIVE CITIZENS, AND OF MANY OF THE EARLY SETTLED FAMILIES. 2 vols. Chicago: J.H. Beers and Co., 1901.

De Vito, Michael D. DIARY OF A TROLLEY ROAD: BEING THE STORY OF THE HARTFORD AND SPRINGFIELD STREET RAILWAY COMPANY AND OTHER STREET RAILWAY COMPANIES OF NORTH CENTRAL HARTFORD COUNTY IN CONNECTICUT. Warehouse Point, Conn.: Valley Chapter of the National Railway Historical Society, 1975. 190 p.

Hartford. CSL, Record Group 3. Main 2. Box 96. Divorce Records 1740-1795. Superior Court.

Hartford. CSL, Record Group 3. Vault 11. Drawer 111-29. Divorce Records 1796-1849. Superior Court.

Hartford. CSL, Record Group 16. Item 13. Divorces granted in 1880. List for Hartford County.

Hartford. CSL, Record Group 3. Vault 11. Drawer 111-29. Loyalist Papers. 1777-1779. Superior Court.

Hartford. CSL, Record Group 3. Main 2. Boxes 298-99. Revolutionary War Pension Applications 1820-1832. Superior Court.

Hartford. CSL, Record Group 3. Vault 11. Drawer 536-62. Revolutionary War Pension Applications 1832-1855. Superior Court.

Hartford. CSL, Record Group 3. Main 2. Row 2. Tavern Keepers. 1796-1799, 1800-1860. Superior Court.

"Items from Hartford County Court Records." TAG 23 (1946-47): 114-16.

Kane, Patricia Ellen. "The Joiners of Seventeenth Century Hartford County." CHSB 35 (1970): 65-85.

_____. "The Seventeenth Century Case Furniture of Hartford County, Connecticut, and Its Makers." Master's thesis, University of Delaware, 1968. 196 p.

Trumbull, J. Hammond. MEMORIAL HISTORY OF HARTFORD COUNTY, CONNECTICUT 1633-1884. 2 vols. Boston: Edward L. Osgood Pub., 1886.

Volkel, Lowell M. AN INDEX TO THE 1800 CENSUS OF FAIRFIELD AND HARTFORD COUNTIES, STATE OF CONNECTICUT. Danville, Ill.: Author, 1968.

WPA Historical Records Survey. INVENTORY OF THE TOWN AND CITY ARCHIVES OF CONNECTICUT, NO. 2, HARTFORD COUNTY, VOL. 1. AVON, BERLIN, BLOOMFIELD. New Haven: Historical Records Survey, 1939. 299 p. (LDS 908,524 Item 1).

LITCHFIELD COUNTY

Organized as a county in 1751 from Fairfield and Hartford Counties.

TOWNS AND CITIES IN LITCHFIELD COUNTY

Barkhamsted, Bethlehem, Bridgewater, Canaan, Colebrook, Cornwall, Goshen, Harwinton, Kent, Litchfield, Morris, New Hartford, New Milford, Norfolk, North Canaan, Plymouth, Roxbury, Salisbury, Sharon, Thomaston, Torrington, Warren, Washington, Watertown, Winchester and Woodbury.

PUBLISHED WORKS AND OTHER RECORDS

BIOGRAPHICAL REVIEW. THIS VOLUME CONTAINS BIOGRAPHICAL SKETCHES OF THE LEADING CITIZENS OF LITCHFIELD COUNTY, CONNECTICUT. Boston: Biographical Review Pub. Co., 1896. 67 p.

Bronson, Elliott B. "The Home of the Western Reserve." CUYAHOGA COUNTY EARLY SETTLERS' ASSOCIATION ANNUAL 6 (6): 16-39.

Calhoun, Newell Meeker. LITCHFIELD COUNTY SKETCHES. Norfolk: Litchfield County View Club, 1906. 177 p.

Cropsey, Joyce MacKenzie. REGISTER OF REVOLUTIONARY SOLDIERS AND PATRIOTS BURIED IN LITCHFIELD COUNTY. Canaan, N.Y.: Phoenix Pub. Co., 1976. 156 p.

Deane, Edgar. "Among the Litchfield Hills." CQ 4 (1898): 86-99.

Deming, Dorothy. SETTLEMENT OF LITCHFIELD COUNTY. Conn. Tercentenary Publication, no. 7. New Haven: Yale University Press, 1933. 16 p.

Finn, William J. "The Mountain County Regiment." THE LURE OF THE LITCHFIELD HILLS 14 (1943): 6-7, 27-28.

"The Following is the Record of Funerals Attended by Me, Z.D. Scokey, During My Ministry. (1845-1878)." DAR MAGAZINE, November 1968, pp. 840-41.

Goodenough, Arthur. CLERY OF LITCHFIELD COUNTY. Winchester: Litchfield County University Club, 1909. 242 p.

Hartford. CSL, Record Group 3, Vault 15. Divorce Records 1752-1922. Superior Court.

Hartford. CSL, Record Group 3. Vault 15. Papers, Confiscated Estates and Loyalists 1753-1876. Superior Court.

Hartford. CSL, Record Group 3. Vault 15. Papers, Confiscated Estates and Loyalists. County Court.

Hartford. CSL, Record Group 3. Vault 15. Papers, Militia. Superior Court.

Hartford. CSL, Record Group 3. Vault 15. Papers, Militia. 1751-1855. County Court.

HISTORY OF LITCHFIELD COUNTY, CONNECTICUT, WITH ILLUSTRATIONS AND BIOGRAPHICAL SKETCHES OF ITS PROMINENT MEN AND PIONEERS. Philadelphia: J.W. Lewis Co., 1881. 730 p. (LDS 496,898).

Kilbourne, Dwight C. THE BENCH AND BAR OF LITCHFIELD COUNTY, CONNECTICUT 1709-1909. BIOGRAPHICAL SKETCHES OF MEMBERS, HISTORY AND CATALOGUE OF THE LITCHFIELD LAW SCHOOL. Historical Notes. Litchfield: Author, 1909, 260 p.

Kilbourne, Payne Kenyon. A BIOGRAPHICAL HISTORY OF THE COUNTY OF LITCHFIELD, CONNECTICUT. New York: Clarke, Austin and Co., 1851. 413 p.

Leete, William White. "Away from the Railroad in Connecticut." CM 5 (1899): 351-61.

Litchfield Historical Society. LITCHFIELD COUNTY FURNITURE, 1730-1850. AN EXHIBITION PRESENTED AT THE LITCHFIELD HISTORICAL SOCIETY, LITCHFIELD, CONNECTICUT, JULY 3RD TO AUGUST 10TH, 1969, ARRANGED TO COMMEMORATE THE TWO HUNDRED AND FIFTIETH ANNIVERSARY OF THE FOUNDING OF LITCHFIELD. Litchfield, Conn.: Litchfield Historical Society, 1969. 124 p.

Morris, James. STATISTICAL ACCOUNT OF SEVERAL TOWNS IN THE COUNTY OF LITCHFIELD. New Haven: Conn. Academy of Arts and Sciences, 1815. 124 p.

THE ONE HUNDRED AND FIFTIETH ANNIVERSARY OF THE LITCHFIELD COUNTY ASSOCIATION, CELEBRATED IN JOINT MEETING OF THE LITCH-FIELD NORTH AND LITCHFIELD SOUTH ASSOCIATION. Litchfield, Conn.: Litchfield Enquirer, 1903.

Peck, Brainerd T. "Early Settlement of Litchfield County, Connecticut." CN 13 (1980): 371-73.

Phelps, Charles Shepherd. RURAL LIFE IN LITCHFIELD COUNTY. Norfolk: Litchfield County University Club, 1917. 317 p.

Richards, Josephine Ellis. HONOR ROLL OF LITCHFIELD COUNTY REVOLU-TIONARY SOLDIERS. Litchfield: May Floyd Tallmadge Chapter, DAR, 1912. 233 p. (LDS 599,295).

Trumbull, H. Clay. "The Achievements of Connecticut Men." CM 8 (1904): 730-37.

_____. "The Evangelization of the World." CM 8 (1904): 505-11.

_____. "Litchfield County: Its Contributions to the Nation's Power and Fame." CM 8 (1903): 225-30.

Vaill, Dudley Landon. THE COUNTY REGIMENT, A SKETCH OF THE SECOND REGIMENT OF CONNECTICUT VOLUNTEER HEAVY ARTILLERY, ORIGINALLY THE NINETEENTH VOLUNTEER INFANTRY, IN THE CIVIL WAR. Litchfield: Litchfield County University Club, 1908. 108 p.

Vaill, Theodore Frelinghuysen. HISTORY OF THE SECOND CONNECTICUT VOLUNTEER HEAVY ARTILLERY, ORIGINALLY THE NINETEENTH CONNECTI-CUT VOLUNTEERS. Winsted: Winsted Printing Co., 1868. 366 p.

Volkel, Lowell M. AN INDEX TO THE 1800 FEDERAL CENSUS OF LITCH-FIELD, NEW HAVEN, TOLLAND AND WINDHAM COUNTIES, STATE OF CONN. Danville, Ill.: Author, 1969.

Willard, L.F. "Connecticut's Northwest Corner." YANKEE 43, no. 3 (March 1979): 76-81.

MIDDLESEX COUNTY

Organized as a county in 1785 from Hartford, New Haven and New London
Counties.

TOWNS AND CITIES IN MIDDLESEX COUNTY

Chester, Clinton, Cromwell, Deep River, Durham, East Haddam, East Hampton,
Essex, Haddam, Killingworth, Middlefield, Middletown, Old Saybrook, Portland, and Westbrook.

HISTORICAL SOCIETY

Middlesex Historical Society, General Mansfield House, 151 Main Street,
Middletown 06457. (203) 346-0746.

PUBLISHED WORKS AND OTHER RECORDS

COMMEMORATIVE BIOGRAPHICAL RECORD OF MIDDLESEX COUNTY, CON-
NECTICUT. CONTAINING BIOGRAPHICAL SKETCHES OF PROMINENT AND
REPRESENTATIVE CITIZENS, AND OF MANY OF THE EARLY SETTLED FAMI-
LIES. Chicago: J.H. Beers Co., 1903. 1,001 p.

COUNTY ATLAS OF MIDDLESEX, CONNECTICUT. New York: F.W. Beers
and Co., 1874. 144 p.

Field, David Dudley. A STATISTICAL ACCOUNT OF THE COUNTY OF
MIDDLESEX IN CONNECTICUT. 1819. Reprint. Haddam: J.T. Kelsey,
1892. 186 p.

Griswold, Glenn E. MIDDLESEX COUNTY, CONNECTICUT, INSCRIPTIONS,
KILLINGWORTH AND CLINTON. Branford, Conn.: 1936. 113 p.

Hartford. CSL, Record Group 3. Vault 15. Divorce Records 1786-1797. Superior Court.

Hartford. CSL, Record Group 3. Vault 15. Papers, Revolutionary War Pension Applications 1785-1855. County Court.

Hartford. CSL, Record Group 3. Vault 15. Papers, Militia. County Court.

Harwood, Pliny LeRoy. HISTORY OF EASTERN CONNECTICUT EMBRACING THE COUNTIES OF TOLLAND, WINDHAM, MIDDLESEX AND NEW LONDON. 3 vols. New Haven: Pioneer Historical Pub. Co., 1932.

HISTORY OF MIDDLESEX COUNTY, CONNECTICUT WITH BIOGRAPHICAL SKETCHES OF ITS PROMINENT MEN. New York: J.B. Beers and Co., 1884. 579 p.

Volkel, Lowell M. AN INDEX TO THE 1800 FEDERAL CENSUS OF MIDDLESEX AND NEW LONDON COUNTIES. Danville, Ill.: Author, n.d. 58 p.

NEW HAVEN COUNTY

Organized as an original county in 1666. Counties organized from New Haven County include Middlesex County.

TOWNS AND CITIES IN NEW HAVEN COUNTY

Ansonia, Beacon Falls, Bethany, Branford, Cheshire, Derby, East Haven, Guilford, Hamden, Madison, Meriden, Middlebury, Milford, Naugatuck, New Haven, North Branford, North Haven, Orange, Oxford, Prospect, Seymour, Southbury, Wallingford, Waterbury, West Haven, Wolcott, Woodbridge.

PUBLISHED WORKS AND OTHER RECORDS

Beers, Frederick W. ATLAS OF NEW HAVEN COUNTY, CONNECTICUT FROM ACTUAL SURVEY. New York: F.W. Beers, A.D. Ellis and G.G. Soule. 1868. 58 p.

COMMEMORATIVE BIOGRAPHICAL RECORD OF NEW HAVEN COUNTY, CONN. CONTAINING BIOGRAPHICAL SKETCHES OF PROMINENT AND REPRESENTATIVE CITIZENS, AND OF MANY OF THE EARLY SETTLED FAMILIES. Chicago: J.H. Beers, 1902. 1563 p. (LDS 22114 pt. 1-3).

CONNECTICUT PRIVATE RECORDS. NEW HAVEN COUNTY. DEATHS AND MARRIAGES 1824-1883. 49 p.

Hartford. CSL, Record Group 3. Vault 11A. Drawer 315-22. Divorce Records, 1712-1798. Superior Court.

Hartford. CSL, Record Group 3. Vault 11A. Drawer 716-52. Divorce Records, 1798-1900. Superior Court.

Hartford. CSL, Record Group 5. Drawer 257-88. Papers-Confiscated Lands and Loyalists. County Court.

Hartford. CSL, Record Group 3. Vault 11A. Drawer 315-22. Papers. Confiscated Lands and Loyalists. Superior Court.

Hartford. CSL, Record Group 3. Vault 11A. Drawer 257-88. Papers. Militia. 1712-1855. County Court.

Hartford. CSL, Record Group 3. Vault 11A. Drawer 257-88. Papers. Revolutionary War Pensions. County Court.

Hartford. CSL, Record Group 3. Vault 11A. Drawer 315-22, 714-15. Papers. Revolutionary War Pensions, 1798-1900. Superior Court.

Hill, Everett Gleason. A MODERN HISTORY OF NEW HAVEN AND EASTERN NEW HAVEN COUNTY. 2 vols. New York: S.J. Clarke, 1918.

ILLUSTRATED REVIEW OF THE NAUGATUCK VALLEY. New York: Sovereign Pub. and Engraving Co., 1891. 98 p. Index.

Mitchell, Mary Hewitt. HISTORY OF NEW HAVEN COUNTY. 3 vols. Chicago: Pioneer Historical Publishing Co., 1930.

Molloy, Leo Thomas. TERCENTENARY PICTORIAL AND HISTORY OF THE LOWER NAUGATUCK VALLEY. Ansonia: Emerson Bros., 1935. 404 p.

Rockey, John L., ed. HISTORY OF NEW HAVEN COUNTY, CONNECTI-CUT. 2 vols. New York: W.W. Preston and Co., 1892. (LDS 845,225).

Sons of the American Revolution. ROSTER OF GRAVES OF, OR MONU-MENTS TO, PATRIOTS OF 1775-1783, AND OF SOLDIERS OF COLONIAL WARS, IN AND ADJACENT TO NEW HAVEN COUNTY. 4 vols. New Haven: 1931-34. (title varies).

Volkel, Lowell M. AN INDEX TO THE 1800 FEDERAL CENSUS OF LITCH-FIELD, NEW HAVEN, TOLLAND AND WINDHAM COUNTIES, STATE OF CONNECTICUT. Danville, Ill.: Author, 1969.

WPA Historical Records Survey. INVENTORY OF THE TOWN AND CITY ARCHIVES OF CONNECTICUT, NO. 5, NEW HAVEN COUNTY, V.8. NORTH BRANFORD, NORTH HAVEN, ORANGE, OXFORD, PROSPECT, SEYMOUR, SOUTHBURY. New Haven: Historical Records Survey, WPA, 1938. 189 p. (LDS 897,354).

Wall, Patricia Q. INDEX TO NEW HAVEN COUNTY MARITIME RECORDS, 1776-1783. New Haven, Conn.: Author, 1975.

Ward, Jessamine, and Guest, Gladys. TERCENTENARY PICTORIAL AND HISTORY OF THE LOWER NAUGATUCK VALLEY. N.p., n.d. 123 p. Index.

NEW LONDON COUNTY

Organized as an original county in 1666. Counties organized from New London County include Middlesex and Windham Counties.

New London Historical Society, 11 Blinman Street, 06320. (203) 443-1209.

Publishes: NEW LONDON COUNTY HISTORICAL SOCIETY QUAR-TERLY BULLETIN, 1953-- ; COLLECTIONS, 1901-- ; OCCASIONAL PUBLICATIONS, 1903-- ; RECORDS AND PAPERS, 1890-1912.

TOWNS AND CITIES IN NEW LONDON COUNTY

Bozrah, Colchester, East Lyme, Franklin, Griswold, Groton, Lebanon, Ledyard, Lisbon, Lyme, Montville, New London, North Stonington, Norwich, Old Lyme, Preston, Salem, Sprague, Stonington, Voluntown, Waterford.

PUBLISHED WORKS AND OTHER RECORDS

Beers, Frederick W. ATLAS OF NEW LONDON COUNTY, CONNECTICUT. New York: F.W. Beers, A.D. Ellis and G.G. Soule, 1868. 35 p.

BIOGRAPHICAL REVIEW. CONTAINING LIFE SKETCHES OF LEADING CITI-ZENS OF NEW LONDON COUNTY, CONNECTICUT. Boston: Biographical Review Publishing Co., 1898. 478 p.

Brown, Barbara W., and Rose, James M., eds. BLACK ROOTS IN SOUTH-EASTERN CONNECTICUT, 1650-1900. Gale Genealogy and Local History Series, vol. 8. Detroit: Gale Research Co., 1980. 722 p. Index.

Cary, William B. "Revival Experiences during the Great Awakening in 1741-44, in New London County." NEW ENGLANDER 62 (1883): 731-39.

CONNECTICUT PRIVATE RECORDS. RECORDS OF NEHEMIAH WATERMAN,

JUSTICE OF THE PEACE, NEW LONDON COUNTY 1712-1801. Hartford: CSL. 30 p.

Ellsberry, Elizabeth Prather. CEMETERY RECORDS OF NEW LONDON COUNTY, CONNECTICUT. 2 vols. Chillicothe, Mo.: 1968.

GENEALOGICAL AND BIOGRAPHICAL RECORD OF NEW LONDON COUNTY, CONNECTICUT. Chicago: J.H. Beers, 1905. 957 p. (LDS 844,968).

Hartford. CSL, Record Group 3. Main 3. Citizenship Declarations, 1854-1873. Superior Court.

Hartford. CSL, Record Group 16. Item 13. Divorce List, 1881.

Hartford. CSL, Record Group 3. Main 3. F-136, F-377. Divorce Records, 1719-1875. Superior Court.

Hartford. CSL, Record Group 3. Main 3. BOX F427-F449. Militia, 1702-1834. County Court.

Hartford. CSL, Record Group 3. Main 3. Box F136-F177. Militia, 1713-1881. Superior Court.

Hartford. CSL, Record Group 3. Records of Trials, 1661-1700. County Court. (LDS 1926).

Hartford. CSL, Record Group 3. Main 3. Box F136-F177. Revolutionary War Pensions, 1713-1881. Superior Court.

Hartford. CSL, Record Group 3. Main 3. Box F427-F449. Revolutionary War Pensions, 1822-1853. County Court.

Harwood, Pliny LeRoy. HISTORY OF EASTERN CONNECTICUT EMBRACING THE COUNTIES OF TOLLAND, WINDHAM, MIDDLESEX AND NEW LONDON. 3 vols. New Haven: Pioneer Historical Pub. Co., 1932.

Hurd, Duane Hamilton. HISTORY OF NEW LONDON COUNTY, WITH BIOGRAPHICAL SKETCHES OF MANY OF ITS PIONEERS AND PROMINENT MEN. Philadelphia: J.W. Lewis and Co., 1882. 768 p.

Marshall, Benjamin Tinkham. A MODERN HISTORY OF NEW LONDON COUNTY, CONNECTICUT. 3 vols. New York: Lewis Historical Publishing Co., 1922.

Volkel, Lowell M. AN INDEX TO THE 1800 FEDERAL CENSUS OF MIDDLE-SEX AND NEW LONDON COUNTIES. Danville, Ill.: Author, n.d. 58 p.

Waterman, Maud Holly. "Marriages Performed by Nehemiah Waterman, Jr., J.P. New London Co., Conn." NGSQ 22 (1934): 53-54.

Waterman, Nehemiah Jr. 1736-1801. New London County Justice of the Peace. Casebook 1788-1789. Marriage Records 1781-1801. Genealogical Records of the Waterman Family from 1733.

TOLLAND COUNTY

Organized in 1785 from Windham County.

TOWNS AND CITIES IN TOLLAND COUNTY

Andover, Bolton, Columbia, Coventry, Ellington, Hebron, Mansfield, Somers, Stafford, Tolland, Union, Vernon and Willington.

PUBLISHED WORKS AND OTHER RECORDS

Cole, J.R. HISTORY OF TOLLAND COUNTY, CONNECTICUT, INCLUDING ITS EARLY SETTLEMENT AND PROGRESS TO THE PRESENT TIME. New York: W.W. Preston and Co., 1888. 992 p.

COMMEMORATIVE BIOGRAPHICAL RECORD OF TOLLAND AND WINDHAM COUNTIES, CONNECTICUT CONTAINING BIOGRAPHICAL SKETCHES OF PROMINENT AND REPRESENTATIVE CITIZENS AND OF THE MANY OF THE EARLY SETTLED FAMILIES. Chicago: J.H. Beers and Co., 1903. 1358 p.

Hartford. CSL, Record Group 3. Box G160-G168. Revolutionary War Pensions.

Hartford. CSL, Record Group 3. Boxes G66-G87. Divorce Records, 1787-1910. Superior Court.

Hartford. CSL, Record Group 3. Boxes G66-G87. Revolutionary War Pension Records.

Harwood, Pliny LeRoy. HISTORY OF EASTERN CONNECTICUT EMBRACING THE COUNTIES OF TOLLAND, WINDHAM, MIDDLESEX AND NEW LONDON. 3 vols. Chicago: The Pioneer Historical Publishing Co., 1931-32.

Lawson, Harvey Merrill. "Revolutionary Soldiers from Tolland Co., Conn." NEHGR 59 (1905): 21-22.

Volkel, Lowell M. AN INDEX TO THE 1800 FEDERAL CENSUS OF LITCH-FIELD, NEW HAVEN, TOLLAND AND WINDHAM COUNTIES, STATE OF CONNECTICUT. Danville, Ill.: Author, 1969.

WINDHAM COUNTY

Organized in 1726 from Hartford and New London Counties.

TOWNS AND CITIES IN WINDHAM COUNTY

Ashford, Brooklyn, Canterbury, Chaplin, Eastford, Hampton, Killingly, Plainfield, Pomfret, Putnam, Scotland, Sterling, Thompson, Windham and Woodstock.

NEWSPAPERS

WINDHAM COUNTY OBSERVER AND PUTNAM PATRIOT. Weekly. 36 South Main Street, Putnam, 06260. (203) 928-2015.

WINDHAM COUNTY TRANSCRIPT. Weekly. 23 Center Street, Danielson, 06239. (203) 774-9357.

PUBLISHED WORKS AND OTHER RECORDS

Bayles, Richard Mather. HISTORY OF WINDHAM COUNTY, CONNECTICUT. New York: W.W. Preston and Co., 1889. 1,204 p.

COMMEMORATIVE BIOGRAPHICAL RECORD OF TOLLAND AND WINDHAM COUNTIES, CONNECTICUT, CONTAINING BIOGRAPHICAL SKETCHES CF PROMINENT AND REPRESENTATIVE CITIZENS AND OF MANY OF THE EARLY SETTLED FAMILIES. Chicago: J.H. Beers and Co., 1903. 1,358 p. Index.

Ellsberry, Elizabeth Prather. CEMETERY RECORDS OF WINDHAM COUNTY, CONNECTICUT. Chilliothe, Mo.: Author, 1968.

Hartford. CSL, Record Group 3. Divorce Records, 1726-1907 (alphabetically arranged). Superior Court.

Hartford. CSL, Record Group 16. Item 16. Windham County. Divorces in 1880.

Hartford. CSL, Record Group 3. Box H. Loyalists. Papers on Confiscated Estates. County Court.

Hartford. CSL, Record Group 3. Box H. Militia Papers, 1728-1759. County Court.

Hartford. CSL, Record Group 3. Box H324-H351. Militia Papers, 1783-1862. Superior Court.

Hartford. CSL, Record Group 3. Boxes H324-H351. Name Changes. 1862-1886.

Hartford. CSL, Record Group 3. Box H. Revolutionary War Pension Applications, 1820-1831.

Hartford. CSL, Record Group 3. Boxes H324-H351. Revolutionary War Pension Applications, 1789. Superior Court.

Harwood, Pliny LeRoy. HISTORY OF EASTERN CONNECTICUT EMBRACING THE COUNTIES OF TOLLAND, WINDHAM, MIDDLESEX AND NEW LONDON. 3 vols. Chicago: Pioneer Historical Publishing Co., 1931-1932.

Larned, Ellen Douglas. HISTORIC GLEANINGS IN WINDHAM COUNTY, CONNECTICUT. Providence, R.I.: Preston and Rounds, 1899. 254 p.

_____. HISTORY OF WINDHAM COUNTY, CONNECTICUT: 2 vols. Worchester, Mass.: Charles Hamilton, 1879.

Lincoln, Allen B. A MODERN HISTORY OF WINDHAM COUNTY, CONNECTICUT. 2 vols. Chicago: J.J. Clarke Pub. Co., 1920.

Sherman, John. A VIEW OF THE ECCLESIASTICAL PROCEEDINGS IN THE COUNTY OF WINDHAM, CONNECTICUT, IN WHICH THE ORIGINAL ASSOCIATION OF THAT COUNTY AND A FEW MEMBERS OF THE FIRST CHURCH IN MANSFIELD WERE CONCERNED. Utica, N.Y.: Asahel Seward, 1806. 110 p.

Tourtellotte, Jerome. A HISTORY OF COMPANY K OF THE SEVENTH CONNECTICUT VOLUNTEER INFANTRY IN THE CIVIL WAR, COMPILED BY A MEMBER WHO WAS SECOND IN RANK IN THE COMPANY WHEN THE REGIMENT LEFT THE STATE FOR THE FRONT AND SECOND IN RANK IN

THE REGIMENT WHEN IT RETURNED TO THE STATE FOR FINAL DISCHARGE. N.p., 1910. 217 p.

Volkel, Lowell M. AN INDEX TO THE 1800 FEDERAL CENSUS OF LITCH-FIELD, NEW HAVEN, TOLLAND AND WINDHAM COUNTIES, STATE OF CONN. Danville, Ill.: Author, 1969.

Wakley, Stephen. HISTORY OF THE SEVENTH CONNECTICUT VOLUNTEER INFANTRY, HAWLEY'S BRIGADE, TERRY'S DIVISION, TENTH ARMY CORPS, 1861-1865. Hartford, Conn.: Author, 1905. 326 p.

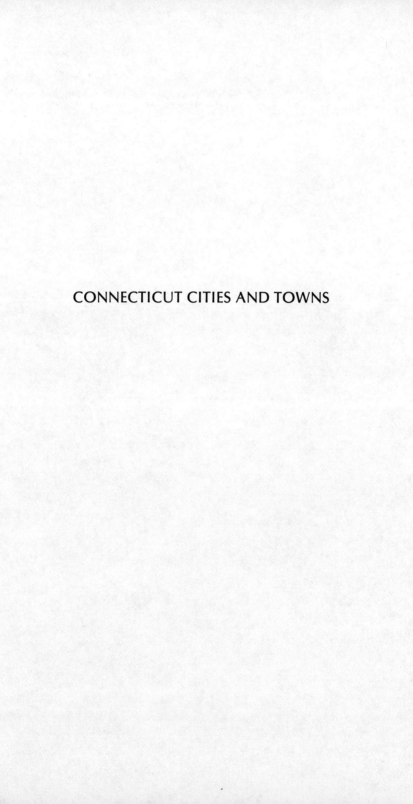

CONNECTICUT CITIES AND TOWNS

ANDOVER

TOLLAND COUNTY. Organized 18 May 1848 from COVENTRY and HEBRON (in 1790 the part of the parish of ANDOVER that was in LEBANON became part of HEBRON).

CEMETERY RECORDS AND CEMETERIES

NAME	ADDRESS	HALE NO.	CITATION
New Andover Cemetery	Near Center, N.W. of Railroad Station	1	1:1-18
Old Andover Cemetery	Near Center, S.E. of Railroad Station	2	1:19-30
Townsend Cemetery	Bishop Road	3	1:31-35
Post Cemetery	Hebron and Bolton Roads	4	1:36
Smith Cemetery	One grave in field by old Baker House. 1 mile West of Village.	5	1:37-38

Index to Hale inscriptions: 1:39-50.

Case, James R. DESCRIPTIONS FROM THE CONGREGATIONAL CHURCH CEMETERY. Typescript. 14 p.

INSCRIPTIONS FROM OLD CEMETERY. N.p., n.d. 14 p.

White, E.D. CEMETERIES OF ANDOVER. N.p., n.d. 20 p.

CHURCH RECORDS

CONGREGATIONAL CHURCH. Minutes, 1747-1917. Vital Records, 1818-1932. (CSL, LDS 1488).

LAND RECORDS

Deeds, 1848-1854. (LDS 1487).

LIBRARY

Andover Public Library, Route 6, 06232. (203) 742-7428.

PROBATE RECORDS

Andover Probate District, Burnap Brook Road, 06232 (203) 742-8510. Also includes BOLTON and COLUMBIA.

> Organized 27 June 1851 from the Hebron Probate District. The part of ANDOVER that was in LEBANON was made a part of HEBRON from May 1790 to 1820.

> ON FILE AT THE CSL: Estate Papers 1787-1946 (includes May 1789 to 27 June 1851 of the Hebron Probate District). Index: 1787-1946. Inventory Control Book: 1787-1946.

SCHOOL RECORDS

List of pupils in various school districts 1820-1864 of BOZRAH, BROOKLYN, ANDOVER, LEBANON and BOLTON. (CSL, LDS 1482).

VITAL RECORDS

Town Clerk, School Road, 06232. (203) 742-7305).

The BARBOUR INDEX covers births and marriages from 1848 to 1851 and deaths from 1848 to 1881. Based on a photocopy of the original records made in 1924, it is on file at the CSL.

ANSONIA

NEW HAVEN COUNTY. Organized April 1889 from DERBY.

CEMETERY RECORDS AND CEMETERIES

NAME	ADDRESS	HALE NO.	CITATION
Pine Grove Cemetery	168 Wakelee Avenue	1	1:1–134
St. Mary Roman Catholic Cemetery. (Office)	185 Division Street 218 New Haven Avenue Derby, 06418 (203) 735-8026	2	1:135–200
Elm Street Cemetery	40 Elm Street	3	1:201–26
Bare Plains Cemetery	166 Wakelee Avenue	4	1:227–34
St. Mary Roman Catholic (Old Cemetery)	177 Wakelee Avenue	5	1:235–44
Merwin Cemetery	(One stone in a printing Office).	6	1:245
Evergreen Cemetery	West Ansonia		(no citation)
Oak Cliff Cemetery	36 Elm Street		(no citation)

Index to Hale inscriptions 1:246–295.

CHURCH RECORDS

CHRIST (EPISCOPAL) CHURCH. Minutes: 1849–1878. Vital Records: 1834–1941 (CSL, LDS 1498).

FIRST CONGREGATIONAL CHURCH. Baptisms: 1850–1961 (CSL, typescript).

MISCELLANEOUS CHURCH RECORDS. (NHCHS, LDS 1455).

HISTORICAL SOCIETY

See DERBY: Derby Historical Society.

LIBRARY

Ansonia Library; 53 South Cliff Street; 06401. (203) 734-6275.

NEWSPAPER

EVENING SENTINEL. Daily. 241 Main St., 06401. (203) 743-2546.
The EVENING SENTINEL has been microfilmed since 19 August 1896.

The PRELIMINARY CHECKLIST lists four newspapers for ANSONIA.

PROBATE RECORDS

ANSONIA is in the Derby Probate District.

VITAL RECORDS

Town Clerk, City Hall, 253 Main Street, 06401. (203) 734-8034.
Earliest birth record 17 April 1889, marriage record 18 April
1889 and death record 26 April 1889.

Birth records of Dr. Josiah Coburn of ORANGE, DERBY and ANSONIA, Conn.
(NHCHS, LDS 1455 pt. 31).

PUBLISHED WORKS AND OTHER RECORDS

Molloy, Leo Thomas. TERCENTENERY PICTORIAL AND HISTORY OF THE
LOWER NAUGATUCK VALLEY. Ansonia: Emerson Bros., 1935. 404 p.

Ward, Jessamine, and Guest, Gladys. TERCENTENARY PICTORIAL AND
HISTORY OF THE LOWER NAUGATUCK VALLEY. N.p., n.d. 123 p.
Index.

ASHFORD

WINDHAM COUNTY. Organized October 1714. Towns organized from ASH-FORD include EASTFORD.

CEMETERY RECORDS AND CEMETERIES

NAME	ADDRESS	HALE NO.	CITATION
Knowlton Cemetery	West Ashford Highway	1	1:1-6
Snow Cemetery	1/4 mile West of Warren-ville on Hartford to Providence Road	2	1:7-21
Warrenville Cemetery	30 rods South of raod from Hartford to Providence in Village	3	1:22-25
Woodward Cemetery	Between Warrenville and Ashford on Hartford and Providence Road	4	1:26-30
Old Ashford Cemetery	Back of Church in Ashford	5	1:31-38
South Cemetery	3/4 mile South of Ashford on Ashford to Chaplin Road	6	1:39-53
Gaylord Cemetery	Gaylord property	7	1:54
Dow Cemetery	3/4 mile North of Ashford	8	1:55-56
Phillips Cemetery	On an abandoned road East of four corners between Ash-ford and Union	9	1:57
Westford Cemetery	Westford Village	10	1:58-77
Westford Hill Cemetery	U.S. 52	11	1:78-100
Swamp Cemetery	U.S. 52-South of Lake Chaffee	12	1:101-103

NAME	ADDRESS	HALE NO.	CITATION
James Cemetery	1 1/2 mile North of Ashford	13	1:104
Whipple Cemetery	1 mile North of Ashford	14	1:105–106
St. Mitchchal Cemetery	Warrenville Cemetery	15	(no citation)
Chaffee Cemetery	1 1/4 mile North of Warrenville	16	(no citation)
Feher Cemetery	Warrenville Cemetery	17	(no citation)
Hughes Cemetery	Old Kidder Farm	18	(no citation)
Two Graves (Young)	East of Mestery Place	19	(no citation)
Child's Grave	Smekal Farm	20	(no citation)
Moore Grave	Fred Chism Farm	21	(no citation)
Baker Grave	Cleworth Property	22	(no citation)

Index to Hale inscriptions: 1:107-26.

Biship, Mary B., Mrs. WESTFORD OLD CEMETERY. N.p.: By the author, 1928. 15 p.

Eno, Joel Nelson. "Connecticut Cemetery Inscriptions: Ashford." NEHGR 66 (1912): 38-39; 69 (1915): 276-80, 334-42; 70 (1916): 239-42.

CHURCH RECORDS

BAPTIST CHURCH AT WEST ASHFORD. Minutes, 1765-1863, Vital Records, 1781-1862. (CSL, LDS 1497).

BAPTIST CHURCH. Minutes, 1846-1903. (CSL, LDS 1496).

CONGREGATIONAL CHURCH. Talcott, Mary Kingsbury. "Record of the Congregational Church, Ashford, Connecticut." CONNECTICUT MAGAZINE 10 (1906): 381-93, 735-45; 1 (1907): 150-60.

FIRST CONGREGATIONAL CHURCH. Marriages, 1719-1799. BAILEY 1:29-34.

RECORDS OF THE ASHFORD CONGREGATIONAL CHURCH. Hartford, Congregation Church, 1906.

SECOND CONGREGATIONAL CHURCH. Marriages, 1768-1783. BAILEY 6:82-84.

WESTFORD CONGREGATIONAL CHURCH. Vital Records, 1768-1932. (CSL, LDS 2232).

INDEX CARDS TO ASHFORD CHURCH RECORDS. (CSL, LDS 1448 p.t 1).

LAND RECORDS

Deeds, 1714-1855. Indexed. (LDS 1494, pt. 1-12).

Proprietor's Records, 1705-1770. (LDS 1493).

LIBRARY

Babcock Library, Route 44, 06278. (203) 429-0287.

NEWSPAPER

The PRELIMINARY CHECKLIST lists one newspaper for ASHFORD.

PROBATE RECORDS

Ashford Probate District, Knowlton Memorial Town Hall, Box 38, Route 44, 06278. (203) 429-7044.

> Organized 4 June 1830 from the Pomfret Probate District. Probate Districts organized from the Ashford Probate District include the Eastford Probate District.

> ON FILE AT THE CSL: Estate Papers, 1865-1944. Index, 1865-1944, Inventory Control Book, 1865-1944 and Court Record Book, 1830-1858 (LDS 1495 pt. 1,2); Index, 1830-1933 (LDS 1495 pt. 1,2).

TAX RECORDS

Tax abstracts, 1821, 1828, 1829-34. (CSL Archives RG62).

VITAL RECORDS

Town Clerk, Town Hall, Route 44, 06278. (203) 429-2750.

> Earliest birth record on file at the town clerk's office is 15 July 1712, marriage record is 28 February 1714/15 and death record 18 September 1714.

The BARBOUR INDEX covers the years 1710-1851 and is based on an index Lucius B. Barbour made to volumes 1-4 and that James N. Arnold of Providence, R.I., made to volumes 5 and 6 of the Ashford Vital Records. The first four volumes are on file at the CSL.

"Connecticut Marriages, Before 1750--Town of Ashford." CN 1 (1969): 75-77; 2 (1969): 15-16, 84-85, 159-60.

Marcy, Thomas Knowlton. "Captain Reuben Marcy." CM 6 (1900): 20-24.

Vital Records. 1880-1905. (CSL, LDS 1483 and 003,662).

AVON

HARTFORD COUNTY. Organized May 1830 from FARMINGTON.

CEMETERY RECORDS AND CEMETERIES

NAME	ADDRESS	HALE NO.	CITATION
Greenwood Cemetery	640 Lovely Street	1	1:1-31
St. Mary Cemetery	644 Huckleberry Hill Road	2	1:32-48
West Avon Cemetery	Country Club Street	3	1:49-69
Avon Cemetery	Simsbury Road	4	1:70-93
Cider Brook Cemetery	359 Waterville Road	5	1:94-104
Pet Cemetery	Huckleberry Hill Road	6	1:105-6
Beth-El Cemetery	Jackson Street		(no citation)
Evergreen Cemetery	76 Climax Road		(no citation)
St. Ann Roman Catholic Cemetery	Arch Road		(no citation)

Index to Hale inscriptions: 1:107-31.

CHURCH RECORDS

CONGREGATIONAL CHURCH (originally the Third Church of Farmington) Minutes, 1818-1921. Vital Records, 1818-1904 (CSL, LDS 1491). CSL Index, 1798-1921 (CSL).

NORTHINGTON CONGREGATIONAL CHURCH. Marriages, 1750-1815. BAILEY. 4:12-20.

WEST AVON CONGREGATIONAL CHURCH. Records. (CSL Index 1751-1941). Minutes, 1840-1889 (CSL, LDS 1492).

LAND RECORDS

Deeds, 1830-1867 (LDS 1490 pt. 1,2).

LIBRARY

Avon Free Public Library, 17 West Main Street, 06001. (203) 678-1262.

PROBATE RECORDS

Avon Probate District, Town Hall (P.O. Box 578), 60 West Main Street, 06001. (203) 677-2634.

Organized May 1844 from the Farmington Probate District. Probate Records 1836-1874. (LDS 1489).

ON FILE AT THE CSL: Estate Papers 1842-1905; Inventory Control Books 1842-1905; Index, 1842-1905; Court Record Books, 1844-74.

SCHOOL RECORDS

School Registers, 1879-80 (CSL Archives RG62).

TAX RECORDS

Tax lists, 1869, 1879 (incomplete). (CSL Archives RG62).

VITAL RECORDS

Town Clerk, Town Hall, 60 West Main Street, 06001. (203) 677-2634.

Vital Records, 1850-1884. (LDS 003,662 and 1483). Abstracts of Vital Records, 1852-1880. (CSL Archives RG62).

The BARBOUR INDEX covers the years 1830-1851. The vital records of AVON prior to 1851 are found scattered through volumes 1, 2 and 4 of the land records. The Barbour Index was created from a photostat of these records on file at the CSL. The citation "LR" with the number of the volume is used to document each event. The cards were not checked against the originals.

PUBLISHED WORKS

INVENTORY OF THE TOWN AND CITY ARCHIVES OF CONNECTICUT, NO. 2, HARTFORD COUNTY, VOL. 1. AVON, BERLIN, BLOOMFIELD. Historical Records Survey. Division of Professional and Service Projects WPA, New

Haven: Historical Records Survey, 1939. 299 p. (LDS 908,524 Item 1).

Wadsworth, S.C. "The Towers of Talcott Mountain." CQ 1 (1895): 180-87.

BARKHAMSTED

LITCHFIELD COUNTY. Organized October 1799.

CEMETERY RECORDS AND CEMETERIES

NAME	ADDRESS	HALE NO.	CITATION
Pleasant Valley Cemetery	South part of town near the New Hartford Town Line	1	(no citation)
Riverside Cemetery	U.S. 51	1	1:1-25
Center Cemetery	Moved in 1939 (now covered by reservoir)	2	1:26-51
Barkhamsted Hollow Cemetery	Town Center	3	1:52-56
Riverview (Riverton) Cemetery	Northwest part of Town	4	1:56-71
Old Riverton Cemetery	Rear of Church in Riverton	5	1:71
Indian Cemetery	1 1/2 miles South of Riverton	6	1:71
Weed Family Cemetery	1 mile North of Pleasant Valley on River Road	7	1:71-72
Philip's Farm Cemetery	Philip's Farm	8	1:72
Moses Family Cemetery	(now under reservoir)	8	(no citation)
Johnson Family Cemetery	Johnson Property	9	1:72
Revolutionary War Cemetery	West Side of Town	10	1:72-73
Lavien Vault	Main Highway and North Road	11	(no citation)
Pleasant Valley Cemetery	New Hartford Townline		(no citation)

Soldiers' Burials

Riverside Cemetery 1:74; Center Cemetery 1:75-76; Barkhamsted Hollow Cemetery 1:76-77; Riverton (Riverton) Cemetery 1:77-78; Philip's Farm Cemetery 1:78-79. Index 1:98-99.

Index to Hale inscriptions: 1:80-97.

Tiffany, Correl H. COPY OF THE ALPHABETICAL LIST OF BURIALS IN THE CENTER AND UNIVERSALIST CEMETERIES. N.p.: Author, 1909. 37 p.

CENSUS RECORDS

State Military Census, 1917. List of male residents with their ages. (CSL Archives RG29 Box 12).

CHURCH RECORDS

"Barkhamsted Church Records." CHSB 8 (1943): 13-16, 18-24; 9 (1944): 26-32; 10 (1945): 3-8, 13-16, 20-24, 29-32.

FIRST CONGREGATIONAL CHURCH. Minutes, 1819-1914. Vital Records, 1781-1909. (CSL, LDS 1526). CSL Card Slip Index, 1781-1914. Vital Records, 1781-1909. (CSL, LDS 1526). Marriages, 1787-1804. BAILEY 7:77-79.

PLEASANT VALLEY METHODIST EPISCOPAL CHURCH. Vital Records, 1850-1952. (CSL, LDS 1525).

ST. PAUL EPISCOPAL CHURCH AT RIVERTON. Vital Records, 1828-1937. (CSL, LDS 1527).

HISTORICAL SOCIETY

Barkhamsted Historical Society, Inc., P.O. Box 9, Pleasant Valley, 06063.

LAND RECORDS

Deeds, 1781-1861. Proprietors' Records, 1729-1833. Index, 1729-1905. (LDS 1523 pt. 1-10).

MILITARY RECORDS

Lee, William Wallace. CATALOGUE OF BARKHAMSTED MEN, WHO SERVED IN THE VARIOUS WARS, 1775 TO 1865. Meriden: Republican Publishing Co., 1897. 100 p.

PROBATE RECORDS

Barkhamsted Probate District, Town Office Building (P.O. Box 185), Route 318, 06063   (203) 379-8665.

Organized 5 June 1834 from the New Hartford Probate District. Probate Records, 1819-1854.   (LDS 1524).

ON FILE AT THE CSL: Estate papers, 1825-1906 (including 27 May 1825-5 June 1834 of the New Hartford Probate District). Indexes, 1825-1906. Inventory Control Books, 1825-1906, Court Record Books, 1825-1854.

VITAL RECORDS

Town Clerk, Town Office Building, Route 318, P.O. Box 185, 06063.   (203) 379-8665.

The town clerk's earliest birth record is about 1767, marriage record 1763 and death record 1777.

The BARBOUR INDEX covers the years 1779-1854 for births and marriages and deaths for the years 1779-1867.   The index cards were made from a manuscript copy of the Barkhamsted Vital Records that has not been compared to the original records.

PUBLISHED WORKS AND OTHER RECORDS

BARKHAMSTED, CONN., AND ITS CENTENNIAL, 1879. TO WHICH IS ADDED A HISTORICAL APPENDIX CONTAINING COPIES OF OLD LETTERS, ANTIQUARIAN, NAMES OF SOLDIERS OF THE REVOLUTION, 1812, 1846 AND 1861, CIVIL OFFICERS, AND OTHER MATTER INTERESTING TO THE PEOPLE OF THE TOWN. N.p., 1881.

"Barkhamsted's Tribute." CQ 3 (1897): 500-501.

Hartford. CSL, Record Group 3. Main 2, Box 548a: Records of Daniel Young, Justice of the Peace.

Sesqui-Centennial Committee of Barkhamsted, Conn. TODAY AND YESTER-DAY IN THE HISTORY OF THE TOWN. Hartford: Case, Lockwood and Brainard, 1930. 111 p.

Wheeler, Richard G., and Hilton, George. BARKHAMSTED HERITAGE: CULTURE AND INDUSTRY IN A RURAL CONNECTICUT TOWN. Barkhamsted: Barkhamsted Historical Society, 1975. 345 p.

BEACON FALLS

NEW HAVEN COUNTY. Organized June 1871 from Bethany, Naugatuck, Oxford and Seymour.

CEMETERY RECORDS AND CEMETERIES

NAME	ADDRESS	HALE NO.	CITATION
Pine Bridge Cemetery	55 Old Turnpike Road	1	2:1-25
Ribbon Hill Cemetery	Old Turnpike Road	2	2:26-27

Index to Hale inscriptions: 2:28-34.

LIBRARY

Beacon Falls Public Library, 10 Maple Avenue, 06403. (203) 729-1441.

NEWSPAPER

The PRELIMINARY CHECKLIST lists one newspaper for BEACON FALLS.

PROBATE RECORDS

BEACON FALLS is in the Naugatuck Probate District.

VITAL RECORDS

Town Clerk, 10 Maple Avenue, 06403. (203) 729-4340.

> The town clerk's earliest birth record is 5 July 1871, marriage record is 1 November 1871 and death record is 30 June 1871.

BERLIN

HARTFORD COUNTY. Organized May 1785 from Farmington, Middletown and Wethersfield. Towns organized from Berlin include New Britain.

CEMETERY RECORDS AND CEMETERIES

NAME	ADDRESS	HALE NO.	CITATION
Maple Grove Cemetery	1160 Worthington Ridge (U.S. 52)	1	2:1-45
Bridge Cemetery	Route 72	2	2:46-58
Beckley Quarter Cemetery	917 Deming Road	3	2:59-71c.
Wilcox Cemetery Association	265 Berlin Street	4	2:72-103
Christian Lane Cemetery	415 Christian Lane	5	2:104-10
Deming Cemetery	Near Christian Lane Cemetery	6	2:111
Ledge Cemetery	Near Railroad Station	7	2:112-123
Dunham Cemetery	Near Railroad Station	8	2:124-129
West Lane Cemetery	720 High Road	9	2:130-146
Blue Hills Cemetery	1-3 miles So. of Kensington (U.S. 53)	10	2:147-171
Hall Corner Cemetery	1900 Orchard Road	11	2:172
Mt. Lamentation Cemetery	Near Mt. Lamentation	12	2:173
Brandegee Cemetery	Near Maple Grove Cemetery	13	2:174
Bowers Cemetery	1 mile South of East Berlin Cemetery	14	2:175
Root Family Cemetery	Opposite William Burnham House	15	2:175

NAME	ADDRESS	HALE NO.	CITATION
Dennison Cemetery	1355 Farmington Avenue		(no citation)
South Meadow Cemetery	744 Norton Road		(no citation)
South Middle Cemetery	Cushman Place		(no citation)
Old Yard	Spruce Brook Road		(no citation)
Church Street Cemetery	Church Street		(no citation)
South Burying Grounds	Southington Road		(no citation)

Index to Hale inscriptions: 2:176-211.

Brandagee, E. "Old Christian Lane Cemetery, Berlin, Connecticut." AMERICAN MONTHLY MAGAZINE 37 (1928): 99-111.

Eardeley, William A.D. CONNECTICUT CEMETERIES. Typescript. Brooklyn, N.Y.: 1917. (LDS 899,935).

Tillotson, Edward Sweetser. WETHERSFIELD INSCRIPTIONS: A COMPLETE RECORD OF THE INSCRIPTIONS IN THE FIVE BURIAL PLACES IN THE ANCIENT TOWN OF WETHERSFIELD, INCLUDING THE TOWNS OF ROCKY HILL, NEWINGTON, AND BECKLEY QUARTER (IN BERLIN), ALSO A PORTION OF THE INSCRIPTIONS IN THE OLDEST CEMETERY IN GLASTONBURY. Hartford: William F.J. Boardman, 1899. 372 p.

Wilson, Kathryn Wethy, Mrs. "Cemetery Inscriptions 'Near Berlin, Conn. No name on Cemetery.'" EARLY SETTLERS OF NEW YORK STATE, THEIR ANCESTORS AND DESCENDANTS 2 (1935-36): 185.

CHURCH RECORDS

EAST BERLIN METHODIST CHURCH. Vital Records, 1871-1939. (CSL, LDS 1518).

FIRST CONGREGATIONAL CHURCH. Vital Records, 1775-1922. (CSL, LDS 1516).

KENSINGTON CONGREGATIONAL CHURCH. Records, 1709-1889 (CSL, LDS 1515). Records, 1709-1889. Index (CSL Card Index LDS 1515).

KENSINGTON METHODIST CHURCH. Records, 1858-1941. (CSL, LDS 1519).

METHODIST CHURCH. Minutes, 1812-1888. (CSL, LDS 1518). Vital Records, 1834-1895. (CSL, LDS 1518).

SECOND CONGREGATIONAL CHURCH OF FARMINGTON AT KENSINGTON. Marriages, 1756-1800. BAILEY 4:3-11.

WORTHINGTON ECCLESIASTICAL SOCIETY. Minutes, 1819-1928. (CSL, LDS 1517). Vital Records, 1772-1818. (CSL, LDS 1517).

Andrews, Alfred. MEMORIAL, GENEALOGY, AND ECCLESIASTICAL HISTORY (OF THE FIRST CHURCH, NEW BRITAIN, CONN.). Chicago: Author, 1867. 538 p. Index.

Eardeley, William A.D. "Kensington Congregational Church Marriages 1800-1806, 1807-February 1820, March 1820-November 1831." CONNECTICUT CEMETERIES. Brooklyn: Author, 1919. (5:45-50, 6:45-52, 8:48-54).

"Record of Deaths in the Society of Kensington in the Town of Berlin. Samuel Peck 1823-1852." CHSB 3 (October 1937): 2-8.

Shepard, James. HISTORY OF ST. MARK'S CHURCH, NEW BRITAIN, CONN. AND OF ITS PREDECESSOR CHRIST CHURCH IN WETHERSFIELD AND BERLIN FROM THE FIRST CHURCH OF ENGLAND SERVICE IN AMERICA TO 1907. New Britain: Tuttle, Morehouse and Taylor, 1907. 707 p.

HISTORICAL SOCIETY

Berlin Historical Society, Inc., 06037.

LAND RECORDS

Deeds, 1783-1850. (LDS 1513 pt. 1-14). Berlin Land Records Volumes 1-29 (through 1850) are kept at the New Britain Town Hall.

LIBRARIES

Berlin Free Library: P.O. Box 187, 06037. (203) 828-3344.

Peck Memorial Library, 305 Main Street, 06037. (203) 828-4310.

NEWSPAPER

BERLIN EAGLE. Weekly. 50 Market Square, Newington, 06111.

The PRELIMINARY CHECKLIST lists three newspapers for BERLIN.

PROBATE RECORDS

Berlin Probate District; 177 Columbus Boulevard, New Britain, Conn. 06051. (203) 225-7687.

Organized 2 June 1824 from FARMINGTON, HARTFORD and MIDDLETOWN Probate Districts. The Berlin Probate District also includes the town of NEW BRITAIN.

Probate Records, 1835-1854. (LDS 1514 pt. 1-2).

ON FILE AT THE CSL: Court Record Books, 1935-1854.

VITAL RECORDS

Town Clerk, Town Hall, 240 Kensington Road, 06037. (203) 828-3501, ext. 21.

The BARBOUR INDEX covers the years 1785-1850 and was based on the James N. Arnold copy made in 1916. The vital records are found in volumes 1, 4, 9 and 12 of the land records and a volume of marriages from 1820 to 1851.

Peck, Samuel. "Record of Deaths in the Society of Kennsington in the Town of Berlin, Conn." CHSB 3 (July 1937): 2-8.

PUBLISHED WORKS AND OTHER RECORDS

Benedict, Arthur J. "Kennsington." CM 6 (1900): 393-410.

Camp, David Nelson. HISTORY OF NEW BRITAIN WITH SKETCHES OF FARMINGTON AND BERLIN, CONNECTICUT. 1640-1889. New Britain: William B. Thomson and Co., 1889. 538 p.

Historical Records Survey. Division of Professional and Service Projects. WPA INVENTORY OF THE TOWN AND CITY ARCHIVES OF CONNECTICUT, NO. 2, HARTFORD COUNTY, VOL. 1. AVON, BERLIN, BLOOMFIELD. New Haven: Historical Records Survey, 1939. 299 p. (LDS 908,524, Item 1).

Moore, Roswell A. "Memoirs of Nathan Cole of Berlin, Connecticut." OLD-TIME NEW ENGLAND 25 (1934): 126-40.

North, Catharine Melinda. HISTORY OF BERLIN, CONNECTICUT. New Haven: Tuttle, Morehouse and Taylor Co., 1916. 294 p.

Pratt, Magee. "Berlin: A Sketch." CM 6 (1900): 167-75.

Robbins, Edward W. HISTORICAL SKETCH OF (KENSINGTON) BERLIN, CONN. DURING THE LAST ONE HUNDRED YEARS. New Britain: W.A. House, 1886. 52 p.

BETHANY

NEW HAVEN COUNTY. Organized May 1832 from WOODBRIDGE. Towns organized from BETHANY include BEACON FALLS, NAUGATUCK.

CEMETERY RECORDS AND CEMETERIES

NAME	ADDRESS	HALE NO.	CITATION
Christ Episcopal Church Cemetery	Amity Road	1	2:1-16
First Congregational Church Cemetery	Amity Road	2	2:17-20
Carrington Cemetery	Rainbow Road	3	2:21-29
Methodist Church Cemetery	Litchfield Turnpike	4	2:30-36
Sperry Cemetery	Litchfield Turnpike	5	2:37-42
Old Bethany Cemetery	U.S. 54	6	2:43-50
Lownsbury Family Cemetery	Beacon Falls Road	7	(no citation)

Index to Hale inscriptions: 2:51-61.

CHURCH RECORDS

CHRIST EPISCOPAL CHURCH. Minutes, 1799-1880. Vital Records, 1813-1896. (CSL, LDS 1546).

CONGREGATIONAL CHURCH. Minutes, 1762-1842. (CSL, LDS 1547).

LAND RECORDS

Deeds, 1832-1881. (LDS 1545 pt. 1-3).

LIBRARY

Clark Memorial Library, Amity Road, 06525. (203) 393-2103.

PROBATE RECORDS

Bethany Probate District, Town Hall, 59 Doolittle Drive, 06525. (203) 393-3744.

Organized 4 July 1854 from the New Haven Probate District.

ON FILE AT THE CSL: Estate Papers, 1833-1950. Indexes, 1833-1950. Inventory Control Books, 1833-1950.

VITAL RECORDS

Town Clerk, Town Hall, 512 Amity Road, 06525. (203) 393-0820.

The town clerk's earliest birth and death records are 1852 and earliest marriage record is 1832.

The BARBOUR INDEX covers the years 1832-1853 and was based on the James N. Arnold copy made in 1916. The Arnold copy has not been compared to the original records.

Humiston, Wallace. "Bethany Mortality List." FAMILIES OF ANCIENT NEW HAVEN 5 (1929): 1272-73.

"Two Private Connecticut Mortuary Lists." TAG 26 (1950): 42-43.

PUBLISHED WORKS AND OTHER RECORDS

Bunton, Alice Bice. BETHANY'S OLD HOUSES AND COMMUNITY BUILDINGS. Bethany: Bethany Library Association, 1972. Unpaged.

Lines, Eliza J. BETHANY AND ITS HILLS. New Haven: Tuttle, Morehouse and Taylor, 1905. 71 p.

Sharpe, William Carvosso. BETHANY SKETCHES AND RECORDS. Seymour, Conn.: Record Print, 1908. 132 p.

_____. BETHANY RECORDS. PART 2. Seymour, Conn.: Record Print, 1913. 55 p.

BETHEL

FAIRFIELD COUNTY. Organized May 1855 from DANBURY.

CEMETERY RECORDS AND CEMETERIES

NAME	ADDRESS	HALE NO.	CITATION
Center Cemetery	South Street	1	2:1-103
Elmwood Cemetery	Newtown Road	2	2:104-11
Congregational Church Cemetery	Main Street	3	2:112-32
St. Mary Cemetery	U.S. 51	4	2:133-140
Stony Hill Cemetery	Walnut Hill Road	5	2:141-147
Wolf Pit Cemetery	Sunset Hill Road	6	2:148-156
St. Mary Roman Catholic Cemetery	At the Church	7	2:157-158

Index to Hale inscriptions: 2:159-97.

CEMETERY RECORDS OF BETHEL. N.p., n.d. (LDS 1680).

CHURCH RECORDS

ST. THOMAS EPISCOPAL CHURCH. Records, 1847-1903. (CSL, LDS 1552).

MANUAL OF THE CONGREGATIONAL CHURCH IN BETHEL, CONN. CONTAINING HISTORICAL SKETCH, ARTICLES OF FAITH, THE COVENANT AND RULES OF THE CHURCH, WITH A CATALOGUE OF OFFICERS AND MEMBERS FROM ITS FOUNDATION, NOVEMBER 25, 1960. Bethel: Congregational Church, 1887.

HISTORICAL SOCIETY

Bethel Historical Society, Inc., Library Place, 06801. (203) 743-5150.

LIBRARY

Bethel Public Library, Library Place, 06801. (203) 743-5150.

NEWSPAPERS

THE BETHEL HOME NEWS. Weekly. 14 P.T. Barnum Square, 06801. (203) 743-9231.

The PRELIMINARY CHECKLIST lists six newspapers for BETHEL.

PROBATE RECORDS

Bethel Probate District, Town Hall, Library Place, 06801. (203) 743-9231.

> Organized 4 July 1859 from the Danbury Probate District.

> ON FILE AT THE CSL: Estate Papers, 1859-1929. Indexes, 1859-1929. Inventory Control Book, 1859-1929.

VITAL RECORDS

Town Clerk, Town Hall, Library Place, 06801. (203) 743-9231.

> The town clerk's earliest birth record is 11 July 1855, marriage record is 13 September 1855 and death record is 8 July 1855.

PUBLISHED WORKS AND OTHER RECORDS

BENJ. HOYT'S BOOK: AN ORIGINAL 1830 MANUSCRIPT. Danbury: Scott-Fanton Museum and Historical Society, 1977. 96 p.

BETHEL CONNECTICUT CENTENNIAL 1855-1955. Bethel, Conn.: n.d. 96 p.

Goodsell, Lerois, and Goodsell, Laura. A HISTORY OF BETHEL, 1759-1976. Bethel: Bethel Historical Society and Bicentennial Commission, 1976. 76 p.

Hulette, Frances S. "Bethel: Growing Too, is Quaint Yet Modern." FAIRFIELD COUNTY 8 (September 1978): 45-47.

BETHLEHEM

LITCHFIELD COUNTY.   Organized May 1787 from WOODBURY.

CEMETERY RECORDS AND CEMETERIES

NAME	ADDRESS	HALE NO.	CITATION
Old Cemetery	Still Hill Road	1	2:1-18
Carmel Hill Cemetery	Eastern Carmel Hill	2	2:19-26
Bethlehem Cemetery	U.S. 56	3	2:27-46
Private Cemetery	Northwest Bethlehem on Leonard Bross Property	4	2:47-48

Index to Hale inscriptions: 2:49-61.

Bissell, Almira A.   OLD NORTH CEMETERY OF BETHLEHEM, LITCHFIELD COUNTY.   N.p.: Author, 1909.   11 p.

CHURCH RECORDS

CHRIST EPISCOPAL CHURCH.   Minutes, 1807-1905.   Vital Records, 1835-1900.   (CSL, LDS 1537).

CONGREGATIONAL CHURCH.   Vital Records, 1738-1850.   (CSL, LDS 1538). Marriages, 1740-1798.   BAILEY.   5:29-33.

METHODIST CHURCH.   Vital Records, 1859-1924.   (CSL, LDS 1539).

WATERTOWN AND BETHLEHEM METHODIST EPISCOPAL CHURCH.   Records, 1820-1826.   (CSL, LDS 2191).

HISTORICAL SOCIETY

Old Bethlehem Historical Society, Inc., P.O. Box 149, 06751.

LAND RECORDS

Deeds, 1787-1904. Indexes, 1787-1925. (LDS 1536 pt. 1-7).

LIBRARY

Bethlehem Public Library, North Main Street, 06751. (203) 266-7792.

PROBATE RECORDS

BETHLEHEM is in the Woodbury Probate District.

VITAL RECORDS

Town Clerk, Town Hall, Main Street, 06751. (203) 266-7510.

> The town clerk's earliest birth record is 16 November 1761, marriage record is 26 October 1785 and death record is 10 September 1771.

The BARBOUR INDEX covers the years 1787-1851 and is based on the 1916 James N. Arnold copy which was not subsequently checked against the original records.

Jacobus, Donald Lines. "Bethlehem (Conn.) Vital Records." NEHRG 77:158.

PUBLISHED WORKS

BETHLEHEM: A PRIMER OF LOCAL HISTORY FROM THE BEGINNING TO 1876 WITH ADDENDUM. Bethlehem: Old Bethlehem Historical Society, 1976.

Cothren, William. HISTORY OF ANCIENT WOODBURY, CONNECTICUT, FROM THE FIRST INDIAN DEED IN 1659 TO 1854 INCLUDING THE PRESENT TOWNS OF WASHINGTON, SOUTHBURY, BETHLEHEM, ROXBURY AND A PART OF OXFORD AND MIDDLEBURY. Waterbury: Bronson Brothers, 1854. 841 p. (LDS 2205).

BLOOMFIELD

HARTFORD COUNTY. Organized May 1835 from WINDSOR.

CEMETERY RECORDS AND CEMETERIES

NAME	ADDRESS	HALE NO.	CITATION
Mt. St. Benedict Cemetery	1 Mt. St. Benedict Avenue (203) 242-0783	1	2:1-77 3:78-484
Latimer Hill Cemetery	10 Latimer Lane	2	3:485-92
Mountainview Cemetery	32 Mountain Avenue	3	3:493-535
Old Bloomfield Cemetery	Granby Road	4	3:536-70
St. Andrew Cemetery	57 Tarniffville Road	5	3:571-601
Mills Cemetery	Near Windsor Town Line	6	3:602-3
Old North Cemetery	28 Tunxis Avenue		(no citation)
Old Wintonbury Cemetery	28 Tunxis Avenue		(no citation)

Index to Hale inscriptions: 3:604-749.

Talcott, Mark Kingsbury, and Barbour, Lucius Barnes. BLOOMFIELD, CON-NECTICUT, WINTONBURY CEMETERY INSCRIPTIONS. Typescript. 1914. Hartford: CSL, 1931. 108 p.

CHURCH RECORDS

CONGREGATIONAL CHURCH. Minutes, 1783-1918. Vital Records, 1738-1916. (CSL, LDS 1522). Marriages, 1738-1800. BAILEY. 4:113-122.

ST. ANDREW EPISCOPAL CHURCH. Minutes, 1743-1922. Vital Records, 1862-1936. (CSL, LDS 1521).

Bates, Albert Carlos. RECORDS OF REV. RANSOM WARNER 1823-1854, RECTOR OF ST. ANDREW'S, SIMSBURY AND BLOOMFIELD; ST. PETER'S, GRANBY: ST. JOHN'S EAST WINDSOR, CONNECTICUT. Hartford: Case, Lockwood and Brainard, Co., 1893. 84 p.

Talcott, Mary Kingsbury. "Records of the Church in Wintonbury Parish (now Bloomfield), Conn." NEHGR 71 (1917): 74-87, 153-66, 271-83, 295-310; 72 (1918): 29-51, 87-107, 166-84.

HISTORICAL SOCIETY

Wintonbury Historical Society, 06002.

LAND RECORDS

Deeds, 1835-1854. (LDS 1520).

LIBRARY

Prosser Public Library, 1 Tunxis Avenue, 06002. (203) 243-9721.

NEWSPAPERS

BLOOMFIELD JOURNAL. Weekly. 176 Broad Street, Windsor, 06095. (203) 688-4984.

The PRELIMINARY CHECKLIST lists two newspapers for BLOOMFIELD.

PROBATE RECORDS

BLOOMFIELD is in the Hartford Probate District.

SCHOOL RECORDS

HARTFORD. CSL, Record Group 29 Box 12. Bloomfield men aged 21-30 from school registers. State Military Census, 1917.

HARTFORD. CSL, Record Group 62. School registers, 1900-1905. School enumeration reports, 1918-1923.

VITAL RECORDS

Town Clerk, Town Hall, 800 Bloomfield Avenue, 06002. (203) 242-6241.

The BARBOUR INDEX covers the years 1835-1853 and was indexed by James N. Arnold in 1916.

The Town clerk's earliest birth record is September 1847, marriage record is October 1835 and death record is August 1847.

PUBLISHED WORKS AND OTHER RECORDS

BLOOMFIELD CONNECTICUT; BICENTENNIAL OF U.S., 1776-1976. Bloomfield: Bloomfield Bicentennial Committee, 1976.

Goodrich, Charlotte R. OVER TUNXIS TRAILS. Bloomfield: Wintonbury Historical Society, 1965.

INVENTORY OF THE TOWN AND CITY ARCHIVES OF CONNECTICUT, NO. 2, HARTFORD COUNTY, VOL. 1, AVON, BERLIN, BLOOMFIELD. Historical Records Survey. Division of Professional and Service Projects, WPA. New Haven: The Historical Records Survey, 1939. 299 p. (LDS 908,524 Item 1).

Stiles, Henry Reed. HISTORY AND GENEALOGIES OF ANCIENT WINDSOR, CONNECTICUT, INCLUDING EAST WINDSOR, SOUTH WINDSOR, BLOOM-FIELD, WINDSOR LAKES AND ELLINGTON. 1635-1891. 2 vols. Hartford: Case, Lockwood and Brainard, 1891. (LDS 417,935).

BOLTON

TOLLAND COUNTY. Organized October 1730. Towns organized from BOLTON include VERNON.

CEMETERY RECORDS AND CEMETERIES

NAME	ADDRESS	HALE NO.	CITATION
Bolton Center Cemetery	Bolton Hill	1	4:1-34
Belknap Cemetery	Quarryville	2	4:35-57

Index to Hale inscriptions: 4:58-69.

Barbour, Lucius Barnes. "Inscriptions from Gravestones at Bolton, Conn." NEHGR 83 (1929): 93-106, 156-64.

CHURCH RECORDS

CONGREGATIONAL CHURCH. Vital Records, 1725-1922. (CSL, LDS 1507). Marraiges, 1725-1779. BAILEY 4:123-125.

BOLTON, CONNECTICUT CONGREGATIONAL CHURCH RECORDS OF BAPTISMS, ADMISSIONS TO MEMBERSHIP AND MARRIAGES 1725-1763. Typescript. Hartford: 1923. 220 p.

Talcott, Mary Kingsbury. "A Copy of the Records of the Rev. Thomas White, The First Pastor of the Church in Bolton, Conn." NEHGR 52 (1898): 180-85, 307-11, 408-20; 53 (1899): 447-49; 54 (1900): 80-85, 253-59; 55 (1901): 34-39, 281-87; 56 (1902): 162-67, 347-56.

HISTORICAL SOCIETY

Bolton Historical Society, 06040.

LAND RECORDS

Deeds, 1719-1851. Index, 1719-1920. (LDS 1506 pt. 1-6).

LIBRARY

Bentley Memorial Library, 206 Bolton Center Road, 06040   (203) 646-7349.

MILITARY RECORDS

"Extracts from Bolton Revolutionary Records, 1774-1784." DAR MAGAZINE 98 (1964): 840-41.

PROBATE RECORDS

BOLTON is in the Andover Probate District.

SCHOOL RECORDS

List of pupils in various school districts 1820-1864 of BOZRAH, BROOKLYN, ANDOVER, LEBANON and BOLTON. (CSL, LDS 1482).

Registers of the West and Southwest schools in BOLTON, 1840-1864. (CSL, LDS 1482 pt. 2).

VITAL RECORDS

Town Clerk, Town Hall, 222 Bolton Center Road, 06040.   (203) 643-4756.

The town clerk has a book of vital records from the earliest records to 1880 arranged by family.

The town clerk's earliest birth record is 29 December 1704, marriage record is 28 November 1705 and death record is 15 April 1708.

VITAL RECORDS OF BOLTON TO 1854 AND VERNON TO 1852. Vital Records of Connecticut, Series 1, Towns. 1. Hartford: Conn. Historical Society, 1909. 291 p. (LDS 823,677).

PUBLISHED WORK

Ronson, Bruce G. BOLTON'S HERITAGE: HISTORICAL SKETCHES OF BOLTON. Essex: Pequot Press, 1970. 220 p.

BOZRAH

NEW LONDON COUNTY. Organized May 1786 from NORWICH.

CEMETERY RECORDS AND CEMETERIES

NAME	ADDRESS	HALE NO.	CITATION
Gardener Cemetery	Near Gardener Lake	1	4:1-6
Johnson Cemetery	Norwich Turnpike U.S. 53	2	4:7-41
Harris Cemetery	Bozrah Street	3	4:42-45
Wightman Cemetery	Bozrah Street	4	4:46
Stark Cemetery	Jobez L. Bailey Farm at Scott Hill	5	4:47
Hough-Harris Cemetery	Colchester Town Line	6	4:48-49
Church Family Cemetery	Bozrah Street	7	4:50
Bailey-Wightman Cemetery	Basham Hill	8	4:51
Old Leffingwell Cemetery	By Ice-house (Bozrah-Montville line)	9	4:52-55
Parker Cemetery	U.S. 53		(no citation)

Index to Hale inscriptions: 4:56-67.

CHURCH RECORDS

BOZRAHVILLE CONGREGATIONAL CHURCH. Vital Records, 1828-1890. (CSL, LDS 1512).

FIRST CONGREGATIONAL CHURCH. Minutes, 1741-1845. Vital Records, 1737-1843. (CSL, LDS 1512). Card File Index, 1737-1845. (CSL). Marriages, 1740-1799. BAILEY 5:50-58.

FITCHVILLE BAPTIST CHURCH. Vital Records, 1887-1932. (CSL, LDS 1510).

UNION CONGREGATIONAL CHURCH. Minutes, 1852-1867. (CSL, LDS 1511).

LAND RECORDS

Deeds, 1786-1850. Indexed. (LDS 1509 pt. 1-3).

PROBATE RECORDS

Bozrah Probate District. Town Hall, 06334 (203) 889-8319.

Organized 3 June 1843 from the Norwich Probate District.

Records from 1843-1889. (LDS 1508).

ON FILE AT THE CSL: Estate Papers, 1833-1930. Indexes, 1833-1930. Inventory Control Books, 1833-1930. Court Record Books, 1943-1889.

SCHOOL RECORDS

List of pupils in various school districts of BOZRAH, BROOKLYN, ANDOVER, LEBANON and BOLTON, 1820-1864. (CSL, LDS 1482).

TAX RECORDS

Tax List of BOZRAH, 1811-1812. (LDS 1482). Rate Books, 1803-1808. (CHS).

VITAL RECORDS

Town Clerk, Town Hall, 06334 (203) 889-8174.

The BARBOUR INDEX covers the years 1786-1871 (incomplete) and was compiled by James N. Arnold in 1910 from the first three volumes of vital records. All births, marriages and deaths were indexed from the first two volumes. In the third volume only were the deaths indexed.

Vital Records of BOZRAH, 1852-1905. Typescript. 55 p. (CSL, LDS 1483 and 003, 662).

PUBLISHED WORK

Dewey, Sherman. "Account of a Hail Storn, which fell on part of the Towns of Lebanon, Bozrah, and Franklin, on the 15th of July, 1799." CM 5 (1899): 647-48.

BRANFORD

NEW HAVEN COUNTY. Organized 1639 from GUILFORD. Towns organized from BRANFORD include NORTH BRANFORD.

CEMETERY RECORDS AND CEMETERIES

NAME	ADDRESS	HALE NO.	CITATION
Old Branford Center Cemetery	Pine Orchard Road	1	4:1-97
St. Mary Roman Catholic Cemetery	55 Monroe Street	2	4:98-110
St. Agnes Roman Catholic Cemetery	Mill Plain Road	3	4:111-27

(St. Agnes and St. Mary Cemeteries Association, Boston Post Road, (203) 488-1950).

NAME	ADDRESS	HALE NO.	CITATION
Tabor Evangelical Lutheran Cemetery	28 Tabor Drive	4	4:128
Mill Plain Cemetery	23 Mill Plain Road	5	4:129-37
Damascus Cemetery	256 Damascus Road	6	4:138-49
Stony Creek Cemetery	414 Leete's Island Road	7	4:150-60
Swedish (Tabor) Cemetery	Green Island Road	8	4:161-65
Goldsmith Farm Cemetery	On Albert Goldsmith Farm (east part of Branford)	9	4:166
Trinity Episcopal Church Cemetery	(Beneath Chancel of the Church)	10	4:167-68
Center Cemetery	Montowese Street		(no citation)
Branford Cemetery Association	Montowese Street (203) 481-2500		(no citation)

Index to Hale inscriptions: 4:169-207.

Hill, Edwin Allston. "Branford, Conn., Gravestone Inscriptions." NEHGR 62 (1908): 143-49.

Norton, Frederick E. "A Pastor of the Church Militant." CM 5 (1899): 468-71.

CENSUS RECORDS

Jacobus, Donald Lines. "Errors in the Census of 1790 (Conn.): Branford." NEHGR 77 (1923): 80.

CHURCH RECORDS

FIRST CONGREGATIONAL CHURCH. Vital Records and Index, 1687-1889. (CSL, LDS 1504). Marriages, 1651-1799. BAILEY 2:99-113.

TRINITY EPISCOPAL CHURCH. Minutes, 1784-1889. Vital Records, 1784-1895. (CSL, LDS 1404).

"Branford Church Records 1688-1706. Transcript of Vital Statistics from Records of First Congregational Society of Branford." TAG 9 (1932): 31-37.

Church Records (Baptisms) of Branford Congregational Church, 1688-1786. (NYGBS, LDS 1501).

Norton, Frederick E. "A Pastor of the Church Militant." CM 5 (1899): 468-71.

Simons, J. Rupert. A HISTORY OF THE FIRST CHURCH AND SOCIETY OF BRANFORD, CONNECTICUT 1644-1919. New Haven: Tuttle, Morehouse and Taylor, n.d. 191 p.

HISTORICAL SOCIETY

Branford Historical Society, P.O. Box 504, 06405.

LAND RECORDS

Deeds, 1645-1851. Index, 1645-1875. (LDS 1504 pt. 1-14).

"Branford Town Records (Excerpts from the First Book of Deeds)." TAG 12 (1935): 112-15.

LIBRARIES

Blackstone Memorial Library, 758 Main Street, 06405 (203) 488-1441.

Harrison, Lynde. "Blackstone Memorial Library at Branford." CM 9 (1905): 493-511.

Wallace Memorial Library, 146 Thimble Islands Road, 06405. (203) 488-8702.

NEWSPAPERS

BRANFORD REVIEW. Weekly. 230 East Main Street, 06405. (203) 488-2535.

The PRELIMINARY CHECKLIST lists four newspapers for BRANFORD.

THE BRANFORD SUBURBAN SPOKESMAN. Weekly. Microfilmed from 10 October 1957 - 9 January 1958.

THE BRANFORD GLEANER. Weekly. Microfilmed from 3 April-29 May 1878.

THE BRANFORD NEWS. Weekly. Microfilmed from 22 March 1878-9 August 1878.

THE BRANFORD OPINION. Weekly. Microfilmed from 4 January 1896-7 March 1913.

THE BRANFORD REVIEW. Weekly. Microfilmed from 13 April 1828-present.

PROBATE RECORDS

Branford Probate District, Town Hall, 1019 Main Street, Box 638, 06405. (203) 488-0318.

Organized 21 June 1850 from Guildford Probate District.

VITAL RECORDS

Town Clerk, Town Hall, 1019 Main Street, 06405. (203) 488-6305.

The BARBOUR INDEX covers the years 1644-1850. The index for BRANFORD was prepared from Miss Ethel L. Scofield's copy of BRNAFORD'S Vital Records she made in 1914. The Vital Records are found in the first two volumes of Land Records and a Book of Town Records and Meetings (1697-1788). Reference to the Land Records is indicated by the numbers 1 and 2, to the Book of Town Records by the number 3, and to the Town Meeting Records by TM3.

"Branford, Connecticut Marriages Before 1750 (Barbour)." CN 2 (1970): 238-40; 3 (1970-71): 25-28, 144-47, 248-51, 387-90; 4 (1971): 32-33.

"Branford (Conn.) Vital Records Contained in the Land Records, Volumes I and II." TAG 12 (1935): 100-111.

"Early Records of Brainford, now Branford, CT." NEHGR 3 (1849): 153-4.

Notebook of John H. Harrison, Branford, Ct. (Deaths, 1852-1886. Births, 1831-1852). (LDS 15031).

PUBLISHED WORKS AND OTHER RECORDS

Baldwin, Elijah C. "Branford Annals." PAPERS OF THE NHCHS 3 (1882): 249-70; 4:299-329.

"The Plantation of Branford, Conn. (Original Signers)." GENEALOGY: A WEEKLY JOURNAL OF AMERICAN ANCESTRY 1 (1912): 11-12.

Roberts, George S. "Anecdote of an Old Time Minister, Reverend Samuel Eells." CM 11 (1907): 609-10.

Seymour, George Dudley. "The General Saltonstall House, Branford." CA 10 (1958): 10-25.

Terry, Roderick. "Experiences of a Minister's Wife in the American Revolution." CM 11 (1907): 523-32.

BRIDGEPORT

FAIRFIELD COUNTY. Organized May 1821 from FAIRFIELD and STRATFORD.

CEMETERY RECORDS AND CEMETERIES

NAME	ADDRESS	HALE NO.	CITATION
St. James Cemetery	139 Grove Street	1	4:1-8
St. Augustine Roman Catholic Cemetery	811 Artic Street	2	4:9-44
Family Cemetery	(Not located)	3	(no citation)
Mountain Grove Cemetery	2675 North Avenue (203) 336-3579	4	5:325-664
Lakeview Cemetery	888 Boston Avenue (203) 335-4912	5	5:665-965
Park Cemetery	620 Lindley Street (203) 334-8165	6	5:966-74 6:157-1106
Old Stratfield Cemetery	8760 Briarwood Avenue	7	6:1107-40
Addath Israel Hebrew Congregation Cemetery	1396 Black Rock Turnpike		(no citation)
Lawncroft Burial Cemetery	955 Main Street (203) 335-2873		(no citation)

Index to Hale inscriptions: 6:1141-1360.

RECORD OF THE TIME OF DEATH AND THE PLACE OF BURIAL OF THE SOLDIERS AND SAILORS OF THE CIVIL WAR WHO SLEEP IN THE CEMETERIES OF BRIDGEPORT AND VICINITY. N.p., 1918. 25 p.

CHURCH RECORDS

UNITED CONGREGATIONAL CHURCH. Records, 1695-1911. (CSL, LDS 1549 pt. 1-4). Index (CSL).

INDEX CARDS TO BRIDGEPORT CONGREGATIONAL CHURCH RECORDS (CSL, LDS 1448 pt. 9).

ANNIVERSARY SERVICES OF THE FIRST PRESBYTERIAN CHURCH, BRIDGE-PORT, CONNECTICUT, OCTOBER 25TH-NOVEMBER 1ST 1853-1903. Bridgeport: First Presbyterian Church, 1903. 158 p.

THE BI-CENTENNIAL CELEBRATION OF THE FIRST CONGREGATIONAL CHURCH AND SOCIETY OF BRIDGEPORT, CONNECTICUT. JUNE 12TH AND 13TH, 1895. New Haven: Tuttle, Morehouse and Taylor, 1895. 234 p.

Lockwood, Helen. TWO HUNDRED AND SEVENTY-FIVE YEARS; THE STORY OF THE UNITED CONGREGATIONAL CHURCH OF BRIDGEPORT 1945-1970. Bridgeport: United Congregational Church, 1970. 236 p.

HISTORICAL SOCIETIES

Museum of Art, Science and Industry, 4450 Park Avenue, 06604. (203) 372-3521.

P.T. Barnum Museum, 820 Main Street, 06604. (203) 576-7320.

LAND RECORDS

Land Records, 1821-1852. (LDS 1548 pt. 1-14).

LIBRARY

Bridgeport Public Library, 925 Broad Street, 06604. (203) 576-7777.

Palmquist, David W. FINAL REPORT OF THE BUSINESS AND LABOR HISTORICAL RECORDS PROJECT APRIL 1, 1977-SEPTEMBER 20, 1978. Bridgeport: City of Bridgeport, 1979. 28 p.

_____. "Notes on the Historical Collections of the Bridgeport Public Library." CONNECTICUT HISTORY NEWSLETTER 20 (October 1977): 2-4.

MILITARY RECORDS

Banit, Thomas F. "The War Machine: Bridgeport, 1914-1918." Master's thesis, University of Bridgeport, 1973.

NEWSPAPERS

BRIDGEPORT POST/BRIDGEPORT TELEGRAM. Daily. 410 State Street, 06602. (203) 366-0161.

The PRELIMINARY CHECKLIST lists seventy-four newspapers for BRIDGEPORT.

The HALE NEWSPAPER INDEX TO DEATHS AND MARRIAGES includes the:

> BRIDGEPORT DAILY STANDARD. 3 January 1861-31 December 1866.
>
> BRIDGEPORT MESSENGER. 26 November 1831-21 November 1832.
>
> BRIDGEPORT REPUBLICAN STANDARD. 21 August 1839-28 December 1852.
>
> BRIDGEPORT SPIRIT OF THE TIMES. 6 October 1830-26 September 1832.
>
> BRIDGEPORT TRI-WEEKLY STANDARD. 16 January 1850-24 July 1854.
>
> CONNECTICUT COURIER. 3 August 1814-12 May 1824.

The Bridgeport Public Library indexes the BRIDGEPORT POST and BRIDGEPORT TELEGRAM for Obituaries since 1935.

PROBATE RECORDS

Bridgeport Probate District. McLevy Hall, 202 State Street, 06604. (203) 333-4165.

> Organized 4 June 1840 from the Stratford Probate District.

Probate districts organized from the Bridgeport Probate District include the Shelton and Trumbull Probate Districts.

> ON FILE AT THE CSL: Estate Papers, 1840-1915. Indexes 1840-1898 (papers from 1898-1915 are arranged alphabetically). Inventory Control Book, 1840-1898. Records from June 11 to October 15, 1840 are in the Stratford Probate District Journal, Volume 9.

VITAL RECORDS

Town Clerk, City Hall, Room 124, 45 Lyon Terrace, 06604. (203) 576-7207.

The BARBOUR INDEX covers the years 1821-1854 and is based on the James A. Arnold copy made in 1915.

"Marriage Records of Bridgeport." 1839-1842 (LDS 1894).

Long, Lewis J. "Marriage Records 1919-1939." Handwritten. (LDS 845, 131).

PUBLISHED WORKS AND OTHER RECORDS

Banks, John W. "The Parks of Bridgeport." CQ 3 (1897): 372-88.

BLACK ROCK: A BICENTENNIAL PICTURE BOOK: A VISUAL HISTORY OF THE OLD SEAPORT OF BRIDGEPORT, CONNECTICUT: 1644 TO 1976. Bridgeport: Black Rock Civic and Business Men's Club, 1976. 144 p.

"Bridgeport, Connecticut: The Story of its Economic and Social Growth." Typescript. WPA Writer's Project (CSL Archives RG33, Boxes 131-137).

"Bridgeport: Fairfield County's 'Guilty City' Works to Make a Vision Come True." FAIRFIELD COUNTY 9 (August 1979): 23-29.

Brilvitch, Charles. "Remnants from a Glittering Age." FAIRFIELD COUNTY 6 (February 1976): 54-55.

Daly, Michael. "Bridgeport: City of People, Parks & P.T. Barnum." FAIRFIELD COUNTY 6 (February 1976): 29-31, 49-53, 56-59.

Danenberg, Elsier Nicholas. THE STORY OF BRIDGEPORT. Bridgeport: Bridgeport Centennial Committee, 1936. 176 p.

Deegan, Paul, and Deegan, Helen. "The Rebirth of Bridgeport." CONNECTICUT 37 (February 1975): 32-46.

Golvin, Anne Castrodale. "Bridgeport's Gothic Ornament: The Harral-Wheeler." SMITHSONIAN STUDIES IN HISTORY AND TECHNOLOGY 18.

Keller, Mollie. "Seth Stratton Builds a House: A Look at Nineteenth Century Methods." CANTIQUARIAN 31 (December 1979): 18-25.

LITHOGRAPH VIEWS OF BRIDGEPORT, CONNECTICUT--1860. Stratford, Conn.: A. Vexierbild Co., 1976. 41 p.

Orcutt, Samuel. A HISTORY OF THE OLD TOWN OF STRATFORD AND THE CITY OF BRIDGEPORT, CONNECTICUT. 2 vols. New Haven: Tuttle, Morehouse and Taylor, 1886. (LDS 899,890).

Roberts, William Willard. PIONEERS AND PATRIOTS OF PEQUANNOCK, 1636-1799. Bridgeport: Author, 1935. 16 p.

Shelton, Philo. STRATFIELD IN 1800. Hartford: Acorn Club of Connecticut, 1949. 9 p.

Sterling, Julian H. "Bridgeport--A Story of Progress." CM 8 (1904): 785-802; 9 (1905): 349-83.

Tomanio, Anthony J., and La Macchia, Lucille N. THE ITALIAN-AMERICAN COMMUNITY IN BRIDGEPORT. Bridgeport Community Area Study, Student Monograph, no. 5. Bridgeport: University of Bridgeport, 1953. 44 p.

Tyler, Betty. "Cultural Life." FAIRFIELD COUNTY 6 (February 1976): 32-35, 60.

_____. "A Rich Ethnic Mixture." FAIRFIELD COUNTY 6 (February 1976): 36-39.

U.S. Custom House Records, 1797-1875 (on file at Bridgeport Public Library).

WPA Ethnic Groups Survey. Bridgeport Office File. Data on Local Ethnic Groups including Biographies, 1936-1940. (CSL Archives RG33 Boxes 109-19).

Waldo, George Curtis. HISTORY OF BRIDGEPORT AND VICINITY. 2 vols. New York: S.J. Clarke Publishing Co., 1917.

_____. THE STANDARD'S HISTORY OF BRIDGEPORT. Bridgeport: Standard Association, 1897. 203 p.

BRIDGEWATER

LITCHFIELD COUNTY. Organized May 1856 from NEW MILFORD.

CEMETERY RECORDS AND CEMETERIES

NAME	ADDRESS	HALE NO.	CITATION
Center Cemetery	Center of Town, Route 133	1	6:1-24
South Cemetery	Christian Street	2	6:25-44

Index to Hale inscriptions: 6:45-56.

Holt, Nellie Beardsley, and Holt, Charles Ebenezer. THE HOP BROOK SECTION. Bridgewater: Authors, 1952. 131 p. (Cemetery inscriptions, pp. 76-102).

CENSUS RECORDS

Holt, Nellie Beardsley, and Holt, Charles Ebenezer. THE HOP BROOK SECTION. Bridgewater: Author, 1952. 131 p. (1860 census index pp. 37-64).

CHURCH RECORDS

CONGREGATIONAL CHURCH. Vital Records, 1809-1919. (CSL, LDS 1554).

ST. MARK EPISCOPAL CHURCH. Vital Records, 1810-1916. (CSL, LDS 1553).

HISTORICAL SOCIETY

Bridgewater Historical Society, 06752.

LIBRARY

Burnham Library, Main Street, 06752.　(203) 354-6937.

NEWSPAPERS

The PRELIMINARY CHECKLIST lists two newspapers for BRIDGEWATER.

PROBATE RECORDS

BRIDGEWATER is in the New Milford Probate District.

VITAL RECORDS

Town Clerk, Town Hall, Main Street, 06752.　(203) 354-5102.
　　The town clerk's earliest birth, marriage and death records are in
　　1856.

PUBLISHED WORKS AND OTHER RECORDS

Holt, Nellie Beardsley, and Holt, Charles Ebenezer.　HOP BROOK SECTION.
Bridgewater: Authors, 1952.　131 p.

Orcutt, Samuel.　HISTORY OF THE TOWNS OF NEW MILFORD AND
BRIDGEWATER CONNECTICUT, 1703-1882.　Hartford: Hartford Co., 1882.
900 p.　Index.　(LDS　476,886).

BRISTOL

HARTFORD COUNTY. Organized May 1785 from FARMINGTON. Towns organized from BRISTOL include BURLINGTON.

CEMETERY RECORDS AND CEMETERIES

NAME	ADDRESS	HALE NO.	CITATION
Forestville (East) Cemetery	60 Circle Street	1	6:1-42
Revolutionary War Soldier Grave	Forestville	2	6:43
Lake Avenue Cemetery	Lake Avenue	3	6:44-52
Bridge Street Cemetery	Bridge Street	4	6:53-68
St. Joseph Roman Catholic Cemetery	31 Queen Street	5	6:69-86
Green Hill Cemetery	Queen Street	6	6:87
St. Thomas Cemetery	54 Curtis Street	7	6:88-120
Old North Cemetery	80 Lewis Street	8	6:121-60
West Cemetery	Cemetery Avenue (West Cemetery Assn., Pound Street, 06010 (203) 583-6133	9	6:161-74
(New) St. Joseph Roman Catholic Cemetery	522 Terryville Avenue (203) 589-2105	10	7:363-77
Oakes Cemetery	New Britain Water Company Property	11	7:378-79
Congregation Beth Israel Cemetery	626 Lake Avenue		(no citation)
South Cemetery	Downs Street		(no citation)

Index to Hale inscriptions: 7:380-465.

"Cemetery Record of Bristol, Hartford County, Connecticut." In CENSUS REC-
ORDS ETC. OF NEW YORK. (Royal Paine Record) p. 33. (LDS 4006).

"Scholars Free School Cemetery, 1812-1814." In CEMETERY AND OTHER
RECORDS OF VARIOUS PLACES IN HARTFORD COUNTY. 2 p. (LDS 1734).

CHURCH RECORDS

FIRST CONGREGATIONAL CHURCH. Minutes, 1742-1876. Vital Records,
1790-1876. (CSL, LDS 1533 pt. 1-2). Card Index, 1742-1897. (CSL).

NEW CAMBRIDGE CHURCH. Records, 1747-1860. (NYGBS, LDS 1884).

PROSPECT METHODIST EPISCOPAL CHURCH. Vital Records, 1849-1916.
(CSL, LDS 1534).

TRINITY EPISCOPAL CHURCH. Minutes, 1834-1949. Vital Records, 1836-
1886. (CSL, LDS 1535).

"Society of North Bristol: List for 1795." In CEMETERY AND OTHER REC-
ORDS OF VARIOUS PLACES IN HARTFORD COUNTY. 14 p. (LDS 1734).

HISTORICAL SKETCH OF THE CONGREGATIONAL SOCIETY AND CHURCH
IN BRISTOL, CONNECTICUT, WITH THE ARTICLES OF FAITH, COVENANT
AND STANDING RULES OF THE CHURCH, TOGETHER WITH A CATALOGUE
OF MEMBERS SINCE ITS GATHERING AND A CATALOGUE OF MEMBERS
APRIL 1ST, 1852. Bristol: Congregational Church, 1852.

Lyon, C.W. A HISTORY OF THE METHODIST EPISCOPAL CHURCH, FOREST-
VILLE, 1864-1889. N.p., n.d. 12 p.

MANUAL OF THE CONGREGATIONAL CHURCH, BRISTOL, CONNECTICUT,
WITH FULL LIST OF ADMISSIONS AND CATALOGUE OF MEMBERS. (Title
varies). Bristol: Church, 1833-- . Annual.

Pond, Edgar LeRoy. THE TORIES OF CHIPPENY HILL, A BRIEF ACCOUNT OF
THE LOYALISTS OF BRISTOL, PLYMOUTH AND HARWINTON, WHO FOUNDED
ST. MATTHEW'S CHURCH IN EAST PLYMOUTH IN 1791. New York: Grafton
Press, 1909. 92 p.

HISTORICAL SOCIETY

Greater Bristol Historical Society, (P.O. Box 1393), 54 Middle Street, 06010.
(203) 538-4381.

Newell, Piera Root. "The Bristol Historical and Scientific Society." CQ 4 (1898): 208-17.

LAND RECORDS

Deeds, 1785-1859. Index, 1785-1865. (LDS 1530 pt. 1-13).

LIBRARY

Bristol Public Library, 5 High Street, 06010. (203) 582-9505.

MILITARY RECORDS

BRISTOL CONNECTICUT IN WORLD WAR II. Bristol: World War II Historical Committee, 1947.

NEWSPAPERS

BRISTOL PRESS. Daily. 99 Main Street, 06010. (203) 584-0501.

The PRELIMINARY CHECKLIST lists seven newspapers for BRISTOL.

PROBATE RECORDS

Bristol Probate District, City Hall, 111 North Main Street, 06010. (203) 584-7641.

> Organized 4 June 1830 from the Farmington Probate District.
>
> ON FILE AT THE CSL: Estate Papers, 1830-1937. Indexes, 1830-1920 (papers from 1920-1937 are arranged alphabetically). Inventory Control Books, 1830-1920. Court Record Book, 1830-1858.

Probate Records, 1830-1852. (LDS 1532 pt. 1-2).

TAX RECORDS

Tax List, 1798. (Henry Whitfield Museum, Guildford).

VITAL RECORDS

Town Clerk, City Hall, 111 North Main Street, 06010. (203) 538-1811, ext. 54.

The town clerk's earliest birth record is 1754, marriage record is 1753 and death record is 1777.

The BARBOUR INDEX covers the years 1785-1854 and is based on the Louis H. Von Sahler copy made in 1914.

Gridley, Silas R., comp. VITAL RECORDS, 1785-1871. N.p., Author, 1948. 69 p. Index. (LDS 1531).

A list of deaths in Bristol from 1793-1859 is on file at the Bristol Public Library.

PUBLISHED WORKS AND OTHER RECORDS

Beals, Carleton. OUR YANKEE HERITAGE: THE MAKING OF BRISTOL. Bristol: Bristol Public Library Association, 1954. 331 p.

Jennings, John Joseph. CENTENNIAL CELEBRATION OF THE INCORPORA-TION OF THE TOWN OF BRISTOL: JUNE 17, 1885. Hartford: Case, Lockwood and Brainard, 1885. 109 p.

Norton, Milo Leon. "Bristol." CM 5 (1899): 4-19.

Peck, Epaphroditus. A HISTORY OF BRISTOL, CONNECTICUT. Hartford: Lewis Street Bookshop, 1932. 362 p.

Phelan, William J. SESQUI-CENTENNIAL CELEBRATION OF THE INCOR-PORATION OF THE TOWN OF BRISTOL JUNE 1935. Bristol: Bristol Press Publishing Co., 1935. 80 p.

Hartford CSL, Record Group 3, Box 549. Records of Simeon Hart. Justice of the Peace, 1799-1800.

Smith, Eddy N., et al. BRISTOL, CONNECTICUT. Hartford: City Printing Co., 1907. 711 p.

BROOKFIELD

FAIRFIELD COUNTY. Organized May 1788 from DANBURY, NEW MILFORD and NEWTOWN.

CEMETERY RECORDS AND CEMETERIES

NAME	ADDRESS	HALE NO.	CITATION
Central Cemetery	Danbury Road	1	7:1-42
Laurel Hill Cemetery	Laurel Hill Road	2	7:43-61
Old South Cemetery	Sunset Hill Road	3	7:62-76
Northrop Cemetery	Near William Blackman's Property	4	7:77-79
Gallows Hill Cemetery	New Milford Town Line	5	7:80-82

Index to Hale inscriptions: 7:83-100.

Eardeley, William A.D. CONNECTICUT CEMETERIES. Brooklyn: Author, 1917. 7:4-46; 8:4-9.

CHURCH RECORDS

ST. PAUL EPISCOPAL CHURCH. Records, 1707-1930. (CSL, LDS 1551 pt. 1-2).

Hawley, Emily Carrie. HISTORICAL SKETCH OF THE FIRST CONGREGA-TIONAL CHURCH OF BROOKFIELD, CONNECTICUT AND OF THE TOWN OF BROOKFIELD. Brookfield: Author, 1907. 169 p.

HISTORICAL SOCIETY

Brookfield Historical Society, Routes 25, 133, P.O. Box 231, Brookfield Center, 06805.

LAND RECORDS

Deeds, 1788-1858. Index, 1788-1927. (LDS 1550 pt. 1-8).

LIBRARY

Brookfield Public Library, Route 25, 06804. (203) 775-6241.

MILITARY RECORDS

"Brookfield Revolutionary Roll." TAG 17 (January 1941): 175-76.

Hoyt, George S. RECORD OF SOLDIERS BURIED IN DANBURY, BROOK-FIELD, NEW FAIRFIELD AND RIDGEFIELD. Hartford: CSL, 1929. 91 p.

NEWSPAPER

BROOKFIELD JOURNAL. Weekly. Route 7, 06804. (203) 775-7523.

The PRELIMINARY CHECKLIST lists one newspaper for BROOKFIELD.

PROBATE RECORDS

Brookfield Probate District, Town Hall, Route 25, 06804. (203) 775-3700.
    Organized 19 June 1850 from The Newtown Probate District.

VITAL RECORDS

Town Clerk, Town Hall, Route 25, 06804. (203) 775-3087.
    The town clerk's earliest birth record is 1765, marriage record is
    1764, and death record is 1792.

The BARBOUR INDEX covers the years 1788-1852 and is based on a copy of them made by Mrs. Julia E.C. Brush in 1915.

PUBLISHED WORK

Hawley, Emily Carrie. ANNALS OF BROOKFIELD FAIRFIELD COUNTY CONNECTICUT. Brookfield: Author, 1929. 656 p.

BROOKLYN

WINDHAM COUNTY. Organized May 1786 from CANTERBURY and POMFRET. Towns organized from BROOKLYN include HAMPTON.

CEMETERY RECORDS AND CEMETERIES

NAME	ADDRESS	HALE NO.	CITATION
South Cemetery	Canterbury Road	1	7:1-84
West Cemetery	Main Street	2	7:85-89
Old Weaver Place	Southwest part of Town	3	7:90
Danes Cemetery	Windham Road	4	7:91
Old Trinity Church Cemetery	Town Center	5	7:92-106
Israel Putnam Grave	Town Center	6	7:107
Sacred Heart	Wauregan Street	7	7:108-36
Whitney Cemetery	Town Center	8	7:137-38
Stetson Cemetery	Stetson Road		(no citation)

Index to Hale inscriptions: 7:139-72.

Barbour, Lucius Barnes. "Connecticut Cemetery Inscriptions, Brooklyn Connecticut Witter Cemetery." NEHGR 100 (1946): 330-31.

Bard, Sidney R. CEMETERY INSCRIPTIONS. N.p.: Author, n.d. 6 p.

_____. CEMETERY INSCRIPTIONS FROM OLD WEAVER PLACE AND CEMETERY ON ROAD NEAR STONE HOUSE. N.p.: Author, 1926. 2 p.

Bishop, Mrs. Mary B. OLD TRINITY CHURCH AND OLD TRINITY CHURCH YARD. N.p.: Author, 1929. 15 p.

"Cemetery Records of Brooklyn." In CENSUS RECORDS ETC. OF NEW YORK Royal Paine Record, p. 78. (LDS 4006).

CHURCH RECORDS

FIRST BAPTIST CHURCH. Minutes, 1828-1934. (CSL, LDS 1543).

FIRST CONGREGATIONAL CHURCH. Minutes, 1731-1870. Vital Records, 1734-1913. (CSL, LDS 1542 pt. 2). Baptisms, 1735-1799. (Transcribed by Mrs. Mary Bigbee Bishop). (CSL). Index, 1731-1913 (CSL).

FIRST TRINITARIAN CONGREGATIONAL CHURCH. Minutes, 1823-1897. Vital Records, 1734-1891. (CSL, LDS 1542 pt. 1).

TRINITY EPISCOPAL CHURCH. Vital Records, 1771-1866 (CSL, LDS 1544). Marriages, 1772-1807. BAILEY 7:28-29.

Kingsley, Louise. "Old Trinity Church, Brooklyn, Connecticut." OLD-TIME NEW ENGLAND 42 (1951): 73-77.

HISTORICAL SOCIETY

Brooklyn Historical Society, 06234.

LAND RECORDS

Deeds, 1786-1852. Index, 1786-1920. (LDS 1540 pt. 1-4).

LIBRARY

Brooklyn Library Association, Route 169, P.O. Box 357, 06234. (203) 774-0649.

NEWSPAPERS

The PRELIMINARY CHECKLIST lists eight newspapers for BROOKLYN.

The HALE NEWSPAPER INDEX TO DEATH AND MARRIAGE RECORDS includes:
    CHRISTIAN MONITOR and COMMON PEOPLE'S ADVISOR, 17
    April 1832-12 August 1833.
    HARRISONIAN, 22 January 1840-16 December 1840.

PROBATE RECORDS

Brooklyn Probate District, Town Hall, 06234.   (203) 774-4507.

> Organized 4 June 1833 from the Plainfield and Pomfret Probate Districts.

> ON FILE AT THE CSL: Estate Papers, 1833-1933. Indexes, 1833-1933. Inventory Control Book, 1833-1933. Court Record Book, 1833-1859.

Probate Records, 1833-1859. (LDS 1541).

SCHOOL RECORDS

List of pupils in various school districts 1820-1864 of Bozrah, Brooklyn, Andover, Lebanon and Bolton." (CSL, LDS 1482).

VITAL RECORDS

Town Clerk, Town Hall, P.O. Box 356, 06234.   (203) 774-9543.

> The town clerk's earliest birth record is 23 October 1758, marriage record is 10 August 1769 and death record is 5 April 1773.

The BARBOUR INDEX covers the years 1786-1850 and includes a list of freemen. The index is based on the James N. Arnold copy of Volumes 1 and 2 and on a photostatic copy of Volumes 3 and 4 on file at the CSL.

PUBLISHED WORKS AND OTHER RECORDS

Browne, George Israel. "A Pilgrimage to Canterbury." CM 10 (1906): 65-76.

A List of Freemen is included in Volume 1 of Brooklyn Vital Records. It has been added as an appendix to the typescript volume of Brooklyn Vital Records, 1921. CSL.

BURLINGTON

HARTFORD COUNTY. Organized May 1806 from BRISTOL.

CEMETERY RECORDS AND CEMETERIES

NAME	ADDRESS	HALE NO.	CITATION
Center Cemetery	Rear of Town Hall	1	7:1-26
Center Street Cemetery	Center Street	2	7:27-36
Milford Street Cemetery	Milford Street	3	7:37-52
Case Cemetery	U.S. 51	4	7:53-58
Seventh Day Baptist Church Cemetery	Northwest part of Town	5	7:59-60
Calvary Cemetery	Collinsville	6	7:61-68

Index to Hale inscriptions: 7:69-84.

HISTORICAL SOCIETY

Burlington Historical Society, 06013.

LAND RECORDS

Deeds, 1806-1857. Index, 1805-1912. (LDS 1528 pt. 1-7).

LIBRARY

Burlington Public Library. RFD 1 (P.O. Box 262), 06013. (203) 673-3331.

PROBATE RECORDS

Burlington Probate District, Burlington Center School, Route, RFD 1, 06013. (203) 673-6689.

> Organized 3 June 1834 from the Farmington Probate District.
>
> ON FILE AT THE CSL: Estate Papers, 1834-1955. Indexes, 1834-1945 (papers from 1945-1955 arranged alphabetically). Inventory Control Book, 1834-1945. Court Record Books, 1835-1861.

Probate Records: 1835-1861. (LDS 1529).

SCHOOL RECORDS

Hartford. CSL, Record Group 62. School Registers, 1808-1926.

VITAL RECORDS

Town Clerk, Route 4, 06013. (203) 673-2108.

The BARBOUR INDEX covers the years 1806-1852.

CANAAN

LITCHFIELD COUNTY. Organized 1739. Towns organized from CANAAN include NORTH CANAAN.

CEMETERY RECORDS AND CEMETERIES

NAME	ADDRESS	HALE NO.	CITATION
Grassy Hill Cemetery	Falls Village	1	8:1-42
Sandy Hill Cemetery	Route 7	2	8:43-54
Under Mountain Cemetery	Under Mountain Road	3	8:55-60
Lower City Cemetery	Under Mountain Road	4	8:61-66
St. Patrick Roman Catholic Cemetery	U.S. 50	5	8:67-81
Barrack Mountain Cemetery	U.S. 50	6	8:82-83
Roote Cemetery	Canaan Mountain	7	8:84-85
Hollabird-Kellog Cemetery	Canaan Mountain	8	8:86
Munson Cemetery	U.S. 56	9	8:87
Phelps Cemetery	Near Canaan Mountain	10	8:88
Wilcox Cemetery	Near Huntsville	11	8:89
Lines Cemetery	Near St. Patrick's Cemetery	12	8:90-91
Hunt Memorial Cemetery	U.S. 50		(no citation)

Index to Hale inscriptions: 8:92-110.

"Cemetery Record of Canaan." In CENSUS RECORDS ETC. OF NEW YORK Royal Paine Record, p. 53. (LDS 4006).

"List of persons buried in the burying ground, deeded by, Benjamin Stevens to School District No. 5 in the Town of Canaan, (Conn.) situated near his dwelling house." DAR MAGAZINE 101 (1967): 813-14.

CHURCH RECORDS

FIRST CONGREGATIONAL CHURCH. Minutes, 1767-1852. Vital Records, 1741-1838. (CSL, LDS 1590). Marriages, 1773-1797. BAILEY 7:72-73.

FALLS VILLAGE CONGREGATIONAL CHURCH. Vital Records, 1858-1941. (CSL, LDS 1591).

CHURCH OF CHRIST CONGREGATIONAL CHURCH. Vital Records, 1752-1817. (CSL, LDS 1589).

SECOND CHURCH OF CHRIST. Vital Records, 1769-1869. (CSL, LDS 1588).

SOUTH CANAAN CONGREGATIONAL CHURCH. Records, 1769-1870. (Rollin H. Cooke Collection, Pittsfield, Mass. (LDS, 030,734 pt. 19).

CHRIST EPISCOPAL CHURCH. Vital Records, 1846-1893. (CSL, LDS 1589).

HISTORICAL SOCIETY

Falls Village, Canaan Historical Society, Main Street, 06018. (203) 824-7478.

LAND RECORDS

Deeds, 1737-1854. Index, 1737-1935. (LDS 1587 pt. 1-11).

LIBRARY

Douglas Library, Main Street, 06018. (203) 824-5441.

NEWSPAPERS

THE WESTERN. Weekly. P.O. Box 428, Litchfield, 06018. (203) 567-8789.

The PRELIMINARY CHECKLIST lists two newspapers for CANAAN.

The HALE NEWSPAPER INDEX TO DEATH AND MARRIAGE NOTICES include: HOUSATONIC REPUBLICAN 10 January 1857-16 August 1862.

PROBATE RECORDS

Canaan Probate District, Town Hall, Main Street (P.O. Box 905), 06018. (203) 824-7114.

Organized 6 June 1846 from the Sharon Probate District. Also includes the town of NORTH CANAAN.

ON FILE AT THE CSL: Estate Papers, 1844-1912. Indexes, 1844-1912. Inventory Control Book, 1844-1912. Court Record Book, 1847-1860.

Probate Records: 1847-1860. (LDS 1586).

VITAL RECORDS

Town Clerk, Town Hall, Main Street, 06018. (203) 824-7931.

The BARBOUR INDEX covers the years 1739-1852 and is based on the James N. Arnold copy of the vital records made in 1915.

PUBLISHED WORKS AND OTHER RECORDS

Adam, Mary Geike. "Canaan." CQ 2 (1896): 105-18.

Gebhard, Elizabeth Louisa. "Canaan--the Land of Promise." AMERICANA 6:304-9.

Lyles, James A. "The Old Lawrence Tavern in Canaan." CA 3 (1951): 26-31.

Randall, Alice Sawtelle. "Connecticut Artists and Their Work: Miss Fedelia Bridges in Her Studio at Canaan." CM 7 (1903): 583-88.

CANTERBURY

WINDHAM COUNTY. Organized October 1703 from PLAINFIELD. Towns organized from CANTERBURY include BROOKLYN and HAMPTON.

CEMETERY RECORDS AND CEMETERIES

NAME	ADDRESS	HALE NO.	CITATION
Carey Cemetery	Route 93	1	8:1-28
Cleveland Cemetery	Canterbury Green	2	8:29-34
Old Smith Cemetery	Across from the New Smith Cemetery. West Canterbury	3	8:35-43
Raymond Cemetery	U.S. 53	4	8:44-49
Packer Cemetery	U.S. 53	5	8:50-66
Baldwin Cemetery	U.S. 43, U.S. 53	6	8:67-72
Plains Cemetery	Canterbury Plains	7	8:73-75
Westminster Cemetery	Westminster	8	8:76-93
Park Cemetery	West of Westminster	9	8:94
Small Cemetery	Next to Simeon Bradford Property	10	8:95
North Parish Cemetery	Simeon Bradford Property	11	(no citation)
New Smith Cemetery	Across the road from the Old Smith Cemetery West Canterbury	12	8:96-100
Wheeler Cemetery	U.S. 53	13	8:101-5
Bennett Cemetery	U.S. 53	14	8:106-7
Hyde Cemetery	Northeast part of Town	15	8:108-13
Bradford Cemetery	U.S. 53	16	8:114-15

NAME	ADDRESS	HALE NO.	CITATION
Dawson Cemetery	North Society Road	17	8:116-17
Farnum Cemetery	Parkville Section	18	8:118
Morse-Ruby Cemetery	Opposite Ruchey Farm	19	8:119
Old Baldwin Cemetery	Near old Railroad Station	20	8:120
Herrington-Stevens Cemetery	South part of Town	21	8:121
Perry Cemetery	South of New Smith Cemetery. West Canterbury	22	8:122-23

Index to Hale inscriptions: 8:124-150.

Dorrance, Sarah Francis. CONNECTICUT CEMETERY INSCRIPTIONS: CANTERBURY. N.p.: Author, n.d. 17 p.

"Inscriptions in the Carey Cemetery, Canterbury, Connecticut." NEHGR 70 (1916): 43-50, 153-61.

Johnson, Alfred. "Inscriptions in the Cleveland Cemetery, Canterbury, Connecticut." NEHGR 70 (1916): 342-46.

The town clerk has the records of the Canterbury Cemetery Association.

CHURCH RECORDS

FIRST CONGREGATIONAL CHURCH. Vital Records, 1711-1821. (CSL, LDS 1604). Marriages, 1712-1771. BAILEY 2:120-126. Card Index, 1711-1821. (CSL, LDS 1448 pt. 10).

SECOND CONGREGATIONAL CHURCH. Vital Records, 1770-1850. (CSL, LDS 1604) (copied by Mrs. J.L. Raymond).

WESTMINSTER CONGREGATIONAL CHURCH. Minutes, 1786-1831. Vital Records, 1770-1878. (CSL, LDS 1604). Card Index, 1770-1850. (CSL, LDS 1448 pt. 10).

Jeffries, John W. "The Separation in the Canterbury Congregational Church: Religion, Family, and Politics in a Connecticut Town." NEQ 52 (1979): 522-49.

RECORDS OF THE CONGREGATIONAL CHURCH IN CANTERBURY, CONNECTICUT 1711-1844. Hartford: Connecticut Historical Society and the Society of Mayflower Descendants in the State of Connecticut, 1932. 217 p. (LDS 823,798).

LAND RECORDS

Deeds, 1703-1855. Index, 1703-1904. (LDS 1602 pt. 1-12).

LIBRARY

Canterbury Public Library, Library Road, 06331. (203) 546-9022.

PROBATE RECORDS

Canterbury Probate District, Town Office Building, Box 45, 06331. (203) 546-9605.

> Organized 27 May 1835 from the Plainfield Probate District.

> ON FILE AT THE CSL: Estate Papers, 1878-1945 (papers from 1835-1878 cannot be found). Indexes, 1878-1945. Inventory Control Book, 1878-1945. Court Record Books, 1935-1849.

Probate Records: 1835-1855. Index, 1835-1849. (LDS 1603 pt. 1-2).

VITAL RECORDS

Town Clerk, Baldwin School, Route 14 (P.O. Box 27), 06331. (203) 546-9377.

> The town clerk's earliest birth record is 1 September 1704, marriage record is December 1706 and death record is July 1709.

The BARBOUR INDEX covers the years 1703-1850 and is based on the James N. Arnold copy of the vital records made in 1910.

"Canterbury Connecticut Marriages Before 1750 (Barbour)." CN 4 (1971): 33-37, 193-95.

Olmstead, M., Mrs. "Canterbury Connecticut Records (Marriages 1706-1813)." PUTNAM'S MONTHLY HISTORICAL MAGAZINE 1 (1906): 272-74.

CANTON

HARTFORD COUNTY. Organized May 1806 from SIMSBURY.

CEMETERY RECORDS AND CEMETERIES

NAME	ADDRESS	HALE NO.	CITATION
Canton Street Cemetery	Canton Street	1	8:1-20
Village Cemetery	U.S. 51	2	8:21-79
St. Patrick Roman Catholic Cemetery	U.S. 51	3	8:80-110
South West Cemetery	U.S. 51	4	8:111-17
Canton Center Cemetery	Canton Center	5	8:118-41
North Canton Cemetery	U.S. 51	6	8:142-58
Dyer Cemetery	On Dyer farm, west side Albany Turnpike	7	8:159-74
New Catholic Cemetery	Collins Road (203) 693-8067	8	8:175-83

Index to Hale inscriptions: 8:184-224.

Barbour, Lucius Barnes. "Inscriptions from Gravestones at Canton, Connecticut." NEHGR 81 (1927): 275-92; 404-18.

"North Canton Cemetery Inscriptions, 1754-1855." CHSB 29 (1964): 59-64; 31 (1966): 58-64, 91-96.

CHURCH RECORDS

CANTON CENTER CONGREGATIONAL CHURCH. Minutes, 1746-1953. Vital Records, 1785-1892. Index, 1785-1890. (CSL, LDS 1609 pt. 1-2).

COLLINSVILLE METHODIST EPISCOPAL CHURCH. Vital Records, 1866-1873. (CSL, LDS 1595).

TRINITY EPISCOPAL CHURCH. Minutes, 1875-1893. Vital Records, 1873-1924.

Adams, Nettie Wright. A SCRAPBOOK HISTORY OF THE NORTH CANTON METHODIST CHURCH. Collinsville: Author, 1972. 104 p.

Alvord, Frederick, and Gridley, Ida R. HISTORICAL SKETCH OF THE CON-GREGATIONAL CHURCH AND PARISH OF CANTON CENTER, CONNECTI-CUT, FORMERLY WEST SIMSBURY. ORGANIZED 1750. Hartford: Case, Lockwood and Brainard Co., 1886. 96 p.

HISTORICAL SOCIETY

Canton Historical Society, 11 Front Street, 06020. (203) 693-2793.

LAND RECORDS

Deeds, 1826-1851. (LDS 1592, pt. 1-3).

Hartford. CSL, Record Group 62. Deeds, attachments and writs.

LIBRARY

Canton Public Library, 26 Center Street, 06019. (203) 693-8266.

MILITARY RECORDS

Hartford. CSL, Record Group 62. Militia Records.

"A Memorial for Canton Soldiers." CQ 2 (1896): 182.

The Town Clerk has a list of soldiers and sailors in the Civil War and World War I.

NEWSPAPERS

The PRELIMINARY CHECKLIST lists four newspapers for CANTON.

PROBATE RECORDS

Canton Probate District, Town Hall, 4 Market Street, 06022. (203) 693-8684.
　　Organized 7 June 1841 from the Simsbury Probate District.

ON FILE AT THE CSL: Estate Papers, 1841-1955. Indexes, 1841-1944 (papers from 1944-1955 arranged alphabetically). Inventory Control Books, 1841-1855.

Probate Records, 1841-1855. (LDS 1593).

SCHOOL RECORDS

Hartford. CSL, Record Group 62. School Records 1813-1870.

VITAL RECORDS

Town Clerk, 4 Market Street, 06022. (203) 693-4112.

The BARBOUR INDEX covers the years 1806-1853 and is based on the James N. Arnold copy of CANTON vital records made in 1916.

VOTER RECORDS

Hartford. CSL. Record Group 62. Voter lists 1848-1880, 1900-1927, 1930. (CSL Archives RG62).

PUBLISHED WORKS AND OTHER RECORDS

Barbour, Sylvester. REMINISCENCES: FIFTY YEARS A LAWYER. Hartford: Case, Lockwood and Brainard Co. for Phoebe Humphrey Chapter of the DAR, 1908. 166 p. (LDS 045,741).

Brown, Abiel. GENEALOGICAL HISTORY, WITH SHORT SKETCHES AND FAMILY RECORDS OF THE EARLY SETTLERS OF WEST SIMSBURY, NOW CANTON, CONNECTICUT. Hartford: Case, Tiffany and Co., 1856. 151 p.

Hartford. CSL, Record Group 62. Town Meeting reports and records, 1849-1940.

Phelps, Noah Amherst. HISTORY OF SIMSBURY, GRANBY AND CANTON FROM 1642 TO 1845. Hartford, Conn.: Case, Tiffany and Burnham, 1845. 176 p.

_____. A HISTORY OF THE COPPER MINES AND NEWGATE PRISON, AT GRANBY, CONNECTICUT. New York: Garland Publishing, 1977. 34 p.

Simonds, William Edgar. "Canton." CQ 1 (1895): 239-49.

Thayer, Albert L. "The Row of Maples." CQ 4 (1898): 394-98.

CHAPLIN

WINDHAM COUNTY. Organized May 1822 from HAMPTON, MANSFIELD and WINDHAM.

CEMETERY RECORDS AND CEMETERIES

NAME	ADDRESS	HALE NO.	CITATION
Center Cemetery	Chaplin Center	1	8:1-25
Chewink Cemetery	U.S. 53	2	8:25-30
Bedlam Cemetery	Bedlam Road	3	8:30-35
New Cemetery	Eastford Road	4	8:35-36
Russ Cemetery	U.S. 53	5	8:36-37
Bare Hill Cemetery	Bare Hill	6	8:37
Tower Hill Cemetery	U.S. 53	7	(no citation)
Clark Cemetery		7	8:37-39
Old Cemetery	Near Chewink Cemetery	8	8:39
Small Pox Cemetery	U.S. 53	9	8:39-40

Soldiers' Burials

Center Cemetery 8:41, Chewink Cemetery 8:42, Bedlam Cemetery 8:42, New Cemetery 8:42-43, Clark Cemetery 8:43-44. Index to Soldiers' burials 8:56-57.

Index to Hale inscriptions: 8:45-55.

CHURCH RECORDS

CONGREGATIONAL CHURCH. Minutes, 1809-1906. (CSL, LDS 1561).

"Chaplin, Connecticut Ecclesiastical Society Records (1809-1890)." ANCES-TRAL NOTES FROM CHEDWATO 14 (1967): 73-75.

LAND RECORDS

Deeds, 1822-1854. (LDS 1560).

LIBRARY

Ross Public Library, Chaplin Street, 06235. (203) 455-9424.

PROBATE RECORDS

Chaplin Probate District, Town Hall, Route 198, 06235. (203) 455-9333.

Organized June 1850 from the Windham Probate District.

ON FILE AT THE CSL: Estate Papers, 1850-1926. Indexes, 1850-1926. Inventory Control Books, 1850-1926.

VITAL RECORDS

Town Clerk, Town Hall, Route 198, 06235. (203) 455-9455.

The town clerk's earliest birth record is 15 July 1797, marriage record is 22 September 1805 and death record is 16 February 1818.

The BARBOUR INDEX covers the years 1822-1861 and is based on the James N. Arnold copy of CHAPLIN vital records made in 1911.

PUBLISHED WORK

Weaver, William L. HISTORY OF ANCIENT WINDHAM, CT., GENEALOGY, CONTAINING A GEANEALOGICAL RECORD OF ALL THE EARLY FAMILIES OF ANCIENT WINDHAM, EMBRACING THE PRESENT TOWNS OF WINDHAM, MANSFIELD, HAMPTON, CHAPLIN AND SCOTLAND. (Part I, A-Bil). Willimantic, Conn.: Weaver and Curtis, 1864. 112 p.

CHESHIRE

NEW HAVEN COUNTY. Organized May 1780 from WALLINGFORD. Towns organized from CHESHIRE include PROSPECT.

CEMETERY RECORDS AND CEMETERIES

NAME	ADDRESS	HALE NO.	CITATION
Hillside Cemetery	Walnut Street	1	8:1-124
St. Peter Episcopal Church Cemetery	40 Horton Avenue	2	8:125-46 9:147-68
(Old) St. Bridget Roman Catholic Cemetery	117 Highland Avenue	3	9:169-76
Cheshire Street Cemetery	1473 Cheshire Street	4	9:177-91
(new) St. Bridget Roman Catholic Cemetery	200 Higgins Road	5	9:192
Johnson Cemetery	Wallingford Road	6	9:193-94

Index to Hale inscriptions: 9:195-237.

"Cheshire Street Cemetery." CN 2 (1969): 122-23.

"Revolutionary Soldiers Buried in Hillside Cemetery. Cheshire, Connecticut." CN 1 (1969): 79-83, 2 (1969): 19-20, 122.

"Town of Cheshire--St. Peter's Church Cemetery." CN 2 (1969): 123.

CENSUS RECORDS

Jacobus, Donald Lines. "Errors in the Census of 1790 (Connecticut)." NEHGR 77 (1923): 80.

"Mortality Schedule. 1850 Census for Cheshire, New Haven Co., Connecticut." ANCESTRAL NOTES FROM CHEDWATO 13 (1966): 56.

CHURCH RECORDS

CONGREGATIONAL CHURCH. Marriages, 1734-1799. BAILEY 3:51-61.

ST. PETER EPISCOPAL CHURCH. Minutes, 1767-1917. Vital Records, 1724-1900. (CSL, LDS 1607 pt. 1-2). Index, (CSL, LDS 448 pt. 1).

HISTORICAL SOCIETY

Cheshire Historical Society, Inc., 06401.

LAND RECORDS

Deeds, 1780-1851. Index, 1780-1931. (LDS 1605 pt. 1-12).

LIBRARY

Cheshire Public Library, 104 Main Street, 06410. (203) 272-2245.

MILITARY RECORDS

Pawson, Florence. "Connecticut Revolutionary Soldiers." CN 1 (1969): 98, 2:19-20, 122-23.

Soule, Sherwood. "A Connecticut Soldier in the French and Indian War, Life of Gideon Hotchkiss, born 1716 at Cheshire, Connecticut." CM 11 (1907): 409-16.

NEWSPAPERS

THE CHESHIRE HERALD. Weekly. 1036 South Main Street, 06410. (203) 272-5316.

The PRELIMINARY CHECKLIST lists eight newspapers for CHESHIRE.

PROBATE RECORDS

Cheshire Probate District, Town Hall, 84 South Main Street, 06410. (203) 272-8247.

Organized 29 May 1829 from the Wallingford Probate District.
The Cheshire Probate District includes CHESHIRE and PROSPECT.

ON FILE AT THE CSL: Estate Papers, 1829–1912. Indexes, 1829–
1912. Inventory Control Books, 1829–1912. Court Record Books,
1829–1858.

Probate Records, 1829–1858. (LDS 1606 pt. 1–2).

SCHOOL RECORDS

Hartford. CSL, Record Group 62. School Tax Lists 1851 and 1852.

VITAL RECORDS

Town Clerk, Town Hall, 84 South Main Street, 06410. (203) 272-2293.

The BARBOUR INDEX covers the years 1780–1840 and is based on town records,
compiled cemetery records, and Joseph P. Beach's HISTORY OF CHESHIRE
(see below).

PUBLISHED WORKS AND OTHER RECORDS

Beach, Joseph Perkins. HISTORY OF CHESHIRE, CONNECTICUT FROM 1694
TO 1840, INCLUDING PROSPECT, WHICH AS COLUMBIA PARISH, WAS A
PART OF CHESHIRE UNTIL 1829. Cheshire: Lady Fenwich Chapter, DAR,
1912. 574 p.

Brown, Edwin Roys. OLD HISTORIC HOMES OF CHESHIRE, CONNECTICUT
WITH AN ACCOUNT OF THE EARLY SETTLEMENT OF THE TOWN, DESCRIP-
TIONS OF THE CHURCHES, ACADEMY AND OLD TOWN CEMETERY. New
Haven: C.H. Ryder, 1895. 138 p.

CHESTER

MIDDLESEX COUNTY. Organized May 1836 from SAYBROOK.

CEMETERY RECORDS AND CEMETERIES

NAME	ADDRESS	HALE NO.	CITATION
Laurel Hill Cemetery	Main Street	1	9:1-11
New Town House Hill Cemetery	Town House Hill	2	9:12-28
Old Town House Hill Cemetery	Town House Hill	3	9:29-34
Cedar Lake Cemetery	Lake Road on bank of Cedar Lake	4	9:35-41
St. Joseph Cemetery	Middlesex Avenue	5	9:42-56

Index to Hale inscriptions: 9:57-73.

Pawson, Florence, comp. "Connecticut Revolutionary War Soldiers, Town of Chester--Cedar Lake Cemetery." CN 2 (1969-70): 193, 270.

CHURCH RECORDS

CONGREGATIONAL CHURCH. Minutes, 1741-1809, 1838-1929. Vital Records, 1742-1881. (CSL, LDS 1578).

FIRST BAPTIST CHURCH. Records, 1886-1941. (CSL, LDS 1579).

THIRD CONGREGATIONAL CHURCH. Marriages, 1759-1799. BAILEY 1:89-94.

ST. LUKE MISSION. Vital Records, 1898-1930. (CSL, LDS 1577).

Rumsey, Jean. "Deaths-Chester, Connecticut, 1786-1836 (taken from Volume 2 of Chester Congregational Church Records)." CN 6 (1974): 631-37.

HISTORICAL SOCIETY

Chester Historical Society, 06412.

LAND RECORDS

Deeds, 1836-1865. (LDS 1576 pt. 1-2).

Proprietors' Records, 1730-1753. (LDS 1941).

LIBRARY

Chester Public Library, West Main Street, 06412. (203) 526-5598.

MILITARY RECORDS

Pawson, Florence. "Connecticut Revolutionary War Soldiers." CN 2 (1969-70): 193, 270.

NEWSPAPER

The PRELIMINARY CHECKLIST lists one newspaper for CHESTER.

PROBATE RECORDS

Saybrook Probate District, Main Street, 06412. (203) 526-2796.

> Organized May 1780 from the Guilford Probate District. Probate Districts organized from the Saybrook Probate District include: the Deep River, Essex and Killingworth Probate Districts.

> ON FILE AT THE CSL: Estate Papers, 1780-1940. Indexes, 1780-1940. Inventory Control Book, 1780-1940. Court Record Book, 1780-1852. (LDS 2038 pt. 1-5).

The Saybrook Probate District now serves only CHESTER.

VITAL RECORDS

Town Clerk, Town Hall, 65 Main Street, 06412. (203) 526-2796.

The BARBOUR INDEX covers the years 1836–1852, and is based on the James N. Arnold copy of CHESTER vital records made in 1913.

PUBLISHED WORKS AND OTHER RECORDS

Clark, Thelma Wright. FOR TWO HUNDRED YEARS THE SAME, AN INTI-MATE AND REVEALING ACCOUNT OF THE BEGINNING AND GROWTH OF THE TOWN OF CHESTER, CONNECTICUT, AND THE PROTESTANT CHURCHES THEREIN. Chester, Conn.: Author, 1948. 79 p.

_____. THE HOUSES AND HISTORY OF CHESTER. Chester, Conn.: Chester Historical Society, 1976. 87 p. Index.

Foster, Theodore, and Lowe, Gertrude C. OLD HOMES OF CHESTER, CON-NECTICUT. West Haven: Church Press, 1936. 109 p.

CLINTON

MIDDLESEX COUNTY. Organized May 1838 from KILLINGWORTH.

CEMETERY RECORDS AND CEMETERIES

NAME	ADDRESS	HALE NO.	CITATION
Clinton Cemetery	Town Center	1	9:1-100
St. Mary Roman Catholic Cemetery	44 Beach Park Road	2	9:101A
Bennett Farm Cemetery	Liberty Street	3	9:101B
Kelsey Farm Cemetery	Liberty Street	4	9:101C
Wright Cemetery	Glenwood Road	5	(no citation)
Beaver Brook Cemetery	Old Westbrook Road		(no citation)
Indian River Cemetery	43 Church Road		(no citation)

Index to Hale inscriptions: 9:102-32.

CHURCH RECORDS

CHURCH OF THE HOLY ADVENT. Minutes, 1873-1936. Vital Records, 1873-1882. (CSL, LDS 1581).

FIRST CONGREGATIONAL CHURCH. Marriages, 1764-1799. BAILEY 6:37-73.

METHODIST EPISCOPAL CHURCH. Minutes, 1829-1885. Vital Records, 1858-1936. (CSL, LDS 1582).

TWO HUNDREDTH ANNIVERSARY OF THE CLINTON CONGREGATIONAL CHURCH. N.p., 1867. 54 p.

HISTORICAL SOCIETY

Clinton Historical Society, Town Hall, 54 East Main Street, 06413.

LAND RECORDS

Deeds, 1838-1873. (LDS 1580 pt. 1-2).

LIBRARY

Hull Library, 10 West Main Street, 06413. (203) 669-2342.

MILITARY RECORDS

Pawson, Florence. "Connecticut Revolutionary War Soldiers." CN 3 (1970): 62-64, 167.

NEWSPAPERS

CLINTON RECORDER. Weekly. Post Office Square, 06413. (203) 669-5727.

The HALE NEWSPAPER INDEX TO DEATH AND MARRIAGE NOTICES includes:
    CLINTON ADVERTISER. 8 March 1861-October 1862.

The PRELIMINARY CHECKLIST lists four newspapers for CLINTON.

PROBATE RECORDS

Clinton Probate District, Town Hall, 54 East Main Street, P.O. Box 130, 06413. (203) 669-6447.
    Organized 5 July 1862 from the Killingworth Probate District.

VITAL RECORDS

Town Clerk, Town Hall, 54 East Main Street, 06413. (203) 669-9101.

Hurd, Aaron G. LIST OF DEATHS IN CLINTON, CONNECTICUT, FROM JANUARY 1, 1809 TO JANUARY 1, 1878. New Haven: Shore Line Times, n.d. 15 p.

The BARBOUR INDEX covers the years 1838-1864 and is based on the James N. Arnold copy of the CLINTON vital records made in 1914. It also includes Hurd's LIST OF DEATHS (see above).

PUBLISHED WORKS AND OTHER RECORDS

Elliott, Robert H. OUR TOWN: SERMONS FROM THE HISTORY OF CLINTON. Clinton: Author, 1928. 88 p.

Hartford. CSL. Record Group 33, Box 138. CLINTON 1663-1937. Typescript. WPA Writer's Project. 1937. 281 p.

Peck, Ellen Brainerd. "Clinton, Once Killingworth." CQ 1 (1895): 233-38.

COLCHESTER

NEW LONDON COUNTY. Organized 1698. Towns organized from COL-CHESTER include MARLBOROUGH and SALEM.

CEMETERY RECORDS AND CEMETERIES

NAME	ADDRESS	HALE NO.	CITATION
Old Cemetery	Rear of Bacon Academy	1	9:1-24
Linwood Cemetery	Linwood Cemetery Road	2	9:25-95
St. Andrew Cemetery	Anston Road	3	9:96-112
St. Andrew Cemetery	Gillette Lane	4	9:113
Colchester Jewish Aid Congregational Cemetery	Gillette Lane	5	9:114-17
Abavath Achim Cemetery	Taintor Hill Road	6	9:118
Keeney Cemetery	New London Turnpike	7	9:119
Newton Ranson Cemetery	West Road near Salem Town Line	8	9:120
Day Cemetery	New London Turnpike	9	9:121
Worthington Cemetery	School Street	10	9:122-23
Wells Cemetery	Param Road	11	9:124
Palmer Cemetery	Chestnut Hill Road	12	9:125
Chestnut Hill Cemetery	Kramer Farm	13	9:126
Buckley Cemetery	Buckley Hollow (all bodies said to be removed)	14	9:127
Scott Hill Cemetery	Norwich Turnpike (5 1/2 miles S.E. of center)	15	9:128-30
Ponemab (Ponemak, Ponoma) Cemetery	River Road	16	9:131-40

NAME	ADDRESS	HALE NO.	CITATION
Bull Hill Cemetery	Bull Hill Road	17	9:141-42
Waterhole Cemetery	1 1/2 miles south of Comstock Bridge in East Hampton	18	9:143-48
Westchester Cemetery	Cemetery Road	19	9:149-64
Scovell Cemetery	Paran Road	20	9:165
Cuckle Hill Cemetery	New London Turnpike	21	9:166
Babcock Farm Cemetery	Cemetery in Salem	22	9:166
Foot Cemetery	Paran Road	23	9:167
St. Joseph Cemetery	Hebron Road	24	9:168
Antioch Cemetery	Salem Town Line	25	9:169-70
St. John Cemetery	Route 85		(no citation)

Index to Hale inscriptions: 9:171-217.

Randall, Frank K. "Memoranda of all the inscriptions in the old burying ground at Colchester, Connecticut. With some notes from the town records." NEHGR 42 (1888): 78-83, 155-59, 264-67, 387-89; 43 (1889): 44-47, 188-91, 253-56, 358-63.

CHURCH RECORDS

BAPTIST CHURCH. Minutes, 1835-1953. (CSL, LDS 1570).

CALVARY EPISCOPAL CHURCH. Vital Records, 1864-1936. (CSL, LDS 1574).

FIRST CONGREGATIONAL CHURCH. Minutes, 1792-1814. Vital Records, 1702-1937. (CSL, LDS 1571 pt. 1). Marriages, 1732-1782. BAILEY 3:97-108. Card Index. 1732-1936. (CSL).

SECOND CONGREGATIONAL CHURCH. Vital Records, 1729-1811. (CSL, LDS 1571 pt. 2). Marriages, 1755-1796. BAILEY 7:112-16.

FIRST BAPTIST CHURCH. Minutes, 1893-1939. Vital Records, 1780-1893. (CSL, LDS 1572).

THIRD BAPTIST CHURCH. Minutes, 1809-1875. (CSL, LDS 1575).

WESTCHESTER ECCLESIASTICAL SOCIETY. Minutes, 1728-1745. Vital Records, 1743-1835. (CSL, LDS 1573).

HISTORICAL SOCIETY

Colchester Historical Society, Inc., 06415.

LAND RECORDS

Deeds, 1703-1862. Index, 1703-1932. (LDS 1568 pt. 1-15).

Proprietor's Records, 1713-1805. (LDS 1567).

LIBRARY

Cragin Memorial Library, 1 Linwood Avenue, 06415. (203) 537-5752.

MILITARY RECORDS

Pawson, Florence. "Connecticut Revolutionary War Soldiers." CN 3 (1970): 167-70, 284-87.

"Richard Lord Jones." CQ 2 (1896): 182.

NEWSPAPERS

The PRELIMINARY CHECKLIST lists three newspapers for COLCHESTER.

PROBATE RECORDS

Colchester Probate District, Town Office Building, Chestnut Hill Road, 06415. (203) 537-2614.

> Organized 29 May 1832 from the East Haddam Probate District. Probate Districts organized from the Colchester Probate District include: Marlborough and Salem Probate Districts.

> ON FILE AT THE CSL: Estate Papers, 1741-1920. Indexes, 1741-1920. Inventory Control Books, 1741-1920. Court Record Books, 1741-1851.

Probate records, 1741-1851. (LDS 1569 pt. 1-5).

Hartford. CSL, Record Group 62. Probate and other papers, 1742-1883.

TAX RECORDS

Hartford. CSL, Record Group 62. Assessment Books, 1819, 1823.

VITAL RECORDS

Town Clerk, Town Hall, 10 Norwich Avenue, (P.O. Box 167), 06415. (203) 537-2393.

Blish, James Knox. AN INDEX TO TAINTOR'S COLCHESTER (CONNECTICUT) RECORDS. Kewanee, Ill.: Kewanee Verdict Steam Print, 1901. 42 p.

Hartford. CSL, Record Group 3, Main 2, Box 549. Records of John Watrons, Justice of the Peace, 1767-1790. Marriages, 1770-1772.

"Note to Colchester Records, Ct." NEHGR 5 (1851): 310.

Taintor, Charles Micaiell. EXTRACTS FROM THE RECORDS OF COLCHESTER, WITH SOME TRANSCRIPTS FROM THE RECORDS OF MICHAEL TAINTOR OF "BRAINFORD," CONNECTICUT. Hartford: Case, Lockwood and Co., 1864. 156 p.

PUBLISHED WORKS AND OTHER RECORDS

Bulkeley, Houghton. "Benjamin Burnham of Colchester, Cabinetmaker." ANTIQUES 76 (July 1959): 62-63.

Loomis, Israel Foote. "Bacon Academy." CQ 2 (1896): 120-39.

Rose, James M., and Brown, Barbara. "The Carter Family of Colchester--A Black Genealogical Tapestry." CA 20 (1977): 32-43.

COLEBROOK

LITCHFIELD COUNTY. Organized October 1799.

CEMETERY RECORDS AND CEMETERIES

NAME	ADDRESS	HALE NO.	CITATION
Center Cemetery	State Road	1	9:1-22
South Cemetery	U.S. 51	2	9:23-34
Baptist Cemetery	North Colebrook, turn right at Phelps Place, go 1/4 mile	3	9:35-46
Hemlock Cemetery	Route 8	4	9:47-55
Spencer Cemetery	Route 8	5	9:56
Colebrook River Cemetery	U.S. 56 near Church	6	9:57-73
Beech Hill Cemetery	Simons Corner	7	9:74-76
Hitchcock Cemetery	Near Baptist Church	8	9:77
Old North Colebrook Cobb City Cemetery	One-half mile east of Church	9	9:78
Hurd Cemetery	North of Spencer Cemetery Route 8	10	9:79-80

Index to Hale inscriptions: 9:81-98.

Union Church Society and Colebrook River Burying Ground Association Records 1828-1884. (CSL, LDS 1584).

CHURCH RECORDS

CONGREGATIONAL CHURCH. Minutes, 1786-1939. Vital Records, 1783-1902. (CSL, LDS 1584). Card Index, 1783-1839. (CSL).

HISTORICAL SOCIETY

Colebrook Historical Inc., Colebrook Town Hall, Colebrook Center, (P.O. Box 54), 06021. (203) 542-5860.

LAND RECORDS

Deeds, 1771-1854. Index, 1771-1938. (LDS 1583 pt. 1-7).

PROBATE RECORDS

COLEBROOK is in the Winchester Probate District.

SCHOOL RECORDS

School register of the West School District, Winter Term 2 December 1839 to Fall/Winter Term 12 October 1859 (LDS 1585).

VITAL RECORDS

Town Clerk, Town Hall, Colebrook Center, 06021. (203) 379-2922.

The town clerk's earliest birth, marriage and death record is 1852.

The BARBOUR INDEX covers the years 1779-1810 and is based on the James N. Arnold copy of COLEBROOK vital records made in 1914.

PUBLISHED WORKS AND OTHER RECORDS

Manchester, Irving Edward. THE HISTORY OF COLEBROOK AND OTHER PAPERS. Winsted: Citizen Printing Co., 1935. 208 p.

Perry, Alfred Tyler, Mrs. "Colebrook, Litchfield County, Conn., People who were removed to New York State or 'West' 1789-1840." NYGBR 54 (1923): 69-73.

Straight, Stephen M. "King Post Bridge." CA 24 (1972): 24.

COLUMBIA

TOLLAND COUNTY. Organized May 1804 from LEBANON.

CEMETERY RECORDS AND CEMETERIES

NAME	ADDRESS	HALE NO.	CITATION
Old Cemetery	Lebanon Road	1	9:1-24
Center Cemetery	Lebanon Road	2	9:25-55
West Street Cemetery (Utley Hill Cemetery)	U.S. 53	3	9:56-62
Root Cemetery	Southwest part of Town	4	9:63
Smith Cemetery	Andover-Willimantic Highway	5	9:64-65
Lone Grave	Boston Post Road	6	no stones

Index to Hale inscriptions: 9:66-80.

Dewey, Louis Marinus. "Descriptions from Old Cemeteries in Connecticut." NEHGR 60 (1906): 370-372.

CHURCH RECORDS

CONGREGATIONAL CHURCH. Minutes, 1737-1880. Vital Records, 1722-1725, 1820-1852, 1839-1917. (CSL, LDS 1564). Card Index, 1722-1917. (CSL). Marriages, 1773-1779. BAILEY 7:74. Minutes and Vital Records, 1804-1841. (LDS 1563).

CATALOGUE OF THE MEMBERS OF THE CONGREGATIONAL CHURCH, COLUMBIA, CONNECTICUT 1720-1882, WITH THE CONFESSION OF FAITH AND COVENANT. Willimantic: W.F. Hanks, 1882. 28 p.

"Rate Bill for the North Parish of Lebanon (now Columbia), Connecticut, for the year 1741." NEHGR 20 (1866): 45-47.

HISTORICAL SOCIETY

Columbia Historical Society, Inc., 06237.

LAND RECORDS

Deeds, 1804-1874. Indexed. (LDS 1562 pt. 1-3).

LIBRARY

Saxton B. Little Free Library, Route 87, 06237. (203) 228-0350.

MILITARY RECORDS

Pawson, Florence. "Connecticut Revolutionary War Soldiers." CN 3 (1971): 422-25.

PROBATE RECORDS

Columbia is in the Andover Probate District.

SCHOOL RECORDS

SCHOOL MEMORIES, COLUMBIA, 1732-1948. Columbia: Columbia Historical Society, 1976. 68 p.

HARTFORD. CSL, Record Group 62. School Records, 1820-1900.

TAX RECORDS

HARTFORD. CSL, Record Group 62. Tax abstracts, 1858-1936. Tax lists, 1910-1936.

VITAL RECORDS

Town Clerk, Yeoman's Hall, Route 87, (P.O. Box 165), 06237. (203) 228-3284.

The town clerk's earliest birth, marriage and death record is 1790.

The BARBOUR INDEX covers the years 1804-1852 and is based on the James N. Arnold copy of COLUMBIA vital records made in 1912.

Hartford. CSL, Record Group 62. Vital Records.

PUBLISHED WORKS AND OTHER RECORDS

THE STORY OF COLUMBIA. Columbia: Women's Guild of the Columbia Congregational Church, 1954. 80 p.

CORNWALL

LITCHFIELD COUNTY. Organized May 1740.

CEMETERY RECORDS AND CEMETERIES

NAME	ADDRESS	HALE NO.	CITATION
Old Wilcox Cemetery	"On Hill west of Ozia's Palmer House."	1	10:1
Calhoun Cemetery	Corner of Routes 7 and 45	2	10:2-20
Sedgwick Cemetery	Route 43	3	10:21-22
New Cornwall Hollow Cemetery	U.S. 50	4	10:23-35
Cornwall Cemetery	U.S. 50	5	10:36-52
Christians Cemetery	Route 7	6	10:53
Old Cemetery	Southwest part of town on old Warren Turnpike	7	10:54
Small Pox Cemetery	"Near North Cornwall Church"	8	10:55
Small Pox Cemetery	"On old Wright farm, on old Sharon to Goshen road"	9	10:56
Puffingham Cemetery	(Same as Hale No. 2 above)	10	10:2-20
Cornwall Cemetery	U.S. 50	11	10:57-100
Allen Cemetery	Route 125, one mile north of town	12	10:101-102

Index to Hale inscriptions: 10:103-20.

CHURCH RECORDS

CORNWALL HOLLOW BAPTIST CHURCH. Minutes, 1843-1935. (CSL, LDS 1601).

FIRST CONGREGATIONAL CHURCH. Minutes, 1789-1904. Vital Records, 1755-1892. (CSL, LDS 1599). Marriages, 1756-1797. BAILEY 5:22-26.

FIRST METHODIST EPISCOPAL CHURCH. Records, 1864-1896. (CSL, LDS 1600).

Andrew, John. "Educating the Heathen: The Foreign Mission School controversy and American Ideals." JOURNAL OF AMERICAN STUDIES 12 (1978): 331-42.

Foster, Stephen. "A Connecticut Separate Church: Strict Congregationalism in Cornwall, 1780-1809." NEQ 39 (1970): 309-33.

Starr, Edward F. "Cornwall, Connecticut, Records of the First Church . . . Account of Deaths, 1776-1777." NEHGR 5 (1897): 70.

CORNWALL. Cornwall Public Library. Church records dating from 1755 to 1904.

HISTORICAL SOCIETY

Cornwall Historical Society, Pine Street, 06753. (203) 672-6800.

LAND RECORDS

Deeds, 1740-1856. (LDS 1598 pt. 1-8).

Proprietor's Records, 1730-1887. (LDS 1597).

"Proprietors of Cornwall, Connecticut (1740, 1742)." GENEALOGY: A WEEKLY JOURNAL OF AMERICAN ANCESTRY 1 (1912): 75.

LIBRARY

Cornwall Public Library, Pine Street, (P.O. Box 3), 06753. (203) 672-6874.

MILITARY RECORDS

CORNWALL. Cornwall Public Library. Militia rolls and lists dating from 1759 to 1919.

NEWSPAPER

The PRELIMINARY CHECKLIST lists one newspaper for CORNWALL.

PROBATE RECORDS

Cornwall Probate District, Route 4, Box 5, 06753. (203) 672-6577.

Organized 15 June 1847 from the Litchfield Probate District.

ON FILE AT THE CSL: Court Record Books, 1847-1860. Probate Records, 1847-1860. (LDS 1596).

TAX RECORDS

CORNWALL, Cornwall Public Library Tax lists, 1754-1800.

Hartford. CSL, Record Group 62. Tax lists, 1885-1924.

VITAL RECORDS

Town Clerk, Town Hall, Pine Street, 06753. (203) 672-6487.

The town clerk's earliest birth record is 1734, marriage record is 1754 and death record is 1756.

The BARBOUR INDEX covers the years 1740-1854 and is based on the James N. Arnold copy of CORNWALL vital records made in 1916.

PUBLISHED WORKS AND OTHER RECORDS

Clark, Harriet Lydia, and Pikosky, Andrew Miles Clark. HISTORY OF EAST CORNWALL AREA. Torrington: Rainbow Press, 1977. 102 p. Index.

CORNWALL: A SAMPLING OF OUR HERITAGE. Cornwall Historical Society. Torrington: Quick Print, 1975. 47 p.

Gold, Theodore S. HISTORICAL RECORDS OF THE TOWN OF CORNWALL, LITCHFIELD COUNTY CONNECTICUT. 2d ed. Hartford: Case, Lockwood and Brainard Co., 1904. 489 p.

Starr, Edward C. A HISTORY OF CORNWALL, CONNECTICUT: A TYPICAL NEW ENGLAND TOWN. New Haven: Tuttle, Morehouse and Taylor Co., 1926. 547 p.

COVENTRY

TOLLAND COUNTY. Organized May 1712. Towns organized from COVENTRY include ANDOVER.

CEMETERY RECORDS AND CEMETERIES

NAME	ADDRESS	HALE NO.	CITATION
Nathan Hale Cemetery	Main Street	1	10:1-67
(Old) Center Cemetery	U.S. 53	2	10:58-75
Silver Street Cemetery	Silver Street	3	10:76-85
St. Mary Roman Catholic Cemetery	South Coventry	4	10:86-91
Warren Cemetery	Flanders District	5	10:92
Strong Cemetery	North Coventry	6	10:93-108
Carpenter Cemetery	West of North Coventry	7	10:109
(New) Center Cemetery	North Coventry	8	10:110-12
Babcock Cemetery	Babcock Hill Road	9	10:113
Mathewson Cemetery	On Joseph Hochberg farm	10	10:113A
Hazen Cemetery	On Hazen farm	11	10:113A-14
French Soldier Camp Site Cemetery	On land owned by Frank Fenton and Judy Hinman	12	(no citation)

Index to Hale inscriptions: 10-115-47.

Pike, Lulu Wright, Mrs. COVENTRY CEMETERY INSCRIPTIONS FROM BROKEN STONES. N.p.: Author, 1929.

CENSUS RECORDS

HARTFORD. CSL, Record Group 29, Box 12. State Military Census 1917. List of Coventry men. Ages included.

CHURCH RECORDS

NORTH COVENTRY SECOND CONGREGATIONAL CHURCH. Minutes, 1740–1910. Vital Records, 1798–1894. (CSL, LDS 1558). Church Records, 1740–1917. Card Index. (CSL).

SOUTH COVENTRY FIRST CONGREGATIONAL CHURCH. Minutes, 1740–1798, 1795–1894. Vital Records, 1763–1936. (CSL, LDS 1559). Marriages, 1763–1799. BAILEY 7:61–68. Card Index to Church Records. (CSL, LDS 1448 pt. 10).

Dimock, Susan Whitney. BIRTHS, MARRIAGES, BAPTISMS AND DEATHS FROM THE RECORDS OF THE TOWN AND CHURCHES IN COVENTRY, CONNECTICUT 1711–1844. New York: Baker and Taylor Co., 1897. 301 p. (LDS 599,303).

HISTORICAL SOCIETY

Coventry Historical Society, Inc., South Street, (P.O. Box 307), 06238.

Nathan Hale Homestead. South Street, 06238. (203) 247-8996.

LAND RECORDS

Deeds, 1710–1854. Index, 1719–1920. (LDS 1555 pt. 1–13).

LIBRARY

Booth G. Dimock Memorial Library, Main Street, (P.O. Box 245), 06238. (203) 742-7606.

NEWSPAPER

The PRELIMINARY CEHCKLIST lists one newspaper for COVENTRY.

PROBATE RECORDS

Coventry Probate District, Town Office Building, Route 31, 06238. (203) 742-6791.

The Coventry Probate District was organized 19 June 1849 from the Hebron Probate District.

ON FILE AT THE CSL: Estate Papers, 1849-1932. Indexes, 1849-1932. Inventory Control Books, 1849-1932. Court Record Books, 1849-1856.

Probate Records, 1849-1856. (LDS 1556).

TAX RECORDS

Hartford. CSL, Record Group 62. Tax abstracts 1855-1916, tax lists 1912-1920.

VITAL RECORDS

Town Clerk, Town Office Building, Route 31, 06238. (203) 742-7966.

The town clerk's earliest birth record is 1 June 1692, marriage record is 5 May 1712 and death record is 18 September 1712.

Hartford. CSL, Record Group 62. Marriage License Book, 1914.

See also: DIMOCK, BIRTHS, above under CHURCH RECORDS.

VOTER RECORDS

Hartford. CSL, Record Group 62. Registers of Voters 1840-1890, 1902, 1906, 1922, 1926.

PUBLISHED WORKS AND OTHER RECORDS

Connolly, Frank B. "DevCo. in Coventry: Connecticut's first (and last) new community proposal." CONNECTICUT GOVERNMENT, Fall 1975, pp. 1-4.

HARTFORD. CSL, Record Group 3, main 2, Boxes 549-50. Records of the Justice of the Peace, 1729-1796, 1845-1905.

Hayward, Kendall Payne. "Notes on Coventry, Connecticut Families." TAG 28 (1952): 65-67, 245-51, 29 (1953): 43-46.

Holman, Winifred Lovering. "Corrections of Coventry (Conn.) Records." TAG 14 (1937): 144.

Peterson, Maude Gridley. HISTORICAL SKETCH OF COVENTRY, CONNEC-TICUT. Coventry: Old Home Week Bicentennial Celebration Committee, 1912. 50 p.

Seymour, George Dudley. "Some Inconsequent Reminiscences of John Singer Sargent, (1856-1925) and Julian Alden Weir (1852-1919)." CA 24 (1972): 13-21.

CROMWELL

MIDDLESEX COUNTY. Organized May 1851 from MIDDLETOWN.

CEMETERY RECORDS AND CEMETERIES

NAME	ADDRESS	HALE NO.	CITATION
Old Cemetery	2 Timber Hill Road	1	10:1-40
Kelsey Cemetery	North Road	2	10:41-52
Old Center (or East) Cemetery	24 Hillside Road	3	10:53-86
New Center Cemetery	"Off Center"	4	10:87-90
Northwest Cemetery	U.S. 52		(no citation)
Quary Cemetery	Ranney Street		(no citation)
Riverside Cemetery	(Not Located)		(no citation)
West Cemetery	29 Hillside Road		(no citation)

Index to Hale inscriptions: 10:91-115.

CHURCH RECORDS

BAPTIST CHURCH (FORMERLY MIDDLETOWN SECOND). Minutes, 1802-1920. Vital Records, 1802-1877. (CSL, LDS 1610).

FIRST CONGREGATIONAL CHURCH. Vital Records, 1715-1875. (CSL, LDS 1611). Card Index, 1715-1875. (CSL).

SECOND CONGREGATIONAL CHURCH. Marriages, 1738-1800. BAILEY 2:87-98, 3:169-170.

Hildreth, Homer Wesky. HISTORY OF THE FIRST CHURCH IN CROMWELL 1715-1915. Middletown: James D. Young Press, 1915. 65 p.

HISTORICAL SOCIETY

Cromwell Historical Society, Inc., 06416.

LIBRARY

Belden Library Association, 346 Main Street, 06416.   (203) 635-4433.

PROBATE RECORDS

CROMWELL is in the Middletown Probate District.

VITAL RECORDS

Town Clerk, 5 West Street, 06416.   (203) 635-5454.

> The town clerk's earliest birth record is 2 September 1850, marriage record 30 May 1852 and death record 5 August 1850.

PUBLISHED WORKS AND OTHER RECORDS

Adams, Charles Collard.   MIDDLETOWN UPPER HOUSES; A HISTORY OF THE NORTH SOCIETY OF MIDDLETOWN. . .1650 TO 1800 WITH GENEALOGICAL AND BIOGRAPHICAL CHAPTERS ON EARLY FAMILIES AND A FULL GENEALOGY OF THE RANEY FAMILY.   N.Y.: Grafton Press, 1908.   847 p.

Dudley, Myron Samuel.   HISTORY OF CROMWELL.   Middletown: Constitution Office, 1880.   36 p.

DANBURY

FAIRFIELD COUNTY. Organized 1685. Towns organized from DANBURY include BETHEL and BROOKFIELD.

CEMETERY RECORDS AND CEMETERIES

NAME	ADDRESS	HALE NO.	CITATION
Wooster Cemetery (Danbury Cemetery Association)	20 Ellsworth Avenue (203) 748-8529	1	10:1-289 11:290-377
Wooster Street Cemetery	Wooster Street	2	11:378-94
North Main Street Cemetery	North Main Street	3	11:395-409
St. James Episcopal Church Cemetery	South Street	4	11:410-14
Kenosia (or Lake) Cemetery	Kenosia Avenue	5	11:416-29
Miry Brook Cemetery	18 Miry Brook Road	6	11:430-33
Great Plain Cemetery (Danbury Cemetery Association	Great Plain Cemetery (203) 748-8529	7	11:434-43
Pembroke Cemetery	Capitola Road	8	11:444-49
Baptist Church Cemetery	King Street		11:450-54
Comes Cemetery	South King Street	10	11:455
Old Westville Cemetery	Middle River Road	11	11:456-58
Upper Starr's Plain Cemetery	Starr's Plain Road	12	11:459-460
Mill Plain Cemetery	U.S. 53	13	11:461-62

NAME	ADDRESS	HALE NO.	CITATION
(New) St. Peter Roman Catholic Cemetery (P.O. Box 425, 06810	Kenosia Avenue (203) 743-9626	14	11:463-548
Children of Israel Cemetery	Miry Brook Road	15	11:549-50
(Old) St. Peter Roman Catholic Cemetery	11 Sheridan Street	16	11:551-76
Immanuel Lutheran Cemetery	Tamarack Avenue Office: 32 West Street	17	11:577-81
Christian Church Cemetery	209 South King Street	18	11:582-87
St. Playton Cemetery	Germantown Road	19	11:588
Old Long Ridge Cemetery	Long Ridge Road	20	11:589
Lower Starr's Plain Cemetery	Starr's Plain Road	21	11:590-96

Index to Hale inscriptions: 11:597-742.

Danbury, Western Conn. State College, Haas Library, Archives. Record Group DVI-139. Cemetery Records, 1887-1949.

Frost, Josephine C. DESCRIPTIONS FROM DANBURY AND NEW FAIRFIELD, CONNECTICUT. Typescript. Brooklyn, N.Y.: Author, 1915. 81 p. (LDS 1612).

Hoyt, George S. RECORD OF SOLDIERS BURIED IN DANBURY, BROOK-FIELD, NEW FAIRFIELD AND RIDGEFIELD. Hartford: CSL, 1929.

CHURCH RECORDS

BAPTIST CHURCH. Records, 1785-1816. (Danbury Public Library).

FIRST CONGREGATIONAL CHURCH. Records, 1754-1930. (CSL, LDS 1616 pt. 1-2). Records, 1754-1930. Index. (CSL).

KING STREET CHRISTIAN CHURCH. Records, 1785-1816.

METHODIST CHURCH. Records, 1848-1945. (CSL, LDS 1615).

ST. JAMES EPISCOPAL CHURCH. Records, 1812-1923. (CSL, LDS 1618).

SECOND CONGREGATIONAL CHURCH. Records, 1851-1906. (CSL, LDS 1616 pt. 3).

HISTORICAL SOCIETY

Danbury Scott-Fanton Museum and Historical Society, 43 Main Street, 06810. (203) 743-5200.

Schnabel, H.H., Jr. "On the Local Scene--Danbury, Connecticut." HISTORY NEWS 18 (1963): 144-46.

LAND RECORDS

Deeds, 1777-1861. Index, 1777-1859. (LDS 1616 pt. 1-18).

Danbury, Western Conn. State College, Haas Library Archives. Record Group DG121, DG208. Miscellaneous Land Records, 1905-1950. Grantor Index, 1850-1917.

Jacobus, Donald Lines. "Danbury, (Conn. Land Records)." TAG 22 (1945-46): 191-192.

LIBRARIES

Danbury Public Library, 170 Main Street, (P.O. Box 1160), 06810. (203) 792-0260.

Western Conn. State College. Ruth A. Haas Library, 181 White Street, 06810. (203) 792-1400, ext. 345.

MILITARY RECORDS

"The British are Burning Danbury." FAIRFIELD COUNTY 5 (December 1975): 52-55, 116-20.

Bayles, Louis B. "The Danbury Raid." NEW CANAAN HISTORICAL SOCIETY ANNUAL 8 (1977-78): 9-15.

Case, James R. AN ACCOUNT OF TRYON'S RAID ON DANBURY IN APRIL, 1777 ALSO THE BATTLE OF RIDGEFIELD AND THE CAREER OF GEN. DAVID WOOSTER. Danbury: Danbury Printing Co., 1927. 56 p.

Danbury, Western Conn. State College, Haas Library Archives. Record Group DM140, 164, 169. Militia enrollment and military service lists, 1861-1923.

Ives, J. Moss. "A Connecticut Battlefield in the American Revolution." CM 7 (1903): 420-50.

Jarvis, Charles M. "An American's Experience in the British Army, Manuscript of Colonel Stephen Jarvis, Born in 1756 in Danbury, Connecticut." CM 11 (1907): 191-215, 477-90.

NEWSPAPERS

DANBURY NEWS TIMES. Daily. 333 Main Street, 06810. (203) 744-5100.

The PRELIMINARY CHECKLIST lists twenty-four newspapers for DANBURY.

The HALE NEWSPAPER INDEX TO DEATHS AND MARRIAGES includes:
>DANBURY FARMERS JOURNAL. 18 March 1790-11 March 1793.
>DANBURY TIMES. 5 July 1837-21 February 1900.
>NEW ENGLAND REPUBLICAN. 29 August 1804-31 July 1805.
>REPUBLICAN FARMER. 31 October 1810-18 December 1857.

PROBATE RECORDS

Danbury Probate District, City Hall, 155 Deer Hill Avenue, 06810. (203) 744-4521.
>Organized May 1744 from the Fairfield Probate District.

>Probate Districts organized from the Danbury Probate District include the Bethel, New Fairfield, New Milford, Newtown, Redding and Ridgefield Probate Districts.

>ON FILE AT THE CSL: Estate Papers, 1756-1891. Indexes, 1756-1891. Inventory Control Books, 1756-1891. Court Record Books, 1739-1851 (also LDS 1614 pt. 1-10).

TAX RECORDS

Danbury, Western Conn. State College. Haas Library Archives. Tax records including grand lists, poll tax lists, etc., 1826-1959.

SCHOOL RECORDS

Danbury, Western Conn. State College. Haas Library Archives. Record Group DSch 172, 174, 195. Miscellaneous Records, 1892-1914.

VITAL RECORDS

Town Clerk, City Hall, 155 Deer Hill Avenue, 06810. (203) 744-7160 ext. 250.

Eardeley, William A. "Danbury, Conn., Town Records of Births, Marriages and Deaths." CQ 4 (1898): 115, 331-33; 5 (1899): 189-90.

The BARBOUR INDEX covers the years 1685-1847 and is based on Mrs. Julia E.C. Brush copy of town and private records made in 1915. The town's records were burned by the British in 1777.

Danbury. Western Conn. State College. Haas Library Archives. Record Group DVI 132. Birth, Marriage and Death records, 1946-1958, 1963-1968.

> Record Group DVI 134. Birth, Marriage and Death Records, 1852-1856.

> Record Group DVI 135. Death Records, 1857-1871.

> Record Group DVI 137. Birth Records, 1857-1896.

> Record Group DVI 138. Marriage Records, 1820-1847, 1857-1870.

> Record Group DVI 136. Index to vital records in Record Groups DVI 134 and DVI 135.

VOTER RECORDS

Danbury, Western Conn. State College, Haas Library Archives. Record Group DG 101, 131, 185. Voter Lists, 1875-1963. Absentee Ballot Lists, 1943-1969. Miscellaneous Records, 1912-1949.

Hartford. CSL, Record Group 62. 1888 voting list.

PUBLISHED WORKS AND OTHER RECORDS

Bailey, James Montomery. HISTORY OF DANBURY, CONN., 1684-1896. New York: Burr Printing House, 1896. 583 p.

BENJ. HOYT'S BOOK: AN ORIGINAL 1830 MANUSCRIPT. Danbury: Scott-Fanton Museum and Historical Society, 1977. 96 p.

"The British are Burning Danbury." FAIRFIELD COUNTY 5 (December 1975): 52-55, 116-20.

Collins, Stephen A. "Fairfield County's New Frontier: Danbury, A City Growing Up." FAIRFIELD COUNTY 8 (September 1979): 28-37.

_____. "Hatting in Danbury." CA 18 (1966): 14-16.

"Danbury." FAIRFIELD COUNTY 5 (September 1975): 36-53.

Danbury. Western Connecticut State College. Haas Library Archives. Record Group DG 133. Registered Physicians, 1893-1937.

Eaton, Edward B. "The Financial History of Danbury." CM 8 (1903): 168-76.

Janick, Herbert. "The Great Awakening: Danbury and Local History." ASSN. FOR THE STUDY OF CONNECTICUT HISTORY NEWSLETTER, Summer 1978, pp. 2-4.

Sikorski, Fran. "Visible Here and There about Town: The Danbury Difference." FAIRFIELD COUNTY 8 (September 1978): 39-44.

DARIEN

FAIRFIELD COUNTY. Organized May 1820 from STAMFORD.

CEMETERY RECORDS AND CEMETERIES

NAME	ADDRESS	HALE NO.	CITATION
Spring Grove Cemetery	2722 Post Road (203) 655-0682	1	11:1-48
Fitch's Home Cemetery	2 Hecker Avenue	2	11:49-75
St. John Roman Catholic Church Cemetery	Hoyt Street (25 Camp Avenue) (203) 322-0495	3	11:76-230
Bates Cemetery	East Lane	4	12:231-35
Mather Cemetery	4 Stephen Mather Road	5	12:236-42
Noroton River Cemetery	Post Road (at Stamford Line)	6	12:243-57
Slasson Cemetery	Hanson Road	7	12:258-64
Andreas Hoyt Cemetery	Middlesex Road (opposite Oxridge Hunt Club)	8	12:265-68
Waterbury Cemetery	Mansfield Avenue (near Oxridge Hunt Club)	9	12:269
Waterbury Cemetery	Hoyt Street	10	12:270
Smith Cemetery	Stamford Avenue (west side near New Canaan line)	11	12:271
Bates Cemetery	Christie Hill Road (near Hollow Tree Road)	12	12:272
Leeds Cemetery	54 Hoyt Street	13	12:273-77
Stevens Cemetery	488 Hoyt Street	14	12:278
Jewish Cemetery (new)	303 Hoyt Street	15	12:279-81

Darien

NAME	ADDRESS	HALE NO.	CITATION
Sammis Cemetery	Hoyt Street (south of Jewish Cemetery)	16	12:282
Jewish Cemetery (old)	305 Hoyt Street	17	12:283
Waterbury Cemetery	Hoyt Street (west side)	18	12:284
Weed Cemetery	Post Road (near Holly Pond)	19	12:285-88
Weed Cemetery	East of Nearwater Lane	20	12:289
Pelton Cemetery	On McCrea property south of Old King's Highway	21	12:290
Raymond Cemetery	Bell Avenue	22	12:291
Lakewood Cemetery	West of Leroy Avenue	23	12:292
Bell Cemetery	Leroy Avenue near Middlesex Road	24	12:293
Fitch Cemetery	St. Luke's Episcopal Church Vault	25	12:294
Howe Cemetery	Corner of Middlesex Road and Hollow Tree Ridge Road	26	12:295
St. John Roman Catholic Church Cemetery	Hoyt Street new section of St. John Cemetery	27	12:296-98

Index to Hale inscriptions: 12:299-377.

Byrnes, H.D., and Banks, William J. CEMETERY INSCRIPTIONS. Typescript. 1934. (LDS 032,593).

Eardeley, William A.D. CONNECTICUT CEMETERIES. Brooklyn, N.Y.: Author, 1916. 2:4-39.

Ford, Mary. "Commission, Volunteers Preserve Historic Cemeteries." STAMFORD ADVOCATE 5 May 1979, B9.

Hunt, Malcolm P. CEMETERY INSCRIPTIONS. Typescript. 1957. (LDS 032,593).

"Report of the Cemetery Committee." DARIEN HISTORICAL SOCIETY ANNUAL 1960, pp. 15-22.

CHURCH RECORDS

FIRST CONGREGATIONAL CHURCH RECORDS. Vols. 1-3. Admissions,

1744-1820, 1838-1875. Baptisms, 1744-1876. Marriages, 1744-1876. Deaths, 1807-1878. (LDS 032,592). Marriages, 1744-1800. BAILEY 6:57-66.

Bibbins, Arthur S. THE STORY OF THE FIRST MEETING HOUSE OF THE SOCIETY OF MIDDLESEX 1739-1837 COMPILED FROM THE RECORDS OF THE FIRST CONGREGATIONAL CHURCH. Darien: Author, 1967. 14 p.

McLean, Louise H. "Middlesex Society of Friends." DARIEN HISTORICAL SOCIETY ANNUAL 2, no. 9 (1973): 4-10.

Mead, Spencer Percival. ABSTRACT OF CHURCH RECORDS OF THE TOWN OF DARIEN, FROM THE EARLIEST RECORDS EXTANT TO 1850. Typescript. 1920. 135 p. (LDS 1619 and 899, 936).

Olson, Virginia H. "Miscellaneous Quaker Notes. Middlesex Parish, Now Darien, Ct." CA 15 (February 1973): 119-21.

Wall, Patricia Q. "Darien's Union Chapel." DARIEN HISTORICAL SOCIETY ANNUAL 2, no. 9 (1973): 11-13.

HISTORICAL SOCIETY

Darien Historical Society, 45 Old King's Highway North, 06820. (203) 655-9233.

Publishes: DARIEN HISTORICAL SOCIETY ANNUAL. 1956-- .

LAND RECORDS

Deeds, 1820-1850. Index, 1832-1850. (LDS 1620 pt. 1-2).

LIBRARY

Darien Library, 35 Leroy Avenue, 06820. (203) 655-2568.

MILITARY RECORDS

McLean, Louise H. "Brothers at War." DARIEN HISTORICAL SOCIETY ANNUAL 3, no. 2 (1976): 5-43.

Montgomery, Marshall H. "Shakers and Soldiers: Some Pre-Darien Background of the Fitch Soldier's Home." DARIEN HISTORICAL SOCIETY ANNUAL, 1, no. 4 (1957): 13-18.

_____. "Shakers and Soldiers. A New Canaan Mystery and Its Aftermath." NEW CANAAN HISTORICAL SOCIETY ANNUAL, 1, no. 2 (1956): 109-14.

NEWSPAPERS

DARIEN NEWS. Weekly. 24 Old Kings Highway South, 06820. (203) 655-7476.

The PRELIMINARY CHECKLIST lists two newspapers for DARIEN.

PROBATE RECORDS

Darien Probate District, Town Hall, 719 Post Road, 06820. (203) 655-0314.
Organized 18 May 1921 from the Stamford Probate District.

VITAL RECORDS

Town Clerk, Town Hall, 719 Post Road, 06820. (203) 655-1170.

Card, Lester P. MARRIAGE RECORDS OF NORWALK AND VICINITY. (LDS 1894).

The BARBOUR INDEX covers the years 1820-1851 and is based on the James N. Arnold copy of DARIEN vital records made in 1914.

PUBLISHED WORKS AND OTHER RECORDS

Armbrister, Mary K. "The Pageant of Darien." DARIEN HISTORICAL SOCIETY ANNUAL, 1, no. 9 (1963): 12-18.

"The Barnard Farm." DARIEN HISTORICAL SOCIETY ANNUAL, 2, no. 3 (1967): 14-15.

"Border Country: No-one in Horseneck, Stamford, or Middlesex was safe from British Raiders." FAIRFIELD COUNTY 5 (December 1975): 60-61, 122-24.

Callahan, Jim. "A Town With the Look and Feel of Success: Darien." FAIRFIELD COUNTY 9 (4): 20-25, 36-40.

Case, Henry Jay, and Cooper, Simon W. THE TOWN OF DARIEN. Darien: Darien Community Assn., 1935. 98 p. Index.

Colgate, Beatrice. OUR INTERESTING NEIGHBORS. Darien: Author, 1957. 176 p.

DARIEN OBSERVED: A GUIDE FOR OUR FUTURE HERITAGE. Darien: Darien Historical Society and the Junior League of Stamford-Norwalk, 1980.

Dreher, Monroe F. "The Andrew Elliot House Fairfield, 1750-1959, Darien since 1959." CA 13 (1961): 19-23.

Halstead, Vera Colton. THE STORY OF FLATT RIDGE, DARIEN. New Canaan: Author, 1949. 36 p.

Jainschigg, Janet T. "Houses that Came to Stay." DARIEN HISTORICAL SOCIETY ANNUAL, 3, no. 1 (1975): 6-12.

McLean, Louise H. "Darien's First Shopping Center." DARIEN HISTORICAL SOCIETY ANNUAL, 1, no. 3 (1957): 4-12.

_____. "Early Darien Seafarers." DARIEN HISTORICAL SOCIETY ANNUAL, 1, no. 2 (1956): 6-11.

_____. "Eighteenth Century Tourist in Fairfield County." DARIEN HISTORICAL SOCIETY ANNUAL, 2, no. 3 (1967): 4-13.

_____. "Goodwives River Road: A Byroad to the Past." DARIEN HISTORICAL SOCIETY ANNUAL, 2, no. 10 (1974): 4-20.

_____. "Moses Mather's Neighbors: The First Families of Brookside Road." DARIEN HISTORICAL SOCIETY ANNUAL, 2, no. 5 (1969): 4-15.

"The Petition of 1820." DARIEN HISTORICAL SOCIETY ANNUAL, 2, no. 4 (1968): 14.

Pierpont, Edith K. "Darien." FAIRFIELD COUNTY 4 (2): 20-28.

Raymond, Edward A. "Darien: The First Hundred Years--1820-1920." DARIEN HISTORICAL SOCIETY ANNUAL, 2, no. 4 (1968): 4-13.

"Report on the 'Historic Darien' Series." DARIEN HISTORICAL SOCIETY ANNUAL, 1, no. 5 (1959): 24-27; (1960): 14; (1961): 20.

Tincker, Alma O. "The Evolution of a New England Town." DARIEN HISTORICAL SOCIETY ANNUAL, 1, no. 8 (1962): 4-12.

Wall, Patricia Q. "Letters by the Sloop." DARIEN HISTORICAL SOCIETY ANNUAL, 2, no. 7 (1971): 4-12.

Walker, Claude F. "In Days Long Past: Repository for Historical Writings and Personal Reminiscences of Middlesex Parish and Darien." DARIEN REVIEW, 1944-45.

DEEP RIVER

MIDDLESEX COUNTY. Organized 1635 as SAYBROOK, name changed 1 July 1947. Towns organized from DEEP RIVER include CHESTER, ESSEX, LYME and WESTBROOK.

CEMETERY RECORDS AND CEMETERIES

NAME	ADDRESS	HALE NO.	CITATION
Fountain Hill Cemetery	25 Essex Road	1	43:1-75
Winthrop Cemetery	Winthrop Road	2	43:76-91
Congregational Church Cemetery	Deep River	3	43:92-94

Index to Hale inscriptions: 43:95-122.

"Connecticut Headstone Inscriptions Before 1800 (Hale)--Town of Saybrook-Winthrop Cemetery." CN 4 (1971): 209-10.

CHURCH RECORDS

"REV. ELISHA CUSHMAN'S RECORD." CHSB 7:30-32, 8:2-8, 12-13.

ST. PETER'S MISSION REGISTER. Vital Records. (CSL, LDS 1626).

SAYBROOK CHURCH RECORDS, kept by the Rev. William Hart. Baptisms, marriages and burials, 1736-1782. (Historical Society of Pennsylvania, LDS 441,390).

SECOND CONGREGATIONAL CHURCH. Marriages, 1726/7-1799. BAILEY 2:113-20.

SECOND ECCLESIASTICAL SOCIETY RECORD OF BAPTISMS AND MARRIAGES 1759-1832. (Historical Society of Pennsylvania, LDS 441,390).

HISTORICAL SOCIETY

Deep River Historical Society Inc., Main Street, 06417. (203) 526-2609.

LAND RECORDS

Deeds, 1648-1859. Index, 1647-1919. (LDS 2039, pt. 1-19).

Index to land records. 40 p. (NYGBS, LDS 2037).

"Items from Saybrook, (Conn.) Land Records." TAG 16 (1940): 240.

LIBRARY

Deep River Public Library, 06417. (203) 526-5674.

NEWSPAPER

The PRELIMINARY CHECKLIST lists one newspaper for DEEP RIVER.

PROBATE RECORDS

Deep River Probate District, Town Hall, Main Street, 06417. (203) 526-5966.
    Organized 5 January 1949 from the Saybrook Probate District (see
    CHESTER: Probate Records).

VITAL RECORDS

Town Clerk, Town Hall, Main Street, 06417. (203) 526-5783.

The BARBOUR INDEX covers the years 1635-1850 and is based on a copy made
by Frederick L. Hommedieu, which is on file at the CSL.

"Connecticut Births before 1730 (Barbour) Town of Saybrook." CN 8 (1975-
76): 334, 634-39; 9 (1976): 6-11, 162-67, 335-38.

VITAL RECORDS OF SAYBROOK 1647-1834. Vital Records of Connecticut,
Series 1: Towns. Vol. 9. Seventh Town. Hartford: Conn. Historical Society
and the Conn. Society of the Order of the Founders and Patriots of America,
1952. 197 p.

PUBLISHED WORKS AND OTHER RECORDS

Connors, Daniel J. DEEP RIVER, THE ILLUSTRATED STORY OF A CONNECT-ICUT RIVER TOWN. Stonington: Pequot Press, 1966. 70 p.

Connors, David, and Connors, Daniel. SAYBROOK AND THE AMERICAN REVOLUTION: THE SAYBROOK TOWN ACTS. 1774-1783. Deep River: Deep River Bicentennial Committee, 1976. 106 p.

Gates, Gilman C. SAYBROOK AT THE MOUTH OF THE CONNECTICUT: THE FIRST ONE HUNDRED YEARS. Orange: Wilson H. Lee Co., 1935. 245 p.

Grant, Marion Hepburn. THE INFERNAL MACHINES OF SAYBROOK'S DAVID BUSHNELL, PATRIOT INVENTOR OF THE AMERICAN REVOLUTION. Old Saybrook: Bicentennial Committee of Old Saybrook, 1976. 66 p.

Holman, Mabel Cassine. "The Romance of a Saybrook Mansion." CM 10 (1906): 46-51.

INDEX CARDS TO JOHN BULL'S PRIVATE ACCOUNT BOOK. (CSL, LDS 2040).

Nash, Sylvester. "Records of Saybrook, Ct." NEHGR 4 (1850): 19-22, 137-41; 5 (1851): 247.

Spallone, Jeanne Field. A WATCH TO KEEP (A HISTORY OF OLD WINTHROP CEMETERY AND BIOGRAPHICAL SKETCHES OF TEN REVOLUTIONARY PA-TRIOTS). Deep River: Deep River Historical Society, 1976. 32 p.

Town and Miscellaneous Records. 269 p. (NYGBS, LDS 2047).

DERBY

NEW HAVEN COUNTY. Organized May 1675. Towns organized from DERBY include ANSONIA, OXFORD, and SEYMOUR.

CEMETERY RECORDS AND CEMETERIES

NAME	ADDRESS	HALE NO.	CITATION
Mount St. Peter Cemetery	219 New Haven Avenue (203) 735-8026	1	12:1-119
Oak Cliff Cemetery	72 Hawthorne Avenue	2	12:120-233
St. Peter and St. Paul Cemeteries	125 Chatfield Street	3	12:234-43
Colonial Cemetery	352 Derby Avenue	4	12:244-74
Three Saints Cemetery	262 Division Street	5	12:275-82
St. Michael Cemetery	Silver Hill Road		(no citation)

Index to Hale inscriptions: 12:283-330.

Bassett, Anne Elizabeth, Mrs. "Inscriptions from Gravestones in the Uptown Burying Ground, Derby, Conn." NEHGR 84 (1930): 134-42.

"Cemetery Record of Birmingham, New Haven County, Conn." In CENSUS RECORDS, ETC. OF NEW YORK (ROYAL PAINE RECORD), p. 31. (LDS 4006).

"Connecticut Headstones Before 1800 (Hale)--Derby." CN 12 (1979): 32-36.

"Inscriptions from the Colonial Cemetery, Derby, Conn." N.p.: Sarah Riggs Humphrey Chapter, DAR, 1929. 36 p.

CENSUS RECORDS

Jacobus, Donald Lines. "Errors in the Census of 1790 (Conn.)." NEHGR 77 (1923): 80.

CHURCH RECORDS

METHODIST EPISCOPAL CHURCH. Vital Records, 1828-1935. (CSL, LDS 1625). Index to Derby Church Records. (CSL, LDS 1448 pt. 2).

Jacobus, Donald Lines. "Records of St. James (Episcopal) Church, Derby, Conn., 1740-1796." NEHGR 76 (1922): 130-53, 170-74.

Miscellaneous Church Records, Derby. 100 p. (NHCHS, LDS 1455).

HISTORICAL SOCIETY

Derby Historical Society, 37 Elm Street, Ansonia, 06401. (Mail: P.O. Box 331) Derby, 06418. (203) 735-6746.

LAND RECORDS

Deeds, 1667-1852. Index, 1667-1860. (LDS 1624, pt. 1-19).

LIBRARY

Derby Public Library, Elizabeth and Caroline Streets, 06418. (203) 734-4173.

NEWSPAPERS

The PRELIMINARY CHECKLIST lists eleven newspapers for DERBY.

The HALE NEWSPAPER INDEX TO DEATH AND MARRIAGE NOTICES includes:
DERBY JOURNAL - 25 December 1846-26 December 1857 (for deaths).
25 December 1846-20 September 1881 (for marriages).

PROBATE RECORDS

Derby Probate District, City Hall, 253 Main Street, Box 192, Ansonia, 06401. (203) 734-1277.

Organized 4 July 1858 from the New Haven Probate District.

Probate districts organized from the Derby Probate District include the Shelton Probate District.

The Derby probate District includes ANSONIA and SEYMOUR.

ON FILE AT THE CSL: Estate Papers, 1858–1900 (papers arranged alphabetically).

VITAL RECORDS

Town Clerk, Town Hall, 35 Fifth Street, 06418. (203) 734-9207.

The BARBOUR INDEX covers the years 1655–1852 and is based on the book TOWN RECORDS OF DERBY by Nancy O. Phillips and the Ethel L. Scofield, a copy of DERBY vital records made in 1914.

Birth records of Dr. Josiah Coburn of Orange, Derby and Ansonia, Conn. (NHCHS, LDS 1455, pt. 51).

"Connecticut Marriages Before 1750 (Barbour) Town of Derby." CN 4 (1971): 195-98, 340-42.

PUBLISHED WORKS AND OTHER RECORDS

Account Book of Lucius S. Osborn, 1832–1882, Humphreyville (Derby), New Haven County, Conn. 156 p. (LDS 1787).

Austin, Mary S. "Pioneer Days in Old Derby and the Naugatuck Valley." CM 12 (1908): 209-22, 337-51.

DERBY CONNECTICUT 300TH ANNIVERSARY COMMEMORATIVE BOOK COMMITTEE, 1675-1975. Derby: Commemorative Book Committee, 1975. 88 p.

Gillespie, Charles Bancroft. SOUVENIR HISTORY OF DERBY AND SHELTON, CONNECTICUT. Derby: Transcript Co., 1896. 74 p.

Hartford. CSL, Record Group 63. Main 2 Box 551. Records of Thomas Clark, Justice of the Peace, 1773–1803.

Molloy, Leo Thomas. TERCENTENARY PICTORIAL AND HISTORY OF THE LOWER NAUGATUCK VALLEY. CONTAINING A HISTORY OF DERBY, ANSONIA, SHELTON, AND SEYMOUR. Ansonia: Emerson Bros. Press, 1935. 409 p.

Orcutt, Samuel, and Beardsley, Ambrose. HISTORY OF THE OLD TOWN OF DERBY, CONNECTICUT, 1642-1880 WITH BIOGRAPHIES AND GENEALOGIES. Springfield, Mass.: Springfield Printing Co., 1880. 844 p.

Phillips, Nancy Pratt Owen. TOWN RECORDS OF DERBY, CONNECTICUT 1655-1710. Derby: Sarah Riggs Humphrey Chapter, DAR, 1901. 497 p.

Ward, Jessamine, and Guest, Gladys. TERCENTENARY PICTORIAL AND HISTORY OF THE LOWER NAUGATUCK VALLEY. CONTAINING A HISTORY OF DERBY, ANSONIA, SHELTON AND SEYMOUR. N.p., n.d. 123 p. Index.

DURHAM

MIDDLESEX COUNTY. Organized May 1704.

CEMETERY RECORDS AND CEMETERIES

NAME	ADDRESS	HALE NO.	CITATION
Old Cemetery	Old Cemetery Road	1	12:1-37
New Cemetery	Town House Road Rear of Town Hall	2	12:38-85
Small Pox Cemetery	South part of town near Mt. Pisgah	3	12:86
Jones Cemetery	New Haven Turnpike	4	12:87-88

Index to Hale inscriptions: 12:89-111.

Benton, Mrs. Frederick H., comp. CEMETERY RECORDS. N.p., n.d. (LDS 850,401).

"Connecticut Headstones Before 1800: Durham." CN 12 (1979): 408-13; 13 (1980): 35-37.

CENSUS RECORDS

Hartford. CSL, Record Group 62. 1810 Census Schedule.

CHURCH RECORDS

"CHURCH AND TOWN RECORDS OF DURHAM. 1713-1845." 44 p. (LDS 1444).
CHURCH OF THE EPIPHANY. Vital Records, 1850-1940. (CSL, LDS 1623).

FIRST CONGREGATIONAL CHURCH. Minutes, 1756-1920. Vital Records, 1800-1938. (CSL, LDS 1622). Card Index, 1758-1938. (CSL).

HISTORICAL SOCIETY

Durham Historical Society, 06422.

LAND RECORDS

Deeds, 1698-1857. Index, 1698-1834. (LDS 1621 pt. 1-10).

LIBRARY

Durham Public Library, Main Street, (P.O. Box 179), 06422. (203) 349-9544.

MILITARY RECORDS

"Smithson's Roll of Men Enlisted Durham August 2, 1746." CHS COLLECTIONS 13 (1911): 272-73.

NEWSPAPER

The PRELIMINARY CHECKLIST lists one newspaper for DURHAM.

PROBATE RECORDS

DURHAM is in the Middletown Probate District.

TAX RECORDS

Hartford. CSL, Record Group 62. Tax Lists 1766-1850.

VITAL RECORDS

Town Clerk, Town Hall, Town House Road, (P.O. Box 246), 06422. (203) 349-3452.

"Index Cards to Durham Death Records." Typescript. (CSL, LDS 2040).

"Connecticut Marriages Before 1750--Town of Durham." CN 4 (1971-72): 343-45, 495-96.

The BARBOUR INDEX covers the years 1708-1852 and is based on Fowler's HISTORY OF DURHAM and the published records of Rev. Nathaniel Chauncey, Rev. Elizur Goodrich and Rev. David Smith.

PUBLISHED WORKS AND OTHER RECORDS

Fowler, William Chauncey. HISTORY OF DURHAM, CONNECTICUT, FROM THE FIRST GRANT OF LAND IN 1662 TO 1866. Hartford: Wiley, Waterman and Eaton, 1894. Reprint. Durham, Conn.: Town of Durham, 1970. 460 p.

EASTFORD

WINDHAM COUNTY. Organized May 1847 from ASHFORD.

CEMETERY RECORDS AND CEMETERIES

NAME	ADDRESS	HALE NO.	CITATION
Deane Cemetery	On road from Sibley Corner to Ashford	1	12:1-2
Palmer-Lewis Cemetery	On road from Sibley Corner to Ashford	2	12:3
Old Cemetery	U.S. 53	3	12:4-20
Grove Cemetery	U.S. 53	4	12:21-32
North Ashford Cemetery	U.S. 53	5	12:33-47
Trowbridge Cemetery	On former farm of Henry Trowbridge near Eastford Village	6	12-48
Snow and Spaulding Cemetery	U.S. 53	7	12:49-50
Latham Cemetery	Phoenixville	8	12:51
De Riva Cemetery	Phoenixville	9	12:52
General Lyon Cemetery	Phoenixville	10	12:53-61
(Abandoned) Cemetery	Pilcher District	11	12:62
Weeks Cemetery	On farm of Frederick Buhler south part of town	12	12:63
Lambert Cemetery	In the State Forest	13	12:64-65

Index to Hale inscriptions: 12:66-82.

Bishop, Mrs. Mary B. INSCRIPTIONS FROM THE BULLARD AND LATHAM

YARD, PHOENIXVILLE, TOWN OF EASTFORD, CONN. N.p.: Author, 1925. 1 p.

_____. INSCRIPTIONS FROM THE GENERAL NATHANIEL LYON YARD, PHOENIXVILLE, TOWN OF EASTFORD, CONN. N.p.: Author, 1925. 10 p.

_____. OLD CEMETERY, FORMERLY IN TOWN OF ASHFORD. N.p.: Author, 1925. 21 p.

CHURCH RECORDS

BAPTIST CHURCH. Minutes, 1850-1938. (CSL, LDS 1671).

CONGREGATIONAL CHURCH. Minutes, 1778-1935. Vital Records, 1778-1935. (CSL, LDS 1670).

Index cards to Eastford Church Records. (CSL, LDS 1448 pt. 2).

Trowbridge, John P. "Eastford Conn., Church Records." NEHGR 63 (1909): 84-90.

HISTORICAL SOCIETY

Eastford Historical Society, 06242.

LIBRARY

Eastford Public Library, Route 198, 06242. (203) 974-0125.

PROBATE RECORDS

Eastford Probate District, Town Hall, Westford Road, 06242. (203) 974-1885.

Organized 21 June 1849 from the Ashford Probate District.

ON FILE AT THE CSL: Estate Papers, 1849-1912. Indexes, 1849-1912. Inventory Control Book, 1849-1912. Court Record Books, 1849-1867. Probate Records, 1847-1867. (LDS 1669).

VITAL RECORDS

Town Clerk, Town Hall, Westford Road, 06242. (203) 974-1885.

The town clerk's earliest birth record is 7 August 1847, marriage record is 25 August 1847 and death record is 9 August 1847.

The BARBOUR INDEX covers the years 1847-1851 and is based on the James N. Arnold copy of the vital records made in 1911.

PUBLISHED WORKS AND OTHER RECORDS

Cameron, Diane Maher. EASTFORD: THE BIOGRAPHY OF A NEW ENGLAND TOWN. Eastford: Eastford Historical Society, 1976. 180 p.

TOWN OF EASTFORD, CENTENNIAL, 1847-1947. Eastford: Eastford Centennial Committee, 1947.

EAST GRANBY

HARTFORD COUNTY. Organized June 1858 from GRANBY and WINDSOR LOCKS.

CEMETERY RECORDS AND CEMETERIES

NAME	ADDRESS	HALE NO.	CITATION
East Granby Cemetery	School Street	1	13:1-29
Elmwood Cemetery	School Street	2	13:30-35
Copper Hill Cemetery	Griffin Road	3	13:36-39
Holcomb Cemetery	Hartford Avenue	4	13:40
Small Pox Cemetery	Tariffville Road	5	13:41
Capt. John Viets Cemetery	Newgate Road	6	13:42
Prisoner's Cemetery	Near Newgate Prison	7	13:43-44
Jewish Cemeteries	Farren Road		(no citation)

Index to Hale inscriptions: 13:45-57.

CHURCH RECORDS

Bates, Albert Carlos. RECORDS OF THE CONGREGATIONAL CHURCH IN TURKEY HILLS, NOW THE TOWN OF EAST GRANBY, CONNECTICUT, 1776-1858. Turkey Hills Series, no. 3. Hartford: Author, 1907. 158 p.

Bates, Albert Carlos. RECORDS OF THE SOCIETY OR PARISH OF TURKEY HILLS, NOW THE TOWN OF EAST GRANBY, CONNECTICUT, 1737-1791. Turkey Hills Series, no. 1. Hartford: Author, 1901. 78 p.

Church Records of Turkey Hills, 1776–1858. 85 p. (NYGBS, LDS 2118).

Index Cards to East Granby (Turkey Hill) Church Records. (CSL, LDS 1448 pt. 2).

LIBRARY

East Granby Library, School Street, 06025. (203) 653-3002.

NEWSPAPER

The PRELIMINARY CHECKLIST lists one newspaper for EAST GRANBY.

PROBATE RECORDS

East Granby Probate District, Town Hall, Center Street, 06026. (203) 653-3434.

> Organized 4 July 1865 from the Granby Probate District.

SCHOOL RECORDS

Bates, Albert Carlos. RECORDS OF THE SECOND SCHOOL SOCIETY IN GRANBY NOW THE TOWN OF EAST GRANBY, CONNECTICUT, 1796–1855. Turkey Hill Series, no. 2. Hartford: Author, 1903. 47 p.

TAX RECORDS

Hartford. CSL, Record Group 62. Tax Lists 1894, 1903–1913.

VITAL RECORDS

Town Clerk, Town Hall, Ceneter Street, 06026. (203) 653-6528.

> The town clerk's earliest birth, marriage and death records are in 1858.

PUBLISHED WORKS AND OTHER RECORDS

Bates, Albert Carlos. HISTORICAL SKETCH OF TURKEY HILLS AND EAST GRANBY, CONNECTICUT. Turkey Hills Series, no. 1. East Granby, Conn.: Author, 1949. 46 p.

_____. SUNDRY VITAL RECORDS OF AND PERTAINING TO THE PRESENT TOWN OF EAST GRANBY, CONNECTICUT, 1737-1886. Turkey Hills Series, no. 4. Hartford: Author, 1947. 236 p.

Owen, Elijah Hunter. "Isaac Owen's Account Book (1729-1773, 1763-1793)." DETROIT SOCIETY FOR GENEALOGICAL RESEARCH MAGAZINE 3 (1939): 11-14.

Phelps, Richard Harvey. NEWGATE OF CONNECTICUT: ITS ORIGINS AND EARLY HISTORY. Hartford: American Publishing Co., 1976. 117 p.

Scanlon, Lawrence. "New Gate, New-Gate or Newgate?" CONNECTICUT HISTORY 19 (1977): 25-37.

Shannahan, John W. "Old New-Gate Prison and Copper Mine." CA 25 (1973): 12-22.

EAST HADDAM

MIDDLESEX COUNTY. Organized 1734 from HADDAM.

CEMETERY RECORDS AND CEMETERIES

NAME	ADDRESS	HALE NO.	CITATION
Cove Cemetery	Route 149	1	13:141
Leesville Cemetery	Leesville	2	13:12-14
Moodus Cemetery	Moodus Road	3	13:15-52
St. Bridget Roman Catholic Cemetery	North Modus Road	4	13:53-57
Tatar Hill Cemetery	Tatar Hill Road	5	13:58-60
Goodspeeds (or Nathan Hale Cemetery)	Nathan Hale School House	6	13:61-85
Bashan Cemetery	Stanley Avenue	7	13:86-91
Wicket Lane Cemetery	Town Street	8	13:92-95
Second Burying Ground	Town Street	9	13:96-99
Warner Cemetery	Town Street	10	13:100-101
Mt. Parnassus Cemetery	Smith Road	11 (20)	13:102-10
Hadlyme Church Cemetery	Hadlyme Church	12	13:111-24
Three Bridges Cemetery	Three Bridges Road	13	13:125-27
Parker Cemetery	1 1/2 mile East of Hadlyme Church	14	13:128-29
Millington Cemetery	Millington Road	16	13:130-40
Ackley (Long Road) Cemetery	Ackley Cemetery Road	17	13:141-44

NAME	ADDRESS	HALE NO.	CITATION
Foxtown Cemetery	Foxtown Cemetery Road	18	13:145-47
Hungerford Cemetery	Mill Road	19	13:148-49
First Church Cemetery	Little Haddam	21	13:150-72
Lake View Cemetery	21 Lake View Street		(no citation)
River View Cemetery	Main Street		(no citation)
Jewish Cemetery	Leesville Road		(no citation)

Index to Hale inscriptions: 13:173-214.

Bashan, Connecticut Cemetery Inscriptions, 1941. (NYGBS, LDS 003,695).

Cemetery Record. Millington Green Cemetery, 44 p. Long Pond Graveyard, 19 p. (NYGBS, LDS 1850).

Cemetery Record. Moodus Cemetery Record. (NYGBS, LDS 1851).

"Cemetery Record of Leesville Cemetery." In CEMETERY, CHURCH RECORDS, ETC. OF CONNECTICUT. 4 p. (LDS 1444).

"Cemetery Record of North Plain Cemetery." In CEMETERY, CHURCH RECORDS, ETC. OF CONNECTICUT. 14 p. (LDS 1444).

"Inscriptions from gravestones at East Haddam, Connecticut." NEHGR 80 (1926): 415.

Wakeman, M.V. INSCRIPTIONS ON THE OLD GRAVE MARKERS IN ALL OF THE BURYING GROUNDS IN EAST HADDAM AND SEVEN OF THOSE IN LYME, BEING ALL THE LEGIBLE RECORDS OF PEOPLE BORN PREVIOUS TO OR DURING THE YEAR 1810. N.p.: Author, 1907. 439 p.

CHURCH RECORDS

BAPTIST CHURCH. Minutes, 1844-1874. (CSL, LDS 1647).

FIRST AND THIRD BAPTIST CHURCH. Minutes, 1809-1875. (CSL, LDS 1575).

FIRST CONGREGATIONAL CHURCH. Minutes, 1734-1866. Vital Records, 1702-1927. (CSL, LDS 1643). Index, (CSL, LDS 1448, pt. 1). Marriages, 1751-1800. BAILEY 6:119-30.

METHODIST CHURCH. Minutes, 1860-1908. Vital Records, 1840-1922. (CSL, LDS 1645).

SECOND CONGREGATIONAL CHURCH. Minutes, 1733–1931. Vital Records, 1733–1931. (CSL, LDS 1646). Marriages, 1736–1799. BAILEY 1:82–89.

Barker, Mrs. W.C.A. RECORD OF THE FIRST CONGREGATIONAL CHURCH OF EAST HADDAM. N.p., n.d. 66 p. (LDS 547,537).

MANUAL OF THE CONGREGATIONAL CHURCH, AND HISTORY OF THE CHURCH AND ITS PARISH IN HADLYME, CONNECTICUT, WITH A LIST OF THE PRINCIPLE OFFICERS AND AN ENTIRE LIST OF THE MEMBERS FROM ITS ORGANIZATION, JUNE 26, 1745, AND A LIST OF PRESENT OFFICERS AND MEMBERS TO DECEMBER 1, 1913. N.p., 1914.

THE TWO HUNDREDTH ANNIVERSARY OF THE FIRST CONGREGATIONAL CHURCH OF HADDAM, CONNECTICUT. Haddam: First Congregational Church, 1902. 360 p.

HISTORICAL SOCIETY

Amasa Day House, Routes 149, 151, 06469. (203) 247-8996.

LAND RECORDS

Deeds, 1704–1860. Index, 1704–1910. (LDS 1641, pt. 1–15).

Patterson, David Williams. "Extracts from the Proprietors' Records of East Haddam, CT." NEHGR 13 (1859): 19–20.

LIBRARIES

East Haddam Public Library (203) 873-8248.

Rathburn Free Library, 06423. (203) 873-8210.

MILITARY RECORDS

Hartford. CSL, Record Group 62. Militia Service Lists, 1860–1865.

McKee, Charles H. "Letters of a Soldier of the American Revolution." CM 10 (1906): 25–27.

Smith, Edward Church, and Smith, Philip Mark. LIST AND RECORD OF CIVIL WAR VETERANS. THOSE WHO ENLISTED FROM, NOW RESIDE IN, OR

ARE BURIED IN THE TOWN OF EAST HADDAM, CONNECTICUT. Moodus, Conn.: Connecticut Valley Advertiser Print, 1899. 35 p.

Smith, Edward Church, and Smith, Philip Mark. "The Roll of an East Haddam, Connecticut, Train-Band." TAG 15 (1939): 167-71.

NEWSPAPERS

The PRELIMINARY CHECKLIST lists two newspapers for EAST HADDAM.

Newspapers indexed in the HALE NEWSPAPER INDEX TO DEATH AND MAR-RIAGE NOTICES include the EAST HADDAM JOURNAL, 12 April 1860-6 April 1861.

PROBATE RECORDS

East Haddam Probate District, Town Office Building, Goodspeed Plaza, 06423. (203) 873-8351.

>   Organized October 1741 from the Hartford Probate District.

>   Probate Districts organized from the East Haddam Probate District include the COLCHESTER, EAST HAMPTON, HEBRON and MIDDLE-TOWN Probate Districts.

>   The records previous to May 1832 are at the Colchester Probate Court.

>   ON FILE AT THE CSL: Estate Papers, 1741-1832 (filed under the Colchester Probate District). Court Record Books, 1832-1855. (LDS 1642).

SCHOOL RECORDS

Hartford. CSL, Record Group 62. School Registers, 1848-1895. School Meeting Minutes 1800-1849.

TAX RECORDS

Hartford. CSL, Record Group 62. Tax books, 1859-1862. Abatement Lists, 1828-1836.

Hartford. Connecticut Historical Society. Tax Rate Book, 1804.

VITAL RECORDS

Town Clerk, Town Office Building, Goodspped Plaza, 06423. (203) 873-8279.

> The town clerk's earliest birth record is 1687, marriage record is 1693 and death record is 1692.

The BARBOUR INDEX covers the years 1743-1857 and is based on the James N. Arnold and Irene H. Mix copy of the EAST HADDAM vital records made in 1913.

"Connecticut Marriages Before 1750 (Barbour) Town of East Haddam." CN 4 (1972): 496-500; 5 (1972): 28-32.

Patterson, David Williams. "First Book East Haddam Land Records. (Certified Copies of all of the records of births, marriages, and deaths, which are to be found in the first book of land records in East Haddam)." NEHGR 11 (1857): 273-78, 311-14; 12 (1858): 42-47.

PUBLISHED WORKS AND OTHER RECORDS

"Account Books of Moses Fox, Merchant, East Haddam, Connecticut, 1795-1821." KANSAS KIN, May 1967, p. 18.

Clemons, W. Harry. "The Legends of Machimoodus." CM 7 (1903): 451-58.

Field, David Dudley. HISTORY OF THE TOWN OF HADDAM AND EAST HADDAM. Middletown: Loomis G. Nichols, 1814. 49 p.

Hartford. CSL, Record Group 3, Main 2, Box 551. Records of the Justices of the Peace, 1857-1864.

Niles, Hosford Buel. OLD CHIMNEY STACKS OF EAST HADDAM, MIDDLE-SEX COUNTY, CONNECTICUT. 1887. Reprint. East Haddam, Conn.: East Haddam Bicentennial Committee and Rathburn Free Public Library, 1976. 146 p. (LDS 051,599).

Palmer, Frederic C. "The John Warner House, ca. 1738 East Haddam, Connecticut." CANTIQUARIAN 24 (1972): 20-25.

Terry, Mrs. Alfred Howe. "The Goodspeed Opera House." CANTIQUARIAN 12 (1960): 26-31.

EAST HAMPTON

MIDDLESEX COUNTY. Organized October 1767 as CHATHAM from MIDDLE-TOWN. The name changed 4 May 1915.

CEMETERY RECORDS AND CEMETERIES

NAME	ADDRESS	HALE NO.	CITATION
Lake View Cemetery	21 Lake View Road	1	13:1-44
St. Patrick Roman Catholic Cemetery	19 Maple Street	2	13:45-50
Skinnerville Cemetery	Young Street and Skinner Street	3	13:51-55
Young Street Cemetery	Lower Young Street and U.S. 52	4	13:56-58
Tartia Cemetery	Tartia Road	5	13:59-62
White Birch Road Cemetery	White Birch Road	6	13:63-64
Waterhole Southwest District Cemetery	Waterhold Road	7	13:65-69
Union Hill Cemetery	Moodus Road	8	13:70-94
Private (Hills) Cemetery	Mrs. Maud West farm, near lake	9	13:95
Hog Hill Cemetery	Hog Hill Road	10	13:96-99
Hurd Cemetery	Near Hurd Park	11	13:100-101
Old Catholic Cemetery	Middletown Road	12	13:102
Griffith Cemetery	On Jacob Anderson farm at Johnsons Bridge	13	13:103
Hall Cemetery	Clark Hill Road	14	13:104-5

Index to Hale inscriptions: 13:106–38.

CHURCH RECORDS

CHRIST CHURCH, EPISCOPAL. Minutes, 1794–1879, 1871–1908. Vital Records, 1794–1823, 1802–1912. (CSL, LDS 1675).

CONGREGATIONAL CHURCH. Minutes, 1747–1911. Vital Records, 1778–1930. (CSL, LDS 1676). Marriage Records. (NYGBS, LDS 1840).

CONGREGATIONAL CHURCH OF CHATHAM. Marriages, 1767–1798. BAILEY 4:96–103.

SECOND CONGREGATIONAL CHURCH of Middle Haddam. Marriages, 1740–1799. BAILEY 3:74–84. Minutes, 1854–1919. Vital Records, 1859–1932. (CSL, LDS 1678).

SECOND CONGREGATIONAL CHURCH of Haddam Neck. Minutes, 1753–1944. Vital Records, 1740–1944. (CSL, LDS 1677).

EARLY RECORDS OF BAPTISMS, MARRIAGES, DEATHS, AND MEMBERSHIP OF THE CONGREGATIONAL CHURCH, EAST HAMPTON, (CHATHAM), CONNECTICUT. Middletown: Pelton and King, 1900. 150 p.

THE ONE HUNDRED AND FIFTIETH ANNIVERSARY 1748–1898 OF THE CONGREGATIONAL CHURCH OF EAST HAMPTON, (CHATHAM), CONNECTICUT. N.p., n.d. 150 p.

HISTORICAL SOCIETY

Chatham Historical Society, 06424.

LAND RECORDS

Deeds, 1767–1873. Index, 1767–1876. (LDS 1566 pt. 1–15).

Hartford. CSL, Record Group 62. Deeds, 1806–1839.

LIBRARIES

East Hampton Public Library, Main Street, 06424. (203) 267-2635.

Middle Haddam Public Library, P.O. Box 202, 06456. (203) 267-9093.

Richmond Memorial Library, R.F.D. 2, 06424. (203) 295-9005.

NEWSPAPERS

The PRELIMINARY CHECKLIST lists two newspapers for EAST HAMPTON.

PROBATE RECORDS

East Hampton Probate District, Town Hall, 20 East High Street, 06424. (203) 267-9262.

> Organized 1 June 1824 from the East Haddam and Middletown Probate Districts.

> Probate Districts formed from the East Hampton Probate District include the HADDAM and PORTLAND Probate Districts.

> ON FILE AT THE CSL: Estate Papers, 1824-1914, are filed under Portland Probate District. Court Record Books, 1824-1853. (LDS 1565).

Name changed from the Chatham Probate District to the East Hampton Probate District 6 January 1915.

TAX RECORDS

Hartford. CSL, Record Group 62. Tax Lists, 1820-1930. Tax Books, 1849-1877.

VITAL RECORDS

Town Clerk, Town Hall, 20 East High Street, 06424. (203) 267-2519.

The BARBOUR INDEX covers the years 1767-1854 under the name CHATHAM and is based on the James N. Arnold copy of the vital records made in 1912.

PUBLISHED WORKS AND OTHER RECORDS

Hartford. CSL, Record Group 3, Main 2, Box 549, Records of NOAH BROOK, Justice of the Peace, 1832-1839.

Loomis, Israel Foote. "The Town of Chatham." CM 5 (1899): 303-19, 370-81.

Price, Carl Fowler. POSTSCRIPT TO YANKEE TOWNSHIP. East Hampton: East Hampton Bicentennial Committee, 1975. 38 p.

_____. YANKEE TOWNSHIP. East Hampton: Citizens Welfare Club, 1941.
212 p.

EAST HARTFORD

HARTFORD COUNTY. Organized October 1783 from HARTFORD. Towns organized from EAST HARTFORD include MANCHESTER.

CEMETERY RECORDS AND CEMETERIES

NAME	ADDRESS	HALE NO.	CITATION
Center Cemetery	944 Main Street	1	13:1-139
Hockanum Cemetery	55 High Street	2	13:140-80
Old Hockanum or Meadowgate Cemetery	Meadow Lane	3	13:181-85
St. Mary Roman Catholic Cemetery	930 Burnside Avenue Office: 360 Broad Street, Manchester, 06040. (203) 646-3772	4	13:186-208
Revolutionary Soldier's graveyard	H. Overton Farm, Willow Brook	5	13:209
Vault	Brewer Place, Station 23, Hockanum	6	13:210
Smallpox Cemetery	Burnham's farm at South Windsor town line	7	13:211
Porter Cemetery	Kenny Property, near Frog Brook	8	13:212
Hillside Cemetery	12 Hillside Street		(no citation)
Old South Cemetery	Meadow Lane		(no citation)

Index to Hale inscriptions: 13:213-79.

Bridgman, Thomas. INSCRIPTIONS ON THE GRAVESTONES IN GRAVEYARDS

OF NORTHAMPTON AND OF OTHER TOWNS IN THE VALLEY OF THE
CONNECTICUT. Northampton, Mass.: Hopkins, Bridgman, and Co., 1850.
227 p.

CENSUS RECORDS

Hartford. CHS. Census list of 1795.

CHURCH RECORDS

FIRST CONGREGATIONAL CHURCH. Minutes, 1699-1895. Vital Records,
1748-1912. (CSL, LDS 1657). Index, 1699-1912. (CSL).

SECOND CONGREGATIONAL CHURCH. Vital Records, 1877-1923, 1925-
1940. (CSL, LDS 1650).

East Hartford, Connecticut. First Congregational Church Vital Records 1723-
1745, kept by Rev. Samuel Woodbridge. W. Herbert Wood, transcriber.
Typescript. (CSL, LDS 003,012).

"East Hartford Church Records (Rev. Andrew Yates 1801-1913)." CHSB 6
(July 1941): 18-24.

Marriage Records Found among the Papers of Rev. Dr. Williams, 1783-1798.
BAILEY 2:85-86.

Tuthill, William Bodle. THE FIRST CONGREGATIONAL CHURCH, EAST
HARTFORD, CONNECTICUT, 1702-1902. Hartford: Hartford Printing Co.,
1902. 117 p.

HISTORICAL SOCIETY

East Hartford Historical Society, 840 Main Street, 06108.

LAND RECORDS

Land Records, 1783-1851. Index, 1783-1851. (LDS 1648 pt. 1-11).

LIBRARY

East Hartford Public Library, 840 Main Street, 06108. (203) 289-6429.

MILITARY RECORDS

Bidwell, Daniel O. EAST HARTFORD'S SHARE IN THE WORLD WAR. East Hartford: Advercraft Press, 1929. 65 p.

INDEX OF NAMES, ETC. FOR EAST HARTFORD'S SHARE IN THE WORLD WAR. Typescript. 17 p.

NEWSPAPERS

EAST HARTFORD GAZETTE. Weekly. 54 Connecticut Boulevard, 06108. (203) 289-6468.

The PRELIMINARY CHECKLIST lists four newspapers for EAST HARTFORD.

PROBATE RECORDS

East Hartford Probate District, Town Hall, 740 Main Street, 06108. (203) 289-2781.

> Organized May 1887 from the Hartford Probate District.

> Probate districts organized from the East Hartford Probate District include the Manchester Probate District.

SCHOOL RECORDS

Hartford. CSL, Record Group 62. School register, 1873-1874. Minutes of the Second South School District, 1839-1871.

TAX RECORDS

Hartford. CSL, Record Group 62. Tax books, 1856-1865. Tax lists, 1869-1878, 1879-1929.

VITAL RECORDS

Town Clerk, Town Hall, 740 Main Street, 06108. (203) 289-2781 ext. 231.

The BARBOUR INDEX covers the years 1783-1853 and is based on the James Lahy copy of the vital records made in 1917.

VOTER RECORDS

Hartford. CSL, Record Group 62. Voter Lists, 1880-1887.

PUBLISHED WORKS AND OTHER RECORDS

Bidwell, Daniel Doane. "A Revolutionary Thanksgiving: A True Story of Olden Time." CQ 4 (1898): 30-32.

"Epitaph for an Old House." CANTIQUARIAN 22, no. 1 (June 1970): 12.

Genealogical Notes on Twenty-four families of East Hartford; also a copy of Capt. Charles Hyde Olmsted's papers. (NHCHS, LDS 1649).

Goodwin, Joseph Olcott. EAST HARTFORD: ITS HISTORY AND TRADITIONS. 1879. Reprint. East Hartford, Conn.: Raymond Library Co., 1976. 249 p.

Paquette, Lee. ONLY MORE SO. THE HISTORY OF EAST HARTFORD 1783-1976. East Hartford, Conn.: Raymond Library Co., 1976. 336 p. Index.

EAST HAVEN

NEW HAVEN COUNTY. Organized 1785 from NEW HAVEN.

CEMETERY RECORDS AND CEMETERIES

NAME	ADDRESS	HALE NO.	CITATION
Old Cemetery	Town Green	1	14:1-53
East Lawn Cemetery	58 River Street (203) 467-0857	2	14:54-89
Green Lawn Cemetery	109 Tyler Street	3	14:90-103
Congregation Shevath Achim Cemetery	16 Brockett Place	4	14:104-15
Congregation Bikar B'nai Abraham Cemetery	16 Brockett Place	5	14:116-27
Hebrew Free Burial Association Cemetery	18-38 Brockett Place	6	14:128-37
Independent Rambam Lodge Cemetery	17 Brockett Place	7	14:138
Independent New Haven Lodge Cemetery	19 Brockett Place	8	14:139
Jewish Cemetery	Brockett Place	9	14:140-42

Index to Hale cemetery inscriptions: 14:143-182.

Cemetery Records at East Haven. (NYGBS, LDS 1627).

CHURCH RECORDS

CHRIST (EPISCOPAL) CHURCH. Minutes, 1788-1889. (CSL, LDS 1630).

FIRST CONGREGATIONAL CHURCH. Minutes, 1755-1905. Vital Records, 1755-1905. (CSL, LDS 1629). Card Index, 1755-1905. (CSL). Marriages, 1755-1799. BAILEY 6:24-34.

Eversull, HARRY K. THE EVOLUTION OF AN OLD NEW ENGLAND CHURCH. BEING THE HISTORY OF THE OLD STONE CHURCH IN EAST HAVEN, CONNECTICUT. N.p., 1924. 176 p.

HISTORICAL SOCIETY

East Haven Historical Society, Inc., 27 Park Place, 06512.

LAND RECORDS

Deeds, 1785-1852. (LDS 1628 pt. 1-6).

LIBRARY

Hagaman Memorial Library, 227 Main Street, 06512. (203) 467-0810.

MILITARY RECORDS

Flood, Phyllis Rice. IN THEIR COUNTRY'S SERVICE, A LISTING OF WAR VETERANS FROM EAST HAVEN, CONNECTICUT FROM COLONIAL TIMES THROUGH WORLD WAR II. N.p., n.d. 28 p.

NEWSPAPERS

The PRELIMINARY CHECKLIST lists two newspapers for EAST HAVEN.

PROBATE RECORDS

East Haven Probate District, Town Hall, 250 Main Street, Box 91, 06512. (203) 469-8055.

Organized 5 January 1955 from the New Haven Probate District.

VITAL RECORDS

Town Clerk, Town Hall, 250 Main Street, 06512. (203) 469-5311 ext. 201.

"Connecticut Marriages Before 1750 (Barbour) Town of East Haven." CN 5 (1972): 32-33.

The BARBOUR INDEX covers the years 1700–1852 and is based on the Ethyl L. Scofield copy of EAST HAVEN Vital Records made in 1914 and Dodd's EAST HAVEN REGISTER (see below).

PUBLISHED WORKS AND OTHER RECORDS

Dodd, Stephen. EAST HAVEN REGISTER, CONTAINING AN ACCOUNT OF THE NAMES, MARRIAGES, AND BIRTHS OF THE FAMILIES WHICH SETTLED OR WHICH HAVE RESIDED IN EAST HAVEN, FROM ITS SETTLEMENT IN 1644 TO THE YEAR 1800. New Haven: Tuttle, Morehouse and Taylor Press, 1910. 168 p.

_____. EAST HAVEN REGISTER: IN THREE PARTS. New Haven: T.G. Woodward and Co., 1824. 200 p.

Hughes, Sarah Eva. HISTORY OF EAST HAVEN. New Haven: Tuttle, Morehouse and Taylor Press, 1908. 324 p.

Welles, Edwin Stanley. "Jacob Hemingway, The First Student of Yale College." CQ 2 (1896): 178–81.

EAST LYME

NEW LONDON COUNTY. Organized May 1839 from LYME and WATERFORD.

CEMETERY RECORDS AND CEMETERIES

NAME	ADDRESS	HALE NO.	CITATION
Old Stone Church Cemetery	U.S. 50	1	14:1-25
Union Cemetery	U.S. 50	2	14:26-63
Banty Cemetery	Southwest part of town near house of C.O. Banty	3	14:64-65
Rogers Cemetery	Whistletown, 3 miles from Flanders	4	14:66-69
Pest Yard Cemetery	Whistletown Road	5	14-70
Center or Riverhead Cemetery	New London Road	6	14:71-75
Calvary Cemetery	Near Mrs. Gushie's home east from Flanders	7	14:76
Huntley Cemetery	Southwest part of town near home of George Huntley	8	14:77
Crocker Cemetery	Butlertown, northwest part of town from highway	9	14:78
Powers Cemetery	Near railroad tracks south of Crescent Beach	10	14:79
Flanders Church Cemetery	Rear of the Flanders School House	11	14:80-100
Taber Cemetery	Near house of John Beckwith	12	14:101
Leech Cemetery	Grassy Hill Road on old Palmer farm	13	14:102

NAME	ADDRESS	HALE NO.	CITATION
Fosdick Cemetery	Near Riverhead Cemetery	14	14:103
Barthrick or Champion Tinker Cemetery	In woods, 1 mile north Wellsweep	15	14:104
Old Fox Farm Cemetery	Walnut Hill Road near Old Fox Place	16	14:106-7
Holmes Cemetery	In rear of James Hatt farm	17	14:108
Tilleson Cemetery	On Walnut Hill Road near house of Joseph Zabana	20	14:109-10
Beebe Cemetery	Whistletown Road	21	14:111
Chadwick Cemetery	On riverbank near Watron Property	22	14:112
Reeve Cemetery	In State Forest, northern part of town	23	14:113-14
Martin Burke Cemetery	On Niantic River near Golden Spur	24	(no citation)

Index to Hale inscriptions: 14:115-40.

Bush, Celeste E. EAST LYME, CONNECTICUT CEMETERY INSCRIPTIONS, 1724-1907. Niantic: Author, 1907.

Cemetery Records. Church Yard Cemetery, 14 p. River View Cemetery, 61 p. (NYGBS, LDS 1733).

"Inscriptions from Gravestones at East Lyme, Connecticut." NEHGR 79 (1925): 66-80.

CHURCH RECORDS

FIRST BAPTIST CHURCH. Minutes, 1752-1797, 1823-1859. Vital Records, 1797-1823. (CSL, LDS 1640).

FIRST CONGREGATIONAL CHURCH. Minutes, 1719-1912. Vital Records, 1828-1914. (CSL, LDS 1639).

Graves, Ross G. HISTORICAL SKETCH OF THE FLANDERS BAPTIST AND COMMUNITY CHURCH OF EAST LYME, CONNECTICUT. KNOWN AS THE LYME SEPARTIST CHURCH 1748-1752, THE FIRST BAPTIST CHURCH OF LYME, 1810-1839; THE FIRST BAPTIST CHURCH OF EAST LYME, 1839-1929. PRESENT NAME, 1929 TO DATE. N.p., 1952.

HISTORICAL SOCIETY

East Lyme Historical Society, Romagna Court, P.O. Box 309, 06357. (203) 739-6070.

LAND RECORDS

Deeds, 1839-1861. (LDS 1638).

LIBRARY

Niantic Public Library, 409 Main Street, 06357. (203) 739-6926.

NEWSPAPER

THE NEWS. Weekly. P.O. Drawer 2, 06357. (203) 739-7504.

The PRELIMINARY CHECKLIST lists one newspaper for EAST LYME.

PROBATE RECORDS

East Lyme Probate District, Town Hall, 108 Pennsylvania Avenue, Box 519, 06357. (203) 739-6931 ext. 18.

Organized 2 June 1843 from the New London Probate District.

ON FILE AT THE CSL: Estate Papers, 1843-1943. Indexes, 1843-1943. Inventory Control Book, 1843-1943. Court Record Book, 1843-1858. Probate Records, 1843-1850. (LDS 1638).

TAX RECORDS

Hartford. CSL, Record Group 62. Tax Assessment Lists 1839-1842, 1840-1849.

VITAL RECORDS

Town Clerk, Town Hall, 108 Pennsylvania Avenue, 06357. (203) 739-6931 ext. 35.

The BARBOUR INDEX covers the years 1839-1853 and is based on the Ernest C. Russell copy of EAST LYME vital records made in 1924.

PUBLISHED WORKS AND OTHER RECORDS

Leibundguth, Shirley Bergman. "McCook Point: A Refuge from Heat and Dust." CANTIQUARIAN 31 (June 1979): 4-17.

Sturtevant, William C. "Two 1761 Wigwams at Niantic, Connecticut." AMERICAN ANTIQUITY 40 (1974): 437-44.

EASTON

FAIRFIELD COUNTY. Organized May 1845 from WESTON.

CEMETERY RECORDS AND CEMETERIES

NAME	ADDRESS	HALE NO.	CITATION
Union Cemetery	Near Baptist Church	1	14:1-36
Aspetuck Cemetery	U.S. 51	2	14:37-46A
Lyon Cemetery	In north part of town, Rock House District	3	14:47-47A
Wheeler Cemetery	On Bridgeport and Danbury Road near Redding Line	4	14:48
(New) Aspetuck Cemetery	U.S. 51	5	14:49-63
Baldwin Cemetery	In west part of town near Redding town line	6	14:64-68
Congregation B'nai Israel Cemetery	237 King's Highway		(no citation)
Congregation Rodeph Sholom Cemetery	225 King's Highway		(no citation)
Perpetual Care Cemetery	U.S. 51		(no citation)
Gilbertown Cemetery	U.S. 51		(no citation)

Index to Hale inscriptions: 14:66-68.

Lacey, Ruth Bradford, and Orcutt, Samuel. "Inscriptions in the Cemetery at Easton, Connecticut, near the Baptist Church." FAIRFIELD COUNTY HISTORICAL SOCIETY ANNUAL REPORT, 1891-92, pp. 63-92.

CHURCH RECORDS

CHRIST EOPISCOPAL CHURCH. Records, 1784-1898. (CSL, LDS 1673).

CONGREGATIONAL CHURCH. Records, 1762-1930. (CSL, LDS 1674).

NORTH CONGREGATIONAL CHURCH. Marriages, 1763-1796. BAILEY 5: 59-63.

HISTORICAL SOCIETY

Historical Society of Easton, Inc., Westport Road (P.O. Box 121), 06612. (203) 268-6291.

Publishes SCHOOLHOUSE SENTINEL. 6 per year.

LAND RECORDS

Land Records, 1845-1860. (LDS 1672).

LIBRARY

Easton Public Library, Morehouse Road, Box 2, 06425. (203) 261-0134.

PROBATE RECORDS

EASTON was in the Weston Probate District until 22 July 1875 when the Easton Probate District was formed. It was discontinued on 4 March 1878 and made a part of the Bridgeport Probate District. In January 1959 EASTON was made a part of the Trumbull Probate District.

VITAL RECORDS

Town Clerk, Town Hall, 274 Center Road, 06612. (203) 268-6291.

The town clerk's earliest birth record is 13 October 1852, marriage record is 14 June 1845 and death record is 1853.

PUBLISHED WORKS AND OTHER RECORDS

Partridge, Helen. EASTON--ITS HISTORY. Collinsville: Lithographics, Inc., 1972. 248 p.

EAST WINDSOR

HARTFORD COUNTY. Organized May 1768 from WINDSOR. Towns organized from EAST WINDSOR include ELLINGTON and SOUTH WINDSOR.

CEMETERY RECORDS AND CEMETERIES

NAME	ADDRESS	HALE NO.	CITATION
Town Street Cemetery	South Main Street	1	14:1-15
Springdale Cemetery	Main Street	2	14:16-38
Warehouse Point Cemetery	On main highway 1/4 mile north Warehouse point	3	14:39-51
Melrose Cemetery	Rockville Road	4	14:52-63
St. Catherine Cemetery	Near Broad Brook, U.S. 53	5	14:54-72
Windsorville Cemetery	Windsorville	6	14:73-99
Scantic Cemetery	Cemetery Road	7	14:100-131

Index to Hale inscriptions: 14:132-68.

CEMETERY AND OTHER RECORDS OF VARIOUS PLACES IN HARTFORD COUNTY. (LDS 1734).

Elmore, Mary Jane. SOUTH WINDSOR CEMETERY INSCRIPTIONS FROM THE EARLIEST INSCRIPTION TO 1900; THE INSCRIPTIONS OF THE CEMETERIES IN SOUTH WINDSOR, EAST WINDSOR HILL AND WIPPING, OLD AND NEW CEMETERIES. Hartford: Author, 1920.

CHURCH RECORDS

BROAD BROOK CONGREGATIONAL CHURCH. Vital Records, 1851-1909. (CSL, LDS 1668).

FIRST CONGREGATIONAL CHURCH. Records, 1695–1853. (CSL, LDS 1666). Vital Records, 1803–1932. (CSL, LDS 1664). Marriage Records, 1761–1783. BAILEY 1:113–116.

GRACE EPISCOPAL CHURCH. Vital Records, 1845–1909. (CSL, LDS 1668).

METHODIST EPISCOPAL CHURCH. Vital Records, 1830–1912. (CSL, LDS 1663).

NORTH OR FOURTH CONGREGATIONAL CHURCH. Minutes, 1752–1933. (CSL, LDS 1665).

ST. JOHN EPISCOPAL CHURCH. Minutes, 1876–1926. Vital Records, 1803–1919. (CSL, LDS 1667).

Bates, Albert Carlos. RECORDS OF REV. RANSOM WARNER, 1823–1854, RECTOR OF ST. ANDREW'S, SIMSBURY AND BLOOMFIELD ST. PETER'S, GRANBY ST. JOHN'S EAST WINDSOR, CONNECTICUT. Hartford: Case, Lockwood and Brainard Co., 1893. 84 p.

HISTORICAL SKETCH OF WAREHOUSE POINT, CONNECTICUT, AND ALSO OF THE METHODIST EPISCOPAL CHURCH FROM 1822 TO THE PRESENT TIME. N.p., 1900. 148 p.

HISTORY OF THE FIRST ECCLESIASTICAL SOCIETY IN EAST WINDSOR, FROM ITS FORMATION IN 1752 TO THE DEATH OF ITS SECOND PASTOR, REV. SHUBAEL BARTLETT, IN 1854, WITH A SKETCH OF THE LIFE OF REV. MR. BARTLETT, AND HIS FAREWELL DISCOURSE. PREPARED FOR THE FIFTIETH ANNIVERSARY OF HIS SETTLEMENT. N.p., 1857.

RECORDS OF REV. RANSOM WARNER 1823–1854 RECTOR OF ST. ANDREW'S, SIMSBURY AND BLOOMFIELD ST. PETER'S, GRANBY ST. JOHN'S, EAST WINDSOR, CONNECTICUT. Hartford: Case, Lockwood and Brainard Co., 1893. 84 p.

HISTORICAL SOCIETY

East Windsor Historical Society, Inc., 06088.

LAND RECORDS

Deeds. Index, 1768–1919. (LDS 1661 pt. 1–17).

LIBRARY

Library Association of Warehouse Point, 107 Main Street, 06088. (203) 623-5482.

MILITARY RECORDS

Hartford. CSL, Record Group 62. Militia Enrollment Books, 1851-1854, 1861, 1862.

NEWSPAPER

The PRELIMINARY CHECKLIST lists one newspaper for EAST WINDSOR.

PROBATE RECORDS

East Windsor Probate District, Town Hall, 1540 Sullivan Avenue, South Windsor, 06074. (203) 644-0211.

Organized May 1782 from the Hartford and Stafford Probate Districts.

The East Windsor Probate District also includes the town of SOUTH WINDSOR.

Probate districts organized from the East Windsor Probate District include the Ellington, Enfield and Hebron Probate Districts.

ON FILE AT THE CSL: Estate Papers, 1782-1899. Indexes, 1782-1899. Inventory Control Books, 1782-1899. Court Record Books, 1781-1855. (CDS 1662 pt. 1-4).

SCHOOL RECORDS

Hartford. CSL, Record Group 62. Second School Society Account Book 1826-1856.

VITAL RECORDS

Town Clerk, Town Hall, 11 Rye Street, 06016. (203) 623-9467.

The town clerk's earliest birth record is 1758, marriage record is 1768 and death record is 1764.

The BARBOUR INDEX covers the years 1768-1860 and is based on a photocopy of the original vital records made in 1914.

VOTER RECORDS

Hartford. CSL, Record Group 62. Voter Lists, 1841-1890 and one undated volume.

PUBLISHED WORKS AND OTHER RECORDS

DeVito, Michael C. EAST WINDSOR, THROUGH THE YEARS. Warehouse Point: East Windsor Historical Society, 1968. 164 p.

Hartford. CSL, Record Group 3, Main 2, Box 551. Records of Joseph Allen and Roswell Grant. Justices of the Peace, 1785–1791, 1798–1801.

Potwin, George Stephen. EAST WINDSOR HERITAGE: TWO HUNDRED YEARS OF CHURCH AND COMMUNITY HISTORY: 1752–1952. East Windsor: First Congregational Church, 1952. 63 p.

Stiles, Henry Reed. HISTORY AND GENEALOGIES OF ANCIENT WINDSOR, CONNECTICUT INCLUDING EAST WINDSOR, SOUTH WINDSOR, BLOOM-FIELD, WINDSOR LOCKS AND ELLINGTON. 1635–1891. 2 vols. Hartford: Case, Lockwood and Brainard, 1891. (LDS 417,435).

Stoughton, John Alden. WINDSOR FARMS. Hartford: Clark and Smith Printers, 1883. 150 p. (LDS 496,751).

ELLINGTON

TOLLAND COUNTY. Organized May 1786 from EAST WINDSOR.

CEMETERY RECORDS AND CEMETERIES

NAME	ADDRESS	HALE NO.	CITATION
Ellington Center Cemetery	Maple Street	1	14:1-71
Jewish Cemetery	Maple Street	2	14:72-73
McKinstry Cemetery	Main Street	3	14:74-75
Crystal Lake Cemetery	Sandy Beach Road	4	14:76-79
Charter Cemetery	Crystal Lake Road	5	14:80-82
Moore-Kibbe Cemetery	On William E. Kibbe farm 3 miles north of center	6	14:83
Ellsworth Cemetery	On Ernest Kupfershind farm south of center	7	14:84
Knight Cemetery	Pinney Street	8	14:85
Shepard Cemetery	On Shepard farm 1 1/2 miles west of Windermere	9	14:86
Old McKinstry Cemetery	Main Street	10	14:87-88
Aborns Cemetery	On farm of Mrs. Edgar Rease Main Road, Somers to Rockville	11	14:88

Index to Hale inscriptions: 14:89-113.

Kimball, Mary. ELLINGTON CEMETERY. Ellington: Sabra Trumbull Chapter, DAR, 1926. 75 p.

_____. MCKINSTRY CEMETERY. Ellington: Sabra Trumbull Chapter, DAR, 1926. 3 p.

Sabra Trumbull Chapter, DAR, CRYSTAL LAKE CEMETERY, DIMMOCK'S CROSSING, ELLINGTON, CONNECTICUT. Ellington: Sabra Trumbull Chapter, DAR, 1926. 5 p.

CHURCH RECORDS

CONGREGATIONAL CHURCH. Records, 1785–1941. Index. (CSL). Minutes, 1785–1940. Vital Records, 1800–1941. (CSL, LDS 1660 pt. 1–2).

HISTORICAL SOCIETY

Ellington Historical Society, Tripp Road, 06029.

LAND RECORDS

Land Records, 1786–1854. Indexed. (LDS 1658 pt. 1–7).

LIBRARY

Hall Memorial Library, Park Street, (P.O. Box 128), 06029. (203) 875–6881.

PROBATE RECORDS

Ellington Probate District, 14 Park Place, Ellington, 06029. (P.O. Box 268, Vernon, 06066.) (203) 872–0519.

> Organized 31 May 1826 from the East Windsor and Stafford Probate Districts.

The Ellington Probate District includes the town of VERNON.

Probate districts organized from the ELLINGTON Probate District include the Somers Probate District.

> ON FILE AT THE CSL: Estate Papers, 1826–1920. Indexes, 1826–1914 (papers from 1914–1920 arranged alphabetically). Inventory Control Books, 1826–1914. Court Record Books, 1826–1854. Probate Records, 1826–1854. (LDS 1657 pt. 1–2).

VITAL RECORDS

Town Clerk, Town Hall, 55 Main Street, (P.O. Box 236), 06029. (203) 875–3190.

The town clerk's earliest birth record is 1737, marriage record is 1761 and death record is 1758.

The BARBOUR INDEX covers the years 1786–1853 and is based on a copy of the vital records made in 1911 and of the James N. Arnold copy made in 1916.

"Record of marriages from 1820–1853." 112 p. (Ellington, LDS 1659).

PUBLISHED WORKS AND OTHER RECORDS

Crane, Darius. BIOGRAPHICAL SKETCHES OF ELLINGTON FAMILIES. Hartford: Star Printing Co., 1889. 80 p.

EARLY ELLINGTON VILLAGE AND SUPPLEMENT: CHANGING TIMES IN ELLINGTON VILLAGE FROM THE MIDDLE 1700'S THROUGH 1975. Ellington: Calendar Staff, Congregational Church, 1975. 270 p.

McKnight, Nellie E. ELLINGTON, GLIMPSES OF EARLIER DAYS. Ellington: Ellington Historical Society, 1975. 38 p.

Pinney, Alice E. "Ellington." CQ 4 (1898): 188–96.

Stiles, Henry Reed. HISTORY AND GENEALOGIES OF ANCIENT WINDSOR, CONNECTICUT INCLUDING EAST WINDSOR, SOUTH WINDSOR, BLOOM-FIELD, WINDSOR LOCKS AND ELLINGTON 1635-1891. 2 vols. Hartford: Case, Lockwood and Brainard, 1891. (LDS 417,935).

ENFIELD

HARTFORD COUNTY. Organized May 1683 as a part of Massachusetts. It was annexed to Connecticut in May 1749.

CEMETERY RECORDS AND CEMETERIES

NAME	ADDRESS	HALE NO.	CITATION
Enfield Street Cemetery	1189 Enfield Street	1	15:1–96
Thompsonville Cemetery	157 Pearl Street	2	15:97–174
(Old) St. Patrick Roman Catholic Cemetery	Pearl Street	3	15:175–231
Old Hazardville Cemetery	300 Hazard Avenue	4	15:232–45
New Hazardville Cemetery	Elm and North Streets	5	15:246–68
St. Bernard Cemetery	Park Street	6	15:269–81
(New) St. Patrick Roman Catholic Cemetery	King Street	7	15:282–87
King Street Cemetery	King Street	8	15:288–96
Shaker Cemetery	Shaker Road	9	15:297
Powder Hollow Cemetery	Old Vault, 1/4 mile from Post Office	10	15:298
Holy Cross Cemetery	723 Enfield Street	11	15:298
St. Adalbert Cemetery	Summer Street	12	15:298
Private Cemetery	Weymouth District, Dr. Pease property	13	15:299
Felician Cemetery	On grounds of Felician Nuns	14	(no citation)

Index to Hale inscriptions: 15:300-381.

BIBLE AND CEMETERY RECORDS. DAR Florida Genealogical Research Committee, 1931. 57 p. (LDS 850,400).

"Connecticut Headstones Before 1800 (Hale--Enfield)." CN 12 (1979): 36-39, 222-26.

Dewey, Louis Marinus. "Inscriptions from Old Cemeteries in Connecticut." NEHGR 60 (1906): 306-307.

CHURCH RECORDS

FIRST CONGREGATIONAL CHURCH. Minutes, 1770-1851. Vital Records, 1782-1707. (CSL, LDS 1655). Marriages 1784-1799. BAILEY 7:79-85.

ST. ANDREW EPISCOPAL CHURCH. Vital Records, 1844-1920. (CSL, LDS 1656).

SHAKER RECORDS. 1782-1940. (Western Reserve Historical Society, NUCMC. M575-1717).

Brainard, Jessie Miriam. "Mother Ann's Children in Connecticut. The Enfield Shakers." CQ 3 (1897): 460-74.

HISTORICAL SOCIETY

Enfield Historical Society, Inc., P.O. Box 328, 06082.

Martha Parson House, 1387 Enfield Street, 06082. (203) 745-6064.

LAND RECORDS

Land Records 1693-1853. Index 1693-1876 (LDS 1653 pt. 1-11). Proprietor's Records 1680-1775. (LDS 1652).

LIBRARY

Enfield Central Library, 104 Middle Road, 06082. (203) 749-0766.

MILITARY RECORDS

Harlow, William Burt. "Courtship of a Sargeant in the War of 1812." CM 10 (1906): 611-14.

NEWSPAPERS

ENFIELD PRESS. Weekly. 71 Church Street, 06082. (203) 745-3348.

The PRELIMINARY CHECKLIST lists three newspapers for ENFIELD.

PROBATE RECORDS

Enfield Probate District, 820 Enfield Street, 06082. (203) 745-0371, ext. 320.

Organized 26 May 1831 from the East Windsor Probate District.

ON FILE AT THE CSL: Estate Papers, 1831-1928 (1873-1928 are only partially indexed and are arranged alphabetically by surname). Indexes, 1831-1898 (1873-1928 are arranged alphabetically). Inventory Control Book 1831-1898. Court Record Book, 1831-1859. The CSL also has a microfilm copy of the Registry of Probate Court Records of Hampshire County, Mass., 1660-1820, which includes Enfield.

Probate Records, 1831-1859. (LDS 1654 pt. 1-2).

VITAL RECORDS

Town Clerk, 820 Enfield Street, 06082. (203) 745-0371 ext. 341.

The town clerk's earliest birth record is 1683, marriage record and death record is 1684.

VOTER RECORDS

Hartford. CHS. Records of Electors, 1814-1836.

PUBLISHED WORKS AND OTHER RECORDS

Allen, Francis Olcott. THE HISTORY OF ENFIELD CONNECTICUT. 3 vols. Lancaster, Pa.: Wickersham Pub. Co., 1900-1905. (LDS 481,068).

Bridge, Ruth. THE CHALLENGE OF CHANGE: THREE CENTURIES OF ENFIELD, CONNECTICUT HISTORY. Canaan, N.H.: Phoenix Publishers, 1977. 327 p. Index.

Fletcher, Henry F. STUDIES IN THE HISTORY OF ENFIELD, CONNECTICUT. Litchfield: Enquirer Press, 1934. 26 p.

Johnson, A. HISTORICAL SKETCH OF THE TOWN OF ENFIELD. Hartford: Case, Lockwood and Brainard, 1876. 26 p.

Knight, C. Terry. "Enfield: Some Beauties Natural and Sketches of an Old New England Town." CQ 2 (1896): 359-74.

ESSEX

MIDDLESEX COUNTY. Organized 13 September 1852 as part of OLD SAY-
BROOK. It was incorporated separately 8 July 1854 as ESSEX.

CEMETERY RECORDS AND CEMETERIES

NAME	ADDRESS	HALE NO.	CITATION
River View Cemetery	96 North Main Street	1	15:1-63
Prospect Hill Cemetery	Prospect Hill, rear of Baptist Church	2	15:65-78
Grove Street Cemetery	Grove Street	3	15:79
Central Burial Grounds	Westbrook Road	4	15:80-104
Chapman Cemetery	1/4 mile northwest of Pound Hill	5	15:105-107

Index to Hale inscriptions: 15:108-39.

CEMETERY INSCRIPTIONS FROM THE TOWN OF ESSEX, 1941. Typescript.
118 p. (NYGBS, LDS 1631).

CHURCH RECORDS

CENTERBROOK CONGREGATIONAL CHURCH. Card Index, 1722-1931. (CSL).

FIRST BAPTIST CHURCH. Minutes, 1810-1896. Vital Records, 1810-1852.
(CSL, LDS 1636).

FIRST CONGREGATIONAL CHURCH. Minutes, 1853-1941. Vital Records,
1852-1941. (CSL, LDS 1634).

ST. JOHN EPISCOPAL CHURCH. Minutes, 1790-1845, 1847-1892. Vital
Records, 1797-1898, 1898-1938. (CSL, LDS, 1632).

Rumsey, Jean. CENTERBROOK CONGREGATIONAL CHURCH IN ESSEX, CONNECTICUT. Oak Park, Ill.: Author, 1976. 28 p.

HISTORICAL SOCIETY

Essex Historical Society, Inc., Prospect Street, 06426.

LIBRARY

Essex Library Association, Inc., South Main Street, 06426. (203) 767-1560.

NEWSPAPERS

The PRELIMINARY CHECKLIST lists four newspapers for ESSEX.

PROBATE RECORDS

Essex Probate District, Town Hall, West Avenue, 06426. (203) 767-8201.

Organized 4 July 1853 as the Old Saybrook Probate District from the Saybrook Probate District (see under CHESTER). Its name was changed to the Essex Probate District in 1859.

The Essex Probate District also includes the towns of OLD SAYBROOK and WESTBROOK.

The Essex Probate District also has the Old Saybrook Probate Records from 4 July 1853 to 4 July 1859.

Probate Districts formed from the Essex Probate District include the Old Saybrook District formed 4 July 1859.

VITAL RECORDS

Town Clerk, Town Hall, West Avenue, 06426. (203) 767-8201.

The town clerk's earliest vital records are from October 1852.

PUBLISHED WORKS AND OTHER RECORDS

Moore, Marie. PORTRAIT OF ESSEX. Barre, Mass.: Barre Pub., 1969. 94 p.

FAIRFIELD

FAIRFIELD COUNTY. Organized 1639. Towns organized from FAIRFIELD include BRIDGEPORT, REDDING, WESTON and WESTPORT.

CEMETERY RECORDS AND CEMETERIES

NAME	ADDRESS	HALE NO.	CITATION
East Cemetery	2370 Old Post Road	1	15:1-36
Oak Lawn Cemetery	1530 Bronson Road (203) 259-0458	2	15:37-109
West Cemetery	2011 Post Road	3	15:110-17
Greenfield Hill Cemetery	2736 Bronson Road	4	15:118-51
St. Thomas Roman Catholic Cemetery	130 North Pine Creek Road	5	15:152-67
Old Cemetery	430 Beach Road	6	16:168-89
Congregation B'nai Israel Cemetery	Kings Highway	7	16:190-206
Congregation Rodeph Sholom Cemetery	36 Ansing Street	8	16:207-12
Lawncroft Cemetery	1740 Black Rock Turnpike	9	16:213-21
Jewish Cemetery	East part of town	10	16:222-40
Eintracht Side Benefit Society Cemetery	63 Shepard Street	11	16:241-46
Wakeman Cemetery	On Danbury Road near Easton	12	16:247-48

Index to Hale inscriptions: 16:249-316.

Cemetery Records of Fairfield. (LDS 1680).

"Connecticut Headstone Inscriptions before 1800 (Hale)." CN 7 (1974): 38-41, 200-205, 347.

Perry, Mrs. Kate E. THE OLD BURIAL GROUND OF FAIRFIELD, CONNECTI-CUT. Hartford: American Publishing Co., 1882. 241 p. Index.

CHURCH RECORDS

CONGREGATIONAL CHURCH AT GREENFIELD HILL. Marriages, 1712-1781. BAILEY 7:29-39. Index, 1668-1878. (CSL, LDS, 448 pt. 3).

FIRST CONGREGATIONAL CHURCH. Records, 1694-1806. (CSL, LDS 1684). Index. (CSL). Marriages, 1726-1799. BAILEY 6:34-47.

ST. PAUL EPISCOPAL CHURCH. Records, 1853-1947. (CSL, LDS 1681).

STRATFIELD BAPTIST CHURCH. Records, 1751-1938. (CSL, LDS 1683).

Guilbert, Edmund. ANNALS OF AN OLD PARISH HISTORICAL SKETCHES OF TRINITY CHURCH, SOUTHPORT, CONNECTICUT 1725 TO 1898. New York: Thomas Whittaker, 1898. 291 p. (LDS 547, 177).

Jennings, George Penfield. GREENS FARMS CONNECTICUT: THE OLD WEST PARISH OF FAIRFIELD. Greens Farms: Congregational Society of Greens Farms, 1933. 152 p.

Merwin, George H. YE CHURCH AND PARISH OF GREENFIELD, THE STORY OF AN HISTORIC CHURCH IN AN HISTORIC TOWN 1725-1913. New Haven: Tuttle, Morehouse and Taylor, 1913. 125 p.

"Rev. Elisha Cushman's Record." (First Baptist Church in Hartford 1813 to 1825; Philadelphia, Pa., 1825-1829; Fairfield, Conn., Sept. 1829-1830; New Haven, 1830-1833; Plymouth, Mass., 1834-1837 and 1840-1863 by son Rev. Elisha Cushman and contains marriages from Willington, Hartford, New Britain and Deep River until 1863). CHSB 7 (1942): 30-32; 8 (1943): 2-8, 12-13.

THE SOUTHPORT CONGREGATIONAL CHURCH, SOUTHPORT, CONNECTI-CUT MARCH 7, 1843-NOVEMBER 30, 1975. New York: N.p., 1915. 178 p.

Talcott, Mary Kingsbury. "Records of the Greenfield Hill Church, Fairfield, Conn." NEHGR 68 (1914): 169-77, 287-300, 375-78; 69 (1915): 39-49, 127-36, 230-42, 364-79; 70 (1916): 33-43.

HISTORICAL SOCIETY

Fairfield Historical Society, 636 Old Post Road, 06432. (203) 259-1598.

Granet, Jocelyn. CATALOGUE OF PAINTINGS, FURNITURE, SILVER, CHINA. Fairfield, Conn.: Fairfield Historical Society, 1972. 18 p.

LAND RECORDS

Land Records, 1649-1851. Index, 1725-1869. (LDS 1692 pt. 1-30). Hartford. CSL, Fairfield Land Records, 1649-1732. Vol. A-4.

Proprietor's Records, 1749-1750. Vol. A-1. (CSL, LDS 1694).

LIBRARIES

Fairfield Public Library, 1080 Old Post Road, 06430. (203) 259-8303.

Pequot Library, 720 Pequot Avenue, 06490. (203) 259-0346.

CATALOGUE OF THE MONROE, WAKEMAN, AND HOLMAN COLLECTION OF THE PEQUOT LIBRARY, SOUTHPORT, CONNECTICUT. DEPOSITED IN THE YAKE UNIVERSITY LIBRARY. New Haven, Conn.: Yale University Press, 1960. 522 p.

NEWSPAPERS

FAIRFIELD CITIZEN NEWS. Weekly. 25 South Benson Road, 06430. (203) 255-4561.

The PRELIMINARY CHECKLIST lists fourteen newspapers for FAIRFIELD.

PROBATE RECORDS

Fairfield Probate District, Town Hall, 611 Old Post Road, 06430. (203) 255-8226.

> The Fairfield Probate District was organized May 1666.

> Probate Districts organized from the Fairfield Probate District include: the Danbury, Norwalk, Stamford, Stratford and Woodbury Probate Districts.

> ON FILE AT THE CSL: Estate Papers, 1648-1911. Indexes, 1648-1911. Inventory Control Book, 1648-1911. Court Record Books, 1648-1755 and 1648-1721.

Probate records: 1648-1759 (Vols. 1-10) (CSL, LDS 1693 pt. 13-15).
1747-1852 (Vols. 11-34) (CSL, LDS 1693 pt. 1-12).

Index to estates, 1666–1728. 4 p. (LDS 1680).

TAX RECORDS

Fairfield. Fairfield Historical Society. Tax Lists, 1805–1898.

VITAL RECORDS

Town Clerk, Town Hall, 611 Old Post Road, 06430. (203) 259-8361.

The BARBOUR INDEX covers the years 1639–1850 and is based on the James N. Arnold copy of FAIRFIELD'S vital records made in 1914.

Wells, Edwin Stanley. BIRTHS, MARRIAGES AND DEATHS RETURNED FROM HARTFORD, WINDSOR AND FAIRFIELD AND ENTERED IN THE EARLY LAND RECORDS OF THE COLONY OF CONNECTICUT. VOLUMES I AND II OF LAND RECORDS AND NO. D OF COLONIAL RECORDS. Hartford: Author, 1898. 73 p. (LDS 823,816).

"Connecticut Marriages before 1750 (Barbour)--Town of Fairfield." CN 5 (June 1972): 33, 199-204, 339-44, 486-91; 6 (June 1973): 17-18.

PUBLISHED WORKS AND OTHER RECORDS

Anderson, Arthur LeRoy. DIVIDED WE STAND: INSTITUTIONAL RELIGION AS A REFLECTION OF PLURALISM AND INTEGRATION IN AMERICA. Dubuque, Iowa: Kendall-Hunt Publishing Co., 1978. 271 p. Index.

Ballen, Mrs. Joan. "Fairfield, Connecticut 1661–1691: A Demographic Study of the Economic, Political, and Social Life of a New England Community." Master's thesis, University of Bridgeport, 1970.

Banks, Elizabeth V.H. THIS IS FAIRFIELD 1639–1940. New Haven: Walker, Radcliff Co., 1960. 270 p.

Brilvitch, Charles W. WALKING THROUGH HISTORY: THE SEAPORTS OF BLACK ROCK AND SOUTHPORT. Fairfield: Fairfield Historical Society, 1977. 54 p.

Chapman, Judy. "The Village of Southport." FAIRFIELD COUNTY 9 (January 1979): 36-37.

Child, Frank Samuel. FAIRFIELD ANCIENT AND MODERN. A HANDBOOK

OF LOCAL HISTORY. Fairfield: Fairfield Historical Society, 1909. 75 p.

_____. AN OLD NEW ENGLAND TOWN: SKETCHES OF LIFE, SCENERY, CHARACTER. New York: Charles Scribner's Sons, 1895. 230 p.

Cortessi, Lawrence. "Was Mercy Desborough in League With the Devil?" CONNECTICUT 35, no. 8 (1972): 26-27, 46-49.

Daniels, Bruce Colin. "Large Town Power Structures in Eighteenth Century Connecticut; An Analysis of Political Leadership in Hartford, Norwich and Fairfield." Ph.D. dissertation, University of Connecticut, 1970. 241 p.

Dreher, Monroe F. "The Andrew Elliot House Fairfield 1750-1959, Darien since 1959." CANTIQUARIAN 13 (July 1961): 19-23.

Havadtoy, Magdalene. DOWN IN VILLA PARK: HUNGARIANS IN FAIRFIELD. West Hartford, Conn.: News Press, 1976. 72 p.

Jacobus, Donald Lines. HISTORY AND GENEALOGY OF THE FAMILIES OF OLD FAIRFIELD. 6 vols. Fairfield: Eunice Dennie Burr Chapter, DAR, 1930. (LDS 599,305-599,307).

Justinius, Ivan O. HISTORY OF BLACK ROCK: 1644-1955. Bridgeport: Black Rock Civic and Business Men's Club, 1955. 171 p.

Lacey, Charlotte Alvord. AN HISTORICAL STORY OF SOUTHPORT, CONNECTICUT. Greens Farms: Modern Books and Crafts, 1929. 69 p.

Lathrop, Cornelia Penfield. BLACK ROCK SEAPORT OF OLD FAIRFIELD, CONNECTICUT, 1644-1870. New Haven: Tuttle, Morehouse and Taylor, Co., 1930. 214 p.

MacKenzie, Ruth. "Connecticut Justice and Mercy." CONNECTICUT BAR JOURNAL 39 (1965): 558-73.

MacRury, Elizabeth Banks. MORE ABOUT THE HILL: GREENFIELD HILL. New Haven: City Printing Co., 1968. 457 p.

Papazian, Rita. "Fairfield: Eleven Varied Neighborhoods form a Viable Interesting Town." FAIRFIELD COUNTY 9 (January 1979): 27-35.

Schneck, Mrs. Elizabeth Hubbell. HISTORY OF FAIRFIELD, FAIRFIELD

COUNTY, CONNECTICUT. FROM THE SETTLEMENT OF THE TOWN IN 1639 TO 1818. 2 vols. New York: J.J. Little and Co., 1889.

Taylor, Mary Darlington. "The People of Old Fairfield." CANTIQUARIAN 1 (June 1949): 9-18.

Washington, D.C. National Archives and Record Service. Port of Fairfield U.S. Customs Passenger Lists.

"Witchcraft at Fairfield, Connecticut, September, 1692." CHS COLLECTIONS 3 (1895): 233-35.

FARMINGTON

HARTFORD COUNTY. Organized December 1645. Towns organized from FARMINGTON include AVON, BERLIN, BRISTOL, PLAINVILLE and SOUTHINGTON.

CEMETERY RECORDS AND CEMETERIES

NAME	ADDRESS	HALE NO.	CITATION
Old Farmington Cemetery	121 Main Street	1	16:1-33
Riverside Cemetery	86 East Windsor	2	16:34-76
Scott's Swamp Cemetery	Scotts Swamp Road	3	16:77-82
Hillside Cemetery	Center of Unionville	4	16:83-95
Indian Cemetery	Near Farmington Station	5	16:96-97

Index to Hale inscriptions: 16:98-126.

Barbour, Lucius B. SCOTT SWAMP CEMETERY. Hartford: Author, 1915. 3 p.

Dewey, Louis Marinus. "Inscriptions from Old Cemeteries in Connecticut." NEHGR 60 (1906): 372.

Hartford. CSL, Record Group 62. New Burial Grounds Papers, 1835-1894.

"The Farmington Cemetery." 10 MAIN STREET, FARMINGTON, CONNECTICUT. Typescript. Farmington: Farmington Village Green and Library Association. 21 p.

CHURCH RECORDS

CHRIST CHURCH, EPISCOPAL, AT UNIONVILLE. Vital Records, 1846-1883. (CSL, LDS 1691).

FIRST CONGREGATIONAL CHURCH. Minutes, 1708-1938. Vital Records, 1652-1877. (CSL, LDS 1689).

ST. JAMES EPISCOPAL CHURCH. Vital Records, 1873-1937. (CSL, LDS 1690).

Gay, Julius. CHURCH MUSIC IN FARMINGTON IN THE OLDEN TIME. Hartford, Conn.: Case, Lockwood and Brainard, 1891. 25 p.

_____. "Church Records of Farmington, Connecticut." NEHGR 12 (1858): 34-38, 147-50, 327-30; 13 (1859): 57-60; 38 (1884): 275-79, 410-13; 39 (1885): 48-52, 118-20, 241-45, 338-41; 40 (1886): 31-33, 155-57, 339-61.

House, Mildred Applegate. "The 300th Anniversary of the First Church of Christ, Congregational." CANTIQUARIAN 4 (December 1952): 16-21.

HISTORICAL SOCIETY

Farmington Historical Society, 1554 Farmington Avenue, P.O. Box 645, 06032.

Farmington Museum, Stanley-Whitman House, 37 High Street, 06032. (203) 677-9222.

LAND RECORDS

Land Records, 1645-1857. Index, 1643-1872. (LDS 1688 pt. 1-29).

Hartford. CSL, Record Group 62. Deeds, 1748-1783. Recorded Deeds, 1753-1894.

Jacobus, Donald Lines. "Farmington, Connecticut Land Records." TAG 11 (1934): 111-13.

LIBRARIES

Farmington Museum, 37 High Street, 06032. (203) 677-9222.

Village Library, 71 Main Street, 06032. (203) 677-1529.

THE LIBRARY OF A FARMINGTON VILLAGE BLACKSMITH, A.D. 1712. Hartford, Conn.: Case, Lockwood and Brainard, 1900. 18 p.

MAGAZINES

FARMINGTON MAGAZINE. 1900-1902.

MILITARY RECORDS

Hartford. CSL, Record Group 62. Military Affairs Papers, 1812-1880.

NEWSPAPERS

FARMINGTON VALLEY PRESS. Daily. P.O. Box 406, 06085. (203) 673-6183.

The PRELIMINARY CHECKLIST lists two newspapers for FARMINGTON.

PROBATE RECORDS

Farmington Probate District, Town Hall, 1 Monteith Drive, 06032. (203) 673-3271.

> Organized January 1769 from the Hartford Probate District.

> Probate Districts formed from the Farmington Probate District include the Avon, Berlin, Bristol, Burlington, Plainville and Southington Probate Districts.

> ON FILE AT THE CSL: Estate Papers, 1769-1948. Indexes, 1769-1908 (papers 1908-1940 and 1940-1948 arranged alphabetically). Inventory Control Book, 1769-1908. Court Record Book, 1769-1860.

Probate Records, 1769-1860. (LDS 1687).

SCHOOL RECORDS

Hartford. CSL, Record Group 62. School returns, tax lists and related papers, 1812-1887. Northeast School District register, 1850-1851.

Gay, Julius. SCHOOLS AND SCHOOLMASTERS IN FARMINGTON IN THE OLDEN TIME. Hartford, Conn.: Case, Lockwood and Brainard, 1892. 24 p.

Seel, Anne G. "She Started a School Neither Practical Nor Necessary." YANKEE 44, no. 9 (September 1980): 109-11, 154, 157-67.

TAX RECORDS

Farmington. Village Library. Tax abatements, 1777-1779.

Hartford. CSL, Record Group 62. Tax Lists, 1817-1819. Tax Returns, 1826-1880.

VITAL RECORDS

Town Clerk, Town Hall, 1 Monteith Drive, 06032. (203) 673-3271.

> The town clerk's earliest birth record is 24 February 1646, marriage record is 14 June 1660 and death record is 25 April 1655.

The BARBOUR INDEX covers the years 1645-1850 and is based on the James N. Arnold copy of the FARMINGTON vital records made in 1915.

"Connecticut Marriages Before 1750 (Barbour)--Town of Farmington." CN 6 (1973-74): 18-22, 186-91, 346-51, 507-11; 7 (1974): 25-31, 178-83.

"Farmington Vital Records in Land Records, Volume I." TAG 9 (1933): 174-82; 11 (1935): 111-13.

Goodwin, Nathaniel. "Records of Farmington in Connecticut." NEHGR 11 (1857): 323-28.

Hartford. CSL, Record Group 62. Reports of births, marriages and deaths. Related Papers, 1851-1896.

Vital Records, 1823-1896. Typescript. (CSL, LDS 003,662 and 1483).

VOTER RECORDS

Hartford. CSL, Record Group 62. Certificates of admissions as electors, 1841-1870. Registration lists and voter checklists, 1836-1890.

PUBLISHED WORKS AND OTHER RECORDS

Bartlett, Ellen Strong. "Bits from Great-Grandmother's Journal." CQ 1 (1895): 265-70.

Bartlett, M.H. "The Farmington River and Its Tributaries." CQ 3 (1897): 324-44.

Blakely, Quincy. FARMINGTON, ONE OF THE MOTHER TOWNS OF CONNECTICUT. Conn. Torcentenary Pubn., no. 38. New Haven: Yale University Press, 1935. 29 p.

Brandegee, Arthur L. FARMINGTON, CONNECTICUT, THE VILLAGE OF BEAUTIFUL HOMES. Farmington, Conn.: Author, 1906. 212 p.

Camp, David Nelson. HISTORY OF NEW BRITAIN, WITH SKETCHES OF FARMINGTON AND BERLIN, CONNECTICUT, 1640-1889. New Britain, Conn.: W.B. Thomson and Co., 1889. 538 p.

Carrington, George H. "In the Tunxis Valley." CQ 1 (1895): 23-32.

Gay, Julius. THE EARLY INDUSTRIES OF FARMINGTON. Hartford, Conn.: Case, Lockwood and Brainard, Co., 1898. 20 p.

_____. FARMINGTON IN THE REVOLUTION. Plainville, Conn.: Plainville Historical Society, 1976. 28 p.

_____. FARMINGTON LOCAL HISTORY--THE CANAL. Hartford, Conn.: Case, Lockwood and Brainard, Co., 1899. 20 p.

_____. FARMINGTON PAPERS. Hartford, Conn.: Case, Lockwood and Brainard, Co., 1929. 338 p.

_____. FARMINGTON TWO HUNDRED YEARS AGO. Hartford, Conn.: Case, Lockwood and Brainard, Co., 1904. 20 p.

_____. OLD HOUSES IN FARMINGTON. Hartford, Conn.: Case, Lockwood and Brainard, Co., 1895. 20 p.

Hartford. CSL, Record Group 62. Correspondence Re: Paupers 1811-1869 and Indentures and Bonds for the Poor 1799-1828.

Hartford. CSL, Record Group 33. Boxes 141-145. Farmington: A New England Town, WPA Writer's Project.

Hartford. CSL, Record Group 62. Liquor dealer bonds, 1815-1823. Liquor and tavern applications, 1832-1888.

Hartford. CSL, Record Group 3. Main 2. Box 551. Records of Noadiah Hooker, Justice of the Peace. 1777-1783.

Hartford. CSL, Record Group 3. Main 2. Box 549. Records of Solomon Whitman, Justice of the Peace. 1763-1769.

Hartford. CSL, Record Group 62. Records of the Justice Court Papers, 1790-1894.

Hartford. CSL, Record Group 62. Town Meeting Records, 1774-1878.

Heinz, Bernard. "The Farmington Canal." CONNECTICUT 42 (December 1979): 34, 36-39.

Hurlburt, Mabel S. FARMINGTON, CHURCH AND TOWN. Stonington, Conn.: Pequot Press, 1967. 110 p.

_____. FARMINGTON TOWN CLERKS AND THEIR TIMES (1645-1940). Hartford: Finlay Bros., 1943. 404 p.

Kane, Patricia Ellen. "Joiners of Middletown and Farmington." CHSB 35 (1970): 81-85.

Kingsbury, Frederick, Jr. "An Ericsson Propeller on the Farmington Canal." CM 7 (1902): 329-33.

Le Vere, Clara M. INDEX TO "FARMINGTON PAPERS" BY JULIUS GAY (COLLECTED EDITION 1929). Typescript. N.d. 56 p.

McBride, John H. "The Farmington Canal." CANTIQUARIAN 1 (November 1949): 28-30.

Reik, Mrs. Susan J. "The Settlement and Development of Colonial Farmington, with Emphasis on the Extent of Social, Economic and Political Democracy, 1640-1750." Master's thesis, Columbia University, n.d.

Reimer, Janice C. A GUIDE TO HISTORIC FARMINGTON, CONNECTICUT. Farmington, Conn.: Farmington Savings Bank, 1976. 24 p.

_____. "History in Towns: Farmington, Connecticut." ANTIQUES 114 (October 1978): 764-75.

Shepard, James. "The Small-Pox Hospital Rock." CQ 1 (1895): 50-55.

Stanley, Martha. "Tunxis Which Is Farmington." CQ 1 (1895): 15-21.

Terry, Mrs. Alfred Howe. "Hill-Stead a Museum in Farmington." CANTI-QUARIAN 6 (June 1954): 17-19.

FRANKLIN

NEW LONDON COUNTY. Organized 2 May 1786 from NORWICH. Towns organized from FRANKLIN include SPRAGUE.

CEMETERY RECORDS AND CEMETERIES

NAME	ADDRESS	HALE NO.	CITATION
New Franklin Plains Cemetery	U.S. 53	1	16:1-10
Pautipaug Cemetery	Northeast of Plains Cemetery	2	16:11-40
Gagertown Cemetery	North part of town near Norwich Road	3	16:41-48
Small Pox Cemetery	West of District School House No. 4. 3 Revolutionary War Officer's graves in the woods	4	16:49
Old Franklin Plains Cemetery	U.S. 53	5	16:50-82
Great Pine Swamp Cemetery	Great Pine Swamp east of town	6	16:82-83

Index to Hale inscriptions: 16:84-100.

Barbour, Lucius Barnes. "Genealogical Data From Connecticut Cemeteries-- Franklin Plains Cemetery, copied 1914." NEHGR 86 (1932): 372-88.

WEST FARMS CEMETERY, FRANKLIN, CONNECTICUT. Hartford: Author, 1914. 16 p.

Hayward, Kendall Payne. "Franklin--Old 8th Society Burying Ground--Cemetery Inscriptions." DETROIT SOCIETY FOR GENEALOGICAL RESEARCH MAGAZINE 16 (1952): 19-21.

Trustee Records of the East Franklin Cemetery. (CSL, LDS 1686).

CHURCH RECORDS

Backus, Joseph W. "A Ministry of a Hundred Years Ago." CQ 3 (1897): 167-77, 276-85.

CONGREGATIONAL CHURCH (formerly Second Church of Norwich). Vital Records, 1718-1932. Minutes, 1730-1833. (CSL, LDS 1686). Index, 1718-1932. (CSL, LDS 1448 pt. 13).

PAUTIPAUG HILL CONGREGATIONAL CHURCH. Deaths, 1763, 1784-1802. Index. (CSL).

SECOND ECCLESIASTICAL SOCIETY. Records, 1813-1864. (CSL, LDS 1686).

WEST FARMS CONGREGATIONAL CHURCH. Marriages, 1719-1799. BAILEY 4:77-86.

THE CELEBRATION OF THE ONE HUNDRED AND FIFTIETH ANNIVERSARY OF THE CONGREGATIONAL CHURCH AND SOCIETY, IN FRANKLIN, CONNECTICUT, OCTOBER 14, 1868. New Haven: Tuttle, Morehouse and Taylor, 1869. 151 p.

RECORDS OF THE CONGREGATIONAL CHURCH, FRANKLIN, CONNECTICUT 1718-1860 AND A RECORD OF DEATHS IN NORWICH EIGHTH SOCIETY, 1763, 1778, 1782, 1784-1802. Hartford: Society of Mayflower Descendants in the State of Connecticut and the Society of the Founders of Norwich, Conn., 1938. 128 p.

HISTORICAL SOCIETY

Franklin Historical Society, 06254.

LAND RECORDS

Land Records, 1716-1858. (LDS 1685 pt. 1-4).

PROBATE RECORDS

FRANKLIN is in the Norwich Probate District.

SCHOOL RECORDS

Hartford. CSL, Record Group 62. School Records, 1830-1831.

TAX RECORDS

Hartford. CSL, Record Group 62. Tax Lists, 1799, 1864.

VITAL RECORDS

Town Clerk, Town Hall, R.F.D. 1, 06254 (203) 642-7352.

The BARBOUR INDEX covers the years 1786-1850 and is based on the James N. Arnold copy of FRANKLIN vital records made in 1910.

PUBLISHED WORKS AND OTHER RECORDS

Dewey, Sherman. "Account of a Hail Storm, Which Fell on Part of the Towns of Lebanon, Bozrah, and Franklin, on the 15th of July, 1799." CM 5 (1899): 647-48.

"Ledger of Levi Dan. 1807-1850 (Revolutionary War Soldier and Merchant." In D.A.R. NEBRASKA. MISCELLANEOUS RECORDS, 1972, pp. 43-72. (LDS 913,003).

Nott, Samuel. FRANKLIN IN 1800. Hartford: Acorn Club of Connecticut, 1949. 12 p.

GLASTONBURY

HARTFORD COUNTY. Organized May 1693 from WETHERSFIELD. Towns organized from GLASTONBURY include MARLBOROUGH.

CEMETERY RECORDS AND CEMETERIES

NAME	ADDRESS	HALE NO.	CITATION
Green Cemetery	1960 Main Street	1	16:1-62
St. James Episcopal Church Cemetery	2580 Main Street	2	16:63-96
Old Church Cemetery	1345 Main Street	3	16:97-122
Still Hill Cemetery	U.S. 53	4	16:123-53
St. Augustine Roman Catholic Cemetery	180 Hopewell Road	5	16:154-60
Wassaic Cemetery	2485 New London Turnpike	6	16:161-70
Nispic Cemetery	1341 Nispic Road	7	16:171-79
Eastbury Cemetery	Manchester Road	8	16:180-89
Buckingham Cemetery	28 Cricket Lane	9	16:190-208
Tom and John Hill Cemetery	2 miles off Buckingham Church	10	16:209-11
Graveyard	Near old driving park	11	16:212
Elijah Miller grave	On James Killian Jr. farm	12	16:213
Hollister graveyard	On H.T. Clark farm	13	16:214
Weir Farm Cemetery	Matson Hill	14	16:215
St. John the Baptist Cemetery	1434 New London Turnpike	15	16:216-17
Old Glastonbury Cemetery	969 Manchester Road		(no citation)

NAME	ADDRESS	HALE NO.	CITATION
Savior of Sorrow (Polish) Cemetery	373 Nipsic Road		(no citation)
South Glastonbury Cemetery	650 Main Street		(no citation)

Index to Hale inscriptions: 16:218-72.

Barbour, Lucius. "Inscriptions from Gravestones at Glastonbury, Connecticut." NEHGR 85 (1931): 57-69, 159-75, 305-21, 401-17; 86 (1932): 46-58, 157-73, 314-23.

Dewey, Louis Marinus. "Inscriptions from Old Cemeteries in Connecticut." NEHGR 60 (1906): 139-41.

Tillotson, Edward Sweetser. WETHERSFIELD INSCRIPTIONS; A COMPLETE RECORD OF THE INSCRIPTIONS IN THE FIVE BURIAL PLACES IN THE ANCIENT TOWN OF WETHERSFIELD, INCLUDING THE TOWNS OF ROCKY HILL, NEWINGTON, AND BECKLEY QUARTER (IN BERLIN), ALSO A PORTION OF THE INSCRIPTIONS IN THE OLDEST CEMETERY IN GLASTONBURY. Hartford: W.F.J. Boardman, 1899. 372 p.

CHURCH RECORDS

BUCKINGHAM CONGREGATIONAL CHURCH. Minutes, 1731-1843. Vital Records, 1769-1873. Index, 1731-1873. (CSL, LDS 1722).

CONGREGATIONAL CHURCH. Marriages, 1760-1799. BAILEY 7:101-11.

FIRST CHURCH OF CHRIST. Minutes, 1731-1924. Vital Records, 1797-1905. (CSL, LDS 1721). Records, 1731-1924. Index. (CSL).

ST. JAMES EPISCOPAL CHURCH. Minutes, 1857-1941. Vital Records, 1857-1940. (CSL, LDS 1720).

ST. LUKE EPISCOPAL CHURCH. Minutes, 1806-1949. Vital Records, 1831-1936. (CSL, LDS 1724).

SECOND CONGREGATIONAL CHURCH. Marriages, 1769-1799. BAILEY 5:103-10.

SOUTH GLASTONBURY CONGREGATIONAL CHURCH. Minutes, 1836-1950. Vital Records, 1836-1863. (CSL, LDS 2108 pt. 1-2). Records, 1836-1916. Index. (CSL).

Hartford. CSL, Record Group 62. Certificates of Church Support, 1840-1841.

Talcott, Mary Kingsbury. "Records of the Church in Eastbury, Connecticut."

NEHGR 60 (1906): 376-83; 61 (1907): 84-90, 190-97, 293-99, 387-92; 62 (1908): 83-90, 192-97, 291-99, 375-80; 63 (1909): 67-72.

HISTORICAL SOCIETY

Historical Society of Glastonbury, 2 Peach Tree Road, 06033. (203) 633-6890.

LAND RECORDS

Land Records, 1690-1853. Index, 1690-1850. (LDS 1719 pt. 1-15).

Proprietor's Records, 1846-1889. (LDS 2109).

Hartford. CSL, Record Group 62. Land Records, 1721-1825. Index, 1695-1857.

LIBRARY

Welles-Turner Memorial Library, 2407 Main Street, 06033. (203) 633-1300.

MILITARY RECORDS

Hartford. CSL, Record Group 62. Military Service Certificates, 1814-1819.

NEWSPAPER

GLASTONBURY CITIZEN. Weekly. P.O. Box 373, 06033. (203) 633-4691.

PROBATE RECORDS

Glastonbury Probate District, Town Hall, 2108 Main Street, 06033. (203) 633-3723.
    Organized 8 January 1975 from the Hartford Probate District.

SCHOOL RECORDS

Hartford. CSL, Record Group 62. School Tax Lists, 1897. Sixteenth School District Records, 1856-1909.

List of School Children in School Districts of South Glastonbury. (CSL, LDS 1484).

TAX RECORDS

Hartford. CSL, Record Group 62. Tax Lists, 1820-1821, 1824, 1829-1866. Tax Record Book, 1871-1874. Assessor's Books, 1882, 1886. Grand Levy Book, 1829. Assessment Lists, 1805-1818. Abatements, 1789-1822.

Hartford. CHS. Tax List, 1779. Rate Books, 1760, 1792.

VITAL RECORDS

Town Clerk, Town Hall, 2108 Main Street, 06033. (203) 633-5231.

The BARBOUR INDEX covers the years 1690-1854 and is based on the James N. Arnold copy of the GLASTONBURY vital records made in 1916.

"Connecticut Marriages Before 1750 (Barbour)--Town of Glastonbury." CN 7 (1974): 338-41.

East Glastonbury Marriage Records, 1769-1799. 13 p. (LDS 1735).

Hartford. CSL, Record Group 62. Marriage Certificates, 1820-1841.

VOTER RECORDS

Hartford. CSL, Record Group 62. Lists of Voters, 1868, 1879-1883, 1885, 1889-1890.

PUBLISHED WORKS AND OTHER RECORDS

Chapin, Alonzo Bowen. GLASTONBURY FOR TWO HUNDRED YEARS: A CENTENNIAL DISCOURSE. Hartford, Conn.: Case, Tiffany and Co., 1853. Reprint. Hartford, Conn.: Findlay Bros., 1976. 282 p.

Curtis, Florence Hollister. GLASTONBURY. Glastonbury: Woman's Club of Glastonbury, 1928. 39 p.

Goslee, Henry Storrs. "Glastonbury Glimpses." CQ 2 (1896): 259-67, 333-41.

Hartford. CSL. Record Group 62. Poor bonds, 1830-1847. Freemen certificates, 1774-1789. Justice of the Peace records, 1782-1854. Indentures, 1779-1806. Minor's lists, 1813-1818. Town Meeting Records, 1804-1818.

Hartford. CSL, Record Group 3, Main 2, Box 552. Records of Elizur Hale, Jr. Justice of the Peace, 1773-1796.

McNulty, J. Bard. "The Welles-Shipman House in Glastonbury, Connecticut." CANTIQUARIAN 19 (December 1967): 14-19.

McNulty, Marjorie Grant. GLASTONBURY FROM SETTLEMENT TO SUBURB. Glastonbury: Historical Society of Glastonbury, 1975. 154 p.

Reynolds, Ronna L. "The Towns of Glastonbury, Rocky Hill, and Newington." ANTIQUES 109 (March 1976): 518-27.

Rhines, Olive S. "Earlier Days in Glastonbury." CANTIQUARIAN 12 (December 1960): 14-25.

Walcott, William S., Jr. "Isaac Tryon's Cherry Highboy." ANTIQUES 20 (August 1931): 99.

GOSHEN

LITCHFIELD COUNTY. Organized October 1739.

CEMETERY RECORDS AND CEMETERIES

NAME	ADDRESS	HALE NO.	CITATION
Center Cemetery	West of Goshen Center	1	17:1-36
West Goshen Cemetery	West of U.S. 50	2	17:37-41
West Side Cemetery	West Side Road	3	17:42-45
East Street Cemetery	East Street	4	17:46-51
Collins Cemetery	East Street	5	17:52
Beach Cemetery	Rear of North Goshen Church	6	17:53
Bentley Cemetery	West Street	7	17:54
Oviatt Cemetery	Malahan farm	8	17:55
Middle Street Cemetery	Old Middle Street	9	17:56-57
Old Cemetery	East of Ludington Corners on old discontinued road	10	17:58
Private Cemetery	East Street	11	17:59
Hall Meadow Cemetery	Hall Meadow Road	12	17:60-63
St. Thomas Roman Catholic Cemetery	North Street	13	17:64-65
Davis Cemetery	On Peter Cyerna Sr. farm south part of town	14	17:66-67
Methodist Cemetery	Milton Road		(no citation)

Index to Hale inscriptions: 17:68-86.

Brooks, Mary E., and Fleig, Harry W. GOD'S ACRE (OLD MIDDLE STREET BURYING GROUND 1745-1905. Waterbury: Mattatuck Press, n.d.

Hall, Lawrence P. GLIMPSES OF GOSHEN. OLD CHURCHES AND BURYING GROUNDS. Ossipee, N.H.: Author, 1978. 44 p.

CHURCH RECORDS

FIRST CONGREGATIONAL CHURCH. Minutes, 1810-1854. Vital Records, 1791-1855. (CSL, LDS 1731). Index, 1791-1855. (CSL, LDS 1731) (and 1448 pt. 13).

NORTH CONGREGATIONAL CHURCH. Minutes, 1828-1853. Vital Records, 1828-1850. (CSL, LDS 1731).

NORTH GOSHEN METHODIST EPISCOPAL CHURCH. Minutes, 1840-1940. Vital Records, 1876-1897. (CSL, LDS 1732).

WEST GOSHEN METHODIST CHURCH. Minutes, 1832-1910. (CSL, LDS 1732).

Case, James R. "Goshen Congregational Church, Records." CN 12 (1979): 392-99.

HISTORICAL SOCIETY

Goshen Historical Society, Old Middle Road, 06756. (203) 491-2665.

LAND RECORDS

Land Records, 1739-1859. Index, 1738-1938. (LDS 1730 pt. 1-12).

LIBRARY

Goshen Public Library, 06756. (203) 491-3234.

MILITARY RECORDS

O'Leary, James P. "Goshen in the Civil War." LURE OF THE LITCHFIELD HILLS 21, no. 2 (1949): 1224-2531.

PROBATE RECORDS

GOSHEN is in the Torrington Probate District.

SCHOOL RECORDS

Litchfield. Litchfield Historical Society. School Records, 1798–1879.

VITAL RECORDS

Town Clerk, Town Hall, Route 63 North, P.O. Box 175, 06756. (203) 491–3647.

The BARBOUR INDEX covers the years 1739–1854 and is based on the James N. Arnold copy of the GOSHEN vital records made in 1915.

See also Hibbard's HISTORY OF THE TOWN OF GOSHEN (below).

PUBLISHED WORKS AND OTHER RECORDS

Capan, Nathan. "A History of Goshen." PROCEEDINGS OF THE VERMONT HISTORICAL SOCIETY, A New Series II, June 1921, pp. 83–108.

Guggenbuhl, Laura. "Gunstock, 1769." CANTIQUARIAN 2 (July 1950): 19–21.

Hartford. CSL. Record Group 63. Main 2. Box 553. Records of the Justice of the Peace, 1795–1820.

Hibbard, Augustine George. HISTORY OF THE TOWN OF GOSHEN, CONNECTICUT, WITH GENEALOGIES AND BIOGRAPHIES. Hartford: Case, Lockwood and Brainard, Co., 1897. 602 p.

Norton, Lewis Mills. GOSHEN IN 1812. Hartford: Acorn Club of Connecticut, 1949. 27 p.

Watkins, Lura Woodside. "The Brooks Pottery in Goshen, Connecticut." ANTIQUES 37 (January 1940): 29–31.

GRANBY

HARTFORD COUNTY. Organized October 1786 from SIMSBURY. Towns organized from GRANBY include EAST GRANBY.

CEMETERY RECORDS AND CEMETERIES

NAME	ADDRESS	HALE NO.	CITATION
Granby Street Cemetery	North Granby Road	1	17:1-61
West Granby Cemetery	54 Simsbury Road	2	17:62-75
Baptist Cemetery	North Granby Road	3	17:76-80
Lee Cemetery	In woods 1/4 mile off road, North Granby	4	17:81-84
Merriman Cemetery	Silver Street	5	17:85
Old Town Farm Cemetery	Just north of the Merriman Cemetery, in the woods	6	17:86
Cossett Cemetery	On Oren Godard farm, North Granby	7	17:87
Day Cemetery	Northeast part of North Granby near old saw mill	8	17:88
Holcomb Cemetery	Newton Holcomb Farm, North Granby	9	17:89
Cooley Cemetery	90 East Street	10	17:90-91
Osborne Cemetery	Suffield Road	11	17:92
Pratt Cemetery	On road to left at Cunningham Corner (1 mile)	12	17:93
Vining Cemetery	On John Robinson farm, West Granby	13	17:94-95

NAME	ADDRESS	HALE NO.	CITATION
Hunt Cemetery	Southeast part of Granby, on farm of Joseph Mazick	14	(no citation)
Universalist Cemetery	284 North Granby Road		(no citation)

Index to Hale inscriptions: 17:96-121.

Godard, George Seymour. "Granby (Conn.) Cemetery Inscriptions." NEHGR 70 (1916): 91-92.

Records of the West Granby Burying Grounds, 1810-1908. (LDS 1729).

CHURCH RECORDS

FIRST CONGREGATIONAL CHURCH. Minutes, 1739-1805, 1811-1857, 1858-1887, 1895-1919. Vital Records, 1753-1875. (CSL, LDS 1728).

FIRST UNIVERSALIST SOCIETY. Minutes, 1832-1881. Vital Records, 1896-1912. (CSL, LDS 1727).

WEST GRANBY METHODIST CHURCH. Minutes, 1844-1879. Vital Records, 1844-1939. (CSL, LDS 1729).

Austin, Ethel Lindstrom. THE STORY OF THE CHURCHES OF GRANBY. N.p., n.d. 56 p.

Bates, Albert Carlos. RECORDS OF REV. RANSOM WARNER 1823-1854. RECTOR OF ST. ANDREW'S, SIMSBURY AND BLOOMFIELD ST. PETER'S GRANBY, ST. JOHN'S EAST WINDSOR, CONNECTICUT. Hartford: Case, Lockwood and Brainard, 1893. 84 p.

HISTORICAL SOCIETY

Salmon Brook Historical Society, 208 Salmon Brook Street, 06035. (203) 653-2165.

LAND RECORDS

Land Records, 1786-1868. (LDS 1726 pt. 1-11).

LIBRARY

Granby Public Library, P.O. Box 4, 248 Salmon Brook Street, 06035. (203) 653-2800.

NEWSPAPERS

The PRELIMINARY CHECKLIST lists two newspapers for GRANBY.

PROBATE RECORDS

Granby Probate District, Town Hall, 32 East Granby Road, 06035. (203) 653-2538.

>   Organized May 1807 from the Hartford and Simsbury Probate Districts.

>   Probate districts organized from the Granby Probate District include the East Granby, Hartland and Suffield Probate Districts.

>   ON FILE AT THE CSL: Estate Papers, 1807-1958. Indexes, 1807-1925 (papers from 1925-1958 are arranged alphabetically). Inventory Control Book, 1807-1925. Court Record Book, 1807-1850.

Probate records, 1807-1850. (LDS 1725).

SCHOOL RECORDS

Bates, Albert Carlos. RECORDS OF THE SECOND SCHOOL SOCIETY IN GRANBY NOW THE TOWN OF EAST GRANBY, CONNECTICUT, 1796-1855. Turkey Hills Series, no. 2. Hartford: Author, 1903. 47 p.

Hartford. CSL, Record Group 62. School Registers, 1927-1943. Reports of the District Commissioner of Schools, 1856-1872.

TAX RECORDS

Hartford. CSL, Record Group 62. Tax Lists, 1857-1858, 1862-1863, 1865, 1876-1948.

VITAL RECORDS

Town Clerk, Town Hall, 15 North Granby Road, 06035. (203) 653-2538.

>   The town clerk's earliest birth record is 3 August 1781, marriage record is 30 June 1768 and death record is 15 November 1800.

The BARBOUR INDEX covers the years 1786-1850 and is based on the Percy Hulbert copy of GRANBY vital records made in 1927.

PUBLISHED WORKS AND OTHER RECORDS

Benjamin, Howard W.   "Scenes in and Around Granby." CQ 1 (1895): 134-40.

THE HERITAGE OF GRANBY. ITS FOUNDING AND HISTORY 1786-1965. Granby: Salmon Brook Historical Society, 1967. 180 p.

Loomis, James Lee.   "The Old Country Store." CANTIQUARIAN 4 (December 1952): 24-32.

Phelps, Noah Amherst. HISTORY OF SIMSBURY, GRANBY AND CANTON FROM 1642 TO 1845. Hartford, Ct.: Case, Lockwood and Brainard, 1845. 176 p. (LDS 897,329).

Williams, F.H.   "Declaration of Support for Revolutionary War with Signers' Names." CQ 3 (1897): 367.

GREENWICH

FAIRFIELD COUNTY.   Organized 1640.

CEMETERY RECORDS AND CEMETERIES

NAME	ADDRESS	HALE NO.	CITATION
Bonnell Cemetery	At Steep Hollow on cross road to North Cos Cob	1	17:1
Lyons Cemetery	North Cos Cob, just south of school house	2	17:2
Church Cemetery	At Stanwich, opposite Church Hall	3	17:3-15
Mead Cemetery	Stanwich Road near North Street	4	17:16
Lockwood-Seward Cemetery	East Stanwich Road 1/2 mile above North Street	5	17:17
Ferris Cemetery	82 Taconic Road	6	17:18
June Cemetery	Within the Old Stanwich Cemetery	7	17:19
Close Cemetery	688 Lake Avenue	8	17:20
Putnam Cemetery	U.S. 51	9	17:21-72
St. Mary Roman Catholic Cemetery	399 North Street (203) 869-7026	10	17:73-126
Town Cemetery	Parsonage Road 1/4 mile from Putnam Cemetery	11	17:127
Calvary Church	402 Round Hill Road	12	17:128-29
Methodist Church	Round Hill Road	13	17:130-31
Knapp Cemetery	Round Hill Road, 1 mile north of the Methodist Church	14	17:132-34

NAME	ADDRESS	HALE NO.	CITATION
Burying Hill	On first cross road to the east north of the Methodist Church	15	17:135
North Greenwich Congregational Church	604 Riversville Road	16	17:137-44
Peck Cemetery	Riversville Road	17	17:145
Brown Cemetery	On Glenville road half way between Greenwich and Glenville	18	17:146
Lyon-Rawson Cemetery	At Byram Shore	19	17:147-49
Mead Cemetery	At Byram Shore, east of Grigg Avenue	20	17:150
Lyons Cemetery	On Post Road, near Byram Hill Removed to #9, Putnam Cemetery	21	17:151
Old Baptist Cemetery	At Glenville, next to Merritt Cemetery	22	17:152-53
Merritt Cemetery	59 Glen Ridge Road	23	17:154-55
Anderson Cemetery	1013 King Street	24	17:156-65
New Baptist Cemetery	1013 King Street	25	17:166-74
Strang Cemetery	At Glenville, on King Street, just north of Baptist Cemetery	26	17:175
Peck Cemetery	371 Riversville Road	27	17:176-77
Green Cemetery	151 Pecksland Road	28	17:178-80
Howe Cemetery	Round Hill Road, just north of Peck Cemetery	29	17:181
North Greenwich Cemetery	649 Riversville Road	30	17:182-90
Mead Cemetery	1 mile south of North Greenwich Congregational Church	31	17:191
Radford Cemetery	Lake Avenue	32	17:192
Mills Cemetery	Clapboard Hill	33	17:193
Peck Cemetery	In lots, south side cross road from Clapboard Ridge to North Street	34	17:194-95

NAME	ADDRESS	HALE NO.	CITATION
Reynolds Cemetery	In lots, south side cross road from Clapboard Ridge to North Street	35	17:196
Selleck Cemetery	South of Episcopal Church at Round Hill	36	17:197
Studwell Cemetery	North Cos Cob, 1 mile north of school house, just north of road Steep Hollow	37	17:198
Union Cemetery	85 Milbank Avenue	38	17:199-233
Davis Cemetery	Davis Street	39	17:234
Second Congregational Church Cemetery	Putnam Avenue	40	17:235-63
Lewis Cemetery	Lafayette Place, near Putnam Avenue	41	17:264
Mead Cemetery	Lafayette Place, near William Street	42	17:265
Old Catholic St. Mary Roman Catholic Cemetery	Corner of William and Church Street	43	17:266
Christ Episcopal Church Cemetery	248 Putnam Avenue	44	17:267-89
Lyons Cemetery	North Cos Cob	45	17:290
Old North Stanwich Cemetery	Junction North Street and Stanwich Road	46	17:291-93
Ingersoll Cemetery	Near Stanwich Church	47	17:294
Reynolds Cemetery	Junction North Street and Stanwich Road	48	17:295
Johns Cemetery	North Cos Cob	49	17:296
Hitchcock Cemetery	10 Sinaway Road	50	17:297
Mead Cemetery	East side of Mill Pond	51	17:298
Old Cos Cob Cemetery	West side of Mill Pond	52	17:299
Timpany Cemetery	Bible Road, near where it begins at Cos Cob	53	17:300
Morrell Cemetery	Bible Road	54	17:301
Fraser Cemetery	Bible Road	55	17:302
Ritch Cemetery	At Steep Hollow, on Stanwich Road, 1 mile above the church	56	17:303

NAME	ADDRESS	HALE NO.	CITATION
Williams Cemetery	West of the Mianus Manufacturing Company	57	17:304
Palmer Cemetery	Stanwich Road, near Ritch Cemetery	58	17:305
Adams Cemetery	Near the Post Road	59	17:306
Old Sound Beach	Sound Beach	60	17:307-14
First Congregational Church Cemetery	North of Sound Beach Railroad Station	61	17:315-56
Merritt Cemetery #2	Weaver Street	62	17:357
Rundell Cemetery	Stanwich Road	63	17:358
Mead-Roscoe Cemetery	Butter Nut Hollow Road	64	17:359
Jewish Cemetery	Memory Lane	65	17:360-73
Finch Cemetery	North Street	66	17:374-75

Index to Hale inscriptions: 17:376-467.

"Connecticut Gravestone Inscriptions (Greenwich)." NEHGR 58 (1904): 405-6.

"Connecticut Headstone Inscriptions Before 1800--Town of Greenwich." CN 7 (1974-75): 348-52, 508.

Davis, Norman C., Jr. "Gravestones of Westchester County, New York and Fairfield County, Conn., Recorded in 1870-1870-1892, with additions and corrections through 1896." CA 15 (1973): 100-105; 16 (1974): 121-23; 17 (1974-75): 15-16, 132.

Eardely, William A.D. CONNECTICUT CEMETERIES. Vol. 9. Brooklyn, N.Y.: Author, 1918.

_____. UNION CEMETERY, GREENWICH. Typescript. Brooklyn, N.Y.: 1912. 36 p.

Mead, Spencer Percival. ABSTRACTS OF RECORDS AND TOMBSTONES OF THE TOWN OF GREENWICH. 2 vols. Typescript. 1913. 281 p. (LDS 899,937).

CENSUS RECORDS

Hartford. CSL, Record Group 29 Box 12. State Military Census, 1917.

CHURCH RECORDS

CHURCH OF ENGLAND, REGISTER BOOK, 1712-1746. (CSL, LDS 2107).

FIRST CONGREGATIONAL CHURCH. Minutes, 1798-1924. Vital Records, 1810-1936. (CSL, LDS 1705).

SECOND CONGREGATIONAL CHURCH. Marriages, 1728-1801. BAILEY 4: 87-95.

STANWICH CONGREGATIONAL CHURCH. Vital Records, 1796-1854. (CSL, LDS 1705).

Clarke, Elizabeth W. THE FIRST THREE HUNDRED YEARS: THE HISTORY OF THE FIRST CONGREGATIONAL CHURCH OF GREENWICH, CONNECTICUT 1665-1965. Greenwich: First Congregational Church, 1967. 300 p.

Ekberg, Peggy L. THE BUILDING OF SAINT BARNABUS CHURCH, ORAL HISTORY WITH PHILIP IVES, JR. Greenwich, Conn.: Greenwich Public Library, 1979. 36 p.

Mead, Spencer Percival. ABSTRACT OF CHURCH RECORDS OF THE TOWN OF GREENWICH. Typescript. 1913. 188 p. (LDS 1703).

HISTORICAL SOCIETY

Historical Society of the Town of Greenwich, Bush-Holly House, 39 Strickland Road, Cos Cob, 06807. (203) 869-9849.

Publishes Greenwich Historical Collections, 1970-- . Irreg.

Bott, Penny. THE GREENWICH HISTORICAL SOCIETY, AS TOLD BY WILLIAM E. FINCH, JR. (GREENWICH ORAL HISTORY PROJECT). Greenwich: Greenwich Library, 1976. 64 p. Index.

Putnam Cottage, 243 East Putnam Avenue, 06830. (203) 869-9697.

LAND RECORDS

Land Records, 1640-1856. Index, 1640-1875. (LDS 1704 pt. 1-16).

LIBRARIES

Greenwich Library, 101 West Putnam Avenue, 06830. (203) 622-7900.

Bott, Penny. THE GREENWICH LIBRARY SINCE 1960: ORAL HISTORY INTER-VIEWS WITH MARIE COLE AND NOLAN LUSHINGTON. Greenwich, Conn.: Friends of the Greenwich Library, 1978. 100 p.

Miller, Mary M. "Public Libraries in Connecticut--Founding and Development of the Public Library at Greenwich, Connecticut." CM 10 (1906): 490-94.

Perrot Memorial Library, 90 Sound Beach Avenue, 06870. (203) 637-1066.

Phillips, Marian. THE PERROT MEMORIAL LIBRARY, 1929-1957. ORAL HISTORY INTERVIEW WITH EDYTHE F. BLACK. Greenwich, Ct.: Greenwich Library, 1978. 37 p.

MILITARY RECORDS

"Border Country: No-one in Horseneck, Stamford or Middlesex was Safe from British Raiders." FAIRFIELD COUNTY 5 (December 1975): 160-61, 122-24.

NEWSPAPERS

GREENWICH TIME. Daily. 20 East Elm Street, 06830. (203) 869-8300.

THE VILLAGE GAZETTE. Weekly. 210 Sound Beach Avenue, 06870. (203) 637-1774.

The Greenwich Library indexes: GREENWICH TIME 1937-- . GREENWICH GRAPHIC 1881-1919. GREENWICH NEWS AND GRAPHIC 1920-1932. DAILY NEWS-GRAPHIC 1932-1937. GREENWICH MAIL 1969-- . GREENWICH OBSERVER 1877-1882. NEWS 1906-1912.

The PRELIMINARY CHECKLIST lists ten newspapers for GREENWICH.

PROBATE RECORDS

Greenwich Probate District, Town Hall, 101 Field Point, 06830. (203) 622-7880.

Organized 4 July 1853 from the Stamford Probate District.

ON FILE AT THE CSL: Estate Papers, 1853-1900 (these are arranged alphabetically with a list).

TAX RECORDS

Hartford. CSL, Record Group 62. Tax abatement book, 1779.

VITAL RECORDS

Town Clerk, Town Hall, Greenwich Avenue, (P.O. Box 455), 06830. (203) 869-8800 ex. 237).

The BARBOUR INDEX covers the years 1640-1848 and is based on the James N. Arnold copy of GREENWICH vital records made in 1915.

Akerly, Lucy D. "Vital Records from the Mss Land Libers of Greenwich, Conn." NYGBR 36 (1905): 196-97.

"Connecticut Marriages Before 1750 (Barbour)--Town of Greenwich." CN 7 (1974-75): 343, 499-503.

"Marriage Records from Greenwich, Conn." DAR MAGAZINE 44 (1910): 322.

Mead, Spencer Percival. ABSTRACT OF BIRTHS, MARRIAGES AND DEATHS OF THE TOWN OF GREENWICH, COUNTY OF FAIRFIELD, AND STATE OF CONNECTICUT, FROM THE EARLIEST TOWN AND LAND RECORDS TO JUNE 1847. Typescript. 1913. 99 p.

Records of Births, marriages, deaths, 1700-1848. (LDS 185,372).

Town Vital Records, 1754-1847. (LDS 25,389).

PUBLISHED WORKS AND OTHER RECORDS

Bott, Penny. BOARD OF ESTIMATE: PEOPLE AND POLICIES: ORAL HISTORY INTERVIEW WITH RICHARD E. DEUTSCH. Greenwich, Conn.: Friends of Greenwich Library, 1977. 59 p.

_____. MEAD'S POINT BOYHOOD: ORAL HISTORY INTERVIEW WITH WHITMAN MEAD REYNOLDS. Greenwich, Conn.: Greenwich Library, 1977. 43 p.

_____. MIANUS AND NORTH MIANUS: ORAL HISTORY INTERVIEW WITH WAKEMAN HARTLEY. Greenwich, Conn.: Greenwich Library, 1976. 43 p.

_____. SETON'S INDIANS: ORAL HISTORY INTERVIEW WITH LEONARD S. CLARK. Greenwich, Conn.: Greenwich Library, 1976. 37 p.

_____. STEAMBOAT ROAD AND NORA STANTON BARNEY: ORAL HISTORY INTERVIEW WITH JOHN BARNEY AND RHODA BARNEY JENKINS. Greenwich, Conn.: Greenwich Library, 1978. 74 p.

_____. THE UNITED NATIONS CONTROVERSY, ORAL HISTORY INTERVIEW

WITH JOHN L. GRAY. Greenwich, Conn.: Greenwich Library, 1976. 45 p.

Charles, Eleanor. "Will The Real Greenwich Please Stand Up?" FAIRFIELD COUNTY 7 (July 1977): 28-31.

Clarke, Elizabeth W. BEFORE AND AFTER 1776: A SECOND EDITION OF THE COMPREHENSIVE CHRONOLOGY OF THE TOWN OF GREENWICH, 1640-1978. 2d ed. Greenwich, Conn.: Historical Society of Town of Greenwich, 1978. 184 p. Index.

Cross, Joe A. "Greenwich." FAIRFIELD COUNTY 4 (September 1974): 32-54.

Curtis, Marge. ISLAND BEACH: ORAL HISTORY INTERVIEW WITH WILLIAM ERDMAN. Greenwich, Conn.: Greenwich Library, 1979. 55 p.

Edwards, Elisha Jay. "Greenwich--A Community of Beautiful Estates." CM 10 (1906): 511-47; 11 (1907): 617-47.

GREENWICH IN 1940: BEING A BRIEF HISTORICAL SKETCH OF THE TOWN WITH VIEWS OF THE PRINCIPAL BUILDINGS AND HOUSES IN THE COMMUNITY AND INCLUDING WHO'S WHO IN GREENWICH. Greenwich: Greenwich Press, 1940. 140 p.

GREENWICH PAST: SOURCES IN LOCAL HISTORY. Greenwich, Conn.: n.p., 1974. 8 p.

Greenwich Town Records, 1648-1848. (LDS 185,372).

Holland, Lydia and Leaf, Margaret. GREENWICH OLD AND NEW. Greenwich: Greenwich Press, 1955. 164 p.

Hubbard, Frederick A. OTHER DAYS IN GREENWICH OR TALES AND REMINISCENSES OF AN OLD NEW ENGLAND TOWN. New York: J.F. Tapley, Co., 1913. 346 p.

Kirkpatrick, Konstance. THE HISTORY OF THE INDIAN HARBOR YACHT CLUB, 1889-1977. Greenwich, Conn.: Indian Harbor Yacht Club, 1978. 238 p.

_____. "Knapp Tavern, Greenwich, Connecticut." DAR MAGAZINE 110 (1976): 23-24.

Levinson, Esther. A SOUND MIND IN A HEALTHY BODY: THE SOKOL SOCIETY OF BYRAM. ORAL HISTORY INTERVIEW WITH ADELAIDE HARTA DARULA. Greenwich, Conn.: Greenwich Library, 1979. 31 p.

Manwarring, Adele, comp. SURNAME INDEX TO A HISTORY OF THE TOWN OF GREENWICH, FAIRFIELD COUNTY, CONN. BY DAVID M. MEAD. (Published 1857). Los Angeles: Los Angeles California Branch Genealogical Library, 1974. 17 p.

Mead, Daniel M. HISTORY OF THE TOWN OF GREENWICH, FAIRFIELD COUNTY, CONN., WITH MANY IMPORTANT STATISTICS. New York: Baker and Goodwin, Printers, 1857. 318 p.

Mead, Spencer Percival. YE HISTORIE OF YE GREENWICH COUNTY OF FAIRFIELD AND STATE OF CONNECTICUT WITH GENEALOGICAL NOTES ON THE ADAMS, AVERY, BANKS, BETTS, BROWN, BRUNDAGE, BRUSH, BUDD, BUSH, CLOSE, DAVIS, DAYTON, DENTON, FERRIS, FINCH, GREEN, HENDRIE, HOBBY, HOLLY, HOLMES, HORTON, HOWE, HUBBARD, HUSTED, INGERSOLL, KNAPP, LOCKWOOD, LYON, MARSHALL, MEAD, MERRITT, MILLS, PALMER, PECK, PURDY, REYNOLDS, RITCH, RUNDLE, SACKETT, SCOFIELD, SELLECK, SEMOUR, SHERWOOD, SLATER, SMITH, STUDWELL, SUTHERLAND, SUTTON, TODD, WARING, WATERBURY, WEBB, WEED, WHITE, WILCOX, WILSON, AND WORDEN FAMILIES. New York: Knickerbocker Press, 1911. 768 p.

McNamara, Catherine, and French, Margaret J. STANWICH ROAD AND THE BOARD OF EDUCATION. ORAL HISTORY INTERVIEWS WITH G. HARRISON HOUSTON, JR. Greenwich, Conn.: Greenwich Library, 1979. 68 p.

Phillips, Marian. THE PUBLIC WORKS DEPARTMENT, 1940-1968. ORAL HISTORY INTERVIEW WITH WALTER F. JOHNSON. Greenwich, Conn.: Greenwich Library, 1979. 62 p.

Roberts, William Willard. PIONEERS AND PATRIOTS OF GREENWICH IN THE COLONIES OF NEW NETHERLANDS, NEW HAVEN AND CONNECTICUT, 1640-1780. Bridgeport: Author, 1936. 23 p.

Talcott, Norman. "The Tavern and the Old Post Road." CM 10 (1906): 647-57.

Yudain, Carol: "Greenwich--Seen as an Enduring Town." FAIRFIELD COUNTY 7 (July 1977): 32-33, 48-55.

GRISWOLD

NEW LONDON COUNTY. Organized October 1815 from PRESTON.

CEMETERY RECORDS AND CEMETERIES

NAME	ADDRESS	HALE NO.	CITATION
Rixtown Cemetery	Southeast part of town, 1 mile southeast from Bethel Church on North Stonington Road	1	18:1-21
Pachaug Cemetery	1 mile east of Pachaug on Voluntown Road	2	18:23-81
Brown Cemetery	On F.S. Brown Estate, 2 miles southeast of Jewett City	3	18:82
Geer Cemetery	On knoll on G.G. Norman farm, near bridge, on old Norwich and Preston Road	4	18:83-88
Cook Cemetery	On Barton Kegiven farm Glasgow	5	18:89-90
Spy Rock Cemetery	One mile northeast of Pachaug River at Hopeville near house of Elmer Starkweather	6	18:91
Kinne Cemetery	East of highway and hidden from road at Glasgow	7	18:92-95
Hopeville Cemetery	U.S. 53	8	18:96-97
Leonard Cemetery	1 mile south of Pachaug on Bethel and Pachaug Road	9	18:98-108
Walton Cemetery	1/4 mile northeast of house on Dorothea Urloff's farm	10	18:109

NAME	ADDRESS	HALE NO.	CITATION
Hatch Cemetery	1/2 mile across field from house of Hohn	11	18:110
Spencer Cemetery	2-1/2 miles south of Jewett City on east road from Jewett City to Norwich	12	18:111-14
Jewett City Cemetery	Anthony Street	13	18:115-57
High Banks Cemetery	At High Banks on Quenebaug River, 1 mile above Jewett City	14	18:158
Phillips Cemetery	Northeast of reservoir on abandoned highway Old Burdick farm	15	18:159
Green Cemetery	On William Briggs farm, near road from Hopeville to Stone Hill	16	18:160-61
Jewett City Baptist Cemetery	In Jewett City, behind the Baptist Church	17	18:162-68
Saunders Cemetery	On Sterry Kinnie farm, on Glasgow to Ashwillet Road	18	18:169
Davis Cemetery	On road from Pero place to Enonk, west of Four Corners	19	18:170
Billings Cemetery	On road from Glasgow to North Stonington, on old Billings farm	20	18:171
Wilcox Cemetery	On Thomas Wilcox farm, west side of Stone Hill	21	18:172
St. Thomas Cemetery	Between Doanville and Glasgow, eastern part of town	22	18:173-76
Tadpole Cemetery	Near Jewett City	23	(no stones)
Indian Cemetery	1/2 mile south of Greer Cemetery farm of S.G. Newman	24	18:177
Hartshorn Cemetery	Off road by Hawkins house	25	18:178
Dawley Cemetery	On Frank Terry farm	26	18:179
Meech Cemetery	Goldstein farm	27	18:180
Indian Cemetery	Norman farm	28	18:181
Reynolds Cemetery	Stanton F. Maine farm	29	18:182-83

NAME	ADDRESS	HALE NO.	CITATION
Tiffany Cemetery	John Desjardies farm	30	18:184

Index to Hale inscriptions: 18:184-219.

Miner, Gilbert H., Sr. CEMETERIES WITH GRAVES OF HONORED DEAD IN TOWN OF GRISWOLD AND VICINITY. Typescript. 1959. 54 p.

Phillips, Daniel Lyon. GRISWOLD CEMETERIES. HISTORICAL AND DESCRIPTIVE SKETCHES OF TWENTY-TWO BURIAL PLACES IN GRISWOLD, CONN. AND ST. MARY'S CEMETERY IN LISBON, CONN., WITH COPIES OF ALL THE INSCRIPTIONS ON THEIR MONUMENTS. N.p., 1918. 385 p.

CHURCH RECORDS

CONGREGATIONAL CHURCH OF LISBON IN JEWETT CITY. Marriages, 1724-1800. BAILEY 5:83-90.

FIRST CONGREGATIONAL CHURCH. Minutes, 1733-1843, 1863-1878. Vital Records, 1720-1857. (CSL, LDS 1716).

SECOND CONGREGATIONAL CHURCH. Index Records, 1720-1881. (CSL).

SECOND CONGREGATIONAL CHURCH AT JEWETT CITY. Vital Records, 1825-1861. (CSL, LDS 1718).

SECOND CONGREGATIONAL CHURCH OF PRESTON. Marriages, 1720-1799. BAILEY 4:32-57; 5:122.

"Portion of the Records of the Second Congregational Church in Griswold, Conn., located at Jewett City." (Dimissions, 1826-1861. Baptisms, 1825-1861). CHSB 3 (January 1937): 2-8; 3 (October 1937): 2-8, 18-24; 4 (July 1938): 25-30; 6 (January 1940): 11.

HISTORICAL SOCIETY

Griswold Historical Society, R.F.D.1, 06351.

LAND RECORDS

Land Records, 1815-1851. Index, 1815-1904. (LDS 1715 pt. 1-3).

LIBRARY

Slater Library, 26 Main Street, 06351. (203) 376-0024.

MILITARY RECORDS

Miner, Gilbert, Sr. IN MEMORY TO THOSE WHO SERVED THEIR COUNTRY. Jewett City: Author, 1949. 35 p.

_____. LIST OF EX-SERVICE MEN FROM THE TOWN OF GRISWOLD WHICH INCLUDES JEWETT CITY, PACHAUG, GLASGOW AND PART OF VOLUNTOWN AS THEY APPEAR ON THE TOWN RECORDS. Typescript. 10 p.

Phillips, Daniel Lyon. THE REVOLUTIONARY MARTYRS OF ANCIENT PA-CHAUG. N.p.: Author, 1903. 15 p.

NEWSPAPERS

The PRELIMINARY CHECKLIST lists two newspapers for GRISWOLD.

PROBATE RECORDS

Griswold Probate District, Town Hall, School Street, Jewett City, 06351. (203) 376-0641.

Organized from the Norwich Probate District.

SCHOOL RECORDS

Hartford. CSL, Record Group 62. Twelfth School District Record Books, 1842-1905.

VITAL RECORDS

Town Clerk, Town Hall, School Street, 06351. (203) 376-2521.

The town clerk's earliest birth record is 1738, marriage record is 1737 and death record is 1754.

The BARBOUR INDEX covers the years 1815-1848 and is based on the James N. Arnold copy of GRISWOLD vital records made in 1909.

PUBLISHED WORKS AND OTHER RECORDS

Burgess, Charles F. JEWETT CITY SOUVENIR COMPRISING HISTORICAL, DESCRIPTIVE AND BIOGRAPHICAL SKETCHES OF JEWETT CITY, CONN. Moosup, Conn.: Graphic, 1896. 38 p.

Phillips, Daniel Lyon. Griswold: A HISTORY, BEING A HISTORY OF THE
TOWN OF GRISWOLD, CONNECTICUT, FROM THE EARLIEST TIMES TO THE
ENTRANCE OF OUR COUNTRY INTO THE WORLD WAR IN 1917. New
Haven: Tuttle, Morehouse and Taylor Co., 1929. 456 p.

GROTON

NEW LONDON COUNTY. Organized 10 May 1705 from NEW LONDON. Towns organized from GROTON include LEDYARD.

CEMETERY RECORDS AND CEMETERIES

NAME	ADDRESS	HALE NO.	CITATION
Col. Ledyard Cemetery	256 Mitchell Street	1	18:1-38
Starr Cemetery	Pleasant Valley Road	2	18:38-82
Wood Cemetery	Pleasant Valley Road	3	18:82-83
2 Graves	Corner of Pleasant Valley Road and Center Groton Road	4	18:83
Perkins Cemetery	Pleasant Valley Road	5	18:83
Knowles Cemetery	Near Old Toll Gate House, center Groton Road	6	18:83-84
Burrows Cemetery #1	Baptist Hill, Mystic	7	18:84-85
Turner Cemetery	Center of Groton	8	18:85-86
Wightman Cemetery	Cold Spring Road	9	18:86-94
Smith Lake Cemetery	Moved to Morgan-Avery Cemetery	10	18:94
Morgan-Avery Cemetery	Poquonock Road	11	18:94-111
Burrows Cemetery #3	Fort Hill	12	18:111-12
Wells Cemetery	Center of Groton Road, west of Old Mystic	13	18:113
Fish Cemetery	Pequot Avenue	14	18:113-15
Niles Cemetery	Fort Hill Road, near center Groton Road	15	18:115

NAME	ADDRESS	HALE NO.	CITATION
St. Patrick Roman Catholic Cemetery	River Road	16	18:115-25
Burrows #2 Cemetery	Baptist Hill, Mystic	17	18:125-26
Packer Cemetery	New London Road	18	18:126-37
Fishtown Cemetery	New London Road	19	18:137-56
Old Town Hill Cemetery	Fort Hill, just north of Burrows #3 Cemetery	20	18:157
Crary Cemetery	385 Packer Road	21	18:157-58
Noank Valley	Elm Street	22	18:159-94
Fish Cemetery #2	Noank Road	23	18:194-95
Binks Cemetery	Poquonock Lake Road	24	18:195
Park Cemetery #1	Parke farm near Burnett's Corner	25	18:196
Park Cemetery #2	Parke farm near Burnett's Corner	26	18:196
Old Cemetery	On former Adams farm north from Fort Hill	27	18:196
Cushman Cemetery	Center Groton Road, near Crary Cemetery	28	18:197
Palmer Cemetery	In woods, on Brown farm, Noank Road	29	18:197-98
Packer Cemetery #2	Southwest of Mystic	30	18:198-99
Adams Cemetery	North of Myers farm	31	18:200
Crouch Cemetery	On old Crouch farm 1/2 mile south of Boston Post Road	32	18:200
Mitchell Cemetery	On road to Old Mystic	33	18:200
Baley Cemetery	Pine Island	34	18:200
Smith Cemetery	Oral School grounds	35	18:200-201
Edgecomb Cemetery	On Edgecomb farm in the woods	36	18:201
Bill Cemetery	Rear of Bill Library	37	18:202

Soldiers' Burials in the first 35 cemeteries are recorded in Volume 18:203-18, with an index in 18:274-77.

Starr Hill Cemetery	Pleasant Valley Road		(no citation)
Congregation Beth El Cemetery	65 Lestertown Road		(no citation)

Index to Hale inscriptions: 18:219-73.

Caulkins, Frances Manwaring. RECORDS OF GROTON. Norwich: Author, 1903. 96 p.

_____. THE STONE RECORDS OF GROTON. Occasional Publications, vol. 1. The New London County Historical Society. Norwich: Free Academy Press, 1903. 96 p.

Anna Warner Bailey Chapter, DAR, EIGHT CEMETERIES LOCATED IN GROTON AND LEDYARD, CONN. Groton: 1929. 11 p.

Meech, Anne and Meech, Susan D. CEMETERY DESCRIPTIONS FROM GROTON, PRESTON, AND STONINGTON, CONN. Typescript. 1920. 68 p.

Stevens, John Austin. "Hartford and Groton Tombstones Illustrative of Genealogical Sketch of Family of Ledyard." NYGBR 7 (1876): 14-16.

CHURCH RECORDS

FIRST BAPTIST CHURCH. Old Mystic. Vital Records, 1754-1899. (CSL, LDS 1698).

FIRST CONGREGATIONAL CHURCH. Vital Records, 1727-1769, 1809-1811. (CSL, LDS 1700).

NOANK BAPTIST CHURCH. Minutes, 1843-1892. (CSL, LDS 1699).

POQUONOCK BRIDGE BAPTIST CHURCH. Minutes, 1856-1921. (CSL, LDS 1702).

ST. MARK EPISCOPAL CHURCH. Mystic. Vital Records, 1859-1920. (CSL, LDS 1701).

A CATALOGUE OF THE DEATHS IN THE SECOND SOCIETY OF GROTON FROM THE YEAR SEVENTEEN HUNDRED AND SEVENTY, TO EIGHTEEN HUNDRED AND FIFTEEN. Windham: Ansil Brown, 1815. 48 p.

Ledyard. Historic District Commission. INDEX TO THE FIRST BAPTIST CHURCH OF GROTON CHURCH RECORDS. Ledyard, Conn.: 1980. 94 p.

HISTORICAL SOCIETY

Noank Historical Society, 17 Sylvan Street, 06340. (203) 536-3021.

LAND RECORDS

Land Records, 1708-1852. Indexed. (LDS 1697 pt. 1-12).

LIBRARIES

Bill Memorial Library, Monument Street, 06340. (203) 445-0392.

Groton Public Library, Route 117, 06340. (203) 448-1552.

MILITARY RECORDS

Burnham, Norman Hammond. THE BATTLE OF GROTON HEIGHTS: A STORY OF THE STORMING OF FORT GRISWOLD, AND THE BURNING OF NEW LONDON, ON THE SIXTH OF SEPTEMBER, 1781. New London, Conn.: Bingham Paper Box Co., 1907. 42 p.

Harris, William Wallace. THE BATTLE OF GROTON HEIGHTS, A COLLECTION OF NARRATIVES, OFFICIAL REPORTS, RECORDS, ETC. OF THE STORMING OF FORT GROTON, THE MASSACRE OF ITS GARRISON, AND THE BURNING OF NEW LONDON BY BRITISH TROOPS UNDER THE COMMAND OF BRIG. GENERAL BENEDICT ARNOLD IN THE SIXTH OF SEPTEMBER, 1781. New London: C. Allyn, 1882. 399 p. Index.

NEWSPAPERS

THE NEWS. Daily. P.O. Box 1126, 06340. (203) 446-1560.

The PRELIMINARY CHECKLIST lists four newspapers for GROTON.

PROBATE RECORDS

Groton Probate District, Town Hall, 45 Fort Hill Road, 06340. (203) 445-4896.

Organized 25 May 1839 from the Stonington Probate District.

ON FILE AT THE CSL: Court Record Books, 1839-1850. Probate Records, 1839-1850. Court Journal, 1839-1850.

TAX RECORDS

Hartford. CHS. Tax Rate Book, 1807.

VITAL RECORDS

Town Clerk, Town Hall, 45 Fort Hill Road, 06340.   (203) 445-8551.

The BARBOUR INDEX covers the years 1704-1853 and is based on the James N. Arnold copy of GROTON vital records made in 1912.

"Connecticut Marriages Before 1750 (Barbour) Town of Groton." CN   7 (1975): 504; 8 (1976): 19-24, 185-90, 341.

PUBLISHED WORKS AND OTHER RECORDS

Burgess, Charles F., ed. HISTORIC GROTON. Moosup: C.F. Burgess, 1909. 101 p.

Hartford. CSL, Record Group 3, Main 2, Box 553. Records of the Justices of the Peace, 1819-1820.

Holman, Mabel Cassine. "The Hive of the Averys." CM 9 (1905): 395-402.

Stark, Charles Rathbone. GROTON, CONNECTICUT 1705-1905. Stonington: Palmer Press, 1922. 444 p.

THE STORY OF ONE CORNER OF CONNECTICUT IN SIXTEEN MAPS. Mystic: Mystic River Historical Society and the Groton Bicentennial Committee, 1976. 16 p.

GUILFORD

NEW HAVEN COUNTY. Organized 1639. Towns organized from GUILFORD include MADISON.

CEMETERY RECORDS AND CEMETERIES

NAME	ADDRESS	HALE NO.	CITATION
Alderbrook Cemetery	On old Post Road 3/4 miles east of Guilford	1	18:1-65
West Side Cemetery	399 Post Road	2	18:66-104
St. George Cemetery	Middletown Road 1 mile north of Guilford	3	18:105-13
North Guilford Cemetery	Ledgehill Road	4	18:113-48
Leete's Island Cemetery	15 Moose Hill Road	5	18:149-53
Nut Plains Cemetery	481 Nut Plains Road	6	18:154-60
Goldsmith Cemetery	1400 Moose Hill Road	7	18:161
Fowler Cemetery	Wallace Fowler farm Moose Hill	8	18:162
Clapboard Hill Cemetery	Clapboard Hill Road, on property of L.E. Montagne	9	18:163
Private Cemetery	Whitfield Street	10	18:164
Murray Cemetery	Nortontown Road	11	18:165
Griswold Cemetery	Charles A. Dudley's farm Clapboard Hill	12	18:166
Foote-Ward Cemetery	Bearhouse Hill Road	13	18:167-69
Griswold-Leete Cemetery	Boston Street	14	18:170
Private Cemetery (moved to Alderbrook Cemetery)	Boston Street	15	18:171

Guilford

NAME	ADDRESS	HALE NO.	CITATION
Fowler Cemetery	In cellar of George W. Hull's house west side	16	18:172
Bluff Cemetery	North part of Guilford near Durham town line	17	18:173-74
Green Cemetery	Guilford Green (no stones)	18	18:175
Frisbie Cemetery	Leete's Island District	19	18:176
Episcopal Church Cemetery	In basement of Episcopal Church	20	18:177
Congregational Church Cemetery	Congregational Church	21	18:178
Godfrey Cemetery	Uncas Point	22	18:179
Parmele Cemetery	Guilford Lakes	23	18:180
		24	18:181
Foot Stone Cemetery	215 State Street	25	18:182
Baldwin Cemetery	Moved to Branford	26	18:183
Fowler Cemetery	Broad and Fair Streets	27	18:184-85
St. John Cemetery	30 Saw Mill Road		(no citation)
Small Pox Cemetery	Clapboard Hill Road		(no citation)

Index to Hale inscriptions: 18:186-90, 19:191-234.

"Burials in North Guilford (1808-1837)." CHSB 6 (January 1940): 14-16.

"Connecticut Headstone Inscriptions Before 1800 (Hale)-Town of Guilford." CN 6 (1973-74): 199-201, 357-62, 514.

"INSCRIPTIONS ON TOMBSTONES IN GUILFORD ERECTED PRIOR TO 1800." NHCHS PAPERS 4 (1888): 405-51; 6 (1900): 375-88.

Royce, Helen. ALDERBROOK CEMETERY, 1700-1816. N.p.: Author, 1929. 7 p.

_____. EPISCOPAL CEMETERY LOT, 1717-1820. N.p.: Author, 1929. 2 p.

CHURCH RECORDS

CHRIST EPISCOPAL CHURCH. Minutes, 1744-1909. Vital Records, 1807-1909. (CSL, LDS 1710).

FIRST CONGREGATIONAL CHURCH. Minutes, 1717-1921. Vital Records, 1717-1921. (CSL, LDS 1714 pt. 1-2).

ST. JOHN EPISCOPAL CHURCH. Minutes, 1805-1868. Vital Records, 1748-1861. (CSL, LDS 1711).

SECOND CONGREGATIONAL CHURCH. Records, 1717-1921. Index. (CSL). Minutes, 1720-1859. Vital Records, 1748-1821. (CSL, LDS 1712). Records, 1720-1859. Index. (CSL).

Miscellaneous Church Records. Guilford. (NHCHS, LDS 1455).

First and Fourth Ecclesiastical Societies' List August 20, 1797. 20 p. (LDS 1706).

Baptisms, 1793-1802, marriages and deaths, 1793 to 1796, of Guilford, Connecticut. 13 p. (Montpelier Vt. Historical Society, LDS 6595).

Fowler, Mrs. Henry Eliot. "Records of the Fourth Church in Guilford, Connecticut 1743-1788." NEHGR 58 (1904): 299-304, 360-64; 59 (1905): 61-67.

"Funerals. Christ's Church in Guilford (1809-1836)." CHSB 6 (October 1940): 3-4.

Index Cards to Guilford 4th Church Records. (CSL, LDS 1448, pt. 3).

"Marriages in Christ Church Parish in Guilford (1808-1835)." CHSB 5 (July 1939): 27-29.

"Marriages in North Guilford (1809-1832)." CHSB 6 (January 1940): 16.

"Register of Baptisms in Christ Church in Guilford (1807-1834)." CHSB 5 (April 1939): 19-24.

"Register of Baptisms in St. John's Church-North Guilford (1808-1850)." CHSB 6 (October 1939): 4-8; 6 (January 1940): 13-14.

Webster, Sophia Riggs. "Guilford Covenant 1 June 1639." NGSQ 1 (1912): 22.

HISTORICAL SOCIETY

Guilford Keeping Society, 171 Boston Street, (P.O. Box 363), 06457. (203) 453-3176.

Henry Whitfield State Historical Museum, Whitfield Avenue, 06437. (203) 453-2457.

LAND RECORDS

Land Records, 1645-1852. Proprietor's Records 1703-1926.

Terrier Records, 1643-1814. Index, 1645-1865. (LDS 1707, pt. 1-23).

Guilford. Henry Whitfield State Historical Museum. Proprietor's Records, 1741-1798.

LIBRARY

Guilford Free Library, 67 Park Street, 06437. (203) 453-3525.

MILITARY RECORDS

Stone, Hiram. "The Experiences of a Prisoner in the American Revolution: Recollections of Thomas Stone." CM 12 (1908): 245-47.

NEWSPAPERS

SHORE LINE TIMES. Weekly, 06437. (203) 453-2711.

The PRELIMINARY CHECKLIST lists three newspapers for GUILFORD.

PROBATE RECORDS

Guilford Probate District, Town Hall, Park Street, 06437. (203) 453-2763.

Organized October 1719 from the New Haven and New London Probate Districts. Probate Districts organized from the Guilford Probate District include the Branford, Madison, Middletown, North Branford, Saybrook and Wallingford Probate Districts.

ON FILE AT THE CSL: Estate Papers, 1719-1900. Indexes, 1719-1900. Court Record Books, 1720-1852.

Probate Records, 1720-1852. (LDS 1709 pt. 1-12).

TAX RECORDS

Guilford. Henry Whitfield State Historical Museum. Lists 1794, 1797, 1798, 1799 and Rate Book First Society 1818.

Hartford. CHS. Tax Lists, 1731-1776.

VITAL RECORDS

Town Clerk, Town Hall, Park Street, 06437. (203) 453-2763.

The BARBOUR INDEX covers the years 1639-1850 and is based on the James N. Arnold copy of GUILFORD vital records made in 1914.

"Connecticut Marriages Before 1750 (Barbour)--Town of Guilford." CN 8 (1975-76): 341-56, 527-32; 9 (1976): 168-74, 346-49.

Early Guilford Vital Records. (NHCHS, LDS 1455).

Ellis, Nettie Barnum. "Death Record of Guilford 1870-1878." 13 p. (NYGBS, LDS 1706).

Jacobus, Donald Lines. "Guilford Vital Records in Town Records Book A, Volume I." TAG 13 (1936-38): 88-98, 181-89, 242-45; 15 (1939): 184-91; 16 (1940): 180-88; 17 (1941-42): 127-28, 191-92, 255-56; 18 (1941): 128; 19 (1942): 33-36.

Olding, Herbert Harris, Jr. "Old Guilford Births and Deaths (From Vol. I of the Guilford, Connecticut Vital Records which were overlooked when the copying of the Guilford town records were completed for the Barbour Collection in the Connecticut State Library)." CN 10 (1977): 160-77.

_____. "Old Guilford Marriage Records (Not in Barbour)." CN 8 (1975): 347-54.

Vital Records of Guilford, 1816-1842, 1865, 1874. Thomas Fitch's Book. (CSL, LDS 1710).

VOTER RECORDS

Hartford. CSL, Record Group 24. Two undated voter lists by party.

PUBLISHED WORKS AND OTHER RECORDS

Andrews, Evangeline Walk. THE HENRY WHITFIELD HOUSE: 1639. Hartford: Prospect Press, 1937. 48 p.

Baker, Mrs. Frederick E. "Charles Gillam and the Guilford Chests." CANTI-QUARIAN 1 (December 1959): 20-22.

Bixby, William. "The Henry Whitfield House: 1639." EARLY AMERICAN LIFE 8 (1977): 40-41, 64.

Brown, Elizabeth Mills. GUILFORD, CONNECTICUT: ITS GREEN AND ITS HISTORIC BUILDINGS. Guilford, Conn.: Guilford Bicentennial Committee, 1975. 32 p.

Griswold, Mary Hoadley. YESTER-YEARS OF GUILFORD. Guilford: Shore Line Times, 1938. 165 p.

GUILFORD AND MADISON EARLY SETTLERS AND DIRECT DESCENDANTS RESIDING IN THOSE TOWNS, JULY 1957. Madison, Conn.: First Congregational Church, 1957. 63 p.

Guilford. Henry Whitfield State Historical Museum, Town Meeting Minutes, 1785-1804.

Hartford. CSL, Record Group 24. Miscellaneous records.

Hartford. CSL, Record Group 3, Main 2, Box 553. Records of the Justice of the Peace, 1810.

Hibbard, Charles D. OLD GUILFORD: INCLUDING THE LAND NOW CON-STITUTING THE TOWNS OF GUILFORD AND MADISON. Guilford: Shore Line Times, 1939. 52 p.

Kelly, John Frederick. THE HENRY WHITFIELD HOUSE 1639. THE JOUR-NAL OF THE RESTORATION OF THE OLD STONE HOUSE, GUILFORD. Guilford: Henry Whitfield State Historical Museum, 1939. 60 p.

Maher, Annie Kelsey. "'John Grave: His Booke'--The Diary of a Common Citizen in 1679." CM 10 (1906): 18-24.

Norton, Frederick Calvin. A YANKEE POST OFFICE, ITS HISTORY AND ITS POST-POSTMASTERS. New Haven: Tuttle, Morehouse and Taylor Co., 1935. 140 p.

318

Rease, Julius Walter. "Adventures of an Early American Sea-Captain." CM 10 (1906): 631-46; 11 (1907): 275-84,

Robinson, Henry Pynchon. GUILFORD PORTRAITS, MEMORIAL EPITAPHS OF ALDERBROOK AND WESTSIDE WITH INTRODUCTORY ELEGIES AND ESSAY. New Haven: Rease-Lavis Co., 1907. 249 p. Index.

_____. "Samuel Johnson Jr., of Guilford and His Dictionaries." CM 5 (1899): 526-31.

Smith, Ralph Dunning. HISTORY OF GUILFORD, CONNECTICUT FROM ITS FIRST SETTLEMENT IN 1639. Albany: J. Munsell, 1877. 219 p.

Steiner, Bernard Christian. A HISTORY OF THE PLANTATION OF MENUNKA-TUCK AND OF THE ORIGINAL TOWN OF GUILFORD, CONNECTICUT, COMPRISING THE PRESENT TOWNS OF GUILFORD AND MADISON. Baltimore: Author, 1897. Reprint. Guilford, Conn.: Guilford Free Library, 1975. 538 p.

Waters, John J. "Patrimony, Succession and Social Stability: Guilford, Connecticut, in the Eighteenth Century." PERSPECTIVES IN AMERICAN HISTORY 10 (1916): 129-60.

Williams, Winston. "Can Guilford Survive the Modern Age?" CONNECTICUT 35 (November 1972): 34-38.

HADDAM

MIDDLESEX COUNTY. Organized October 1668. Towns organized from HADDAM include EAST HADDAM.

CEMETERY RECORDS AND CEMETERIES

NAME	ADDRESS	HALE NO.	CITATION
Haddam New Cemetery	Middlesex Turnpike	1	19:1-15
Haddam Old Cemetery	By Town Hall	2	19:16-33
Tylerville Cemetery	On Camp Bethel Road	3	19:34-52
Turkey Hill Cemetery	Turkey Hill	4	19:53-56
Beaver Meadow Cemetery	Beaver Meadow Road	5	19:57-58
Burr District Cemetery	Killingworth Road	6	19:59-64
New Rock Landing Cemetery	Rock Landing Road	7	19:65-70
Higganum Cemetery	Maple Avenue	8	19:71-111
Old Rock Landing Cemetery	Old Rock Landing Road	9	19:112-27
Old Ponsett Cemetery	Pokorny Road	10	19:128-36
Emmons Cemetery	1 grave near Reservoir	11	19:137
Little City Cemetery	Little City Road	12	19:138-45
Dickinson Cemetery	Near Center	13	19:146
Clark Cemetery	Saybrook Road	14	19:147
Andrews Cemetery	Haddam Neck	15	(no citation)
New Ponsett Cemetery	Killingworth Road (U.S. 52)	16	19:148-55

NAME	ADDRESS	HALE NO.	CITATION
Old Little City	West part of town	17	19:156-57
Thirty Mile Island Plantation Cemetery	Middlesex Turnpike		(no citation)

Index to Hale inscriptions: 19:158-95.

"Connecticut Headstone Inscriptions before 1800 (Hale)." CN 10 (1977): 409-414.

CHURCH RECORDS

EPISCOPAL HADDAM MISSION. Vital Records, 1876-1934. (CSL, LDS 1750).

FIRST CONGREGATIONAL CHURCH. Minutes, 1739-1908. Vital Records, 1700-1880. (CSL, LDS 1747). Index, 1739-1908. (CSL, LDS 1448 pt. 14-15). Marriages, 1756-1799. BAILEY 1:44-52, 3:169. Frederick L'Hommedieu copy of Vital Records, 1756-1799. (CSL, LDS 1747).

HIGGANUM CONGREGATIONAL CHURCH. Vital Records, 1844-1893. (CSL, LDS 1783).

ST. JAMES EPISCOPAL CHURCH. Vital Records, 1860-1931. (CSL, LDS 1748).

WEST HADDAM METHODIST-EPISCOPAL CHURCH. Vital Records, 1619-1930. (CSL, LDS 1749).

THE TWO HUNDREDTH ANNIVERSARY OF THE FIRST CONGREGATIONAL CHURCH OF HADDAM, CONNECTICUT, OCTOBER 14TH AND 17TH, 1900. CHURCH ORGANIZED 1696; PASTOR INSTALLED 1700. N.p., 1902. 360 p. Index. (LDS 823, 572).

HISTORICAL SOCIETY

Haddam Historical Society, 06438.

LAND RECORDS

Land Records, 1673-1857. Index, 1662-1920. (LDS 1746 pt. 1-16).

LIBRARY

Brainerd Memorial Library, Main Street, 06438. (203) 345-2204.

PROBATE RECORDS

Haddam Probate District, Town Hall, Main Street, 06438.   (203) 345-4994.

> Organized 3 June 1830 from the Chatham and Middletown Probate Districts.
>
> ON FILE AT THE CSL: Estate Papers, 1830-1934. Indexes, 1830-1934. Inventory Control Book, 1830-1934. Court Record, 1830-1855. Probate Records, 1830-1855. (LDS 1745).

VITAL RECORDS

Town Clerk, Town Hall, Main Street, (P.O. Box 87), 06438.   (203) 345-4555.

> The town clerk's earliest birth record is 1662, marriage record is 1699 and death record is 1733.

The BARBOUR INDEX covers the years 1668-1852 and is based on the James N. Arnold copy of HADDAM vital records of 1913.

"Connecticut Marriages Before 1750 (Barbour)--Town of Haddam." CN 9 (1976-77): 349-51, 518-30.

PUBLISHED WORKS AND OTHER RECORDS

Brainerd, Eveline Warner. "Haddam Since the Revolution." CM 5 (1899): 591-604.

_____. "The Plantation of Thirty Mile Island." CM 5 (1899): 543-52.

Brooks, Lillian Kruger. LIFE FLOWS ALONG LIKE A RIVER: A HISTORY OF HADDAM NECK. Haddam: Haddam Neck Genealogical Group, 1972. 132 p.

Burr, Nelson Rollin. THE EPISCOPAL CHURCH IN HADDAM. Hartford, Conn.: Church Missions Publishing Co., 1942. 32 p.

Clark, Levi H. HADDAM IN 1808. Hartford: Acorn Club of Conn., 1949. 10 p.

Field, David Dudley. A HISTORY OF THE TOWNS OF HADDAM AND EAST HADDAM. Middletown: Loomis and Richards, 1814. 49 p.

Knowles, William C. BY GONE DAYS IN PONSETT-HADDAM, MIDDLESEX COUNTY, CONNECTICUT. New York: Author, 1914. 65 p.

Parker, Francis H. "The Nathan Hale School House in East Haddam." CM 6 (1900): 243-46.

Phipps, Frances. HADDAM TERCENTENARY EXHIBITION, HADDAM HISTORICAL SOCIETY, JUNE 29-JULY 28, 1962. Higganum, Conn.: Haddam Historical Society, 1962. 36 p.

_____. "The Thankful Arnold House, Haddam, Connecticut." CANTIQUARIAN 18 (December 1966): 17-24.

_____. "The Wilhelmina Ann Arnold Barnhart Memorial Gardens at Haddam." CANTIQUARIAN 26 (July 1974): 13-19.

HAMDEN

NEW HAVEN COUNTY. Organized May 1786 from NEW HAVEN.

CEMETERY RECORDS AND CEMETERIES

NAME	ADDRESS	HALE NO.	CITATION
State Street Cemetery	2139 State Street	1	19:1-8
Whitneyville Cemetery	1266 Whitney Avenue	2	19:9-40
Hamden Plains Cemetery	248 Circular Avenue	3	19:41-94
Centerville Cemetery	347 Washington Avenue	4	19:95-127
St. Mary Roman Catholic Cemetery	3126 Whitney Avenue	5	19:128-39
Mt. Carmel Cemetery	3801 Whitney Avenue	6	19:140-62
Congregation B'nai Scholom Cemetery	25 Allen Street	7	19:163-72
Congregation B'nai Cemetery	55 Warner Street	8	19:173-84
Doolittle Cemetery	Bethany Road	9	19:185-87
West Woods Cemetery	Gaylord Mountain Road		(no citation)
Woodin Street Cemetery	606 Woodin Street		(no citation)
Beaverdale Memorial Park Cemetery	599 Fitch Street (203) 387-6601		(no citation)

Index to Hale inscriptions: 19:188-237.

"Hamden Plains Cemetery." FAMILIES OF ANCIENT NEW HAVEN 7 (1931): 1792-1804.

CENSUS RECORDS

Jacobus, Donald Lines. "Errors in the Census of 1790 (Conn.) Hamden."
NEHGR 77 (1923): 81.

CHURCH RECORDS

CONGREGATIONAL CHURCH. Mt. Carmel. Marriages, 1783-1790. BAILEY
7:74-75. Whitneyville. Minutes, 1795-1915. (CSL, LDS 1785). Vital
Records, 1795-1915. (CSL, LDS 1786). Index. Records, 1795-1915. (CSL,
LDS 1448).

GRACE EPISCOPAL CHURCH. Minutes, 1790-1924. Vital Records, 1821-
1927. (CSL, LDS 1785).

PLAINS METHODIST EPISCOPAL CHURCH. Minutes, 1897-1903, 1927-1933.
(CSL, LDS 1784).

Coley, James Edward. HISTORY OF GRACE CHURCH, HAMDEN, CONNECT-
ICUT FROM ITS ORGANIZATION, MARCH 1, 1790 TO JULY 1, 1912. New
Haven: n.p., 1913. 71 p.

HISTORICAL SOCIETY

Hamden Historical Society, Mt. Carmel Avenue, 06518.

LAND RECORDS

Land Records, 1786-1861. Index, 1786-1870. (LDS 1783 pt. 1-14).

LIBRARY

Hamden Library, 2914 Dixwell Avenue, 06518. (203) 248-7747.

MILITARY RECORDS

HISTORY OF HAMDEN MEN IN THE WORLD WAR FROM INFORMATION
COLLECTED BY THE HAMDEN WAR BUREAU. WITH A BRIEF SUMMARY OF
THE ACTIVITIES OF THE BUREAU. New Haven: Tuttle, Morehouse and
Taylor Co., n.d. 184 p.

"Revolutionary War Pay Roll, 1777." NGSQ 9 (1920): 45.

NEWSPAPERS

HAMDEN CHRONICLE. Weekly. 2821 Dixwell Avenue, 06518. (203) 288-1661.

The PRELIMINARY CHECKLIST lists three newspapers for HAMDEN.

PROBATE RECORDS

Hamden Probate District, Town Hall, 2372 Whitney Avenue, 06518. (203) 248-3561.

Organized 22 July 1945 from the New Haven Probate District.

TAX RECORDS

Hartford. CSL, Record Group 62. Tax List. East Plain Society, 1798.

VITAL RECORDS

Town Clerk, Town Hall, 2372 Whitney Avenue, 06518. (203) 288-5641 ext. 211.

The BARBOUR INDEX covers the years 1786-1867 and is based on the Ethel L. Scofield and Irene H. Mix copy of HAMDEN vital records made in 1914.

Stiles, Mr., and Nelson, Mrs. "Gilbert Mortality List." NEW HAVEN GENE-ALOGY MAGAZINE 4 (1927): 1015-24; 5 (1929): 1249-66; 6 (1930): 1529-30.

PUBLISHED WORKS AND OTHER RECORDS

Blake, William P. HISTORY OF THE TOWN OF HAMDEN, WITH AN AC-COUNT OF THE CENTENNIAL CELEBRATION, JUNE 15TH, 1886. New Haven: Price, Lee and Co., 1888. 350 p.

Dickerman, John H. COLONIAL HISTORY OF THE PARISH OF MOUNT CARMEL. New Haven: Ryder's Printing House, 1904. 109 p.

_____. "Hamden." CQ 4 (1898): 376-90.

Hartley, Rachel M. HISTORY OF HAMDEN, CONNECTICUT 1786-1959. Hamden: Shoe String Press, 1959. 506 p.

_____. THE STORY OF HAMDEN, LAND OF THE SLEEPING GIANT. Hamden: Shoe String Press, 1966. 98 p.

HAMPTON

WINDHAM COUNTY. Organized October 1786 from BROOKLYN, CANTER-
BURY, MANSFIELD, POMFRET and WINDHAM. Towns organized from HAMP-
TON include CHAPLIN.

CEMETERY RECORDS AND CEMETERIES

NAME	ADDRESS	HALE NO.	CITATION
Hammond or North Cemetery	1 mile north of Hampton Center	1	19:1-37
South Cemetery	1 1/2 miles south of Hampton Center	2	19:38-68
Litchfield Cemetery	In field, east of East Road U.S. 53	3	19:69-72
Grow Cemetery	Half in Pomfret and Hampton	4	19:73-75
Litchfield Incorporated Cemetery	On East Road, south of Brooklyn Road	5	19:76-80
Calvin-Burnham Cemetery	On Burnham farm. Goshen District near Clark Corners	6	19:81-82

Index to Hale inscriptions: 19:83-102.

Cary, Mrs. Irving L. BURNHAM CEMETERY INSCRIPTIONS. Hampton:
Author, 1930. 1 p.

_____. NORTH CEMETERY INSCRIPTIONS FROM HEADSTONES. Hampton:
Author, 1930. 34 p.

_____. SOUTH CEMETERY INSCRIPTIONS TAKEN FROM HEADSTONES.
Hampton: Author, 1930. 29 p.

CHURCH RECORDS

BAPTIST CHURCH. Minutes, 1770-1844. (CSL, LDS 1739).

CONGREGATIONAL CHURCH. Minutes, 1761-1879. Vital Records, 1723-1855. (CSL, LDS 1738). Records. Index, 1723-1855. (CSL, LDS 1448). Canadian Society. Marriages, 1734-1789. BAILEY 4:69-76.

SECOND SOCIETY RATE BILLS, 1747-1803. (CSL Archives RG62).

HISTORICAL SOCIETY

Hampton Antiquarian and Historical Society, 06247.

LAND RECORDS

Land Records 1786-1855. (LDS 1736 pt. 1-5).

LIBRARY

Fletcher Memorial Library, P.O. Box 11, 06247. (203) 445-9295.

PROBATE RECORDS

Hampton Probate District, Town Office Building, Windham Turnpike, 06247. (203) 455-9132.

Organized 2 June 1836 from the Windham Probate District.

ON FILE AT THE CSL: Estate Papers, 1836-1936. Indexes, 1836-1936. Inventory Control Book, 1836-1936. Court Record Books, 1836-1858.

Probate Records 1836-1858. (LDS 1737).

TAX RECORDS

Hartford. CSL, Record Group 62. Grand Lists 1852-1929.

VITAL RECORDS

Town Clerk, Town Office Building, Old Route 6, P.O. Box 143, 06247. (203) 455-9132.

The BARBOUR INDEX covers the years 1786-1851 and is based on the James N. Arnold copy of HAMPTON vital records made in 1911.

PUBLISHED WORKS AND OTHER RECORDS

Davis, Alison.   HAMPTON REMEMBERS; A SMALL TOWN IN NEW ENGLAND, 1885-1950. Danielson: Racine Printing Co., 1976.   173 p.

Griggs, Susan J.   EARLY HOMESTEADS OF POMFRED AND HAMPTON. Danielson: Ingalls Printing Co., 1950.   118 p.

Weaver, William Lawton.   HISTORY OF ANCIENT CT., GENEALOGY, CONTAINING A GENEALOGICAL RECORD OF ALL THE EARLY FAMILY OF ANCIENT WINDHAM, EMBRACING THE PRESENT TOWNS OF WINDHAM, MANSFIELD, HAMPTON, CHAPLIN AND SCOTLAND. Part I. A-Bil. Willimantic: Weaver and Curtiss, 1864.   112 p.   (LDS 2146).

HARTFORD

HARTFORD COUNTY. Organized 1635. Towns organized from HARTFORD include EAST HARTFORD and WEST HARTFORD.

CEMETERY RECORDS AND CEMETERIES

NAME	ADDRESS	HALE NO.	CITATION
Old Burial Ground (Center)	Rear of Center Church	1	19:1-19
Old South Cemetery	430 Maple Avenue	2	19:20-28
Old North Cemetery	1821 Main Street	3	20A:1-231 21:232-36
Spring Grove Cemetery	2035 Main Street (203) 247-1548	4	20A:1-32 21:33-397
Zion Hill Cemetery	Corner of 195 Ward and 548 Zion Streets	5	19:29-100 20:100-229
Mt. Pleasant Cemetery	Southern part of Zion Hill Cemetery	6	20:230-301
Congregation Beth Israel Cemetery	153 Ward Street (203) 247-2679	7	20:302-24
Holy Trinity Cemetery	Rear part of Old North Cemetery	8	21:1-12
St. Patrick Roman Catholic Cemetery	470 Garden Street	9	21:1-135
Small Pox Cemetery	Sigourney Park	10	20:325
Morison Cemetery	Market Street (St. Anthony's Church) Grave of Dr. Morison, King George War Veteran	11	20:326

NAME	ADDRESS	HALE NO.	CITATION
Soldier's Memorial Arch	Bushnell Park	12	20:307
Cedar Hill Cemetery	453 Fairfield Avenue (203) 522-4630	13	21:1-306
Jewish Center Cemetery	Garden Street near Tower Avenue	14	20:328-29
Congregation Aguas Achim Cemetery	Garden Street Extension near Tower Avenue	15	20:330
Peddlers 1909 Cemetery	Garden Street Extension near Tower Avenue	16	20:331
Aaron Lodge Cemetery	Garden Street Extension near Tower Avenue	17	20:332
First Ludmir Benevolent Association Cemetery	Garden Street Extension near Tower Avenue	18	20:333
Hope of Zion Cemetery	Garden Street Extension near Tower Avenue	19	20:334
Jewish Cemetery	Garden Street Extension near Tower Avenue	20	20:335
Workingman Circle (Branch No. 326) Cemetery	Garden Street Extension near Tower Avenue	21	20:336
Jewish Cemetery	Garden Street Extension near Tower Avenue	22	20:337
Jewish Cemetery	Garden Street Extension near Tower Avenue	23	20:338
Shevig Mishnay Cemetery	Garden Street Extension near Tower Avenue	24	20:339
Jewish Cemetery	Garden Street Extension near Tower Avenue	25	20:340
Jewish Cemetery	Garden Street Extension near Tower Avenue	26	20:341
Jewish Cemetery	Garden Street near Mahl Avenue	27	20:342
St. Joseph Cathedral Cemetery	Farmington Avenue	28	20:343
St. Patrick Roman Catholic Church Cemetery	Church Street	29	20:344
Capitol City Lodge Cemetery	Zion Hill	30	20:345-52

NAME	ADDRESS	HALE NO.	CITATION
Workingmens S.B. Association Cemetery	Zion Hill	31	20:353-56
Moses Montifner Lodge Cemetery	Zion Hill	32	20:357-61
Hartford City Lodge Cemetery	Zion Hill	33	20:362-67
Dreyfus Lodge Cemetery	Zion Hill	34	20:368-70
Agudater Achim Association Cemetery	Zion Hill	35	20:371-77
Hartford Lodge Cemetery	Zion Hill	36	20:378-79
Congregation Adas Israel Cemetery	Zion Hill	37	20:380-94
Jewish Cemetery	Zion Hill	38	20:395-99
Rothschild Cemetery	Zion Hill	39	20:400
Hartford Hebrew Association Cemetery	Zion Hill	40	20:401-02
Jewish Cemetery	Mahl Avenue	41	20:403
Workingman Circle Cemetery	Mahl Avenue	42	20:404-05
Workingman Circle Cemetery	Mahl Avenue	43	20:406-08
Jewish Cemetery	Mahl Avenue	44	20:409-10
Hartford Mutual Society Cemetery	Mahl Avenue	45	20:411
Hartford Peddlers Lodge Cemetery	Mahl Avenue	46	20:412-13
Hartford Free Burial Association Cemetery	Mahl Avenue	47	20:414-19
Austrian Hebrew Congregation Cemetery	1st, 2d and 3d section within Old North Cemetery	48	20:420-25
All Jewish Cemetery	Zion Hill	49	20:426-31
First Burial Yard Cemetery	Northeast of Old State House, near 80 State Street	50	20:432
Town House Cemetery	Vine House	51	20:433
(Unnamed Cemetery)	71 Capitol Avenue	52	20:434
International Workers Order Cemetery	Garden Street Extension near Tower Avenue	53	20:435

NAME	ADDRESS	HALE NO.	CITATION
Young Friends Progressive Association Cemetery	Garden Street Extension near Tower Avenue	54	20:436
Jonathan Welfare Cemetery	Tower Avenue	55	20:437
(Single Grave)	Near No. 55	56	20:438-39

Index to Hale inscriptions: 21:398-510. 20:440-551.

CEDAR HILL CEMETERY HARTFORD CONNECTICUT 1863-1903. Hartford: Cedar Hill Cemetery, 1903. 57 p.

"Connecticut Headstone Inscriptions Before 1800 (Hale)--Town of Hartford." CN 4 (1971): 40-46, 206-9.

DAR Wisconsin. Genealogical Records Committee. "Cemetery Records of . . . Center Church in Hartford." BIBLE AND CEMETERY RECORDS 1800-1940 (LDS 848,696).

"Hartford South Burying Ground Inscriptions." CHSB 7 (1941): 15-16, 20-30.

Holcombe, Emily S.G. "The Ancient Burying Ground of Hartford." CQ 4 (1898): 73-85.

"List of Interments by William Goodwin (1689-1698)." CHSB 3 (November 1936): 2-8.

Names from Gold Street Cemetery. (LDS 1964).

RESTORATION OF THE ANCIENT BURYING GROUND OF HARTFORD AND THE WIDENING OF GOLD STREET. Hartford: Ruth Wyllop Chapter, DAR, 1904. 794 p.

Stevens, John Austin. "Hartford and Groton Tombstones Illustrative of Genealogical Sketch of Family of Ledyard." NYGBR 7 (1876): 14-16.

Talcott, Mary Kingsbury: "The Center Church Burying Ground and Its Associations." CQ 1 (1895): 43-45.

_____. "List of Burials or 'Sexton's List' of the Center Church Burying Ground, Hartford." CQ 4 (1898): 180-87, 264-71, 417-20; 5 (1899): 118-19, 186-87, 242-43, 290-91, 336-38, 382-85, 426-28, 481-84, 520-25.

CHURCH RECORDS

ASYLUM STREET BAPTIST CHURCH. Minutes, 1869-1936. (CSL, LDS 1769, pt. 5).

BLUE HILLS BAPTIST CHURCH. Minutes, 1816-1899. Vital Records, 1810-1894. (CSL, LDS 1770).

CENTRAL BAPTIST CHURCH. Minutes, 1923-1931. (CSL, LDS 1769 pt. 4).

CHRIST (EPISCOPAL) CHURCH. Minutes, 1795-1840. Vital Records, 1848-1877. Index. (CSL, LDS 1780 LDS 1448 pt. 6-7). Vital Records, 1887-1927. (CSL, LDS 1772).

CHURCH OF THE GOOD SHEPHERD (EPISCOPAL). Minutes, 1866-1935. Vital Records, 1864-1923. (CSL, LDS 1773 pt. 1-2).

FIRST BAPTIST CHURCH. Vital Records, 1789-1909. (CSL, LDS 1769 pt. 1).

FIRST CONGREGATIONAL CHURCH. Index (CSL, LDS 1448 pt. 4).

FIRST INDEPENDENT UNIVERSALIST CHURCH. Vital Records, 1824-1923. (CSL, LDS 1779).

FIRST PRESBYTERIAN CHURCH. Minutes, 1851-1924. (CSL, LDS 1778).

FOURTH CONGREGATIONAL CHURCH. Vital Records, 1832-1907. (CSL, LDS 1766).

GRACE (EPISCOPAL) CHURCH. Minutes, 1890-1937. Vital Records, 1863-1937. (CSL, LDS 1765).

NORTH AND PARK CONGREGATIONAL CHURCH. Minutes, 1824-1926. Vital Records, 1824-1887. (CSL, LDS 1771 pt. 1).

NORTH METHODIST CHURCH. Minutes, 1871-1880. Vital Records, 1871-1926. (CSL, LDS 1767).

PEARL STREET CONGREGATIONAL CHURCH. Vital Records, 1851-1913. (CSL, LDS 1779).

ST. JAMES (EPISCOPAL) CHURCH. Minutes, 1868-1878. Vital Records, 1868-1947. (CSL, LDS 1775).

ST. JOHN'S (EPISCOPAL) CHURCH. Minutes, 1841-1925. Vital Records, 1842-1922. (CSL, LDS 1774 pt. 1-2).

ST. PAUL'S (EPISCOPAL) CHURCH. Minutes, 1856-1879. Vital Records, 1850-1878. (CSL, LDS 1776).

ST. THOMAS (EPISCOPAL) CHURCH. Vital Records, 1871-1920. (CSL, LDS 1776).

SECOND CONGREGATIONAL CHURCH. Minutes, 1868-1896. Vital Records 1792-1862, 1873-1914. (CSL, LDS 1764). Index. (CSL, LDS 1448 pt. 5).

SOUTH BAPTIST CHURCH. Minutes, 1834-1928. (CSL, LDS 1769 pt. 2-3).

TRINITY (EPISCOPAL) CHURCH. Minutes, 1859-1936. Vital Records, 1861-1926. (CSL, LDS 1777 pt. 1-2).

WETHERSFIELD AVENUE CONGREGATIONAL CHURCH. Minutes, 1858-1896. Vital Records, 1873-1914. (CSL, LDS 1768).

WINDSOR AVENUE CONGREGATIONAL CHURCH. Minutes, 1865-1908. Vital Records, 1870-1905. (CSL, LDS 1771 pt. 2).

ADDITIONAL CONTRIBUTIONS TO THE HISTORY OF CHRIST CHURCH, HARTFORD WITH THE RECORDS OF BAPTISMS, CONFIRMATIONS, COMMUNICANTS, MARRIAGES AND BURIALS 1760-1900. VOL. 2. Hartford: Belknap and Warfield, 1908. 517 p.

A BRIEF HISTORY OF THE FIRST BAPTIST CHURCH, HARTFORD, WITH THE ARTICLES OF FAITH, THE CHURCH COVENANT, GENERAL REGULATIONS AND LIST OF MEMBERS. Hartford: Case, Lockwood and Brainard Co., 1876. 44 p. (LDS 823,648).

CONTRIBUTIONS TO THE HISTORY OF CHRIST CHURCH, HARTFORD. Hartford: Belknap and Warfield, 1895. 787 p.

"Falling Section of the Steeple of the Pearl Street Church, Hartford." CM 5 (1899): 645-48.

A HALF-CENTURY HISTORY OF THE FARMINGTON AVENUE CONGREGATIONAL CHURCH ORGANIZED AS THE PEARL STREET CONGREGATIONAL CHURCH IN HARTFORD, CONNECTICUT, 1851-1901. Hartford: Farmington Avenue Congregational Church, 1901. 84 p.

Congregation of the Sisters of Mercy. TRIBUTES TO OUR FOUNDRESS FOR THE CENTENNIAL OF THE FOUNDATION OF THE CONGREGATION OF THE SISTERS OF MERCY. 1831-1931. Hartford, Conn.: Author, 1931. 396 p.

HISTORICAL CATALOGUE OF THE FIRST CHURCH IN HARTFORD 1633-1885. Hartford: First Congregational Church, 1885. 274 p. (LDS 1782).

"The Hooker Memorial Window in Center Church, Hartford." CM 6 (1900): 430-40.

"Papers Relating to the Controversy in the Church in Hartford 1656-1659." CHS COLLECTIONS 2 (1870): 51-125. (LDS 897,068).

Parker, Edwin Pond. HISTORY OF THE SECOND CHURCH OF CHRIST IN HARTFORD. Hartford: Belknap and Warfield, 1892. 435 p. Index.

"The Pearl Street Ecclesiastical Society." CM 5 (1899): 434-35.

Pierce, William J. HISTORY OF THE ADVENT CHRISTIAN CHURCH OF HARTFORD, FROM THE FIRST MEETINGS IN 1838 TO JANUARY 1ST 1906, AS GATHERED FROM THE RECORDS. Boston: Advent Christian Publication Society, 1907. 184 p.

A RECORD OF DEATHS FOUND IN THE DIARY, 1737-1747 OF THE REV. DANIEL WADSWORTH, SEVENTH PASTOR OF THE FIRST CHURCH IN HART-FORD, CONNECTICUT. Hartford: n.p., n.d. 6 p.

"Rev. Elisha Cushman's Record." (First Baptist Church in Hartford 1813 to 1825, Philadelphia, Pennsylvania 1825-1829, Fairfield, Connecticut September 1829-1830, New Haven 1830-1833, Plymouth Massachusetts 1834-1837, 1840-1863 by son Rev. Elisha Cushman and contains marriages from Willington, Hartford, New Britain and Deep River until 1863.) CHSB 7 (July 1941): 30-32; 8 (October 1941): 2-8; 8 (January 1942): 12-13.

Silverman, Morris. HARTFORD JEWS 1659-1970. Hartford: CHS, 1970. 449 p.

Wadsworth, Daniel. DIARY OF REV. DANIEL WADSWORTH, SEVENTH PAS-TOR OF THE FIRST CHURCH OF CHRIST IN HARTFORD. Hartford, Conn.: Case, Lockwood and Brainard, Co., 1849.

Walker, George Leon. HISTORY OF THE FIRST CHURCH OF HARTFORD 1633-1883. Hartford: Brown and Gross, 1884. 503 p. Index.

Warren, William Lamson. "Who Designed Hartford's Center Church?" CANTI-QUARIAN 7 (December 1955): 19-27.

Weld, Stanley Burnham. HARTFORD: THE HISTORY OF IMMANUEL CHURCH 1824-1967. Hartford: Immanuel Congregational Church, 1968. 115 p. Index.

CITY DIRECTORY

DIRECTORY FOR THE CITY OF HARTFORD FOR THE YEAR 1799, CONTAIN-ING THE NAMES OF THE BUSINESS MEN AND OTHER RESIDENTS, THEIR OCCUPATION AND LOCATION WHEN KNOWN, TO THE NUMBER OF NEARLY EIGHT HUNDRED. Vineland, N.J.: Frank DeWitte Andrews, 1910. 34 p.

HISTORICAL SOCIETY

Butler-McCook Homestead, 396 Main Street, 06106. (203) 522-1806.

Connecticut Historical Society. (See HISTORICAL SOCIETIES).

Hartford Architecture Conservancy, 130 Washington Street, 06106. (203) 525-0279. Publishes HAC NEWS. Bimonthly.

LAND RECORDS

Land Records, 1685-1851. Proprietor's Records, 1639-1688. Index, 1639-1865. (CSL, LDS 1761 pt. 1-42).

Proprietor's Records. North Meadow Association, 1792-1931. (CSL, LDS 1781).

Proprietor's Records. Vols. 1 and 2, 1659-1857. (CSL, LDS 1763).

"Original Distribution of the Lands in Hartford Among the Settlers 1639." CHS COLLECTIONS 14 (1912): 1-571. (LDS 897,073).

Woodhouse, Levi, et al. GENERAL INDEX OF THE LAND RECORDS OF THE TOWN OF HARTFORD, FROM THE YEAR 1639 TO THE YEAR 1839. VOLUMES 1 AND 61 INCLUSIVE. Hartford: Wiley, Waterman and Eaton, 1873. 1,326 p.

LIBRARIES

Connecticut State Library. (See LIBRARIES).

Hartford Public Library. 500 Main Street, 06103. (203) 525-9121.

Stowe-Day Library. 77 Forest Street, 06105. (203) 522-9258.

Wadsworth Atheneum. 600 Main Street, 06103. (203) 278-2670.

Published: WADSWORTH ATHENEUM BULLETIN. 1965-1972. 3/4 year.

Maynard, Henry P. "The Wadsworth Atheneum and Wallace Nutting." CANTIQUARIAN 13 (December 1961): 13-20.

MILITARY RECORDS

CHS. HARTFORD LISTS AND REFORMS OF CONNECTICUT MEN IN THE REVOLUTION, 1775-1783. Hartford: Author, 1909.

CITY GUARD REGISTER, BEING A COMPLETE ROSTER OF THE HARTFORD CITY GUARD SINCE ITS ORGANIZATION IN 1861. Hartford: Case, Lockwood and Brainard, 1880. 43 p.

NEWSPAPERS

CATHOLIC TRANSCRIPT. Weekly. 785 Asylum Avenue, 06105. (203) 527-1175.

CONNECTICUT JEWISH LEDGER. Weekly. P.O. Box 923, 06101. (203) 233-2148.

HARTFORD COURANT. Daily. 285 Broad Street, 06115. (203) 249-6411.

The PRELIMINARY CHECKLIST lists 133 newspapers for HARTFORD.

HARTFORD TIMES. Genealogical Department. Genealogical Questions and Answers. A Weekly Feature. 1918-1967. Index, 1956-1967. (LDS 496,526 - 496,531; 496,627 - 496,632. 599,106. 824,280. 873,815. 873,822. 496,532).

Newspapers included in the HALE INDEX TO DEATHS AND MARRIAGES include:

AMERICAN MERCURY. deaths and marriages 12 July 1784-24 December 1832.

CALENDAR. deaths and marriages 4 January 1845-23 December 1865.

CHARTER OAK. deaths 4 June 1846-14 December 1848 and marriages April 1839-14 December 1848.

CHRISTIAN SECRETARY. deaths and marriages 1 February 1823- 6 March 1867.

COLUMBIAN REGISTER. deaths and marriages 1 December 1812- 30 December 1865.

CONGREGATIONALIST AND NO. WATCHMAN. deaths and marriages 4 January 1836-26 December 1840.

CONNECTICUT FOUNTAIN. deaths and marriages 1 January 1848-22 December 1848.

CONNECTICUT MIRROR. deaths and marriages 10 July 1809-15 December 1832.

CONNECTICUT OBSERVER. deaths and marriages 4 January 1825- 21 May 1842.

CONNECTICUT PRESS. deaths and marriages 8 March 1856-29 December 1866.

EPISCOPAL WATCHMAN. deaths 26 March 1827–8 May 1832. marriages 24 May 1831–8 May 1832.

FREEMAN'S CHRONICLE. deaths 29 September 1783–10 November 1783.

HARTFORD COURANT. deaths 29 October 1764–30 December 1865. marriages 28 December 1767–30 December 1865.

HARTFORD DAILY POST. deaths and marriages 4 July 1865–26 February 1866.

HARTFORD EVENING COURIER. deaths and marriages 29 July 1839–4 September 1840.

HARTFORD EVENING PRESS. deaths and marriages 28 February 1856–31 December 1866.

HARTFORD PATRIOT AND DEMOCRAT. deaths and marriages 7 March 1835–15 October 1836.

HARTFORD TIMES. deaths and marriages 1 January 1817–29 December 1866.

HARTFORD WEEKLY POST. deaths and marriages 5 June 1858–29 December 1866.

NEW ENGLAND RELIGIOUS HERALD. deaths and marriages 2 February 1847–23 December 1848.

NEW ENGLAND REVIEW. deaths and marriages 14 July 1834–17 October 1840.

RELIGIOUS INQUIRER. deaths and marriages 10 November 1821–7 November 1835.

REPUBLICAN. deaths and marriages 11 January 1849–31 December 1852.

John Elliot Bowman also indexed the following two newspapers and the index cards have been added to the BARBOUR INDEX.

CONNECTICUT OBSERVER. deaths and marriages 1820–1837.

HARTFORD GAZETTE. deaths 1792–1800.

The Connecticut Historical Society has an index to the CONNECTICUT COURANT for the years 1764–1820.

Cawley, Peter. "Behind the COURANT Sale." CONNECTICUT 42 (November 1979): 116–17.

McNulty, John Band. OLDER THEN THE NATION: THE STORY OF THE HARTFORD COURANT. Stonington: Pequct Press, 1964. 231 p.

Spaulding, E. Wilder. "The CONNECTICUT COURANT, A Representative Newspaper in the Eighteenth Century." NEQ 3 (1930): 443-63.

PROBATE RECORDS

Hartford Probate District, Municipal Building, 550 Main Street, 06103. (203) 566-6550. Organized May 1666.

> Probate districts organized from the Hartford Probate District include the Berlin, East Haddam, East Hartford, East Windsor, Farmington, Glastonbury, Granby, Litchfield, Middletown, Newington, Simsbury, Stafford, Suffield, Waterbury, Windham, Windsor and Windsor Locks Probate Districts.

> The Hartford Probate District also includes the towns of BLOOMFIELD and WEST HARTFORD.

> ON FILE AT THE CSL: Estate Papers, 1641-1940. Indexes, 1641-1920 (papers from 1920-1940 arranged alphabetically). Inventory Control Book, 1641-1814. Court Record Books, 1677-1850. Journal, 1829-1832. Ledger, 1863-1884. Decrees, 1863-1887.

Probate Records, 1635-1850. (CSL, LDS 1762 pt. 1-22).

Probate Records, 1649-1850. (CSL, LDS 4,550-4,572).

Probate Records Index, 1800-1920. (CSL, LDS 22787 pt. 1-11).

Manwaring, Charles William. A DIGEST OF THE EARLY CONNECTICUT PROBATE RECORDS. HARTFORD DISTRICT 1635-1750. 3 vols. Hartford: R.S. Peck and Co., 1904, 1904, 1906. (LDS 599,296).

RECORDS OF THE PARTICULAR COURT OF THE COLONY OF CONNECTICUT. ADMINISTRATION OF SIR EDMOND ANDROS, ROYAL GOVERNOR 1687-1688. Hartford: Case, Lockwood and Brainard Co., 1935. 43 p.

SCHOOL RECORDS

Eaton, Edward Bailey. "Hartford's Educational Institutions." CM 3 (1905): 610-16.

Hartford. CHS. Northwest School District. Tax List, 1808-1819.

Rathbun, J.G. "Hartford Public High School." CM 5 (1899): 649.

TAX RECORDS

Hartford. CSL, Record Group 62. Tax Registers, Abstracts, Etc., 1850-1920.

VITAL RECORDS

Town Clerk, Municipal Building, 550 Main Street, 06103. (203) 566-6400.

The BARBOUR INDEX covers the years 1635-1855 and is based on the Frank Farnsworth Starr copy of Hartford vital records "Original Distribution of the Lands in Hartford Among the Settlers 1639" and BIRTHS, MARRIAGES AND DEATHS by Edwin Stanley Welles (see below).

Bottwood, Lucius M. "Births, Marriages and Deaths Contained in the Volume Lettered ORIGINAL DISTRIBUTION OF THE TOWN OF HARTFORD (CT.) AMONG THE SETTLERS 1639." NEHGR 12 (1858): 173-75, 196-98, 331-36; 13 (1859): 48-54, 141-48.

_____. "Births, Marriages and Deaths, from Book Lettered RECORDS OF TOWN OF HARTFORD, 1685-1709, NO. I." NEHGR 13 (1859): 239-44, 343-46.

_____. "Records of Town of Hartford, 1709-1716." NEHGR 20 (1861): 234-37; 22 (1868): 192-95; 23 (1869): 42-46.

"Connecticut Marriages Before 1750 (Barbour)--Town of Hartford." CN 9 (1977): 520-23; 10 (1978): 27-32, 199-204, 401-5.

Dana, Elizabeth Ellery. "Vital Records Kept by William Watson of Hartford, Connecticut, 1819-1834." NEHGR 79 (1925): 150-70, 298-310, 401-9; 80 (1926): 54-72.

Death Records, 1794-1837. Rollin H. Cooke Collection. Pittsfield, Mass. (LDS 30734 pt. 17).

"Early Hartford Vital Records." CHS COLLECTIONS 14 (1912): 573-716.

Hinman, Ralph Royal. A PART OF THE EARLY MARRIAGES, BIRTHS AND BAPTISMS IN HARTFORD, CT. Hartford, Conn.: n.p., 1910. 336 p.

"Midwife Records, 1815-1849 Kept by Mrs. Jennet Boardman of Hartford." CHSB 33 (1968): 64-69, 132-36; 34 (1969): 26-31, 119-26.

"Some Connecticut Records Hartford, Connecticut (Various Newspapers)."
NGSQ 5 (1916): 41-42.

Welles, Edwin Stanley. BIRTHS, MARRIAGES AND DEATHS RETURNED FROM
HARTFORD, WINDSOR AND FAIRFIELD AND ENTERED IN THE EARLY LAND
RECORDS OF THE COLONY OF CONNECTICUT. VOLUMES I AND II OF
LAND RECORDS AND NO. D OF COLONIAL RECORDS. Hartford: Author,
1898. 73 p. (LDS 823,816).

VOTER RECORDS

Alvarez, David J., and Ture, Edmond J. "Critical Elections and Partisan Re-
alignment: An Urban Test-Case." POLITY 5 (1973): 563-76.

Hartford. CSL, Record Group 62. Electors Lists, 1874-1910, 1936.

"Hartford Town Votes 1635-1716." CHS COLLECTIONS, vol. 6, 1898. (LDS
897,069).

PUBLISHED WORKS AND OTHER RECORDS

"Aaron Chapin, Hartford Cabinetmaker." ANTIQUES 24 (September 1933):
97-98.

Adams, Sherman W. "The Hartford Park System." CQ 1 (1895): 67-71,
171-79.

Allyn, Adeline Bartlett. BLACK HALL TRADITIONS AND REMINISCENCES.
Hartford: Case, Lockwood and Brainard, Co., 1908. 89 p.

"The Amos Bull House." CANTIQUARIAN 22 (December 1970): 28-29.

Andrews, Charles McLean. THE RIVER TOWNS OF CONNECTICUT: A STUDY
OF WETHERSFIELD, HARTFORD AND WINDSOR. 1889. Reprint. New
York: Johnson Reprint Corp., 1973. 126 p.

Arms, H. Phelps. "Hartford's Empty Reservoirs." CM 6 (1900): 25-32.

"Autumn in Hartford's Parks." CM 4 (1905): 701-15.

"Bear in Hartford. September 22, 1766." CQ 2 (1896): 99.

"Beautiful Homes of Hartford." CM 3 (1905): 603-9; 4 (1905): 860-72.

Benjamin, Howard W. "The Pope and Pond Parks and their Donors." CQ 1 (1895): 336-44.

Bradstreet, Howard. HARTFORD BACKGROUNDS. PART I. Hartford: Pyne-Davidson Co., 1930. 70 p.

Brainard, Newton Cass. THE ANDRUS BINDRY, A HISTORY OF THE SHOP, 1831-1839. Hartford, Conn.: Case, Lockwood and Brainard, Co., 1940. 45 p.

Buffalo, John, and Clay, Carl. "Black Hartford 1843-1860." Paper for University of Hartford Summer Session, 1972. 39 p.

Campbell, John R. "Governor Talcott's Mansion and the City of Hartford's Claim." CM 6 (1900): 359-61.

Cave, Henry. "The Automobile Industry in the U.S.A. Birth in Hartford 1897." CANTIQUARIAN 2 (November 1950): 22-28.

Chapman, Louise J.R. "A Visit to Mrs. Sigourney." CQ 1 (1895): 47-49.

Clovette, Bruce. "Antebellum Urban Renewal: Hartford's Bushnell Park." CONNECTICUT HISTORY 18 (1976): 1-21.

Daniels, Bruce Colin. "Large Town Power Structures in Eighteenth Century Connecticut: An Analysis of Political Leadership in Hartford, Norwich and Fairfield." Ph.D. dissertation, University of Connecticut, 1970. 241 p.

Eaton, Edward Bailey. "Financial History of Hartford." CM 9 (1905): 889-912.

_____. "Hartford the Stronghold of Insurance." CM 9 (1905): 617-44, 873-88.

_____. "Inventions and Manufactures in Hartford." CM 9 (1905): 913-21.

Eaton, Leonard K. "Eli Todd and the Hartford Retreat." NEQ 26 (1953): 435-53.

"Edward Sheffield Bartholomew." CQ 2 (1896): 202-14.

"First Connecticut Heavy Artillery Monument." CM 7 (1902): 395.

Giddings, Emory B. "Historical Sketch of the Putnam Phalanx." CM 6 (1900): 335-47.

Grant, Ellsworth Strong, and Grant, Marion Hepburn. PASSBOOK TO A PROUD PAST AND A PROMISING FUTURE: 1819-1969. 150TH ANNIVER-SARY. Hartford, Conn.: Society for Savings, 1969. 97 p.

Grant, Marion Hepburn. IN AND ABOUT HARTFORD: TOURS AND TALES. Hartford: Connecticut Historical Society, 1978. 360 p. Index.

Grumman, W.E. "Old Books Printed in Connecticut." CM 11 (1907): 574-76.

Harding, Dorothy Huggins. THE FOUNDER'S MONUMENT AT HARTFORD, CONNECTICUT: OUR LINES OF DESCENT FROM EARLY SETTERS WHOSE NAMES ARE INSCRIBED ON IT. N.p., 1966. (LDS 496, 485).

_____. MORE HARTFORD ANCESTORS, A SUPPLEMENT TO THE FOUNDER'S MONUMENT AT HARTFORD, CONNECTICUT. N.p., 1968. 16 p. (LDS 824,107).

Harlow, Thompson Ritner. EARLY HARTFORD PRINTERS. Hartford: Columbia Club of Connecticut, 1940. 12 p.

Hartford. CSL, Record Group 33 Box 120-126 and scrapbooks. WPA Ethnic Groups Survey. Hartford Office File, 1936-1940. Includes newspaper articles, biographies, etc.

"Hartford as a Shopping Center." CM 9 (1905): 922-24.

"Hartford Loses Another." CANTIQUARIAN 29 (June 1977): 34-35.

"Hartford's New Theatre in 1795." CQ 2 (1896): 183.

"The Hearthstone Club of Hartford." CQ 3 (1897): 121.

Henney, William Franklin. "The Building of a Model Municipality." CM 9 (1905): 555-602.

_____. "Modern Factors in Municipal Progress." CM 9 (1905): 813-60.

HISTORY OF HARTFORD STREETS, THEIR NAMES, WITH ORIGIN AND DATES OF USE. Publications of the Municipal Art Society of Hartford Connecticut Bulletin, no. 9. Hartford: Municipal Art Society of Hartford, n.d. 88 p.

Hoadley, Charles J. "A Case of Witchcraft in Hartford." CM 5 (1899): 551-61.

Holman, Mabel Cassine. "American Citizens in Embryo, The Good Will Club of Hartford." CM 10 (1906): 271-86.

Hoopes, Penrose R. "Notes on Some Colonial Cabinetmakers of Hartford." ANTIQUES 23 (May 1933): 171-72.

Kane, Patricia Ellen. "Joiners of Hartford." CHSB 35 (1970): 66-73.

Kuckro, Anne Crofoot. HARTFORD ARCHITECTURE. 2 vols. Hartford, Conn.: Hartford Architecture Conservancy, 1978-80.

Landau, Sarah Bradford. "The Colt Industrial Empire in Hartford." ANTIQUES 109 (March 1976): 568-79.

"List of Families in Hartford With Quantity of Grain in Possession of Each." (1670). CHS COLLECTIONS 21 (1924): 195-97.

Love, William DeLoss. THE COLONIAL HISTORY OF HARTFORD. Hartford: Hartford Conn. Printers, 1935. 369 p.

McCook, Frances A. "Main Street Now and Then." CANTIQUARIAN 37 (December 1975): 13-21.

_____. "Our Old Homestead." CANTIQUARIAN 23 (June 1971): 5-10.

McManus, James. "The History of Anaesthesia." CQ 1 (1895): 56-66.

"Mister Huntsinger and His College." CQ 2 (1896): 406-7.

"The Morse Business College." CM 5 (1899): 444-45.

Norton, Frederick Calvin. "Henry Barnard, Educator." CQ 4 (1898): 122-37.

Page, John F. "The Hartford State House." CANTIQUARIAN 18 (July 1966): 5-8.

Pawlowski, Robert E. HOW THE OTHER HALF LIVED: AN ETHNIC HISTORY OF THE OLD EAST SIDE AND SOUTH END OF HARTFORD. West Hartford, Conn.: Author, 1973. 91 p.

Phipps, Frances. "Connecticut's Printmakers: The Kelloggs of Hartford." CANTIQUARIAN 21 (June 1969): 19-26.

Porter, William Smith. HISTORICAL NOTICES OF CONNECTICUT. Hartford: E. Geer's Press, 1842.

Potwine, Elizabeth B. "Hartford in an Old Account Book." OLD TIME NEW ENGLAND 53 (Summer 1962): 17-22.

Randall, Herbert. "Beautiful Homes of Connecticut: Colonial Lines Embodied in Modern Architecture--Residence of George L. Chase, of Hartford, and its Artistic Treatment." CM 8 (1903): 395-400.

Ransom, David S. "Keney Tower in Hartford." CANTIQUARIAN 27 (July 1975): 5-9.

Rathbun, Julius G. "Backward Glances at Hartford." CM 5 (1899): 42-51, 99-112, 218-25, 339-45.

Smith, Anna L. Wetmore. "The Birth of a Commonwealth." CM 7 (1901): 162-68.

"The Smiths, Hartford Saddlers." CHSB 31 (1966): 76-83.

"Summertime in Hartford's Parks." CM 3 (1905): 461-69.

Twitchell, Willis I. HARTFORD IN HISTORY. Hartford: Plimpton Manufacturing Co., 1907. 268 p.

Warren, William Lamson. "The Talcott Settle." CANTIQUARIAN 29 (June 1977): 23-33.

Washington, D.C. National Archives and Records Service. U.S. Customs Passenger Lists. Hartford 1832. Immigration Passenger Lists February 1929-December 1943.

Weaver, Glen. THE HARTFORD ELECTRIC LIGHT COMPANY. Hartford, Conn.: Hartford Electric Light Co., 1969. 259 p.

_____. HARTFORD FOUNDATION FOR PUBLIC GIVING: THE FIRST FIFTY YEARS. Hartford, Conn.: The Foundation, 1975. 95 p. Index.

_____. THE HARTFORD STEAM BOILER INSPECTION AND INSURANCE COMPANY, 1866-1966. Hartford, Conn.: Hartford Steam Boiler Inspection and Insurance Co., 1966. 151 p.

_____. THE HISTORY OF TRINITY COLLEGE. Hartford, Conn.: Trinity College Press, 1967.

Wheeler, George. "Additions and Corrections for Families of Early Hartford, Connecticut, by Lucius Barnes Barbour." CN 13 (1980): 212.

White, B.S. HARTFORD IN 1912: STORY OF THE CAPITOL CITY PRESENT AND PROSPECTIVE. Hartford: Hartford Post, 1912. 275 p.

White, David O. "Amos Bull and that House that Would Not Die." CANTI-QUARIAN 25 (June 1973): 4-11.

Woodward, Patrick Henry. 1792-1892. ONE HUNDRED YEARS OF THE HARTFORD BANK, NOW THE HARTFORD NATIONAL BANK OF HARTFORD, CONNECTICUT. Hartford, Conn.: Case, Lockwood and Brainard Co., 1892. 176 p.

_____. STATUE OF COLONEL THOMAS KNOWLTON: CEREMONIES AT THE UNVEILING. Hartford, Conn.: Case, Lockwood and Brainard Co., 1895. 53 p.

Wright, George Edward. CROSSING THE CONNECTICUT. Hartford: Smith-Linsley Co., 1908. 159 p.

HARTLAND

HARTFORD COUNTY. Organized May 1761.

CEMETERY RECORDS AND CEMETERIES

NAME	ADDRESS	HALE NO.	CITATION
East Hartland Cemetery	Next to East Hartland Congregational Church	1	22:1-30
West Hartland Cemetery	West Hartland Baptist Church	2	22:31-41
Hartland Hollow Cemtery	Moved in 1941. The old site is now under water.	3	22:42-49
Tiffany Farm Cemetery	Moved to West Hartland Cemetery	4	22:50
Newton Cemetery	Moved to West Hartland Cemetery	5	22:51
Peters Cemetery	1 mile northwest of Hartland	6	22:52
Bates Cemetery	2 miles north of Riverton, near Colebrook line	7	22:53
Wright Cemetery	Near Granby town line	8	22:54
Searles Cemetery	Near Massachusetts State Line	9	22:55
Holcomb Cemetery	Near Massachusetts State Line	10	22:56
Coe Cemetery	Moved to West Hartland Cemetery	11	22:57-58
Miller Cemetery	Family Lot in woods	12	(no citation)

Index to Hale inscriptions: 22:59-72.

Hartford. CSL, Record Group 62. Burial Reports, 1901.

CENSUS RECORDS

Hartford. CSL, Record Group 29, Box 11. State Military Census, 1917-1918. List of Hartland men who registered in June 1917 and September 1918.

CHURCH RECORDS

FIRST CONGREGATIONAL CHURCH. Records, 1768-1913. (CSL). Marriages, 1768-1799. BAILEY 5:77-82. Records, 1768-1913. Index. (CSL, LDS 1448).

SECOND CONGREGATIONAL CHURCH. Minutes, 1779-1889. Vital Records, 1780-1890. (CSL, LDS 2228).

West Hartford, Second Society, Baptisms, Marriages and Deaths and Church Members, 1762-1901. (LDS 2228).

WEST HARTFORD CONGREGATIONAL CHURCH. Records, 1779-1899. (CSL, LDS 1448).

Gaines, David W. First and Second Congregational Church Vital Records, 1768-1922. (LDS 1756).

Keep, Helen Elizabeth. "Hartland, Conn., Church Records." NEHGR 60 (1906): 392-99; 61 (1907): 31-35.

Tiffany, Conell H. The First Congregational Church, 1731-1896; Second Congregational Church, 1781-1912. Records. (CSL, LDS 1755).

HISTORICAL SOCIETY

Hartland Historical Society, 06027.

LAND RECORDS

Land Records, 1760-1838. Proprietor's Records, 1734-1760. Index, 1734-1906. (LDS 1751 pt. 1-7).

Hartford. CSL, Record Group 62. Land Records, 1764-1901.

LIBRARY

Hartland Public Library, Center Street, 06091. (203) 379-4800.

MILITARY RECORDS

Hartford. CSL, Record Group 62. Military Records 1897-1910.

HARTLAND PATRIOTIC CELEBRATION JUNE 17, 1930. East Hartland: n.p., 1930. 18 p.

Jones, Edward Payson. LIST OF 334 (sic, 354) OFFICERS AND ENLISTED MEN IN THE REVOLUTIONARY ARMY FROM EAST HARTLAND, CONNECTICUT. Typescript. Winsted: Author, 1930. 79 p. (LDS 1755).

PROBATE RECORDS

Hartland Probate District, South Road, 06027. (203) 653-3073.

Organized 3 June 1836 from the Granby Probate District.

ON FILE AT THE CSL: Estate Papers, 1836-1921. Indexes, 1836-1921. Inventory Control Book, 1836-1921. Court Record Book, 1838-1859. Probate Records, 1836-1850. (LDS 1752).

TAX RECORDS

Hartford. CSL, Record Group 62. Tax Abstracts, Lists, etc. 1779-1909.

VITAL RECORDS

Town Clerk, Town Hall, South Road, 06027. (203) 653-3542.

The BARBOUR INDEX covers the years 1761-1848 and is based on the Lucius B. Barbour copy of HARTLAND vital records.

Vital Records. Typescript. 25 p. (CSL, LDS 1483).

PUBLISHED WORKS AND OTHER RECORDS

Account Book of Marsh Emmons, a Tailor. 1830-1858. (CSL).

Ransom, Stanley Austin. HISTORY OF HARTLAND. THE 69TH TOWN IN THE COLONY OF CONNECTICUT. Winsted: Dowd Printing Co., 1961. 189 p.

HARWINTON

LITCHFIELD COUNTY. Organized October 1737.

CEMETERY RECORDS AND CEMETERIES

NAME	ADDRESS	HALE NO.	CITATION
Old Cemetery	Second Street	1	22:1-5
South Cemetery	South Road	2	22:6-28
North Cemetery	North Road	3	22:29-35
West Cemetery	Cemetery Road	4	22:36-49
East or Jones Cemetery	Terryville Road	5	22:50-56
Scoville Cemetery	Wild Cat Hill Road	6	22:57
Haden Cemetery	Wild Cat Hill Road	7	22:58-59

Index to Hale inscriptions: 22:60-76.

Andrews, Frank DeWette. TOMBSTONE INSCRIPTIONS IN THE OLD BURYING GROUND AT HARWINTON, CONNECTICUT. Vineland, N.J.: Author, 1913. 21 p.

CHURCH RECORDS

FIRST CONGREGATIONAL CHURCH. Vital Records, 1791-1861. (CSL, LDS 1760). Index. (CSL, LDS 1448 pt. 15).

HISTORICAL SOCIETY

Harwinton Historical Society, Inc., Hungerford Memorial Library, Burlington Road, P.O. Box 84, 06790. (203) 482-5113.

LAND RECORDS

Land Records, 1738-1879. Index, 1738-1935. (LDS 1758 pt. 1-9). Proprietor's Records, 1729-1748. (LDS 1757).

LIBRARY

Hungerford Memorial Library, Burlington Road, 06790. (203) 482-5113.

NEWSPAPER

The PRELIMINARY CHECKLIST lists one newspaper for HARWINTON.

PROBATE RECORDS

Harwinton Probate District, Consolidated School Building, 06790. (203) 482-3852.

> Organized 27 May 1835 from the Litchfield Probate District.

> ON FILE AT THE CSL: Estate Papers, 1835-1924. Indexes, 1835-1924. Inventory Control Books, 1835-1924. Court Record Books, 1835-1854. Probate Records, 1835-1854. (LDS 1759).

VITAL RECORDS

Town Clerk, Town Hall, Hutchings Road, 06790. (203) 489-9212.

> The town clerk's earliest birth record is 6 February 1733, marriage record is 6 January 1736 and death record is 29 April 1742.

The BARBOUR INDEX covers the years 1737-1854 and is based on the James N. Arnold copy of HARWINTON vital records made in 1916.

Vital Records, 1738-1921. (LDS 1757).

PUBLISHED WORKS AND OTHER RECORDS

Bentley, Raymond George. HISTORY OF HARWINTON FROM THE TIME IT WAS SETTLED THROUGH THE MID 1960'S. Winsted: Dowd Printing Co., 1970. 166 p.

Chipman, Richard Manning. THE HISTORY OF HARWINTON, CONNECTICUT. Hartford: Williams, Wiley and Taylor, 1860. 152 p.

HARTLAND PATRIOTIC CELEBRATION. EAST HARTLAND, CONNECTICUT. JUNE 17, 1930. (Program: has a list of all who served in the military from colonial times)

Pond, Edgar LeRoy. THE TORIES OF CHIPPENY HILL; A BRIEF ACCOUNT OF THE LOYALISTS OF BRISTOL, PLYMOUTH AND HARWINTON, WHO FOUNDED ST. MATTHEWS CHURCH IN EAST PLYMOUTH IN 1791. New York: Grafton Press, 1909. 92 p.

HEBRON

TOLLAND COUNTY. Organized 26 May 1708. Towns organized from HEBRON include ANDOVER and MARLBOROUGH.

CEMETERY RECORDS AND CEMETERIES

NAME	ADDRESS	HALE NO.	CITATION
Old Cemetery	Andover Road	1	22:1-13
Gilead Cemetery	Gilead Hill, 1/4 mile South Gilead Church	2	22:14-39
Church of England Cemetery	Bolton Road	3	22:40-42
Jones Street Cemetery	Jones Street	4	22:43-49
Burroughs Cemetery	At Burroughs Hill, 2 miles west of Villa, 3/4 miles south of Hebron and Middletown Road	5	22:50-54
Gott Cemetery	3 miles south of Village near old Colchester Road	6	22:55-56
Sumner Cemetery	Bolton Road	7	22:57
Jones Cemetery	3 miles south of Village, near Gott Cemetery	8	22:58
St. Peter's Episcopal Cemetery	Rear of Church in center of Village	9	22:59-80
Stark Cemetery	Near Burroughs Hill Cemetery	10	22:81
Rollo Cemetery	1 grave on old road west from Godfrey Hill, south side of road	11	22:82

Index to Hale inscriptions: 22:83-105.

Bissell, Frederic Clarence. HEBRON CEMETERY INSCRIPTIONS. N.p., n.d.

CENSUS RECORDS

Printed list of Persons over 70 and living in Hebron. (LDS 1742).

CHURCH RECORDS

CONGREGATIONAL CHURCH. Minutes, 1787-1915. (CSL, LDS 1742).

GILEAD CONGREGATIONAL CHURCH. Vital Records, 1752-1943. (CSL, LDS 1742. Index. (CSL, LDS 1448).

GILEAD ECCLESIASTICAL SOCIETY. Minutes, 1748-1941. (CSL, LDS 1743).

ST. PETER EPISCOPAL CHURCH. Minutes, 1787-1853. Vital Records, 1822-1905. (CSL, LDS 1744).

SECOND CONGREGATIONAL CHURCH. Gilead. Marriages, 1752-1797. BAILEY 3:91-97.

"Hebron, Connecticut-Gilead Congregational Church--Baptisms in the year 1752-Elijah Lathrup, Pastor." ANCESTRAL NOTES FROM CHEDWATO 15 (1968): 84-88.

"Some Records from the Gilead Congregational Church at Harwinton, Connecticut. Vol. 1 (1752)." ANCESTRAL NOTES FROM CHEDWATO 13 (1966): 75-77.

Warner, Will J. CONNECTICUT PRIVATE RECORDS, HEBRON BAPTISMS-MARRIAGES-DEATHS 1752-1876. Typescript. Hartford: CSL, 1931. 72 p.

HISTORICAL SOCIETY

Hebron Historical Society, 06248.

LAND RECORDS

Land Records, 1713-1851. Index 1713-1856. (LDS 1740 pt. 1-10).

LIBRARY

Douglas Library Association, Route 66, 06248. (203) 228-9312.

PROBATE RECORDS

Hebron Probate District, Town Office Building, Route 85, Box 167, 06248.
(203) 228-3832.

> Organized May 1789 from the East Haddam, East Windsor and Windsor
> Probate Districts. Probate districts organized from the Hebron Probate
> District include the Andover and Coventry Probate Districts.
>
> ON FILE AT THE CSL: Estate Papers, 1851-1897 (papers from
> 1789-27 June 1851 are at the Andover Probate District). Indexes,
> 1851-1897. Inventory Control Book, 1851-1897. Court Record Books,
> 1789-1851. Probate Records, 1789-1851. (LDS 1741 pt. 1-10).

TAX RECORDS

Hartford. CSL, Record Group 62. Tax Lists 1797, 1814-1824, 1828.

VITAL RECORDS

Town Clerk, Town Office Building, Route 8, P.O. Box 156, 06248. (203) 228-9406.

Cemetery, Church Records, etc., of Connecticut. Marriages 1752-1797. N.p.,
n.d. 10 p. (LDS 1444).

The BARBOUR INDEX covers the years 1708-1854 and is based on the Mrs.
Anne C. Gilbert copy of HEBRON vital records made in 1921.

VOTER RECORDS

Hartford. CSL, Record Group 62. Voter Lists, 1859-1873, 1906-1907.

PUBLISHED WORKS AND OTHER RECORDS

Bissell, Frederic Clarence. HEBRON, CONNECTICUT BICENTENNIAL AUGUST
23D TO 25TH, 1908. AN ACCOUNT OF THE CELEBRATION OF THE TWO HUN-
DREDTH ANNIVERSARY OF THE INCORPORATION OF THE TOWN, 1708-1908.
Hebron, Conn.: Bicentennial Committee, 1910. 77 p.

Ricketts, Rowland J. "Hebron, Connecticut: The Emergence of a Connecticut
Community 1704-1748." Master's thesis, Trinity College, 1971.

Siburn, John. OUR TOWN'S HERITAGE 1708-1958, HEBRON, CONNECTICUT.
Hebron: Douglas Library of Hebron, 1975. 199 p.

KENT

LITCHFIELD COUNTY. Organized October 1739. Towns organized from KENT include WARREN and WASHINGTON.

CEMETERY RECORDS AND CEMETERIES

NAME	ADDRESS	HALE NO.	CITATION
Congregational Church Cemetery	Kent Village	1	23:1-20
St. Andrews Church Cemetery	Kent Village	2	23:21-43
Good Hill Cemetery	Route 7	3	23:44-71
Skiff Mountain Cemetery	Skill Mountain Road	4	23:72-75
Indian Reservation Cemetery	Schaghtikoke	5	23:76
Bull's Bridge Cemetery	Bull's Bridge	6	23:77-86
Kent Hollow Cemetery	Kent Hollow-1 1/4 mile west of Lake Waramaug	7	23:87-97
Morehouse Cemetery	Kent Mountain	8	23:98
Fanton Cemetery	1 mile east of South Kent	9	23:99
Alder City Cemetery	1 grave only, John Rodgers, Civil War Veteran	10	23:100-101

Index to Hale inscriptions: 23:83-105.

BURYING GROUNDS OF SHARON, CONNECTICUT. Amenia, N.Y.: Walsh, Griffon and Horpradt Printers, 1903. 248 p. (Inscriptions from Skiff Mountain Cemetery, pp. 99-101). (LDS 4039).

CHURCH RECORDS

CONGREGATIONAL CHURCH. Vital Records, 1739-1915. (CSL, LDS 1798). Records. Index. 1741-1859. (CSL, LDS 1448). Marriages, 1741-1757. BAILEY 5:19-20.

HISTORICAL SOCIETY

Kent Historical Society, Inc., 06757.

LAND RECORDS

Land Records, 1735-1856. Index, 1735-1921. (LDS 1796 pt. 1-12).

Proprietor's Records, 1758-1802. (LDS 1795).

Grant, Charles S. "Land Speculation and the Settlement of Kent, 1738-1760." NEQ 28 (1955): 51-71.

"Original Proprietary Shares (Kent, 1738)." DAR MAGAZINE 97 (1963): 152-53, 215-16.

LIBRARY

Kent Library Association, Main Street, P.O. Box 127, 06757. (203) 927-3761.

NEWSPAPER

KENT GOOD TIMES DISPATCH. Weekly. Bluff Road, 06757. (203) 922-3776.

The PRELIMINARY CHECKLIST lists one newspaper for KENT.

PROBATE RECORDS

Kent Probate District, Town Hall, South Main Street, Box 277, 06757. (203) 927-3729.

> Organized 26 May 1831 from the New Milford Probate District.

> ON FILE AT THE CSL: Estate Papers, 1831-1928. Indexes, 1831-1928. Inventory Control Book, 1831-1928. Court Record Book, 1837-1858.

Probate Records, 1837-1858, 1847-1858. (LDS 1797).

TAX RECORDS

Love, Helen D. "Tax List, Kent, Connecticut 1744." TAG 11 (1934): 57-59.

VITAL RECORDS

Town Clerk, Town Hall, R.F.D. Box M5, South Main Street, 06757. (203) 927-3433.

The BARBOUR INDEX covers the years 1739-1852 and is based on the James N. Arnold copy of KENT vital records made in 1915.

PUBLISHED WORKS AND OTHER RECORDS

Atwater, Francis. HISTORY OF KENT, CONNECTICUT, INCLUDING BIO-GRAPHICAL SKETCHES OF MANY OF ITS PRESENT OR FORMER INHABITANTS. Meriden: Journal Publishing Co., 1897. 176 p.

Cables, Myron E. "Lake Waramaug." CQ 3 (1897): 227-34.

Davis, Ann Soper. KENT 1776: A CONNECTICUT TOWN TWO CENTURIES AGO. Kent: Bicentennial Commission, 1976. 112 p.

Goodenough, G.F. A GOSSIP ABOUT A COUNTRY PARISH OF THE HILLS AND ITS PEOPLE. Amenia, N.Y.: Times Press, 1900. 129 p.

Grant, Charles S. DEMOCRACY IN THE CONNECTICUT FRONTIER TOWN OF KENT. Columbia Studies in History, Economics and Public Law, no. 601. New York: Columbia University, 1961. 227 p.

Seymour, Maker. A LAWYER OF KENT: BARZILLA SLOSSON AND HIS ACCOUNT BOOKS 1794-1812. Connecticut Tercentenary Publishing, no. 47. New Haven: Yale University Press, 1935. 35 p.

KILLINGLY

WINDHAM COUNTY. Organized May 1708. Towns organized from KILLINGLY include PUTNAM and THOMPSON.

CEMETERY RECORDS AND CEMETERIES

NAME	ADDRESS	HALE NO.	CITATION
Babbitt Cemetery	Northeast past of town on Putnam line	1	23:1-2
Covell Cemetery	Northeast part of town	*2	23:3-4
Harrington Cemetery	Northeast part of town	3	23:5
Pasto-Spencer Cemetery	Northeast part of town	*4	23:6
Bartlett Cemetery	Northeast part of town	5	23:7
Adams-Smith Cemetery	North part of town	*6	23:8
Old Chestnut Hill Cemetery (Bateman Cemetery)	Chestnut Hill	*7	23:9-11
Wescott Cemetery	Chestnut Hill	*8	23:12
Durfee Cemetery	Chestnut Hill	9	23:13
Burgess Cemetery #1	East of East Killingly	10	23:14
Mathewson Cemetery	East of East Killingly	*11	23:15
Alvah Chase Cemetery	East of East Killingly	12	23:16
Simmons Cemetery	East of East Killingly	13	23:17A
Tucker Cemetery	Near East Killingly	*14	23:17B
Bartlett Cemetery #1	East Killingly	*15	23:18-33A
Smith-Mason Cemetery	East Killingly	*16	23:33B-34
Angell Cemetery	South of East Killingly	*17	23:35

NAME	ADDRESS	HALE NO.	CITATION
Henry Cemetery	South of East Killingly	*18	23:36
Chase Cemetery #1	South of East Killingly	*19	23:37
Aldrich Cemetery	South of East Killingly	20	23:38
Sparks Cemetery	South of East Killingly near Rhode Island line	*21	23:39
Smith-Aldrich Cemetery	South of East Killingly near Rhode Island line	*22	23:40-41
Fuller Cemetery	East part of town on Rhode Island line	23	23:42
Smith Cemetery	East part of town near Rhode Island line	*24	23:43
Slater Cemetery #1	East part of town near Rhode Island line	25	23:44-45
Fiske Cemetery	East of South Killingly near Rhode Island line	*26	23:46
Burgess Cemetery #2	East of South Killingly on Rhode Island line	27	23:47
Hall Cemetery	East of South Killingly on Rhode Island line	28	23:48
Old South Killingly Cemetery	South Killingly	*29	23:49-62
Young Cemetery #1	North of South Killingly	30	23:63
Mashentuck Cemetery #1	Mashentuck	*31	23:64-65
Mashentuck Cemetery #2	Mashentuck	*32	23:66
Burlingame Cemetery	North of Mashentuck	33	23:67
Slater Cemetery #2	East of Killingly Center	*34	23:68
Cleveland Cemetery	East of Killingly Center	*35	23:69
Chase Cemetery	East of Killingly Center	*36	23:70-72
Warren Cemetery	East of Killingly Center	37	23:73
Brainard Cemetery	East of Killingly Center	*38	23:74
Breakneck Cemetery	Breakneck Hill	*39	23:75
Mitchell Cemetery	Near Breakneck Hill	*40	23:76
Mathews Cemetery	Near Breakneck Hill	*41	23:77
Chase-Haines Cemetery	North part of town	42	23:78
Whitmore Cemetery	Attawangan	*43	23:79

NAME	ADDRESS	HALE NO.	CITATION
St. Joseph Church Cemetery	U.S. 55	*44	23:80-97
Cross Roads Cemetery	Near Dayville	*45	23:98-101
Old Westfield Cemetery	Danielson	*46	23:102-88
St. James Church Cemetery	Danielson	*47	23:189-220
Holy Cross Cemetery	U.S. 55	*48	23:221-31
Hutchins Street Cemetery	Danielson	*49	23:232
Hutchins-Franklin Street Cemetery	Danielson	*50	23:233-34
Young Cemetery #2	East of Killingly Center	51	23:235
Town Farm Cemetery	Dayville	52	23:236
High Street Cemetery	Dayville	*53	23:237-58
Fairmont Cemetery	On Cherry Farm south of South Killingly	54	23:259
New Westfield Cemetery	Danielson	*55	23:260-87
New South Killingly Cemetery	South Killingly	*56	23:288-97
Mowry Cemetery	East of East Killingly	57	23:298
Brown Cemetery	East of East Killingly	23	23:299
O'Brien Cemetery	Northeast part of town near Rhode Island line	*59	23:300
Benajah Mathers Cemetery	North part of town	*60	23:301
Allen Cemetery	West of Dayville	*61	23:302
Pray Cemetery	Near Chestnut Hill	62	23:303
Shippee Cemetery	South of East Killingly	*63	23:304
Dexter-Adams Cemetery	South of East Killingly	64	23:305
Gilbert-Baker Cemetery	East part of town near Rhode Island line	65	23:306
Fairmont Cemetery	South of South Killingly	*66	23:307
Private Cemetery	East of Killingly Center	67	23:308
Law-Bennett Cemetery	3/4 mile east of Ballouville Post Office	68	23:309-10
Field stones only	North Alexander Lake, Dunn farm	69	(no citation)

NAME	ADDRESS	HALE NO.	CITATION
Old Cemetery	Field Stones		(no citation)

Soldiers buried in cemeteries are marked with an (*) asterisk.

Index to Hale inscriptions: 23:311-86.

Barbour, Lucius Barnes. "Connecticut Cemetery Inscriptions." NEHGR 100 (1946): 328-330.

Eardeley, William A.D. CONNECTICUT CEMETERIES. Vols. 2 and 7. Brooklyn, N.Y.: Author, 1916. (LDS 899, 935).

"Headstones - Killingly - Hale." CN 13 (1980): 37-40, 215-16.

CHURCH RECORDS

CONGREGATIONAL CHURCH RECORDS. 1746-1835. (Copied by Mrs. J.L. Raymond). (CSL, LDS 1802).

SOUTH CONGREGATIONAL CHURCH. Minutes, 1769-1838. Vital Records. (CSL, LDS 1972).

SOUTH KILLINGLY CONGREGATIONAL CHURCH. Minutes, 1790-1858. (CSL, LDS 2106).

WESTFIELD CONGREGATIONAL CHURCH. Minutes, 1805-1936. Vital Records, 1801-1930. (CSL, LDS 1801 pt. 102).

"Killingly Church Records, The Old Church on Putnam Heights." THE PATRIOT (newspaper). N.d.

"Killingly, Connecticut Church Records." PUTNAM'S MONTHLY HISTORICAL MAGAZINE 3 (1907): 224-27, 259-60, 295-96; 4 (1908): 26-27, 77-80, 207-8; 5 (1908): 74-78, 174-78; 7 (1910): 72-76.

Talcott, Mary Kingsbury. "Records of Breakneck Hill Congregational Church, Killingly, Connecticut." NEHGR 66 (1912): 337-40.

_____. "Records of the Church in South Killingly, Connecticut." NEHGR 66 (1912): 129-41.

HISTORICAL SOCIETY

Killingly Historical Society, 06239.

LAND RECORDS

Land Records, 1709-1851. Index, 1709-1908. (LDS 1800 pt. 1-7).

LIBRARY

Bugbee Memorial Library, 06239. (203) 774-9429.

NEWSPAPERS

WINDHAM COUNTY TRANSCRIPT. Weekly. 23 Center Street, 06239.

The PRELIMINARY CHECKLIST lists ten newspapers for KILLINGLY.

PROBATE RECORDS

Killingly Probate District, Town Hall, 127 Main Street, 06239. (203) 774-8601.

> Organized 4 June 1830 from Plainfield and Pomfret Probate District.

> ON FILE AT THE CSL: Estate Papers, 1845-1945. (The records from 1830-1845 were burned, according to a note in the inventory control book). Indexes, 1845-1914. Inventory Control Book, 1845-1914. Court Record Books, 1849-1854.

Probate records, 1849-1854. (LDS 1799).

SCHOOL RECORDS

HISTORY OF EDUCATION, TOWN OF KILLINGLY, 1650-1976. Killingly, Conn.: Killingly Historical Society, 1976. 52 p.

VITAL RECORDS

Town Clerk, Town Hall, 127 Main Street, P.O. Box 707, 06239. (203) 774-2333.

Chamberlain, George Walter. "Killingly (Conn.) Marriages." NEHGR 69 (1915): 90.

The BARBOUR INDEX covers the years 1708-1850 and is based on the James N. Arnold copy of KILLINGLY vital records made in 1908.

PUBLISHED WORKS AND OTHER RECORDS

Arnold, Henry Vernon. THE MAKING OF DANIELSON. AN OUTLINE HIS-
TORY OF THE BOROUGH OF DANIELSON, CONNECTICUT. Larimore,
N.D.: Author, 1905. 228 p.

Larned, Ellen D. "Three Killingly Boys." CQ 3 (1897): 221-25.

Weaver, Margaret M., et al. MILES OF MILLSTREAMS; A CHRONICLE OF
KILLINGLY. Killingly: American Revolution Bicentennial Commission of
Killingly, 1976. 242 p. Index.

KILLINGWORTH

MIDDLESEX COUNTY. Organized May 1667. Towns organized from KILLING-
WORTH include CLINTON.

CEMETERY RECORDS AND CEMETERIES

NAME	ADDRESS	HALE NO.	CITATION
Old Cemetery	West part of town	1	23:1-6
Union Cemetery	U.S. 51	2	23:7-25
New South West Cemetery	Southwest part of town	3	23:26
Nettleton Cemetery	Parker Hill District, north-east part of town	4	23:27-34
Evergreen Cemetery	U.S. 51	5	23:35-47
Pine Orchard Cemetery	U.S. 52	6	23:48-49
Stone House Cemetery	Country Road	7	23:50-57
Old South West Cemetery	U.S. 51	8	23:58-66
Lane Cemetery	U.S. 52	9	23:67-79
Parker Hill Cemetery	Parker Hill Road		(no citation)

Index to Hale inscriptions: 23:70-85.

CHURCH RECORDS

CONGREGATIONAL CHURCH. Minutes, 1735-1893. Vital Records, 1737-
1851. Index, 1735-1893. (CSL, LDS 1792, and LDS 1448 p. 16).

EMMANUEL EPISCOPAL CHURCH. Vital Records, 1800-1883. (CSL, LDS
1793).

SECOND CONGREGATIONAL CHURCH. Marriages, 1739-1799. BAILEY 3:
30-42.

Second Parish. Killingworth. 1739-1839. (NYGBS, LDS 1789).

"Funerals at North Killingworth. (1809-1853)." CHSB 7 (January 1941): 12-14.

Hartford. CSL, Record Group 62. Second Society Tax List, 1815-1817.

"Marriages at North Killingworth. (1808-1830)." CHSB 7 (January 1941): 14-15.

"Register of Baptisms in Union Church in North Killingworth. (1807-1836)." CHSB 7 (January 1941): 5-8.

HISTORICAL SOCIETY

Killingworth Historical Society, 06417.

LAND RECORDS

Land Records, 1664-1854. Index, 1664-1947. (LDS 1790 pt. 1-15).

Jacobus, Donald Lines. "Killingworth (Conn.) Land Records." TAG 22 (1945-46): 113-14.

LIBRARY

Killingworth Library, Routes 80 and 81, P.O. Box 41, 06417. (203) 663-2000.

PROBATE RECORDS

Killingworth Probate District, Town Office Building, Route 81, 06417 (203) 663-2505.

> Organized 3 June 1834 from the Saybrook Probate District (see under CHESTER.)

> Probate districts organized from the Killingworth Probate District include the Clinton Probate District.

> From 28 May 1838 to 1 June 1842 it was known as the Clinton Probate District.

> ON FILE AT THE CSL: Estate Papers, 1834-1921. Indexes, 1834-1921. Inventory Control Book, 1834-1921. Court Record Books, 1834-1852.

Probate Records, 1834–1852. (LDS 1791).

TAX RECORDS

Hartford. CSL, Record Group 62. Tax Lists, 1777–1785, 1831–1932.

VITAL RECORDS

Town Clerk, Town Office Building, Route 81, 06417. (203) 663-1616.
> The town clerk's earliest birth and marriage records are 1665 and death record is 1669.

The BARBOUR INDEX covers the years 1667–1850 and is based on the James N. Arnold copy of KILLINGWORTH vital records made in 1914.

"Connecticut Marriages Before 1750 (Barbour)--Town of Killingworth." CN 10 (1977): 405-6, 584-89; 11 (1978): 208-13, 388-91.

Jacobus, Donald Lines. "Killingworth Vital Records in Land Records, Volume I." TAG 12 (1935): 35-50; 23 (1946): 113-14.

Rumsey, Jean. "Errors in the Barbour Collection." CN 11 (1978): 226-27, 379.

Whitman, Roger Bradbury. "Vital Records of Genealogical interest abstracted from the diaries of Josiah Bishop Andrews of Connecticut, New York and New Jersey." NYGBR 57 (1926): 236-39.

PUBLISHED WORKS AND OTHER RECORDS

Lentry, Thomas, et al. PICTORIAL HISTORY OF KILLINGWORTH. Killingworth: Killingworth Historical Society, 1976.

Notebooks of Deacon Abraham Pierson, 1787–1802. (CSL, LDS 1794).

LEBANON

NEW LONDON COUNTY. Organized October 1700. Towns organized from LEBANON include COLUMBIA.

CEMETERY RECORDS AND CEMETERIES

NAME	ADDRESS	HALE NO.	CITATION
Liberty Hill Cemetery	On Trumbull Highway, near Liberty Hill	1	23:1-10
Exeter Cemetery	Exeter District	2	23:11-33
Lebanon Center Cemetery	Exeter Road	3	23:34-60.
Old Cemetery	3/4 miles east of Lebanon Street	4	23:61-87
New South Cemetery	Southwest of Lebanon Street	5	23:88-92
Goshen Cemetery	U.S. 53	6	23:93-100 24:101-8
Geer Cemetery	Southwest part of town	7	24:109
Scoville-Buckingham Cemetery	Lebanon Village	8	24:110-12
Segar Cemetery	(not located)	9	24:113
Greenman Cemetery	Northeast part of town	10	24:114
Loomis Cemetery	Cheese Factory Hill	11	24:115
Bliss Cemetery	William Gorsky farm	12	24:116
Mackall Cemetery	On Waterman farm	13	24:117
Fowler Cemetery	Andrew Jello farm	14	24:118
Young Cemetery	Albert O. Schwester farm	15	24:119
Webster Cemetery	Lone grave 20 feet from road	16	24:120
Lone soldier grave	Opposite Lebanon Center	17	24:121

Index to Hale inscriptions: 24:122-55.

Dewey, Louis Marinus. "Inscriptions from Old Cemeteries in Connecticut." NEHGR 60 (1906): 370.

Eno, Joel Nelson. "Connecticut Cemetery Inscriptions." NEHGR 74 (1920): 53-67, 108-14; 98 (1944): 300-303.

"Headstones." CN 13 (1980): 216-20, 394-99.

Pearce, Albert E. THE TURNBULL CEMETERY, LEBANON, CONNECTICUT. Lebanon: Lebanon Historical Society, 1978. 15 p.

Woodward, Ashbel. "Ancient Grave Yard at Lebanon, Connecticut." NEHGR 12 (1858): 55-63.

CHURCH RECORDS

EXETER CONGREGATIONAL CHURCH. Minutes, 1784-1887. Vital Records, 1709-1914. (CSL, LDS 1816).

FIRST CONGREGATIONAL CHURCH. Minutes, 1721-1839. Vital Records, 1700-1804. Alphabetical list of members, 1700-1873. (CSL, LDS 1814). Marriages, 1712-1775. BAILEY 2:38-50.

GOSHEN CONGREGATIONAL CHURCH. Minutes, 1728-1851. Vital Records, 1729-1895. (CSL, LDS 1816).

ORANGE BAPTIST CHURCH. Minutes, 1818-1881. (CSL, LDS 1815).

SECOND CONGREGATIONAL CHURCH. Marriages, 1730-1799. BAILEY 5:41-50.

Champe, Howard C. "The Old Meeting House at Lebanon, Connecticut." OLD-TIME NEW ENGLAND 30 (January 1940): 82-85.

"Church Records. Lebanon, Connecticut-Goshen Congregational Church." (1729-1782). ANCESTRAL NOTES FROM CHEDWATO 15 (1968): 13-15, 109-10.

"Record of the First Congregational Church in Lebanon December 1711-1714." CHSB 1 (1935): 3-6.

HISTORICAL SOCIETY

Lebanon Historical Society, 06249.

LAND RECORDS

Land Records, 1685-1869. Index, 1685-1788. (LDS 1812 pt. 1-16).

LIBRARY

Jonathan Trumbull Library. Route 207, 06249. (203) 642-7763.

PROBATE RECORDS

Lebanon Probate District, Town Hall, Route 207, 06249. (203) 642-7429.

> Organized 2 June 1826 from the Windham Probate District. The part of the parish of ANDOVER, belonging to LEBANON, became part of HEBRON from the May session, 1790, until about 1820. Since then it has been in LEBANON.

> ON FILE AT THE CSL: Estate Papers, 1826-1922. Indexes, 1826-1922. Inventory Control Books, 1826-1922. Court Record Books, 1826-1853.

Probate Records, 1826-1853. (LDS 1813).

SCHOOL RECORDS

Hartford. CSL, Record Group 62. School Lists, 1820-1850, 1856. District Returns, 1850-1885.

"List of pupils in various school districts 1820-1864 of Bozrah, Brooklyn, Andover, Lebanon and Bolton." (CSL, LDS 1482).

TAX RECORDS

Hartford. CSL, Record Group 62. Lists and other records, 1790-1928.

VITAL RECORDS

Town Clerk, Town Hall, Route 207, 06249. (203) 642-7319.

"Connecticut Marriages Before 1750 (Barbour)--Town of Lebanon." CN 11 (1978-79): 391-93, 576-81; 12 (1979): 22-29, 210-217, 400-405.

Kingsley, Walter G. Vital Records 1638-1883 (including Baptisms 1715-1813, deaths 1702-1888 and an index to marriages 1671-1883). (LDS 1817).

Thomas, Milton Halsey. "Marriages by Peleg Thomas (Justice of the Peace) of Lebanon, Connecticut." NEHGR 91 (1937): 196-98.

The BARBOUR INDEX covers the years 1700-1854 and is based on the James N. Arnold copy of LEBANON vital records made in 1912.

PUBLISHED WORKS AND OTHER RECORDS

"The Celebration at Lebanon." CQ 2 (1896): 306.

Dewey, Sherman. "Account of a Hail Storm, which Fell on Part of the Towns of Lebanon, Bozrah, and Franklin, on the 15th of July, 1799." CM 5 (1899): 647-48.

EARLY LEBANON. AN HISTORICAL ADDRESS DELIVERED IN LEBANON, CONNECTICUT, BY REQUEST ON THE NATIONAL CENTENNIAL, JULY 4, 1876 BY REV. ORLO D. HIME, PASTOR OF THE FIRST CHURCH. WITH AN APPENDIX OF HISTORICAL NOTES, BY NATHANIEL H. MORGEN OF HART- FORD, CONNECTICUT. Hartford: Case, Lockwood and Brainard Co., 1880. 176 p. (LDS 476,933).

HISTORIC LEBANON, HIGHLIGHTS OF AN HISTORIC TOWN. Lebanon: First Congregational Church, 1950. 79 p.

Hooker, Mrs. Martha Williams. "Booklovers of 1738--One of the First Libraries in America." CM 10 (1906): 715-23.

Huntington, Mary Clarke. "Early Lebanon." CQ 2 (1896): 247-58.

Stark, Bruce Puriaton. "Freemanship in Lebanon, Connecticut: A Case Study." CONNECTICUT HISTORY 15 (1975): 27-48.

_____. "Lebanon, Connecticut: a Study of Society and Politics in the Eigh- teenth Century." Ph.D. dissertation, University of Connecticut, 1970. 524 p.

Warren, William Lamson. ISAAC FITCH OF LEBANON, CONNECTICUT MASTER JOINER 1734-1791. Hartford: Antiquarian and Landmark Society, 1978. 74 p.

_____. "Isaac Fitch of Lebanon Master Joiner 1734-1791." CANTIQUARIAN 28 (June 1976): 3-50; 28 (December 1976): 13-26.

_____. "Isaac Fitch Revisited (as cabinetmaker)." CANTIQUARIAN 31 (June 1979): 19-27.

LEDYARD

NEW LONDON COUNTY. Organized May 1836 from GROTON.

CEMETERY RECORDS AND CEMETERIES

NAME	ADDRESS	HALE NO.	CITATION
Allen Cemetery	Sandy Hollow Road	1	24:1
Allyn's Point Cemetery	At Allyn's Point, Thames River	2	24:1-3
B.T. Avery Cemetery	1 mile south of Avery Hill	3	24:3-7
Fanning Cemetery	1/2 mile south of Long Pond U.S. 52	4	24:7
Bill Cemetery	1 mile north of Ledyard Center	5	24:7-8
Brown Cemetery	R.F.D. 7	6	24:8-11
Gales Ferry Cemetery	At Gales Ferry, Military Highway	7	24:11-32
Bolles Cemetery	Military Highway	8	24:32
Lamb Town Cemetery	Lamb Town Road	9	24:33-35
Gallup Hill Cemetery	Gallup Hill Road	10	24:35-39
Lamb Cemetery	Stones and bodies removed to Groton	11	24:39
Center Cemetery	Groton Road	12	24:39-47
Maintown Cemetery	Near Lantern Hill Pond	13	24:48
Morgan Cemetery #1	Sandy Hollow Road	14	24:48-51
Morgan Cemetery #2	Sand Hollow	15	24:52
Morgan Cemetery #3	North of Morgan Pond	16	24:52-53

NAME	ADDRESS	HALE NO.	CITATION
Myers or Williams Cemetery	North part of town	17	24:53-55
Newton Cemetery	Whalehead Road	18	24:55-56
Quakertown Cemetery #2	Quakertown Road	19	24:56-61
Roach Cemetery	Sandy Hollow Road	20	24:61
Spicer Cemetery	Col. Ledyard Highway	21	24:61-63
Stoddard Cemetery	On bank of Thames River, 1 mile north of Allyn's Point Cemetery	22	24:63-64
Stoddard Cemetery	At Stoddard Hill	23	24:64
Williams Cemetery #1	In woods, opposite Morgan Pond	24	24:65
Williams Cemetery #2	Same as Myers or Williams Cemetery #17	25	24:65
Williams Cemetery	East part of town	26	24:65-66
Avery Cemetery	Near Norwich Road	27	24:66
Avery Hill Cemetery	Avery Hill	28	24:67-68
Eldredge Cemetery	Near Old Mystic	29	24:68-69
Lee Cemetery	1/2 mile west of Brown Cemetery RD 7	30	24:69
Geer Cemetery	1 mile north of Center	31	24:69-70
Gray Cemetery	1/2 mile north of Brown Cemetery	32	24:70
Holdredge Cemetery	Near Maintown Cemetery	33	24:70
Hallet Cemetery	North part of town	34	24:71
Hewitt Cemetery	East part of town	35	24:72
Hurlbut Cemetery	Near Gales Ferry	36	24:72-73
Kate Swamp	Near Gray Cemetery (not found)	37	24:73
Indian (Mashantucket) Cemetery	Near Long Pond and Fanning Road	38	24:73
Indian Cemetery	Near Gales Ferry	39	24:73
Woodbridge Cemetery	Southeast part of Ledyard	40	24:74
Lester Cemetery	Vinegar Hill near Royal Oak Tree	41	24:74
Quakertown Cemetery #2	Next to Quakertown #1 Cemetery	42	24:74-75

NAME	ADDRESS	HALE NO.	CITATION
Bailey Cemetery	In field, 1 mile south of Center-U.S. 52	43	24:75
Private Cemetery	In field near Bailey Cemetery	44	24:75
Thomas Main Cemetery	Near upper end of Long Pond	45	24:75-76
Rogerene Cemetery	In woods near the Woodbridge Cemetery	46	(no citation)
Lamb Cemetery (field stones only)	On Austin Lamb's farm	47	(no citation)
Rose Hill Cemetery (field stones only)	Opposite Calvin Main's old house	48	(no citation)
Single Grave	In swamp near Calvin Main's house	49	(no citation)
McGuire Cemetery	North of Quakertown Cemetery	50	(no citation)
Chapman Cemetery	Near Stoddard's wharf	51	(no citation)
Allyn Cemetery	2 miles north of Ledyard Center	52	(no citation)
Bellows Cemetery	Near Allyn no. 52 Cemetery		(no citation)
Williams Cemetery #4	On Town farm		(no citation)

Index to Hale inscriptions: 24:87-106.

List of Soldiers buried in the Hale List of Cemeteries 24:77-86, Index 24:107-8.

"Inscriptions at Allyn's Point, the terminus of the Worcester and Norwich Railroad, on the east side of the River Thames, seven miles below Norwich, Connecticut." NEHGR 3 (1849): 125.

Ledyard Cemetery Committee. CEMETERIES AND BURIALS IN THE TOWN OF LEDYARD INCLUDING DECEASED VETERANS OF ALL WARS. Ledyard: Town of Ledyard, 1965. 66 p.

CHURCH RECORDS

FIRST CONGREGATIONAL CHURCH. Vital Records, 1810-1897. Index. (CSL, LDS 1820).

CATALOG OF THE DEATHS IN THE SECOND SOCIETY OF GROTON FROM THE YEAR 1790 TO 1815. Windham: Ansil Brown, 1815. 48 p.

HISTORICAL SOCIETIES

Ledyard Historical Society, 06339.

Nathan Lester House, Long Cove and Vinegar Hill Roads, 06339. (203) 464-0266.

LAND RECORDS

Land Records, 1834-1853. (LDS 1819 pt. 1-2).

LIBRARIES

Ledyard Public Library, Col. Ledyard Highway, P.O. Box 225, 06339. (203) 464-9912.

Gales Ferry Library, Hurlburt Road, 06339. (203) 464-6943.

PROBATE RECORDS

Ledyard Probate Districts, Town Hall, Ledyard Center, Box 38, 06339. (203) 464-9550.

> Organized 6 June 1837 from the Stonington Probate District. Ledyard records from May 1666 to October 1766 are at the New London Probate District. From October 1766 to 6 June 1837, they are at the Stonington Probate District.

> ON FILE AT THE CSL: Estate Papers, 1837-1934. Indexes, 1837-1934. Inventory Control Book, 1837-1934. Court Record Books, 1837-1857.

Probate Records, 1837-1857. (LDS 1818).

SCHOOL RECORDS

Hartford. CSL, Record Group 62. District 3 Register 1839-1840; District 13 Register 1856-1858.

VITAL RECORDS

Town Clerk, Town Hall, Ledyard Center, 06339.   (203) 464-8140.

The BARBOUR INDEX covers the years 1836-1855 and is based on the James N. Arnold copy of LEDYARD vital records made in 1911.

"List of some of the Vital Records of Ledyard, Connecticut."   (1801-1858). CHSB   3 (April 1937):   3-8; 4 (July 1938):   30-32; 5 (January 1939):   10; 6 (January 1940):   11-13.

PUBLISHED WORKS AND OTHER RECORDS

Avery, John. HISTORY OF THE TOWN OF LEDYARD. 1650-1900. Nor-wich: Bulletin Co., 1901. 334 p. Index.

Gallup, Mrs. Herbert W.   A SUPPLEMENTARY INDEX OF JOHN AVERY'S HISTORY OF LEDYARD, CONNECTICUT 1650-1900. Typescript. Norwich: Author, 1929. 29 p.

HISTORIC LEDYARD: VOL. 1: GAIL FERRY VILLAGE. Ledyard: Ledyard Historic District Commission, 1976.   136 p.

Ledyard Historic District Commission. INDEX, TOWN MEETING RECORDS OF LEDYARD, CONNECTICUT, 1836-1891. Ledyard, Conn.: 1979. 77 p.

LISBON

NEW LONDON COUNTY. Organized May 1786 from NORWICH. Towns organized from LISBON include SPRAGUE.

CEMETERY RECORDS AND CEMETERIES

NAME	ADDRESS	HALE NO.	CITATION
Ames Cemetery	Near Taftville	1	24:1-16
Read-Haskell Cemetery	Near Lisbon Station	2	24:17-33
St. Mary Roman Catholic Cemetery	Near Jewett City	3	24:34-57
Kinsman Cemetery	Near Versailles	4	24:58-62

Index to Hale inscriptions: 24:63-81.

Barbour, Lucius Barnes. "Genealogical data from Connecticut Cemeteries. Lisbon-Kinsman Cemetery (1914)." NEHGR 86 (October 1932): 388-390.

Phillips, Daniel Lyon. GRISWOLD CEMETERIES. HISTORICAL AND DESCRIPTIVE SKETCHES OF TWENTY-TWO BURIAL PLACES IN GRISWOLD, CONNECTICUT, AND ST. MARY'S CEMETERY IN LISBON, CONNECTICUT, WITH COPIES OF ALL THE INSCRIPTIONS ON THEIR MONUMENTS. N.p., Author, 1918.

CHURCH RECORDS

NEWENT CONGREGATIONAL CHURCH. Minutes, 1734-1872. Miscellaneous Records, 1736-1873. Vital Records, 1924-1932. (CSL, LDS 1811). Marriages, 1724-1800. BAILEY 5:83-90.

HISTORICAL SOCIETY

Lisbon Historical Society, Inc. 06351.

LAND RECORDS

Land Records, 1786–1852. Index, 1786–1812 (1835–1852 is partially indexed). (LDS 1810 pt. 1–3).

PROBATE RECORDS

LISBON is in the Norwich Probate District.

SCHOOL RECORDS

School lists of Bagwell, 1796–1798. In CEMETERY, CENSUS, CHURCH RECORDS, ETC. OF HOMER, CORTLAND CO., NEW YORK, 2 p. (LDS 4225).

TAX RECORDS

Hartford. CSL, Record Group 62. Tax Books, Lists from 1888–1941.

VITAL RECORDS

Town Clerk, Town Office Building, R.F.D. 2, 06351. (203) 376-2708.

> The town clerk's earliest birth, marriage and death records date from 1771.

The BARBOUR INDEX covers the years 1786–1875 and is based on the James N. Arnold copy of 1909. The births and marriages go to 31 December 1850 and deaths to 29 July 1875.

VOTER RECORDS

Hartford. CSL, Record Group 62. Voter Lists, 1877–1908.

PUBLISHED WORKS AND OTHER RECORDS

Bishop, Henry Fitch. HISTORICAL SKETCH OF LISBON, CONNECTICUT FROM 1786 TO 1900. New York: H.F. Bishop, 1903. 84 p.

Fitch, Dorothy. HISTORY OF LISBON. Lisbon: American Revolution Bicentennial Commission, 1976. 63 p.

Hale, David. PRESTON IN 1801. LISBON IN 1800 AND LISBON IN 1801. Hartford: Acorn Club of Connecticut, 1961. 32 p.

HISTORICAL SKETCHES OF EARLY LISBON AND HISTORY OF THE NEWENT CONGREGATIONAL CHURCH 250TH ANNIVERSARY 1723-1973. N.p., n.d.

LITCHFIELD

LITCHFIELD COUNTY. Organized May 1719. Towns organized from LITCH-
FIELD include MORRIS and WASHINGTON.

CEMETERY RECORDS AND CEMETERIES

NAME	ADDRESS	HALE NO.	CITATION
West Cemetery	South Lake Street	1	24:1-40
East Cemetery	Lincoln Place	2	24:41-101
Bantam Cemetery	Banton Road	3	24:102-32
Northfield Cemetery	U.S. 56	4	24:133-63
Milton Cemetery	Blue Swamp Road	5	24:164-83
Headquarters Cemetery	U.S. 56	6	24:184-91
Stone Cemetery	3 stones of Stone Family	7	24:192
Smith-Roberts Cemetery	At East Litchfield	8	24:193
St. Anthony Roman Catholic Cemetery	South Lake Street	9	24:194-208
Beach Cemetery	Beach Street	10	24:209
Osborn Cemetery	3 miles northwest of Litchfield Center	11	24:210-11

Index to Hale inscriptions: 24:212-71.

Payne, Charles Thomas. LITCHFIELD AND MORRIS INSCRIPTIONS. A REC-
ORD OF INSCRIPTIONS UPON THE TOMBSTONES IN THE TOWNS OF
LITCHFIELD AND MORRIS, CONNECTICUT. Litchfield: Dwight C. Kilbourn,
1905. 304 p. (LDS 823,773).

CHURCH RECORDS

FIRST CONGREGATIONAL CHURCH. Minutes, 1886-1938. (CSL, LDS 1826). Minutes, 1768-1927. (CSL, LDS 1824).

LITCHFIELD SOUTH ASSOCIATION (CONGREGATIONAL). Minutes, 1795–1930. (CSL, LDS 1828).

MILTON CONGREGATIONAL CHURCH. Minutes, 1799-1881. Vital Records, 1798-1898. (CSL, LDS 1825).

ST. MICHAEL EPISCOPAL CHURCH. Minutes, 1784-1896. Vital Records, 1750-1870. (CSL, LDS 1830). Records, 1750-1870. Index. (CSL, LDS 1448 pt. 17).

ST. PAUL EPISCOPAL CHURCH. Vital Records, 1832-1862, 1866-1916. (CSL, LDS 1829).

ST. PAUL TRINITY EPISCOPAL CHURCH. Vital Records, 1799-1866. Mrs. Alomia A. Bissell Copy. (CSL, LDS 1880).

TRINITY EPISCOPAL CHURCH. Minutes, 1793-1892. Vital Records, 1835-1880. (CSL, LDS 1833).

Adams, Marjorie. "Communicants, St. Paul's Church, Banton Falls, Connecticut (Rev. D.E. Brown)." FLINT GENEALOGICAL SOCIETY QUARTERLY 7 (1965): 16-17.

_____. "Marriages of St. Paul's Parish, Bantam Falls, Connecticut. 1853-1857." FLINT GENEALOGICAL SOCIETY QUARTERLY 7 (1965): 17.

THE ANNIVERSARY OF THE NORTHFIELD CONGREGATIONAL CHURCH. (JAN. 1, 1882-JUNE 26, 1889). Litchfield: Congregational Church (newspaper).

"Baptisms of Trinity Church, Milton, Connecticut by Rev. Brown (1833-1856)." FLINT GENEALOGICAL SOCIETY QUARTERLY 7 (1965): 66.

Brewster, Mary B. ST. MICHAEL'S PARISH (EPISCOPAL), LITCHFIELD, CONNECTICUT 1745-1954. Litchfield: St. Michael's Parish, 1954. 186 p. Index.

"Funerals attended by Rev. D.E. Brown." FLINT GENEALOGICAL SOCIETY QUARTERLY 7 (1965): 67.

"Marriages in Trinity Church, Milton, Connecticut 1844-1857." FLINT GENEALOGICAL SOCIETY QUARTERLY 7 (1965): 67.

"Parish Record of Trinity Church, Milton, Connecticut Communicants." FLINT
GENEALOGICAL SOCIETY QUARTERLY 7 (1965): 45.

HISTORICAL SOCIETY

Litchfield Historical Society, P.O. Box 385, on the Green, 06759. (203) 546-
5862.

CATALOGUE OF BOOKS, PAPERS AND MANUSCRIPTS OF THE LITCHFIELD
HISTORICAL SOCIETY. Litchfield, Conn.: Litchfield Historical Society,
1906. 115 p.

LAND RECORDS

Land Records, 1719-1853. Index, 1719-1871. (LDS 1823 pt. 1-24).

Proprietor's Records, 1723-1807. (LDS 1822).

LIBRARY

Oliver Wolcott Library, South Street, 06759. (203) 567-8030.

NEWSPAPERS

LITCHFIELD ENQUIRER. Weekly. P.O. Box 547, 06759. (203) 567-8766.

The PRELIMINARY CHECKLIST lists sixteen newspapers for LITCHFIELD.

The HALE NEWSPAPER INDEX TO DEATH AND MARRIAGE NOTICES include:
> AMERICAN EAGLE. 9 September 1822-13 July 1826.
> DEMOCRAT. 2 November 1833-13 September 1834.
> DEMOCRAT AND WATCHMAN. 20 January 1844-6 April 1844.
> GAZETTE. 16 March 1808-17 May 1809.
> LITCHFIELD ENQUIRER. 4 July 1826-27 December 1866.
> LITCHFIELD REPUBLICAN. 12 May 1819-30 September 1852.
> MERCURY. 16 January 1840-7 April 1842.
> MISCELLANY. 25 August 1821-24 July 1822.
> SENTINEL. 10 February 1865-29 December 1865.
> SUN. 7 February 1835-20 April 1839.
> WEEKLY MONITOR. 21 December 1784-22 July 1807 (deaths) 21
> December 1784-29 July 1807 (marriages).
> WITNESS. 21 August 1805-24 June 1807.

The Litchfield Historical Society has indexed:

> AMERICAN EAGLE 1822-1826, DEMOCRAT 1833-1834, DEMOCRAT WATCHMAN 1844, LITCHFIELD COUNTY POST 1826-1827, LITCHFIELD ENQUIRER 1829-1822, SUN 1835-1839, WEEKLY MONITOR 1786-1807, WITNESS 1805-1807.

The PRELIMINARY CHECKLIST lists sixteen newspapers for LITCHFIELD.

PROBATE RECORDS

Litchfield Probate District, Town Office Building, West Street, 06759. (203) 567-8065.

> Organized October 1742 from the Hartford, New Haven and Woodbury Probate Districts.

> The Litchfield Probate District also include the towns of MORRIS and WARREN.

> Probate districts organized from the Litchfield Probate District include the Cornwall, Harwinton, Norfolk, Sharon, Torrington, and Washington Probate Districts.

> ON FILE AT THE CSL: Estate Papers, 1743-1924. Indexes, 1743-1924. Inventory Control Book, 1743-1924. Court Record Books, 1743-1850.

Probate Records, 1743-1850. (LDS 1821 p. 1-9).

SCHOOL RECORDS

Fisher, Samuel Herbert. THE LITCHFIELD LAW SCHOOL, 1775-1833. New Haven, Conn.: Yale University Press, 1933. 31 p.

_____. LITCHFIELD LAW SCHOOL, 1774-1833, BIOGRAPHICAL CATALOGUE OF STUDENTS. New Haven, Conn.: Yale University Press, 1946. 142 p.

Hartford. CSL, Record Group 62. School Records, lists, etc. 1848-1863, 1889.

Morris, James. MR. MORRIS' ADDRESS TO HIS PUPILS, AT THE CLOSE OF HIS SCHOOL, DELIVERED AT LITCHFIELD (SOUTH FARMS SOCIETY) MARCH 11TH, A.D. 1802. Litchfield, Conn.: Thomas Collier, 1802. 20 p.

Vanderpool, Emily Nayes. CHRONICLES OF A PIONEER SCHOOL, FROM 1792 TO 1833 BEING THE HISTORY OF MISS SARAH PIERCE AND HER LITCHFIELD SCHOOL. Cambridge: University Press, 1903. 465 p.

_____. MORE CHRONICLES OF A PIONEER SCHOOL FROM 1792 TO 1833. N.p., 1927. 376 p.

VITAL RECORDS

Town Clerk, Town Hall, West Street, 06759. (203) 567-9461.

The town clerk's earliest birth record is 28 July 1721, marriage record is January 1723 and death record is 8 July 1723.

The BARBOUR INDEX covers the years 1719-1854 and is based on the James N. Arnold copy of the LITCHFIELD vital records made in 1916.

PUBLISHED WORKS AND OTHER RECORDS

Bostwick, Arthur E. INDEX TO ALAIN C. WHITE'S HISTORY OF LITCHFIELD. N.p., 24 p.

Boswell, George C. THE LITCHFIELD BOOK OF DAYS. Litchfield: Alex B. Shumway, 1899. 221 p. Index.

Bulkeley, Alice Talcott. HISTORIC LITCHFIELD, 1721-1907. Hartford: Hartford Press, 1907. 37 p.

DeForest, John L. "Tapping Reeve--Lawyer Extraordinary." CANTIQUARIAN 8 (December 1956): 16-25.

Egler, Frank E., and Niering, William A. THE NATURAL AREAS OF THE WHITE MEMORIAL FOUNDATION. Litchfield, Conn.: Friends of the Litchfield Nature Center and Museum, 1976. 34 p.

Eraclito, Frank B., and Hall, Joseph J. THIS IS LITCHFIELD: A BRIEF ACCOUNT OF THE HOUSES OF LITCHFIELD. Elizabeth, N.J.: Collotype Press, 1953.

Fisher, Samuel Herbert. "List of Virginia Students at the Litchfield Law School with Year of their Registration and all Known Data." WILLIAM AND MARY QUARTERLY 21 (1964): 35-36.

_____. THE PUBLICATIONS OF THOMAS COLLIER, PRINTER, 1784-1808. Litchfield, Conn.: Litchfield Historical Society, 1933. 98 p.

Fryer, Aaron G. "Litchfield: An American Heritage." ANTIQUES 68 (July 1955): 57-59.

Kilbourne, Dwight C. "Litchfield." CQ 2 (1896): 215-29.

Kilbourne, Payne Kenyon. SKETCHES AND CHRONICLES OF THE TOWN OF LITCHFIELD, CONNECTICUT, HISTORICAL, BIOGRAPHICAL, AND STATISTICAL, TOGETHER WITH A COMPLETE REGISTER OF THE TOWN. Hartford: Case, Lockwood Co., 1859. 264 p.

LITCHFIELD, CONNECTICUT, 250TH ANNIVERSARY 1719-1969. Lakeville: Lakeville Journal, 1969. 110 p.

Litchfield Historical Society. SOME HISTORIC SITES OF LITCHFIELD, CONNECTICUT, 1933. Reprint. Litchfield, Conn.: Litchfield Historical Society, 1951. 12 p.

Shepherd, Henry L. LITCHFIELD, PORTRAIT OF A BEAUTIFUL TOWN. Litchfield: Author, 1969. 152 p.

TALES OF OLD LITCHFIELD. Vol. I. Reprinted from Litchfield Enquirer, 1933. 40 p.

Thompson, Marvin Gardner. "Litchfield, Connecticut and an Analysis of its Political Leadership, 1719 to 1784." Ph.D. dissertation, University of Connecticut, 1977. 187 p.

White, Alain Campbell. HISTORY OF THE TOWN OF LITCHFIELD, CONNECTICUT 1720-1920. Litchfield: Litchfield Enquirer, 1920. 360 p.

THE WHITE MEMORIAL FOUNDATION INCORPORATED, LITCHFIELD, CONNECTICUT 1913-1938. Hartford: Prospect Press, 1938. 102 p.

Woodruff, George Catlin. A GENEALOGICAL REGISTER OF THE INHABITANTS OF THE TOWN OF LITCHFIELD, CONNECTICUT. Hartford: Case, Lockwood and Brainard Co., 1900. 267 p.

LYME

NEW LONDON COUNTY. Organized May 1665 from DEEP RIVER. Towns organized from LYME include EAST LYME, OLD LYME and SALEM.

CEMETERY RECORDS AND CEMETERIES

NAME	ADDRESS	HALE NO.	CITATION
Sterling Cemetery	U.S. 52	1	24:1-2
Congregational Church Cemetery	Hamburg	2	24:3-17
Bill Hill Cemetery	On Capt. James A. Bill's farm	3	24:18-20
Sterling Cemetery	2 stones on farm of Ely Harding	4	24:21
Marvin Cemetery	Route 156	5	24:22-26
Brockway Cemetery	On farm of Zebulon Warner	6	24:27-28
Joshuatown	Near house of Willis Banning	7	24:29-35
Selden Cemetery	Hadlyme, south of Center, near Dr. John Morgan	8	24:36-43
Cove Cemetery	1/2 mile west of Hadlyme	9	24:44-48
Luther Cemetery	1 stone, 1 mile from Hadlyme Ferry near Edward Wilcox	10	24:49-50
Daniels Cemetery	2 stones Joshuatown, near Jerod Daniels	11	24:51
Indian Grave	Eastern part of Town near Cedar Pond	12	24:52
Beckitt Hill Cemetery	Eastern part of town near house of Paul Dessar	13	24:53

NAME	ADDRESS	HALE NO.	CITATION
Gillette Cemetery	Grassy Hill	14	24:54
Grassy Hill Cemetery	Grassy Hill, near Congregational Church	15	24:55-58
Colt Cemetery	Beaver Brook Road	16	24:59-62
Beebe Cemetery	U.S. 52	17	24:63
Griffin Cemetery	Eastern part of town, near Lucius Stark	18	24:64-68
Sisson Cemetery	Northern part of town, near Salem line	19	24:69
Pleasant View Cemetery	Route 156	20	24:70-79
North Lyme Baptist Cemetery (moved to Pleasant View)	Near Baptist Church, North Lyme	21	24:70-79
Ely Cemetery	Ferry Road	22	24:80-87
Lord Cemetery	Southern part of town near Bill Hill School	23	24:88-89
Hall Cemetery (moved to Grassy Hill Cemetery)	Southeast part of town, near W. Hall house	24	24:90
Richards Cemetery	1/2 mile east of Hadlyme	25	24:91-92

Index to Hale inscriptions: 24:93-114.

"Connecticut Headstones Before 1800-Lyme Connecticut." CN 9:534-35.

French, Elizabeth. "Inscriptions from the Old Burying Ground, Meeting House Hill, Lyme, Connecticut." NEHGR 61 (1907): 75-79.

"Cemetery Records of Hadlyme." 4 p. In CEMETERY, CHURCH RECORDS, ETC. OF CONNECTICUT. (LDS 1444).

"Inscriptions from Gravestones at Lyme, Connecticut." NEHGR 78 (1924): 365-87.

Wakeman, M.V. INSCRIPTIONS ON THE OLD GRAVE MARKERS IN ALL THE BURYING GROUNDS IN EAST HADDAM AND SEVEN OF THOSE IN LYME, BEING ALL THE LEGIBLE RECORDS OF PEOPLE BORN PREVIOUS TO OR DURING THE YEAR 1810. Lyme: Author, 1907. 439 p.

CHURCH RECORDS

FIRST CONGREGATIONAL CHURCH. Marriages, 1731-1799. BAILEY 3:132-44, 5:122. RECORDS. 1787-1932. Index. (CSL, LDS 1448 pt. 8).

HADLYME CONGREGATIONAL CHURCH. Minutes, 1742-1890. Vital Records, 1742-1932. (CSL, LDS 1807).

NORTH LYME BAPTIST CHURCH. Minutes, 1810-1903. (CSL, LDS 1807).

Church Records, 1731-1780. 12 p. (NYGBS, LDS, 1804).

"North Lyme Separate Congregational Church: An Extract of Records from Lyme Book 1801." CHSB 5 (January 1939): 11-16.

Wood, Nora Bethel. "Rev. Abner Wood's Record of Marriages and Funerals, 1825-1846." NEHGR 81 (1927): 271-75.

HISTORICAL SOCIETY

Lyme Historical Society, Florence Griswold House, Lyme Street, Old Lyme, 06371. (203) 434-5542.

LAND RECORDS

Land Records, 1662-1748. Index, 1662-1800. (LDS 1805 pt. 1-20).

Jacobus, Donald Lines. "Lyme (Conn.) Land Records." TAG 22 (1946): 260-62.

LIBRARY

Lyme Public Library, Route 156, 06371. (203) 434-2272.

NEWSPAPERS

The PRELIMINARY CHECKLIST lists two newspapers for LYME.

PROBATE RECORDS

Lyme Probate District, Town Hall, Route 156, 06371. (203) 434-7733.

Organized 5 July 1869 from The Old Lyme Probate District. Lyme records from 1 May 1666 to 4 June 1830 are at the New London Probate Court. From 4 June 1830 to 4 July 1869 they are at the Old Lyme Probate Court. After that they are at the Lyme Probate Court.

ON FILE AT THE CSL: Estate Papers, 1869-1937. Indexes, 1869-1937. Inventory Control Books, 1869-1937.

TAX RECORDS

Hartford. CSL, Record Group 62. Tax Lists, 1781-1793.

VITAL RECORDS

Town Clerk, Town Hall, Route 156, 06371. (203) 434-7733.

The BARBOUR INDEX covers the years 1667-1852 and is based on the James N. Arnold copy of the LYME vital records made in 1912.

Clapham, F.W. "Births, Marriages and Deaths in Lyme, Connecticut." NEHGR 24 (1870): 425-29; 25 (1871): 30-32; 31 (1877): 211-12; 32 (1878): 32-84; 33 (1879): 438-39; 34 (1880): 37-41.

Hall, Verne M., and Plimpton, Elizabeth B. VITAL RECORDS OF LYME, CONNECTICUT TO THE END OF THE YEAR 1850. Lyme: American Revolution Bicentennial Commission of Lyme, Connecticut, 1976. 403 p.

Jacobus, Donald Lines. "Lyme, Conn.: Deaths 1731-1736." TAG 24 (1948): 62-63.

"Lyme (Conn.) Vital Records from Town Records, Book I." TAG 10 (1933-34): 217-25; 12 (1935-36): 64; 22 (1945-46): 260-62.

"Marriages-Town of Lyme-Barbour pre. 1750." CN 13 (1980): 27-34, 204-5.

PUBLISHED WORKS AND OTHER RECORDS

Brown, Mrs. Barbara W. "Genealogical Material from the Account Book of Dr. Samuel Mather of Lyme, Connecticut." CHSB 38 (1973): 54-59.

Burr, Jean Chandler. LYME RECORDS 1667-1730. A LITERAL TRANSCRIPTION OF THE MINUTES OF THE TOWN MEETINGS WITH MARGINAL NOTATION, TO WHICH HAVE BEEN APPENDED LAND GRANTS AND EAR MARKS. Stonington: Pequot Press, 1968. 190 p.

Chadwick, Ernest. "The Evolution of Aestheticism." CM 8 (1903): 201-4.

Harding, James Ely. LYME AS IT WAS AND IS. Lyme: American Revolution Bicentennial Commission of Lyme, 1975. 84 p.

_____. LYME YESTERDAYS, HOW OUR FOREFATHERS MADE A LIVING ON THE CONNECTICUT SHORE. Stonington, Conn.: Pequot Press, 1967. 71 p.

Stark, Bruce Purinton. Lyme, CONNECTICUT FROM FOUNDING TO INDE-PENDENCE. Lyme: American Revolution Bicentennial Commission of Lyme, 1976. 121 p.

Williams, George J. Jr. A LYME MISCELLANY 1776-1976. Middletown: Wesleyan University Press, 1976. 288 p.

MADISON

NEW HAVEN COUNTY. Organized May 1826 from GUILFORD.

CEMETERY RECORDS AND CEMETERIES

NAME	ADDRESS	HALE NO.	CITATION
Hammonassett Cemetery	96 River Road	1	25:1-17
West Cemetery	399 Boston Post Road	2	25:18-90
Summer Hill Cemetery	604 Route 80	3	25:91-94
Rockland Cemetery	County Road	4	25:102-11
West Side Cemetery	47 Race Hill Road	5	25:112-14
Old Summer Hill Cemetery	Wood Road leaving main North Madison Road	6	25:115-16
Johnson Cemetery	1/2 mile southeast of Summer Hill Cemetery, on land of Owen Shepard Sr.	7	(no citation)

Index to Hale inscriptions: 25:117-49.

Griswold, Glenn E. NEW HAVEN COUNTY, CONNECTICUT INSCRIPTIONS, MADISON. N.p., 1936. 90 p.

"Inscriptions on Tombstones in Madison, Connecticut. Erected Prior to 1880." NHCHS PAPERS 6 (1900): 39-419.

CHURCH RECORDS

FIRST CONGREGATIONAL CHURCH. Minutes, 1714-1917. Vital Records, 1741-1917. (CSL, LDS 1537 pt. 1-2). Records, 1707-1917. Index. (CSL).

NORTH MADISON CONGREGATIONAL CHURCH. Minutes, 1754-1877. Vital Records, 1757-1827. (CSL, LDS 1966). Marriages, 1757-1798. BAILEY 1:101-104. Records. Index, 1754-1877. (CSL).

NORTH MADISON IMANUEL LUTHERAN CHURCH. Minutes, 1702-1922. Vital Records, 1898-1922. (CSL, LDS 1838).

METHODIST EPISCOPAL CHURCH. Vital Records, 1839-1923. (CSL, LDS 1839).

ROCKLAND EPISCOPAL CHURCH. Vital Records, 1833-1906. (CSL, LDS 1839).

Allen, Louise R. "Early Church Records of Madison, Connecticut 1791-1822." 65 p. Index. (NYGBS, LDS 1834).

HISTORICAL SOCIETY

Madison Historical Society, 833 Boston Post Road, 06443. (203) 245-4567.

LAND RECORDS

Land Records, 1826-1894. (LDS 1836 pt. 1-4).

LIBRARY

Scranton Memorial Library, 801 Boston Post Road, P.O. Box 631, 06443. (203) 245-7365.

MILITARY RECORDS

MADISON. HER SOLDIERS, MEMORIAL SUNDAY SERVICES HELD IN THE FIRST CONGREGATIONAL CHURCH, MADISON, CONNECTICUT, MAY 25, 1890. Madison: Evening Post, 1890.

RECORD OF LISTED NAMES, MEN AND WOMEN OF MADISON, CON-NECTICUT. PARTICIPANTS IN ARMED FORCES . . . WORLD WAR I UP TO SEPTEMBER 1ST, 1972. Madison: American Legion, Griswold Post no. 79, n.d.

NEWSPAPER

The PRELIMINARY CHECKLIST lists one newspaper for MADISON.

PROBATE RECORDS

Madison Probate District, Town Hall, P.O. Box 205, 06443. (203) 245-2614.

Organized 22 May 1834 from the Guilford Probate District.

ON FILE AT THE CSL: Court Record Books, 1834-1856.

Probate Records, 1834-1856. (LDS 1835).

TAX RECORDS

Hartford. CSL, Record Group 62. Highway tax list of 1832.

VITAL RECORDS

Town Clerk, Town Hall, P.O. Box 605, 06443. (203) 245-2465.

The town clerk's earliest birth record is 1776, marriage record is 1827 and death record 1815.

The BARBOUR INDEX covers the years 1826-1850 and is based on the James N. Arnold copy of MADISON vital records made in 1914.

Allen, Louise R. MADISON, CONNECTICUT VITAL RECORDS FROM TOWN RECORDS TO 1852. New York: Author, 1935. 125 p. Index.

PUBLISHED WORKS AND OTHER RECORDS

Allen, Louise R. MADISON, CONNECTICUT TOWN RECORDS, 1727-1882. New York: 1935. Indexed. (NYGBS, LDS 1834).

Bushnell, Jane Finch. "An Old Neighborhood, Boston Street, Madison, Connecticut." CQ 3 (1897): 307-15.

GUILFORD AND MADISON EARLY SETTLERS AND DIRECT DESCENDANTS RESIDING IN THOSE TOWNS, JULY 1957. Madison, Conn.: First Congregational Church, 1957. 63 p.

Harder, Peter J. "An Analysis of the Evolution of Public Responsibility for Secondary Education in the Town of Madison, Connecticut, 1821-1922." Master's thesis, University of Connecticut, 1977. 267 p.

Hartford. CSL, Record Group 33 Box 146. Watrons, Louise E. Dew. MADISON 1645-1938. WPA Writer's Project. Typescript. 515 p.

Hibbard, Charles D. OLD GUILFORD: INCLUDING THE LAND NOW CONSTITUTING THE TOWNS OF GUILFORD AND MADISON. Guilford: Shore Line Times, 1939. 52 p.

Oedel, Howard T. DANIEL HAND OF MADISON, CONNECTICUT 1801-1891. Madison: Madison Historical Society, 1973. 58 p. Index.

Platt, Philip S. MADISON'S HERITAGE. Madison: Madison Historical Society, 1964. 296 p.

Ryerson, Kathleen Hulser. A BRIEF HISTORY OF MADISON, CONNECTICUT. New York: Pageant Press, 1960. 75 p.

Steiner, Bernard Christian. A HISTORY OF THE PLANTATION OF MENUNKA-TUCK AND OF THE ORIGINAL TOWN OF GUILFORD, CONNECTICUT, COMPRISING THE PRESENT TOWNS OF GUILFORD AND MADISON. Baltimore: Author, 1897. 538 p.

MANCHESTER

HARTFORD COUNTY. Organized May 1823 from EAST HARTFORD.

CEMETERY RECORDS AND CEMETERIES

NAME	ADDRESS	HALE NO.	CITATION
East Cemetery	240 East Center Street	1	25:1-164
West Cemtery	375 Spencer Street	2	25:165-92
Northwest Cemetery	U.S. 52	3	25:193-241
St. James Roman Catholic Cemetery	368 Broad Street, 06040 (203) 646-3772	4	25:242-62
St. Bridget Roman Catholic Cemetery	186 Oakland Street (office: 360 Broad Street, 06040) (203) 642-3772	5	25:263-301
Cheney Association Cemetery	Next to East Cemetery	6	25:302-5
St. John Roman Catholic Cemetery	Jefferson Street	7	25:306
St. James Cemetery	St. James Church Main Street	8	25:307-8
Buckland Cemetery	1190 Tolland Turnpike		(no citation)
Temple Beth Scholom Cemetery	68 Autumn Street		(no citation)

Index to Hale inscriptions: 25:309-97.

CHURCH RECORDS

FIRST CONGREGATIONAL CHURCH. Minutes, 1772-1863. Vital Records,

1779-1917. (CSL, LDS 1867 pt. 1). Records, 1772-1931. Index. (CSL).

METHODIST CHURCH. Vital Records, 1850-1941. (CSL, LDS 1869).

ST. MARY EPISCOPAL CHURCH. Vital Records, 1876-1924. (CSL, LDS 1868).

SECOND CONGREGATIONAL CHURCH. Minutes, 1851-1911. Vital Records, 1851-1913.

HISTORICAL SOCIETY

Manchester Historical Society, 106 Hartford Road, 06040. (203) 643-5588.

LAND RECORDS

Land Records, 1823-1871. Index, 1823-1916. (LDS 1866 pt. 1-6).

LIBRARIES

Manchester Public Library, 586 Main Street, 06040. (203) 643-2471.

Manchester Community College Library, 60 Bidwell Street, P.O. Box 1046, 06040. (203) 646-4900 ext. 321.

MILITARY RECORDS

Kilpatrick, Archie. WORLD WAR II HISTORY OF MANCHESTER, CONNECTICUT. New York: Hobson Book Press, 1946. 148 p.

NEWSPAPERS

JOURNAL INQUIRER. Daily. 306 Progress Drive, 06040. (203) 646-0500.

MANCHESTER EVENING HERALD. Daily. P.O. Box 591, 06040. (203) 643-2711.

THE LEADER. Weekly. P.O. Box 1207, 06040. (203) 728-0202.

The PRELIMINARY CHECKLIST lists five newspapers for MANCHESTER.

PROBATE RECORDS

Manchester Probate District, Town Hall, 41 Center Street, 06040. (203) 647-3227.

Organized 22 June 1850 from the East Hartford Probate District.

VITAL RECORDS

Town Clerk, Town Hall, 41 Center Street, 06040. (203) 649-5281.

The BARBOUR INDEX covers the years 1823-1853 and is based on the James Lahy copy of MANCHESTER vital records made in 1918.

PUBLISHED WORKS AND OTHER RECORDS

Buckley, William E. A NEW ENGLAND PATTERN: THE HISTORY OF MAN-CHESTER, CONNECTICUT. N.p., 1973. 372 p.

Lewis, Thomas Reed, Jr. "The 19th Century Marine Propeller Industry in Manchester, Connecticut." CHSB 45 (1980): 90-96.

_____. SILK ALONG STEEL: THE STORY OF THE SOUTH MANCHESTER RAILROAD. Chester, Conn.: Pequot Press, 1976. 64 p. Index.

Spiess, Mathias, and Bidwell, Percy Wells. HISTORY OF MANCHESTER, CON-NECTICUT. Manchester: Centennial Committee of the Town of Manchester, 1924. 306 p.

Valcherville, Marie de. "Highland Park Manchester." CQ 1 (1895): 298-301.

MANSFIELD

TOLLAND COUNTY. Organized October 1702 from WINDHAM.

CEMETERY RECORDS AND CEMETERIES

NAME	ADDRESS	HALE NO.	CITATION
Old Mansfield Center Cemetery	Mansfield Road	1	25:1-21
New Mansfield Center Cemetery	Mansfield Road	2	25:22-31
Atwoodville Cemetery	Ashford Road	3	25:32-38
Mt. Hope Cemetery	Ashford Road	4	25:39-44
Wormwood Hill Cemetery	Wormwood Hill, near Ashford town line	5	25:45-46
Gurleyville (Pink) Cemetery	West of Gurleyville	6	25:47-54
New Storrs Cemetery	West of Old Storrs Cemetery	7	25:55-74
Old Storrs Cemetery	At University of Connecticut	8	25:75-83
Gurley Cemetery	Between Storrs and Mansfield Railroad station	9	25:84-99
Spring Hill Cemetery	South of Spring Hill	10	25:100-111
Pleasant Valley Cemetery	Near Windham town line	11	25:112-114
Ridges Cemetery	Stafford Springs Road, near Windham town line	12	25:115-117
Jewish Cemetery	Stafford Road, north of Ridges Cemetery	13	25:118-119
Durkee Cemetery	On Alexander Nick farm	14	25:120
Barrows Cemetery	(Not located)	15	25:121

NAME	ADDRESS	HALE NO.	CITATION
Old Abbe Cemetery	(Not located)	16	25:122
Tilden Cemetery	On Waldo Homestead	17	25:123
Foss Cemetery	North of Mansfield Depot	18	25:124
Old Dunham Cemetery	Moved	19	25:125A
Farwell Cemetery	Moved	20	25:125B
Holley Cemetery	Moved from property of John Plimpton	21	25:125C
Parker Cemetery	On A. Chasser farm	22	25:125D
Thompson Cemetery	On William Chabot farm	23	25:125E

Index to Hale inscriptions: 25:126–61.

Crandall, Adelaide Blanchard. LIST OF INSCRIPTIONS IN THE GRAVEYARD AT STORRS, CONNECTICUT. Typescript. 7 p.

_____. LIST OF INSCRIPTIONS IN THE GRAVEYARD AT THE RIDGES, NEAR THE WILLIMANTIC LINE. Typescript. 2 p.

_____. LIST OF INSCRIPTIONS IN THE "PINK" OR GURLEY CEMETERY. Typescript. 1930. 13 p.

CHURCH RECORDS

FIRST CONGREGATIONAL CHURCH. Minutes, 1737–1894. Vital Records, 1710–1893. (CSL, LDS 1857). Marriages, 1744–1785. BAILEY 2:126–31. Records, 1710–1892. Index. (CSL, LDS 1448).

SECOND CONGREGATIONAL CHURCH. Minutes, 1737–1921. Vital Records, 1744–1929. (CSL, LDS 1858). Records Kept by Rev. Moses Cook Welch, 1784–1824. (CSL, LDS 1858).

Barnett, James H., and Barnett, Esther D. ON THE TRAIL OF A LEGEND: THE SEPARTIST MOVEMENT IN MANSFIELD, CONNECTICUT, 1745–1769. Storrs: Parousta Press, 1978. 76 p.

Benton, Sarah Adelaide. RECORDS OF A HUNDRED YEARS OF THE METHODIST EPISCOPAL CHURCH, SOUTH MANCHESTER, CONNECTICUT, WITH NAMES OF THE PASTORS, PRESIDING ELDERS, AND PRESENT OFFICIARY. Manchester: Herald Printery, 1894. 53 p.

Slafter, Edmund F. "Inscriptions on Gravestones in North Mansfield, Connecticut." NEHGR 22 (1868): 387-88.

Southwick, G.O. HISTORY OF THE CONGREGATIONAL CHURCH, NORTH MANSFIELD, CONNECTICUT 1744-1879. Mansfield: W.P. Hanks Steam Job Printer, 1879. 67 p.

HISTORICAL SOCIETY

Mansfield Historical Society, 898 Stafford Road, 06268.

Barnett, James H., and Munsell, Ruth V. "Historical Collections of the Mansfield Historical Society." ASCH NEWSLETTER, Spring 1979, pp. 5-8.

LAND RECORDS

Proprietor's Records, 1702-1752. (LDS, 004,865).

Land Records, 1702-1852. Index, 1702-1900. (LDS 004,866 - 004,881).

Copies of Proprietor's Records, 1702-1752. Land Records, 1702-1841. Index, 1702-1900. (CSL, LDS 1856 pt. 1-13).

LIBRARIES

Mansfield Library, 54 Warrenville Road, P.O. Box 206, 06250. (203) 423-2501.

UCONN-Wilbur Cross Library, 06268. (203) 486-2219.

MILITARY RECORDS

Hartford. CSL, Record Group 62. Militia papers, lists of eligibles, etc.

Washington, D.C. Library of Congress. Connecticut Miscellany 4 Boxes 1646-1837. Item 205. A list of Minutemen in Mansfield, Connecticut.

PROBATE RECORDS

Mansfield Probate District, 4 South Eagleville Road, 06268. (203) 429-3313.
    Organized 30 May 1831 from the Windham Probate District.

ON FILE AT THE CSL: Estate Papers, 1831-1953. Indexes, 1831-1953. Inventory Control Book, 1831-1953. Court Record Book, 1831-1851.

Probate Records, 1831-1851. (LDS 1855).

SCHOOL RECORDS

Hartford. CSL, Record Group 62. School records, returns 1823-1917.

TAX RECORDS

Hartford. CSL, Record Group 62. Tax abstracts, lists, grand lists 1810-1912.

VITAL RECORDS

Town Clerk, Town Hall, 9545 Stone Road, 06268. (203) 429-1963.

The town clerk's earliest birth record is 19 June 1704, marriage record is 30 October 1707 and death record is 8 June 1713.

Dimock, Susan Whitney. BIRTHS, BAPTISMS, MARRIAGES AND DEATHS FROM THE RECORDS OF THE TOWN AND CHURCHES IN MANSFIELD, CONNECTICUT 1703-1850. New York: Baker and Taylor, 1898. 475 p. (LDS 823,814).

Hartford. CSL, Record Group 62. Vital Record Abstracts.

PUBLISHED WORKS AND OTHER RECORDS

CHRONOLOGY OF MANSFIELD, CONNECTICUT 1702-1972. Mansfield: Mansfield Historical Society, 1974. 198 p.

PRESENT MANSFIELD; A PASSING SKETCH OF THE VILLAGE WITH OCCASIONAL JOTTINGS OF ITS FORMER HISTORY, PRESENT ASPECT AND PROSPECTIVE GREATNESS FROM 1685 TO 1879. Willimantic: Journal Steam Job Print, 1880.

Weaver, William L. HISTORY OF ANCIENT WINDHAM, CONNECTICUT GENEALOGY, CONTAINING A GENEALOGICAL RECORD OF ALL THE EARLY FAMILY OF ANCIENT WINDHAM, EMBRACING THE PRESENT TOWNS OF WINDHAM, MANSFIELD, HAMPTON, CHAPLIN, AND SCOTLAND. Part I: A-Bil. Willimantic: Weaver and Courtiss, 1864. 112 p. (LDS 2146).

MARLBOROUGH

HARTFORD COUNTY. Organized October 1803 from COLCHESTER, GLAS-
TONBURY and HEBRON.

CEMETERY RECORDS AND CEMETERIES

NAME	ADDRESS	HALE NO.	CITATION
Old Cemetery	At Center	1	26:1-15
New Cemetery	1/2 mile west of Center on East Hampton Road	2	26:16-25
Fawn Brook Cemetery	On New London Highway 2 1/2 miles south of Center	3	26:26
Jones Hollow Cemetery	Northeast part of town near Hebron line	4	26:27-29

Index to Hale inscriptions: 26:30-38.

CHURCH RECORDS

Harvey, Cora Alford. "Connecticut Church Records-Baptisms in Church of
Marlborough, Connecticut 1749-1833." DAR MAGAZINE 87 (1953): 57-59,
163-65.

Jones, Myrtle A. CONGREGATIONAL CHURCH RECORDS. 1718-1900.
Index. (CSL, LDS 1860).

HISTORICAL SOCIETY

Marlborough Historical Society, RFD 5, 06424.

LAND RECORDS

Land Records, 1803-1878. Index, 1803-1936. (LDS 1859 pt. 1-3).

LIBRARY

Richmond Memorial Library, North Main Street, 06424.

NEWSPAPER

The PRELIMINARY CHECKLIST lists one newspaper for MARLBOROUGH.

PROBATE RECORDS

Marlborough Probate District, Town Hall, North Main Street and Route 66, 06447. (203) 295-9547.

Organized 11 June 1846 from the Colchester Probate District.

ON FILE AT THE CSL: Estate Papers, 1846-1938. Indexes, 1846-1938. Inventory Control Book, 1846-1938.

VITAL RECORDS

Town Clerk, Town Hall, North Main Street and Route 66, 06424. (203) 295-9547.

The town clerk's earliest birth record is 1762, marriage record is 1790 and death record is 1852.

The BARBOUR INDEX covers the years 1803-1852 and is based on the James N. Arnold copy of MARLBOROUGH vital records made in 1912.

Marlborough deaths, 1718-1900. (LDS 1860).

Vital Records, 1881-1905. Typescript. (CSL, LDS 003,662 and 1483).

Curray, Kate S. "Death Records copied from the Marlboro, Connecticut Town Books." NGSQ 15 (1927): 14.

PUBLISHED WORKS AND OTHER RECORDS

Hal, Mary. REPORT OF THE CELEBRATION OF THE CENTENNIAL OF THE INCORPORATION OF THE TOWN OF MARLBOROUGH. AUGUST 23RD AND

25TH, 1903. Hartford: Case, Lockwood and Brainard, 1904. 96 p.

Whittles, Lee Jay. "Saddler's Ordynary: John Saddler: Second Connecticut Innkeeper." CANTIQUARIAN 5 (June 1953): 5-19.

MERIDEN

NEW HAVEN COUNTY.   Organized May 1806 from WALLINGFORD.

CEMETERY RECORDS AND CEMETERIES

NAME	ADDRESS	HALE NO.	CITATION
Broad Street Cemetery	402 Broad Street	1	26:1-25
Indian, Buckwheat Hill Cemetery	Southeast of Center	2	26:26-27
Walnut Grove Cemetery	280 New Hanover Avenue	3	26:28-211
St. Laurent Cemetery	1351 Hanover Avenue	4	26:212-24
St. Stanilaus Roman Catholic Cemetery	156 Yale Avenue	5	26:225-36
East Cemetery	45 East Main Street	6	26:237-95
St. Patrick Roman Catholic Cemetery	94 Wall Street office: 250 Gypsy Lane, 06450. (203) 237-3226	7	26:296-353
Sacred Heart Roman Catholic Cemetery	206 South Broad Street office: 250 Gypsy Lane, 06450. (203) 237-3226	8	26:354-413
Meriden Hebrew Cemetery	114 Corrigan Avenue	9	26:414-20
West Cemetery	202 Hanover Avenue	10	26:421-83
Gethsemane Cemetery	76 Bee Street	11	26:484-97
St. Boniface Cemetery	Old Colony Road	12	26:498-511
Workman Circle Cemetery (same as No. 9)	Near Meriden Hebrew Cemetery	13	26:512
St. Peter & St. Paul Russian Orthodox Cemetery	362 Westfield road	14	26:513-14

NAME	ADDRESS	HALE NO.	CITATION
Old Roman Catholic Cemetery	1/4 mile south of Sacred	15	26:515-16
Soldier's burials in cemeteries 1-12			27:662-80
Academy Burying Ground	Market Street		(no citation)

Index to Hale inscriptions: 27:517-661.

CHURCH RECORDS

CENTER CONGREGATIONAL CHURCH.   Minutes, 1846-1915. Vital Records, 1848-1900. (CSL, LDS 1864 pt. 1).

FIRST BAPTIST CHURCH. Minutes, 1786-1852. (CSL, LDS 1863).

FIRST CONGREGATIONAL CHURCH. Vital Records, 1729-1937. (CSL, LDS 1864 pt. 2). Marriages, 1729-1793. BAILEY 4:104-12, 5:122.

MAIN STREET BAPTIST CHURCH. Vital Records, 1861-1936. (CSL, LDS 1863).

ST. ANDREW EPISCOPAL CHURCH. Minutes, 1789-1929. Vital Records, 1816-1893. (CSL, LDS 1865).

WEST MERIDEN BAPTIST CHURCH. Minutes, 1861-1886. (CSL, LDS 1863).

THE 175TH ANNIVERSARY OF THE FIRST CONGREGATIONAL CHURCH, MERIDEN, CONNECTICUT OCTOBER 22ND, 23RD AND 24TH, 1904. Meriden: First Congregational Church, 1904.

HISTORICAL SOCIETY

Meriden Historical Society, 424 West Main Street, P.O. Box 641, 06450. (203) 237-5079

LAND RECORDS

Land Records, 1806-1854. (LDS 1861 pt. 1-7).

LIBRARY

Meriden Public Library, 105 Miller Street, 06450. (203) 238-2344.

NEWSPAPERS

MORNING RECORD AND JOURNAL. Daily. 11 Crown Street, 06450. (203) 235-1661.

The PRELIMINARY CHECKLIST lists twenty-four newspapers for MERIDEN.

PROBATE RECORDS

Meriden Probate District, City Hall, 142 East Main Street, 06450. (203) 235-4325.

> Organized 3 June 1826 from the Wallingford Probate District.
>
> ON FILE AT THE CSL: Court Record Books, 1836-1854.

Probate Records, 1836-1854. (LDS 1862).

VITAL RECORDS

Town Clerk, Town Hall, 142 East Main Street, P.O. Box 804, 06450. (203) 634-003.

> The town clerk's earliest birth, marriage and death records date from 1762.

The BARBOUR INDEX covers the years 1806-1853 and is based on the Ethel L. Scofield copy of MERIDEN vital records made in 1915.

PUBLISHED WORKS AND OTHER RECORDS

Arms, H. Phelps. "Hubbard Park." CM 5 (1899): 66-76.

Breckenridge, Mrs. Frances A. "Memories of Meriden." CQ 1 (1895): 352-54; 2 (1896): 67-71; 4 (1898): 49-54.

_____. RECOLLECTIONS OF A NEW ENGLAND TOWN. Meriden: Journal Publishing Co., 1899. 222 p.

Curtis, George Munson. "Meriden and Wallingford in Colonial and Revolutionary Days." PAPERS NHCHS 7 (1908): 298-327.

General Centennial Committee. CENTENNIAL OF MERIDEN JUNE 10-16, 1906, REPORT OF THE PROCEEDINGS, WITH FULL DESCRIPTION OF THE

MANY EVENTS OF ITS SUCCESSFUL CELEBRATION. Meriden: Journal Publishing Co., 1906. 400 p.

Gillespie, Charles Bancroft. AN HISTORIC RECORD AND PICTORIAL DESCRIPTION OF THE TOWN OF MERIDEN, CONNECTICUT AND MEN WHO MADE IT. FROM EARLIEST SETTLEMENT TO CLOSE OF ITS FIRST CENTURY OF INCORPORATION. Meriden: Journal Publishing Co., 1906. 1,226 p.

ART SOUVENIR EDITION OF THE MERIDEN DAILY JOURNAL ILLUSTRATING THE CITY OF MERIDEN, CONNECTICUT, IN THE YEAR 1895. Meriden: Journal Publishing Co., 1895. 87 p.

ONE HUNDRED YEARS OF MERIDEN. Meriden: City of Meriden, 1956. 316 p.

Perkins, George William. HISTORICAL SKETCHES OF MERIDEN. West Meriden: Franklin E. Hinman, 1849. 117 p.

SILVER CITY. Meriden: E.A. Horton and Co., 1893.

MIDDLEBURY

NEW HAVEN COUNTY. Organized October 1807 from SOUTHBURY, WATER-BURY and WOODBURY.

CEMETERY RECORDS AND CEMETERIES

NAME	ADDRESS	HALE NO.	CITATION
Middlebury Cemetery	Cemetery Road	1	27:1-37

Index to Hale inscriptions: 27:38-48.

CHURCH RECORDS

FIRST CONGREGATIONAL CHURCH. Minutes, 1800-1871. Vital Records, 1796-1915. (CSL, LDS 1871). Records Index, 1790-1915. (CSL).

METHODIST EPISCOPAL CHURCH. Minutes, 1834-1890. Vital Records, 1836-1922. (CSL, LDS 1872).

Kingsbury, Frederic John. A NARRATIVE AND DOCUMENTARY HISTORY OF ST. JOHN'S PROTESTANT EPISCOPAL CHURCH (FORMERLY ST. JAMES) OF WATERBURY, CONNECTICUT; WITH SOME NOTICE OF ST. PAUL'S CHURCH, PLYMOUTH, CHRIST CHURCH, WATERTOWN, ST. MICHAEL'S CHURCH, NAUGATUCK, A CHURCH IN MIDDLEBURY, ALL SAINTS CHURCH, WOL-COTT, ST. PAUL'S CHURCH, WATERVILLE, TRINITY CHURCH, WATERBURY, (ALL COLONIES OF ST. JOHN'S). New Haven: Price, Lee and Adkins, 1907. 181 p. Index.

PAPERS CONNECTED WITH THE CENTENNIAL OF THE CONGREGATIONAL CHURCH IN MIDDLEBURY, CONNECTICUT OBSERVED MAY 27, 1896. Hartford: D.S. Moseley, Printer, n.d. 47 p.

Smith, Walton B., et al. THE MIDDLEBURY CONGREGATIONAL CHURCH. 1796-1946. Middlebury: Church, 1946. 64 p.

HISTORICAL SOCIETY

Middlebury Historical Society, Inc., 06762.

LAND RECORDS

Land Records, 1807-1873. (LDS 1870 pt. 104).

LIBRARY

Middlebury Public Library, Crest Road, 06762. (203) 758-2634.

MILITARY RECORDS

List of War Veterans through World War I, in land records. (LDS 1870 pt. 4).

PROBATE RECORDS

MIDDLEBURY is in the Waterbury Probate District.

VITAL RECORDS

Town Clerk, Town Hall, 1212 Whittemore Road, 06762. (203) 758-2557.

> The town clerk's earliest birth record is 25 April 1853, marriage record is 26 November 1854 and death record is 2 May 1853.

The BARBOUR INDEX covers the years 1807-1850 and is based on the James N. Arnold copy of MIDDLEBURY vital records made in 1915.

Humiston, Wallace. "Two Private Connecticut Mortuary Lists--Middlebury, Connecticut." TAG 26 (1950): 44-49.

PUBLISHED WORKS AND OTHER RECORDS

Bronson, Henry. HISTORY OF WATERBURY, CONNECTICUT. THE ORIGINAL TOWNSHIP EMBRACING PRESENT WATERTOWN AND PLYMOUTH, AND PARTS OF OXFORD, WOLCOTT, MIDDLEBURY, PROSPECT AND NAUGA-TUCK. WITH AN APPENDIX OF BIOGRAPHY, GENEALOGY AND STATIS-TICS. Waterbury: Bronson Bros., 1858. 583 p. Index. (LDS 599,254).

Cothren, William. HISTORY OF ANCIENT WOODBURY, CONNECTICUT, FROM THE FIRST INDIAN DEED IN 1659 TO 1854. INCLUDING THE PRES-ENT TOWNS OF WASHINGTON, SOUTHBURY, BETHLEHEM, ROXBURY, AND A PART OF OXFORD AND MIDDLEBURY. Waterbury: Bronson Bros., 1854. 841 p. (LDS 2205).

MIDDLEFIELD

MIDDLESEX COUNTY. Organized June 1866 from MIDDLETOWN.

CEMETERY RECORDS AND CEMETERIES

NAME	ADDRESS	HALE NO.	CITATION
North Cemetery	Jackson Hill Road	1	27:1-12
Middlefield Cemetery	Main Street	2	27:13-46
St. Sebastian Cemetery	Meriden Road (203) 346-4815		(no citation)

Index to Hale inscriptions: 27-47-60.

CHURCH RECORDS

CONGREGATIONAL CHURCH. Minutes, 1744-1940. Vital Records, 1808-1892. (CSL, LDS 1882).
ST. PAUL EPISCOPAL CHURCH. Vital Records, 1873-1911. (CSL, LDS 1881).

HISTORICAL SOCIETY

Middlefield Historical Society, 06455.

LIBRARY

Coe Library Association, Main Street, 06455. (203) 349-3857.

PROBATE RECORDS

Middlefield is in the Middletown Probate District.

VITAL RECORDS

Town Clerk, Town Hall, Jackson Hill Road, P.O. Box 179, 06455.   (203) 349-3446.

> The town clerk's earliest birth, marriage and death records date from 1866.

PUBLISHED WORKS

Atkins, Thomas. HISTORY OF MIDDLEFIELD AND LONG HILL. Hartford: Case, Lockwood and Brainard Co., 1883. 175 p.

MIDDLETOWN

MIDDLESEX COUNTY. Organized 11 September 1651. Towns organized from MIDDLETOWN include BERLIN, CROMWELL, EAST HAMPTON, and MIDDLE-FIELD.

CEMETERY RECORDS AND CEMETERIES

NAME	ADDRESS	HALE NO.	CITATION
Indian Hill Cemetery	383 Washington Street	1	27:1-153
Pine Grove Cemetery	South Main Street (203) 346-0271	2	27:154-207
Mortimer Cemetery	557 Main Street	3	27:208-66
Old East Street Cemetery	East Street	4	27:267-69
Miner Cemetery	Miner Street	5	27:270-91
New Farm Hill Cemetery	502 Ridge Road	6	27:292-319
Old Farm Hill Cemetery	522 Ridge Road	7	27:320-23 28:334-64
Maromas Cemetery	River Road	8	28:335-71
St. John Roman Catholic Cemetery (New)	65 Johnson Street	9	28:372-494
St. John Roman Catholic Cemetery (Old)	St. John's Square	10	28:495-531
Connecticut State Hospital Cemetery	Rear of the State Hospital	11	28:532-79
Washington Street Cemetery	349 Washington Terrace	12	28:580-613
Wesleyan University Cemetery	Wesleyan University	13	28:614-15

NAME	ADDRESS	HALE NO.	CITATION
Old Highland Cemetery	Highland District	14	28:616-20
New Highland Cemetery	Highland District	15	28:621-28
Congregation Adath Israel Cemetery	River Street	16	28:629-30
Middletown Jewish Association Cemetery	Pine Street	17	28:631
New Connecticut State Hospital Cemetery	Opposite Old Cemetery State Hospital	18	28:632
McDonough Cemetery	Near Railroad Station	19	28:633-49
Prior Cemetery	1/3 mile south of Maromas Station, 100 ft. east of railroad	20	28:650
Old South Side Cemetery	Westfield	21	28:651-52
Industrial School Cemetery	Rear of Long Lane Farm	22	28:653
Bonn Cemetery	Intersection of Asylum Street & Saybrook Road	23	28:654-55
Calvary Cemetery	Bow Lane	24	(no citation)

Index to Hale inscriptions: 28:656-837.

"Connecticut Headstone Inscriptions Before 1800 (Hale)--Town of Middletown."
CN 7 (1975-76): 512-3; 8 (1976-77): 29-34, 201-6, 355-60, 544-48.

Derby, Alice Gray Southmayd. "The Riverside Cemetery. A Sketch of the
Old Burying Ground in Middleton." CQ 2 (1896): 377-85; 4 (1898): 329.

Hubbard, Pascal E. "Epitaphs copied from the Old Burying Ground, on the
Bank of the River, Middletown, Connecticut." NEHGR 11 (1857): 80-82.

THE INDIAN HILL CEMETERY, MIDDLETOWN, CONNECTICUT BY-LAWS,
REGULATIONS AND C. 1873. Middletown: Charles H. Pelton Printer, 1873.
55 p.

"The Old Burying Ground in Middletown, Connecticut." NEHGR 2 (1848):
70-75.

Parsons, Samuel H. "Epitaphs in the Old Burying Place." NEHGR 15
(1861): 161-67.

CHURCH RECORDS

CHRIST CHURCH (HOLY TRINITY). Vital Records, 1801-1839. (CSL, LDS 1847). Minutes, 1762-1947. Vital Records, 1750-1937. (CSL, LDS 1844). Records, 1750-1937. Index. (CSL).

FIRST BAPTIST CHURCH. Minutes, 1805-1858, 1862, 1914. Vital Records, 1795-1828, 1840-1897. (CSL, LDS 1845).

FIRST CONGREGATIONAL CHURCH. Minutes, 1732-1871. Vital Records, 1668-1816. (CSL, LDS 1846). Marriages, 1762-1799. BAILEY 6:92-119. Vital Records, 1697-1853. 20 p. (NYGBS, LDS 1841). Records, 1668-1871. Index. (CSL).

FIRST UNIVERSALIST CHURCH. Minutes, 1846-1911. (CSL, LDS 1847).

SECOND CONGREGATIONAL CHURCH. Covenant, 1828. 9 p. (NYGBS, LDS 1841).

SOUTH CONGREGATIONAL CHURCH. Minutes, 1827-1868. Vital Records, 1787-1844, 1869-1909. (CSL, LDS 1848).

THIRD CONGREGATIONAL CHURCH. Minutes, 1787-1894. Vital Records, 1773-1916. (CSL, LDS 1849).

Hazen, Anzel Washburn. A BRIEF HISTORY OF THE FIRST CHURCH OF CHRIST IN MIDDLETOWN, CONNECTICUT, FOR TWO CENTURIES AND A HALF: 1668-1918. N.p., n.d. 165 p. Index.

A HISTORICAL SKETCH OF THE PARISH OF THE CHURCH OF THE HOLY TRINITY (FORMERLY CHRIST CHURCH), MIDDLETOWN, CONNECTICUT. Middletown: Pelton and King Printers, 1887. 52 p.

Lindenthal, Jacob Jay. "Early History of the Jews of Middletown, Connecticut." Ph.D. dissertation, Yeshiva University, 1973. 516 p.

Richter, Mrs. Louis Eugene. FAITHFUL REMNANT CHURCH OF THE HOLY TRINITY, MIDDLETOWN, CONNECTICUT FROM ARCHIVES AND RECORDS 1724-1874 AND OTHER MIDDLESEX COUNTY DATA. 2 vols. N.p.: Author, 1969.

VITAL RECORDS FROM REV. SAMUEL F. JARVIS' MANUSCRIPT. CHRIST CHURCH. MIDDLETOWN 1836-1839. Typescript. Hartford: CSL, 1929. 5 p.

HISTORICAL SOCIETY

The Middlesex County Historical Society, General Mansfield House, 15 Main Street, 06457. (203) 346-0746.

LAND RECORDS

Land Records, 1640-1853. (LDS 004,792 - 004,831).

Index, 1654-1855. (LDS 004,788 - 004,791).

Copy of Deeds, 1640-1853. Index, 1654-1855. (CSL, LDS 1842, pt. 1-44).

Jacobus, Donald Lines. "Middletown (Conn.) Proprietors, 1673." TAG 10 (1933): 109.

LIBRARIES

Godfrey Memorial Library, 134 Newfield Street, 06457. (203) 346-4375.

Russell Public Library, 119 Broad Street, 06457. (203) 347-2528.

Wesleyan University, Olin Library. Archives. Church Street, 06457. (203) 347-9411 ext. 456.

NEWSPAPERS

MIDDLETOWN PRESS. Daily. 472 Main Street, 06457. (203) 347-3331.

The HALE NEWSPAPER INDEX to deaths and marriages includes:
> AMERICAN SENTINEL & WITNESS. 1 January 1823-23 December 1866.
> MIDDLESEX GAZETTE. 8 November 1785-27 November 1883.
> MIDDLESEX REPUBLICAN. 29 January 1857-15 October 1857.
> MIDDLETOWN CONSTITUTION. 3 January 1838-26 December 1866.
> MIDDLETOWN NEWS AND ADVERTISER. 4 January 1851-29 December 1854.
> RAINBOW AND OASIS. 26 January 1850-August 1860.

The PRELIMINARY CHECKLIST lists thirty-four newspapers for MIDDLETOWN.

PROBATE RECORDS

Middletown Probate District, Marino Professional Building, 94 Court Street, P.O. Box 1143, 06457. (203) 347-7424.

Organized May 1752 from the East Haddam, Guilford and Hartford Probate Districts.

Probate districts organized from the Middletown Probate District include the Berlin, East Hampton and Haddam Probate Districts.

ON FILE AT THE CSL: Estate Papers, 1752-1831. Indexes, 1752-1831. Inventory Control Book, 1752-1831. Court Record Book, 1752-1855.

Probate Records, 1752-1855. (LDS 1843 pt. 1-9).

TAX RECORDS

Hartford. CSL, Record Group 62. Tax Lists, 1860-1949.

VITAL RECORDS

Town Clerk, Town Hall, DeKoven Drive and Court Street, P.O. Box 141, 06457. (203) 347-4671, ext. 224.

The town clerk's earliest birth record is April 1640, marriage record is February 1654 and death record is April 1655.

The BARBOUR INDEX covers the years 1651-1854 and is based on the James N. Arnold copy of MIDDLETOWN vital records made in 1913.

"Connecticut Births Before 1730 (Barbour)--Town of Middletown." CN 1 (1969-70): 77-79; 2 (1969-70): 13-14, 82-83, 156-58, 233-35; 3 (1970-71): 16-19, 132-35, 239-42, 374-77; 4 (1971-72): 18-23, 176-81, 326-31, 484.

Jacobus, Donald Lines. "Middletown (Conn.) Vital Records in Land Records, Volume I." TAG 12 (1936): 155-70, 210-22; 13 (1936): 32-45.

"Marriages." CN 13 (1980): 206-9, 384-89.

Parsons, Samuel H. "Record of the Births, Marriages and Deaths of the First Proprietors of Lands in Middletown, Connecticut (Copied from the records of Middletown, Connecticut, Vol. I.)." NEHGR 14 (1860): 63-68, 133-39.

PUBLISHED WORKS AND OTHER RECORDS

Adams, Charles Collard. MIDDLETOWN UPPER HOUSES, A HISTORY OF THE NORTH SOCIETY OF MIDDLETOWN, CONNECTICUT, FROM 1650 TO 1800, WITH GENEALOGICAL AND BIOGRAPHICAL CHAPTERS ON EARLY FAMILIES AND A FULL GENEALOGY OF THE RANEY FAMILY. New York: Grafton Press, 1908. 847 p.

Brainerd, A. MIDDLETOWN ILLUSTRATED. N.p., n.d. 28 p.

Chafee, Grace Irene. "Middletown." CQ 4 (1898): 10-29.

Cox, Ally. "The Wall Paintings of the Alsop House." ANTIQUES 58 (September 1950): 172, 174-76.

Donahue, William C., Jr. "The Greater Middletown Preservation Trust." CANTIQUARIAN 37 (December 1975): 22-25.

Field, David Dudley. CENTENNIAL ADDRESS WITH HISTORICAL SKETCHES OF CROMWELL, PORTLAND, CHATHAM, MIDDLE-HADDAM, MIDDLETOWN AND ITS PARISHES. Middletown: William B. Casey, 1853. 296 p.

Gilman, Emma C. "Hero of Battleship 'Saratoga' MacDonough of Connecticut." CM 11 (1907): 553-59.

Jackson, Margaret Ellen. "Some Old Mattabeseck Families." CM 7 (1903): 473-82; 8 (1903): 101-7.

Kane, Patricia Ellen. "Joiners of Middletown and Farmington." CHSB 35 (1970): 81-85.

"List of Freemen in Middletown." (LDS 897,076).

"List of Freemen in Middletown (1669)." CHS COLLECTIONS 21:190.

"List of the Householders and Proprietors, as taken March 22nd, 1670." NEHGR 14 (1860): 139.

Sangre, Walter H. "Mel Hyblaeum: A Study of the People of Middletown of Sicilian Extraction." Master's thesis, Wesleyan University, 1952. 142 p.

Van Dusen, Albert Edward. MIDDLETOWN AND THE AMERICAN REVOLUTION. Middletown: Middlesex County Historical Society, 1950. 36 p.

Wallace, Willard Mosher. MIDDLETOWN TERCENTENARY, 1650-1950. N.p.: 1950. 44 p.

Wyllis Papers. GOVERNOR GEORGE WYLLYS OF CONNECTICUT 1590-1796. Hartford: Hartford Historical Society, 1924. 567 p. Index.

MILFORD

NEW HAVEN COUNTY. Organized 1639. Towns organized from MILFORD include ORANGE and WOODBRIDGE.

CEMETERY RECORDS AND CEMETERIES

NAME	ADDRESS	HALE NO.	CITATION
Milford Center Cemetery	35 Gulf Stream (203) 874-8998	1	28:1-144 29:145-48
St. Mary Roman Catholic Cemetery	305 Buckingham Avenue	2	29:149-60
New Roman Catholic Cemetery	Boston Post Road	3	29:161
Founders Cemetery	Milford Memorial Bridge	4	29:162-66
Kings Highway Cemetery	281 Cherry Street (203) 874-8998	5	(no citation)

Index to Hale inscriptions: 29-87-109.

Abbott, Morris Woods. INDEX TO ACCOMPANY CHART OF THE OLDEST PORTION OF THE MILFORD CEMETERY, MILFORD, CONNECTICUT. Typescript. 1943. 23 p.

_____. "Inscriptions on Tombstones in Milford, Connecticut." TAG 26 (1950): 36-41.

_____. MILFORD TOMBSTONE INSCRIPTIONS WITH GENEALOGICAL NOTES. Milford: Author, 1967. 138 p. Index. (LDS 897,321).

_____. OLD TOMBSTONES IN MILFORD CEMETERY, OR STYLES IN STELLES. Milford: Author, 1974. 17 p.

Buckingham, Leah, and Abbott, Morris W. INSCRIPTIONS COPIED FROM HEADSTONES IN MILFORD, CONNECTICUT CEMETERY. Milford, Conn.: W. Abbott, 1977. 28 p.

"Connecticut Headstone Inscriptions Before 1800 (Hale)--Town of Milford." CN 5 (1972-73): 364-68, 508-13; 6 (1973): 196-99.

Diamond, Frederica Craft. "Grotesque inscriptions in God's Acre Tombs of the dead decorated with quaint sculpture and epitaphs-moss covered and crumbling stones marking the resting places of the forefathers in the little burying ground at Milford, Connecticut." CM 9 (1905): 262-68.

Greene, Maria Louise. "Milford Cemetery." CM 5 (1899): 430-33, 485-89.

"Inscriptions on Tombstones in Milford." NHCHS PAPERS 5 (1894): 1-69c.

CHURCH RECORDS

FIRST CONGREGATIONAL CHURCH. Minutes, 1804-1889. Vital Records, 1784-1926. (CSL, LDS 1875). Marriages, 1784-1799. BAILEY 5:7-11. Records, 1639-1926. Index. (CSL).

MARY TAYLOR MEMORIAL METHODIST CHURCH. Records, 1790s-- . (Milford Historical Society).

PLYMOUTH SECOND CONGREGATIONAL CHURCH. Minutes, 1899-1926. Vital Records, 1851-1898. (CSL, LDS 1876). Marriages, 1747-1799. BAILEY 5:11-14. Records, 1747-1926. Index. (CSL).

ST. PETER EPISCOPAL CHURCH. Minutes, 1764-1843. Vital Records, 1832-1868. (CSL, LDS 1877).

Abbot, Mrs. Morris Woods. RECORDS OF PLYMOUTH CONGREGATIONAL CHURCH, FORMERLY SECOND CHURCH, MILFORD, CONNECTICUT. BAPTISMS, MARRIAGES, BURIALS, DEATHS, 1747-1885. Milford: Freelove Baldwin Stow Chapter, DAR, 1949. Index. (LDS 823,816).

Hartford. CSL, Record Group 62. First Ecclesiastical Society. Rate Book, 1875-1829, 1831-1834.

Jacobus, Donald Lines. "Milford Church Records Admissions, First Church, 1639-1687." TAG 16 (1940): 28-38.

PROCEEDINGS AT THE CELEBRATION OF THE TWO HUNDRED AND FIFTIETH ANNIVERSARY OF THE FIRST CHURCH OF CHRIST, IN MILFORD, CONNECTICUT, AUGUST 25TH, 1889. Ansonia: Evening Sentinal, 1890. 189 p.

Moran, Gerald Francis. "Religious Renewal, Puritan Tribalism, and the Family in Seventeenth Century Milford, Connecticut." WILLIAM AND MARY QUARTERLY 36 (April 1979): 236-54.

HISTORICAL SOCIETY

Milford Historical Society, 32-34 High Street, Box 337, 06460. (203) 874-2664. Publishes: WHARF LANE NEWSLETTER. Bimonthly.

LAND RECORDS

Land Records, 1639-1852. Index, 1639-1862. (LDS 1873 pt. 1-18).

Jacobus, Donald Lines. "Milford, Connecticut, Land Records . . . ." TAG 10 (1933): 34-35; 12 (1936): 170-75; 16 (1940): 238-40.

Labaree, Leonard Woods. MILFORD, CONNECTICUT THE EARLY DEVELOPMENT OF A TOWN AS SHOWN IN ITS LAND RECORDS. Connecticut Tercentenary Publication, no. 13. New Haven: Yale University Press, 1933. 29 p.

LIBRARIES

Milford Public Library, 3 Broad Street, 06469. (203) 874-7659.

Green, Maria Louise. "Taylor Library Milford, Connecticut." CM 5 (1899): 266-71.

NEWSPAPERS

MILFORD CITIZEN. Daily. 117 Broad Street, 06460. (203) 874-1691.

The PRELIMINARY CHECKLIST lists seven newspapers for MILFORD.

PROBATE RECORDS

Milford Probate District, City Hall, River Street, Box 414, 06460. (203) 878-1731 ext. 69.

>   Organized 30 May 1832 from the New Haven Probate District.
>   ON FILE AT THE CSL: Court Record Books, 1832-1853.

Probate Records, 1832-1853. (LDS 1874).

VITAL RECORDS

Town Clerk, City Hall, River Street, 06460. (203) 878-1731.

> The town clerk's earliest birth, marriage and death records date from 1639.

The BARBOUR INDEX covers the years 1640-1850 and is based on the James N. Arnold copy of MILFORD vital records made in 1914.

"Connecticut Births Before 1730 (Barbour)--Town of Milford." CN 4 (1972): 484-89; 5 (1972-73): 9-14, 326-31, 475-79; 7 (1974): 11-14.

"Milford (Conn.) Vital Records." TAG 9 (1932-33): 100-120, 159-73.

PUBLISHED WORKS AND OTHER RECORDS

Abbott, Morris Woods. MEDICAL MEN OF MILFORD. Milford, Conn.: Milford Medical Society, 1965. 40 p.

Abbott, Susan Emma Woodruff. FAMILIES OF EARLY MILFORD, CONNECTI-CUT. Baltimore: Genealogical Publishing Co., 1979. 875 p. Index.

_____. FIRST FAMILIES OF MILFORD, CONNECTICUT. 2 vols. Milford: Author, 1976.

Account Book of Joseph Tibbals. (LDS 441,390).

"Associate Library in Milford (1761)." CHSB 13 (1948): 12-16.

Ford, George Hare. HISTORICAL SKETCHES OF THE TOWN OF MILFORD. New Haven: Tuttle, Morehouse and Taylor, 1914. 80 p.

Greene, Maria Louise. "Milford 1689-1900." CM 5 (1899): 570-84.

Hartford. CSL. Record Group 33. Boxes 147-53. Materials related to HISTORY OF MILFORD; CONNECTICUT 1639-1939.

HISTORY OF MILFORD, CONNECTICUT 1639-1939. Bridgeport: Federal Writers Project, WPA, 1939. 210 p.

Labaree, Leonard Woods. MILFORD, CONNECTICUT: THE EARLY DEVELOPMENT OF A TOWN AS SHOWN IN ITS LAND RECORDS. Connecticut Tercentenary Publication, no. 13. New Haven: Yale University Press, 1933. 32 p.

Moran, Gerald Francis. "Religious Renewal, Puritan Tribalism, and the Family in Seventeenth-Century Milford, Connecticut." WILLIAM AND MARY QUARTERLY 36 (April 1979): 236-56.

O'Donnell, William G. "Race Relations in a New England Town." NEQ, 14 (1941): 235-42.

Pond, Mrs. Nathan Gillette. "Journal of 'Sir' Peter Pond--Born in Milford, Connecticut, in 1740." CM 10 (1906): 235-59.

Pond, Nathan Gillette. "Milford Families." (NHCHS, LDS 1455).

Stevenson, Malcolm. "A Yankee Continental, Sergeant Joseph Martin." NEW ENGLAND GALAXY 20, no. 3 (1979): 44-51.

Stowe, Nathan, and Newton, Harrison. SIXTY YEARS' RECOLLECTIONS OF MILFORD, AND ITS CHRONOLOGY FROM 1637 UP TO AND INCLUDING 1916. Milford: N.p., n.d. 95 p.

Walker, Gladys. "My Lifelong Love Affair with a Haunted Island." CONNECTICUT 35 (July 1972): 30-33.

MONROE

FAIRFIELD COUNTY. Organized May 1823 from SHELTON.

CEMETERY RECORDS AND CEMETERIES

NAME	ADDRESS	HALE NO.	CITATION
Elm Street Cemetery	Northeast of Lower Stepney	1	29:1-17
East Village Cemetery	East Village Road	2	29:18-34
Stepney Cemetery	21 Pepper Street	3	29:35-65
Walker's Farm Cemetery	Near Newtown Town Line U.S. 53	4	29:66-69
Center Cemetery	Old Tannery Road	5	29:70-86
Potsford Cemetery	Hammertown Road		(no citation)
Cutler's Farm Cemetery	Cross Hill Road		(no citation)

Index to Hale inscriptions: 29:87-109.

"Cutler's Farms Graveyard, Monroe, Connecticut." TAG 11 (1934): 53-55.

"Inscriptions, Upper Stepney, Monroe, Connecticut." TAG 12 (1935): 51-55.

Sarah Riggs Humphreys Chapter, DAR. INSCRIPTIONS IN THE EAST VILLAGE CEMETERY WEST OF ZOAR BRIDGE, CONNECTICUT. N.p.: Author, n.d. 28 p.

CHURCH RECORDS

CONGREGATIONAL CHURCH. Records, 1762-1812. (CSL, LDS 1879).
ST. PETER EPISCOPAL CHURCH. Minutes, 1823-1908. (CSL, LDS 1880).

HISTORICAL SOCIETY

Monroe Historical Society, Monroe Center, 06468. (203) 261-3097.

LAND RECORDS

Land Records, 1823-1858. Index, 1823-1924. (LDS 1878 pt. 1-4).

LIBRARY

Monroe Center Public Library, 7 Fan Hill Road, 06468. (203) 261-3651.

NEWSPAPER

The PRELIMINARY CHECKLIST lists one newspaper for MONROE.

PROBATE RECORDS

MONROE is in the Trumbull Probate District.

TAX RECORDS

Hartford. CSL, Record Group 62. Abstracts or Grand Lists for 1871-1872, 1876-1879, 1881-1884, 1886-1889, 1891-1954.

VITAL RECORDS

Town Clerk, Town Hall, 11 Fan Hill Road, 06468. (203) 261-3651, ext. 26.

>   The town clerk's earliest birth, marriage and death records date from 1847.

The BARBOUR INDEX covers the years 1823-1854 and is based on the James N. Arnold copy of MONROE vital records made in 1917.

PUBLISHED WORKS AND OTHER RECORDS

Coffey, Edward Nichols. A GLIMPSE OF OLD MONROE. Derby: Bacon Publishing Co., 1974. 118 p.

MONTVILLE

NEW LONDON COUNTY. Organized 12 October 1786 from NEW LONDON.
Towns organized from MONTVILLE include SALEM.

CEMETERY RECORDS AND CEMETERIES

NAME	ADDRESS	HALE NO.	CITATION
Comatook Cemetery	107 Depot Road	1	29:1-39
St. Patrick Roman Catholic Cemetery	126 Depot Road	2	29:40-44
Chesterfield Cemetery	Route 161	3	29:45-55
Raymond Hill Cemetery	Route 163	4	29:56-71
Shantok Cemetery	Fort Shantock (Mohegan Indian)	5	29:72
Maples Cemetery #1	Montville Hill	6	29:73
Maples Cemetery #2	Montville Hill	7	29:74
Parker Cemetery	Montville Hill (not located)	8	29:75
Brainard Cemetery	Chapel Hill	9	29:76
Dolbear Cemetery	Fitch Corners	10	29:77
Smith Cemetery	Massapeag	11	29:78
Lewis Cemetery	Palmertown	12	29:79
Rogers Cemetery #1	Montville Hill	13	29:80
Rogers Cemetery #2	1/2 mile north of Montville Center Road	14	29:81
Johnson Cemetery	On Norwich and New London Road	15	29:82
Indian Cemetery		16	29:83

NAME	ADDRESS	HALE NO.	CITATION
Gay Cemetery	18 Depot Road	17	29:84
Smith Cemetery	Palmertown	18	29:85
Fox Cemetery	Near Fair Oaks	19	29:86
Raymond Cemetery	Route 163	20	29:87
Miner Cemetery	Near Oxoboxo Lake	21	29:88
Champlin Cemetery	Near Oxoboxo Lake	22	29:89
Chester Cemetery	On Salem Road	23	29:90
Thompson Cemetery	South of Champlin Cemetery	24	29:91
Maynard Cemetery	South of Champlin Cemetery	25	29:92
Allen Cemetery	Opposite Maynard Cemetery	26	29:93
Baker Cemetery	South of Maynard Cemetery	27	29:94
Chapel Cemetery	1 mile south of Baker Cemetery	28	29:95
Mosier Cemetery #1	Next to Brainard Cemetery Chapel Hill	29	29:96
Jewish Cemetery	Chesterfield Road	30	29:97
Gilbert Cemetery	Near Chesterfield	31	29:98
DeWolf Cemetery	Near Chesterfield	32	29:99
Martenus Cemetery	Near Chesterfield (2 stones)	33	29:100
Latimer Cemetery	Back of DeWolf Cemetery near Chesterfield	34	29:101
Cemetery removed to Waterford		35	29:102
Comstock Cemetery	South of Chapel Hill	36	29:103
Douglass Cemetery	On Harrison Daniels farm south part of town	37	29:104
Chapman Cemetery	413 Chapel Hill Road	38	29:105-6
Street-Gongdon Cemetery	Waterford Road	39	29:107-9
(Cemetery not named)		40	29:110
Baker Cemetery #1	Montville Hill Road	41	29:111
Baker Cemetery #2	Montville Hill	42	29:112
Jewish Cemetery	Leffingwell Road	43	29:113
Rogers Cemetery #3	Near Norwich town line	44	29:114

NAME	ADDRESS	HALE NO.	CITATION
Indian Cemetery	415 Massapeag Side Road	45	29:115
Smith-Rogers Cemetery	Near Thames River	46	29:116
Spicer Cemetery	75 Massapeag Side Road	47	29:117
Rogers Cemetery #4	Near Thames River	48	29:118-19
Stoddard Cemetery	Near Thames River	49	29:120
White Cemetery	Near Thames River	50	29:121
Haughton Cemetery	1 mile north of Uncasville	51	29:122
Dolbear Cemetery	At Fort Shantok	52	29:123
Rogers Cemetery #5	At Trading Cove	53	29:124
St. John the Baptist (Greek Orthodox) Church Cemetery	Route 85		(no citation)

Index to Hale inscriptions: 29:126-52.

Barbour, Lucius Barnes. "Connecticut Cemetery Inscriptions." NEHGR 98 (1944): 286-88.

Raymond, Mrs. Edith. TRANSCRIPT OF RECORDS OF THE NORTH CON-GREGATIONAL SOCIETY IN NEW LONDON, 1722-1819, GRAVESTONE INSCRIPTIONS FROM FIVE MONTVILLE CEMETERIES TO 1850 AND ALL REMAINING RECORDS OF THE CHESTERFIELD CONGREGATIONAL SOCIETY, 1769-1820. Montville: Author, n.d. 199 p.

CHURCH RECORDS

BAPTIST CHURCH. Minutes, etc., 1749-1827. (Western Reserve Historical Society NUCMUC M375-1340).

CONGREGATIONAL CHURCH. Minutes, 1722-1909. Vital Records, 1722-1827. (CSL, LDS 1854).

CONGREGATIONAL CHURCH (FORMERLY NEW LONDON NORTH PARISH.) Minutes, 1721-1837. (CSL, LDS 1854).

CONGREGATIONAL CHURCH. Records, 1722-1909. Index. (CSL). Marriages, 1724-1738. BAILEY 1:69-70.

Baker, Henry Augustus. "Record of Baptisms and Marriages by Rev. Royel Cook, Third Pastor of the Second Church in the North Parish of New London, (Now Montville), Conn., from 1784-1798." MAGAZINE OF NEW ENGLAND HISTORY 1 (1891): 186-89, 212-15.

_____. "Record of the Second Church in the North Parish of New London, (now Montville) Conn., from 1722 to 1740." MAGAZINE OF NEW ENGLAND HISTORY 1 (1891): 42-50, 186-89, 213-15.

HISTORICAL SOCIETY

Montville Historical Society, P.O. Box 1786, 06353.

LIBRARY

Raymond Library, Raymond Hill Road, 06382. (203) 848-9943.

NEWSPAPERS

The PRELIMINARY CHECKLIST lists two newspapers for MONTVILLE.

PROBATE RECORDS

Montville Probate District, Town Hall, 310 Norwich-New London Turnpike, 06382. (203) 848-9847.

> Organized 27 June 1851 from the New London Probate District.

> ON FILE AT THE CSL: Estate Papers, 1850-1935. Index, 1850-1935. Inventory Control Book, 1850-1935.

TAX RECORDS

Hartford. CSL, Record Group 62. Tax Abstracts or Grand Lists 1891-1929.

VITAL RECORDS

Town Clerk, Town Hall, 310 Norwich-New London Turnpike, 06382. (203) 848-1349.

> The town clerk's earliest birth record is 1770, marriage record is 1769 and death record is 1793.

The BARBOUR INDEX covers the years 1786-1850 and is based on the original records which have been damaged. The book HISTORY OF MONTVILLE (see below) included many of the town's vital records. It was published in 1876 and probably was based on the original records which had been lost. Henry A. Baker was a Montville Town Clerk. The original records that we now have were found in 1925 and are in the CSL.

Marriage Records, 1820-1855. (LDS 1854).

PUBLISHED WORKS AND OTHER RECORDS

Baker, Henry Augustus. HISTORY OF MONTVILLE, CONNECTICUT FORMERLY THE NORTH PARISH OF NEW LONDON FROM 1640 TO 1896. Hartford: Case, Lockwood and Brainard, Co., 1876. 727 p.

Gallup, Mrs. Herbert W. COMPLETE INDEX TO HENRY A. BAKER'S HISTORY OF MONTVILLE, CONNECTICUT. Hartford: Author, 1930. 106 p.

MORRIS

LITCHFIELD COUNTY. Organized June 1859 from LITCHFIELD.

CEMETERY RECORDS AND CEMETERIES

NAME	ADDRESS	HALE NO.	CITATION
Morris Cemetery	In Center	1	29:1-28
Footville Cemetery	At West Morris 2 miles west of Morris Center	2	29:29-37
Town Poor Cemetery	On farm of L and S Whittlesey, east side of Bantam Lake	3	29:38
Stone		4	29:39

Index to Hale inscriptions: 29:40-51.

Payne, Charles Thomas. LITCHFIELD AND MORRIS INSCRIPTIONS. A RECORD OF INSCRIPTIONS UPON THE TOMBSTONES IN THE TOWNS OF LITCHFIELD AND MORRIS, CONNECTICUT. Litchfield: Dwight C. Kilbourn, 1905. 304 p. (LDS 823,773).

CHURCH RECORDS

CONGREGATIONAL CHURCH. Minutes, 1854-1892. Vital Records, 1767-1854. (CSL, LDS 1883). Records, 1767-1892. Index. (CSL). Marriages, 1787-1799. BAILEY 6:84-86.

HISTORICAL SOCIETY

Morris Historical Society, 06763.

LIBRARY

Morris Public Library, Route 61, 06763. (203) 567-0160.

NEWSPAPER

The PRELIMINARY CHECKLIST lists one newspaper for MORRIS.

PROBATE RECORDS

MORRIS is in the Litchfield Probate District.

SCHOOL RECORDS

Hartford. CSL, Record Group 62. Miscellaneous Records, 1839-1858.

Strong, Barbara Nolan. THE MORRIS ACADEMY 1790-1888. PIONEER IN COEDUCATION. Morris: Morris Bicentennial Committee, 1976. 135 p. Index.

VITAL RECORDS

Town Clerk, Town Hall, 06763. (203) 567-5387.

> The town clerk's earliest birth, marriage and death record is dated 1859.

Record of Deaths, 1767-1789 at South Farms now in the Town of Morris. 20 p. (NYGBS, LDS 1803).

PUBLISHED WORKS AND OTHER RECORDS

Choate, Mrs. Washington. "Memoirs of a Connecticut Patriot, Life Story of James Morris as told in his Own Manuscript." CM 11 (1907): 449-55.

1976 EARLY HOMES OF SOUTH FARMS (NOW MORRIS) A BICENTENNIAL SURVEY OF HOMES BUILT BEFORE 1859 AND STILL OCCUPIED. Morris: Bicentennial Committee on Historic Homes, Morris Public Library, 1976. 66 p.

Weik, Laura Stoddard. "ONE HUNDRED YEARS"--HISTORY OF MORRIS, CONNECTICUT 1859-1959. Morris: Morris Centennial Committee, 1959. 250 p.

NAUGATUCK

NEW HAVEN COUNTY. Organized May 1844 from BETHANY, OXFORD and WATERBURY. Towns organized from NAUGATUCK include BEACON FALLS.

CEMETERY RECORDS AND CEMETERIES

NAME	ADDRESS	HALE NO.	CITATION
Grove Cemetery	U.S. 54	1	29:1-57
St. James Roman Catholic Cemetery	Riverside Drive office: 2324 East Main Street Waterbury, 06705 (203) 754-9105	2	29:58-124
Gunntown Cemetery	Gunntown Road	3	29:125-37
Ancient Cemetery	In cellar of church on green	4	29:138
Hillside Cemetery	U.S. 54	5	29:139-234
St. Francis Roman Catholic Cemetery	High Street office: 2324 East Main Street Waterbury, 06705 (203) 754-9105	6	29:235-60
Wooster Cemetery	Route 68	7	29:261-62
Polish National Catholic Cemetery	New Haven Road	8	29:263
Oak Street Cemetery	Oak Street	9	29:264-66
Old Salem Cemetery	30 Oak Street		(no citation)

Index to Hale inscriptions: 29:267-323.

Jillson, Myrtle M. "Those Buried in Gunntown Cemetery, Naugatuck, Connecticut." TAG 13 (1936-37): 21-31, 166-80.

CHURCH RECORDS

CONGREGATIONAL CHURCH. Vital Records, 1781-1901. (CSL, LDS 1944).

FIFTIETH ANNIVERSARY 1887-1937, SALEM NAUGATUCK LUTHERAN CHURCH, A BRIEF HISTORY OF THE CHURCH AND ITS ORGANIZATIONS. Naugatuck: Salem Lutheran Church, 1937. 86 p.

A NARRATIVE AND DOCUMENTARY HISTORY OF ST. JOHN'S PROTESTANT EPISCOPAL CHURCH (FORMERLY ST. JAMES) OF WATERBURY, CONNECTI-CUT. WITH SOME NOTICE OF ST. PAUL'S CHURCH, PLYMOUTH, CHRIST CHURCH, WATERTOWN, ST. MICHAEL'S CHURCH, NAUGATUCK, A CHURCH IN MIDDLEBURY, ALL SAINT'S CHURCH, WOLCOTT, ST. PAUL'S CHURCH WATERVILLE, TRINITY CHURCH, WATERBURY, (ALL COLONIES OF ST. JOHN'S). New Haven: Price, Lee, and Adkins, 1907. 187 p.

HISTORICAL SOCIETY

Naugatuck Historical Society, 144 Meadow Street, P.O. Box 317, 06770.

LAND RECORDS

Land Records, 1844-1854. (LDS 1943 pt. 1-2).

LIBRARY

Whittenmore Memorial Library, 243 Church Street, 06770. (203) 729-3212.

MILITARY RECORDS

THE RECORD OF THE ERECTION AND DEDICATION OF THE SOLDIERS' MONUMENT, NAUGATUCK, CONNECTICUT DECORATION DAY, 1885, WITH SOME ACCOUNT OF THE WAR HISTORY OF THE TOWN. Naugatuck: The Committee, 1885. 48 p.

"Revolutionary War Pay Roll, 1777." (Transcript from a book of Stephen Goodyear). NGSO 9 (1920): 45.

NEWSPAPERS

NAUGATUCK DAILY NEWS. Daily. 195 Water Street, 06770. (203) 729-2228.

The PRELIMINARY CHECKLIST lists ten newspapers for NAUGATUCK.

PROBATE RECORDS

Naugatuck Probate District, Town Hall, 229 Church Street, 06770. (203) 729-4571.

Organized 4 July 1863 from the Waterbury Probate District.

The Naugatuck Probate District includes BEACON FALLS.

SCHOOL RECORDS

Hartford. CSL, Record Group 62. Registers, 1852-1871.

Ward, William. THE EARLY SCHOOLS OF NAUGATUCK, A BRIEF HISTORY OF OUR SCHOOLS, TEACHERS, TEXT BOOKS, ETC. FROM 1730 TO 1850. Naugatuck: Perry Press, 1906. 95 p.

VITAL RECORDS

Town Clerk, Town Hall, 229 Church Street, 06770. (203) 729-4571.

The BARBOUR INDEX covers the years 1844-1853 and is based on the Percy E. Hulbert copy of NAUGATUCK vital records made in 1927.

PUBLISHED WORKS AND OTHER RECORDS

Bronson, Henry. HISTORY OF WATERBURY, CONNECTICUT. THE ORIGINAL TOWNSHIP EMBRACING PRESENT WATERTOWN AND PLYMOUTH, AND PARTS OF OXFORD, WOLCOTT, MIDDLEBURY, PROSPECT AND NAUGATUCK. WITH AN APPENDIX OF BIOGRAPHY, GENEALOGY AND STATISTICS. Waterbury: Bronson Bros., 1858. 583 p. Index. (LDS 599,254).

Leuchars, William G. NAUGATUCK STORIES AND LEGENDS. Naugatuck: Naugatuck Historical Society, 1969. 110 p.

_____. NAUGATUCK STORIES AND LEGENDS II. Naugatuck: Author, 1977. 125 p.

McLaughlin, Constance Green. HISTORY OF NAUGATUCK. Naugatuck: Author, 1948. 331 p.

_____. HISTORY OF NAUGATUCK. New Haven: Yale University Press, 1949. 383 p.

Roth, Leland M. "Three Industrial Towns by McKin, Mead and White." JOURNAL OF THE SOCIETY OF ARCHITECTURAL HISTORIANS 38 (1979): 317-47.

NEW BRITAIN

HARTFORD COUNTY. Organized May 1850 from BERLIN.

CEMETERY RECORDS AND CEMETERIES

NAME	ADDRESS	HALE NO.	CITATION
Fairview Cemetery	120 Stanley Street	1	30:1-326
St. Mary Roman Catholic Cemetery (New)	1309 Stanley Street (203) 225-1938	2	30:327-466
St. Mary Roman Catholic Cemetery (Old)	44 Beatty Street	3	30:467-508
Sacred Heart Cemetery	2180 Osgood Street	4	30:509-31
Congregation Beth Alom Cemetery	60 Allen Street (203) 223-8663	5	30:532-46
Holy Trinity Greek Catholic Cemetery	249 Osgood Avenue	6	30:547-50
Andrews Cemetery	53 Sefton Drive	7	30:551
Russian Orthodox Cemetery	280 Wells Street	8	30:552
Beth Mishka Cemetery	60 Chapman Street	9	30:553
Town Farm Cemetery	Kelsey Street	10	30:554-57

Index to Hale inscriptions: 30:558-706.

CHURCH RECORDS

FIRST BAPTIST CHURCH. Minutes, 1832-1922. Vital Records, 1821-1836. (CSL, LDS 1967).

FIRST CHURCH OF CHRIST, New Britain. Records, etc., 1754-1931. (Central Connecticut State College, Burritt Library).

Andrews, Alfred. MEMORIAL, GENEALOGY AND ECCLESIASTICAL HISTORY. Chicago: A.H. Andrews, 1867. 538 p.

Blejwas, Stanislaus A. "A Polish Community in Transition: the Origins and Evolution of Holy Cross Parish, New Britain, Connecticut." POLISH AMERICAN STUDIES 35 (Spring-Autumn 1978): 23-53.

Jerzierski, Bronislas A. "Father Lucian Bejnowski 1868-1960." POLISH AMERICAN STUDIES 16 (1959): 99-107.

A HALF CENTURY OF THE SOUTH CONGREGATIONAL CHURCH NEW BRITAIN, CONNECTICUT 1842-1892. New Britain: South Congregational Church, 1893. 196 p.

ONE HUNDRED AND FIFTIETH ANNIVERSARY, FIRST CHURCH OF CHRIST, NEW BRITAIN, APRIL 25, 26 AND 27, 1908. New Britain: Adkins Printing Co., 1908. 125 p.

"Rev. Elisha Cushman's Record." (First Baptist Church in Hartford 1813 to 1825, Philadelphia, Pennsylvania 1825-1829, Fairfield, Connecticut September 1829-1830, New Haven 1830-1833, Plymouth, Massachusetts 1834-1837, 1840-1863 lay son Rev. Elisha Cushman and contains marriages from Willington, Hartford, New Britain and Deep River until 1863). CHSB 7 (1942): 30-32; 8 (1943): 2-8, 12-13.

Shepard, James. HISTORY OF SAINT MARK'S CHURCH, NEW BRITAIN, CONNECTICUT, AND ITS PREDECESSOR CHRIST CHURCH, WETHERSFIELD AND BERLIN, FROM THE FIRST CHURCH OF ENGLAND SERVICE IN AMERICA TO NINETEEN HUNDRED AND SEVEN. New Britain, Conn.: Tuttle, Morehouse and Taylor Co., 1907. 707 p.

HISTORICAL SOCIETY

Historical Society of New Britain, 06051.

LIBRARIES

New Britain Public Library, 20 High Street, P.O. Box 1291, 06050. (203) 224-3155.

Central Conn. State College. Elihu Burritt Library, Wells Street, 06050. (203) 827-7524.

Camp, David Nelson. "Public Libraries in Connecticut--The Founding and Development of the Institute Library in New Britain." CM 4 (1905): 780-94.

NEWSPAPERS

THE HERALD. Daily. 1 Herald Square, 06050. (203) 225-4601.

The PRELIMINARY CHECKLIST lists twenty-eight newspapers for NEW BRITAIN.

PROBATE RECORDS

NEW BRITAIN is in the Berlin Probate District.

TAX RECORDS

Andrews, Frank DeWette. NAMES OF THE RESIDENTS OF NEW BRITAIN, CONNECTICUT IN THE YEAR 1797 WHO PAID TAXES WITH THE AMOUNT OF THEIR LIST PRINTED FROM THE ORIGINAL MANUSCRIPT IN THE POS-SESSION OF FRANK D. ANDREWS. Vineland, N.J.: Frank D. Andrews, 1910. 11 p.

_____. "Taxpayers of New Britain, Conn." GENEALOGY: A WEEKLY JOUR-NAL OF AMERICAN ANCESTRY 1 (1912): 107-8.

Hartford. CSL, Record Group 62. Tax abstracts, 1822-1879.

VITAL RECORDS

Town Clerk, City Hall, 17 West Main Street, 06051. (203) 224-2491.
    The town clerk's birth, marriage and death records date from 1847.

PUBLISHED WORKS AND OTHER RECORDS

Andrews, Alfred. MEMORIAL, GENEALOGY, AND ECCLESIASTICAL HISTORY. Chicago: A.H. Andrews, 1867. 538 p. Index.

Atwell, George C. "New Britain." CM 6 (1900): 124-42.

Camp, David Nelson. HISTORY OF NEW BRITAIN WITH SKETCHES OF FARMINGTON AND BERLIN, CONNECTICUT 1640-1889. New Britain: William B. Thomson and Co., 1889. 538 p.

Donuzio, Albert F. NEW BRITAIN AND THE CIVIL WAR: WITH A SHORT COMMENTARY ON LINCOLN AND THE EMANCIPATION PROCLAMATION. New Britain, Conn.: Author, 1977. 160 p.

Fowler, Herbert E. A CENTURY OF TEACHER EDUCATION IN CONNECTI-
CUT; THE STORY OF THE NEW BRITAIN STATE NORMAL SCHOOL AND
TEACHERS' COLLEGE OF CONNECTICUT, 1849-1949. New Britain, Conn.:
n.p., 1949. 125 p.

_____. HISTORY OF NEW BRITAIN. New Britain: New Britain Historical
Society, 1960. 294 p.

Hartford. CSL, Record Group 33. Boxes 154-155. Materials for a History of
New Britain. WPA Writers' Project.

Hartford. CSL, Record Group 33. Boxes 127-130. WPA Ethnic Groups Survey. New Britain Office Files, 1936-1940. Reports on individuals and ethnic
groups.

Larson, Kenneth A. A WALK AROUND WALNUT HILL, NEW BRITAIN, CON-
NECTICUT. New Britain, Conn.: Art Press, 1975. 99 p.

"Our First Woman's Club." CQ 2 (1896): 284.

Parker, C.J. "New Britain in the Days of the Revolution." CQ 1 (1895):
379-90; 2 (1896): 72-80.

Tyron, Lillian Hart. STORY OF NEW BRITAIN, CONNECTICUT. Hartford:
Finlay Brothers, 1925. 132 p.

NEW CANAAN

FAIRFIELD COUNTY. Organized May 1801 from NORWALK and STAMFORD.

CEMETERY RECORDS AND CEMETERIES

NAME	ADDRESS	HALE NO.	CITATION
Talmadge Hill Cemetery	Stamford Avenue, foot of Talmadge Hill Road	1	31:1
Smith Cemetery	Jelliffe Mill Road	2	31:2-3
Stevens Cemetery	Weed Street	3	31:4
Weed Cemetery	Frogtown Road	4	31:5-9
Parade Ground Cemetery	Near Oenoke Avenue	5	31:10-16
Lakeview Cemetery	352 Main Street	6	31:17-108
Park Street Cemetery	South of Maple Street	7	31:109-10
Old Cemetery (moved to Lakeview Cemetery)	Carter and Buttery Road	8	31:111
Crissy Cemetery	Stamford Avenue near C.E.T. Fairty's farm	9	31:112-13
Old Cemetery (moved)	Rose Brook Road	10	31:114
Crissy Cemetery	Ponus Ridge Road	11	31:115
Young Cemetery	Ponus Ridge Road	12	31:116
Crissy Cemetery	Ponus Ridge Road	13	31:117
Selleck's Corner Cemetery	17 Barnegat Road	14	31:118-24
Church Hill Cemetery	West Road	15	31:125-28
Carter Cemetery	300 Carter Street	16	31:129-30
Valley Road Cemetery	Valley Road	17	31:131-35

NAME	ADDRESS	HALE NO.	CITATION
Hickock Cemetery	Valley Road	18	31:136
Seely-Stevens Cemetery	Ponus Ridge Road	19	31:137
Silvermine Cemetery	Silvermine Road	20	31:138-43
White Oak Shade Cemetery	White Oak Shade Street	21	31:144
Crissey-Young Cemetery	Ponus Ridge Road	22	31:145
Hoyt Cemetery	Ponus Ridge Road	23	31:146
Crissey Cemetery	Ponus Ridge Road	24	31:147
New Richards Cemetery	Comstock Road	25	31:148-54
Old Richards Cemetery	Next to New Richards Cemetery	26	31:155
Old Mather Cemetery	Post Road, next to Darien line	27	31:156-57
Waters Cemetery	Laurel Reservoir covers this Cemetery	28	31:158
Clinton Cemetery	Near intersection of Norwalk, New Canaan and Visla Roads	29	31:159-60
St. Mark Church Cemetery	West Road		(no citation)

Index to Hale inscriptions: 31:161-202.

CEMETERIES IN AND NEAR NEW CANAAN. Typescript. 131 p. (LDS 1885).

Eardeley, William A.D. CONNECTICUT CEMETERIES. Brooklyn: Author, 1916. (2:45-53.)

INDEX. RURAL CEMETERIES IN NEW CANAAN, CONNECTICUT (1931). INCLUDING REVOLUTIONARY SOLDIERS, MEXICAN SOLDIERS, AND CIVIL WAR SOLDIERS. New Canaan: N.p., n.d. 74 p.

INDEX. RUSSELL HALL'S BURIAL BOOKS 2-4. (CANOE HILL CEMETERY, PARADE HILL CEMETERY, TOWN FARM. NAMES NOT IN RURAL CEME-TERIES OF NEW CANAAN.) New Canaan: N.p., n.d. 7 p.

Menett, Helen. "Smith Family Cemetery. Old Stamford Road, Talmadge Hill Road, New Canaan, Connecticut." DAR MAGAZINE 108 (1974): 866.

CENSUS RECORDS

Bayless, Lois B. TOWN OF NEW CANAAN CENSUS 1790-1800. New Canaan: Author, 1969.

_____. TOWN OF NEW CANAAN CENSUS 1810-1840. New Canaan: Author, 1968. 89 p.

_____. TOWN OF NEW CANAAN CENSUS 1850. New Canaan: Author, 1968. 71 p.

_____. TOWN OF NEW CANAAN CENSUS 1860. New Canaan: Author, 1968. 83 p.

_____. TOWN OF NEW CANAAN CENSUS 1870. New Canaan: Author, n.d. 74 p.

_____. TOWN OF NEW CANAAN CENSUS 1880. New Canaan: Author, 1969. 81 p.

Card, Lester. 1820 CENSUS OF NEW CANAAN, CONNECTICUT. South Norwalk, Conn.: Author, 1941. 17 p.

"New Canaan Heads of Families in 1810." NEW CANAAN HISTORICAL SOCIETY ANNUAL (1954): 272-74.

"New Canaan Heads of Families in 1820." NEW CANAAN HISTORICAL SOSIETY ANNUAL (1954): 275-78.

CHURCH RECORDS

CONGREGATIONAL CHURCH. Records, 1733-1899. Index. (CSL, LDS 1887). Marriages, 1742-1800. BAILEY 4:21-31.

Bacon, Edwin Lex. "The People's Union." NEW CANAAN HISTORICAL SOCIETY ANNUAL, 1974, pp. 12-18.

Benedict, Theodore W. INDEX OF VOLUME II OF THE CHURCH REGISTER OF ST. MARK'S PARISH, NEW CANAAN, CONNECTICUT 1871-1913. New Canaan: Author, 1952. 92 p.

_____. INDEX OF VOLUME III OF THE CHURCH REGISTER OF ST. MARK'S PARISH, NEW CANAAN, CONNECTICUT 1901-1904. New Canaan: Author, 1951. 110 p.

_____. INDEX TO VOLUME IV OF THE CHURCH REGISTER OF ST. MARK'S PARISH, NEW CANAAN, CONNECTICUT 1913-1943. New Canaan: Author, 1951. 44 p.

_____. INDEX OF THE REGISTER OF THE METHODIST CHURCH, NEW CANAAN, CONNECTICUT VOL. I-V (1787-1945). New Canaan: Author, 1953. 139 p.

CANAAN PARISH 1733-1933, BEING THE STORY OF THE CONGREGATIONAL CHURCH OF NEW CANAAN, CONNECTICUT. New Canaan: New Canaan Advertiser, 1935. 265 p.

Connecticut Genealogical Records Committee. "Members of the Congregational Church, New Canaan, Connecticut, June 1833." DAR MAGAZINE 75 (1968): 35-36.

DEATH RECORDS OF NON-CONGREGATIONALISTS KEPT BY REV. WILLIAM BONNEY 1813-1829. N.p., n.d. 8 p.

Eardeley, William A.D. "Marriages January 1, 1800 to November 1832 from the Records of the Congregational Church at New Canaan." In CONNECTICUT CEMETERIES. Brooklyn: 1916. 4:36-50.

_____. NEW CANAAN CONGREGATIONAL CHURCH RECORDS 1733-1850. 2 vols. Brooklyn: Author, 1923.

Fitzgerald, Mrs. John B. RECORDS OF AN OLD REGISTER OF THE CONGREGATIONAL CHURCH IN NEW CANAAN, CONNECTICUT FROM 1739 TO 1850 INCLUSIVE. Typescript. 24 p.

Greenleaf, Joseph, and Davenport, Amonzi B. HISTORICAL ACCOUNT OF THE CELEBRATION OF THE ONE HUNDRED AND FIFTIETH ANNIVERSARY OF THE ORGANIZATION OF THE CONGREGATIONAL CHURCH OF NEW CANAAN, CONNECTICUT JUNE 20, 1883. Stamford: Gillespie Brothers, n.d. 141 p.

Hall, Clifford W. THE EARLY HISTORY OF THE METHODIST EPISCOPAL SUNDAY SCHOOL OF NEW CANAAN, CONNECTICUT. N.p., n.d. 15 p.

Halstead, Vera Colton. "Index to Deaths and Notes, New Canaan Congregational Church Records. Pages 28-98, Vol. 1A, March 14, 1808-May 19, 1853." NEW CANAAN HISTORICAL SOCIETY ANNUAL, 1955, pp. 31-55.

_____. "Newly found New Canaan Records, Congregational Church." NEW CANAAN HISTORICAL SOCIETY ANNUAL, 1955, pp. 26-31.

HISTORICAL ACCOUNT OF THE CELEBRATION OF THE ONE HUNDRED AND FIFTIETH ANNIVERSARY OF THE ORGANIZATION OF THE CONGREGATIONAL CHURCH OF NEW CANAAN, CONNECTICUT JUNE 20, 1883. Stamford: Gillespie Brothers, 1883. 141 p.

Hubbard, G. Evans. "Records of Marriages as copied from Wilton Congregational Church Records." (New Canaan Couples 1778-1780). NEW CANAAN HISTORICAL SOCIETY ANNUAL, 1955. 36 p.

MEMORIAL YEARBOOK AND CHURCH DIRECTORY 1948. New Canaan: Methodist Church of New Canaan, 1948. 48 p.

Pennypacker, John G. ST. MARK'S AND ITS FOREBEARERS 1764-1964. New Canaan: Author, 1964. 175 p.

Schnurbush, Helen M., and Morrill, Grant A. THE HISTORY OF ST. MARK'S PARISH 1964-1971. New Canaan: Authors, 1971. 77 p.

HISTORICAL SOCIETY

New Canaan Historical Society, 13 Oenoke Ridge, 06840 (203) 966-1776.

PUBLISHES THE NEW CANAAN HISTORICAL SOCIETY ANNUAL June 1943-- .

Mitchell, Allan. "Two Living Centuries in New Canaan: A Photo Essay on the New Canaan Historical Society." NEW CANAAN HISTORICAL SOCIETY ANNUAL, 1972, pp. 1-34.

Montgomery, Marshall. "Indexes of the New Canaan Historical Society Library." NEW CANAAN HISTORICAL SOCIETY ANNUAL, 1965, pp. 57-59.

Palmquist, David W. "The Noyes Collection." New Canaan, Connecticut: New Canaan Historical Society, 1969. 82 p.

SUBJECT INDEX, NEW CANAAN HISTORICAL SOCIETY PUBLICATIONS. (READINGS IN NEW CANAAN HISTORY, ANNUALS 1943-1960, CANAAN PARISH, LANDMARKS OF NEW CANAAN, SCRAPBOOK SERIES 2, VOL. 1, VOL. 2). New Canaan: N.p., n.d. 50 p. Index.

LAND RECORDS

Land Records, 1801-1857. Index, 1801-1937. (LDS 1886 pt. 1-10).

"The Division of Common Land in Canaan Parish." NEW CANAAN HISTORICAL SOCIETY ANNUAL, 1944, pp. 11-24.

Hoyt, Stephen B. "The Map of the Industrial Period of New Canaan." NEW CANAAN HISTORICAL SOCIETY ANNUAL, 1944, pp. 29-36.

"The Map of the Homesteading Period of Canaan Parish circa 1772." NEW CANAAN HISTORICAL SOCIETY ANNUAL, 1944 pp. 25-28.

LIBRARY

New Canaan Library, 151 Main Street, 06840. (203) 966-1985.

MILITARY RECORDS

Bayless, Louis B. "Canaan Parish and the American Revolution." NEW CANAAN HISTORICAL SOCIETY ANNUAL, 1976. 124 p.

"Canaan Parish Patriots War of the Revolution." NEW CANAAN HISTORICAL SOCIETY ANNUAL, 1951. 19 p.

"Exerpts from the letters written by New Canaan Men and Women in the Armed Service." NEW CANAAN HISTORICAL SOCIETY ANNUAL, 1943, pp. 31-39.

THE GOLD STAR BOOK OF NEW CANAAN. RECORDS OF WORLD WAR II. 5 vols. New Canaan: War Records Committee of the Town of New Canaan and the New Canaan Historical Society, 1948, 1951.

Montgomery, Marshall H. "Shakers and Soldiers: A New Canaan Mystery and Its Aftermath." NEW CANAAN HISTORICAL SOCIETY ANNUAL, 1956, pp. 109-14.

New Canaan's Part in the War of 1812." NEW CANAAN HISTORICAL SOCIETY ANNUAL, 1954, pp. 279-81.

Pennoyer, Henry F. "Letters from the Front 1861-1865." NEW CANAAN HISTORICAL SOCIETY ANNUAL, 1956, pp. 118-28.

NEWSPAPERS

NEW CANAAN ADVERTISER. Weekly. P.O. Box 605, 06840. (203) 966-9541.

The PRELIMINARY CHECKLIST lists seven newspapers for NEW CANAAN.

The New Canaan Historical Society has indexed the NEW CANAAN-ADVER-TISER 1908-- . NEW CANAAN ERA 1868-1871, and the NEW CANAAN MESSENGER 1877-1913.

Montgomery, Marshall. "New Canaan Newspapers 1818-1973." NEW CA-NAAN HISTORICAL SOCIETY ANNUAL, 1973, pp. 12-24.

_____. "Society Indexes, New Canaan Newspapers." NEW CANAAN HIS-TORICAL SOCIETY ANNUAL, 1956. 132 p.

PROBATE RECORDS

New Canaan Probate District, Town Hall, Main Street, P.O. Box 326, 06840. (203) 966-1530.
    Organized 22 June 1937 from the Norwalk Probate District.

Nelson, Carl V. "Probate Records of New Canaan." NEW CANAAN HIS-TORICAL SOCIETY ANNUAL, 1957. 171 p.

SCHOOL RECORDS

Baldwin, Faith. "Clapboard Hill District of New Canaan, Connecticut." NEW CANAAN HISTORICAL SOCIETY ANNUAL, 1949, pp. 5-9.

Cutler, Isabel C. "A History of the Fourth or Old Church, School District of Canaan Parish and New Canaan." NEW CANAAN HISTORICAL SOCIETY ANNUAL, 1948, pp. 5-55.

Dunn, Mrs. Robert D. "Old School District No. 6 (The Talmadge Hill Re-gion)." NEW CANAAN HISTORICAL SOCIETY ANNUAL, 1946, pp. 29-46.

Geacock, Harvey F. "The Rock School: A Progress Report." NEW CANAAN HISTORICAL SOCIETY ANNUAL, 1973, pp. 6-11.

Hoyt, Stephen B. "School District Number Three, Better Known as the Carter Street or Clapboard Hill District." NEW CANAAN HISTORICAL ANNUAL, 1949, pp. 10-45.

Lee, Winifred Traske. "Notes on Silvermine (Old School District No. 9)." NEW CANAAN HISTORICAL SOCIETY ANNUAL, 1946, pp. 48-66.

"Mrs. William C. Esty's Story of School District No. 7 (The Old Olmstead District)." NEW CANAAN HISTORICAL SOCIETY ANNUAL, 1946, pp. 13-28.

Pennypacker, John G. "Smith Ridge and the Fifth School District." NEW CANAAN HISTORICAL SOCIETY ANNUAL, 1945, pp. 27-74.

Rockwell, Minerve W. COPY OF RECORDS OF SCHOOL DISTRICT NO. 1 1816-1855. New Canaan: Author, 1939. 139 p.

_____. COPY OF RECORDS OF SCHOOL DISTRICT NO. 1 1855-1894. New Canaan: Author, n.d.

Salmon, Genevieve Cartwright. "The Hundred Years of School District One of New Canaan, Connecticut." NEW CANAAN HISTORICAL SOCIETY AN-NUAL, 1945, pp. 14-26.

Schafer, Katherine Morgan. "A Neighborhood Story of Old White Oak Shade School District Number Eight." NEW CANAAN HISTORICAL SOCIETY AN-NUAL, 1947, pp. 18-27.

Tunney, Mary D., and Rockwell, Minerve W. PRIVATE SCHOOLS AND PUB-LIC SCHOOLS, NEW CANAAN, CONNECTICUT. New Canaan: Authors, 1938.

TAX RECORDS

"New Canaan Town Tax, A.D. 1838." NEW CANAAN HISTORICAL SOCIETY ANNUAL, 1953, pp. 188-91.

VITAL RECORDS

Town Clerk, Town Hall, Main Street, P.O. Box 447, 06840. (203) 966-3539.

The BARBOUR INDEX covers the years 1801-1854 and is based on the Mrs. Julia E.C. Brush copy of NEW CANAAN vital records made in 1926.

PUBLISHED WORKS AND OTHER RECORDS

Abbot, Charles R. "A Sketch of Captain Stephen Betts." NEW CANAAN HISTORICAL SOCIETY ANNUAL, 1951, pp. 13-18.

Adam, Sydney. "The Benedict-Lockwood-Fischer Estate." NEW CANAAN HISTORICAL SOCIETY ANNUAL, 1970, pp. 16-20.

Argus, I. "New Canaan Footnotes." FAIRFIELD COUNTY 8 (November 1978): 36-37.

Ballots, Joan H. "The Italo-Americans in New Canaan." NEW CANAAN HISTORICAL SOCIETY ANNUAL, 1975, pp. 28-39.

Bartow, Edith M. "Dan Town: The Lost District." NEW CANAAN HISTORICAL SOCIETY ANNUAL, 1947, pp. 29-39.

Bayles, Lois B. "Cody's Drug Store 1919-1965." NEW CANAAN HISTORICAL SOCIETY ANNUAL, 1966, pp. 49-51.

_____. COMPARATIVE EMPLOYMENT STATISTICS FROM NEW CANAAN CENSUS RECORDS. 1850 THROUGH 1880. New Canaan: Author, 1974.

_____. "Journal of a Family Visitation." NEW CANAAN HISTORICAL SOCIETY ANNUAL, 1974, pp. 19-27.

_____. "New Canaan's Oldest Drug Store: 1845-1855." NEW CANAAN HISTORICAL SOCIETY ANNUAL, 1966, pp. 37-39.

_____. "The Story of Husted Lane." NEW CANAAN HISTORICAL SOCIETY ANNUAL, 1965, pp. 53-55.

Bayles, Lois B.; King, Mary Louise; and Lapham, David F. "The Story of Waveny." NEW CANAAN HISTORICAL SOCIETY ANNUAL, 1969, pp. 12-27.

Bell, Robert B. "Airplanes on South Avenue and the Story of Aeronautics in New Canaan." NEW CANAAN HISTORICAL SOCIETY ANNUAL, 1975, pp. 12-75.

Benedict, Theodore W. "Before the Turn of the Century--Main and Elm Streets." NEW CANAAN HISTORICAL SOCIETY ANNUAL, 1960, pp. 86-95.

_____. "The Shoe Industry in New Canaan, Connecticut." NEW CANAAN HISTORICAL SOCIETY ANNUAL, 1955, pp. 39-55.

Bye, George T. "Dan Town: The Lost District." NEW CANAAN HISTORICAL SOCIETY ANNUAL, 1947, 28 p.

Chrostowski, Ed. "New Canaan: The Town with the Careful Conscience." FAIRFIELD COUNTY 8 (November 1978): 25-26, 29-30, 32-35.

"David Ogden's Voyage on the Kalamazo." NEW CANAAN HISTORICAL SOCIETY ANNUAL, 1967, pp. 28-37.

Eberhart, Jean Christopher. "Orchard Farm." NEW CANAAN HISTORICAL SOCIETY ANNUAL, 1971, pp. 12-17.

_____. "Stepping Stones: The Hatfield Estate." NEW CANAAN HISTORICAL SOCIETY ANNUAL, 1970, pp. 11-15.

Ely, Jean. "New Canaan Modern: The Beginning 1947-1952." NEW CANAAN HISTORICAL SOCIETY ANNUAL, 1967, pp. 8-19.

Eskesen, Hal. "New Canaan, A Colloidal View." FAIRFIELD COUNTY 3 (October 1973): 15-24.

"The First Hundred Years--New Canaan Savings Bank, 1859-1959." NEW CANAAN HISTORICAL SOCIETY ANNUAL, 1959, pp. 6-15.

Garcia-Mata, Lucy Appleton. "Seventeen Days Dead, Seek and You Will Find a Victorian Murder Case." NEW CANAAN HISTORICAL SOCIETY ANNUAL, 1970, pp. 6-10.

Halstead, Paul B. "'New Canaan' or 'N. Canaan.'" NEW CANAAN HISTORICAL SOCIETY ANNUAL, 1955, pp. 37-38.

Hersam, V. Donald, Jr. "The Early Years of Fire Companies in New Canaan." NEW CANAAN HISTORICAL SOCIETY ANNUAL, 1971, pp. 18-29.

_____. "History of the New Canaan Fire Company No. 1, Part 2, 1896-1912." NEW CANAAN HISTORICAL SOCIETY ANNUAL, 1973, pp. 25-36.

Hill, Carlton. "New Canaan's 150th Birthday." NEW CANAAN HISTORICAL SOCIETY ANNUAL, 1952, pp. 86-97.

"Honor Roll-Fifty Years or More New Canaan's Oldest Active Businesses." NEW CANAAN HISTORICAL SOCIETY ANNUAL, 1959, pp. 61-62.

Hoyt, Stephen B. "From the Connecticut to the Rippowam: A Story of Joanas Weed and his Descendants of Old Canaan Parish and New Canaan." NEW CANAAN HISTORICAL SOCIETY ANNUAL, 1943, pp. 19-30.

Humason, H. Monroe. "The New Canaan Drug Store." NEW CANAAN HISTORICAL SOCIETY ANNUAL, 1966, pp. 39-48.

Hunt, Malcolm P. NAMES AND PLACES OF OLD NORWALK; WITH POR-
TIONS OF WILTON, WESTPORT AND NEW CANAAN. Norwalk, Conn.:
Friends of Lockwood House, 1976. 98 p.

"The Journal of Sarah Davenport: May 1, 1849 through May 16, 1852."
NEW CANAAN HISTORICAL SOCIETY ANNUAL, 1950, pp. 25-109.

Kelly, Walter. NEW CANAAN FROM THE EYE OF THE HISTORICAL GEOG-
RAPHER. New Canaan: Author, n.d.

King, Mary Louise. "New Canaan No Longer is Provincial: The Paving of
Main Street." NEW CANAAN HISTORICAL SOCIETY ANNUAL, 1960, pp.
96-101.

_____. "Some of the Houses Around God's Acre." NEW CANAAN HISTOR-
ICAL SOCIETY ANNUAL, 1965, pp. 39-45.

"Landmarks of New Canaan." NEW CANAAN HISTORICAL SOCIETY ANNUAL,
1951, pp. 1-505.

"(List of) Founders of Canaan Parish and Settlers Previous to 1750." NEW CA-
NAAN HISTORICAL SOCIETY ANNUAL, 1943, pp. 3-4.

Labozza, Carl. "Introduction . . . The Italo-Americans in New Canaan."
NEW CANAAN HISTORICAL SOCIETY ANNUAL, 1975, pp. 26-27.

Marvin, Arba B. "A Child of Canaan Parish." NEW CANAAN HISTORICAL
SOCIETY ANNUAL, 1950, pp. 110-19.

Mead, Stanley P. "Discussion of the Title to the Church Green: 'Whose
Shall These Things Be.'" NEW CANAAN HISTORICAL SOCIETY ANNUAL,
1965, pp. 46-51.

Mitchell, David H. "Hanford-Silliman House." NEW CANAAN HISTORICAL
SOCIETY ANNUAL, 1974, pp. 28-29.

Montgomery, Marshall H. "The Branch's Best Customer in New Canaan: the
100 Year History of Weeds." NEW CANAAN HISTORICAL SOCIETY AN-
NUAL, 1968, pp. 24-28.

Mulligan, Carina Englesfield. "Sunset Hill--The Child Estate." NEW CA-
NAAN HISTORICAL SOCIETY ANNUAL, 1970, pp. 26-29.

"New Canaan, Incorporated, May 4, 1801." NEW CANAAN HISTORICAL
SOCIETY ANNUAL, 1965, pp. 23-38.

"New Canaan Postmasters." NEW CANAAN HISTORICAL SOCIETY ANNUAL, 1957, pp. 176-77.

"New Canaan Railroad." NEW CANAAN HISTORICAL SOCIETY ANNUAL, 1968, pp. 4-24.

"Ninety-one years of Fellowship: New Canaan Organizations 1868-1959." NEW CANAAN HISTORICAL SOCIETY ANNUAL, 1959, pp. 48-59.

"No Business Like Shoe Business: Smaller Manufacturers." NEW CANAAN HISTORICAL SOCIETY ANNUAL, 1955, pp. 55-68.

Noble, Henry S. "The Mill." NEW CANAAN HISTORICAL SOCIETY ANNUAL, 1971, pp. 6-11.

"An Old Road, a Glimpse of Its Past." NEW CANAAN HISTORICAL SOCIETY ANNUAL, 1966, pp. 8-37.

Palmquist, David W. "A Note on the Noyes Collection." NEW CANAAN HISTORICAL SOCIETY ANNUAL, 1969, pp. 28-29.

Pennypacker, John. "The McLanes." NEW CANAAN HISTORICAL SOCIETY ANNUAL, 1970, pp. 21-25.

Prescott, Orville. "The Crusader Returns: Anthony Comstock." NEW CANAAN HISTORICAL SOCIETY ANNUAL, 1969, pp. 8-11.

Raymond, Percy E., and Hoyt, Stephen B. "The Pre-History of New Canaan: A Geological Sketch." NEW CANAAN HISTORICAL SOCIETY ANNUAL, 1952, pp. 102-33.

"Readings in New Canaan History." NEW CANAAN HISTORICAL SOCIETY ANNUAL, 1941. 290 p.

Salmon, Genevieve C. "From Common Land to Common Land: A History of the Susan Dwight Bliss Estate." NEW CANAAN HISTORICAL SOCIETY ANNUAL, 1959, pp. 34-46.

"Selectmen of New Canaan." NEW CANAAN HISTORICAL SOCIETY ANNUAL, 1957, pp. 189-92.

Selinger, Jerome. "The Historic District of New Canaan: The History of Church Hill." NEW CANAAN HISTORICAL SOCIETY ANNUAL, 1965, pp. 7-21.

"Silver Mine Present Residents 1946 (and Map)." NEW CANAAN HISTORICAL SOCIETY ANNUAL, 1946. 71 p.

"This Leaves Us All Well. Letters of Mrs. Henry B. Rogers--1886." NEW CANAAN HISTORICAL SOCIETY ANNUAL, 1959, pp. 16-32.

"Town Clerks of New Canaan." NEW CANAAN HISTORICAL SOCIETY ANNUAL, 1957. 189 p.

"(A Town History)." NEW CANAAN HISTORICAL SOCIETY ANNUAL, 1958, pp. 215-78.

"Undertakers' Records. R.L. Hall & Brother, New Canaan, Connecticut 1872-1882." CA 13 (1970-71): 43-45, 86, 89, 115-19.

Wade, Mrs. Leo. "Drugs for Another Era: The Cody Drug Store." NEW CANAAN HISTORICAL SOCIETY ANNUAL, 1971, pp. 30-31.

Wendell, Mrs. Chester. "Undertakers' Records of Russell Hall (R.L. Hall & Brother), New Canaan, Connecticut Book 1. November 1854-January 1872." CA 15 (1972-73): 21-28, 59-68, 108-14, 136-40; 16 (1973): 23-27.

"What's in a Name?--How New Canaan named its Roads." NEW CANAAN HISTORICAL SOCIETY ANNUAL, 1960, pp. 102-41.

NEW FAIRFIELD

FAIRFIELD COUNTY. Organized May 1740. Towns organized from NEW FAIRFIELD include SHERMAN.

CEMETERY RECORDS AND CEMETERIES

NAME	ADDRESS	HALE NO.	CITATION
New Fairfield Cemetery	Near Methodist Church	1	31:1-11
Old Cemetery	Northeast part of town	2	31:12-19
Gerow Cemetery	Quaker Road	3	31:20-27
Balls Pond Cemetery	Ball Pond Road	4	31:28-32
Mountain View Cemetery	Route 37	5	31:33-44
Beaver Bog Cemetery	Route 37		(no citation)
Congregational Church Cemetery	Brush Hill Road		(no citation)
Union Cemetery	Route 37A		(no citation)

Index to Hale inscriptions: 31:45-55.

CEMETERY INSCRIPTIONS AND MARRIAGES OF NEW FAIRFIELD, CONNECTICUT. (NHCHS, LDS 1455 pt. 31).

CEMETERY RECORDS OF HAVILAND HOLLOW, DUTCHESS CO., NEW YORK AND NEW FAIRFIELD, FAIRFIELD COUNTY, CONNECTICUT. (LDS 4228).

CEMETERY RECORDS OF NEW FAIRFIELD. (LDS 4138).

Eardeley, William A.D. CONNECTICUT CEMETERIES. Brooklyn: Author, 1914.

Frost, Josephine C. CEMETERY INSCRIPTIONS FROM DANBURY AND NEW FAIRFIELD, CONNECTICUT. Typescript. Brooklyn, N.Y.: 1915. 81 p. (LDS 1612).

Hoyt, George S. RECORD OF SOLDIERS BURIED IN DANBURY, BROOK-FIELD, NEW FAIRFIELD AND RIDGEFIELD. Hartford: CSL, 1929. 91 p.

Pearce, Edward H. "Union Cemetery at Ball's Pond Prior to 1850." CQ 3 (1897): 236-37.

CHURCH RECORDS

CONGREGATIONAL CHURCH. Records, 1754-1790 (1885 copy). (Danbury Public Library). Minutes, 1755-1900. Vital Records, 1742-1897. Records, 1742-1900. (CSL, LDS 1968). Index. (CSL, LDS 1448 pt. 15).

Heireth, Imogene O. "Congregational Church Records of New Fairfield, Connecticut." CA 19 (1976-77): 86-91, 141-45, 183-88; 20 (1977): 24-31.

_____. "Earliest Congregational Church Records of New Fairfield, Connecticut (1758-1785)." CA 20 (1977-78): 89-94, 145-50.

Miscellaneous Church Records. (NHCHS, LDS 1455).

"Record of Congregational Church in New Fairfield 1742." CQ 3 (1897): 486.

HISTORICAL SOCIETY

New Fairfield Historical Society, P.O. Box 156, 06810.

LIBRARY

New Fairfield Free Library, 06810. (203) 746-9297.

NEWSPAPERS

The HALE NEWSPAPER INDEX TO DEATH AND MARRIAGE NOTICES includes:
AMERICAN TELEGRAPH: 10 June 1795-14 September 1803 (deaths), 18 May 1796-14 September 1800 (marriages).

PROBATE RECORDS

New Fairfield Probate District, Town Hall, Route 39, 06810. (203) 746-4500.

Organized 8 January 1975 from the Danbury Probate District.

SCHOOL RECORDS

Hartford. CSL, Record Group 62. Centerville School District Records, 1869–1909.

TAX RECORDS

Hartford. CSL, Record Group 62. Book of Taxes collected 1892.

VITAL RECORDS

Town Clerk, Town Hall, Route 39, 06810. (203) 746-1234.

The town records burned in 1867.

"Cemetery Inscriptions and Marriages of New Fairfield, Connecticut." (NHCHS, LDS 1455 pt. 31).

Eardeley, William A.D. "Record of Marriages by Ephraim Hubbell, Justice of the Peace in the North Society of New Fairfield, at the time of all the following marriages, but now the town of Sherman." NYGBR 39 (1908): 213-17.

Hubbell, Ephraim, comp. (Justice of the Peace). Connecticut Private Records. New Fairfield Marriages, 1746-1791. 11 p. (CSL, LDS 002,883).

PUBLISHED WORKS AND OTHER RECORDS

Simon, Irving Bernard. OUR TOWN: THE HISTORY OF NEW FAIRFIELD. New Fairfield: New Fairfield Bicentennial Commission, 1975. 56 p.

NEW HARTFORD

LITCHFIELD COUNTY. Organized October 1738.

CEMETERY RECORDS AND CEMETERIES

NAME	ADDRESS	HALE NO.	CITATION
Town Hill Cemetery	Town Hill	1	31:1-17
North Village Cemetery	West of Village	2	31:18-46
Immaculate Conception Church Cemetery	Near Village Cemetery	3	31:47-67
Pine Grove Cemetery	Route 219 East	4	31:68-80
Old Nepaug Cemetery	Collinsville to Torrington Road	5	31:81-94
New Nepaug Cemetery	Collinsville to Torrington Road	6	31:95
Pine Meadow Cemetery	Pine Meadow	7	31:96-101
Sakerville Cemetery	Near Torrington Road	8	31:102-5
Community House Cemetery	Stone used as step-stone	9	31:106-7
New Roman Catholic Church Cemetery	Town Hill	10	

South East Cemetery. Covered by Nepaug Reservoir.

Index to Hale inscriptions: 31:108-37.

Barbour, Lucius Barnes. "Inscriptions from gravestones at New Hartford, Connecticut." NEHGR 82 (1928): 375-80, 453-56.

CHURCH RECORDS

BAKERSVILLE METHODIST EPISCOPAL CHURCH. Minutes, 1827–1858. Vital Records, 1861–1930. (CSL, LDS 1936).

FIRST CONGREGATIONAL CHURCH. Minutes, 1767–1867. Vital Records, 1739–1854. (CSL, LDS 1937). Marriages, 1743–1794. BAILEY 3:144–51.

ST. JOHN EPISCOPAL CHURCH. Vital Records, 1850–1904. (CSL, LDS 1938).

Index Cards to New Hartford Church Records. (CSL, LDS 1448 pt. 18).

HISTORICAL SOCIETY

New Hartford Historical Society, 06057.

LAND RECORDS

Land Records, 1739–1853. Index, 1739–1895. (LDS 1934 pt. 1–10).

LIBRARIES

Bakerville Library, Maple Hollow Road, 06057. (203) 482–8806.

New Hartford Free Library, Main Street, 06057. (203) 379–8121.

NEWSPAPERS

FOOTHILLS TRADER. Weekly. Central Avenue, 06057. (203) 379–0082.

The PRELIMINARY CHECKLIST lists two newspapers for NEW HARTFORD.

PROBATE RECORDS

New Hartford Probate District, Town Hall, Main Street, 06057. (203) 379–3254.

Organized 27 May 1825 from the Simsbury Probate District.

Probate districts organized from the New Hartford Probate District include the Barkhamsted Probate District.

The Records previous to 5 June 1834 are at the Barkhamsted Probate District.

ON FILE AT THE CSL: Estate Papers, 1834-1902. Indexes, 1854-1902. Inventory Control Book, 1834-1902. Court Record Books, 1834-1852.

Journal and ledger of R.M.D. Cleaveland, 1877-1899.

Probate Records, 1834-1852. (LDS, 1935); 1825-1833. (LDS 1524).

TAX RECORDS

Hartford. CSL, Record Group 62. Abstracts, 1850-1957.

VITAL RECORDS

Town Clerk, Town Hall, Main Street, 06057. (203) 379-3254.

The town clerk's earliest birth record is 3 February 1716, marriage record is 11 May 1739, and death record 8 February 1734.

The BARBOUR INDEX covers the years 1740-1854 and is based on the James N. Arnold copy of NEW HARTFORD vital records made in 1917.

PUBLISHED WORKS AND OTHER RECORDS

Hall, Eileen Creevey. NEW HARTFORD, CONNECTICUT IN 1775 AND 1852. New Hartford: Esperanza Press, 1976. 47 p. Index.

Mills, Lewis Sprague. LEGENDS OF BARKHAMSTED LIGHTHOUSE AND SATAN'S KINGDOM IN NEW HARTFORD. Hamden, Conn.: Shoe String Press, 1961. 326 p.

Simonds, Mrs. William Edgar. "In Satan's Kingdom." CQ 2 (1896): 230-43, 320-32.

SKETCHES OF THE PEOPLE AND PLACES OF NEW HARTFORD IN THE PAST AND PRESENT. New Hartford: Tribune, 1883. 33 p.

NEW HAVEN

NEW HAVEN COUNTY. Organized April 1638. Towns organized from NEW HAVEN include EAST HAVEN, HAMDEN, NORTH HAVEN, ORANGE and WOODBRIDGE.

CEMETERY RECORDS AND CEMETERIES

NAME	ADDRESS	HALE NO.	CITATION
Grove Street Cemetery	227 Grove Street (203) 787-1443	1	31:1-266
Evergreen Cemetery	92 Winthrop Avenue (203) 624-5505	2	32:932-1029
Mapledale Cemetery	Winthrop Avenue, junction of Oak Street	3	33:932-1029
Fair Haven Union Cemetery	149 Grand Avenue (203) 562-8315	4	33:1030-1150
Center Church Crypt Cemetery	250 Temple Street	5	33:1151-56
St. Bernard Cemetery	520 Columbus Avenue corner of Boulevard Street (203) 624-3980	6	33:1157-1411
Westville Cemetery	639 Walley Avenue	7	33:1412-1500
Beaverdale Memorial Park	599 Fitch Street (203) 387-6601	8	33:1501-10
Congregation Mishkan Israel Cemetery	639 Whalley Avenue near Jewell Street	9	33:1511-42
Independent Israel Society Cemetery	Jewell Street	10	33:1543-53
B'nai Jacob Cemetery	30 Jewell Street	11	33:1554-68

NAME	ADDRESS	HALE NO.	CITATION
Independent Connecticut Lodge Cemetery No. 1	32 Jewell Street	12	33:1569-71
Old Potters Field	Blake Street	13	33:1572
Independent Connecticut Lodge Cemetery No. 2	Jewell Street	14	33:1573-79
Herzl Cemetery	Jewell Street	15	33:1580-85
Congregation Beth Israel Cemetery	46 Jewell Street	16	33:1586-88
Independent Wilner Lodge Cemetery	Jewell Street	17	33:1589
Warshaver Relief Society Cemetery	Jewell Street	18	33:1590-92
Independent Adas Israel Cemetery	52 Jewell Street	19	33:1593-98
Mt. Sinai Memorial Park	58 Jewell Street (203) 777-3317	20	33:1599-1600
United Independent (1934) Cemetery	Fitch Street near Onyx Street	21	33:1601
Blake Street Cemetery	Forest Road	22	34:1602-73
Dog Cemetery	Forest Road	23	34:1674
Asbusin Vault	In vault at Hayes and Pierce, 38 High Street	24	34:1675
Col. John Trumbell	Yale University, Art School	25	34:1676-77
Congregation Shara Torah Cemetery	Farwell Avenue		(no citation)
Farband Labor Zionist Order Cemetery	65 Fitch Street		(no citation)

Index to Hale inscriptions: 34:1678-2157.

Bartlett, Ellen Strong. "The Grove Street Cemetery, New Haven." CQ 2 (1896): 272-83.

"Connecticut Headstone Inscriptions Before 1800 (Hale)--New Haven." CN 4 (1971-72): 210-11, 350-55, 521-26; 5 (1972): 52-57, 221-26, 363-64.

Dexter, Franklin Bowditch. "Inscriptions on Tombstones in New Haven, Erected Prior to 1800." PAPERS OF THE NEW HAVEN COLONY HISTORICAL SOCIETY 3 (1882): 471-614; 8 (1914): 351-56.

New Haven. New Haven Colony Historical Society. Bills for town burials 1777-1831.

Townshend, Henry Hotchkiss. "The Grove Street Cemetery." PAPERS OF THE NEW HAVEN COLONY HISTORICAL SOCIETY 10 (1951): 119-146.

CENSUS RECORDS

Hartford. CSL, Record Group 29. Box 25. State Military Census, 1917. List of New Haven residents who are citizens, alphabetized by occupation.

Jacobus, Donald Lines. "Errors in the Census of 1790 (Connecticut)." NEHGR 77 (1923): 81.

_____. "New Haven Census, 1704." FAMILIES OF ANCIENT NEW HAVEN 6 (1930): 1531-34.

CHURCH RECORDS

CHAPEL STREET CONGREGATIONAL CHURCH. Minutes, 1855-1933. Vital Records, 1838-1840, 1871-1908. (CSL, LDS 1958).

CHRIST EPISCOPAL CHURCH. Minutes, 1856-1939. Vital Records, 1837-1913. (CSL, LDS 1955 pt. 1-2).

FAIR HAVEN CONGREGATIONAL CHURCH. Vital Records, 1830-1894. (CSL, LDS 1954). Marriages, 1751-1782. BAILEY 6:7-15.

FIRST BAPTIST CHURCH. Minutes, 1824-1941. Vital Records, 1816-1902. (CSL, LDS 1953 pt. 1-3).

FIRST CONGREGATIONAL CHURCH. Vital Records, 1639-1911. (CSL, LDS 1960). Minutes, 1715-1866. Vital Records, 1715-1880. (CSL, LDS 1952). Marriages, 1758-1789. BAILEY 1:7-28, 3:169.

FIRST PRESBYTERIAN CHURCH. Minutes, 1873-1875. (Presbyterian Historical Society, LDS 503,607).

HOPE BAPTIST CHURCH. Vital Records, 1887-1902. (CSL, LDS 1953 pt. 5).

ST. PAUL EPISCOPAL CHURCH. Vital Records, 1845-1940. (CSL, LDS 1956).

ST. THOMAS EPISCOPAL CHURCH. Minutes, 1848-1925. Vital Records, 1848-1931. (CSL, LDS 1957 pt. 1-2).

SECOND BAPTIST CHURCH. Minutes, 1842-1865. Vital Records, 1842-1863. (CSL, LDS 1953).

THE CHURCH OF JESUS CHRIST OF LATTER-DAY SAINTS. Early records to 1941. (LDS 1131 pt. 134,247).

TRINITY EPISCOPAL CHURCH. Vital Records, 1767-1939. Index, 1767-1814. (CSL, LDS 1959 pt. 1-2). Burials of Males, 1815-13 March 1858. (CSL, LDS 1483).

Male Memberships, 1815-13 March 1858. (CSL, LDS 3,662). Marriages, 1768-1800. BAILEY 7:22-28.

UNITED CHURCH. Burials. Males, 1888-1929. (CSL, LDS 1483). Male Memberships, 1815-1931. (CSL, LDS 3,662). Marriages, 1751-1782. BAILEY 6:7-15.

Bacon, Theodore Davenport. LEONARD BACON A STATESMAN IN THE CHURCH. New Haven: Yale University Press, 1931. 563 p.

Bartlett, Ellen Strong. "A New Haven Church." CQ 3 (1897): 123-41.

Brooks, Mrs. Kate B. "A History of the South Congregational Church from its Separation in 1842 to January 1, 1930." NEHGR.

DEATH RECORDS OF MALES ONLY, TAKEN FROM MEMBERSHIP RECORDS, UNITED CHURCH PARISH HOUSE, NEW HAVEN, CONNECTICUT. Hartford, Conn.: Connecticut State Library, 1975. 12 p.

Dexter, Franklin Bowditch. HISTORICAL CATALOGUE OF THE MEMBERS OF THE FIRST CHURCH OF CHRIST IN NEW HAVEN, CONNECTICUT (CENTER CHURCH). A.D. 1639-1914. New Haven: First Church of Christ in New Haven, 1914. 469 p.

Dickerman, John H. COLONIAL HISTORY OF THE PARISH OF MOUNT CARMEL AS READ IN ITS GEOLOGIC FORMATIONS, RECORDS AND TRADITIONS. New Haven: Press of Ryders Printing House, 1904. 109 p.

Hallock, Gerald. HISTORY OF THE SOUTH CONGREGATIONAL CHURCH, NEW HAVEN, FROM ITS ORIGIN IN 1852 TILL JANUARY 1, 1865. New Haven: Tuttle, Morehouse and Taylor, 1865. 257 p.

Heinz, Bernard. WELCOME TO CENTER CHURCH, NEW HAVEN, CONNECTICUT. New Haven, Conn.: First Church of Christ, 1976. 32 p.

LEONARD BACON: PASTOR OF THE FIRST CHURCH IN NEW HAVEN. New Haven: Tuttle, Morehouse and Taylor, 1882. 260 p.

Lyon, Josephine A. THE CHRONICLE OF CHRIST CHURCH. New Haven: Author, 1941. 166 p.

Mitchell, Mary Hewitt. HISTORY OF THE UNITED CHURCH OF NEW HAVEN: United Church, 1942. 286 p.

"Rev. Elisha Cushman's Record." (First Baptist Church in Hartford 1813 to 1825, Philadelphia, Pennsylvania 1825-1829, Fairfield, Connecticut September 1829-1830, New Haven 1830-1833, Plymouth, Massachusetts 1834-1837, 1840-1863 by son Rev. Elisha Cushman and contains marriages from Willington, Hartford, New Britain and Deep River until 1863). CHSB 7 (July 1941): 30-32; 8 (October 1941): 2-8; 8 (January 1942): 12-13.

Scofield, Ethel Lord. "The Baptismal Record of the Societies of Whitehaven and Fairhaven, now the United Church (Congregational), New Haven, Connecticut." NYGBR 42 (1911): 28-50.

White, Henry. "List of Baptisms in New Haven, Connecticut, During the Ministry of Rev. John Davenport, from November 1639 to November 1666, Taken from the Church Records and Arranged Alphabetically." NEHGR 9 (1855): 357-64.

Zilberberg, Nahum. "The George Street Synagogue of Congregation B'nai Jacob." Master's thesis, Yale University, 1961. 77 p.

HISTORICAL SOCIETY

Jewish Historical Society of New Haven, 119 Davenport Avenue, 06519. (203) 787-3183.

New Haven Colony Historical Society, 114 Whitney Avenue, 06510. (203) 562-4183.

Publishes NEW HAVEN COLONY HISTORICAL SOCIETY JOURNAL. March 1952-- . Semiannual. Indexed.

PAPERS OF THE NEW HAVEN COLONY HISTORICAL SOCIETY. 1865-- . Annual.

ANNUAL REPORT. 1901-- .

Koel, Otillia. "The Library of the New Haven Colony Historical Society." LEAGUE BULLETIN 32 (September 1980): 7-12.

New Haven Colony Historical Society. COLLECTIONS OF THE NEW HAVEN COLONY HISTORICAL SOCIETY, NEW HAVEN, CONNECTICUT. New Haven, Conn.: New Haven Colony Historical Society, 1907. 98 p.

_____. THE PAINTING COLLECTION OF THE NEW HAVEN COLONY HISTORICAL SOCIETY. New Haven, Conn.: New Haven Colony Historical Society, 1971. 100 p.

LAND RECORDS

Land Records, 1679-1849. Index, 1679-1850. (LDS 1949 pt. 1-69).

Proprietor's Records, 1724-1771. (LDS 1950).

Jacobus, Donald Lines. "Division of New Haven Lands (Proprietor's Records)." FAMILIES OF ANCIENT NEW HAVEN 4 (1927): 137-38.

LIBRARIES

New Haven Free Public Library, 133 Elm Street, 06510. (203) 562-0151.

Yale University Library, 120 High Street, 06520. (203) 436-8335.

Stetson, Willis K. "Public Libraries in Connecticut, Founding and the Development of the Free Public Library in New Haven." CM 10 (1906): 129-38.

MILITARY RECORDS

Dexter, Franklin Bowditch. "Notes on Some of the New Haven Loyalists, Including Those Graduated at Yale." NHCHS PAPERS 9 (1918): 29-45.

Greene, M. Louise. "New Haven Defenses in the Revolution and in the War of 1812." CQ 4 (1898): 272-90.

Hedden, James Spencer. COLONIAL WARS OF AMERICA. A SYNOPSIS OF THE MILITARY AND CIVIL RECORDS OF SOME OF THE NEW HAVEN MEN ORIGINALLY BURIED ON NEW HAVEN GREEN WHOSE GRAVE STONES WERE LATER REMOVED EITHER INSTALLED IN THE CRYPT OF CENTER CHURCH OR REMOVED TO GROVE STREET CEMETERY. New Haven: Author, 1944. 20 p.

Jacobus, Donald Lines. LIST OF OFFICIALS CIVIL, MILITARY, AND ECCLESIASTICAL OF CONNECTICUT COLONY FROM MARCH 1636 THROUGH 11 OCTOBER 1677 AND OF NEW HAVEN COLONY THROUGHOUT ITS SEPARATE EXISTENCE ALSO SOLDIERS IN THE PEQUOT WAR WHO THEN SUBSEQUENTLY RESIDED WITHIN THE PRESENT BOUNDS OF CONNECTICUT. New Haven: Roland Mather Hooker, 1935. 65 p.

_____. "List of Officials Military and Civil Who Served from March 1636 to December 1665 in the Colonies of Connecticut and New Haven." NEW HAVEN GENEALOGICAL MAGAZINE 4 (1927): 961-1010.

_____. "War Service Records." NEW HAVEN GENEALOGICAL MAGAZINE 1 (1923): 238-54; 2 (1924): 485-503.

Lucke, Jerome Bonaparte. HISTORY OF THE NEW HAVEN GRAYS FROM SEPTEMBER 13, 1816 TO SEPTEMBER 13, 1876. New Haven: Tuttle, Morehouse and Taylor, 1876. 540 p.

Osterweis, Rollin Gustav. THE NEW HAVEN GREEN AND THE AMERICAN BICENTENNIAL. Hamden: Archon Books, 1976. 129 p.

REVOLUTIONARY CHARACTERS OF NEW HAVEN, THE SUBJECT OF ADDRESSES AND PAPERS DELIVERED BEFORE THE GENERAL DAVID HUMPHREY'S BRANCH NO. 1, CONNECTICUT SOCIETY, SONS OF THE AMERICAN REVOLUTION. ALSO, LIST OF MEN, SO FAR AS THEY ARE KNOWN, FROM THE TERRITORY EMBRACED IN THE TOWN OF NEW HAVEN, CONNECTICUT, WHO SERVED IN THE CONTINENTAL ARMY AND MILITIA AND ON CONTINENTAL AND STATE VESSELS AND PRIVATEERS, AND THOSE WHO RENDERED OTHER PATRIOTIC SERVICES DURING THE WAR OF THE REVOLUTION, AND A RECORD OF KNOWN CASUALTIES; TOGETHER WITH THE LOCATION OF KNOWN GRAVES IN AND ABOUT NEW HAVEN OF PATRIOTS OF 1775-1783, AND CATALOGUE OF THE OFFICERS AND MEMBERS OF GENERAL DAVID HUMPHREY'S BRANCH SINCE ITS ORGANIZATION. New Haven: General David Humphrey's Chapter, SAR, 1911.

NEWSPAPERS

NEW HAVEN JOURNAL COURIER/NEW HAVEN REGISTER. Daily. 367 Orange Street, 06503. (203) 562-3131.

The PRELIMINARY CHECKLIST lists ninety-six newspapers for NEW HAVEN.

Newspapers included in the HALE INDEX TO DEATHS AND MARRIAGES include:

BELLES-LETTRES REPOSITORY, deaths and marriages 5 March 1808.

COLUMBIAN REGISTER, deaths and marriages 1 December 1812 - 30 December 1865.

CONNECTICUT GAZETTE, deaths and marriages 12 April 1755-19 February 1768.

CONNECTICUT HERALD, deaths and marriages 1 November 1803-27 December 1851.

CONNECTICUT JOURNAL, deaths and marriages 23 October 1767–7 April 1835.

FEDERAL GAZETEER, deaths 26 July 1776, marriages 17 May 1796–1 February 1797.

MESSENGER, deaths and marriages 1 January 1800–16 August 1802.

NATIONAL PILOT, deaths and marriages 6 September 1821–15 May 1823.

NATIONAL REPUBLICAN, deaths and marriages 23 July 1831–17 March 1832.

NEW HAVEN ADVERTISER, deaths and marriages 1 May 1829–11 February 1831.

NEW HAVEN CHURCHMAN'S MAGAZINE, deaths and marriages January 1804–October 1809.

NEW HAVEN CHRONICLE, deaths and marriages 3 March 1827–30 August 1828.

NEW HAVEN DEMOCRAT, deaths and marriages 21 April 1845–20 April 1846.

NEW HAVEN GAZETTE AND CONNECTICUT MAGAZINE, deaths 13 May 1784–29 June 1791, marriages 16 February 1786–13 November 1788.

NEW HAVEN LITERARY EMPORIUM, deaths and marriages 16 August 1835–4 August 1838.

NEW HAVEN LITERARY TABLET, deaths and marriages 14 April 1832–29 March 1834.

NEW HAVEN PALLADIUM, deaths and marriages 7 November 1829–30 December 1865.

NEW HAVEN RECORD, deaths and marriages 23 February 1839–27 June 1840.

NEW HAVEN RELIGIOUS INTELLIGENCER, deaths 5 April 1817–11 February 1837, marriages 9 January 1836–11 February 1837.

VISITOR, deaths 30 October 1802–8 November 1804, marriages 11 January 1803–8 November 1804.

Scott, Kenneth, and Conway, Rosanne. GENEALOGICAL DATA FROM COLONIAL NEW HAVEN NEWSPAPERS. Baltimore: Genealogical Publishing Co., 1979. 547 p. Index.

PROBATE RECORDS

New Haven Probate District, City Hall, 161 Church Street, 06504. (203) 787-2118.

Organized May 1666. The New Haven Probate District also includes WOODBRIDGE.

Probate Districts organized from the New Haven Probate District
include the Bethany, Derby, East Haven, Guilford, Hamden, Litchfield, Milford, North Haven, Orange, Oxford, Wallingford, West
Haven and Woodbury Probate Districts.

ON FILE AT THE CSL: Estate Papers, 1683-1922. Indexes, 1683-
1912. Court Record Books, 1647-1852.

Probate Records, 1647-1914. Index, 1647-1781. (LDS 1951 pt. 1-35).

Alcorn, Mrs. Winifred S. "Abstracts of the Early Probate Records of New Haven, Book I, Part I, 1647-1687." NEHGR 81 (1927): 121-35.

SCHOOL RECORDS

CATALOGUE OF THE TRUSTEES, RECTORS, INSTRUCTORS AND ALUMNI OF
THE HOPKINS GRAMMAR SCHOOL OF NEW HAVEN, CONNECTICUT 1660-
1902. New Haven: Dorman Lithographing Co., 1902. 183 p.

Gould, Isabelle. "The Challenge of 1866." LEAGUE BULLETIN 32 (May
1980): 5-8, 20.

TAX RECORDS

Hartford. CSL, Record Group 62. Abstracts, 1795-1899.

VITAL RECORDS

Town Clerk, Hall of Records, 200 Orange Street, 06510. (203) 562-0151.
Marriages, 1835-1854. Vol. 6 (CSL, LDS 1961).

Dexter, Franklin Bowditch. ANCIENT TOWN RECORDS. NEW HAVEN
TOWN RECORDS 1649-1662. New Haven: New Haven Colony Historical
Society, 1917. 548 p.

_____. ANCIENT TOWN RECORDS. NEW HAVEN TOWN RECORDS 1662-
1684. New Haven: New Haven Colony Historical Society, 1919. 457 p.

Jacobus, Donald Lines. "Errors in New Haven Vital Records." FAMILIES OF
ANCIENT NEW HAVEN 2 (1921): 504-8.

_____. "Extracts from New Haven County Court Records." TAG 35 (July 1959): 136.

_____. "New Haven County Court Records Marriage and Birth Evidences." TAG 34 (January 1958): 54-64.

Powers, Zara Jones. ANCIENT TOWN RECORDS. NEW HAVEN TOWN RECORDS 1684-1769. New Haven: New Haven Colony Historical Society, 1962. 884 p.

"Record of Deaths in New Haven in 1820." NEW HAVEN GENEALOGICAL MAGAZINE 8 (1932): 2054-57.

Scofield, Ethel Lord. "Record of Deaths in New Haven in 1820." FAMILIES OF ANCIENT NEW HAVEN 8 (1932): 2054-57.

VITAL RECORDS OF NEW HAVEN 1649-1850. Vital Records of Connecticut Series I. Towns IV Part I and II. 2 vols. Hartford: Connecticut Society of the Order of the Founders and Patriots of America, 1917, 1924. (LDS 599, 303 and 599,304).

PUBLISHED WORKS AND OTHER RECORDS

Andrews, Charles McLean. THE RISE AND FALL OF THE NEW HAVEN COLONY. Connecticut Tercentenary Commission, no. 48. New Haven: Yale University Press, 1936. 56 p.

Anthony, N.B. Garvan. ARCHITECTURE AND TOWN PLANNING IN COLONIAL CONNECTICUT. New Haven, Conn.: Yale University Press, 1951. 116 p.

Archer, John. "Puritan Town Planning in New Haven." JOURNAL OF THE SOCIETY OF ARCHITECTURAL HISTORIANS 34 (May 1975): 140-49.

ATLAS OF THE CITY OF NEW HAVEN, CONNECTICUT. Philadelphia: G.M. Hopkins, 1888.

Atwater, Edward Elias. HISTORY OF THE CITY OF NEW HAVEN: TO THE PRESENT TIME. New York: W.W. Munsell and Co., 1887. 702 p.

_____. HISTORY OF THE COLONY OF NEW HAVEN TO ITS ABSORPTION INTO CONNECTICUT. New Haven: Author, 1881. Reprint. Meriden, Conn.: Journal Publishing Co., 1902. 767 p.

Baker, Christina H. "Sidelights on the New Haven Green." CA 7 (1955): 26-30.

Barber, John Warner, and Anderson, Lemuel S. HISTORY AND ANTIQUITIES OF NEW HAVEN, FROM ITS EARLIEST SETTLEMENT TO THE PRESENT TIME. New Haven: Authors, 1856. 180 p.

Bartlett, Ellen Strong. "Hillhouse Avenue, New Haven." CQ 3 (1897): 47-64.

_____. HISTORICAL SKETCHES OF NEW HAVEN. New Haven, Conn.: Tuttle, Morehouse and Taylor, 1897. 98 p.

_____. "The New Haven Green." CQ 1 (1895): 315-25.

_____. "A Patriarch of American Portrait Painters--Nathaniel Jocelyn." CM 7 (1903): 589-601.

Beecher, Edward C. "Reminiscences of Three Quarters of a Century in New Haven." CM 10 (1906): 679-91.

Broaddus, Margaret. "Thomas P. Rossiter: In Pursuit of Diversity." AMERICAN ART AND ANTIQUES 2 (1979): 106-13.

Brown, Elizabeth Mills. NEW HAVEN: A GUIDE TO ARCHITECTURE AND URBAN DESIGN. New Haven: Yale University Press, 1976. 238 p. Index.

Calder, Isabel MacBeath. "John Cotton and the New Haven Colony." NEQ 3 (1930): 82-94.

_____. THE NEW HAVEN COLONY. 1934. Reprint. Hamden, Conn.: Archon Books, 1970. 301 p. Index.

Davis, Cochran, Miller, Noyes Architects. PRESERVATION OF THE ELI WHITNEY GUN FACTORY SITE AND ITS POTENTIAL DEVELOPMENT AS AN HISTORICAL SITE MUSEUM. Guilford, Conn.: Author, 1974. 167 p.

De Motte, Charles M. "Family and Social Structure in Colonial New Haven." CR 9 (November 1975): 82-95.

Dexter, Franklin Bowditch. "New Haven in 1784." PAPERS OF THE NEW HAVEN COLONY HISTORICAL SOCIETY 4 (1888): 117-38.

Dwight, Timothy. STATISTICAL ACCOUNT OF THE CITY OF NEW HAVEN. New Haven: Author, 1811. 60 p.

Ford, George H. "Town of New Haven, 1638-1789." CM 5 (1899): 627-43.

Garrard, John A. "The History of Local Political Power: Some Suggestions for Analysis." POLITICAL STUDIES 25 (1977): 252-69.

Hegel, Richard. CARRIAGES FROM NEW HAVEN, NEW HAVEN'S NINE-TEENTH CENTURY CARRIAGE INDUSTRY. Hamden: Shoe String Press, 1914. 103 p.

_____. NINETEENTH-CENTURY HISTORIANS OF NEW HAVEN. Hamden, Conn.: Archon Books, 1972. 105 p.

Hill, Everett Gleason. A MODERN HISTORY OF NEW HAVEN AND EAST-ERN NEW HAVEN COUNTY. 2 vols. New York: S.J. Clarke Publishing Co., 1918.

Hoadly, Charles Jeremy. RECORDS OF THE COLONY AND PLANTATION OF NEW HAVEN FROM 1638 TO 1649. Hartford: Case, Tiffany and Co., 1857. 547 p.

_____. RECORDS OF THE COLONY, OR JURISDICTION OF NEW HAVEN, FROM MAY, 1653, TO THE UNION. Hartford: Case, Lockwood and Co., 1858. 626 p.

Hornstein, Harold. NEW HAVEN CELEBRATES THE BICENTENNIAL. New Haven, Conn.: New Haven Bicentennial Commission, 1976. 148 p.

Horowitz, Daniel. "The Meaning of City Biographies: New Haven in the Nineteenth and Early Twentieth Centuries." CHSB 29 (1964): 65-75.

Jacobus, Donald Lines. FAMILIES OF ANCIENT NEW HAVEN. 8 vols. New Haven: Author, 1922-32. (LDS 823,840 and 1963).

_____. "Notes on New Haven Families." NEHGR 46 (1892): 308-11.

_____. "Old Record Book, New Haven." TAG 20 (1943-44): 122-25.

Kane, Patricia E. FURNITURE OF THE NEW HAVEN COLONY: THE SEV-ENTEENTH CENTURY STYLE. New Haven, Conn.: New Haven Colony His-torical Society, 1973. 93 p.

Keyes, John A. MANUAL OF THE CITY GOVERNMENT. New Haven, Conn.: New Haven City-Town Clerk, 1980. 84 p. Index.

Krynine, Dmitri Pavlovich. "History of an Old New Haven Landmark." CONNECTICUT SOCIETY OF CIVIL ENGINEERS ANNUAL REPORT, 1948, pp. 73-98.

Lambert, Edward Radolphus. HISTORY OF THE COLONY OF NEW HAVEN BEFORE AND AFTER THE UNION WITH CONNECTICUT. New Haven, Conn.: Hitchcock and Stafford, 1834. 216 p.

Levermore, Charles H. REPUBLIC OF NEW HAVEN. Baltimore: Johns Hopkins University Press, 1886. 342 p.

New Haven. Chamber of Commerce. THE INDUSTRIES AND OPPORTUNITIES OF NEW HAVEN, CONNECTICUT. New Haven, Conn.: 1910. 50 p.

New Haven. Colony Historical Society. AN EXHIBITION OF CHINA TRADE PORCELAIN DESIGNED TO ILLUSTRATE THE WARES IMPORTED TO THE PORT OF NEW HAVEN. New Haven, Conn.: 1968. 199 p.

_____. AN EXHIBITION OF EARLY SILVER BY NEW HAVEN SILVERSMITHS. New Haven, Conn.: 1967. 99 p.

_____. THE NEW HAVEN SCENE; AN EXHIBITION OF PAINTINGS, WATERCOLORS AND DRAWINGS, APRIL 19 THROUGH JUNE 14, 1970. New Haven, Conn.: 1970.

_____. SHALLOPS, SLOOPS, AND SHARPIES: A MARITIME HISTORY OF NEW HAVEN. New Haven, Conn.: 1976. 62 p.

New Haven. New Haven Colony Historical Society. Lists of Town's Poor, 1817-- . Indentures of Town's poor children.

NEW HAVEN ORPHAN ASYLUM: HISTORICAL SKETCH READ AT THE SEMI-CENTENNIAL. NORTH CHURCH FEBRUARY 26, 1883. New Haven: D.A. Dorman, 1883. 31 p.

Newton, Roger Hale. "'Sachem's Wood,' New Haven, Connecticut, One of the Earliest Greek Revival Mansions in the United States." OLD TIME NEW ENGLAND 33 (October 1942): 33-36.

Osterweis, Rollin Gustav. CHARTER NUMBER TWO: THE CENTENNIAL HISTORY OF THE FIRST NEW HAVEN NATIONAL BANK. New Haven: n.p., 1963. 103 p.

_____. THREE CENTURIES OF NEW HAVEN, 1638-1988. New Haven: Yale University Press, 1953. 541 p.

_____. "The Three Houses of Ralph Isaacs, Jr.: Colonial Merchant of New Haven." CANTIQUARIAN 7 (July 1955): 18-25.

Palmer, Harry H. "Some of New Haven's Colonial Houses." CQ 2 (1896): 90-97.

Pearson, Ralph L., and Wrigley, Linda. "Before Mayor Richard Lee: George Dudley Seymour and the City Planning Movement in New Haven, 1907-1924." JOURNAL OF URBAN PLANNING 6 (1980): 297-319.

PROCEEDINGS OF THE GRAND LODGE OF CONNECTICUT. HELD AT MASON'S HALL IN THE TOWN OF NEW HAVEN. N.p., 1822. 18 p.

Register of Seamen, 1801. Miscellaneous Papers, 1826-1830. (CSL, LDS 1962).

Rindler, Edward Paul. "The Migration from the New Haven Colony to Newark, East New Jersey: a Study of Puritan Values and Behavior, 1630-1720." Ph.D. dissertation, University of Pennsylvania, 1977. 448 p.

Scofield, Ethel Lord. "Town Poor, New Haven, 1786." FAMILIES OF ANCIENT NEW HAVEN 6 (1930): 1535-36.

Seymour, George Dudley. NEW HAVEN, A BOOK RECORDING THE VARIED ACTIVITIES OF THE AUTHOR IN HIS EFFORTS OVER MANY YEARS TO PROMOTE THE WELFARE OF THE CITY OF HIS ADOPTION SINCE 1883, TOGETHER WITH SOME RESEARCHES INTO ITS STORIED PAST AND MANY ILLUSTRATIONS. New Haven, Conn.: Tuttle, Morehouse and Taylor, 1942. 805 p.

Seymour, Jack M. SHIPS, SAILORS, AND SAMARITANS: THE WOMAN'S SEAMAN'S FRIEND SOCIETY OF CONNECTICUT 1859-1976. New Haven: Woman's Seaman's Friend Society of Connecticut, 1976. 157 p.

Smith, Charles H. "Early Struggles in American Education." CM 8 (1903): 179-92.

Smith, George V. "The First Theocratic Government in the New World." CM 8 (1903): 256-63.

Solenberger, Willard E. ONE HUNDRED YEARS OF CHILD CARE IN NEW HAVEN: THE STORY OF THE NEW HAVEN ORPHAN ASYLUM AND THE CHILDREN'S COMMUNITY CENTER 1833-1933. New Haven: Children's Community Center of the New Haven Orphan Asylum, 1933. 110 p.

Townshend, Charles Hervey. "New Haven Harbor." CQ 2 (1896): 161-66.

Townshend, Henry Hotchkiss. NEW HAVEN AND THE FIRST OIL WELL. New Haven, Conn.: Yale University Press, 1934. 40 p.

Trowbridge, Thomas Rutherford. "History of the Ancient Maritime Interests of New Haven." NHCHS PAPERS 3 (1882): 85-205.

Warner, Robert Austin. NEW HAVEN NEGROES, A SOCIAL HISTORY. London: Oxford University Press, 1940. 309 p.

Washington, D.C. National Archives and Record Service. U.S. Customs Passenger lists. Port of New Haven 1820-1873. State Department Transcripts 1822-1831.

Woodward, Sarah Day. EARLY NEW HAVEN. New Haven, Conn.: Price, Lee and Adkins Co., 1912. 119 p.

Woolsey, Theodore S. "The Old New Haven Bank." NHCHS PAPERS 8 (1914): 310-28.

NEWINGTON

HARTFORD COUNTY. Organized 10 July 1871 from WETHERSFIELD.

CEMETERY RECORDS AND CEMETERIES

NAME	ADDRESS	HALE NO.	CITATION
Newington Cemetery	Rear of the Congregational Church	1	34:1-38
Church Street Cemetery	Church Street	2	34:39-42

Index to Hale inscriptions: 34:43-55.

Tillotson, Edward Sweetser. WETHERSFIELD INSCRIPTIONS. Hartford: William F.J. Boardman, 1899. 372 p.

Wilson, Mrs. Katherine Wethy. "Newington, Connecticut (Cemetery) across from Veteran's Hospital." In EARLY SETTLERS OF NEW YORK STATE, pp. 169-70.

CENSUS RECORDS

Welles, Edwin Stanley. A CENSUS OF NEWINGTON, CONNECTICUT TAKEN ACCORDING TO HOUSEHOLDS IN 1776 BY JOSIAH WILLARD TOGETHER WITH SOME DOCUMENTS RELATING TO THE EARLY HISTORY OF THE PARISH. Hartford: Frederic B. Hartranft, 1909. 41 p. (LDS 823,819).

CHURCH RECORDS

CONGREGATIONAL CHURCH. Minutes, 1716-1927. Vital Records, 1769-1861. (CSL, LDS 1969).

GRACE EPISCOPAL CHURCH. Minutes, 1871-1938. Vital Records, 1874-1940. (CSL, LDS 1970).

Welles, Roger. EARLY ANNALS OF NEWINGTON, COMPRISING THE FIRST RECORDS OF THE NEWINGTON ECCLESIASTICAL SOCIETY, AND OF THE CONGREGATIONAL CHURCH, CONNECTED THEREWITH: WITH DOCUMENTS AND PAPERS RELATING TO THE EARLY HISTORY OF THE PARISH. Hartford: Case, Lockwood and Brainard Co., 1874. 204 p. (LDS 823,580).

HISTORICAL SOCIETY

Newington Historical Society, 06111.

LIBRARY

Wells Library, 95 Cedar Street, 06111. (203) 666-9350.

MILITARY RECORDS

Welles, Roger. THE REVOLUTIONARY WAR LETTERS OF CAPTAIN ROGER WELLES OF WETHERSFIELD AND NEWINGTON, CONNECTICUT, WITH FOUR SUCH LETTERS FROM THREE NEWINGTON SOLDIERS. Hartford, Conn.: n.p., 1932. 40 p.

NEWSPAPERS

NEWINGTON TOWN CRIER. Weekly. 50 Market Square, 06111. (203) 666-8477.

The PRELIMINARY CHECKLIST lists four newspapers for NEWINGTON.

PROBATE RECORDS

Newington Probate District, Town Hall, 131 Cedar Street, 06111. (203) 666-4661 ext. 247.

 Organized January 1975 from the Hartford Probate District.

The Newington Probate District also includes the towns of ROCKY HILL and WETHERSFIELD.

TAX RECORDS

Town Clerk, Town Hall, 131 Cedar Street, 06111. (203) 666-4661.

The town clerk's earliest birth is recorded in 1705, marriage and death records date from 1871.

PUBLISHED WORKS AND OTHER RECORDS

Baxter, Elizabeth Sweetser. THE CENTENNIAL HISTORY OF NEWINGTON, CONNECTICUT 1970. Hartford: Finlay Brothers, 1971. 316 p.

Little, Henry Gilman. EARLY DAYS IN NEWINGTON, CONNECTICUT 1833-1836. Newington: Privately printed, 1937. Reprint. Evansville, Ind.: Unigraphic, 1977. 122 p.

Reynolds, Ronna L. "The Towns of Glastonbury, Rocky Hill, and Newington." ANTIQUES 109 (March 1976): 518-27.

Welles, Edwin Stanley. "Newington." CQ 3 (1897): 389-402.

WPA Historical Records Survey. INVENTORY OF THE TOWN AND CITY ARCHIVES OF CONNECTICUT NO. 2 HARTFORD COUNTY. Vol. 7, NEWINGTON. New Haven: Connecticut Historical Records Survey, WPA, 1939. 98 p.

NEW LONDON

NEW LONDON COUNTY. Organized 1646. Towns organized from NEW LONDON include GROTON, MONTVILLE and WATERFORD.

CEMETERY RECORDS AND CEMETERIES

NAME	ADDRESS	HALE NO.	CITATION
Cedar Grove Cemetery	688 Broad Street	1	35:1-345
Ancient Cemetery	Hill Center	2	35:346-63
Gardner Cemetery	712 Ocean Avenue	3	35:364-71
St. Mary Roman Catholic Cemetery	On Hartford & Waterford line. Office: 666 Jefferson Avenue, 06320 (203) 443-3465	4	

Index to Hale inscriptions: 35:372-468.

Allyn, Mrs. Mary H. "Allyn Burial Ground." NGSQ 16 (1928): 25-27.

Caulkins, Frances Manwaring. "Ancient Burial Ground at New London, Connecticut." NEHGR 11 (1857): 21-30.

Cemetery Records of New London. (LDS 1444).

Prentice, Edward. YE ANCIENT BURIAL PLACE OF NEW LONDON, CONNECTICUT. New London: Day Publishing Co., 1899. 40 p.

PUBLICATIONS OF CEDAR GROVE CEMETERY. Vol. 1, 1936-1941.

CHURCH RECORDS

CONGREGATIONAL CHURCH. Marriages, 1691-1800. BAILEY 2:7-38.

FEDERAL STREET METHODIST EPISCOPAL CHURCH. Minutes, 1893-1897. Vital Records, 1816-1918. (CSL, LDS 1924.

FIRST BAPTIST CHURCH. Minutes, 1804-1909. Vital Records, 1804-1869. (CSL, LDS 1925).

FIRST CHURCH OF CHRIST (CONGREGATIONAL). Minutes, 1865-1888. Vital Records, 1670-1888. Index, 1670-1888. (CSL, LDS 1922).

FIRST CONGREGATIONAL CHURCH. Minutes, 1726-1780, 1865-1903, 1908-1916. Vital Records, 1670-1767, 1860-1896. (CSL, LDS 1920).

SECOND CONGREGATIONAL CHURCH. Minutes, 1835-1905. Vital Records, 1835-1922. (CSL, LDS 1923).

ST. JAMES EPISCOPAL CHURCH. Minutes, 1725-1850. Vital Records, 1792-1874. (CSL, LDS 1921).

Baker, Henry Augustus. "Record of Baptisms and Marriages by Rev. Royel Cook, Third Pastor of the Second Church in the North Parish of New London (now Montville), Connecticut, from 1784 to 1798." MAGAZINE OF NEW ENGLAND HISTORY 1 (1891): 186-89, 212-15.

_____. "Record of the Second Church in the North Parish of New London, (now Montville), Connecticut, from 1722-1740." MAGAZINE OF NEW ENGLAND HISTORY 1 (1891): 42-50.

Ballam, Robert A. ANNALS OF ST. JAMES' CHURCH, NEW LONDON, FOR ONE HUNDRED AND FIFTY YEARS. Hartford: H.H. Mallory and Co., 1873. 120 p.

Blake, Silas LeRoy. THE EARLY HISTORY OF THE FIRST CHURCH OF CHRIST, NEW LONDON, CONNECTICUT. New London: Day Publishing Co., 1897. 327 p.

_____. THE LATER HISTORY OF THE FIRST CHURCH OF CHRIST, NEW LONDON, CONNECTICUT. New London: Day Publishing Co., 1900. 559 p.

Dart, Dorothy Ripley. INDEX TO BAPTISMS IN THE LATER HISTORY OF THE FIRST CONGREGATIONAL CHURCH OF CHRIST (CONGREGATIONAL) NEW LONDON, CONNECTICUT 1670-1821. Typescript. N.p.: Author, 1933. 71 p.

THE FIRST CHURCH OF CHRIST IN NEW LONDON, THREE HUNDREDTH ANNIVERSARY, MAY 10, 17, 31 AND OCTOBER 11, 1942. New London: First Church of Christ, 1946. 116 p.

Jensen, Mrs. Carl. INDEX TO THE LATER HISTORY OF THE FIRST CON-
GREGATIONAL CHURCH OF CHRIST, NEW LONDON, CONNECTICUT.
Typescript. Bloomfield: Author, n.d. 80 p.

A LIST OF ALL THOSE WHO ARE KNOWN TO HAVE BEEN MEMBERS OF
THE FIRST CHURCH OF CHRIST IN NEW LONDON, FROM THE BEGINNING
TO JANUARY 1, 1901. New London: Clarke and Keach, 1900. 51 p.

Raymond, Mrs. Edith. TRANSCRIPT OF RECORDS OF THE NORTH CONGRE-
GATIONAL SOCIETY IN NEW LONDON, 1722-1819, GRAVESTONE IN-
SCRIPTIONS FROM FIVE MONTVILLE CEMETERIES TO 1850, AND ALL RE-
MAINING RECORDS OF THE CHESTERFIELD CONGREGATIONAL SOCIETY,
1769-1820. Montville: Author. 199 p.

Smith, Philip M. "Early New London Churchmen." (Episcopalian) TAG 9
(1932): 233-34.

HISTORICAL SOCIETY

See New London County Historical Society.

LAND RECORDS

Land Records, 1664-1854. Index, 1646-1903. (LDS, 1917 pt. 1-28).

Deshon-Allyn House, 613 Williams Street, 06320. (203) 443-2545.

Hempsted House, 11 Hempsted Street, 06320. (203) 443-8996.

Birdsall, Richard D. "The Significance of Hempsted House." CANTIQUARIAN
11 (July 1959): 6-9.

Clark, Delphina L.H. "Joshua Hempsted and His House." CANTIQUARIAN
6 (June 1954): 5-10.

Cogan, Lillian Blankley. "Furnishing the Hempsted House: Joshua Hempsted's
Diary, Valuable Guide." CANTIQUARIAN 11 (December 1959): 10-19.

"Nathaniel Hempsted House." CANTIQUARIAN 24 (June 1972): 17-18.

Palmer, Frederic. "Hempsted House in New London." CANTIQUARIAN 10
(July 1958): 6-33.

Shaw Mansion, 11 Blinman Street, 06320. (203) 443-1209.

Small, Carleton F. "The Shaw Family and the Shaw Mansion." CANTIQUAR-IAN 20 (June 1968): 14-16.

Tale of the Whale Museum, 3 Whale Oil Row, 06320. (203) 442-8191.

LIBRARIES

Public Library of New London, 63 Huntington Street, 06320. (203) 447-1411.

Gay, Helen Kilduff. "Public Libraries in Connecticut--The Benefaction of a Pioneer Alaskan Trader." CM 11 (1907): 139-44.

MILITARY RECORDS

Burnham, Norman Hammond. THE BATTLE OF GROTON HEIGHTS: A STORY OF THE STORMING OF FORT GRISWOLD, AND THE BURNING OF NEW LONDON, ON THE SIXTH OF SEPTEMBER, 1781. New London, Conn.: Bingham Paper Box Co., 1907. 42 p.

"Muster Roll of Captain Abial Peese's Company at New London in the year 1776." AMERICAN MONTHLY MAGAZINE 29 (1936): 264-65.

Rogers, Ernest Elias. "Connecticut's Naval Office at New London during the War of the American Revolution, including the Mercantile Letter Book of Nathaniel Shaw, Jr." COLLECTIONS OF THE NEW LONDON COUNTY HISTORICAL SOCIETY 2 (1933): 1-358.

_____. SESQUICENTENNIAL OF THE BATTLE OF GROTON HEIGHTS AND THE BURNING OF NEW LONDON, CONNECTICUT, SEPTEMBER 6 AND 7, 1931. Hartford: Case, Lockwood and Brainard Co., 1932. 186 p.

NEWSPAPERS

THE DAY. Daily. 47-53 Eugene O'Neill Drive, 06320. (203) 443-2882.

The PRELIMINARY CHECKLIST lists thirty-four newspapers for NEW LONDON.

The HALE NEWSPAPER INDEX to deaths and marriages includes the following newspapers:

> NEW LONDON BEE, deaths 13 September 1797-5 July 1803. Marriages 13 September 1797-10 May 1803.

NEW LONDON DAILY STAR, deaths 3 July 1850–28 December 1867. Marriages 3 July 1850–10 June 1869.

NEW LONDON DEMOCRAT, deaths and marriages 22 March 1845–17 November 1866.

NEW LONDON MORNING NEWS, deaths and marriages 17 November 1847–25 April 1848.

NEW LONDON GAZETTE, deaths and marriages 2 August 1765–28 December 1836.

NEW LONDON SUMMARY & WEEKLY ADVERTISER, deaths 29 September 1738–23 September 1763, marriages 29 September 1758–26 July 1763.

NEW LONDON WEEKLY CHRONICLE, deaths and marriages 5 May 1848–18 May 1867.

PEOPLE'S ADVOCATE, deaths and marriages 26 August 1840–26 April 1848.

REPUBLICAN ADVOCATE, deaths and marriages 6 January 1819–10 December 1828.

SPRINGER'S WEEKLY ORACLE, deaths and marriages 28 November 1797–29 September 1801.

PROBATE RECORDS

New London Probate District, Municipal Building, 181 State Street, 06320. (203) 443-7121.

Organized May 1666; the New London Probate District also includes the town of WATERFORD. Probate Districts organized from the New London Probate District include the Guilford, Montville, New London, Norwich, Old Lyme, Salem, Stonington and Windham Probate Districts.

ON FILE AT THE CSL: Estate Papers, 1675-1850. CSL has a special index to Vols. 1-7, 1667-1700.

Probate Records, 1675-1872. (LDS 1918 pt. 1-11).

Jacobus, Donald Lines. "New London, (Conn.) Probate Records. Abstract of Records Before 1710." TAG 9 (1932-33): 230-33; 10 (1933-34): 35-40, 101-104, 166-70, 215-17; 11 (1934-35): 30-31, 103-5, 153-57; 12 (1935-36): 33-34, 115-16, 151-54; 13 (1936-37): 106-110, 164-66, 246-47; 14 (1937-38): 16-18, 103-104, 184-86, 246-48; 15 (1938-39): 104-106; 17 (1941-42): 118-20.

"Oldest Wills Extant in America." CM 10 (1906): 474.

TAX RECORDS

Hartford. CSL, Record Group 62. Individual Tax Lists, 1807-1860, Town Tax Notebooks, 1857-1869. Abstracts, 1733-1849.

VITAL RECORDS

Town Clerk, Municipal Building, 181 State Street, 06320. (203) 443-2861.

The BARBOUR INDEX covers the years 1646-1854 and is based on the James N. Arnold copy of NEW LONDON vital records made in 1911.

"Connecticut Births Before 1730 (Barbour)--Town of New London." CN 5 (1973-74): 480; 6 (1974-75): 7-12, 175-80, 336-41, 493-98.

Hartford. CSL, Record Group 62. Vital Records, 1869-1878 (incomplete).

VOTER RECORDS

Hartford. CSL, Record Group 62. List of Electors, 1836-1932 (incomplete).

PUBLISHED WORKS AND OTHER RECORDS

Bodenwein, Gordon. "New London, Connecticut, Silversmiths." OLD-TIME NEW ENGLAND 33 (1942): 57-60.

Bolles, John Rogers. NEW LONDON, A SEAPORT FOR THE NORTH AND WEST, AND OUT PORT OF NEW YORK: ITS GREAT COMMERCIAL ADVANTAGES, CONVENIENT, AMPLE AND CHEAP WHARF ROOM, MANUFACTURING FACILITIES, ABUNDANT SUPPLY OF PURE WATER, HEALTHFULNESS ETC. New London, Conn.: Power Press of George E. Starr, 1877. 24 p.

Caulkins, Frances Manwaring. HISTORY OF NEW LONDON, CONNECTICUT FROM THE FIRST SURVEY IN 1612, TO 1852. Hartford: Case, Tiffany and Co., 1852. New London: H.D. Utley, 1895. 696 p. (LDS 896,732).

"The Celebration at New London." CQ 2 (1896): 305.

Colby, Barnard Ledward. NEW LONDON WHALING CAPTAINS. Westerly, R.I.: Utter Co., 1936. 41 p.

Decker, Robert Owen. "The New London Merchants: 1645-1909: The Rise and Decline of a Connecticut Port." Ph.D. dissertation, University of Connecticut, 1970. 412 p.

_____. THE WHALING CITY: A HISTORY OF NEW LONDON. Chester: Pequot Press, 1976. 415 p.

_____. WHALING INDUSTRY OF NEW LONDON. York, Pa.: Liberty Cap Books, 1973. 202 p.

DIARY OF JOSHUA HEMPSTEAD OF NEW LONDON, CONNECTICUT, COVERING A PERIOD OF FORTY-SEVEN YEARS, FROM SEPTEMBER 1711, TO NOVEMBER 1758, CONTAINING VALUABLE GENEALOGICAL DATA RELATING TO MANY NEW LONDON FAMILIES, REFERENCES TO THE COLONIAL WARS, TO THE SHIPPING AND OTHER MATTERS OF INTEREST PERTAINING TO THE TOWN AND THE TIMES, WITH AN ACCOUNT OF THE JOURNEY MADE BY THE WRITER FROM NEW LONDON TO MARYLAND. New London: New London County Historical Society, 1901. 750 p.

Feldman, Patricia, and Barnes, Constance. "Joshua Hempsted, 1678-1758." CANTIQUARIAN 5 (December 1953): 27-31.

Gorton, Elizabeth. "A Backward Glance." NEW LONDON COUNTY HISTORICAL SOCIETY RECORD 3 (1912): 167-74.

Griswold, Cecilia. INDEX TO "HISTORY OF NEW LONDON, CONNECTICUT FROM THE FIRST SURVEY OF THE COAST IN 1612, TO 1852 BY FRANCES MANWARING CAULKINS." New London: Trustees of the Public Library of New London, 1950. 134 p.

Hahn, Charles Curtis. "In Unknown Seas: Being the Story Told by Captain Frank Reynolds, who sailed from New London, Connecticut, on the Francis Allyn, in 1872." CM 6 (1900): 475-80.

Hartford. CSL, Record Group 63. Main 2. Boxes 502-503. New London City Court. Declarations of intent to become naturalized American citizens 1819-1871.

Hartford. CSL, Record Group 62. New London Town Records. Miscellaneous. 1760-1930.

Harwood, Pliny LeRoy, and Harwood, Rowena Mossette. THE POETS OF NEW LONDON; AN ANTHOLOGY. New London, Conn.: Authors, 1933. 163 p.

Hine, F.E. "Fisher's Island: Its History and Development." NEW LONDON COUNTY HISTORICAL SOCIETY RECORD 3 (1912): 178-204.

Holloway, Charlotte Molyneux. "A Daughter of Puritans." CQ 3 (1897): 3-18.

_____. "The Old Whaling Port." CQ 3 (1897): 206-21.

Johnson, Hazel A. A CHECKLIST OF NEW LONDON, CONNECTICUT IM-PRINTS, 1709-1800. Charlottesville: Published for the Bibliographical Society of America by the University Press of Virginia, 1979. 493 p. Index.

Lyman, Lila Parrish. "A New London House." CANTIQUARIAN 9 (July 1957): 20-25.

NEW LONDON HISTORIC DISTRICT; DISTRICT STUDY, 1978. New London, Conn.: Herman and Joncus, 1978. 48 p.

Parkhurst, Charles Dyer. PARKHURST MANUSCRIPT ON EARLY FAMILIES OF NEW LONDON AND VICINITY. Index. (NHCHS, LDS 1919 pt. 1-9).

Phipps, Frances. "Joshua Hempsted's Journey to Maryland." CANTIQUARIAN 22 (December 1970): 12-17; 23 (June 1971): 13-26.

PICTURESQUE NEW LONDON AND ITS ENVIRONS, GROTON, MYSTIC, MONTVILLE, WATERFORD AT THE COMMENCEMENT OF THE TWENTIETH CENTURY. New London: American Book Exchange, 1901. 192 p.

Rogers, Ernest Elias. NEW LONDON'S PARTICIPATION IN CONNECTICUT'S TERCENTENARY, 1935. New London, Conn.: New London County Historical Society, 1935. 121 p.

Starr, William Holt. CENTENNIAL HISTORICAL SKETCH OF THE TOWN OF NEW LONDON. New London: G.E. Starr, 1876.

Warch, Richard. "The Shepherd's Tent: Education and Enthusiasm in the Great Awakening." AMERICAN QUARTERLY 30 (1978): 177-98.

Washington, D.C. National Archives and Record Service. U.S. Customs Passenger Lists. Port of New London, 1820-1847. State Department transcripts 1820, 1823-1827, 1829, 1831.

Williams, C.A. "Early Whaling Industry in New London." NEW LONDON HISTORICAL SOCIETY COLLECTIONS 2 (1933): 1-22.

NEW MILFORD

LITCHFIELD COUNTY. Organized October 1712. Towns organized from NEW MILFORD include BRIDGEWATER, BROOKFIELD and WASHINGTON.

CEMETERY RECORDS AND CEMETERIES

NAME	ADDRESS	HALE NO.	CITATION
Center Cemetery	Poplar Street	1	35:1-120
St. Francis Xavier Cemetery	84 Fort Hill Street	2	35:121-43
Morningside Cemetery	50 Kent Road	3	35:144-48
Gaylordsville Cemetery	Gaylord Road	4	35:149-61
Quaker Cemetery	268 Danbury Road	5	35:162-71
Pickett District Cemetery	49 Danbury Road	6	35:172-78
Lower Merryall Cemetery	Lower Merryall	7	35:179-91
Northville Cemetery	Route 25	8	35:192-212
Upper Merryall Cemetery	Chermiske Road	9	35:213-26
Long Mountain Cemetery	Bass Road	10	35:227-30
Gallows Hill Cemetery	Danbury Road	11	35:231-38
Fanton Cemetery	1 mile south of South Kent	12	36:239
Old Lanesville Cemetery	Rear of Quaker Lanesville	13	36:240-41
Grave of Chief Waramaug	Lovers Leap	14	36:242
Holy Cross Cemetery	187 Danbury Road		
West Meeting House Cemetery	West Meeting House Road		

Index to Hale inscriptions: 36:243-311.

"Tombstone Inscriptions, Long Mountain Cemetery, New Milford, Conn." DAR GENEALOGICAL RECORDS, 1954. 16 p. (CSL, LDS 1401).

CHURCH RECORDS

FIRST CONGREGATIONAL CHURCH. Minutes, 1753-1938. Vital Records, 1812-1938. (CSL, LDS 1948). Marriages, 1717-1799. BAILEY 3:108-23.

NORTHVILLE BAPTIST CHURCH. Minutes, 1814-1939. (CSL, LDS 1947).

Heireth, Imogene. "Quaker Records from New Milford, Connecticut. Vital Statistics." CA 18 (1976): 88-93.

HISTORICAL SOCIETY

New Milford Historical Society, 6 Aspetuck Avenue, P.O. Box 566, 06776. (203) 354-3069.

LAND RECORDS

Land Records, 1707-1858. Index, 1707-1866. (LDS 1945 pt. 1-27).

LIBRARY

New Milford Public Library, 24 Main Street, 06776. (203) 355-1191.

NEWSPAPERS

NEW MILFORD TIMES. Weekly. P.O. Box 539, 06776. (203) 354-2261.

The PRELIMINARY CHECKLIST lists four newspapers for NEW MILFORD.

PROBATE RECORDS

New Milford Probate District, Town Hall, 10 Main Street, 06776. (203) 354-4629.

Organized May 1787 from the Danbury, Sharon and Woodbury Probate Districts.

The New Milford Probate District also includes the town of BRIDGEWATER.

Probate districts organized from the New Milford Probate District include the Kent Probate District.

ON FILE AT THE CSL: Estate Papers, 1787-1947. Indexes, 1787-1947. Inventory Control Books, 1787-1947. Court Record Books, 1787-1853.

Probate Records, 1787-1853. (LDS 1946 pt. 1-8).

TAX RECORDS

Hartford. CSL, Record Group 62. Grand List, 1813. Rate Book, 1848.

VITAL RECORDS

Town Clerk, Town Hall, 06776. (203) 354-4478.

The town clerk's earliest birth record is 1707, and marriage and death record is 1728.

The BARBOUR INDEX covers the years 1712-1860 and is based on the Mrs. Julia E.C. Brush copy of NEW MILFORD vital records made in 1915.

"Connecticut Births Before 1730 (Barbour)--Town of New Milford." CN 6 (1973-74): 498.

PUBLISHED WORKS AND OTHER RECORDS

Barlow, Charles Beach. EDITH NEWTON'S NEW MILFORD. New Milford: New Milford Historical Society, n.d. 87 p.

Davenport, Daniel. THE TWO HUNDREDTH ANNIVERSARY OF THE SETTLE-MENT OF THE TOWN OF NEW MILFORD, CONNECTICUT JULY 17TH, 1907. Bridgeport: Buckingham, Brewer and Platt Co., 1907. 20 p.

Giddings, Minot S. TWO CENTURIES OF NEW MILFORD, CONNECTICUT; AN ACCOUNT OF THE BICENTENNIAL CELEBRATION OF THE FOUNDING OF THE TOWN HELD JUNE 15, 16, 17 AND 18, 1907. New York: Grafton Press, 1907. 307 p.

Kilbourn, Dwight C. "New Milford." CM 5 (1899): 499-519.

Orcutt, Samuel. HISTORY OF THE TOWNS OF NEW MILFORD AND BRIDGE-WATER, CONNECTICUT, 1703-1882. Hartford: Case, Lockwood and Brainard Co., 1882. 909 p. (LDS 476,886).

TWO CENTURIES OF NEW MILFORD, CONNECTICUT (1707-1907). New York: Grafton Press, 1907. 307 p.

NEWTOWN

FAIRFIELD COUNTY. Organized October 1711. Towns organized from NEW-
TOWN include BROOKFIELD.

CEMETERY RECORDS AND CEMETERIES

NAME	ADDRESS	HALE NO.	CITATION
Town Plot Cemetery	In Center of Town	1	36:1-66
Village Cemetery	26 Elm Drive	2	---
Land's End Cemetery	Hawleyville Road	3	36:67-85
Berkshire Cemetery	Formerly known as Zoar Farm	4	36:86-108
Taunton Cemetery	Taunton Lake Road	5	36:109-18
Huntington Cemetery	Brushy Hill Road	6	36:119-34
Sandy Hook Cemetery	Riverside Road	7	36:135-46
Flat Swamp Cemetery #1	Near School House	8	36:147-49
Flat Swamp Cemetery #2	On a triangular piece of ground between 3 roads	9	36:150-51
Bradleyville Cemetery	Half Way River District	10	36:152-53
Hopewell Cemetery	Hollow Road	11	36:154
Platt's Cemetery	In Palestine near Morgan Four Corners	12	36:155
Old Morgan's Cemetery	On cross road from Hope-well to Gregory's Orchard, stones in wall	13	36:156
Botsford Cemetery	Cold Spring	14	36:157-60
St. Rose Roman Catholic Cemetery	Cherry Street	15	36:161-91

NAME	ADDRESS	HALE NO.	CITATION
Soldiers Monument Cemetery	In Center of town	16	36:192-97
McCartan Cemetery	Front of St. Rose Roman Catholic Church	17	36:198
Bennetts Cemetery	Near Bennett Bridge	18	36:199-200
Resurrection Roman Catholic Cemetery	Office: P.O. Box 425, Danbury (203) 743-9626		(no citation)
Dodgingtown Cemetery	Cemetery Road		(no citation)
Hattertown Road Cemetery	Hattertown Road		(no citation)
Middle Gate Cemetery	Botsford Hill Road		(no citation)
St. Peter Cemetery	South Main Street		(no citation)
Zoar Cemetery	Berkshire Road		(no citation)

Index to Hale inscriptions: 36:201-55.

Sarah Riggs Humphreys Chapter, DAR. RIVERSIDE CEMETERY AT ZOAR. N.p.: Sarah Riggs Humphreys Chapter, DAR, n.d. 15 p.

CHURCH RECORDS

FIRST CONGREGATIONAL CHURCH. Minutes, 1715-1946. Index. (CSL, LDS 1893). Marriages, 1743-1799. BAILEY 2:131.

METHODIST EPISCOPAL CHURCH. Vital Records, 1743-1887. (CSL, LDS 1891).

ST. JOHN EPISCOPAL CHURCH. Parish Register, 1880-1913. (CSL, LDS 1892).

TRINITY EPISCOPAL CHURCH. Minutes, 1764-1792. Vital Records, 1818-1921. (CSL, LDS 1892).

Lucas, Mary R. NEWTOWN CONGREGATIONAL CHURCH, 250TH ANNIVERSARY YEAR, 1714-1964. Newtown: Newtown Congregational Church, 1964. 114 p. Index.

Mappen, Marc Alfred. "Anatomy of a Schism: Anglican Dissent in the New Community of Newtown, Connecticut, 1708-1765." Ph.D. dissertation, Rutgers University, 1976. 217 p.

HISTORICAL SOCIETY

Newtown Historical Society, Main Street, P.O. Box 189, 06470. (203) 426-5937.

Publishes THE ROOSTER'S CROW. Quarterly.

LAND RECORDS

Land Records, 1712-1852. Index, 1707-1933. (LDS 1889 pt. 1-23).

LIBRARY

Booth Library, 25 Main Street, 06470. (203) 426-4533.

MILITARY RECORDS

"Newtown and the American Revolution." CH 20 (1979): 6-26.

"Newtown Soldiers in the Continental Army." CH 20 (1979): 19-23.

NEWSPAPERS

NEWTOWN BEE. Weekly. 5 Church Hill Road, 06470. (203) 426-3141.

The PRELIMINARY CHECKLIST lists three newspapers for NEWTOWN.

PROBATE RECORDS

Newtown Probate District, Town Hall, 45 Main Street, 06470. (203) 426-2675.

Organized May 1820 from the Danbury Probate District. Probate Districts formed from the Newtown Probate District include the Brookfield Probate District.

ON FILE AT THE CSL: Estate Papers, 1820-1931. Indexes, 1820-1931. Inventory Control Book, 1820-1931. Court Record Books, 1820-1850.

Probate Records, 1810-1850. (LDS 1890 pt. 1-4).

SCHOOL RECORDS

Hartford. CSL, Record Group 62. School Census, 1886-1902 (incomplete).

VITAL RECORDS

Town Clerk, Town Hall, 45 Main Street, 06470. (203) 426-8131.

> The town clerk's earliest birth and marriage records are 1705 and death record is 1715.

The BARBOUR INDEX covers the years 1711-1870 and is based on the James N. Arnold copy of NEWTOWN vital records made in 1915.

Barber, Mrs. W.A., comp. Vital Records, about 1740-1871. 157 p. Index. (CSL, LDS 823,815).

PUBLISHED WORKS AND OTHER RECORDS

Boyle, John Nevile. NEWTOWN: 1708-1758. HISTORICAL NOTES AND MAPS. Newtown: Bee Publishing Co., n.d. 83 p.

George, James Hardin, et al. NEWTOWN'S BICENTENNIAL 1705-1905. New Haven: Tuttle, Morehouse and Taylor Co., 1906. 177 p.

Johnson, Jane Eliza. NEWTOWN'S HISTORY AND HISTORIAN, EZRA ELIZA JOHNSON. Newtown: Author, 1917. 453 p. (LDS, 844,900).

McGrath, Stephen B. "Connecticut's Tory Towns: The Loyalty Struggle in Newtown, Redding and Ridgefield 1774-1783." CHSB 44 (1979): 88-96.

Mappen, Marc A. "Anatomy of a Schism: American Dissent in the New England Community of Newtown, Connecticut, 1708-1876." Ph.D. dissertation, Rutgers University, 1975. 207 p.

"Newtown and the American Revolution." CH 20 (1979): 6-26.

NEWTOWN CONNECTICUT PAST AND PRESENT. Newtown: League of Women Voters of Newtown, 1955. 107 p.

Smith, Betty. "A Place You'd Never Believe . . . Newtown, Fairfield County's Largest (60 Sq.Mi.) Small Town." FAIRFIELD COUNTY 8 (October 1978): 30-37.

Town Records, 1700-1875. Typescript. 146 p. (LDS 1888).

NORFOLK

LITCHFIELD COUNTY. Organized October 1758.

CEMETERY RECORDS AND CEMETERIES

NAME	ADDRESS	HALE NO.	CITATION
Center Cemetery	Old Colony Road	1	36:1-58
St. Mary Roman Catholic Cemetery	Old Colony Road	2	36:59-70
South Norfolk Cemetery	Litchfield Road	3	36:71-79
Huxley Cemetery	Over Massachusetts State Line	4	36:80-87
Grantville Cemetery	Near Grantville	5	36:88-93
Dickinson Cemetery	On Goshen Road near South Norfolk	6	36:94
Meekertown Cemetery	Southwest part near Canaan line	7	36:95
Benedict Cemetery	Near Doolittle Lake, northeast part of town	8	36:96-99
St. Mary Roman Catholic Cemetery (new)	North of St. Mary Roman Catholic Cemetery (old)	10	36:101-7
Stoekel Cemetery	On Stoekel Estate in Center	11	36:108-9
Merrill Cemetery	Doolittle Drive		(no citation)

Index to Hale inscriptions: 36:110-39.

CHURCH RECORDS

CONGREGATIONAL CHURCH. Minutes, 1760-1896. Vital Records, 1760-

1928. Index 1760-1814. (CSL, LDS 1942). Marriages 1762-1800. BAILEY 1:63-69. (Church of Christ). 1760-1769. (NYGBS, LDS 1803).

CHURCH OF CHRIST (CONGREGATIONAL) NORFOLK, CONNECTICUT: TWO HUNDRED YEARS 1760-1960. N.p., n.d. 108 p.

BAPTISMS, MARRIAGES, BURIALS AND LIST OF MEMBERS TAKEN FROM THE CHURCH RECORDS OF THE REVEREND AMMI RUBAMAH ROBBINS, FIRST MINISTER OF NORFOLK, CONNECTICUT, 1761-1813. N.p., 1910. 141 p. (LDS 31098).

Hartford. CSL, Record Group 62. Ecclesiastical Society Rate Book, 1819-1821.

HISTORICAL SOCIETY

Norfolk Historical Society, Village Green, 06058. (203) 542-5761.

LAND RECORDS

Land Records, 1758-1855. Index, 1758-1898. (LDS 1939 pt. 1-9). Proprietors' Records, 1754-1772. (LDS 1941).

LIBRARY

Norfolk Library, Greenwoods Road, 06058. (203) 542-5075.

NEWSPAPERS

The PRELIMINARY CHECKLIST lists three newspapers for NORFOLK.

PROBATE RECORDS

Norfolk Probate District, Town Hall, Greenwoods Road, 06058. (203) 542-5134.

Organized May 1779 from the Litchfield and Simsbury Probate Districts. Probate Districts organized from the Norfolk Probate District include the Winchester Probate District.

ON FILE AT THE CSL: Estate Papers, 1779-1900. Indexes, 1779-1900. Inventory Control Book, 1779-1900. Court Record Book, 1778-1856.

Probate records, 1778-1856. (LDS 1940).

SCHOOL RECORDS

Hartford. CSL, Record Group 62. South Norfolk School Register, 1867; Robbins School Register, 1903-1911.

VITAL RECORDS

Town Clerk, Town Hall, Greenwoods Road, 06058. (203) 542-5679.

> The town clerk's earliest birth record is 1740, marriage record is 1756, and death record is 1762.

The BARBOUR INDEX covers the years 1758-1850 and is based on the Irene H. Mix and James N. Arnold copy of NORFOLK vital records made in 1916.

PUBLISHED WORKS AND OTHER RECORDS

Crissey, Theron Wilmot. HISTORY OF NORFOLK, LITCHFIELD COUNTY, CONNECTICUT 1744-1900. Everett, Mass.: Massachusetts Publishing Co., 1900. 648 p.

Dennis, Frederick Shepard. NORFOLK VILLAGE GREEN. New York: Beer Publishing Co., 1917. 137 p.

Greene, Adele. "Norfolk and that Neighborhood." CQ 1 (1895): 109-22.

Roys, Auren. A BRIEF HISTORY OF THE TOWN OF NORFOLK FROM 1738 TO 1844. New York: Henry Ludwig, 1847. 89 p.

Waldecker, Alice V. NORFOLK, CONNECTICUT 1900-1975. Winsted: Winchester Press, 1976. 294 p. Index.

NORTH BRANFORD

NEW HAVEN COUNTY. Organized May 1831 from BRANFORD.

CEMETERY RECORDS AND CEMETERIES

NAME	ADDRESS	HALE NO.	CITATION
Bare Plain Cemetery	Foxon Road	1	36:1-15
Zion Episcopal Church Cemetery	Foxon Road	2	36:16-18
Congregational Church Cemetery	North Branford Center	3	36:19-38
Old Northford Cemetery	Spruce Street	4	36:39-75
New Northford Cemetery	Spruce Street	5	36:76-81

Index to Hale inscriptions: 36:82-104.

CHURCH RECORDS

FIRST CONGREGATIONAL CHURCH. Vital Records, 1768-1805, 1807-1867. (CSL, LDS 1929).

NORTHFORD CONGREGATIONAL CHURCH. Minutes, 1780-1926. Vital Records 1750-1926. (CSL, LDS 1971). Records, 1750-1926. Index. (CSL, LDS 1448 pt. 2). Marriages, 1750-1800. BAILEY 5:14-19. Baptisms, Marriages and Deaths, 1750-1825. Edith M.A. Raymond, comp. (CSL, LDS 1971).

ST. ANDREW EPISCOPAL CHURCH. Minutes, 1763-1872. Vital Records, 1843-1863, 1866-1899. (CSL, LDS 1930).

ZION EPISCOPAL CHURCH. Vital Records, 1812-1875. (CSL, LDS 1928).

HISTORICAL SOCIETY

Northford Historical Society, 06472.

LAND RECORDS

Land Records, 1831-1854. (LDS 1927 pt. 1-2).

LIBRARY

North Branford Library, 1720 Foxon Road, P.O. Box 258, 06471. (203) 488-8353.

PROBATE RECORDS

North Branford Probate District Administration Building, Route 80, P.O. Box 203, 06471. (203) 488-2501.

> Organized 14 April 1937 from the Guilford and Wallingford Probate Districts.

SCHOOL RECORDS

Hartford. CSL, Record Group 62. North School District Minute Book, 1841-1905.

VITAL RECORDS

Town Clerk, Administration Building, Route 80, 06471. (203) 488-8353.

The BARBOUR INDEX covers the years 1831-1854 and is based on Ethel L. Scofield copy of NORTH BRANFORD vital records made in 1914.

PUBLISHED WORKS AND OTHER RECORDS

WPA Historical Records Survey. INVENTORY OF THE TOWN AND CITY ARCHIVES OF CONNECTICUT, NO. 5, NEW HAVEN COUNTY, VOL. 8, NORTH BRANFORD, NORTH HAVEN, ORANGE, OXFORD, PROSPECT, SEYMOUR, SOUTHBURY. New Haven: Historical Records Survey, 1938. 189 p. (LDS 897,354).

NORTH CANAAN

LITCHFIELD COUNTY. Organized May 1858 from CANAAN.

CEMETERY RECORDS AND CEMETERIES

NAME	ADDRESS	HALE NO.	CITATION
Lower Cemetery	Canaan Village	1	36:1-44
Hillside Cemetery	East Canaan	2	36:45-66
Canaan Valley Cemetery	Canaan Valley	3	36:67-79
Quaker Cemetery	Canaan Valley	4	36:80
George Adam, Private Cemetery	Lower road, East Canaan	5	36:81-82
St. Joseph's Cemetery	Canaan	6	36:83-92
Stevens-Pease Cemetery	Near Norfolk Line	7	36:93
East Canaan Cemetery	Near of East Canaan Church	8	36:94-96
Austen Cemetery	Charles Goodwin farm	9	36:97
Clayton Cemetery	At Clayton, Massachusetts on the state line	10	36:98
Ashley Falls Cemetery	Ashley Falls, Massachusetts just over the state line	11	36:99-109
Mountain View Cemetery	U.S. 58		(no citation)

Index to Hale inscriptions: 36:110-41.

CHURCH RECORDS

CONGREGATIONAL CHURCH. Marriages, 1770-1775. BAILEY 5:21-22.

NEWSPAPER

The PRELIMINARY CHECKLIST lists one newspaper for NORTH CANAAN.

PROBATE RECORDS

NORTH CANAAN is in the Canaan Probate District.

VITAL RECORDS

Town Clerk, Town Hall, Pease Street, P.O. Box 338, Canaan, 06018. (203) 824-7246.

> The town clerk's earliest birth record is 9 October 1858, marriage record 24 January 1859 and death record 9 February 1859.

Vital Records, 1886-1897, 1907, 1909. (CSL, LDS 003,662 and 1483).

NORTH HAVEN

NEW HAVEN COUNTY. Organized October 1786 from NEW HAVEN.

CEMETERY RECORDS AND CEMETERIES

NAME	ADDRESS	HALE NO.	CITATION
Center Cemetery	24 Elm Street	1	37:1-50
Old Center Cemetery	Center	2	37:51-74
Montowese Cemetery	150 Quinipac Avenue	3	37:75-98
All Saints Cemetery	700 Middletown Avenue (203) 239-2557		(no citation)

Index to Hale inscriptions: 37:99-126.

CHURCH RECORDS

FIRST CONGREGATIONAL CHURCH. Minutes, 1784-1858. Vital Records, 1716-1910. (CSL, LDS 1933). Marriages, 1760-1799. BAILEY 6:15-24.

ST. JOHN EPISCOPAL CHURCH. Minutes, 1784-1858. Vital Records, 1759-1858. (CSL, LDS 1932).

Flood, Phyllis Rice. HISTORY OF THE BAPTIST CHURCH IN MONTOWESE. North Haven, Conn.: North Haven Baptist Church, 1976. 24 p.

MONTOWESE BAPTIST CHURCH. SESQUICENTENNIAL HISTORY. 1811-1961; JUNE 10-12, 1961. N.p., n.d. 30 p.

Stiles, H. Nelson. A CHRONICLE OF TWO HUNDRED YEARS OF ST. JOHN'S CHURCH. North Haven: n.p., 1959. 103 p.

CENSUS RECORDS

Jacobus, Donald Lines. "Errors in the Census of 1790 (Conn.): North Haven."
NEHGR 77 (1923): 81.

HISTORICAL SOCIETY

North Haven Historical Society, 06973.

LAND RECORDS

Land Records, 1779-1877. Index, 1779-1877. (LDS 1931).

LIBRARY

North Haven Memorial Library, 17 Elm Street, 06473. (203) 239-5803.

MILITARY RECORDS

DEDICATION OF THE SOLDIERS' MONUMENT, NORTH HAVEN. New Haven: New Haven Printing Co., 1905. 48 p.

Pearsall, Thomas I. NORTH HAVEN IS THE REVOLUTION. North Haven: North Haven Bicentennial Commission, 1976. 92 p.

NEWSPAPERS

NORTH HAVEN POST. Weekly. P.O. Box 9, 06492. (203) 269-1464.

The PRELIMINARY CHECKLIST lists two newspapers for NORTH HAVEN.

PROBATE RECORDS

North Haven Probate District, Town Hall, 18 Church Street, P.O. Box 175, 06473. (203) 239-5321, ext. 69.

Organized 5 January 1955 from New Haven Probate District.

SCHOOL RECORDS

Allen, D.C. THREE CENTURIES OF NORTH HAVEN SCHOOL HISTORY. Winstead: Dowd Printing Co., 1956. 246 p.

VITAL RECORDS

Town Clerk, Town Hall, 18 Church Street, P.O. Box 336, 06473. (203) 239-5321 ext. 41.

The BARBOUR INDEX covers the years 1786-1854 and is based on the James N. Arnold copy of NORTH HAVEN vital records made in 1914.

PUBLISHED WORKS AND OTHER RECORDS

Flood, Phyllis Rice. INDEX TO SHELDON B. THORPE'S "ANNALS OF NORTH HAVEN." 1892. North Haven: Author, 1973. 51 p.

Thorpe, Sheldon Brainerd. NORTH HAVEN ANNALS. A HISTORY OF THE TOWN FROM ITS SETTLEMENT 1680 TO ITS FIRST CENTENNIAL 1886. New Haven: Price, Lee and Adkins Co., 1882. 422 p.

_____. NORTH HAVEN IN THE NINETEENTH CENTURY, A MEMORIAL. N.p.: 1901. 207 p.

WPA Historical Records Survey. INVENTORY OF THE TOWN AND CITY AR-CHIVES OF CONNECTICUT, NO. 5, NEW HAVEN COUNTY, VOL. 8, NORTH BRANFORD, NORTH HAVEN, ORANGE, OXFORD, PROSPECT, SEY-MOUR, SOUTHBURY. New Haven: Historical Records Survey, 1938. 189 p. (LDS 897,354).

NORTH STONINGTON

NEW LONDON COUNTY. Organized May 1807 from STONINGTON.

CEMETERY RECORDS AND CEMETERIES

NAME	ADDRESS	HALE NO.	CITATION
	The distances and directions are given from the Town Hall		
Browning Cemetery	Northwest 7 miles	1	37:1
Denison Cemetery	Northwest 5 3/4 miles	2	37:1
Prentice Cemetery	Northwest 5 1/2 miles	3	37:2
Browning Cemetery	Northwest 5 1/4 miles	4	37:2-3
Denison Cemetery	Northwest 5 1/2 miles	5	37:3
Swan Cemetery	Northwest 4 3/4 miles	6	37:3-4
Baldwin Cemetery	North 5 miles	7	37:4-5
Main Cemetery	North 5 1/4 miles	8	37:5
Billings Cemetery	North 5 miles	9	37:5
Eccleston Cemetery	North 4 1/2 miles	10	37:6-9
Field Stones	North 4 miles	11	37:9
Crandall Cemetery	North 5 miles	12	37:9
Chapman Hill Cemetery	North 3 1/2 miles	13	37:9-10
Pendleton Hill Cemetery	North 5 miles	14	37:11-16
Palmer Cemetery	North 4 1/2 miles	15	37:16
Thompson Cemetery	North 4 1/2 miles	16	37:17-18
Park Cemetery	North 4 miles	17	37:18-19
York Cemetery	North 3 3/4 miles	18	37:19

NAME	ADDRESS	HALE NO.	CITATION
Bliven Cemetery	North 4 1/4 miles	19	37:20
Field Stones	East 4 1/2 miles	20	37:20
Gongdon Cemetery	North 5 1/4 miles	21	37:20
Palmer Cemetery	North 5 1/4 miles	22	37:20
Wilcox Cemetery	North 5 miles	23	37:20
Holdredge Cemetery	North 4 1/2 miles	24	37:20
Lewis Cemetery	East 5 1/4 miles	25	37:21
Field Stones	East 4 1/2 miles	26	37:21
York Cemetery	East 4 miles	27	37:21
Family Cemetery	East 4 miles	28	37:21
Burdick Cemetery	Northeast 4 miles	29	37:21-22
Maine Cemetery	Northeast 3 miles	30	37:22
Breed or Brown Cemetery	Northeast 3 1/4 miles	31	37:22-23
Crumb Cemetery	Northeast 3 miles	32	37:23
York Cemetery	Northeast 2 1/2 miles	33	37:23
Chapman Cemetery	Northeast 3 miles	34	37:24
Chapman Cemetery	North 3 1/4 miles	35	37:24
Field Stones	North 2 miles	36	37:24
Holmes Cemetery	North 1 3/4 miles	37	37:24-25
Coats Cemetery	North 2 miles	38	37:25
Stewart Hill Cemetery	North 2 3/4 miles	39	37:25-26
Hewitt Cemetery	North 3 miles	40	37:26
Hewitt Cemetery	North 2 1/4 miles	41	37:26
Family Cemetery	Northwest 2 miles	42	37:27
Children's Cemetery	Northwest 2 1/2 miles	43	37:27
Wheeler Cemetery	Northwest 3 1/4 miles	44	37:27
Field Stones	Northwest 4 miles	45	37:27
Woodward Cemetery	Northwest 5 miles	46	37:28
Ayer Cemetery	West 3 3/4 miles	47	37:28-29
Hewitt Cemetery	West 2 1/2 miles	48	37:29-31
Avery Cemetery	West 2 3/4 miles	49	37:31
Hewitt Cemetery	West 2 3/4 miles	50	37:31-32

NAME	ADDRESS	HALE NO.	CITATION
Indian Reservation Cemetery	West 3 miles	51	37:32
Phelps Cemetery	West 2 miles	52	37:32
Stanton Cemetery	West 2 miles	53	37:33
Edgecomb Cemetery	West 1 3/4 miles	54	37:33
Hillard Cemetery	Northwest 1 1/2 miles	55	37:33–34
Indian Cemetery	West 3 miles	56	37:34
Great Plain Cemetery	Northwest 3/4 miles	57	37:34–43
Wheeler Cemetery	West 1 1/2 miles	58	37:43–47
Hull Cemetery	West 1/2 miles	59	37:47–48
Grant Cemetery	Southwest 1 1/2 miles	60	37:48
Munsell Cemetery	South 1 1/4 miles	61	37:48
Wheeler Cemetery	West 1/2 miles	62	37:49–53
Pitcher Cemetery	North 1/2 miles	63	37:53
Williams Cemetery	North 1 1/4 miles	64	37:54
Crary Cemetery	Northeast 2 1/4 miles	65	37:55–58
Holmes Cemetery	East 2 miles	66	37:58
Main Cemetery	East 1 1/4 miles	67	37:59
Frink Cemetery	East 1 1/2 miles	68	37:59
Brown Cemetery	Southeast 1 1/4 miles	69	37:60
Brown-Randall Cemetery	South 1 3/4 miles	70	37:60–61
Brown Cemetery	East 1 3/4 miles	71	37:61–64
Union Cemetery	East 2 1/4 miles	72	37:64–88
Partlow Cemetery	East 2 3/4 miles	73	37:88
Stanton Cemetery	East 3 miles	74	37:88
Lewis Cemetery	East 3 3/4 miles	75	37:88–89
Miner Cemetery	East 3 3/4 miles	76	37:89
Miner Cemetery	East 4 miles	77	37:90
Weed Cemetery	Northwest 4 miles	78	37:90
Brown Cemetery	East 3 1/4 miles	79	37:90–91
Kenyon Cemetery	East 2 1/2 miles	80	37:91
Spalding Cemetery	East 2 1/2 miles	81	37:92–93
Field Stones	East 3 1/4 miles	82	37:93

NAME	ADDRESS	HALE NO.	CITATION
Field Stones	East 4 miles	83	37:93
Austin Cemetery	East 4 1/4 miles	84	37:93
Babcock Cemetery	Northeast 5 1/2 miles	85	37:93
Park Cemetery	North 3 miles	86	37:93
York Cemetery	Northwest 3 3/4 miles	87	37:94
Clark Cemetery	Northeast 5 1/2 miles	88	37:94-95
Thompson Cemetery	Northeast 5 miles	89	37:95
Family (Crumb) Cemetery	East 2 3/4 miles	90	37:95
Chapman Cemetery	North 5 miles	91	37:95
Field Stones	Northwest 1 mile	92	37:95
Family Cemetery	Northeast 4 3/4 miles	93	37:95
Parks Cemetery	East 4 miles	94	37:95
Randall Cemetery	Southeast 2 1/4 miles	95	37:95
Allen Cemetery	Southeast	96	37:96
Field Stones	Southeast	97	37:96
Field Stones	Southeast	98	37:96

List of Soldiers Burial Places, 37:97-107.

Index to Hale inscriptions: 37:108-32.

CHURCH RECORDS

CONGREGATIONAL CHURCH. Minutes, 1720-1846. Vital Records, 1727-1887. (CSL, LDS 1915). Admissions, baptisms, marriages, 1727-1828 (copied by Mrs. J.L. Raymond). (CSL, LDS 1914). Marriages, 1733-1781. BAILEY 1:53-63.

FIRST BAPTIST CHURCH. Minutes, 1754-1905. Vital Records, 1762-1886, 1883-1904. (CSL, LDS 1913).

FIRST BAPTIST CHURCH NORTH STONINGTON, CONNECTICUT. Westerly, R.I.: Utter Co., 1936. 145 p. Index.

HISTORICAL SOCIETY

North Stonington Historical Society, 06359.

LAND RECORDS

Land Records, 1813–1850. Index, 1818–1943. (LDS 1911 pt. 104).

LIBRARY

Wheeler Library, Route 2, P.O. Box 217, 06359. (203) 535-0383.

MILITARY RECORDS

Hartford. CSL, Record Group 62. Service certificates and records pertaining to support of soldiers' families, 1826–1865.

PROBATE RECORDS

North Stonington Probate District, Town Hall, Main Street, P.O. Box 91, 06359. (203) 535-2877.

> Organized 4 June 1835 from the Stonington Probate District.

> ON FILE AT THE CSL: Estate Papers, 1835–1912. Indexes, 1835–1912. Inventory Control Book, 1835–1912. Court Record Books, 1835–1858. Probate Records, 1835–1852. Court Journal, 1835–1858. Records. (LDS 1912).

SCHOOL RECORDS

Hartford. CSL, Record Group 62. Returns, records, etc., 1827–1909.

TAX RECORDS

Hartford. CSL, Record Group 62. Abstracts, lists, etc., 1810–1891.

VITAL RECORDS

Town Clerk, Town Hall, Main Street, 06359. (203) 535-2877.

> The town clerk's earliest birth record is 1758, marriage record is 1765 and death record is 1779.

The BARBOUR INDEX covers the years 1807–1852 and is based on the James N. Arnold copy of NORTH STONINGTON vital records made in 1912.

Vital Records, 1880–1905. (CSL, LDS 003,662).

Hartford.   CSL, Record Group 62.   Marriage Certificates, 1836–1850.

VOTER RECORDS

Hartford.   CSL, Record Group 62.   Voter lists, 1827–1839, 1850.

PUBLISHED WORK

Holmes, Jeremiah.   "The Voyages of an Old Sea Captain."   CM   11 (1907): 65–80.

NORWALK

FAIRFIELD COUNTY. Organized 11 September 1651. Towns organized from NORWALK include NEW CANAAN, WESTPORT and WILTON.

CEMETERY RECORDS AND CEMETERIES

NAME	ADDRESS	HALE NO.	CITATION
Norwalk Cemetery	Union Avenue and Ward Street	1	37:1-125
Riverside Cemetery	81 Riverside Avenue (203) 847-7422	2	37:126-241
St. Mary Roman Catholic Cemetery	5 Broad Street	3	37:242-317
Union Cemetery	409 Rowayton Avenue	4	37:318-50
Pine Island Cemetery	Crescent Street	5	37:351-84
East Norwalk Cemetery	243 East Avenue	6	37:385-412
Town House Cemetery	Town House Hill	7	37:413-19
Jewish Cemetery	Turnpike	8	37:420
Silvermine Cemetery	Silvermine Avenue, partly in New Canaan	9	37:421
St. Paul Cemetery	East Avenue	10	38:422-38
Reed Cemetery	West Norwalk, west side of Brookside Avenue, north of Stephen Mather Road, Darien	11	38:439-40
Raymond Cemetery	Rowayton, near Cudlipp Street	12	38:441-43
Gregory Cemetery	93 Chestnut Hill Avenue	13	38:444
Jewish Cemetery	Richards Avenue	14	38:445-49

NAME	ADDRESS	HALE NO.	CITATION
St. John Roman Catholic Cemetery	223 Richards Avenue (203) 838-4271	15	38:450-54
Old Five Mile River Cemetery	Near Union Cemetery	16	38:455-58
Bouton or Huguenot Cemetery	Rowayton	17	38:439
Smith Cemetery	Weed & Millard Streets West Norwalk	18	38:460
Ferndale Cemetery	Holy Ghost Fathers at Ferndale	19	38:461
2 stones on Sheffield Island	Sheffield Island	20	38:462
Reid Cemetery	Flax Hill Road	21	38:463
Kellogg Comstock Cemetery	Corner of Nursery & Ponus Avenue	22	38:464-65
Bolton Hoyt Cemetery	128 Witch Lane		(no citation)
Rowayton Cemetery	212 Rowayton Avenue		(no citation)

Index to Hale inscriptions: 38:466-608.

Card, Lester. NORWALK CEMETERIES. Typescript. Norwalk: Author, 1948. 158 p. Index.

Corriea, Robert. "Pine Island Cemetery is Victim of Vandalism, Lack of Funding." NORWALK HOUR, 31 July 1979, p. 29.

Hunt, Malcolm P. CEMETERY INSCRIPTIONS. OLD ROWAYTON, 1957. (LDS 32593).

Martin, Harold Secor. THE RECORD OF INSCRIPTIONS AND EPITAPHS FOUND ON THE MONUMENTS AND HEADSTONES IN EAST NORWALK HISTORICAL CEMETERY, THE OLDEST CEMETERY IN NORWALK. 1655 TO 1971. Norwalk: Author, 1971. 60 p.

Van Hoosear, David Hermon. A COMPLETE COPY OF THE INSCRIPTIONS FOUND ON THE MONUMENTS, HEADSTONES, ETC. IN THE OLDEST CEMETERY IN NORWALK, CONNECTICUT, SEPTEMBER, 1892. Bridgeport: Standard Association, Printers, 1895. 47 p. (LDS 823,677).

CHURCH RECORDS

EPISCOPAL CHURCH. Register, 1742-1746. (CSL, LDS 2107).

ST. PAUL EPISCOPAL CHURCH. Minutes, 1741-1925. Vital Records, 1830-1906. (CSL, LDS 1897 pt. 1-2).

SOUTH NORWALK CONGREGATIONAL CHURCH. Sunday School Minutes, 1838-1847. (CSL, LDS 2107).

TRINITY EPISCOPAL CHURCH. Vital Records, 1867-1948. (CSL, LDS 1898).

ADDRESS BY REV. CHARLES M. SELLECK, A.M., AT THE CENTENARY OF ST. PAUL'S CHURCH, NORWALK, CONNECTICUT, JULY 15, 1886. Norwalk: THE HOUR, 1886. 126 p. Index.

Martin, Harold Edgar. HISTORICAL PAPERS CONCERNING THE FIRST CONGREGATIONAL CHURCH ON THE GREEN, NORWALK. Norwalk: First Congregational Church, 1955. 44 p.

HISTORICAL SOCIETY

Norwalk Historical Society, P.O. Box 335, 06852.

Rowayton Historical Society, Rowayton Avenue, 06853.

Lockwood House, 141 East Avenue, 06850. (203) 866-0202.

Lockwood-Mathews Mansion, Museum, 295 West Avenue, 06850. (203) 838-1434.

LAND RECORDS

Green, Erma F. "Public Land System of Norwalk, Connecticut, 1654-1704: A Structural Analysis of Economic and Political Relationships." Master's thesis, University of Bridgeport, 1972. 179 p.

Hartford. CSL, Record Group 62. Land Records, 1815-1843.

Land Records, 1652-1853. Index, 1652-1856. (LDS 1896 pt. 1-20).

LIBRARY

Norwalk Public Library, One Belden Avenue, 06850. (203) 866-5559.

MILITARY RECORDS

McLean, Louise H. "Brothers at War." DARIEN HISTORICAL SOCIETY AN-NUAL (1976): 5-43.

28TH ANNIVERSARY ROSTER OF BUCKINGHAM POST NO. 12. DEPARTMENT OF CONNECTICUT, G.A.R. AND BUCKINGHAM W.R.C. AUXILIARY TO THE POST. Norwalk: Buckingham Post, G.A.R., n.d.

NEWSPAPERS

THE HOUR. Daily. 346 Main Avenue, 06851. (203) 846-3281.

The PRELIMINARY CHECKLIST lists nineteen newspapers for NORWALK.

Card, Lester. DEATHS FROM THE NORWALK GAZETTE 1818-1844. Norwalk: Author: n.d. 149 p. Index.

Card, Lester. MARRIAGES FROM THE NORWALK GAZETTE 1818-1848. Norwalk: Author: n.d. 321 p.

PROBATE RECORDS

Norwalk Probate District, Norwalk Court House, 105 Main Street, Box 2009, 06852. (203) 847-1443.

Organized May 1802 from the Fairfield and Stamford Probate Districts. Probate districts organized from the Norwalk Probate District include the New Canaan Probate District. The Norwalk Probate District also includes WILTON.

ON FILE AT THE CSL: Index, 1802-1920. Court Record Books, 1802-1851.

Probate Records, 1810-1850. (LDS 1895 pt. 1-4).

Card, Lester. PROBATE RECORDS OF NORWALK 1802-1808. South Norwalk: Author, n.d. 197 p. Index. (LDS 1894).

SCHOOL RECORDS

Norwalk. Lockwood House, First School Society Records, 1799.

TAX RECORDS

Hartford. CSL, Record Group 62. Assessment List, 1829.

VITAL RECORDS

Town Clerk, Town Hall, North Main Street, 06854. (203) 838-7531, ext. 245.

"Connecticut Births Before 1730 (Barbour)-Town of Norwalk." CN 7 (1974): 14-16, 168-73, 328-31.

MARRIAGE RECORDS OF NORWALK AND VICINITY. (LDS 1894).

The BARBOUR INDEX covers the years 1651-1850 and is based on the James N. Arnold copy of NORWALK vital records made in 1915.

PUBLISHED WORKS AND OTHER RECORDS

Beard, Augustus Field. "The Building of Norwalk." NEW CANAAN HISTORICAL SOCIETY ANNUAL, 1957, pp. 158-70.

Beard, Patten. THE CHRONOLOGY OF NORWALK 1640-1940. WPA. (CSL Archives RG33 Box 156).

Byington, A.H. "Ancient and Modern Norwalk." CQ 1 (1895): 281-87.

THE COLONIAL REVOLUTIONARY HOMES OF WILTON, NORWALK, WESTPORT, DARIEN AND VICINITY. Norwalk: Norwalk Chapter, DAR, 1901. 113 p.

Comstock, Eliza. "The Bill of Sale of a Negro Slave in 1721." CM 10 (1906): 692.

_____. "The Will of a Negro Slave in 1773." CM 10 (1906): 693.

D'Amico, Anthony J. ITALIANS IN WESTPORT, A PERSONAL ACCOUNT FOR AN ETHNOHISTORY OF THE WESTPORT-NORWALK AREA FROM 1900 TO TODAY. New Haven: Connecticut Humanities Council, 1979. 16 p.

Danenberg, Elsie Nichols. THE ROMANCE OF NORWALK. New York: States History Co., 1929. 514 p.

Hunt, Malcolm P. NAMES AND PLACES OF OLD NORWALK: WITH POR-TIONS OF WILTON, WESTPORT AND NEW CANAAN. Norwalk: Friends of the Lockwood House, 1976. 98 p.

Lobozza, Carl. NORWALK, CONNECTICUT. PICTURES FROM THE PAST. Norwalk: Norwalk Historical Society, 1974. 80 p.

Mahar, John L. HISTORY OF IMMIGRANT GROUPS FOR AN ETHNOHISTORY OF THE WESTPORT-NORWALK AREA FROM 1900 TO TODAY. New Haven: Conn. Humanities Council, 1979. 19 p.

Mead, Stanley P. "Roton Point." NEW CANAAN HISTORICAL SOCIETY ANNUAL, 1956, pp. 90-100.

Parks, Jane, and Bescia, Patsy. "Norwalk, a City for All Seasons." Vol. 1 and Supplement, FAIRFIELD COUNTY, February 1979, pp. 25-31, 42-46.

Rasmussen, James A. "Norwalk, Connecticut Manumissions." TAG 53 (January 1977): 9-11.

Ray, Deborah Wing, and Stewart, Gloria P. NORWALK: BEING AN HISTORICAL ACCOUNT OF THAT CONNECTICUT TOWN. Canaan, N.H.: Phoenix Publishing, 1979. 243 p. Index.

Selleck, Charles Melbourne. NORWALK. Norwalk: Author, 1896. 482 p.

TRANSCRIPTS OF ORAL HISTORIES FOR AN ETHNOHISTORY OF THE WEST-PORT-NORWALK AREA FROM 1900 TO TODAY. New Haven: Conn. Humanities Council, 1979.

Vassos, John V. "This is Norwalk." FAIRFIELD COUNTY 7 (February 1977): 26-28, 31-32.

Weed, Samuel Richards. NORWALK AFTER TWO HUNDRED AND FIFTY YEARS. South Norwalk: C.A. Freeman, 1901. 387 p.

Winton, Andrew L., and Winton, Kate B. "Norwalk Potteries." OLD-TIME NEW ENGLAND 24 (1933): 75-92, 111-28.

Walden, Grace. "Rowayton." FAIRFIELD COUNTY 4 (February 1974): 28-29.

NORWICH

NEW LONDON COUNTY. Organized 1659. Towns organized from NORWICH include BOZRAH, FRANKLIN and LISBON.

CEMETERY RECORDS AND CEMETERIES

NAME	ADDRESS	HALE NO.	CITATION
Maplewood Cemetery	184 Salem Turnpike (203) 887-2623	1	38:1-64
St. Joseph Roman Catholic Cemetery	768 Boswell Avenue (203) 887-1019	2	38:65-100
St. Mary Roman Catholic Cemetery	815 Boswell Avenue (203) 887-1019	3	38:101-228
Yantic Cemetery	68 Lafayette Street	4	38:229-500 39:501-57
Sacred Heart Cemetery	Hartland Road	5	39:558-71
Gifford Cemetery (No. 6 and 16 are the same)	Old Salem Road	6	39:572
Ray-Yerrington Cemetery	362 Canterbury Turnpike	7	39:573-75
Old Norwich Town Cemetery	40 East Town Street	8	39:576-622
City Cemetery	32 Arcadia Street	9	39:623-83
Greenville Cemetery	202 Hickory Street	10	39:684-711
West Plain Cemetery	318 Salem Turnpike	11	39:712-26
Hamilton Avenue Cemetery	420 Hamilton Avenue	12	39:727-40
St. Nicholas Cemetery	South part of city, near Montville town line	13	39:741-44

NAME	ADDRESS	HALE NO.	CITATION
Uncas Cemetery	26 Sachem Street	14	39:745
Mason (oldest) Cemetery	Norwich Town	15	39:746-47
Gifford Cemetery (No. 16 and 6 are the same)	Old Salem Road	16	39:748-49
Durr Cemetery	Next to Church-Norwich Town	17	39:750
Divine Providence Cemetery	750 New London Turnpike	18	39:751-53
Maples Cemetery	West Side	19	39:754
Beebe Cemetery	In center of Maplewood Cemetery	20	39:755-56
Jewish Cemetery	Lois Street	21	39:757-59
Brumbley Cemetery	Within St. Joseph Cemetery	22	39:760
Miantonomo (Indian) Cemetery	North of St. Mary Cemetery	23	39:761
Bingham Cemetery	West Town Street, Norwich Town	24	39:762
Riverside or Town Poor Cemetery	Asylum Street Almshouse	25	39:763
Christ Church Cemetery	765 Washington Street	26	39:764-65
Oak Street Cemetery	37 Oak Street		(no citation)

Index to Hale inscriptions: 39:766-1005.

Index Cards to Cemetery inscriptions. Christ Church. (CSL, LDS 2040).

Benes, Peter. "Lt. John Hartshorn: Gravestone Maker of Haverhill and Norwich." ESSEX INSTITUTE HISTORICAL COLLECTIONS 109 (1973): 152-64.

"Connecticut Headstone Inscriptions before 1800 (Hale)--Town of Norwich Connecticut." CN 8 (1976): 549; 9 (1976): 119-23, 175-81, 371-76.

Case, William S. DISPUTE SURVEYOR'S BLUE PRINT ON LOCATING OLD BURYING GROUND. Norwich: Norwich Bulletin, 1929.

_____. LOCATING THE POST-GAGER CEMETERY. Norwich: Bulletin Print, 1929.

_____. THE FIRST BURYING GROUND IN NORWICH. Norwich: Bulletin Print, 1929.

Porter, George Shepard. "Inscriptions from Gravestones in Christ Church, Norwich, Connecticut." NEHGR 60 (1906): 16-19.

_____. INSCRIPTIONS FROM GRAVESTONES IN CHRIST CHURCH, NORWICH, CONNECTICUT. Boston: David Clapp and Son, 1906. 6 p.

_____. INSCRIPTIONS FROM GRAVESTONES IN THE OLD BURYING GROUND NORWICH TOWN, CONNECTICUT. Norwich: Bulletin Press, 1933. 177 p.

_____. "Inscriptions from the Burying-Ground in Norwich, Connecticut." NEHGR 2 (1848): 404-7.

Wilson, Edith Huntington. LETTERS TO THE EDITOR OF THE NORWICH BULLETIN ABOUT THE POST-GAGER CEMETERY. Norwich: Bulletin Print, 1929.

CHURCH RECORDS

CHRIST CHURCH. Minutes, 1746-1863. Vital Records, 1768-1901. (CSL, LDS 1902).

FIFTH CONGREGATIONAL CHURCH. Record of marriages, deaths, admissions. (NYGBS, LDS 1899).

FIRST BAPTIST CHURCH. Minutes, 1800-1923. Vital Records, 1800-1944. (CSL, LDS 1904 pt. 1).

FIRST CONGREGATIONAL CHURCH. Vital Records, 1660-1916. (CSL, LDS 1906). Marriages, 1769-1799. BAILEY 6:86-92.

FIRST SOCIETY. Deaths, 1826-1830, 1832-1846 in Sermon Book of Mary Ann Huntington. (CSL, LDS 1908).

GREENVILLE CONGREGATIONAL CHURCH. Vital Records, 1833-1857. (CSL, LDS 1905).

NORWICH FALLS CONGREGATIONAL CHURCH. Minutes, 1827-1842. (CSL, LDS 1909).

SECOND CONGREGATIONAL CHURCH. Minutes, 1832-1918. Vital Records, 1760-1831. (CSL, LDS 1907).

TAFTVILLE CONGREGATIONAL CHURCH. Minutes, 1867-1916. Vital Records, 1867-1901. (CSL, LDS 1910).

Bumsted, J.M. "Revivalism and Separatism in New England: The First Society of Norwich, Connecticut, as a Case Study." WILLIAM AND MARY QUARTERLY 24 (1967): 588-612.

Clark, Edgar F. THE METHODIST EPISCOPAL CHURCHES OF NORWICH, CONNECTICUT. Norwich: n.p., 1867. 270 p.

CONNECTICUT BAPTISMAL RECORDS PERFORMED BY REV. D.D. LYONS AS RECORDED IN HIS JOURNAL DURING THE YEARS 1843-87. Typescript. Norwich: Faith Trumbull, DAR. 13 p. Index.

Denison, Frederic. NOTES OF THE BAPTISTS, AND THEIR PRINCIPLES IN NORWICH, CONNECTICUT, FROM THE SETTLEMENT OF THE TOWN TO 1850. Norwich: Manning Printer, 1857. 91 p.

Gallup, Jennie Tefft. RECORDS OF BAPTISMS, MARRIAGES, DEATHS AND CHURCH ADMISSIONS OF THE FIFTH CHURCH OF NORWICH, CONNECTI- CUT FROM 1739 TO 1824. N.p., n.d. 88 p.

Goldberg, Arthur. "The Jew in Norwich, Connecticut: A Century of Jewish Life." RHODE ISLAND JEWISH HISTORICAL NOTES 7 (1975): 79-103.

THE JEW IN NORWICH A CENTURY OF JEWISH LIFE. Norwich: Norwich Jewish Tercentenary Committee, 1956. 57 p.

Kumor, Boleslaw. DZIEJE PARAFII SW. JOZEFA W POLSKIEJ RZYMSKO- KATOLICKIEJ NORWICH, CONNECTICUT 1904-1979. Norwich, Conn.: Author, 1980. 320 p.

"Membership List of the Norwich, Connecticut Second Church (Chelsea dated March 1, 1832." ANCESTRAL NOTES FROM CHEDWATO, July 1968, pp. 110-11.

RECORDS OF THE CONGREGATIONAL CHURCH, FRANKLIN, CONNECTI- CUT 1718-1860, AND A RECORD OF DEATHS IN NORWICH EIGHTH SOCI- ETY 1763, 1778, 1782, 1784-1802. Hartford: Society of Mayflower Descen- dants in the State of Connecticut and the Society of the Founders of Norwich, Connecticut, 1938. 128 p.

Sawyer, M. Norwich. CONNECTICUT FIFTH CONGREGATIONAL CHURCH RECORDS OF BAPTISMS, MARRIAGES, DEATHS AND CHURCH ADMISSIONS OF THE FIFTH CHURCH OF NORWICH, CONNECTICUT FROM 1739-1824. Hartford; CSL, 1929. 101 p.

"Vital Statistics of Norwich, New London and Montville, Connecticut, Church Book, North Parish, New London." BOSTON EVENING TRANSCRIPT, May 15, 20, 22, 1912.

HISTORICAL SOCIETY

Society of the Founders of Norwich, Connecticut, 348 Washington Street, 06360. (203) 887-3880.

Faith Trumbull Chapter, DAR Museum and Chapter House, 42 Rockwell Street, 06360. (203) 887-8737.

LAND RECORDS

Land Records, 1659-1850. Index, 1659-1881. (LDS 1900 pt. 1-31).

LIBRARIES

Otis Library, 261 Main Street, 06360. (203) 889-2365.

Trumbull, Jonathan. "Public Libraries in Connecticut--Founding and Development of Otis Library at Norwich." CM 10 (1906): 345-49.

MILITARY RECORDS

Dana, Malcolm McGregor. THE ANNALS OF NORWICH, NEW LONDON COUNTY, CONNECTICUT IN THE GREAT REBELLION OF 1861-1865. Norwich: J.H. Jewett and Co., 1873. 395 p.

"McCall's Company of Veteran Guards--1775 Petition Payroll 1776." DAR MAGAZINE 96 (1962): 710; 97 (1963): 949-50.

Nafie, Joan. TO THE BEAT OF A DRUM: A HISTORY OF NORWICH, CONNECTICUT DURING THE AMERICAN REVOLUTION. Norwich: Old Town Press, 1975. 169 p. Index.

NEWSPAPERS

NORWICH BULLETIN. Daily. 66 Franklin Street, 06360. (203) 887-9211.

The HALE NEWSPAPER INDEX TO DEATH AND MARRIAGE NOTICES include the following:

CANAL OF INTELLIGENCE, 28 May 1828-18 November 1829.
NATIVE AMERICAN, 3 June 1812-20 January 1813.
NORWICH AURORA, 15 May 1839-29 December 1866.
NORWICH BULLETIN, 15 December 1858-30 December 1865.
NORWICH COURIER, 30 November 1796-28 December 1865.

NORWICH PACKET, 4 November 1773-30 September 1812.
NORWICH REPUBLICAN, 1 October 1828-2 April 1836.
WEEKLY REGISTER, 29 November 1791-9 December 1794.
WEEKLY REVILLE, 1 October 1858-7 January 1859.

The PRELIMINARY CHECKLIST lists forty-four newspapers for NORWICH.

THE NORWICH COURIER and NORWICH SPECTATOR were indexed for death notices from 1820-1837 by John Elliot Bowman. These cards were included in the BARBOUR INDEX.

PROBATE RECORDS

Norwich Probate District, City Hall, P.O. Box 38, 06360. (203) 887-2160.

The Norwich Probate district was organized October 1748 from the New London Probate District. The Norwich Probate District also includes the FRANKLIN, GRISWOLD, LISBON, PRESTON, SPRAGUE and VOLUNTOWN Probate Districts.

Probate districts organized from the Norwich Probate District include the Bozrah Probate District.

ON FILE AT THE CSL: Estate Papers, 1748-1896. Indexes, 1748-1896. Inventory Control Book, 1748-1896. Court Record Book, 1748-1852.

Probate Records, 1748-1852. Indexed. (LDS 1901 pt. 1-10).

Gallup, Mrs. Herbert W. ABSTRACTS OF THE FIRST PROBATE RECORDS OF NORWICH 1748-1763. (CSL).

SCHOOL RECORDS

Hartford. CSL, Record Group 62. First District School Registers, 1839-1851.

Gilman, Emily S. "An Ancient School-Dame." CM 5 (1899): 472-77.

Williams, Charles Allyn. "Norwich, Connecticut, Heads of Families (School List 1775)." NEHGR 103 (1949): 152.

TAX RECORDS

Hartford. CSL, Record Group 62. Grand Lists, 1752-1754. Rate books, 1730-1743. Abstracts, 1825-1900 incomplete.

VITAL RECORDS

Town Clerk, City Hall, Room 214, 06360. (203) 889-8408.

The BARBOUR INDEX covers the years 1847-1851 and is based on the James N. Arnold copy of NORWICH vital records made in 1910. It also includes index references to the obituary notices from 1820-1837 of the NORWICH COURIER and the NORWICH SPECTATOR, as indexed by John Elliot Bowman.

"A Record of Marriages Performed by me, Walter King, in Chelsea, in Norwich, Connecticut." (1787-1795). ANCESTRAL NOTES FROM CHEDWATO, July 1968, pp. 111-12.

VITAL RECORDS OF NORWICH 1659-1848. Vital Records of Connecticut Series I, Towns II, Part I and II. 2 vols. Hartford: Society of Colonial Wars in the State of Connecticut, 1913.

PUBLISHED WORKS AND OTHER RECORDS

Benes, Peter. "Lt. John Hartshorn: Gravestone Maker of Haverhill and Norwich." ESSEX INSTITUTE HISTORICAL COLLECTIONS 109 (1973): 152-64.

Birdsall, Richard D. "The Leffingwell Inn: Past and Present." CANTIQUARIAN 12 (July 1960): 12-16.

Bulkeley, Houghton. "The Norwich Cabinetmakers." CHSB 29 (1964): 76-85.

Burnham, Rufus Bradford. "Vignettes from a New England Boyhood." NEW ENGLAND GALARY 7 (1965): 12-20.

Caulkins, Frances Manwaring. HISTORY OF NORWICH, CONNECTICUT. FROM ITS POSSESSION BY THE INDIANS, TO THE YEAR 1866. Hartford: Case, Lockwood and Co., 1866. 704 p.

Chase, Ida R. "Old Clocks in Norwich, Connecticut." ANTIQUES 27 (March 1935): 99-101.

_____. "History in Towns: Norwich, Connecticut." ANTIQUES 79 (June 1961): 560-64.

Cogswell, Alice W. "Art Education in the 'Rose of New England.'" CQ 4 (1898): 201-7.

Cohen, Sheldon S. "Norwich Remonstrance." CHSB 29:43-48.

CRAFTSMEN AND ARTISTS IN NORWICH. Stonington: Society of the Founders of Norwich and Friends of the Slater Museum, 1965. 67 p.

Daniels, Bruce Colin. "Large Town Power Structure in Eighteenth Century Connecticut: An Analysis of Political Leadership in Hartford, Norwich and Fairfield." Ph.D. dissertation, University of Connecticut, 1970. 241 p.

Farnham, Elmer F. THE QUICKEST ROUTE, THE HISTORY OF THE NORWICH AND WORESTER RAILROAD. Chester: Pequot Press, 1973. 210 p.

"First Settlers of Norwich, Connecticut." NEHGR 1 (1847): 314-17.

Gilman, Daniel Coit. A HISTORICAL DISCOURSE DELIVERED IN NORWICH, CONNECTICUT SEPTEMBER 7, 1859, AT THE BI-CENTENNIAL CELEBRATION OF THE SETTLEMENT OF THE TOWN. Boston: George C. Rand and Avery City Printers, 1859. 128 p.

Gilman, William C. CELEBRATION OF THE TWO HUNDRED AND FIFTIETH ANNIVERSARY OF THE SETTLEMENT OF THE TOWN OF NORWICH, CON- NECTICUT, AND OF THE INCORPORATION OF THE CITY, THE ONE HUN- DRED AND TWENTY-FIFTH, JULY 4, 5, 6, 1909. Norwich: n.p., 1912. 244 p.

Hyde, Burrell W. "Reminiscence of Bean Hill, Norwich." CQ 3 (1897): 294-305, 441-51.

INDEX: HISTORY OF NORWICH, CONNECTICUT. N.p.: 1976. 25 p.

Jacobs, Carl. "The Danforths of Connecticut Merchants Extraordinary." CAN- TIQUARIAN 9 (December 1957): 21-23.

Johnson, Philip A. "The Silversmiths of Norwich, Connecticut." ANTIQUES 79:570-71.

Keith, Elmer D. "The Leffingwell Inn at Norwich." CANTIQUARIAN 8 (December 1956): 26-30.

Lacey, Barbara E. "Women in the Era of the American Revolution: The Case of Norwich, Connecticut." NEQ 53 (1980): 527-43.

New London County Mutual Fire Insurance Co. PARTNERS FOR 100 YEARS;

A CHRONICLE IN WHICH THE SPIRIT OF FRIENDLINESS AND COOPERATION PLAYS AN IMPORTANT PART IN THE GROWTH OF A FIRE INSURANCE COMPANY. Norwich, Conn.: Author, 1940. 109 p.

Norwich Board of Trade. NORWICH, CONNECTICUT: ITS IMPORTANCE AS A BUSINESS AND MANUFACTURING CENTRE AND AS A PLACE OF RESIDENCE. Norwich: Press of the Bulletin, 1888. 111 p.

NOTES ON PERSONS AND PLACES IN THE ANCIENT TOWN OF NORWICH IN CONNECTICUT. Norwich: Bulletin Print, 1909. 31 p.

O'Keefe, Marian K., et al. NORWICH HISTORIC HOMES AND FAMILIES. Stonington: Pequot Press, 1967. 112 p.

Perkins, Mary Elizabeth. OLD FAMILIES OF NORWICH, 1600-1800. Norwich: n.p., 1900. 50 p.

_____. OLD HOUSES OF THE ANCIENT TOWN OF NORWICH 1660-1800. WITH MAPS, ILLUSTRATIONS, PORTRAITS AND GENEALOGIES. Norwich: Bulletin Co., 1895. 621 p.

Read, Eleanor P., and Nettles, Diane. NORWICH CENTURY OF GROWTH. Norwich, Conn.: Franklin Press, 1978. 41 p.

Sherman, John W. NORWICH JUBILEE, A REPORT OF THE CELEBRATION AT NORWICH, CONNECTICUT ON THE TWO HUNDREDTH ANNIVERSARY OF THE SETTLEMENT OF THE TOWN, SEPTEMBER 7TH AND 8TH, 1859. Norwich: n.p., 1859. 304 p.

OLD LYME

NEW LONDON COUNTY. Organized 13 February 1665 from SAYBROOK, LYME. Name changed from SOUTH LYME in 1857.

CEMETERY RECORDS AND CEMETERIES

NAME	ADDRESS	HALE NO.	CITATION
Duck River Cemetery	U.S. 51	1	39:1-62
Layville Cemetery	2 miles northeast from Lyme Village near Rogers Lake	2	39:63-68
Peck Cemetery	U.S. 51	3	39:69
Black Hall Schoolhouse	Near Black Hall Schoolhouse	4	39:70
Champion Cemetery #1	Easternpart of town 1/3 miles from highway	5	39:71-73
Wait Cemetery	Eastern part of town	6	39:74
Champion Cemetery #2	Near South Lyme Railroad Station	7	39:75
Old Meeting House Hill Cemetery	Top Meeting House Hill	8	39:76-84
Griswold Cemetery	U.S. 51	9	39:85-86
Wait Cemetery	In South Lyme	10	39:87-89
Chadwick Cemetery	Near Episcopal Church in South Lyme	11	39:90
One stone	Near house of Richard W. Chadwick, South Lyme	12	39:91
Slate Cemetery	Hatchetts Reef Club Grounds	13	39:92-93

Index to Hale inscriptions: 39:94-118.

"Inscriptions from Gravestones at Old Lyme, Connecticut." NEHGR 77 (1923): 194-213; 78 (1924): 250-55.

CHURCH RECORDS

FIRST BAPTIST CHURCH. Minutes, 1842-1924. Vital Records, 1842-1888. (CSL, LDS 1976).

FIRST CONGREGATIONAL CHURCH. Minutes, 1721-1876. Vital Records, 1731-1874. (CSL, LDS 1975 pt. 1-2). Vital Records, 1731-1874. Index. (CSL, LDS 1448 pt. 22).

HISTORICAL SOCIETY

Lyme Historical Society, Lyme Street, 06371. (203) 434-5542.

LIBRARY

Noyes Library, Lyme Street, 06371. (203) 434-1684.

NEWSPAPERS

THE GAZETTE. Weekly. P.O. Box 528, 06371. (203) 434-1631.

The PRELIMINARY CHECKLIST lists two newspapers for OLD LYME.

THE OLD LYME GAZETTE has been indexed since 1977 by the Noyes Library.

PROBATE RECORDS

Old Lyme Probate District, Town Hall, 52 Lyme Street, 06371. (203) 434-1406.

Organized 24 July 1868 by a name change from the Lyme Probate District.

Papers concerning OLD LYME from 1 May 1666 to 4 June 1830 to the present are at the New London Probate District. From 4 June 1830 to the present they are at the Old Lyme Probate Court.

ON FILE AT THE CSL: Estate Papers, 1830-1945. Indexes, 1830-1945. Inventory Control Book, 1830-1945. Court Record Book, 1829-1866.

Probate districts organized from the Old Lyme Probate Districts include the Lyme Probate District.

Probate Records, 1829-1866.   Indexed.   (LDS 1974).

SCHOOL RECORDS

James, Mary Hall.   THE EDUCATIONAL HISTORY OF OLD LYME, CONNECT-
ICUT 1635-1935.   New Haven: New Haven Colony Historical Society, 1939.
259 p.

VITAL RECORDS

Town Clerk, Town Hall, Lyme Street, 06371.   (203) 434-1655.

> The town clerk's earliest birth record is 6 January 1856, marriage
> record is 31 March 1856 and death record is 4 January 1856.

PUBLISHED WORK

LYME, A CHAPTER OF AMERICAN GENEALOGY.   Old Lyme, Conn.:   Old
Lyme Bicentennial Commission, 1976.   51 p.

OLD SAYBROOK

Middlesex County. Organized 8 July 1854 from ESSEX.

CEMETERY RECORDS AND CEMETERIES

NAME	ADDRESS	HALE NO.	CITATION
Cypress Cemetery	84 College Street	1	39:1-36
Upper or Junction Cemetery	37 North Main Street	2	39:37-67
St. John Roman Catholic Cemetery	Old Middlesex Turnpike	3	39:68-74
River View Cemetery	61 Sheffield Street	4	39:75-86
Small Pox Cemetery	West of the Railroad Station	5	39:87-88

Index to Hale inscriptions: 39:89-113.

CEMETERY INSCRIPTIONS. (NYGBS, LDS 2037).

CHURCH RECORDS

CONGREGATIONAL CHURCH. Minutes, 1792-1876. Vital Records, 1736-1935. (CSL, LDS 1984).

Chapman, Edward Mortimer. THE FIRST CHURCH OF CHRIST IN SAYBROOK, 1646-1946. New Haven, Conn.: Author, 1947. 192 p.

FREDERICK L'HOMMEDIEU COPY - Old Saybrook Congregational Church, 1736-1782. Centerbrook Congregational Church, 1759-1832. Chester Congregational Church, 1759-1835. (CSL, LDS 2041).

GENEALOGICAL SOCIETY OF PENNSYLVANIA COPY. Old Saybrook Congregational Church, 1736-1842. (CSL, LDS 2047).

GRACE EPISCOPAL CHURCH. Vital Records, 1815-1948. (CSL, LDS 1983).

"Church Records, Old Saybrook, Connecticut." ANCESTRAL NOTES FROM CHEDWATO, November 1968, pp. 206-9.

HISTORICAL SOCIETY

Old Saybrook Historical Society. P.O. Box 4, 06475. (203) 388-2622. Publishes OLD SAYBROOK HISTORICAL SOCIETY BULLETIN. 1973-- . Quarterly.

LIBRARY

Acton Public Library, 60 Old Boston Post Road, 06475. (203) 388-2037.

NEWSPAPER

THE NEW ERA. Weekly. 61 Main Street, 06475. (203) 388-3441.

The PRELIMINARY CHECKLIST lists one newspaper for OLD SAYBROOK.

PROBATE RECORDS

Old Saybrook Probate District, Town Hall, 302 Main Street, 06475. (203) 388-5390.

Organized 4 July 1853 from the Essex Probate District. Probate Districts organized from the Old Saybrook Probate District includes Westbrook Probate District.

ON FILE AT THE CSL: Estate Papers, 1859-1927. Indexes, 1859-1927. Inventory Control Book, 1859-1927.

TAX RECORDS

Hartford. CSL, Record Group 62. Tax Lists, etc., 1854-1968.

VITAL RECORDS

Town Clerk, Town Hall, 302 Main Street, 06475. (203) 388-2029.

The town clerk's earliest birth and death records are from August
1854 and marriage records from 30 September 1854.

PUBLISHED WORKS AND OTHER RECORDS

"At Old Saybrook." CQ 2 (1896): 306.

Brainard, Newton Case. FENWICK. Hartford: Case, Lockwood and Brainard
Co., 1944. 52 p.

Grant, Marion Hepburn. THE FENWICK STORY. Hartford: Connecticut Historical Society, 1974. 244 p.

Hart, Samuel. "Yale College in Old Saybrook: The First Graduating Class
was a 'Class of One,' Receiving Bachelor's Degree from the Institution in
1703." CM 7 (1902): 266–72.

Holman, Mabel Cassine. THE WESTERN NECK: THE STORY OF FENWICK.
Hartford: Case, Lockwood and Brainard Co., 1930. 46 p.

Washington, D.C. National Archives and Records Service. U.S. Customs Passenger Lists. Saybrook, 1820.

ORANGE

NEW HAVEN COUNTY. Organized May 1822 from MILFORD and NEW HAVEN. Towns organized from ORANGE include WEST HAVEN.

CEMETERY RECORDS AND CEMETERIES

NAME	ADDRESS	HALE NO.	CITATION
Orange Cemetery	Orange Center Road	1	40:1-30
Hebrew Cemetery	833 Derby Avenue	2	40:31-37

Index to Hale inscriptions: 40:38-49.

CHURCH RECORDS

CONGREGATIONAL CHURCH. Minutes, 1804-1929. Vital Records, 1805-1910. (CSL, LDS 1978).

HISTORICAL SOCIETY

Orange Historical Society, 06477.

LAND RECORDS

Land Records, 1822-1858. Index, 1822-1861. (LDS 1977 pt. 1-4).

LIBRARY

Orange Public Library, Orange Center Road, 06477. (203) 795-0288.

NEWSPAPERS

The PRELIMINARY CHECKLIST lists three newspapers for ORANGE.

PROBATE RECORDS

Orange Probate District, Town Hall, 617 Orange Center Road, 06477. (203) 795-0751, ext. 36.

> Organized 8 January 1975 from the New Haven Probate District.

VITAL RECORDS

Town Clerk, Town Hall, 617 Orange Center Road, 06477. (203) 799-2359.

> The town clerk's earliest birth record is 9 July 1921, marriage record is 5 September 1921 and death record is 19 August 1921.

> Birth records of Dr. Josiah Coburn of Orange, Derby and Ansonia, Connecticut. (NHCHS, LDS 1455 pt. 31).

The BARBOUR INDEX covers the years 1822-1850 and is based on the James N. Arnold copy of ORANGE vital records made in 1914.

PUBLISHED WORKS AND OTHER RECORDS

MISCELLANEOUS RECORDS. (NHCHS, LDS 1455 pt. 31).

WPA Historical Records Survey. INVENTORY OF THE TOWN AND CITY ARCHIVES OF CONNECTICUT, NO. 5, NEW HAVEN COUNTY, VOL. 8. NORTH BRANFORD, NORTH HAVEN, ORANGE, OXFORD, PROSPECT, SEYMOUR, SOUTHBURY. New Haven: Historical Records Survey, 1938. 189 p. (LDS 897,354).

Woodruff, Mary K. HISTORY ORANGE, NORTH MILFORD, CONNECTICUT 1639-1949. Orange: Town of Orange, 1949. 177 p.

OXFORD

NEW HAVEN COUNTY. Organized October 1798 from DERBY and SOUTH-BURY. Towns organized from OXFORD include BEACON FALLS and NAUGA-TUCK.

CEMETERY RECORDS AND CEMETERIES

NAME	ADDRESS	HALE NO.	CITATION
Congregational Church Cemetery	Governor's Hill Road	1	40:1-10
St. Peter Roman Catholic Cemetery	Governor's Hill Road	2	40:11-19
Southford Cemetery	Litchfield Turnpike	3	40:20-34
Quaker Farms Cemetery #1	Upper Quaker Farms	4	40:35-40
Quaker Farms Cemetery #2	Lower Quaker Farms	5	40:41-48
Riverside Cemetery	Freeman Road	6	40:49-57
Jack's Hill Cemetery	7 North Larkey Road	7	40:58-64
Brookside Cemetery	30 Edmonds Road		(no citation)
Hillside Cemetery	45 Captain Wooster Road		(no citation)

Index to Hale inscriptions: 40:65-81.

CHURCH RECORDS

CHRIST CHURCH. Vital Records, 1845-1948. (CSL, LDS 1981).

FIRST CONGREGATIONAL CHURCH. Minutes, 1741-1886. Vital Records, 1745-1929. (CSL, LDS 1980).

ST. PETER EPISCOPAL CHURCH. Vital Records, 1769-1948. (CSL, LDS 1982).

Litchfield, Norman. A HISTORY OF CHRIST CHURCH, QUAKER FARMS IN OXFORD, CONNECTICUT. Ann Arbor, Mich.: Edwards Brothers, 1954. 200 p.

_____. HISTORY OF ST. PETER'S CHURCH IN OXFORD, CONNECTICUT. Ann Arbor, Mich.: Edwards Brothers, 1958. 119 p.

LAND RECORDS

Land Records, 1798-1858. Index, 1798-1897. (CSL, LDS 1979 pt. 1-9).

LIBRARY

Oxford Public Library, Route 67, Seymour, 06483. (203) 888-6944.

PROBATE RECORDS

Oxford Probate District, Town Hall, 429 Oxford Road, 06483. (203) 888-2543.

    Organized 4 June 1846 from the New Haven Probate District.

    ON FILE AT THE CSL: Estate Papers, 1846-1908. Inventory Control Book, 1846-1908.

SCHOOL RECORDS

Hartford. CSL, Record Group 62. Registers, minutes, etc., 1825-1902.

VITAL RECORDS

Town Clerk, Town Hall, 429 Oxford Road, 06483. (203) 888-4551.

The BARBOUR INDEX covers the years 1798-1850 and is based on the James N. Arnold copy of OXFORD vital records made in 1917.

PUBLISHED WORKS AND OTHER RECORDS

Bronson, Henry. HISTORY OF WATERBURY, CONNECTICUT. THE ORIGINAL TOWNSHIP EMBRACING PRESENT WATERTOWN AND PLYMOUTH, AND PARTS OF OXFORD, WOLCOTT, MIDDLEBURY, PROSPECT AND NAUGATUCK. WITH AN APPENDIX OF BIOGRAPHY, GENEALOGY AND STATISTICS. Waterbury: Bronson Brothers, 1858. 583 p. Index. (LDS 599,254).

Cothren, William. HISTORY OF ANCIENT WOODBURY, CONNECTICUT, FROM THE FIRST INDIAN DEED IN 1659 TO 1854, INCLUDING THE PRESENT TOWNS OF WASHINGTON, SOUTHBURY, BETHLEHEM, ROXBURY, AND A PART OF OXFORD AND MIDDLEBURY. Waterbury: Bronson Brothers, 1854. 841 p. (LDS 2205).

EARLY HOUSES OF OXFORD. Oxford: Historic House Committee of the Bi-centennial Commission, 1976. 61 p. Index.

Litchfield, Norman, and Hoyt, Sabina Connolly. HISTORY OF THE TOWN OF OXFORD, CONNECTICUT. N.p.: Author, 1960. 325 p.

Sharpe, William Carvosso. HISTORY OF OXFORD. 2 vols. Seymour: Record Print, 1885, 1910.

PLAINFIELD

WINDHAM COUNTY. Organized May 1699. Towns organized from PLAIN-
FIELD include CANTERBURY.

CEMETERY RECORDS AND CEMETERIES

NAME	ADDRESS	HALE NO.	CITATION
Bennett Cemetery	Canterbury Road, rear of Cornell Cemetery	1	40:1
Cornell-Munroe Cemetery	Canterbury Road	2	40:2-3
Randall Farm Cemetery	South of Cornell Cemetery	3	40:4
North Davis Farm Cemetery	South part of town	4	40:5
South Davis Farm Cemetery	South part of town	5	40:6
Gallup Cemetery	South part of town	6	40:7-12
One stone near Flat Rock School	South part of town	7	40:13
Neighborhood Lot Cemetery	In pasture south part of town	8	40:14
Parke Cemetery	Near neighborhood Lot, south part of town	9	40:15
Spalding Cemetery	Near Parke Cemetery, south part of town	10	40:16
Hammett Cemetery	Green Hollow Road, near Killingly town line	11	40:17-19
Small Cemetery	On Alexander Hill Farm, northeast part of town	12	40:20

NAME	ADDRESS	HALE NO.	CITATION
Hopkins Cemetery	Inclosed in a stone wall, east part of town	13	40:21
Rood Cemetery	Inclosed in a stone wall, southwest part of town	14	40:22
Joseph Roode Farm Cemetery	Jewett City Road, near Griswold town line	15	40:23-24
Union Cemetery	Moosup	16	40:25-84
All Hollows Cemetery	Green Hollow Road	17	40:85-95
Evergreen Cemetery	Central Village	18	40:96-153
Old Plainfield Cemetery	Canterbury Road	19	40:154-69
New Plainfield Cemetery	Canterbury Road, next to Old Plainfield Cemetery	20	40:170-90
St. John Cemetery	Jewett City Road, 1 mile south of Central Village	21	40:191-93
Locke Farm Cemetery	Field stones only, east part of town	22	40:194
Briggs Cemetery	Opposite cellar hole, south part of town	23	40:195
Kinne Cemetery	Near Canterbury town line	24	40:196-97

Index to Hale inscriptions: 40:198-248.

Dorrance, Sarah Frances. THE BURIAL PLACES OF THE TOWN OF PLAINFIELD, CONNECTICUT. 1921. 9 p.

_____. CONNECTICUT CEMETERY INSCRIPTIONS: PLAINFIELD. N.p.: n.d. 36 p.

Prior, John Eben. "Inscriptions from Gravestones at Plainfield, Connecticut." NEHGR 71 (1917): 33-44.

Weld, Emma Finney. "Gravestone Inscriptions. Plainfield 1720-1880 (approx.)." (Historical Society of Pennsylvania, LDS 441,390).

CHURCH RECORDS

CENTRAL VILLAGE CONGREGATIONAL CHURCH. Vital Records, 1846-1941. (CSL, LDS 2006).

FIRST CONGREGATIONAL CHURCH. Minutes, 1799-1879. Vital Records,

1747-1838. (CSL, LDS 2004). Records, 1747-1832. Index. (CSL, LDS 1448 pt. 8,23). Marriages, 1748-1800. BAILEY 2:66-72.

METHODIST EPISCOPAL CHURCH (MOOSUP). Vital Records, 1842-1932. (CSL, LDS 2008).

NORTH PLAINFIELD ECCLESIASTICAL SOCIETY. Minutes, 1845-1941. (CSL, LDS 2005).

PACKERVILLE BAPTIST CHURCH. Minutes, 1828-1900. Vital Records, 1828-1928. (CSL, LDS 2009).

ST. PAUL EPISCOPAL CHURCH. Vital Records, 1856-1893. (CSL, LDS 2003).

UNION BAPTIST CHURCH. Minutes, 1834-1840, 1890-1931. Vital Records, 1792-1833, 1840-1906. (CSL, LDS 2010).

WAUREGAN CONGREGATIONAL CHURCH. Vital Records, 1856-1941. (CSL, LDS 2007).

Talcott, Mary Kingsbury. "Records of the First Congregational Church, Plainfield, Connecticut." NEHGR 70 (1916): 171-81, 220-32, 309-17.

HISTORICAL SOCIETY

Plainfield Historical Society, 06374.

LAND RECORDS

Land Records, 1701-1851. Index, 1701-1924. (LDS 2001 pt. 1-9).

LIBRARIES

Aldrich Free Library, 299 Main Street, 06374. (203) 564-8760.

Plainfield Public Library, 8 Community Avenue, 06374. (203) 564-7769.

MILITARY RECORDS

"Extracts from Plainfield, Connecticut, Revolutionary Records 1774-1784." DAR MAGAZINE 101 (June 1967): 25-26.

NEWSPAPERS

THE JOURNAL PRESS. Weekly. 66 Franklin Street, 06360. (203) 887-9211.

The PRELIMINARY CHECKLIST lists three newspapers for PLAINFIELD.

PROBATE RECORDS

Plainfield Probate District, Town Hall, 8 Community Avenue, 06374. (203) 564-2052.

Organized May 1747 from the Windham Probate District.

Probate Districts organized from the Plainfield Probate District include the Brooklyn, Canterbury, Killingly, Pomfret and Sterling Probate Districts.

ON FILE AT THE CSL: Estate Papers, 1747-1854. Indexes, 1747-1854. Inventory Control Book, 1747-1854. Court Record Books, 1747-1850.

Probate Records, 1747-1850. Index (partly 1747-1762, and 1815-1830), 1762-1815, 1830-1850. (LDS 2002 pt. 1-9).

VITAL RECORDS

Town Clerk, Town Hall, 8 Community Avenue, 06374. (203) 564-5925.

The town clerk's earliest birth record is 25 March 1694, marriage record is 27 May 1696 and death record is 16 June 1699.

The BARBOUR INDEX covers the years 1699-1852 and is based on the James N. Arnold copy of PLAINFIELD vital records made in 1909.

"Connecticut Births before 1730 (Barbour)-Town of Plainfield." CN 7 (1974-75): 331-33, 486-91; 8 (1975): 9-12.

Prior, John Ebsen. "Record of Deaths kept by Manuel Kinne of Plainfield, Connecticut." NEHGR 71 (1917): 133-44.

PUBLISHED WORKS AND OTHER RECORDS

Burgess, Charles F. PLAINFIELD SOUVENIR COMPRISING HISTORICAL, DESCRIPTIVE AND BIOGRAPHICAL SKETCHES IN THE TOWN OF PLAINFIELD AND VICINITY FROM "GRAPHIC" SOUVENIR ISSUES. Mossup: Author, 1895. 83 p.

Morse, Abner. "Early Settlers of Plainfield, Connecticut." NEHGR 15 (1861): 53.

PLAINFIELD BICENTENNIAL (1879) A SOUVENIR VOLUME. Norwich: Bulletin Co., 1899. 122 p.

PLAINVILLE

HARTFORD COUNTY. Organized July 1869 from FARMINGTON.

CEMETERY RECORDS AND CEMETERIES

NAME	ADDRESS	HALE NO.	CITATION
West Cemetery	6 Carter Road	1	40:1-58
East Cemetery	East Street	2	40:59-66
St. Joseph Roman Catholic Cemetery	Farmington Road	3	40:67-83
Congregational Church Cemetery	Park Street		(no citation)
Plainville Cemetery Association	North Washington Street (203) 747-2314		(no citation)

Index to Hale inscriptions: 40:84-110.

CHURCH RECORDS

CONGREGATIONAL CHURCH. Minutes, 1839-1926. Vital Records, 1840-1869. (CSL, LDS 2013).

FIRST BAPTIST CHURCH. Minutes, 1851-1934. (CSL, LDS 2014).

HISTORICAL SOCIETY

Plainville Historical Society, P.O. Box 24, 06062. (203) 747-0705.

LIBRARY

Plainville Public Library, 56 East Main Street, 06062. (203) 747-9626.

NEWSPAPERS

The PRELIMINARY CHECKLIST lists two newspapers for PLAINVILLE.

PROBATE RECORDS

Plainville Probate District, Municipal Center, 1 Central Square, 06062. (203) 747-0221.

> Organized May 1909 from the Farmington Probate District.

VITAL RECORDS

Town Clerk, Municipal Center, 1 Central Square, P.O. Box 250, 06062. (203) 747-2781.

> The town clerk's earliest birth record is 12 July 1869, marriage record is 6 August 1869 and death record is 29 July 1869.

PUBLISHED WORKS AND OTHER RECORDS

Castle, Henry Allen. THE HISTORY OF PLAINVILLE, CONNECTICUT 1640-1918. Chester, Conn.: Pequot Press, 1972. 205 p.

Hummel, Ruth Sharp. "Plainville." LEAGUE BULLETIN 32 (September 1980): 4, 18-19.

PLYMOUTH

LITCHFIELD COUNTY. Organized May 1795 from WATERTOWN. Towns organized from PLYMOUTH include THOMASTON.

CEMETERY RECORDS AND CEMETERIES

NAME	ADDRESS	HALE NO.	CITATION
Old Cemetery	Wolcott Road	1	40:1-5
East Plymouth Cemetery	Terryville	2	40:6-18
Allentown Cemetery	Terryville	3	40:19-22
Hillside Cemetery	57 North Main Street	4	40:23-53
St. Mary Roman Catholic Cemetery	Poland Brook Road	5	40:54-66
St. John Roman Catholic Cemetery	70 South Main Street	6	40:67-70
Greek Catholic Cemetery	Terryville	7	40:71
Greek Orthodox Cemetery	Terryville	8	40:72
Old Cemetery	Plymouth	9	40:73-93
West Cemetery	Plymouth	10	40:94-133
St. Matthew Episcopal Cemetery	East Plymouth Road		(no citation)

Index to Hale Inscriptions: 40:134-73.

St. Matthew Episcopal Church. Sexton Records, 1822-1891. (CSL, LDS 1995).

Shepard, James. MR. JUNIS PRESTON'S RECORD OF TWO HUNDRED NINE-TEEN BURIALS IN ST. MATTHEW'S CEMETERY, EAST PLYMOUTH, CONNECTI-CUT SEPTEMBER 8, 1846 TO SEPTEMBER 9, 1886. Hartford: CSL, 1929.

CHURCH RECORDS

FIRST CONGREGATIONAL CHURCH. Vital Records, 1765–1810. (CSL, LDS 1996). Index. (CSL, LDS 1448 pt. 23).

ST. MATTHEW EPISCOPAL CHURCH. Vital Records, 1747–1877. (CSL, LDS 1995).

ST. PETER EPISCOPAL CHURCH. Minutes, 1784–1890. Vital Records, 1810–1910, 1915–1919. (CSL, LDS 1997).

Leach, Marshall W. ANNALS OF AN OLD NEW ENGLAND CHURCH. TWO HUNDRED YEARS OF THE FIRST CONGREGATIONAL CHURCH, PLYMOUTH, CONNECTICUT, 1739–1939. Brattleboro: Vermont Publishing Co., 1939. 125 p.

Lumpkin, Elizabeth Welton. HISTORY OF AN OLD HILL-TOWN PARISH OF ST. PETER'S, PLYMOUTH, CONNECTICUT 1740–1796, 1796–1915, 1915–1940. N.p., n.d. 74 p.

A NARRATIVE AND DOCUMENTARY HISTORY OF ST. JOHN'S PROTESTANT EPISCOPAL CHURCH (FORMERLY ST. JAMES) OF WATERBURY, CONNECTI-CUT. WITH SOME NOTICE OF ST. PAUL'S CHURCH, PLYMOUTH, CHRIST CHURCH, WATERTOWN, ST. MICHAEL'S CHURCH, NAUGATUCK, A CHURCH IN MIDDLEBURY, ALL SAINT'S CHURCH, WOLCOTT, ST. PAUL'S CHURCH, WATERVILLE, TRINITY CHURCH, WATERBURY, (ALL COLONIES OF ST. JOHN'S). New Haven: Price, Lee and Adkins, 1907. 187 p.

Pond, Edgar LeRoy. THE TORIES OF CHIPPENY HILL, A BRIEF ACCOUNT OF THE LOYALISTS OF BRISTOL, PLYMOUTH AND HARWINTON, WHO FOUNDED ST. MATTHEWS CHURCH IN EAST PLYMOUTH IN 1791. New York: Gafton Press, 1909. 92 p.

HISTORICAL SOCIETY

Plymouth Historical Society, 06782.

LAND RECORDS

Land Records, 1795–1857. Index, 1795–1865. (LDS 1994 pt. 1–9).

LIBRARIES

Plymouth Library Association, 13 East Main Street, 06782. (203) 283-5977.

Terryville Public Library, 132 Main Street, 06786. (203) 582-3121.

NEWSPAPER

The PRELIMINARY CHECKLIST lists one newspaper for PLYMOUTH.

PROBATE RECORDS

Plymouth Probate District, Town Hall, 118 Main Street, 06786. (203) 589-6122.

> The Plymouth Probate District was organized 31 May 1833 from the Waterbury Probate District.

> ON FILE AT THE CSL: Estate Papers, 1833-1926. Indexes, 1833-1926. Inventory Control Book, 1833-1926. Court Record Books, 1833-1855.

Probate records, 1833-1855. (LDS, 1993 pt. 1-2).

SCHOOL RECORDS

Hartford. CSL, Record Group 62. First School District Records, 1844-1867.

TAX RECORDS

Hartford. CSL, Record Group 62. Grand List 1795, Rate Bill 1798, Lists 1924-1944.

VITAL RECORDS

Town Clerk, Town Hall, 19 East Main Street, 06786. (203) 589-6330.

The BARBOUR INDEX covers the years 1795-1850 and is based on the James N. Arnold copy of PLYMOUTH vital records made in 1915.

PUBLISHED WORKS AND OTHER RECORDS

Atwater, Francis. HISTORY OF THE TOWN OF PLYMOUTH, CONNECTICUT WITH AN ACCOUNT OF THE CENTENNIAL CELEBRATION MAY 14 AND 15, 1895. Meriden: Journal Publishing Co., 1895. 448 p.

_____. SOUVENIR HISTORY, PLYMOUTH, CONNECTICUT, 1795-1895. Meriden, Conn.: Journal Publishing Co., 1895. 91 p.

Bowles, Ella S. "A Trio of Plymouths." YANKEE 2 (August 1936): 29-33.

Bronson, Henry. HISTORY OF WATERBURY, CONNECTICUT. THE ORIGINAL TOWNSHIP EMBRACING PRESENT WATERTOWN AND PLYMOUTH, AND PARTS OF OXFORD, WOLCOTT, MIDDLEBURY, PROSPECT, AND NAUGATUCK. WITH AN APPENDIX OF BIOGRAPHY, GENEALOGY AND STATISTICS. Waterbury, Conn.: Bronson Brothers, 1858. 583 p. Index. (LDS 599,254).

POMFRET

WINDHAM COUNTY. Organized May 1713. Towns organized from POMFRET include BROOKLYN, HAMPTON and PUTNAM.

CEMETERY RECORDS AND CEMETERIES

NAME	ADDRESS	HALE NO.	CITATION
Chandler Cemetery	North part of Pomfret	1	40:1
Pomfret Street Cemetery	Pomfret Street	2	40:2-11
Episcopal Church Cemetery	Rear of Episcopal Church	3	40:12-13
Savin Cemetery	Near the Pomfret railroad station	4	40:14-47
New Abbington Cemetery	Near Abbington four corners	5	40:48-50 41:51-68
Old Abbington Cemetery	South of Church at Abbington	6	41:69-82
Bruce Cemetery	In eastern part of town	7	49:83-87
Dennis Cemetery	West of Pomfret Center Schoolhouse	8	49:88
Baker-Hollow Cemetery	In Baker Hollow	9	49:89
Randall-Botham Cemetery	Ragged Hill	10	49:90
Field Cemetery	J.D. Johnson farm	11	49:91
Benson Cemetery	On Young farm, on Road Pomfret to Brooklyn	12	49:92
Quaker Cemetery	West of Pomfret Hill, old abandoned road	13	49:93-94

Index to Hale inscriptions: 49:95-119.

"Inscriptions in the Wappaquians Burial Ground, Pomfret, Connecticut, 1723–1861." NEHGR 73 (1919): 105–24.

CHURCH RECORDS

ABINGTON CONGREGATIONAL CHURCH. Minutes, 1749-1790. Vital Records, 1753-1923. (CSL, LDS 1499).

CATHOLIC REFORMED CHRISTIAN CHURCH. Vital Records, 1792-1798. (CSL, LDS 2000).

CHRIST EPISCOPAL CHURCH. Vital Records, 1826-1889. (CSL, LDS 2000).

SECOND CONGREGATIONAL CHURCH. Marriages, 1753-1799. BAILEY 1:76-82.

"Church Records from Pomfret, Connecticut." ANCESTRAL NOTES FROM CHEDWATO, March 1967, pp. 25-27; May 1967, pp. 51-52.

"Deaths Recorded on Records of Congregational Church. Abington in Pomfret, Connecticut 1783-84." CQ 3 (1897): 354, 482-83; 4 (1898): 329-30; 5 (1899): 188, 246-47, 440-42.

HISTORICAL SOCIETY

Pomfret Historical Society, 06258.

LAND RECORDS

Land Records, 1686-1852. Index, 1686-1857. (LDS 1999 pt. 1-9).

LIBRARIES

Pomfret Free Library, Route 44, 06258. (203) 928-3475.

Abington Library, P.O. Box 118, Route 97, 06230. (203) 974-0415.

MILITARY RECORDS

A RECORD OF THOSE WHO SERVED IN THE CIVIL WAR 1861-1865 FROM THE TOWN OF POMFRET, CONNECTICUT. Pomfret: Ralph J. Sabin, 1916. 32 p.

NEWSPAPER

The PRELIMINARY CHECKLIST lists one newspaper for POMFRET.

PROBATE RECORDS

Pomfret Probate District, Town Hall, Route 44, 06259. (203) 974-0186.

> The Pomfret Probate district was organized May 1752 from the Plainfield and Windham Probate Districts. Probate districts organized from the Pomfret Probate District include the Ashford, Brooklyn, Killingly, Stafford, Thompson and Woodstock Probate Districts.

> ON FILE AT THE CSL: Estate Papers, 1752-1935. Indexes, 1752-1935. Inventory Control Book, 1752-1935. Court Record Book, 1753-1857.

Probate Records, 1753-1857. Indexes. (LDS 1998 pt. 1-9).

TAX RECORDS

Hartford. CSL, Record Group 62. Abstracts, 1797-1932.

VITAL RECORDS

Town Clerk, Town Hall, Route 44, 06259. (203) 974-0343.

The BARBOUR INDEX covers the years 1705-1850 and is based on the James N. Arnold copy of POMFRET vital records amde in 1910.

"Connecticut Births before 1730 (Barbour)--Town of Pomfret." CN 8 (1975): 12-14, 173-78, 329.

Leavitt, Emily Wilder. "Marriages at Pomfret, Connecticut 1706-1753." NEHGR 67 (1913): 371-76.

PUBLISHED WORKS AND OTHER RECORDS

Benes, Peter. "The Templeton 'Run' and the Pomfret 'Cluster': Patterns of Diffusion in Rural New England Meetinghouse Architecture, 1647-1822." OLD-TIME NEW ENGLAND 68, nos. 3-4 (1978): 1-21.

Griggs, Susan J. EARLY HOMESTEADS OF POMFRET AND HAMPTON. Danielson: Ingalls Printing Co., 1950. 118 p.

Hartford. CSL, Record Group 62. Town Records. Abstracts, 1852–1897. Election Returns, 1788–1886. Indentures, 1753–1841. Justice Files, 1800–1903. Registration Lists, 1837–1882.

Porter, John Addison. "Picturesque Pomfret." CQ 2 (1896): 3–24.

TOWN OF POMFRET--TWO HUNDRED FIFTIETH ANNIVERSARY CELEBRATION ISSUE. N.p.: 1963.

Wetherbee, Olive Pike. THE OLD FULLING MILL OF POMFRET, CONNECTICUT. Worcester, Mass.: E.W. Farnum Printing Co., 1971. 148 p.

PORTLAND

MIDDLESEX COUNTY. Organized May 1841 from EAST HAMPTON. Formerly called CONWAY; name changed in 1841.

CEMETERY RECORDS AND CEMETERIES

NAME	ADDRESS	HALE NO.	CITATION
Trinity Church Cemetery	343 Main Street	1	41:1-49
Center Cemetery	Bartlett Street	2	41:50-107
Swedish Cemetery	William Street	3	41:108-19
St. Mary Roman Catholic Cemetery	Riverside Street	4	41:120-45
Old Cemetery	At Quarry's, they were moved to Trinity Church Cemetery	5	41:146-54
Phelps Cemetery	Moved to Trinity Church Cemetery	6	41:155
Jewish Cemetery	Near Swedish Cemetery	7	41:156
Bidwell Cemetery	On Fred C. Cornwell Estate north part of town	8	41:156A-57

Index to Hale inscriptions: 41:158-201.

THE PORTLAND BURYING GROUND ASSOCIATION AND ITS CEMETERY. Portland: Middlesex County Printing Co., 1897. 77 p.

CHURCH RECORDS

CENTRAL CONGREGATIONAL CHURCH. Vital Records, 1851-1888. (CSL, LDS 1992).

FIRST CONGREGATIONAL CHURCH. Minutes, 1710-1923. Vital Records, 1721-1925. (CSL, LDS 1991). Records, 1698-1883. Index. (CSL, LDS 1448 pt. 24).

HISTORICAL SOCIETY

Portland Historical Society, 06480.

LAND RECORDS

Land Records, 1841-1857. (LDS 1900 pt. 1-2).

LIBRARY

Buck Library, 263 Main Street, 06480. (203) 342-1841.

NEWSPAPERS

The PRELIMINARY CHECKLIST lists two newspapers for PORTLAND.

PROBATE RECORDS

Portland Probate District, Town Hall, 265 Main Street, 06480. (203) 342-2880.
    Organized 22 April 1913 from the East Hampton Probate District.

SCHOOL RECORDS

Hartford. CSL, Record Group 62. School District Assessment Lists, 1867-1869.

TAX RECORDS

Hartford. CSL, Record Group 62. Assessment Book of Nelson Pelton, Collector, 1863.

VITAL RECORDS

Town Clerk, Town Hall, 265 Main Street, 06480. (203) 342-2880.

The BARBOUR INDEX covers the years 1841-1850 and is based on the James N. Arnold copy of PORTLAND vital records made in 1912.

PUBLISHED WORKS AND OTHER RECORDS

HISTORY OF PORTLAND, CONNECTICUT. Portland: Portland Historical Society for the Nation's Bicentennial Program, 1976. 66 p.

Murphy, Frances Solomon. HISTORY OF PORTLAND. Middletown: Stewart Press, 1969. 180 p.

PRESTON

NEW LONDON COUNTY. Organized October 1687. Towns organized from PRESTON include GRISWOLD.

CEMETERY RECORDS AND CEMETERIES

NAME	ADDRESS	HALE NO.	CITATION
Preston City Cemetery	Preston City	1	41:1-43
Avery Cemetery	Southeast part of town, near Avery Pond	2	41:43-54
New Poquetaunke Cemetery	Poquetaunke	3	41:54-82
Long Society Cemetery	Preston City Road	4	41:82-86
Palmer Cemetery	North part of town, near Griswold town line	5	41:87-91
Gates Cemetery	Westerly Road	6	41:91-94
Guile Cemetery	On old turnpike road, east part of town	7	41:94
Old Cemetery	Preston City Road	8	41:94-95
Davis Cemetery	On John Lucas farm, eastern part of town	9	41:95-96
Gore Cemetery	Westerly Road	10	41:96
Carey Cemetery	On Joseph Griffing farm, northeast part of town	11	41:96
Brown Cemetery	Near house of Ernest Luther eastern part of town	12	41:96-97
Brewster Cemetery	Brewster Neck, on Groton Road near Hospital	13	41:97-107

NAME	ADDRESS	HALE NO.	CITATION
Jewish Cemetery	Next to Brewster Neck Cemetery	14	41:107-9
Killam Cemetery	On Calvin Miner farm	15	41:109
Bentley Cemetery	Poquetaunke Road	16	41:109-10
Old Poquetaunke Cemetery	Poquetaunke Road	17	41:110-12
Safford Cemetery	In rear of Guile Cemetery eastern part of town	18	41:112
Brothers of Joseph Cemetery	Next to Brewster Neck	19	41:113-17
Norwich Hebrew Association Cemetery	Next to Brothers of Joseph Cemetery	20	41:117-22

Index to Hale inscriptions: 41:131-64.

HALE LIST OF BURIAL PLACE OF SOLDIERS: 41:123-30. HALE INDEX 41: 165-67.

CEMETERIES AND BURIALS IN THE TOWN OF PRESTON INCLUDING DECEASED VETERANS. Preston: Preston Historical Society, 1967.

Porter, George Shepherd. INSCRIPTIONS FROM THE LONG SOCIETY BURYING GROUND, PRESTON, CONNECTICUT. Boston: David Clapp and Son, 1906. 6 p.

_____. "Inscriptions from the Long Society Burying Ground, Preston, Connecticut." NEHGR 60 (1906): 121-25.

CHURCH RECORDS

CHURCH OF THE HOLY TRINITY (EPISCOPAL). Minutes, 1762-1799, 1812-1947. Vital Records, 1786-1811. (CSL, LDS 1988 pt. 3-6).

FIRST CONGREGATIONAL CHURCH. Minutes, 1716-1887. Vital Records, 1698-1883. (CSL, LDS 1989). Marriages, 1744-1798. BAILEY 7:40-47. Vital Records, 1698-1883. Index. (CSL). Baptisms, 1665-1754. Index. (NYGBS, LDS 1985).

FIRST CONGREGATIONAL CHURCH OF PRESTON, CONNECTICUT 1698-1898 TOGETHER WITH STATISTICS OF THE CHURCH TAKEN FROM THE CHURCH RECORDS. Preston: First Congregational Church, 1900. 201 p. (LDS 476, 900).

LONG SOCIETY RECORDS. 1757-1938. (CSL, LDS 1987).

ST. JAMES EPISCOPAL CHURCH. Minutes, 1814-1899. Vital Records, 1840-1883. Sunday School Minutes, 1845-1847. (CSL, LDS 1988).

Anderson, Ruby Parke. PARKE SCRAPBOOK. 3 vols. N.p., n.d. (Records of the Separate Church by Rev. Paul Parke from 1747 to 1800).

Palmer, Frank. "Church Records of Preston, Connecticut." NEHGR 45 (1891): 24-27.

HISTORICAL SOCIETY

Preston Historical Society, R.F.D. 1, 06360.

LAND RECORDS

Land Records, 1687-1854. Index, 1687-1940. (LDS 1986 pt. 1-12).

LIBRARY

Preston Public Library, R.F.D. 1, 06360. (203) 886-1010.

PROBATE RECORDS

PRESTON is in the Norwich Probate District.

SCHOOL RECORDS

Hartford. CSL, Record Group 62. Accounts and Records, 1805-1909.

TAX RECORDS

Hartford. CSL, Record Group 62. Abstracts, Abatements, Lists, 1800-1928.

VITAL RECORDS

Town Clerk, R.F.D. 1, 06360. (203) 887-9831.
> The town clerk's earliest birth record is 1675, marriage record is 1672 and death records is 1704.

The BARBOUR INDEX covers the years 1687-1850 and is based on the James N. Arnold copy of PRESTON vital records made in 1910.

Palmer, Frank. "Marriages by Samuel Mott, Justice of the Peace, of Preston, Connecticut (1769-1811)." NEHGR 55 (1901): 176-80.

PRESTON FIRST BOOK OF MARRIAGES. N.p., n.d. 145 p. Index. (also contains birth dates of children born to couples).

Youngs, Florence E., and Tracy, Dwight. ABSTRACT OF PRESTON, CONNECTICUT VITAL STATISTICS. Hartford: CSL, 1920. 146 p.

VOTER RECORDS

Hartford. CSL, Record Group 62. Lists, 1883-1900. Certificates, 1885-1934. Applicants for Admission as Voters, 1899-1906. Register of Women Voters, 1893-1897.

PUBLISHED WORKS AND OTHER RECORDS

Hale, David. PRESTON IN 1801 . . . . Hartford: Acorn Club of Connecticut, 1961. 32 p.

Hall, Marion White. PRESTON EARLY HOMES AND FAMILIES. Stonington: Stonington Printing and Publishing Co., 1968.

_____. PRESTON-HOMES AND FAMILIES. 3 vols. N.p., n.d.

Johnson, Helen Haase, ed. NINE DOLLARS PER MONTH AND BOARD: REMINISCENCES OF LEWIS R. PECKHAM, 1882-1967. Preston, Conn.: Preston Historical Society, 1975. 83 p.

Norman, Diane A. MEET OUR CRAFTSMEN: A PRESENTATION OF 18TH CENTURY PRESTON CABINETMAKERS. Preston, Conn.: Preston Historical Society, 1976. 32 p.

PRESTON IN REVIEW. Preston: Preston Historical Society, 1971. 236 p.

Town Records. 1706-1743. Indexed. (NYGBS, LDS 1985).

PROSPECT

NEW HAVEN COUNTY. Organized May 1827 from CHESHIRE and WATERBURY.

CEMETERY RECORDS AND CEMETERIES

NAME	ADDRESS	HALE NO.	CITATION
Old Cemetery	Prospect Center	1	41:1-16
New Cemetery	Prospect Center	2	41:17-20

Index to Hale inscriptions: 41:21-27.

CHURCH RECORDS

CONGREGATIONAL CHURCH   Minutes, 1797-1937. Vital Records, 1797-1937. (CSL, LDS 2012).

Cowdell, Nellie H. A HISTORY OF THE CONGREGATIONAL CHURCH, PROSPECT, CONNECTICUT, FORMERLY COLUMBIA PARISH 1798-1973. N.p., n.d. 64 p.

HISTORICAL SOCIETY

Prospect Historical Society, Inc., Center Street, 06712. (Mailing address: 31 Summit Road, 06712).

LAND RECORDS

Land Records, 1827-1854. (LDS 2011 pt. 1-2).

LIBRARY

Prospect Public Library, Center Street, 06712. (203) 758-4687.

MILITARY RECORDS

Soule, Sherwood. "A Connecticut Soldier in the French and Indian War, Life of Gideon Hotchkiss, Born 1716 at Cheshire, Connecticut." CM 11 (1907): 409-16.

NEWSPAPER

The PRELIMINARY CHECKLIST lists one newspaper for PROSPECT.

PROBATE RECORDS

PROSPECT is in the Cheshire Probate District.

VITAL RECORDS

Town Clerk, Town Hall, Center Street, 06712. (203) 758-4461.

The BARBOUR INDEX covers the years 1827-1853 and is based on the James N. Arnold copy of PROSPECT vital records made in 1916.

PUBLISHED WORKS AND OTHER RECORDS

Beach, Joseph Perkins. HISTORY OF CHESHIRE, CONNECTICUT FROM 1694 TO 1840. INCLUDING PROSPECT, WHICH AS COLUMBIA PARISH, WAS A PART OF CHESHIRE UNTIL 1829. Cheshire: Lady Fenwick Chapter, DAR, 1912. 574 p.

Bronson, Henry. HISTORY OF WATERBURY, CONNECTICUT. THE ORIGINAL TOWNSHIP EMBRACING PRESENT WATERTOWN AND PLYMOUTH, AND PARTS OF OXFORD, WOLCOTT, MIDDLEBURY, PROSPECT AND NAUGA-TUCK. WITH AN APPENDIX OF BIOGRAPHY, GENEALOGY AND STATIS-TICS. Waterbury: Bronson Bros., 1858. 583 p. Index. (LDS 599,254).

Clapp, Mrs. PROSPECT, CONNECTICUT FAMILY RECORDS. (NHCHS, LDS 1455 pt. 32).

Jacobus, Donald Lines. "Inhabitants of Columbia Society (now Prospect) Connecticut, 1805." TAG 14 (1938): 183-84.

WPA Historical Records Survey. INVENTORY OF THE TOWN AND CITY
ARCHIVES OF CONNECTICUT, NO. 5, NEW HAVEN COUNTY, VOL. 8,
NORTH BRANFORD, NORTH HAVEN, ORANGE, OXFORD, PROSPECT, SEY-
MOUR, SOUTHBURY. New Haven: Historical Records Survey, 1938. 189 p.
(LDS 897,354).

PUTNAM

WINDHAM COUNTY. Organized May 1855 from KILLINGLY, POMFRET and THOMPSON.

CEMETERY RECORDS AND CEMETERIES

NAME	ADDRESS	HALE NO.	CITATION
Grove Street Cemetery	Grove Street	1	41:1-121
Putnam Heights Cemetery	Putnam Heights	2	41:122-40
Munyan Cemetery	East Putnam	3	41:141-57
Wheelock Cemetery	On hill near mill, west side of river	4	41:158
Malbone Cemetery	Northwest part of city	5	41:158
Carpenter-Dresser Cemetery	Southwest part of city	6	41:158-59
Day Cemetery	Eastern part of town	7	41:160
Babbitt Cemetery	East part of town, near Killingly town line	8	41:160
Aspinwall Cemetery	Grove Street, south of Grove Street Cemetery	9	41:160-74
St. Mary Cemetery	Northwest part of city	10	41:175-220 42:221-41
Malbone Cemetery	West part of town near Pomfred town line	11	42:242
Bowen Cemetery	South of Day Cemetery	12	42:243-44

Index to Hale inscriptions: 42:245-314.

Eardeley, William A.D. CONNECTICUT CEMETERIES. Brooklyn: Author, 1916. 3:59.

CHURCH RECORDS

EAST CONGREGATIONAL CHURCH. Minutes, 1836-1903. Vital Records, 1715-1904. (CSL, LDS 2016).

FIRST CONGREGATIONAL CHURCH. Minutes, 1909-1933. Vital Records, 1848-1928. (CSL, LDS 2015). Records 1715-1904. Index. (CSL, LDS 1448, pt. 25). Marriages 1715-1799. BAILEY 5:33-41. Baptisms, Marriages, Deaths, 1711-1829. Mrs. Mary B. Bishop and Mrs. William H. Mansfield Copy. (CSL, LDS 2017).

HISTORICAL SOCIETY

Aspinock Historical Society of Putnam, Inc., P.O. Box 465, 06260.

LIBRARY

Putnam Public Library, 225 Kennedy Drive, 06260. (203) 928-6489.

NEWSPAPERS

WINDHAM COUNTY OBSERVER AND PUTNAM PROSPECT. Weekly. 36 South Main Street, 06260. (203) 928-2015.

The PRELIMINARY CHECKLIST lists six newspapers for PUTNAM.

PROBATE RECORDS

Putnam Probate District, 135 Main Street, 06260. (203) 928-2723.

   The Putnam Probate District was organized 5 July 1856 from the Thompson Probate District.

VITAL RECORDS

Town Clerk, 126 Church Street, 06260. (203) 928-5529.

   The town clerk's earliest birth, marriage and death records date from July 1855.

PUBLISHED WORKS AND OTHER RECORDS

Weaver, Margaret M. PERSPECTIVES OF PUTNAM: A HISTORY OF PUTNAM, CONNECTICUT. Putnam: Aspinock Historical Society of Putnam, 1980. 144 p. Index.

REDDING

FAIRFIELD COUNTY. Organized May 1767 from FAIRFIELD.

CEMETERY RECORDS AND CEMETERIES

NAME	ADDRESS	HALE NO.	CITATION
Old Cemetery	Near Congregational Church, Redding Center	1	42:1-5
Umpawaug Cemetery	Umpawaug Road	2	42:6-32
Center Cemetery	Redding Center	3	42:33-36
Isaac Hamilton Cemetery	Lonetown District	4	42:37-38
Christ Church Cemetery	Black Rock Turnpike	5	42:39-44
Hull Cemetery	Redding Road	6	42:45-55
Ridge Cemetery	Black Rock Turnpike	7	42:56-69
Sanford Cemetery	Ethan Allen Highway	8	42:70-71
Ferry Cemetery	Valley Road	9	42:72
Putnam Cemetery	Lonetown Road	10	42:73
Family Cemetery	Redding Ridge, in Easton	11	42:74
Gould Cemetery	Lonetown District	12	42:75
Marchant Cemetery	Marchant Road	13	42:76
Hill Cemetery	Henry Hill farm	14	42:77-78

Index to Hale inscriptions: 42:79-98.

THE EIGHT CEMETERIES IN THE TOWN OF REDDING, FOUNDED 1767.
N.p., n.d.

CHURCH RECORDS

CONGREGATIONAL CHURCH. 1729-1881. Index. (CSL, LDS 1448 pt. 26). Marriages, 1734-1780. BAILEY 1:70-76. Baptisms, 1750-1780. Marriages. (CSL, LDS 1735).

METHODIST EPISCOPAL CHURCH. Vital Records, 1779-1850. (CSL, LDS 2027).

HISTORICAL SOCIETY

Redding Historical Society, P.O. Box 23, 06875. (203) 938-2377.

LAND RECORDS

Land Records, 1767-1861. Index, 1767-1921. (LDS 2020 pt. 1-11).

LIBRARY

Mark Twain Library, Route 53, P.O. Box 9, 06875. (203) 938-2240.

MILITARY RECORDS

Foster, Sandra C. "Connecticut's Valley Forge." CONNECTICUT 36 (February 1973): 34-37.

Grumman, William Edgar. THE REVOLUTIONARY SOLDIERS OF REDDING, CONNECTICUT AND THE RECORD OF THEIR SERVICES, WITH MENTION OF OTHERS WHO RENDERED SERVICE OR SUFFERED LOSS AT THE HANDS OF THE ENEMY DURING THE STRUGGLE FOR INDEPENDENCE 1775-1783; TOGETHER WITH SOME ACCOUNT OF THE LOYALISTS OF THE TOWN AND VICINITY; THEIR ORGANIZATION, THEIR EFFORTS AND SACRIFICES IN BEHALF OF THE CAUSE OF THEIR KING, AND THEIR ULTIMATE FATE. Hartford: Case, Lockwood and Brainard, 1904. 208 p.

NEWSPAPERS

THE REDDING PILOT. Weekly. P.O. Box 394, 06829. (203) 544-8823.

The PRELIMINARY CHECKLIST lists four newspapers for REDDING.

PROBATE RECORDS

Redding Probate District, Town Hall, Route 107, Redding Center, Box 125, 06875. (203) 938-2326.

Organized 24 May 1839 from the Danbury Probate District.

ON FILE AT THE CSL: Estate Papers, 1839-1902. Indexes, 1839-1902. Inventory Control Books, 1839-1902. Court Record Books, 1839-1856. Probate Records, 1839-1856. (LDS 2021).

TAX RECORDS

Hartford. CSL, Record Group 62. Tax lists 1883, 1888-1890, 1895-1899, 1902-1938.

VITAL RECORDS

Town Clerk, Town Hall, Route 107, Redding Center, 06885. (203) 938-2377.

The BARBOUR INDEX covers the years 1767-1852 and is based on the Irene H. Mix copy of REDDING vital records made in 1915.

Redding Marriage Records, 1750-1780. (LDS 1735).

PUBLISHED WORKS AND OTHER RECORDS

Beach, Rebecca Donaldson. "The Redding Loyalists." NHCHS PAPERS 7 (1908): 218-36.

McGrath, Stephen B. "Connecticut's Tory Towns: The Loyalty Struggle in Newtown, Redding, and Ridgefield 1774-1783." CHSB 44 (1979): 88-96.

Squire, C.B. "The Greenest Town of All." FAIRFIELD COUNTY 4 (August 1974): 32-39.

Todd, Charles Burr. THE HISTORY OF REDDING, CONNECTICUT. FROM ITS FIRST SETTLEMENT TO THE PRESENT TIME. Newburgh, N.Y.: Newburgh Journal Co., 1906. 303 p.

_____. "An Old Mansion at Redding, Connecticut, Where Aaron Burr Visited." CM 10 (1906): 359-60.

RIDGEFIELD

FAIRFIELD COUNTY. Organized 1708.

CEMETERY RECORDS AND CEMETERIES

NAME	ADDRESS	HALE NO.	CITATION
Old Town Cemetery	54 North Salem Road	1	42:1
St. Mary Roman Catholic Cemetery	Copps Hill Road	2	42:2-12
Branchville Cemetery	Brooklane Road	3	42:13-27
Beers Cemetery	U.S. 51	4	42:28
Davis Cemetery	Silver Spring Road on Wilton line (back from road, east side)	5	42:29
Seymour Cemetery	Olmstead Lane, Flat Rock District	6	42:30
Gamaliel Smith Cemetery	West Lane District (near Swords Place)	7	42:31
Old Florida Cemetery	Route 7	8	42:32
Florida Cemetery	Route 7	9	42:33-36
Selleck Bennett's Farm Cemetery	In Bennett's Farm District	10	42:37
Ridgebury Cemetery	Ridgebury Road	11	42:38-52
Town Cemetery	In Titicus District, also as part of Town Cemetery	12	42:53-155
Mapleshade Cemetery	In Titicus District, also as part of Town Cemetery	13	42:53-155
Scott's Cemetery	In Titicus District, also as part of Town Cemetery	14	42:53-155

NAME	ADDRESS	HALE NO.	CITATION
Hurlbutt Cemetery	In Titicus District, also as part of Town Cemetery	15	42:53-155
Lounsbury Cemetery	In Titicus District, also as part of Town Cemetery	16	42:53-155
Fair Lawn Cemetery	48 North Salem Road	17	42:53-155
Smith Cemetery	Northwest part of town, half in New York State	18	42:156
Old Episcopal Cemetery	In triangle top Ridgebury Hill	19	42:157-58
Revolutionary War Battle Ground Cemetery	Main Street	20	42:159-60

Index to Hale inscriptions: 42:161-203.

CHURCH RECORDS

CHURCH OF ENGLAND. Registry Book. 1742-1746. (CSL, LDS 2107).

FIRST CONGREGATIONAL CHURCH. Minutes, 1761-1915. Vital Records, 1820-1913. (CSL, LDS 2031). Records, 1761-1931. Index. (CSL).

RIDGEBURY CHURCH OF CHRIST. Records, 1769-1863. (Danbury Public Library).

SECOND CONGREGATIONAL CHURCH. Marriages, 1769-1800. BAILEY 3: 84-90.

Brush, Mrs. Julia. "Marriages, Ridgebury, Connecticut, Church Records." TAG 19 (1943): 211-217.

Hanson, Muriel R. A HISTORY OF THE FIRST CONGREGATIONAL CHURCH OF RIDGEFIELD 1712-1962. Ridgefield: First Congregational Church of Ridgefield, 1962. 56 p.

Heireth, Imogene O. "Ridgebury, Connecticut, Church Records." CA 23 (1980): 53-56.

HISTORICAL SOCIETY

Keeler Tavern, 132 Main Street, 06877. (203) 438-5485

LAND RECORDS

Land Records, 1709-1854. Index, 1708-1855. (LDS 2029 pt. 1-13).

LIBRARY

Ridgefield Library, 472 Main Street, 06877. (203) 438-2282.

MILITARY RECORDS

Case, James R. AN ACCOUNT OF TRYON'S RAID ON DANBURY IN APRIL, 1777, ALSO THE BATTLE OF RIDGEFIELD AND THE CAREER OF GENERAL DAVID WOOSTED. Danbury: Danbury Printing Co., 1927. 56 p.

Foster, Sandra. "The Battle of Ridgefield." CONNECTICUT 35 (September 1972): 28-31, 56.

Hoyt, George S. RECORD OF SOLDIERS BURIED IN DANBURY, BROOK-FIELD, NEW FAIRFIELD AND RIDGEFIELD. Hartford: CSL, 1929. 91 p.

Prickett, Effie M. RIDGEFIELD MEN IN THE WAR OF THE AMERICAN REV-OLUTION, WAR OF 1812, MEXICAN WAR, CIVIL WAR AND SPANISH AMERI-CAN WAR. Hartford: CSL, 1921.

Smith, Philip M. "Ridgefield (Conn.) Patriots, 1776." TAG 10 (1943): 49-50.

NEWSPAPERS

THE RIDGEFIELD PRESS. Weekly. P.O. Box 397, 06877. (203) 438-6545.

The PRELIMINARY CHECKLIST lists two newspapers for RIDGEFIELD.

PROBATE RECORDS

Ridgefield Probate District, Town Hall, 400 Main Street, 06877. (203) 438-7301, ext. 7.

>   The Ridgefield Probate District was organized 10 June 1841 from the Danbury Probate District.

>   ON FILE AT THE CSL: Record Books, 1841-1855.

Probate Records, 1841-1855. (LDS 2030).

SCHOOL RECORDS

Hartford. CSL, Record Group 62. Registers, 1844–1859. Visitor's Record, 1856–1896.

VITAL RECORDS

Town Clerk, Town Hall, 400 Main Street, 06877. (203) 438-7301, ext. 56.

> The town clerk's earliest birth, marriage and death records date from 1708.

The BARBOUR INDEX covers the years 1709–1850 and is based on the James N. Arnold copy of RIDGEFIELD vital records made in 1915.

"Connecticut Births Before 1730 (Barbour)--Town of Ridgefield." CN 8 (1975): 329–34.

PUBLISHED WORKS AND OTHER RECORDS

Bassett, Preston R. "The Towns in the Ridges: The Story of Wilton and Ridgefield." CA 17 (1965): 6–10.

Bicentennial Committee. 1708-RIDGEFIELD, CONNECTICUT--1908. BICENTENNIAL CELEBRATION. Hartford: Case, Lockwood and Brainard Co., 1908. 96 p.

Casagrande, Gordon. "Ridgefield: A Changing Constance." FAIRFIELD COUNTY 4 (July 1974): 25–36.

Cummings, Parke. "Ridgefield--Past and Present." FAIRFIELD COUNTY 9 (May 1979): 40–43.

Goodrich, Samuel. RIDGEFIELD IN 1800. Hartford: Acorn Club of Connecticut, 1954. 21 p.

Le Menager, Jack. "Ridgefield: A Bucolic Fairfield County Town Battens Down for the Future." FAIRFIELD COUNTY 9, no. 5 (May 1979): 24–29, 38–39.

McGrath, Stephen B. "Connecticut's Tory Towns: The Loyalty Struggle in Newtown, Redding, and Ridgefield 1774–1783." CHSB 44 (1979): 88–96.

Rockwell, George Lounsbury. HISTORY OF RIDGEFIELD, CONNECTICUT. Ridgefield, Conn.: Author, 1927. Reprint. Harrison, N.Y.: Harbor Hill Books, 1979. 583 p.

Rockwell, Mary Everest. "1708--Ridgefield Bi-Centennial 1908." CM 12 (1908): 1-35.

Teller, Daniel W. THE HISTORY OF RIDGEFIELD, CONNECTICUT FROM ITS SETTLEMENT TO THE PRESENT TIME. Danbury: T. Donovan, 1878. 251 p.

Welsh, Glenna M. THE PROPRIETORS OF RIDGEFIELD, CONNECTICUT. Ridgefield: Caudatowa Press, 1976. 188 p.

ROCKY HILL

Organized May 1843 from WETHERSFIELD.

CEMETERY RECORDS AND CEMETERIES

NAME	ADDRESS	HALE NO.	CITATION
Rocky Hill or Center Cemetery	On Main Highway, 1/4 mile south of Center	1	42:1-71
Graveyard Cemetery	At the Valley Railroad Crossing Wethersfield line, one grave under tree	2	42:72
Rose Memorial Cemetery	West Rocky Hill Road	3	42:73-78
Bulkley Cemetery	In cellar of Hand's General Store at center of town	4	42:79

Index to Hale inscriptions: 42:80-101.

Tillotson, Edward Sweetser. WETHERSFIELD INSCRIPTIONS. Hartford: William F.J. Boardman, 1899. 372 p.

CHURCH RECORDS

CONGREGATIONAL CHURCH. Records, 1722-1855. (CSL, LDS 2024). Marriages, 1766-1799. BAILEY 6:73-82.

HISTORICAL SOCIETY

Rocky Hill Historical Society, 785 Old Main Street, P.O. Box 185, 06067. (203) 529-9673. Publishes NEWSLETTER OF THE ROCKY HILL HISTORICAL SOCIETY. 1964-- . Frequency varies.

Confederation of Connecticut River History Societies, 460 Old Main Street, 06067. Publishes THE RANGELIGHT. Frequency varies.

LAND RECORDS

Land Records, 1843-1866. (LDS 2023).

LIBRARY

Belden Library, 33 Church Street, 06067. (203) 529-2379.

PROBATE RECORDS

ROCKY HILL is in the Newington Probate District.

SCHOOL RECORDS

Hartford. CSL, Record Group 62. School Returns, 1819-41.

TAX RECORDS

Hartford. CSL, Record Group 62. List 1843, Abstracts, 1848-1909, 1917.

VITAL RECORDS

Town Clerk, Town Hall, 699 Old Main Street, 06067. (203) 563-1451.

The BARBOUR INDEX covers the years 1765-1854 and is based on the James N. Arnold copy of ROCKY HILL vital records made in 1917.

Vital Records, 1865-1879. (CSL, LDS 1483 and 003,662).

PUBLISHED WORK

Reynolds, Ronna L. "The Towns of Glastonbury, Rocky Hill, and Newington." ANTIQUES 109 (March 1976): 518-27.

ROXBURY

LITCHFIELD COUNTY. Organized October 1796 from WOODBURY.

CEMETERY RECORDS AND CEMETERIES

NAME	ADDRESS	HALE NO.	CITATION
Roxbury Center Cemetery	Hemlock Road	1	42:1-40
Old South Cemetery	2 miles south of Center	2	42:41-48
Old Cemetery	Squire Road	3	42:49-50
North Cemetery	1 mile north of Center	4	42:51-53
Beardsley-Levenworth Cemetery	Lord Hill	5	42:54
Warner Cemetery	Under Soldiers' Monument in Roxbury Center	6	42:55-56

Index to Hale inscriptions: 42:57-73.

"Leavenworth." NEHGR 72 (1918): 77-78.

Worthington, Elmer H. ROXBURY CEMETERIES 1743-1745. N.p., n.d.

CHURCH RECORDS

CONGREGATIONAL CHURCH. Vital Records, 1871-1889. Rev. David E. Jones Copy. (CSL, LDS 2022).

FIRST CONGREGATIONAL CHURCH. Minutes, 1785-1930. Vital Records, 1742-1888. (CSL, LDS 2088). Records, 1742-1930. Index. (CSL).

FIRST ECCLESIASTICAL SOCIETY. Minutes, 1729-1766. Vital Records, 1733-1882. (CSL, LDS 2027).

Jacobus, Donald Lines. "Church Records of Roxbury, Connecticut." TAG 33 (1957): 25-35.

HISTORICAL SOCIETY

Roxbury Historical Society, Blue Stone Ridge, 06783. (203) 354-7612.

LAND RECORDS

Land Records, 1796-1855. Index, 1796-1935. (LDS 2025 pt. 1-8).

LIBRARY

Hodge Memorial Library, Route 67, 06783. (203) 354-6135.

MILITARY RECORDS

ROXBURY IN THE CIVIL WAR. Roxbury: Civil War Centennial Committee, 1963. 29 p.

PROBATE RECORDS

Roxbury Probate District, Town Hall, South Street, 06783. (203) 354-3328.

> The Roxbury Probate District was organized 6 June 1842 from the Woodbury Probate District.

> ON FILE AT THE CSL: Estate Papers, 1842-1921. Indexes, 1842-1921. Inventory Control Book, 1842-1921. Court Record Book, 1842-1859.

Probate Records, 1842-1859. (LDS 2026).

VITAL RECORDS

Town Clerk, Town Hall, South Street, 06783. (203) 354-3328.

The BARBOUR INDEX covers the years 1796-1835 and is based on the James N. Arnold copy of ROXBURY vital records made in 1915.

Cothren, William. HISTORY OF ANCIENT WOODBURY (see below). Includes a section of ROXBURY vital records, pp. 582-650.

PUBLISHED WORKS AND OTHER RECORDS

Cothren, William. HISTORY OF ANCIENT WOODBURY, CONNECTICUT, FROM THE FIRST INDIAN DEED TO 1659 TO 1854. INCLUDING THE PRESENT TOWNS OF WASHINGTON, SOUTHBURY, BETHLEHEM, ROXBURY, AND A PART OF OXFORD AND MIDDLEBURY. Waterbury: Bronson Bros., 1854. 841 p. (LDS 2205).

Hartford. CSL, Record Group 62. Town Records Book, 1796–1832.

SALEM

NEW LONDON COUNTY. Organized May 1819 from COLCHESTER, LYME and MONTVILLE.

CEMETERY RECORDS AND CEMETERIES

NAME	ADDRESS	HALE NO.	CITATION
Woodbridge Cemetery	South part of town, on the Mitchell Place	1	42:1
Baptist Cemetery	East part of town, near Gardner Lake	2	42:2-4
Dolebear Place Cemetery (same as #19)	East part of town near Gardner Lake	3	42:5
Lathrop Cemetery	Northeast part of town, near Gardner Lake	4	42:6
Old Rathbone Cemetery	Northeast part of town, near Gardner Lake	5	42:7-8
Old Rathbone Cemetery	Northeast part of town, opposite Rathbone home	6	42:9
Wesley Brown Cemetery	Near Wesley Brown home	7	42:10-18
Newton-Ransom Cemetery	Northwest part of town, half in Colchester	8	42:19
Niles Cemetery	South from Salem Street	9	42:20-21
Gilbert Cemetery	In lots east from Morgan home	10	42:22
Hillard Cemetery	1/4 mile east from Salem Street	11	42:23-25
Harris Cemetery	Norwich Road	12	42:26
Palmer Plot (1 stone)	East part of town, on Luther Forsythe Place	13	42:27

NAME	ADDRESS	HALE NO.	CITATION
Miner Cemetery	East part of town on D.Y. Miner property	14	42:28
Raymond Cemetery	Southeast part of town, near Olando Raymond property	15	42:29-30
1 stone	Southeast part of town, near Siegel property	16	42:31
Rogers Cemetery	Southeast part of town, near Reservoir	17	42:32
Mosswood Glen Cemetery	Music Vale, Salem Street	18	42:33
Fox Cemetery	East part of town, 1/4 mile in woods near Gardner Lake	19	42:34
Whittlesey Cemetery (same as #19)	Near Music Vale, west of Salem Street	20	42:35
Fish Cemetery	Northeast part of town, near Colchester Line	21	42:36
Way Cemetery	Northeast part of town, near Colchester Line	22	42:37
Loomis Cemetery	Southeast part of town, near Horse Pond	23	42:38
DeWolf Farm Cemetery #1	Near Gardner Lake	24	42:39
DeWolf Farm Cemetery #2	On Clark Property	25	42:40
Rogers Cemetery	Salem Turnpike	26	42:41
Single Grave	On Senator Bingham's farm	27	42:42
Dolbeare Cemetery	Southwest of Baptist Cemetery	28	42:43
9 Field stones	Back of store across from Harris Place	29	42:44
Cuckle Hill Cemetery	Cuckle Hill	30	42:45
Babcock Cemetery	Babcock farm	31	42:46-47

Index to Hale inscriptions: 42:48-54.

Barbour, Lucius Barnes. "Inscriptions from Gravestones at Salem, Connecticut." NEHGR 80 (1926): 186-94; 89 (1935): 243-58.

Taintor, Charles Micaiell. "Inscriptions from Salem, Connecticut." NEHGR 12 (1858): 54.

HISTORICAL SOCIETY

Salem Historical Society, Route 85, 06415. (Mailing address: R.F.D. 4). (203) 859-1307.

LAND RECORDS

Land Records, 1819-1880. Indexed. (LDS 2055 pt. 1-2).

LIBRARY

Salem Free Public Library, Route 85, R.F.D. 4, 06415. (203) 859-1333.

NEWSPAPER

The PRELIMINARY CHECKLIST lists one newspaper for SALEM.

PROBATE RECORDS

Salem Probate District, Town Office Building, Route 85, 06415. (203) 859-1100.

> The Salem Probate District was organized 9 July 1841 from the Colchester and New London Probate Districts.

> ON FILE AT THE CSL: Estate Papers, 1834-1956. Indexes, 1834-1956. Inventory Control Book, 1834-1956. Court Record Books, 1842-1872.

Probate Records, 1842-1872. (LDS 2056).

VITAL RECORDS

Town Clerk, Town Office Building, Route 85, 06415. (203) 859-0593.

> The town clerk's earliest birth record is 15 October 1818, marriage record is 5 November 1817 and death record is 24 February 1827.

The BARBOUR INDEX covers the years 1836-1852 and is based on the James N. Arnold copy of SALEM vital records made in 1912.

Vital Records, 1856-1903. (LDS 003,662).

PUBLISHED WORKS AND OTHER RECORDS

Perkins, Mary Elizabeth. CHRONICLE OF A CONNECTICUT FARM, 1769–1905. Boston: Author, 1905. 298 p.

Thompson, Florence Whittlesey. "Music Vale." CQ 3 (1897): 19-22.

SALISBURY

LITCHFIELD COUNTY. Organized October 1741.

CEMETERY RECORDS AND CEMETERIES

NAME	ADDRESS	HALE NO.	CITATION
Center Cemetery	Rear of Town Hall	1	42:1-9
Chapinville Cemetery	East of Chapinville	2	42:10-15
Dutchess Bridge Cemetery	Canaan Road	3	42:16-19
Mt. Riga Cemetery	Near Forge Pond	4	42:20-23
Town Hill Cemetery	1 mile south of Lakeville	5	42:24-37
Lime Rock Cemetery	At Lime Rock	6	42:38-62
Salisbury Cemetery	Salisbury Center	7	42:63-84
New Cemetery	New part of Salisbury Cemetery	8	43:85-130
Catholic Cemetery	North of Salisbury Cemetery	9	43:131-38
Walton Cemetery (3 stones)	Lime Rock Road	10	43:139
Private Cemetery (2 stones)	Lime Rock Road	11	43:139
Reed Cemetery	1 1/2 miles north of Salisbury Center	12	43:140
Swan Farm Cemetery	Swan Farm	13	43:141
Indian Cemetery	On shore of Lake Riga	14	43:142
Surdam Farm Cemetery	Mt. Riga	15	43:143
(No records on file in Hale Collection)		16	(no citation)

NAME	ADDRESS	HALE NO.	CITATION
Marsh Cemetery	Reservoir Road	17	43:145
Bayliss Family Cemetery	Near Town Hall	18	43:146
Bushnell Cemetery	North of Bushnell Farm	19	43:147
Amesville Cemetery	Not located	20	43:148
Cande Cemetery	On Massachusetts State Line	21	43:149
Bryant Cemetery	1/2 mile from J.W. Sherwood property	22	43:150
Evarts Cemetery	Millerton Road	23	43:151-52

Index to Hale inscriptions: 43:153-95.

"Cemetery Records." HISTORICAL COLLECTIONS RELATING TO THE TOWN OF SALISBURY. 1 (1913): 81-123; 2 (1916): 123-66.

Rudd, Malcolm Day. INSCRIPTIONS AT SALISBURY CENTER, LIME ROCK, ETC. Boston: David Clapp and Son, 1898. 16 p.

CHURCH RECORDS

CONGREGATIONAL CHURCH. Minutes, 1804-1941. Vital Records, 1818-1892. (CSL, LDS 2035). Records, 1740-1891: Rollin H. Cooke Collection, Pittsfield, Massachusetts. (LDS 30,754 pt. 17). Records, 1764-1817. (NYGBS, LDS 2032).

ST. JOHN EPISCOPAL CHURCH. Minutes, 1846-1853. Vital Records, 1823-1862. (CSL, LDS 2036).

THE ONE HUNDRED AND FIFTIETH ANNIVERSARY OF THE CONGREGA-TIONAL CHURCH IN SALISBURY, CONNECTICUT. Hartford: Case, Lock-wood and Brainard, 1895. 82 p.

Pettee, Julia. THE REV. JONATHAN LEE AND HIS EIGHTEENTH CENTURY SALISBURY PARISH. THE EARLY HISTORY OF THE TOWN OF SALISBURY, CONNECTICUT. Salisbury: Salisbury Association, 1957. 242 p.

HISTORICAL SOCIETY

Salisbury Association, 06068. (203) 435-9511.

LAND RECORDS

Hartford. CSL. Record Group 62. Towns Deeds, notes from land records, 1756–1882.

Land Records, 1741–1861. Proprietor's Records, 1739–1835. Index, 1739–1898. (LDS 2033 pt. 1–14).

Land Records, 1747–1762. Index, 1720–1749. (NYGBS, LDS 2032).

"Land Records, Vol. 1." HISTORICAL COLLECTIONS RELATING TO THE TOWN OF SALISBURY 2 (1916): 173–96.

LIBRARY

Scoville Memorial Library, Route 44, 06068. (203) 435-2838.

MILITARY RECORDS

"Civil War Soldiers found in 'New' Cemetery." HISTORICAL COLLECTIONS RELATING TO THE TOWN OF SALISBURY 2 (1916): 167–68.

Hartford. CSL, Record Group 62. Papers, 1851–1865.

Norton, Thomas Lunt. SALISBURY IN WAR TIME. N.p., 1910. 34 p.

Rome, Adam Ward. CONNECTICUT'S CANNON: THE SALISBURY FURNACE IN THE AMERICAN REVOLUTION. Hartford: American Revolution Bicentennial Commission in Connecticut, 1977. 60 p. Index.

NEWSPAPER

LAKEVILLE JOURNAL. Weekly. 06039. (203) 435-2541.

The PRELIMINARY CHECKLIST lists one newspaper for SALISBURY.

PROBATE RECORDS

Salisbury Probate District, Town Hall, Main Street, 06068. (203) 435-9513.

    The Salisbury Probate District was organized 16 June 1847 from the Sharon Probate District.

    ON FILE AT THE CSL: Court Record Books, 1847–1856.

Probate Records, 1847-1856. (LDS 2034).

SCHOOL RECORDS

Eaton, Edward Bailey. "Lakeville--Its Educational and Commercial Interests." CM 8 (1903): 372-84.

"Enumerations of Children in School Districts, 1820." and "School Record." HISTORICAL COLLECTIONS RELATING TO THE TOWN OF SALISBURY, Vols. 3 and 4.

Hartford, CSL, Record Group 62. Records, accounts, abatements, tax lists, 1816-1896.

TAX RECORDS

Hartford. CSL, Record Group 62. Abatement lists, 1778-1784. School Tax List, 1896.

Litchfield. Litchfield Historical Society. Grand Lists, 1762-1765. (Data from 1763-1764 also includes lists of people who moved or died before they paid taxes.)

Tax Lists, 1746-1761. (NYGBS, LDS 2032).

VITAL RECORDS

Town Clerk, Town Hall, Main Street, 06068. (203) 435-9511.

> The town clerk's earliest birth record is 16 September 1728, marriage record is 4 June 1747 and death record is 28 May 1746.

The BARBOUR INDEX covers the years 1741-1846 and is based on the James N. Arnold copy of SALISBURY vital records made in 1915.

"Vital Records . . . to 1770." HISTORICAL COLLECTIONS RELATING TO THE TOWN OF SALISBURY 1 (1913): 2-79; 2 (1916): 2-122.

PUBLISHED WORKS AND OTHER RECORDS

Allen, Morse. "Place-names in Salisbury, Connecticut." NAMES 6 (June 1958): 97-111.

Bartlett, Ellen Strong. "Salisbury." CQ 4 (1898): 344-71.

DuBois, Mrs. Howard J. "Freeman's List, 1784-1849--Town Meeting Records." DAR MAGAZINE, January 1966, pp. 29-30.

Gesner, R.H. "In the Connecticut Highlands." CM 8 (1904): 689-703.

Kimball, Richard A. COMMEMORATIVE GUIDE, BICENTENNIAL CELEBRATION, 1776-1976. Salisbury: Salisbury Association, 1976. 89 p.

Rome, Adam Ward. CONNECTICUT'S CANNON. THE SALISBURY FURNACE IN THE AMERICAN REVOLUTION. Connecticut Bicentennial Series, no. 24. Hartford: American Revolution Bicentennial of Connecticut, 1977. 60 p. Index.

Rudd, Malcolm Day. AN HISTORICAL SKETCH OF SALISBURY, CONNECTICUT. New York: n.p., 1899. 23 p.

_____. "Lakeville--In the American Switzerland." CM 8 (1903): 337-71.

SCOTLAND

WINDHAM COUNTY. Organized May 1857 from WINDHAM.

CEMETERY RECORDS AND CEMETERIES

NAME	ADDRESS	HALE NO.	CITATION
Old Scotland Cemetery	1 mile south of Center	1	43:1-28
New Scotland Cemetery	Next to Old Scotland Cemetery	2	43:29-45
Palmertown Cemetery	2 miles southwest of Center	3	43:46-50
Fuller Cemetery	Center	4	43:51-52

Index to Hale inscriptions: 43:53-67.

CHURCH RECORDS

BRUNSWICK SEPARATE CHURCH. Minutes, 1746-1846. Index. (CSL, LDS 2110).

FIRST CONGREGATIONAL CHURCH. Minutes, 1732-1759. Vital Records, 1735-1915. (CSL, LDS 2110).

Rev. Tallman's Notebook, 1844-1869. (CSL, LDS 2110). Marriages, 1735/6-1800. BAILEY 3:43-51.

HISTORICAL SOCIETY

Scotland Historical Society, Waldo Road, 06264. (203) 456-0077.

LIBRARY

Scotland Public Library, Route 97, 06264. (203) 423-0925.

PROBATE RECORDS

SCOTLAND is in the Windham Probate District.

VITAL RECORDS

Town Clerk, Route 97, P.O. Box 122, 06264. (203) 423-9634.

> The town clerk's earliest birth, marriage and death records date from 1857.

PUBLISHED WORKS AND OTHER RECORDS

Jones, Charles Edwin. "The Impolitic Mr. Edwards: the Personal Dimension of the Robert Breck Affair." NEQ 51 (1978): 64-79.

Weaver, William L. HISTORY OF ANCIENT WINDHAM, CONNECTICUT, GENEALOGY, CONTAINING A GENEALOGICAL RECORD OF ALL THE EARLY FAMILY OF ANCIENT WINDHAM, EMBRACING THE PRESENT TOWNS OF WINDHAM, MANSFIELD, HAMPTON, CHAPLIN AND SCOTLAND. Part I. A-Bil. Willimantic: Weaver and Curtiss, 1864. 112 p. (LDS 2146).

SEYMOUR

NEW HAVEN COUNTY. Organized May 1850 from DERBY. Towns organized from SEYMOUR include BEACON FALLS.

CEMETERY RECORDS AND CEMETERIES

NAME	ADDRESS	HALE NO.	CITATION
Union Cemetery	115 Derby Avenue	1	43:1-36
Trinity Cemetery	40 West Street	2	43:37-69
St. Augustine Roman Catholic Cemetery	Bissell Place	3	43:70-77
Congregational Church Cemetery	150 South Main Street	4	43:78-83
Methodist Church Cemetery	90 Pearl Street	5	43:84-87
Squantic Cemetery	386 Roosevelt Drive	6	43:88-89
St. Kirylot and St. Meftody Cemetery	South of St. Augustine Cemetery	7	43:90
Great Hill Cemetery	175 Cemetery Road	8	43:91-102

Index to Hale inscriptions: 43:103-28.

CHURCH RECORDS

ALBERT SWAN MEMORIAL HALL DEDICATION 1789-1908. Seymour: Congregational Church, 1908. 36 p.

Sharpe, William Carvosso. ANNALS OF THE METHODIST EPISCOPAL CHURCH OF SEYMOUR, CONNECTICUT. Seymour: Record Print, 1885. 131 p.

Thorpe, Sheldon Brainerd. "Records of Trinity Episcopal Church, Humphreysville, Connecticut (now Seymour)." In GENEALOGICAL NOTES ON BARRETT AND ALLIED FAMILIES, Vol. 6 (CSL, LDS, LDS 002,993).

HISTORICAL SOCIETY

Seymour Historical Society, Inc., 06483.

LIBRARY

Seymour Public Library, 46 Church Street, 06483. (203) 888-3903.

NEWSPAPERS

The PRELIMINARY CHECKLIST lists four newspapers for SEYMOUR.

PROBATE RECORDS

SEYMOUR is in the Derby Probate District.

SCHOOL RECORDS

Seymour. Seymour Public Library. School Records from 1875-1884.

VITAL RECORDS

Town Clerk, Town Hall, 1 First Street, 06483. (203) 888-0519.

> The town clerk's earliest birth record is May 1849, marriage record is September 1849 and death record is August 1849.

Jacobus, Donald Lines. "Records kept by Thomas Gilyard of Deaths mainly in the Naugatuck Valley, Connecticut." TAG 32 (1956): 245-49.

Sharpe, William Carvosso. VITAL STATISTICS OF SEYMOUR, CONNECTICUT, 1849-1914. 5 vols. Seymour: Record Print, 1883-1923.

PUBLISHED WORKS AND OTHER RECORDS

Bassett, Frank G. "The Town of Seymour." CM 6 (1900): 310-34.

Campbell, Hollis Andrew. "Old Landmarks of Seymour." CM 6 (1900): 491-513.

Campbell, Hollis Andrew; Sharpe, William Carvosso; and Bassett, Frank G. SEYMOUR PAST AND PRESENT. Seymour: W.C. Sharpe, 1902. 613 p. (LDS 599,304).

Molloy, Leo Thomas. TERCENTENARY PICTORIAL AND HISTORY OF THE LOWER NAUGATUCK VALLEY. Ansonia: Emerson Bus., 1935. 404 p.

Sharpe, William Carvosso. HISTORY OF SEYMOUR, CONNECTICUT, WITH BIOGRAPHIES AND GENEALOGIES. Seymour: Record Print, 1879. 244 p.

_____. SEYMOUR AND VICINITY. Seymour: Record Print, 1878. 148 p.

WPA Historical Records Survey: INVENTORY OF THE TOWN AND CITY ARCHIVES OF CONNECTICUT, NO. 5, NEW HAVEN COUNTY, VOL. 8. NORTH BRANFORD, NORTH HAVEN, ORANGE, OXFORD, PROSPECT, SEYMOUR, SOUTHBURY. New Haven: Historical Records Survey, 1938. 189 p. (LDS 897,354).

Ward, Jessamine, and Guest, Gladys. TERCENTENARY PICTORIAL AND HISTORY OF THE LOWER NAUGATUCK VALLEY. Typescript. 123 p.

SHARON

LITCHFIELD COUNTY. Organized October 1739.

CEMETERY RECORDS AND CEMETERIES

NAME	ADDRESS	HALE NO.	CITATION
Sharon Burying Ground	Sharon Street	1	43:1-73
Hillside Cemetery	Part of Sharon Burying Ground	2	
Cartwright Cemetery	East Street	3	43:74-78
Boland Cemetery	Halfway between Sharon (on west side of road) and Amenia	4	43:79-89
Pine Swamp Cemetery	On Road from Sharon to West Cornwall on left hand side of road	5	43:90
Malcuit Farm Cemetery	2 stones on farm of Charles Malcuit, Sharon Mountain	5	43:91
Ticknor's Woods Cemetery (same as #13)	East Street	6	43:92
Amenia Union Cemetery	On road to Skiff Mountain	7	43:93-99
Ellsworth Cemetery	On south side of road between the two churches	8	43:100-122
St. Bridget Cemetery	Cornwall Bridge	9	43:123-28
Moravian Cemetery	1 stone, that of David Bruce on center shore of Lake Wequadnach	10	43:129
Catholic Cemetery	1 mile west of Sharon Center	11	43:130-36
Roberts Cemetery	2 miles north of Ellsworth	12	43:137

NAME	ADDRESS	HALE NO.	CITATION
Amenia Union Cemetery	Next to Amenia Union Cemetery	13	43:138-47
Leedsville Cemetery	On Ford farm	14	43:148-51
Smith-Cartwright Cemetery	Pine Swamp	16	43:152-56
Town Poor Farm Cemetery	On Hamlin Farm	17	43:157
Pine Cemetery	Sharon to Cornwall Road	18	43:158
Town Poor Farm Cemetery	On farm next to Hamlin Farm	19	43:159
Hatch Farm Cemetery	On Old Hatch Farm	20	43:160-61

Index to Hale inscriptions: 43:162-203.

BURYING GROUNDS OF SHARON, CONNECTICUT, AMENIA AND NORTH EAST, NEW YORK. BEING AN ABSTRACT OF INSCRIPTIONS FROM THIRTY PLACES OF BURIAL IN THE ABOVE NAMED TOWNS. Amenia, N.Y.: Walsh, Griffen and Horpradt Printers, 1903. 248 p. (LDS 4039).

CHURCH RECORDS

CHRIST CHURCH (EPISCOPAL). Minutes, 1809-1932. (CSL, LDS 2069).

FIRST CHURCH OF CHRIST (CONGREGATIONAL). Minutes, 1799-1847. Vital Records, 1755-1879. (CSL, LDS 2068).

HISTORICAL SOCIETY

Sharon Historical Society, Gay-Hoyt House, Main Street, 06069. (203) 364-5688.

LAND RECORDS

Hartford. CSL. Record Group 62. Land Records, 1860-1878.

Land Records, 1739-1865. Index, 1739-1938. (LDS 2066 pt. 1-16).

Proprietor's Records, 1739-1871. (LDS 2065).

Sharon Historical Society. THE ORIGINAL HOME LOTS OF THE TOWN OF SHARON, CONNECTICUT; HISTORY OF THE SALE AND SETTLEMENT OF SHARON TOGETHER WITH A MAP. Sharon, Conn.: 1963. 43 p.

LIBRARY

Hotchkiss Library, Upper Main Street, P.O. Box 277, 06069. (203) 364-5041.

NEWSPAPERS

The PRELIMINARY CHECKLIST lists two newspapers for SHARON.

PROBATE RECORDS

Sharon Probate District, Town Hall, Main Street, 06069. (203) 364-5224.

The Sharon Probate District was organized October 1775 from the Litchfield Probate District.

Probate districts organized from the Sharon Probate District include the Canaan, New Milford and Salisbury Probate Districts.

ON FILE AT THE CSL: Estate Papers, 1755-1939. Indexes, 1755-1939. Inventory Control Book, 1755-1939. Court Record Books, 1757-1855.

Probate Records, 1757-1855. (LDS 2067 pt. 1-10). Indexes. (LDS 22,788).

Burr, Mrs. Sharon A.W. "Sharon (Conn.) Probate Records." TAG 10 (1934): 170-74.

Jacobus, Donald Lines. "Sharon (Conn.) Probate Records." TAG 22 (1946): 192-93.

TAX RECORDS

Hartford. CHS List, 1781-1783, 1786, 1794-1798.

Hartford. CSL, Record Group 62. Lists, 1916-1917, 1919-1928.

VITAL RECORDS

Town Clerk, Town Hall, Main Street, P.O. Box 224, 06069. (203) 364-5224.

The town clerk's earliest birth record is 25 February 1738, marriage record is 1 January 1739 and death record is 22 April 1740.

The BARBOUR INDEX covers the years 1739-1865 and is based on the James N. Arnold copy of SHARON vital records made in 1917.

Van Alstyne, Lawrence. BORN, MARRIED AND DIED IN SHARON, CON-NECTICUT. A RECORD OF BIRTHS, MARRIAGES AND DEATHS IN THE TOWN OF SHARON, CONNECTICUT FROM 1721 TO 1879. Sharon: Author, 1897. 143 p. (LDS 496,869).

PUBLISHED WORKS AND OTHER RECORDS

Benton, Myron B. "The Rose of Sharon." CM 5 (1899): 448-67.

Goodenough, E.F. A GOSSIP ABOUT A COUNTRY PARISH OF THE HILLS AND ITS PEOPLE. Amenia, N.Y.: Times Press, 1900. 129 p.

Jensen, Mrs. Carl. INDEX TO HISTORY OF ELLSWORTH, CONNECTICUT BY G.F. GOODENOUGH, 1900. Typescript. Bloomfield.

"Manufacturing in Sharon." AMERICANA 11 (1916): 197-202, 320-31, 462-68.

Sedgwick, Charles Frederick. GENERAL HISTORY OF THE TOWN OF SHARON, LITCHFIELD COUNTY, CONNECTICUT FROM ITS FIRST SETTLEMENT. Amenia, N.Y.: Charles Walsh, 1898. 204 p.

Van Alstyne, Lawrence. MANUFACTURING IN SHARON. Poconnuck Historical Society Collection, no. 1. Lakeville: Lakeville Journal, 1912.

SHELTON

FAIRFIELD COUNTY. Organized January 1789 from STRATFORD. Name changed from Huntington 15 April 1919.

CEMETERY RECORDS AND CEMETERIES

NAME	ADDRESS	HALE NO.	CITATION
Old Coram Cemetery	540 River Road	1	43:1-2
Riverview Cemetery	Swedish part of Coram Hill Cemetery	2	43:3-4
Riverside Cemetery	308 River Road	3	43:5-35
Upper White Hills Cemetery	North part of town	4	43:36-38
Lower White Hills Cemetery	82 Maple Avenue	5	43:39-47
Long Hill Cemetery	275 Long Hill Avenue	6	44:48-61
Lawn Cemetery	16 Lane Street	7	44:62-71
Congregational Sons of Israel Cemetery	18 Ladas Place	8	44:72
St. Paul Cemetery	Huntington Center	9	44:72A-100
Old Huntington Center Cemetery	38 Church Street	10	44:101-101A

Index to Hale inscriptions: 44:102-31.

Beard, Anna, and Beard, Lavina. MAP AND BURIAL RECORD, HUNTINGTON OLD CEMETERY. N.p., 1974.

CHURCH RECORDS

CONGREGATIONAL CHURCH. Vital Records, 1892-1922. (CSL, LDS 2093).

HUNTINGTON CONGREGATIONAL CHURCH. Minutes, 1717-1946. Vital Records, 1773-1904. (CSL, LDS 2092, pt. 1-2). Marriages, 1773-1800. BAILEY 7:86-92.

ST. PAUL EPISCOPAL CHURCH. Minutes, 1784-1888. Vital Records, 1755-1907. (CSL, LDS 2095). Marriages, 1787-1792. BAILEY 7:14-15.

WHITE HILLS BAPTIST CHURCH. Minutes, 1838-1932. (CSL, LDS 2094).

HISTORICAL SOCIETY

Huntington Historical Society, 70 Ripton Road, P.O. Box 2155, Huntington Station, 06484.

Tree Farm Archives, 272 Israel Hill Road, 06484. (203) 929-0126.

LAND RECORDS

Land Records, 1789-1856. Index, 1789-1901. (LDS 2091 pt. 1-8).

LIBRARY

Plumb Memorial Library, 65 Wooster Street, 06484. (203) 734-3386.

NEWSPAPERS

SUBURBAN NEWS. Weekly. P.O. Box 33, 06484. (203) 735-6424.

The PRELIMINARY CHECKLIST lists five newspapers for SHELTON.

PROBATE RECORDS

Shelton Probate District, Town Hall, 40 White Street, P.O. Box 127, 06484. (203) 734-8462.

> The Shelton Probate District was organized May 1889 from the Bridgeport and Derby Probate Districts.

VITAL RECORDS

Town Clerk, Town Hall, 54 Hill Street, 06484. (203) 736-9231.

The town clerk's earliest birth record is 24 September 1848, marriage record is 11 October 1848 and death record is 25 September 1848.

The BARBOUR INDEX covers the years 1789-1850 and is based on the Irene H. Mix copy of SHELTON vital records made in 1912. It is listed under the original name of Huntington.

PUBLISHED WORKS AND OTHER RECORDS

Gillespie, Charles Bancroft. SOUVENIR HISTORY OF DERBY AND SHELTON, CONNECTICUT. Derby: Transcript Co., 1896. 74 p.

Molloy, Leo Thomas. TERCENTENARY PICTORIAL AND HISTORY OF THE LOWER NAUGATUCK VALLEY. Ansonia: Emerson Bros., 1935. 404 p.

Ward, Jessamine, and Guest, Gladys. TERCENTENARY PICTORIAL AND HISTORY OF THE LOWER NAUGATUCK VALLEY. Index. Typescript. 123 p.

White Hills Civic Club. THE WHITE HILLS OF SHELTON. Essex: Pequot Press, 1968. 63 p.

SHERMAN

FAIRFIELD COUNTY. Organized October 1802 from NEW FAIRFIELD.

CEMETERY RECORDS AND CEMETERIES

NAME	ADDRESS	HALE NO.	CITATION
Graves Cemetery	Route 39	1	44:1
North Sherman Cemetery	Church Road	2	44:2-16
Center Cemetery	Route 37	3	44:17-31
Leach Cemetery	Leach Hollow, near Creek Bridge	4	44:32-35
Graveyard Cemetery	On farm of Stevens Constable west side of Creek Pond	5	44:32-35
Wanzer Cemetery	Near Mauwehoo Lake	6	44:36
Pepper Cemetery	Near Mauwehoo Lake	7	44:36
Old Graveyard	Near Sherman Center, moved	8	44:46
Briggs Cemetery	On Mrs. Walsh's farm	9	44:47
Hungerford Cemetery	On the Irwin Atchinson Farm	10	44:48-49

Index to Hale inscriptions: 44:50-63.

Frost, Josephine C. CEMETERY INSCRIPTIONS FROM SHERMAN, CONNECT-ICUT. Brooklyn: Author, 1912. 118 p. Index. (LDS 2042).

Platt, Wilford C. "Inscriptions from Gravestones in Lieutenant Henry Bennett's Burying Ground in Sherman, Connecticut." CQ 4 (1898): 114-333.

CHURCH RECORDS

CONGREGATIONAL CHURCH. Minutes, 1786–1949. Vital Records, 1799–1949. (CSL, LDS 2044).

NORTH CONGREGATIONAL CHURCH. Minutes, 1744–1777, 1782–1921. Vital Records, 1744–1881. (CSL, LDS 2044). Records, 1744–1921. Index. Records, 1799–1941. Index. (CSL).

HISTORICAL SOCIETY

Sherman Historical Society, P.O. Box 293, 06784.

LAND RECORDS

Land Records, 1803–1855. Index, 1804–1931. (LDS 2043 pt. 1–4).

LIBRARY

Sherman Library, Route 37, 06784. (203) 354–2455.

NEWSPAPER

The PRELIMINARY CHECKLIST lists one newspaper for SHERMAN.

PROBATE RECORDS

Sherman Probate District, Town Hall, Sherman Center, 06784. (203) 355–1821.

The Sherman Probate District was organized 4 June 1846 from the New Milford Probate District.

ON FILE AT THE CSL: Estate Papers, 1846–1946. Indexes, 1846–1946. Inventory Control Book, 1846–1946.

VITAL RECORDS

Town Clerk, Town Hall, Sherman Center, 06784. (203) 354–5281.

The town clerk's earliest birth record is 1852, marriage and death records 1853.

The BARBOUR INDEX covers the years 1802–1850 and is based on the James N. Arnold copy of SHERMAN vital records made in 1917.

Eardeley, William A.D. "Record of Marriages by Ephraim Hubbell, Justice of the Peace in the North Society of New Fairfield, at the time of all the following marriages, but now the town of Sherman, Connecticut." NYGBR 39 (1908): 213-17.

PUBLISHED WORKS AND OTHER RECORDS

Rogers, Ruth. HISTORICAL LANDMARKS IN THE TOWN OF SHERMAN, CONNECTICUT. Quaker Hill Series, no. 17. Quaker Hills, N.Y.: Quaker Hill Conference Association, 1907. 26 p.

SIMSBURY

HARTFORD COUNTY. Organized May 1670. Towns organized from SIMSBURY include CANTON and GRANBY.

CEMETERY RECORDS AND CEMETERIES

NAME	ADDRESS	HALE NO.	CITATION
Hop Meadow (or Center) Cemetery	759 Hopmeadow Street	1	44:1-82
Bushy Hill Cemetery	2 Wildwood Road	2	44:83-86
Town Farm Cemetery	Between Simsbury and Tariffville	3	44:87
Non-Sectarian (or Tariffville) Cemetery	76 Winthrop Street	4	44:88-101
St. Bernard Roman Catholic Cemetery	70 Winthrop Street	5	44:102-23
Russell Cemetery	Next to raod east of Simsbury Cemetery	6	44:124-25

Index to Hale inscriptions: 44:126-59.

"Connecticut Headstone Inscriptions Before 1800 (Hale)." CN 10 (1977-78): 414, 592-95.

CHURCH RECORDS

METHODIST CHURCH. Vital Records, 1857-1926. (CSL, LDS 2059).

PRESBYTERIAN CHURCH. Sessional Minutes and Register, 1844-1860. (Presbyterian Historical Society, LDS 468,364).

TRINITY EPISCOPAL CHURCH. Vital Records, 1849-1936. (CSL, LDS 2060).

Bates, Albert Carlos. RECORDS OF REV. ROGER VIETS, RECTOR OF ST. ANDREWS, SIMSBURY, CONNECTICUT, 1763-1800. Hartford: Case, Lockwood and Brainard, 1893. 84 p.

_____. REV. DUDLEY WOODBRIDGE, HIS CHURCH RECORD AT SIMSBURY, IN CONNECTICUT, 1697-1710. Hartford, Conn.: Case, Lockwood and Brainard Co., 1894. 32 p.

Index Cards to Simsbury First Church and St. Andrews Church Records. (CSL, LDS 1448, pt. 8).

HISTORICAL SOCIETY

Simsbury Historical Society, 800 Hopmeadow Street, 06070. (203) 658-2500.

Publishes ECHO II.

LAND RECORDS

Land Records, 1666-1860. Index, 1666-1850. (LDS 2057 pt. 1-20).

LIBRARY

Simsbury Public Library, 749 Hopmeadow Street, 06070. (203) 658-5382.

NEWSPAPER

FARMINGTON VALLEY HERALD. Weekly. 1 Old Mill Lane, 06070. (203) 658-4471.

The PRELIMINARY CHECKLIST lists one newspaper for SIMSBURY.

PROBATE RECORDS

Simsbury Probate District, Town Office Building, 760 Hopmeadow Street, P.O. Box 454, 06070. (203) 651-3751.

> The Simsbury Probate District was organized May 1769 from the Hartford Probate District.

> Probate Districts organized from the Simsbury Probate District include the Canton, Granby, New Hartford, and Norfolk Probate Districts.

> ON FILE AT THE CSL: Estate Papers, 1769-1906. Indexes, 1769-

1906. Inventory Control Book, 1769-1906. Court Record Book, 1769-1852.

Probate Records, 1769-1852. (LDS 2058 pt. 1-7).

TAX RECORDS

Hartford. CSL, Record Group 62. Tax Lists, 1778-1811. Assessor's Books, 1807-1812, 1841-1844.

VITAL RECORDS

Town Clerk, Town Office Building, 760 Hopmeadow Street, 06070. (203) 658-4455.

The BARBOUR INDEX covers the years 1670-1855 and is based on Albert C. Bates' SIMSBURY, CONNECTICUT BIRTHS (see below) and on Percy E. Hulbert's copy of SIMSBURY vital records made in 1927.

"Connecticut Births Before 1730 (Barbour)--Town of Simsbury." CN 9 (1976-77): 338-40, 504-09; 10 (1977): 13-18, 212-14.

Bates, Albert Carlos. SIMSBURY, CONNECTICUT BIRTHS, MARRIAGES AND DEATHS TRANSCRIBED FROM THE TOWN RECORDS. Hartford: Case, Lockwood and Brainard, 1898. 345 p. (LDS 896,756).

PUBLISHED WORKS AND OTHER RECORDS

Barber, Lucius Israel. A RECORD AND DOCUMENTARY HISTORY OF SIMSBURY. Simsbury: Abigail Phelps Chapter, DAR, 1974. 429 p.

"A Colonial Ecclesiastical Suit." CQ 2 (1896): 286-87.

Ellsworth, John Edwards. SIMSBURY, BEING A BRIEF HISTORICAL SKETCH OF ANCIENT AND MODERN SIMSBURY 1642-1935. Simsbury: Simsbury Committee for the Tercentenary, 1935. 190 p.

HISTORIC SIMSBURY HOMES: FIFTY HOMES DATING FROM THE COLONIAL ERA 1717-1834. Simsbury: Simsbury Historical Society, n.d.

McLean, John B. "Simsbury." CQ 1 (1895): 141-50.

Phelps, Noah Amherst. HISTORY OF SIMSBURY, GRANBY AND CANTON FROM 1642 TO 1845. Hartford: Case, Lockwood and Brainard, Co., 1845. 176 p. (LDS, 897,329).

Vibert, William M. THREE CENTURIES OF SIMSBURY. Simsbury: Simsbury Tercentenary Committee, 1970. 272 p.

SOMERS

TOLLAND COUNTY. Organized July 1734. Part of Massachusetts until May 1749.

CEMETERY RECORDS AND CEMETERIES

NAME	ADDRESS	HALE NO.	CITATION
West Cemetery	1/2 mile west of Center	1	44:1-58
North Cemetery	1/2 mile north of Center	2	44:59-99
South Cemetery	Same as North Cemetery	3	44:59-99

Index to Hale inscriptions: 44:100-28.

Dewey, Louis Marinus. "Inscriptions from Old Cemeteries in Connecticut." NEHGR 60 (1906): 307-8.

CENSUS RECORDS

Hartford. CSL, Record Group 62. Census of all males, 1852-1854.

CHURCH RECORDS

CONGREGATIONAL CHURCH. Minutes, 1822-1884. Vital Records, 1727-1890. (CSL, LDS 2076). Marriages, 1727-1799. BAILEY 5:90-99. Records, 1727-1890. Index. (CSL).

SOMERVILLE CONGREGATIONAL CHURCH. Minutes 1871-1939. Index. (CSL, LDS 2077). Index 1871-1939. (CSL).

HISTORICAL SOCIETY

Somers Historical Society, Inc., 574 Main Street (Mailing address: 177 Gulf Road), 06071. (203) 749-7273.

LAND RECORDS

Hartford. CSL, Record Group 62. Land Records, 1758-1933.

Land Records, 1729-1854. Index, 1729-1750. (LDS 2075 pt. 1-6).

LIBRARY

Somers Public Library, Main Street, P.O. Box 368, 06071. (203) 749-8845.

MILITARY RECORDS

Barnes, A.T. "Somers, Connecticut Men in the 1762, 'Expedition to the Havanah.'" NEHGR 55 (1901): 109.

Hartford. CSL, Record Group 62. Returns and Reports, 1802-1914. Militia Enrollment Books, 1854-1904. World War I Service Books and Honor Roll, 1917-1919.

PROBATE RECORDS

Somers Probate District, Town Hall, 600 Main Street, 06071. (203) 749-7012.

> The Somers Probate District was organized 3 June 1834 from the Ellington Probate District.

> ON FILE AT THE CSL: Estate Papers, 1834-1941. Indexes, 1834-1941. Inventory Control Book, 1834-1941. Court Record Book, 1834-1851.

Probate Records, 1834-1853. (LDS 2074).

The CSL also has a microfilm copy of the Registry of Probate Court Records for Hampshire County, Massachusetts, which included Somers between 1660-1820.

SCHOOL RECORDS

Hartford. CSL, Record Group 62. Records, Registers, 1796-1936.

TAX RECORDS

Hartford. CSL, Record Group 62. Lists, 1797-1820, 1826. Grand Lists and other records, 1801-1933.

VITAL RECORDS

Town Clerk, Town Hall, 600 Main Street, 06071. (203) 749-8351.

> The town clerk's earliest birth record is 1729, marriage record is 1727 and death record is 1735.

The BARBOUR INDEX covers the years 1734-1850 and is based on the James N. Arnold copy of SOMERS vital records made in 1912.

Hartford. CSL, Record Group 62. Abstracts of vital records, 1852-1897.

VOTER RECORDS

Hartford. CSL, Record Group 62. Lists of electors, 1840-1937. Voter lists, 1838-1844.

PUBLISHED WORKS AND OTHER RECORDS

Davis, Fred Cady. SOMERS, THE HISTORY OF A CONNECTICUT TOWN. Somers: Somers Historical Society, 1973. 92 p.

DeBell, Jeanne K., and Mercier, Judith E. SOMERS, CONNECTICUT, THRU THE CAMERA'S EYE. Somers: Somers Historical Society, 1978. 106 p.

SOUTHBURY

NEW HAVEN COUNTY. Organized May 1787 from WOODBURY. Towns organized from SOUTHBURY include MIDDLEBURY and OXFORD.

CEMETERY RECORDS AND CEMETERIES

NAME	ADDRESS	HALE NO.	CITATION
Pierce Hollow Cemetery	1 mile north of South Britain	1	44:1-12
South Britain Cemetery	South Britain Road	2	44:13-31
George's Hill Cemetery	East of George's Hill	3	44:32
Pine Hill Cemetery	Pine Hill Road	4	44:33-40
White Oak Cemetery	Main Street	5	44:41-55
Sacred Heart Cemetery	Near Woodbury Town Line	6	44:56-58
Warner Cemetery	Wapping District, in front of George Oehler's house	7	44:58:A
French Family Vault	Located between numbers 1 and 2 above	8	44:59
Old Middle Cemetery	Town Center	9	44:60-69
Lone Grave Farm	In Southford section on farm owned by Mr. Udelmesser	10	44:70-71

Index to Hale inscriptions: 44:72-91.

CHURCH RECORDS

CHURCH OF THE EPIPHANY (EPISCOPAL). Vital Records, 1863-1940. (CSL, LDS 2105).

CONGREGATIONAL CHURCH RECORDS. Minutes, 1732-1778. Vital Records, 1759-1922. (CSL, LDS 2105).

METHODIST EPISCOPAL CHURCH. Vital Records, 1847-1938. (CSL, LDS 2105).

MISSION OF THE GOOD SHEPHERD. Vital Records, 1921-1929. (CSL, LDS 2103).

SOUTH BRITAIN CONGREGATIONAL CHURCH. Minutes, 1766-1884. Vital Records, 1808-1851. (CSL, LDS 2104).

Southbury Church Records (NHCHS, LDS 1455 pt. 31).

Hartford. CSL, Card Drawer 51. Record of Southbury Baptisms, Dimissions and Deaths.

Pastor's Record Book Kept by Rev. John Hartwell, Southbury, Connecticut 1872-1878. (CSL, LDS 3559).

HISTORICAL SOCIETY

Southbury Historical Society, Inc. 06488.

LAND RECORDS

Land Records, 1786-1882. Index 1786-1882. (LDS 2102 pt. 1-8).

LIBRARY

Southbury Public Library, Main Street, P.O. Box 414, 06488. (203) 264-6373.

MILITARY RECORDS

Mitchell, Mrs. Frank H. "A Southbury (Conn.) Militia Company, 1774." TAG 19 (1942): 21-22.

NEWSPAPER

VOICES. Weekly. P.O. Box 383, 06488. (203) 263-2116.

The PRELIMINARY CHECKLIST lists one newspaper for SOUTHBURY.

PROBATE RECORDS

Southbury Probate District, Town Hall, Peter Road, P.O. Box 674, 06488. (203) 264-0606.

> The Southbury Probate District was organized 4 January 1967 from the Woodbury Probate District.

SCHOOL RECORDS

Hartford. CSL, Record Group 62. Records, 1788-1909.

TAX RECORDS

Hartford. CSL, Record Group 62. Tax Lists, 1791-1929.

VITAL RECORDS

Town Clerk, Town Hall, Peter Road, P.O. Box 155, 06488. (203) 264-8682.

> The town clerk's earliest birth record is 1755, marriage record is 1760, death record is 1725.

The BARBOUR INDEX covers the years 1787-1830 and is based on the James N. Arnold copy of SOUTHBURY vital records made in 1915.

The book, HISTORY OF ANCIENT WOODBURY (see below) by William Cothren includes a section of SOUTHBURY vital records, pp. 427-527.

PUBLISHED WORKS AND OTHER RECORDS

Clark, Howard. SAGA OF POMPERAUG PLANTATION; 1673-1973. Southbury: Southbury Tercentennial Committee, 1973. 77 p.

Cothren, William. HISTORY OF ANCIENT WOODBURY, CONNECTICUT, FROM THE FIRST INDIAN DEED IN 1659 TO 1854. INCLUDING THE PRESENT TOWNS OF WASHINGTON, SOUTHBURY, BETHLEHEM, ROXBURY, AND A PART OF OXFORD AND MIDDLEBURY. Waterbury: Bronson Brothers, 1854. 841 p. (LDS 2205).

Sharpe, William Carvosso. SOUTH BRITAIN SKETCHES AND RECORDS. Seymour: Record Print, 1898. 167 p.

WPA Historical Records Survey. INVENTORY OF THE TOWN AND CITY ARCHIVES OF CONNECTICUT, NO. 5, NEW HAVEN COUNTY, VOL. 8. NORTH BRANFORD, NORTH HAVEN, ORANGE, OXFORD, PROSPECT, SEYMOUR, SOUTHBURY. New Haven: Historical Records Survey, 1938. 189 p. (LDS 897-354).

SOUTHINGTON

HARTFORD COUNTY. Organized October 1779 from FARMINGTON. Towns organized from SOUTHINGTON include WOLCOTT.

CEMETERY RECORDS AND CEMETERIES

NAME	ADDRESS	HALE NO.	CITATION
South End Cemetery	South End Road	1	44:1-42
Oak Hill Cemetery	North Main Street	2	44:43-140
St. Thomas Roman Catholic Cemetery	331 Meriden Avenue	3	44:141-60 45:161-83
Quinnipiac Cemetery	Marion Avenue	4	45:184-235
Mount Vernon Cemetery	West Center Street	5	45:236-39
Wonx Spring Cemetery	591 Marion Avenue	6	45:240-53
Merriam Cemetery	Near Wonx Spring Cemetery	7	45:254-55
Holy Trinity Cemetery	Prospect Street	8	45:256-57
Bradley Graveyard	East part of town, on mountain	9	45:258
Dunham Cemetery	Queen Street	10	45:259
Barnabas Power's Yard	Near home of Adriah Neal	11	45:260
Bunce Yard	Near Homes Bunce home	12	45:261
St. Mary Roman Catholic Cemetery	Next to St. Mary Roman Catholic Church	13	45:262
Immaculate Conception Roman Catholic Cemetery	South End Road	14	45:263-64

Index to Hale inscriptions: 45:265-328.

Upson, W., and Deion, Mrs. Walter. INSCRIPTIONS IN THE GRAVEYARD SOUTH OF WONX SPRINGS CEMETERY, SOUTHINGTON, CONNECTICUT CALLED THE MERRIMAN BURYING GROUND. N.p.: Hannah Worthington Chapter, DAR, 1928. 3 p.

CHURCH RECORDS

FIRST CONGREGATIONAL CHURCH. Minutes, 1728-1837, 1876-1930. Vital Records, 1779-1876. (CSL, LDS 2063). Records, 1728-1876. Index. (CSL, LDS 1448 pt. 27-28).

ST. PAUL EPISCOPAL CHURCH. Minutes 1919-1941. Vital Records 1876-1939.

Miscellaneous Church Records (NHCHS, LDS 1455).

Timlow, Heman Rowlee. ECCLESIASTICAL AND OTHER SKETCHES OF SOUTHINGTON, CONNECTICUT. Hartford: Case, Lockwood and Brainard, Co., 1875. 570 p.

HISTORICAL SOCIETY

Southington Historical Society, 06489.

LAND RECORDS

Land Records, 1779-1851. Index, 1779-1862. (LDS 2061 pt. 1-10).

LIBRARY

Southington Public Library, 255 Main Street, 06489. (203) 628-0947.

NEWSPAPERS

The PRELIMINARY CHECKLIST lists eight newspapers for SOUTHINGTON.

PROBATE RECORDS

Southington Probate District, Town Office Building, 75 Main Street, P.O. Box 165, 06489. (203) 628-5903.

> The Southington Probate District was organized 24 May 1825 from the Farmington Probate District.

ON FILE AT THE CSL: Estate Papers, 1825-1907. Indexes, 1825-1907. Inventory Control Books, 1825-1907. Court Record Books, 1825-1851.

Probate Records, 1825-1851. (LDS 2062).

TAX RECORDS

Hartford. CSL, Record Group 62. Abstracts, 1792 and undated.

VITAL RECORDS

Town Clerk, Town Office Building, 75 Main Street, P.O. Drawer 152, 06489. (203) 628-5523.

The BARBOUR INDEX covers the years 1658-1857 and is based on an index to SOUTHINGTON vital records made by Louis H. Von Sahler and Percy E. Hulbert.

PUBLISHED WORKS AND OTHER RECORDS

Atwater, Francis. HISTORY OF SOUTHINGTON, CONNECTICUT. Meriden: Journal Press, 1924. 549 p.

Newell, Elisha A. "Glimpses of Southington, Past and Present." CM 6 (1900): 3-16.

Roys, Mrs. Nancy Cowles. "Early Reflections of Mrs. Nancy Roys--Born in 1792." CM 10 (1906): 77-79.

SOUTH WINDSOR

HARTFORD COUNTY. Organized May 1845 from EAST WINDSOR.

CEMETERY RECORDS AND CEMETERIES

NAME	ADDRESS	HALE NO.	CITATION
Center South Windsor Cemetery	Main Street	1	45:1-40
Old South Windsor	On Main Highway next to Masonic Temple	2	45:41-57
East Windsor Hill Cemetery	Off Main Highway, rear of Dixieland building	3	45:58-63
Watson lot Cemetery	In lot north of East Windsor Hill	4	45:64
Rye Street Cemetery	Broad Brook Highway	5	45:65-66
Old Wapping Cemetery	Rear of Church at Wapping	6	45:67-79
New Wapping Cemetery	1/4 mile east of Church at Wapping	7	45:80-110
Single Graves	King Street	8	(no citation)
Dog Cemetery	On Troy farm, 3/4 mile east of Wapping	9	(no citation)

Index to Hale inscriptions: 45:111-40.

Benton, Mrs. Frederick H. "Cemetery at the First Congregational Church, South Windsor." In CEMETERY RECORDS, pp. 28-41. (LDS 850,401).

DAR Wisconsin Genealogical Records Committee. "Cemetery Records of . . . South Windsor, Connecticut . . . ." BIBLE AND CEMETERY RECORDS, 1800-1940. (LDS 848,696).

Elmore, Durary Janette. SOUTH WINDSOR CEMETERY INSCRIPTIONS FROM THE EARLIEST INSCRIPTION TO 1900; THE INSCRIPTIONS OF THE CEME- TERIES IN SOUTH WINDSOR, EAST WINDSOR HILL AND WAPPING, OLD AND NEW CEMETERIES. Hartford: Author, 1920.

CHURCH RECORDS

FIRST CONGREGATIONAL CHURCH. Minutes, 1694-1898. Vital Records, 1736-1854. (CSL, LDS 2087).

SECOND CONGREGATIONAL CHURCH. Minutes, 1861-1881. Vital Records, 1830-1936. (CSL, LDS 2089).

WAPPING FEDERATED CHURCH. Records, 1924-1936. (CSL, LDS 2089).

WAPPING METHODIST EPISCOPAL CHURCH. Vital Records, 1843-1936. (CSL, LDS 2079).

HISTORICAL SOCIETY

South Windsor Historical Society, 06074.

LAND RECORDS

Land Records, 1841-1878. (LDS 2078).

LIBRARY

South Windsor Public Library, 993 Sullivan Avenue, 06074. (203) 644-1541.

NEWSPAPER

The PRELIMINARY CHECKLIST lists one newspaper for SOUTH WINDSOR.

PROBATE RECORDS

SOUTH WINDSOR is in the East Windsor Probate District.

SCHOOL RECORDS

Hartford. CSL, Record Group 62. Registers, Records, 1814-1913.

TAX RECORDS

Hartford. CSL, Record Group 62. Abstracts, Abatements, Liens, 1845-1920.

VITAL RECORDS

Town Clerk, Town Hall, 1540 Sullivan Avenue, 06074. (203) 644-2511, ext. 10.

The BARBOUR INDEX covers the years 1845-1851 and is based on the Percy E. Hulbert copy of SOUTH WINDSOR vital records made in 1927.

VOTER RECORDS

Hartford. CSL, Record Group 62. Electors and applicants lists, 1904-1922.

PUBLISHED WORKS AND OTHER RECORDS

Elmore, Mary Janette. LONG HILL, SOUTH WINDSOR, CONNECTICUT. "REMINISCENCES:" A FAMILY RECORD OF EARLY AMERICAN LIFE. South Windsor, Conn.: South Windsor Historical Society, 1976. 125 p.

Starr, Mary Seabury. "The Home of Timothy and Jonathan Edwards." CQ 4 (1896): 33-43.

Stiles, Henry Reed. A SUPPLEMENT TO THE HISTORY AND GENEALOGIES OF ANCIENT WINDSOR. CONTAINING CORRECTIONS AND ADDITIONS. Albany: J. Munsell, 1863. 134 p.

_____. THE HISTORY AND GENEALOGIES OF ANCIENT WINDSOR, CON-NECTICUT. INCLUDING EAST WINDSOR, SOUTH WINDSOR, BLOOMFIELD, WINDSOR LOCKS AND ELLINGTON 1635-1891. 2 vols. Hartford: Case, Lockwood and Brainard, 1891. (LDS 417,935).

SPRAGUE

NEW LONDON COUNTY. Organized May 1861 from FRANKLIN and LISBON.

CEMETERY RECORDS AND CEMETERIES

NAME	ADDRESS	HALE NO.	CITATION
Lovett Cemetery	Versailles	1	45:1-5
New Hanover Cemetery	Hanover	2	45:6-18
St. Mary Roman Catholic Cemetery	Baltic	3	45:19-39
Old Hanover Cemetery	Hanover	4	45:40-50
Old Lovett-Parkins Cemetery	Near Lovett Cemetery	5	45:51-52

Index to Hale inscriptions: 45:53-68.

CHURCH RECORDS

CONGREGATIONAL CHURCH. Records, 1760-1899. Index. (CSL, LDS).

HISTORICAL SOCIETY

Sprague Historical Association, 06330.

NEWSPAPER

The PRELIMINARY CHECKLIST lists one newspaper for SPRAGUE.

PROBATE RECORDS

SPRAGUE is in the Norwich Probate District.

SCHOOL RECORDS

Hartford. CSL, Record Group 62. Registers, 1902, 1917-1921, 1925-1938.

TAX RECORDS

Hartford. CSL, Record Group 62. Abstracts, 1861-1919.

VITAL RECORDS

Town Clerk, Town Hall, 1 Main Street, 06330. (203) 822-6223.

The town clerk's earliest birth, marriage and death records date from 1861.

STAFFORD

TOLLAND COUNTY. Organized in 1719.

CEMETERY RECORDS AND CEMETERIES

NAME	ADDRESS	HALE NO.	CITATION
Springs Cemetery	Stafford Springs	1	45:1-55
St. Edward Cemetery	Stafford Springs	2	45:56-76
Center Cemetery	West Stafford	3	45:77-85
Old Cemetery	West Stafford Hill	4	45:86-97
Belcher Cemetery	Northeast part of town	5	45:97A-100
Crystal Lake Cemetery	Crystal Lake	6	45:101-7
Hillside Cemetery	Stafford Hollow	7	45:108-24
Staffordville Cemetery	Staffordville	8	45:125-39
Old Stafford Village Cemetery	Stafford Village	9	45:140-47
West Village Cemetery	Village Hill	10	45:148-49
Old Cemetery	Stafford Street	11	45:150-54
New Cemetery	Stafford Street	12	45:155-80
Old Springs Cemetery	Stafford Springs	13	45:181-84
New Cemetery	West Stafford Hill	14	45:185-90
Dimick Cemetery	Near Crystal Lake	15	45:191-93
Woodworth Cemetery	1/2 mile west of West Stafford	16	45:194
Childs Cemetery	Near State Police Station	17	45:195
St. Edwards Cemetery	Catholic Church Yard	18	45:196

NAME	ADDRESS	HALE NO.	CITATION
Washburn Cemetery	Near Haydenville	19	45:197
Davis Cemetery	On Fletcher Farm	20	45:198
Old Bush Farm Cemetery	Wales Road	21	45:199
Merrill Cemetery	Near Grove Hill in woods	22	45:200-201

Index to Hale inscriptions: 45:202-57.

"Cemetery Inscriptions in Stafford, Connecticut, Hill District Cemetery."
NEHGR 101 (1947): 73-75.

Bummer, Mrs. Karl J. "Cemetery Inscriptions in West Stafford, Connecticut."
NEHGR 101 (1947): 255-57.

Eno, Joel Nelson. "Connecticut Cemetery Inscriptions: Stafford Street Old
Cemetery." NEHGR 66 (1912): 39-42.

Chapman, Grace Olive. "Stafford Springs, Connecticut: Cemetery Inscriptions." NEHGR 102 (1948): 151-53.

CHURCH RECORDS

FIRST CONGREGATIONAL CHURCH. Minutes, 1797, 1803-1892. Vital Records, 1757-1817, 1840-1879. (CSL, LDS 2113).

FIRST UNIVERSALIST CHURCH. Minutes, 1814-1917. Vital Records, 1847-
1913. (CSL, LDS 2090).

METHODIST EPISCOPAL CHURCH (CRYSTAL LAKE). Vital Records, 1792-
1894, 1898-1949. (CSL, LDS 2008).

METHODIST EPISCOPAL CHURCH (STAFFORD SPRINGS). Minutes, 1890-
1946. Vital Records, 1866-1944. (CSL, LDS 2086). Minutes, 1844-1866,
1938-1940. Vital Records, 1830-1849. (CSL, LDS 2089).

SECOND CONGREGATIONAL CHURCH. Vital Records, 1780-1848, 1864-
1895. (CSL, LDS 2085).

STAFFORD SPRINGS CONGREGATIONAL CHURCH. Minutes, 1850-1936.
Vital Records, 1850-1900. (CSL, LDS 2112 pt. 1).

STAFFORDVILLE CONGREGATIONAL CHURCH. Minutes, 1852-1941. (CSL,
LDS 2087).

Barlow, Claude W. RECORDS OF THE BAPTIST CHURCH OF STAFFORD,
CONNECTICUT 1809-1909. Worcester, Mass.: 1974. 37 p. Index.

Grobel, Kendrick. HISTORY OF THE FIRST CHURCH OF STAFFORD, CON-
NECTICUT KNOWN AS THE STAFFORD STREET CONGREGATIONAL CHURCH
FROM ITS BIRTH 1723 TO ITS DEATH 1892. Stafford Springs: Women's Coun-
cil of the Congregational Church, 1942. 87 p. Index.

HISTORICAL SOCIETY

Stafford Historical Society, P.O. Box 56, 06075. (203) 684-7244.

LAND RECORDS

Land Records, 1727-1852. Indexed. (LDS 2083 pt. 1-14).

The CSL has a microfilm copy of STAFFORD land records from 1727-1852,
1894-1938, and a card file index to them.

LIBRARY

Stafford Public Library, 5 Spring Street, 06076. (203) 684-2852.

NEWSPAPERS

THE STAFFORD PRESS. Weekly. P.O. Box 26, 06076. (203) 684-2306.

The PRELIMINARY CHECKLIST lists four newspapers for STAFFORD.

The HALE NEWSPAPER INDEX to death and marriage notices includes the
STAFFORD NEWS & PALMER JOURNAL. Deaths 20 April 1850-27 December
1867; Marriages 6 April 1850-27 December 1867.

PROBATE RECORDS

Stafford Probate District, Town Hall, P.O. Box 63, 06076. (203) 684-3423.
> The Stafford Probate District was organized May 1759 from the
> Hartford and Pomfret Probate Districts.
>
> ON FILE AT THE CSL: Estate Papers, 1759-1933. Indexes, 1759-
> 1933. Inventory Control Book, 1759-1933. Court Record Books,
> 1759-1852.

The Stafford Probate District also includes the town of UNION.

Probate districts formed from the Stafford Probate District include the East Windsor, Ellington and Tolland Probate Districts.

SCHOOL RECORDS

Witt, Earl M. HISTORY OF THE SCHOOLS OF STAFFORD, CONNECTICUT. Stafford: Stafford Teachers Club, 1946. 100 p.

TAX RECORDS

Hartford. CSL, Record Group 62. Lists, 1879-1883, 1892. (B-C only) Tax Collector's Book, 1896.

VITAL RECORDS

Town Clerk, Town Hall, P.O. Box 11, 06076. (203) 684-2532.

> The town clerk's earliest birth record is 3 September 1709, marriage record is 6 October 1708 and death record is 11 August 1730.

The BARBOUR INDEX covers the years 1719-1850 and is based on the James N. Arnold copy of STAFFORD vital records made in 1912.

Hartford. CSL, Record Group 62. Vital Records, 1848-1895.

Smith, Philip M. "Marriages by Justice Foote, Stafford, Connecticut." TAG 13 (1937): 248-49.

VOTER RECORDS

Hartford. CSL, Record Group 62. Lists of Electors, 1894, 1896.

PUBLISHED WORKS AND OTHER RECORDS

Manion, Helen Rose. "Admitted Freemen, between the years 1775 and 1783, Town of Stafford, Connecticut." NGSQ 15 (1927): 4-8.

STAFFORD HISTORICAL HIGHLIGHTS 1776-1976. Stafford: Stafford Heritage Committee, 1976. 74 p.

STAMFORD

FAIRFIELD COUNTY. Organized 1641. Towns organized from STAMFORD include DARIEN and NEW CANAAN.

CEMETERY RECORDS AND CEMETERIES

NAME	ADDRESS	HALE NO.	CITATION
Woodland Cemetery (Old)	536 Bedford Street (moved)	1	46:1
Simsbury Cemetery	North Stamford Avenue	2	46:2-3
Old Cemetery	Roxbury Road	3	46:4
Temple Beth El Cemetery	360 Roxbury Road	4	46:5-11
Roxbury Cemetery	514 Roxbury Road	5	46:12-23
Westover Cemetery	571 Westover Road	6	46:24-25
Palmer Hill Cemetery	Between Westover and Palmer Hill Road	7	46:26
Stillwater Road Cemetery #1	Stillwater Road	8	46:27
Stillwater Road Cemetery #2	Stillwater Road	9	46:28
Northfield Cemetery	110 North Street	10	46:29-49
St. Andrew Episcopal Church Cemetery	42 Franklin Street	11	46:50-74
St. John Episcopal Church Cemetery	42 Franklin Street	12	46:50-74
West Stamford Cemetery	Greenwich Avenue	13	46:75-80
Long Ridge Cemetery	170 Erskine Road	14	46:81-114
High Ridge Cemetery	2970 High Ridge Road	15	46:115-40

NAME	ADDRESS	HALE NO.	CITATION
North Stamford Cemetery	Lakeside Drive	16	46:141-50
Scofieldtown and Lockwood Cemetery #4	365 Scofieldtown Road	17	46:151-53
Turn of River Cemetery	195 Turn of River Road	18	46:154-55
Newfield Cemetery	1600 Newfield Avenue	19	46:156-60
Belltown Cemetery	118 Toms Road	20	46:161
Scofield Cemetery #1	976 Hope Street	21	46:162
Emmanuel Chapel Cemetery	977 Hope Street	22	46:163-70
Hoyt Cemetery #1	Hope Street	23	46:171
Brush Cemetery	East Middle Patent Road, 1/2 mile from New York State line	24	46:172
Rundle (same as #44) Cemetery	Farms Roads	25	46:173
Hoyt Cemetery #2	Hope Street	26	46:174
Green Cemetery	Hope Street, next to Hoyt Cemetery	27	46:175-76
Agudath-Sholom Cemetery	600 West Hill Road	28	46:177
Woodland Cemetery (New)	54 Woodland Place (203) 323-2681	29	46:178-342
Smith Cemetery	Near Roxbury Cemetery	30	46:343
Scofield (same as #2) Cemetery	North Stamford Avenue	31	46:344
Knapp Cemetery	Stillwater Road, south of Roxbury School	32	46:345
June Cemetery	Junction of Bengal and Den Roads	33	46:346
Scofield Cemetery #3	526 Haviland Road	34	46:347
Dean (same as #53) Cemetery	Scofieldtown Road	35	46:348
Hebard (same as #49) Cemetery	Turn of River Union Church Old North Stamford Road	36	46:349
Belltown Cemetery #2	35 Oaklawn Avenue	37	46:350
Hunting Ridge Cemetery #1	East Hunting Ridge Road corner of Haviland Road	38	46:351
Webb's Hill Cemetery	287 Webb's Hill Road	39	46:352

NAME	ADDRESS	HALE NO.	CITATION
Hunting Ridge #2	Hunting Ridge Road	40	46:353
Lockwood Cemetery #1	Long Ridge Road, 1/2 mile north of Roxbury School	41	46:354
Hunting Ridge Cemetery #3	West side of Hunting Ridge Road, opposite Haviland Road	42	46:355
Lockwood Cemetery #2	Riverbank Road	43	46:356
Hait Cemetery (same as #25)	Farms Road	44	46:375
Hoyt-Miller Cemetery	In woods east side of Stanwich Road, south of East Middle Patent Road	45	46:358
Lockwood Cemetery (same as #24)	In orchard 1/8 mile from Riverbank Road. Road opposite junction of Farms Road	46	46:359
Scofield Cemetery #4	Newfield Avenue above Weed Avenue	47	46:360
Lockwood Cemetery #4 (same as #17)	Junction High Ridge Road and Scofieldtown Road	48	46:361
Hebard Cemetery (same as #36)	Turn of River Union Church Old North Stamford Road	49	46:362
Knapp Cemetery	Sherwood Homestead, North Stamford Road	50	46:363
Weed Cemetery #1	Cedar Heights Road and Wire Mill Road	51	46:364
Lockwood Cemetery #5	Cedar Heights Road, rear of Yellow Farm	52	46:365
Dean Cemetery (same as #35)	Scofieldtown Road near Wall Homestead	53	46:366
Smith Cemetery	Riverbank Road opposite Revolutionary Rock	54	46:367
Weed Cemetery	On H.I. Dan's farm, North Stamford Road	55	46:368-69
Fairfield Memorial Park	230 Oaklawn Avenue (203) 325-1315	56	(no citation)

Index to Hale inscriptions: 46:370-463.

"Connecticut Headstone Inscriptions Before 1800--Town of Stamford." CN 7 (1975): 508-12.

Eardeley, William A.D. CONNECTICUT CEMETERIES. Vols. 4, 5, 6, 7, 8, 9. Brooklyn, N.Y.: Author, 1916. (LDS 899,935).

Hale, Charles R. HALE COLLECTION. HEADSTONE INSCRIPTIONS. TOWN OF STAMFORD. Hartford: Author, 1939. 381 p. (LDS 899,935).

Majdalany, Jeanne, and Mulkerin, Jean. POEMS ON STONE IN STAMFORD, CONNECTICUT. Stanford: Stamford Historical Society, 1980. 188 p. Index.

Morrell, Samuel W. "My Search for Veteran's Graves." STAMFORD HISTOR-IAN 1 (1957): 135-38.

Putcamp, Luise, Jr. "Memorial Service in the Making. (Long Ridge Memorial Cemetery)." ADVOCATE 2 June 1979, p. A8.

CHURCH RECORDS

FIRST CONGREGATIONAL CHURCH. Minutes, 1836-1907. Vital Records, 1747-1890. (CSL, LDS 2048). Marriages, 1747-1800. BAILEY 6:247-56.

METHODIST EPISCOPAL CHURCH. Minutes, 1838-1896. Vital Records, 1788. (CSL, LDS 2049).

NORTH STAMFORD CONGREGATIONAL CHURCH. Minutes, 1782-1962. Vital Records, 1854-1928. (CSL, LDS 2050).

ST. JOHN EPISCOPAL CHURCH. Registry Book, 1742-1746. (CSL, LDS 2107). Marriages, 1758-1800. BAILEY 7:15-21.

Buczek, Daniel S. "Ethnic to American: Holy Name of Jesus Parish, Stam-ford, Connecticut." POLISH AMERICAN STUDIES 37 (Autumn 1980): 1-32.

Daniels, Nina W. REFLECTIONS . . . UNION BAPTIST CHURCH. Stamford: Union Baptist Church, 1978. Unpaged.

Eardeley, William A.D. "Marriages on Records of St. John's Protestant Epis-copal Church, Stamford and Greenwich." CQ 4 (1898): 115-16, 332-33.

_____. STAMFORD RECORDS OF THE CONGREGATIONAL CHURCH (1746-1846). 6 vols. Brooklyn, N.Y.: Author, 1914. (LDS 899,936).

Koenig, Samuel. AN AMERICAN JEWISH COMMUNITY: THE STORY OF THE JEWS IN STAMFORD, CONNECTICUT. N.p.: Author, 1940. (CSL Archives RG 33 Box 102).

McGown, Russell M. "Rippowam Ripples--a Story of the Relations of Church and Town in the Beginning of Stamford." STAMFORD HISTORIAN 1 (1957): 111-16.

McLean, Louise. "The Middlesex Society of Friends." DARIEN HISTORICAL SOCIETY ANNUAL, 1973, pp. 4-10.

Mead, Spencer Percival. ABSTRACT OF CHURCH RECORDS OF THE TOWN OF STAMFORD, COUNTY OF FAIRFIELD; AND STATE OF CONNECTICUT, FROM THE EARLIEST RECORDS EXTANT TO 1850. Greenwich: Author, 1924. 499 p. (LDS 899,936).

SEVENTY FIVE YEARS CHURCH AND A PEOPLE. Charlotte, N.C.: Delmar Co., 1979. 176 p.

Wicks, Edith M. "Journal of Reverend F.M. Ayres 14 October 1879 Long Ridge, Connecticut." CA 18 (1976): 79-80.

_____. "Pastor's Record for Private Use. Arranged by Rev. W.T. Beatly." CA 18 (1976): 81-83.

GENEALOGICAL SOCIETY

The Stamford Genealogical Society, P.O. Box 249, Stamford, 06904.

Publishes CONNECTICUT ANCESTRY. Vol. 14. No. 2, November 1971-- . Quarterly. Formerly known as: The BULLETIN OF THE STAMFORD GENEA-LOGICAL SOCIETY. 1958-1971. Entire collection is kept at the Ferguson Library in Stamford.

Carder, Robert Webster, and Hubbell, Harold Berresford, Jr. INDEX: BULLE-TIN OF THE STAMFORD GENEALOGICAL SOCIETY, Volumes 1-5, 1958-1963. Stamford: Stamford Genealogical Society, 1963. 23 p.

Ralston, Mrs. Lloyd W. SUBJECT AND NAME INDEXES TO VOLUMES 6-13 (1963-1971) OF THE BULLETIN OF THE STAMFORD GENEALOGICAL SOCI-ETY. Stamford: Stamford Genealogical Society, 1974. 76 p.

Wicks, Edith M. "Query Name Index." CA 22 (November 1979): 73-88; 22 (February 1980): 149-55; 22 (May 1980): 183-94; 23 (September 1980): 45-49; 23 (November 1980): 99-103.

_____. "Stamford Genealogical Society." STAMFORD HISTORIAN 1, no. 2 (1957): 184-85.

HISTORICAL SOCIETY

Stamford Historical Society, 713 Bedford Street, 06901. (203) 323-1975.

Published STAMFORD HISTORIAN, 1954-57.

"Catalogue of the Permanent Collection of the Stamford Historical Society." STAMFORD HISTORIAN 1 (1954): 76-79, 171-72.

Gershman, Elizabeth, and Pendery, Joyce. "Woman at Work: How Stamford's Exhibit Traces the Professional Development of Women." HISTORY NEWS 35 (August 1980): 12-14.

Hilliard, Mary P. "Contributions of the Historical Society to Stamford." STAMFORD HISTORIAN 1 (1954): 70-79.

Mead, B.H. "Acquisition of the Betsy Barnum Home." STAMFORD HISTORIAN 1 (1954): 19-20.

Otto, Robert W. "History of the Stamford Historical Society Especially the First Twenty Years." STAMFORD HISTORIAN 1 (1954): 21-36.

LAND RECORDS

Land Records, 1630-1852. (LDS 2047 pt. 1-19).

Fuller, Clement A. "History of the Southern Commons or Sequest Land in Stamford, Connecticut Part I." STAMFORD HISTORIAN 1 (1954): 41-56.

Sinnott, Edward W., Jr. "Indian Deeds and Related Documents of Stamford." LEAGUE BULLETIN 19 (1967): 13-15.

Wicks, Edith M. "Genealogical References in Stamford Land Records Vols. A Through G. 1666-1767." CA 18 (1976): 119-28; 19 (1976-77): 11-20, 63-72, 108-18, 165-74; 20 (1977-78): 11-20, 75-84, 133-42, 188-96; 21 (1978-79): 8-18, 77-88, 131-40, 177-86; 22 (1979): 13-22, 55-67.

LIBRARY

Ferguson Library, 96 Broad Street, 06901. (203) 964-1000.

Kemp, Thomas Jay. GENEALOGIES IN THE FERGUSON LIBRARY. Stamford, Conn.: Little Factory Press, 1981. 143 p.

MILITARY RECORDS

"Border Country: No-one in Horseneck, Stamford or Middlesex was safe from British Raiders." FAIRFIELD COUNTY 5 (December 1975): 60-61, 122-24.

Clark, Henry Austin. "A Connecticut Revolutionary Roll." NEHGR 50 (1896): 31.

Hodge, Harriett Woodbury. "Mary Lockwood, Second Wife of Nathan Knapp. (A Correction to STAMFORDS' SOLDIERS)." CA 22 (1979): 69-70.

Huntington, Elijah Baldwin. STAMFORD SOLDIERS' MEMORIAL. Stamford: Author, 1869. 166 p.

Keeler, E. Wesley B. "Corrections, STAMFORDS' SOLDIERS." CA 22 (1979): 68-69.

"List of Stamford Men Registered for Selective Service." STAMFORD ADVO-CATE, 28 October 1940, Sec. D, 16 p.

McLean, Louise H. "Brothers at War." DARIEN HISTORICAL SOCIETY AN-NUAL, 1976, pp. 5-43.

Marcus, Ronald M. FORT STAMFORD. Stamford: Stamford Historical Society, 1973. 24 p.

_____. SERVICE RECORD OF STAMFORD, CONNECTICUT BLACK SOLDIERS DURING THE CIVIL WAR. Stamford: Stamford Historical Society, 1972.

STAMFORD'S WELCOME TO THE SOLDIERS AND SAILORS OF THE GREAT WAR OCTOBER 10, 11, 12 and 13, 1919. Stamford: Guillespie Bros., 1919.

"Theodore Delacroix, First Civil War Enlistee." STAMFORD HISTORIAN 1, no. 2 (1957): 138.

Wicks, Edith M. "Stamford Revolutionary Soldier Records." BULLETIN OF THE STAMFORD GENEALOGICAL SOCIETY 9 (1966-67): 7-13, 16-22, 74-78, 103-7; 10 (1967-68): 8-20, 47-59, 77-88, 118-24; 11 (1968-69): 16-24, 45-53, 68-78, 94-100; 12 (1969-70): 12-22, 60-67, 96.

Wicks, Edith M., and Olson, Virginia H. STAMFORD'S SOLDIERS GENEA-LOGICAL BIOGRAPHIES OF REVOLUTIONARY WAR PATRIOTS FROM STAM-FORD, CONNECTICUT. New Orleans: Polyanthos Press, 1976. 407 p.

NEWSPAPERS

ADVOCATE. Daily. 75 Tresser Boulevard, 06901. (203) 964-2200.

STAMFORD WEEKLY MAIL AND SHOPPER. Weekly. 60 Crescent Street, 06906 (203) 327-2550.

The PRELIMINARY CHECKLIST lists forty-four newspapers for STAMFORD.

Newspapers included in the HALE INDEX TO DEATHS AND MARRIAGES are the STAMFORD ADVOCATE, deaths 22 June 1830-25 January 1867; marriages 8 December 1829-28 December 1866.

INDEX (CHRONOLOGY) OF EARLY STAMFORD NEWSPAPERS. STAMFORD SENTINEL 1830-1837, STAMFORD DEMOCRATIC SENTINEL 1838-1839. STAMFORD FARMER'S ALMANAC 1840-1842, STAMFORD FARMER AND ME-CHANICS ALMANAC 1843-1853. New Canaan: New Canaan Historical Society, n.d. 25 p.

Kemp, Thomas Jay. "Stamford's Newspapers." CA 20 (1978): 185-87.

Walmsley, Grace Hope, and Roberts, Marguerite. INDEX STAMFORD ADVO-CATE TERCENTENARY EDITION TOWN OF STAMFORD 1641-1941. Stamford: Ferguson Library, 1941. 21 p.

PROBATE RECORDS

Stamford Probate District, Old Town Hall, 175 Atlantic Street, 06901. (203) 323-2149.

> The Stamford Probate District was organized May 1728 from the Fairfield Probate District.

> Probate districts organized from the Stamford Probate District include the Darien, Greenwich and Norwalk Probate Districts.

> ON FILE AT THE CSL: Estate Papers, 1760-1870. Court Record Books, 1728-1851.

Probate Records, 1728-1851. (LDS 2046 pt. 1-8).

Mead, Spencer Percival. ABSTRACTS OF PROBATE RECORDS FOR THE DIS-TRICT OF STAMFORD, COUNTY OF FAIRFIELD AND STATE OF CONNECTI-CUT. Greenwich: Author, 1919. 425 p. (LDS 2045).

_____. ABSTRACTS OF PROBATE RECORDS FOR THE DISTRICT OF STAM-FORD, COUNTY OF FAIRFIELD, AND STATE OF CONNECTICUT, 1803-1848. Greenwich: Author, 1924. 503 p. (LDS 2045).

SCHOOL RECORDS

Betts, Charlotte E. "The Betts Family and Their Academy." STAMFORD HISTORIAN 1, no. 2 (1957): 163-68.

TAX RECORDS

Marcus, Ronald M. STAMFORD CONNECTICUT GRAND LIST OF 1780. Stamford: Stamford Historical Society, 1970. 29 p.

VITAL RECORDS

Town Clerk, Old Town Hall, 175 Atlantic Street, P.O. Box 891, 06904. (203) 358-4054.

The BARBOUR INDEX covers the years 1641-1852 and is based on the James N. Arnold copy of STAMFORD vital records made in 1915. (LDS 899,934).

"Connecticut Births Before 1730 (Barbour)--Stamford." CN 10 (1977-78): 214-17, 387-92, 567-72; 11 (1978-79): 13-18, 198-203, 379-82.

Harris, Jay. GOD'S COUNTRY: A HISTORY OF POUND RIDGE, NEW YORK. Chester: Pequot Press, 1976. 541 p. Index.

Huntington, Elijah Baldwin. REGISTRATION OF BIRTHS, MARRIAGES AND DEATHS OF STAMFORD FAMILIES, INCLUDING EVERY NAME, RELATION-SHIP AND DATE NOW FOUND IN THE STAMFORD REGISTERS, FROM THE FIRST RECORD DOWN TO THE YEAR 1825. Stamford: William W. Gillespie and Co., 1874. 140 p. (LDS 05,592 and 2051).

"Stamford's First Baby." STAMFORD HISTORIAN 1, no. 2 (1957): 179.

PUBLISHED WORKS AND OTHER RECORDS

"A Bibliographical List of Books and Pamphlets Relating to or Printed in Stamford, Fairfield County, Connecticut." BIBLIOGRAPHIC SOCIETY OF AMERICA PAPERS 7 (1910): 22-32.

Blokhine, Margery Todahl. "Concerning the Knap House, Stillwater Road." STAMFORD HISTORIAN 1, no. 2 (1957): 157-62.

Day, Lloyd N. "Stamford in Who's Who." STAMFORD HISTORIAN 1, no. 2 (1957): 117-28.

Dreher, Monroe F. "The Richard Webb House." STAMFORD HISTORIAN 1, no. 1 (1954): 57-69.

Feinstein, Estelle S. STAMFORD FROM PURITAN TO PATRIOT: THE SHAPING OF A CONNECTICUT COMMUNITY 1641-1774. Stamford: Stamford Bicentennial Corp., 1976. 236 p.

_____. STAMFORD IN THE GILDED AGE: THE POLITICAL LIFE OF A CONNECTICUT TOWN, 1868-1893. Stamford: Stamford Historical Society, 1973. 319 p.

Hawley, Charles W. "Family Names of Stamford." STAMFORD HISTORIAN 1, no. 2 (1957): 186-91.

Huntington, Elijah B. HISTORY OF STAMFORD, CONNECTICUT, FROM ITS SETTLEMENT IN 1641, TO THE PRESENT TIME, INCLUDING DARIEN, WHICH WAS ONE OF ITS PARISHES UNTIL 1820. Stamford: William W. Gillespie and Co., 1868. 492 p.

Kemp, Thomas Jay. "Stamford's First City Directory, 1872." CA 21 (May 1979): 194.

Koehler, Mathilda A. "Stamford's 50-Year Firms." STAMFORD HISTORIAN 1, no. 2 (1957): 104-10.

Lobozza, Carl. CHANGING FACE OF STAMFORD, CONNECTICUT. Stamford: Stamford Historical Society, 1978. 80 p.

_____. JOURNEY THROUGH TIME. Stamford: Stamford Historical Society, 1971. 81 p.

_____. PICTURES FROM THE PAST. Stamford: Stamford Historical Society, 1970. 81 p.

McCann, Guy. "A Renaissance." FAIRFIELD COUNTY 4, no. 5 (May 1974): 28-47.

McLean, Louise H. "The Sellecks of Early Stamford." CANTIQUARIAN 14 (July 1962): 9-16.

"The Making of Modern Stamford." Manuscript. 118 p. Related materials including biographical notes, ethnic studies, bibliographies, etc. (CSL Archives RG 33 Boxes 157-169).

Majdalany, Jeanne. THE EARLY HISTORY OF LONG RIDGE VILLAGE, 1700-1800. Stamford: Stamford Historical Society, 1977. 60 p.

_____. THE HISTORY OF THE COVE IN STAMFORD, CONNECTICUT. Stamford: Stamford Historical Society, 1979. 122 p. Index.

Marcus, Ronald M. STAMFORD REVOLUTIONARY WAR DAMAGE CLAIMS. Essex: Pequot Press, 1969. 83 p.

Martin, Edward Warren. "Stamford Street Railroad Co." TRANSPORTATION BULLETIN, no. 83 (January-December 1976): 1-80.

Otto, Virginia Darling. "Early Mills at Stamford." STAMFORD HISTORIAN 1, no. 2 (1957): 139-46.

Penfield, Jone. "Will of Jeffery Ferris, 1641 Stamford Pioneer." STAMFORD HISTORIAN 1, no. 2 (1957): 180-83.

Pershing, George Orr. "Washington's Visits to Stamford." STAMFORD HISTORIAN 1, no. 2 (1957): 129-34.

Powell, Julie Adams. "Stamford--1641-1900." CM 6 (1900): 209-23.

Scofield, Edward C. "Story of the Cove." STAMFORD HISTORIAN 1, no. 2 (1957): 147-51.

_____. "Wallack's Point Near the Cove." STAMFORD HISTORIAN 1, no. 2 (1957): 152-53.

Scofield, Mrs. Edward C., and Hawley, Charles W. "Stamford Pioneer and Descendants." STAMFORD HISTORIAN 1, no. 2 (1957): 173-77.

Sherwood, Herbert Francis. THE STORY OF STAMFORD. New York: States History Co., 1930. 379 p. Index.

Simick, Phyllis. "Stamford: Turning Up for Tomorrow." FAIRFIELD COUNTY 7 (February 1977): 24-31, 34.

Snead, Lorcise Willis. SILVER AND GOLD. Stamford: Stamford Trust Co., 1916. 58 p.

"Stamford (Conn.) Town Records." TAG 10 (1933-34): 40-45, 110-18, 174-83; 11 (1934-35): 32-41, 87-98, 157-66, 220-29.

"Stamford Issue." COUNTY 15 (August 1968): 60.

Toner, Joseph R. "Town Records of Stamford." STAMFORD HISTORIAN 1, no. 2 (1957): 178-79.

Town Records, 1630-1806. (LDS 899,934).

TWENTY-FIVE YEARS OF PROGRESS, 1910-1935. Stamford: Instituto Italiano, 1953. 100 p.

Wicks, Edith M. "List of Oath of Fidelity 16 September 1777." CA 17 (1975): 123-25.

STERLING

WINDHAM COUNTY. Organized 4 May 1794 from VOLUNTOWN.

CEMETERY RECORDS AND CEMETERIES

NAME	ADDRESS	HALE NO.	CITATION
Parker Hill Cemetery	Northwest part of town	1	46:1-3
Card-Clark Cemetery	Northwest part of town	2	46:4-5
Ames Cemetery	North part of town	3	46:6
Field Stones	North part of town	4	46:7
Bennett Cemetery	Northeast part of town	5	46:8
Card-Hill Cemetery	Northwest part of town	6	46:9
Hall-Fuller Cemetery	North part of town	7	46:10
Young Cemetery	Northeast part of town	8	46:11
Arnold Cemetery	Northwest part of town	9	46:12
French Cemetery	Northeast part of town	10	46:13
Griffiths Cemetery	Northeast part of town	11	46:14
Williams Cemetery	West part of town	12	46:15
Potter Cemetery	North part of Center of town	13	46:16
Dixon Cemetery	North part of Center of town	14	46:17
Kenyon Cemetery	West of Center	15	46:18
Sheldon Cemetery	Center of town	16	46:19-20
Riverside Cemetery	Center of town	17	46:21-53
Hunt Cemetery	South of Center	18	46:54

NAME	ADDRESS	HALE NO.	CITATION
Gallup Cemetery	South of Center	19	46:55-62
Cedar Swamp Cemetery	South part of town	20	46:63-66
Benadam Gallup Cemetery	South part of town	21	46:67
Ball Cemetery	Outside of Riverside Cemetery	22	46:68
French-Green Cemetery	1/2 mile from Main Road	23	46:69
Wright Cemetery	Near #7 Hall-Fuller	24	46:70-71

Index to Hale inscriptions: 46:72-87.

Bard, Sidney R. INSCRIPTIONS FROM CARD-CLARK CEMETERY. STERLING, CONNECTICUT. N.p.: 1928. 3 p.

CHURCH RECORDS

STERLING CONGREGATIONAL CHURCH. Minutes, 1727-1889. Vital Records, 1723-1914. (CSL, LDS 2137 pt. 1-2). Index, 1723-1905. (CSL, LDS 1448 pt. 8, 433).

HISTORICAL SOCIETY

Sterling Historical Society, 06373.

LAND RECORDS

Land Records, 1794-1859. Index, 1794-1946. (LDS 2082 pt. 1-4).

LIBRARY

Sterling Public Library, Route 14-A, 06373. (203) 564-2492.

PROBATE RECORDS

Sterling Probate District, R.F.D. #1, 06354. (203) 564-2098.

The Sterling Probate District was organized 17 June 1852 from the Plainfield Probate District.

ON FILE AT THE CSL: Estate Papers, 1852-1920. Indexes, 1852-1920. Inventory Control Books, 1852-1920.

VITAL RECORDS

Town Clerk, Route 14A, 06373. (203) 564-2657.

> The town clerk's earliest birth record is 16 July 1768, marriage
> record is 3 September 1767 and death record is 8 December 1791.

The BARBOUR INDEX covers the years 1794-1867 and is based on the James
N. Arnold copy of STERLING vital records made in 1909. The births and marriages date to 31 December 1850 and deaths to 23 September 1867.

STONINGTON

NEW LONDON COUNTY. Organized 1649. Towns organized from STON-INGTON include NORTH STONINGTON.

CEMETERY RECORDS AND CEMETERIES

NAME	ADDRESS	HALE NO.	CITATION
Wheeler-Bentley Cemetery	North Stonington Road	1	47:1
Sherry Cemetery	In front of Catholic Church Pawcatuck	2	47:1
Old St. Michael Cemetery	Near of St. Michael's Church	3	47:1-23
New St. Michael Cemetery	Stillmanville	4	47:24-47
Stanton Cemetery	2 1/2 miles south of Pawcatuck	5	47:47
Davis Cemetery	Near Stanton Cemetery	6	47:47-50
Burdick-Culver Cemetery	Barren Island Road	7	47:50-51
Old Wequetequock	Wequetequock	8	47:51-63
Slack Cemetery	Near Wequetequock Cemetery	9	47:63
Robinson Cemetery	In field near Post Road	10	47:63-64
Noyes Cemetery	1 mile west of Hinckley Hill	11	47:64-65
Rhodes Cemetery	Near Noyes Cemetery	12	47:66
Robinson Cemetery	Stonington	13	47:67-72
Richmond Cemetery	1/2 mile north of Stonington	14	47:72
Stonington Borough Cemetery	1 mile north of Stonington	15	47:72-154

NAME	ADDRESS	HALE NO.	CITATION
St. Mary Cemetery	1 mile west of Stonington	16	47:154-68
Thomas Miner Cemetery	Next to Quiambog Cove	17	47:168-72
Industrial Cemetery	Boston Post Road	18	47:172-74
Denison Cemetery	Boston Post Road	19	47:174-77
Elm Grove Cemetery	Old Mystic Road	20	47:177-317
White Hall Cemetery	Old Mystic Road, north of Elm Grove Cemetery	21	47:317-23
Williams Cemetery	1/2 mile north of Old Mystic	22	47:323-25
Hillard Cemetery	Near Congregational Church Center of Stonington	23	47:325-34
Jonathan Wheeler Cemetery	Near Town Farm	24	47:334-37
Old Tangwank Cemetery	1 1/2 miles east of Town Farm	25	47:337-38
Breed Cemetery	East of Merritt Hill	26	47:338-39
Brown or Cogswell Cemetery	Howard Perry's farm	27	47:339
Frink or Williams Cemetery	Near Ralph Wheeler's property	28	47:340-42
Wheeler Cemetery	1/2 mile south of Ralph Wheeler's property	29	47:342
Babcock Cemetery	1 mile south of Pawcatuck	30	47:342-43
Helome Cemetery	West of (Old) St. Michael's Cemetery	31	47:343-44
Hallam Cemetery	Side of Railroad, Wamphassuc Neck	32	47:344-45
Hempstead Cemetery	2 1/2 miles north of Old Mystic	33	47:345-46
Bennett Cemetery	1 mile north of Hempstead Cemetery	34	47:346
Cranston Cemetery	1 1/2 miles southeast of Hempstead Cemetery	35	47:346
Bennett Cemetery	2 miles north of Old Mystic	36	47:346-47
Whittlesey Cemetery	1 1/4 miles north of Old Mystic	37	47:347
John Wheeler Cemetery	1 1/2 miles northeast of Whittlesey Cemetery	38	47:347

NAME	ADDRESS	HALE NO.	CITATION
Bentley Cemetery	1 mile northeast of John Wheeler Cemetery	39	47:348
Paul Wheeler Cemetery	1/2 mile south of Ralph Wheeler's property	40	47:348-50
Stanton-Hull Cemetery	1 mile north of Town farm	41	47:350-52
Town Farm Cemetery	1/4 mile from Town farm	42	47:352
Pendleton Cemetery	North of Robin-Cemetery	43	47:352
Warren Palmer Cemetery	1 mile northeast of Stonington	44	47:352-55
Chesebrough Cemetery	East of Velvet Mill	45	47:355
Richardson Cemetery	1 stone, west part of Pawcatuck	46	47:356
Small Pox Cemetery	West side Dean Pond	47	47:356
Oliver Denison Cemetery	Moved to Denison and Elm Grove Cemetery	48	47:356
William Miner Cemetery	West side of Quiambog Cove	49	47:356-57
Miner Cemetery	Stones and remains moved to Thomas Miner Cemetery	50	47:357
Baker Cemetery	East side of Quiambog Cove	51	47:357
Family Cemetery	1/2 mile on road, 1 mile east of Old Mystic	52	47:357
Joseph Denison Cemetery	1 mile north of Hillard Cemetery	53	47:358
Beebe-David Cemetery	1/2 mile north of Town farm	54	47:359
Hinckley Hill Cemetery	Hinckley Hill	55	47:359
Quaker Cemetery	Next to Wheeler-Bentley Cemetery North Stonington Road	56	47:360
Burdick-Frink Cemetery	North of Wheeler-Bentley Cemetery	57	47:360
William Vinson Cemetery	Moved to River Bend Cemetery Westerly, Rhode Island	58	47:360
Shaw Cemetery	Opposite States Cemetery North Stonington Road	59	47:360
States Cemetery	North Stonington Road	60	47:360-61
Miner Cemetery	North part of town near North Stonington Town Line	61	47:361-63

Index to Hale inscriptions: 47:386-487.

List of Soldiers buried in the above Cemeteries: 47:364-85. Index 47:488-94.

Champlin, J.D. "Ancient Burial-Ground at Stonington, Connecticut." NEHGR 13 (1859): 23-29.

Meech, Anne, and Meech, Susan B. CEMETERY INSCRIPTIONS FROM GROT-ON, PRESTON, AND STONINGTON, CONNECTICUT. Typescript. 1920. 68 p. (LDS 1695 and 599,838).

STONINGTON GRAVEYARDS: A GUIDE. Stonington: Stonington Historical Society, 1980. 184 p.

CHURCH RECORDS

FIRST CONGREGATIONAL CHURCH. Minutes, 1674-1892. Vital Records, 1674-1925. (CSL, LDS 2054 pt. 1-3). Vital Records, 1674-1925. Index. (CSL, LDS 1448 pt. 30).

SECOND CONGREGATIONAL CHURCH. Vital Records, 1809-1929. (CSL LDS 2054 pt. 4). Index. (CSL).

FIRST BAPTIST CHURCH, NORTH STONINGTON, CONNECTICUT. THE PAPERS AND ADDRESSES DELIVERED ATH THE DEDICATION OF THE GRANITE MEMORIAL ON THE SITE OF THE FIRST CHURCH EDIFICE SEPTEMBER 23, 1934. Westerly, R.I.: Utter Co., 1936. 145 p. Index.

Galley, Mrs. Jennie Tefft. INDEX TO WHEELER'S HISTORY OF THE FIRST CONGREGATIONAL CHURCH, STONINGTON, CONNECTICUT 1674-1874. N.p., 1929. 55 p.

Wheeler, Richard Anson. HISTORY OF THE FIRST CONGREGATIONAL CHURCH, STONINGTON, CONNECTICUT, 1674-1874. WITH THE REPORT OF BICENTENNIAL PROCEEDINGS, JUNE 3, 1874. WITH APPENDIX CON-TAINING STATISTICS OF THE CHURCH. Norwich: T.H. Davis and Co., 1875. 300 p. (LDS 547,508).

HISTORICAL SOCIETY

Stonington Historical Society, Whitehall Mansion, Whitehall Avenue, 06378. (203) 535-1440.

Publishes HISTORICAL FOOTNOTES: 1963-- . Quarterly. Indexed.

Mystic Seaport, Inc., Greenmanville Avenue, 06355. (203) 536-2631, ext. 261.

Publishes LOG OF MYSTIC SEAPORT. 1948-- . Quarterly with annual index.

Schultz, Charles R. "Manuscript Collections of the Marine Historical Association (Mystic Seaport)." AMERICAN NEPTUNE 25 (1965): 99-111.

LAND RECORDS

Land Records, 1665-1850. Index. (LDS 2052 pt. 1-12).

Wheeler, Richard Anson. "Land in Stonington, Connecticut, Sold for the Use of the Pequot Indians, 1683." MAGAZINE OF NEW ENGLAND HISTORY 2 (1892): 128-33.

LIBRARIES

G.W. Blunt White Library, Mystic Seaport, Inc., Greenmanville Avenue, Mystic, 06355. (203) 536-2631.

Stonington Free Library Association, P.O. Box 188, 06378. (203) 535-0658.

MAPS

THE STORY OF ONE CORNER OF CONNECTICUT IN 16 MAPS. Stonington: Mystic River Historical Society and Groton Bicentennial Committee, 1976. 16 p.

NEWSPAPERS

THE COMPASS COVENANT. Weekly. P.O. Box 37, 06355. (203) 536-2616.

The PRELIMINARY CHECKLIST lists nineteen newspapers for STONINGTON.

The HALE NEWSPAPER INDEX TO DEATH AND MARRIAGE NOTICES includes AMERICA'S FRIEND. 22 July 1807-29 June 1808, and MYSTIC PIONEER 12 March 1859-2 March 1867.

PROBATE RECORDS

Stonington Probate District, Town Hall, Elm Street, P.O. Box 312, 06378. (203) 535-0747.

> The Stonington Probate District was organized October 1766 from the New London Probate District.

Probate districts organized from the Stonington Probate District include the Groton, Ledyard and North Stonington Probate Districts.

ON FILE AT THE CSL: Estate Papers, 1766–1875. Indexes, 1766–1875. Inventory Control Book, 1766–1875. Court Record Books, 1767–1855.

Probate Records, 1767–1855. (LDS 2053 pt. 1–9).

TAX RECORDS

Hartford. CHS. Account Book, 1792–1830.

VITAL RECORDS

Town Clerk, Town Hall, Elm Street (P.O. Box 191), 06378. (203) 535–0182.

The town clerk's earliest birth record is 30 September 1656, marriage record is 20 November 1662 and death record is 24 January 1660.

The BARBOUR INDEX covers the years 1658–1854 and is based on the James N. Arnold copy of STONINGTON vital records made in 1912.

"Births Before 1730 (Barbour)." CN 11 (1978–79): 382–85, 565–70; 12 (1979): 7–14, 194–201, 386–91.

PUBLISHED WORKS AND OTHER RECORDS

Anderson, Virginia B. MARITIME MYSTIC. Mystic: Marine Historical Association, 1962. 88 p. Index.

Baughman, James P. THE MALLORYS OF MYSTIC: SIX GENERATIONS IN AMERICAN MARITIME ENTERPRISE. Middletown: Wesleyan University Press, 1972. 496 p.

Bray, Maynard. MYSTIC SEAPORT MUSEUM WATERCRAFT. Mystic: Mystic Seaport Museum, 1979. 280 p. Index.

Cutler, Carl C. MYSTIC: THE STORY OF A SMALL NEW ENGLAND SEAPORT. Mystic: Mystic Seaport Museum, 1980. 24 p. Index.

DIARY OF THOMAS MINER, STONINGTON, CONNECTICUT, 1653–1684. New London: Day Publishing Co., 1899. 221 p. Index.

Dickerman, Marion. "Mystic Seaport. The Williamsburg of the Sea." NEW CANAAN HISTORICAL SOCIETY ANNUAL, 1950, pp. 5–11.

Frank, Stuart M. "Mystic Seaport Harbor of Craftsmen and their Craft." OCEANS 11 (September 1978): 38–43.

Dodge, David. STEAMBOAT SABINO. Mystic, Conn.: Mystic Seaport, 1974. 16 p.

Gallup, Mrs. Herbert W. SUPPLEMENTARY INDEX TO WHEELER'S HISTORY OF STONINGTON, CONNECTICUT. Norwich: Author, 1928.

Gordon, George A. "A Contribution to the Early History of Stonington, Connecticut." NEHGR 47 (1893): 459–60.

Haynes, Williams. "Silks, Sandalwood and Seal Skins: The South Seas Voyages of Edmund Fanning." CANTIQUARIAN 11 (July 1959): 15–25.

_____. 1649–1949: STONINGTON CHRONOLOGY: BEING A YEAR-BY-YEAR RECORD OF THE AMERICAN WAY OF LIFE IN A CONNECTICUT TOWN. Stonington: Pequot Press, 1949. 151 p.

_____. "Too Many Fanning Homes." CANTIQUARIAN 12 (July 1960): 17–22.

Jones, Richard Michael. "Stonington Borough: A Connecticut Seaport in the Nineteenth Century." Ph.D. dissertation, City University of New York, 1976. 43 p.

Leavitt, John F. THE CHARLES W. MORGAN. Mystic, Conn.: Mystic Seaport, 1973. 131 p.

"Mystic Vision of Everett Scholfield: A Connecticut Photographer's Record of Life in a Shipbuilding Town." AMERICAN HERITAGE 31 (1980): 24–33.

"Names of Persons appearing in Asa Spaulding's Account Book, (Doctor) October 3, 1774–March 20, 1776, residing in the vicinity of Stonington, Connecticut, and Hopkinton, Rhode Island." DAR MAGAZINE 102 (January 1968): 34–35.

Palmer, Henry R., Jr. "Amazons on the Warpath." LEAGUE BULLETIN 31 (1979): 45–47, 60.

_____. STONINGTON BY THE SEA. 1913. Reprint. Stonington: Palmer Press, 1957. 95 p.

Read, Eleanor B. MYSTIC MEMORIES. Mystic: Author, 1980. 84 p.

Stackpole, Edouard A. "A House of Two Centuries The Buckingham House at Mystic Seaport." CANTIQUARIAN 13 (December 1961): 20-23.

Stanton, Mrs. Harriet A. "Aged Residents of Stonington, Connecticut, 1893." NEHGR 48 (1894): 322.

Steers, B. MacDonald, and Reed, Barbara. A TIME TO REMEMBER: ART AND ARTISTS OF THE MYSTIC, CONNECTICUT AREA, 1700-1950. Mystic: Mystic River Historical Society, 1976. 34 p.

"Stonington, Connecticut, where the Colonial Atmosphere is Preserved to a Marked Degree." ARCHITECTURAL RECORD 32 (1912): 230-37.

Wheeler, Grace Dennison. HOMES OF OUR ANCESTORS IN STONINGTON, CONNECTICUT. Salem, Mass.: Newcomb and Gauss Printers, 1903. 286 p.

Wheeler, Richard Anson. HISTORY OF THE TOWN OF STONINGTON, COUNTY OF NEW LONDON, CONNECTICUT, FROM THE FIRST SETTLE-MENT IN 1649 TO 1900, WITH A GENEALOGICAL REGISTER OF STONING-TON FAMILIES. New London: Day Publishing Co., 1900. 754 p. (LDS 847,758).

Wilbur, William Allen. "Mystic." CM 5 (1899): 398-419.

STRATFORD

FAIRFIELD COUNTY. Organized 1639. Towns organized from STRATFORD include BRIDGEPORT, HUNTINGTON, SHELTON, and TRUMBULL.

CEMETERY RECORDS AND CEMETERIES

NAME	ADDRESS	HALE NO.	CITATION
Union Cemetery	23 Temple Court (203) 375-4932	1	48:1-88
St. Michael Roman Catholic Cemetery	2205 Stratford Avenue (203) 378-0404	2	48:89-488
Congregational Church Cemetery	2207 Main Street	3	48:489-521
Episcopal Church Cemetery	Rear of Episcopal Church, Monument Place	4	48:522-32
St. John Orthodox Cemetery	Nichols Avenue (203) 375-0109	5	48:533-51
Putney Cemetery	Main Street	6	48:552-62
St. Joseph Roman Catholic Cemetery	1170 Stratford Road	7	48:563-65

Index to Hale inscriptions: 48:566-713.

"Connecticut Headstone Inscriptions Before 1800 (Hale)." CA 6 (1974): 514-20; 7 (1974): 36-38.

"Finding List for Congregational Burying Ground: Indexes, Stratford, Connecticut." MISCELLANEOUS RECORDS 1975-1976. CONNECTICUT DAR, pp. 22-45.

CHURCH RECORDS

CHRIST (EPISCOPAL) CHURCH. Minutes, 1726–1904. Vital Records, 1722–1932. (CSL, LDS 2099 pt. 2). Marriages, 1723–1800. BAILEY 7:9–14.

FIRST CONGREGATIONAL CHURCH. Minutes, 1847–1914. (CSL, LDS 2100). Records, 1688–1927. (CSL, LDS 2099). Marriages, 1733–1800. BAILEY 5:99–103. Baptisms and Marriages 1814–1849, copied by Mrs. Mary Chaffee Hart. (CSL, LDS 2099 pt. 3).

FIRST CONGREGATIONAL CHURCH OF HUNTINGTON (RIPTON PARISH). Baptisms, 1773–1781. (LDS 1455). Marriages, 1773–1800. BAILEY 7:86–92.

FIRST CONGREGATIONAL CHURCH AND CHRIST (EPISCOPAL) CHURCH. Index to Baptisms, Marriages and Deaths 1692–1820. (CSL, LDS 2099 pt. 1).

FIRST METHODIST EPISCOPAL CHURCH. Minutes, 1833–1853, 1908–1924 and Vital Records 1813–1931. (CSL, LDS 2101).

UNITY CONGREGATIONAL CHURCH. Marriages, 1747–1774. BAILEY 7:93–100.

Jacobus, Donald Lines. "Stratford, (Conn.) Congregational Church Records." TAG 13 (1937): 270–72; 14 (1937): 126–30.

HISTORICAL SOCIETY

Stratford Historical Society, 967 Academy Hill (P.O. Box 382), 06497. (203) 378–0630.

LAND RECORDS

Land Records, 1652–1857. (LDS 2096 pt. 1–21).

"Proprietors of Stratford, Connecticut." TAG 11 (1934): 56–57.

LIBRARY

Stratford Library Association, 2203 Main Street, 06497. (203) 378–7345.

NEWSPAPERS

STRATFORD BARD. Weekly. 720 Barnum Avenue, 06497. (203) 377–3809. The STRATFORD BARD is indexed by the Stratford Library Association.

The PRELIMINARY CHECKLIST lists six newspapers for STRATFORD.

PROBATE RECORDS

Stratford Probate District, Town Hall, 2725 Main Street, 06497. (203) 375-5621 ext. 271

> The Stratford Probate District was organized May 1782 from the Fairfield Probate District.

> Probate districts formed from the Stratford Probate District include the Bridgeport Probate District.

> From 1782 to June 1840 the probate district was located in Bridgeport. The Bridgeport Probate District was formed at that time and it has the court records and books for those early years, 1782-1840.

> ON FILE AT THE CSL: Estate Papers, 1798-1898. Indexes, 1798-1898. Inventory Control Book, 1798-1898, Probate Court Journal, 1811-1840. Court Journal and Record Book 1782-1788, 1805-1813, 1829-1836, 1840-1851.

Probate Records, 1782-1851. (LDS 2098 pt. 1-6). 1840-1853. (LDS 2097).

VITAL RECORDS

Town Clerk, Town Hall, 2725 Main Street, 06497. (203) 375-5621, ext. 291.

The BARBOUR INDEX covers the years 1639-1852 and is based on the James N. Arnold Copy of vital records made in 1914 and the Mrs. Kate Hammond Fogarty copy of 1924.

"Births--Town of Stratford. Barbour pre 1730." CN 13 (1980): 11-16, 192-97, 374-79.

Cothren, William. HISTORY OF ANCIENT WOODBURY . . . includes a section of STRATFORD vital records, pp. 651-92.

See also Orcutt's HISTORY OF THE OLD TOWN OF STRATFORD, below.

PUBLISHED WORKS AND OTHER RECORDS

Cohen, Sharon L. "Stratford, a Town where Families Beget Families, Where 'Newcomers' Rarely Leave." FAIRFIELD COUNTY 9 (August 1979): 32-34.

Cothren, William. HISTORY OF ANCIENT WOODBURY, CONNECTICUT, FROM THE FIRST INDIAN DEED IN 1659 TO 1854 INCLUDING THE PRESENT TOWNS OF WASHINGTON, SOUTHBURY, BETHLEHEM, ROXBURY, AND A PART OF OXFORD AND MIDDLEBURY. Waterbury, Conn.: Bronson Press, 1854. 841 p. (LDS 2205).

Cuncliffe, Richard. "Dr. Richard William Samuel Johnson of Stratford, Connecticut." LEAGUE BULLETIN 32 (September 1980): 8-9, 12-13.

DeMille, George E., and Gerlach, Don R. "Samuel Johnson, Parson of 'Stratford in New England.'" CHSB 45 (1980): 97-114.

"Early Settlers of Stratford, Connecticut." NEHGR 27 (1873): 62-63.

Manion, Helen Rose. "Admitted Freemen, Between the Years 1775 and 1783, Town of Stratford, Connecticut." NGSQ 15 (1927): 4-8.

Orcutt, Samuel. HISTORY OF THE OLD TOWN OF STRATFORD AND THE CITY OF BRIDGEPORT, CONNECTICUT. 2 vols. New Haven: Tuttle, Morehouse and Taylor, 1886. (LDS 899,890).

Smith, H. Monmouth. "George Smith of Stratford, Connecticut; Some Relics of His Family." OLD-TIME NEW ENGLAND 36 (1945): 74-80.

Weld, Stanley Burnham. "History of Medicine in Stratford in its Early Days." CONNECTICUT STATE MEDICAL JOURNAL 15 (1950): 305-8

Wilcoxson, William Howard. HISTORY OF STRATFORD, CONNECTICUT 1639-1939. Stratford: Stratford Tercentenary Commission, 1939. 827 p.

SUFFIELD

HARTFORD COUNTY. Organized May 1674 in Massachusetts and annexed to Connecticut May 1749.

CEMETERY RECORDS AND CEMETERIES

NAME	ADDRESS	HALE NO.	CITATION
Old Center Cemetery	Rear of Church at Center	1	49:1-56
Woodlawn Cemetery	491 Bridge Street	2	49:57-97A
West Suffield Cemetery	1140 Mountain Road	3	49:98-139
Phelps-Warner Cemetery	West Suffield, near Granby Line	4	49:140-48
Hastings Hill Cemetery	Next to Church	5	49:149-63
Sikes Cemetery	Revolutionary Soldier buried on Hendee Farm	6	49:164
Austin Cemetery	Riverview Boulevard, 1/4 mile north of Thompsonville and Suffield bridge on right hand side near the road	7	49:165
Harrlow Cemetery	1 mile north of Stony Brook Bridge on East Street on the Old Patrick Quinn farm on left side of road going north and 500 feet in from road beside a shed	8	49:166
Pease Cemetery	Miller Farm, at Lake Cognomond	9	49:167
Clark Cemetery	1/8 mile north of East Granby-Suffield town line	10	49:167A-168
St. Joseph Cemetery	595 Hill Street		(no citation)

Index to Hale inscriptions: 49:169-218.

"Connecticut Headstones Before 1800 (Hale)--Suffield." CN 11 (1978-79): 401-403, 586-91; 12 (1979): 32.

Dewey, Louis Marinus. "Inscriptions from Old Cemeteries in Connecticut: Suffield." NEHGR 60 (1906): 305-8.

Lathrop, Samuel G. RECORDS OF THE "OLD CEMETERY" SUFFIELD, CONNECTICUT. N.p., 1948.

_____. RECORDS OF THE SUFFIELD OLD CEMETERIES. N.p., 1956. 87 p.

Priest, Alice L. "Suffield, Connecticut Inscriptions: Corrections." NEHGR 100 (1946): 331.

CHURCH RECORDS

CALVARY (EPISCOPAL) CHURCH. Minutes and Vital Records, 1865-1933. (CSL, LDS 2073).

FIRST CONGREGATIONAL CHURCH. Records, 1776-1812. (CSL, LDS 2073).

SECOND ECCLESIASTICAL SOCIETY. Minutes, 1792-1858. (CSL, LDS 2073).

RECORDS OF THE CONGREGATIONAL CHURCH IN SUFFIELD, CONNECTICUT (EXCEPT CHURCH VOTES) 1710-1836. Vital Records of Connecticut Series II. Churches; Vol. 7, Town 5. Hartford: CHS, 1941. 224 p.

HISTORICAL SOCIETY

Hatheway House, Main Street, 06078. (203) 668-0055.

Suffield Historical Society, 541 North Main Street, 06078. (203) 668-2581.

Clark, Delphina L.H. "The Burbank Kitchen of the Hatheway House: Its Changes and Its Re-Creation." CANTIQUARIAN 20 (December 1968): 15-19.

"The Phelps-Hatheway House in Suffield." CANTIQUARIAN 14 (July 1962): 6-8.

"Some Notes on the Hatheway House in Suffield." CANTIQUARIAN 17 (December 1965): 19.

LAND RECORDS

Land Records, 1677-1722, 1754-1858. (LDS 2071). Index, 1754-1885. (LDS 2070 pt. 1-13).

LIBRARY RECORDS

Kent Memorial Library, 50 North Main Street, 06078. (203) 668-2325.

MILITARY RECORDS

Kent. Kent Memorial Library. Muster Rolls and other Military Records from 1744-1781.

PROBATE RECORDS

Suffield Probate District, Town Hall, Mountain Road, P.O. Box 234, 06078. (203) 668-5335.

> Organized May 1821 from the Granby and Hartford Probate Districts.

> ON FILE AT THE CSL: Estate Papers, 1821-1952. Indexes, 1821-1947 (papers from 1945-1952 are arranged alphabetically). Inventory Control Book 1821-1947. Court Record Book, 1821-1853. Also the records of the Registry of the Probate Court of Hampshire County, Massachusetts from 1660-1820 are on microfilm.

Records, 1821-1853. (LDS 2072).

VITAL RECORDS

Town Clerk, Town Hall, Mountain Road, 06078. (203) 668-7391.

The BARBOUR INDEX covers the years 1674-1850 and is based on the James N. Arnold copy of SUFFIELD vital records made in 1913.

The Kent Memorial Library has the original volume of vital records.

RECORDS OF CASES OF MIDWIFERY OF E.G. UFFORD, PRACTICED AT SUFFIELD 1827-1837. (LDS 25390 and 185,373).

VITAL RECORDS, BIRTHS 1668-1692. MARRIAGES 1679-1694. DEATHS 1675-1692 OF SUFFIELD. KEPT PRIVATELY BY WILLIAM AND JOHN PYNCHON. N.p., n.d.

PUBLISHED WORKS AND OTHER RECORDS

Alcorn, Robert Hayden. BIOGRAPHY OF A TOWN, SUFFIELD, CONNECTI-
CUT: 1670-1970. Suffield: Three Hundredth Anniversary Committee of the
Town of Suffield, 1970. 366 p.

Bissell, Charles S. ANTIQUE FURNITURE IN SUFFIELD, CONNECTICUT,
1670-1835. Hartford: Connecticut Historical Society, 1956. 144 p. Index.

CELEBRATION OF THE TWO HUNDRED AND FIFTIETH ANNIVERSARY OF
THE SETTLEMENT OF SUFFIELD, CONNECTICUT, OCTOBER 12, 13 AND 14,
1920, WITH SKETCHES FROM ITS PAST AND SOME RECORD OF ITS LAST
HALF-CENTURY AND OF ITS PRESENT. Suffield: General Executive Committee, 1921. 204 p.

Clark, Delphina L.H. "The Bultolph-Williams House." CANTIQUARIAN 1
(November 1949): 11-21.

_____. "Iron in the Woods of Suffield." CANTIQUARIAN 21 (June 1969):
7-12.

_____. "Two Speculators and Two Surveyors of Suffield." CANTIQUARIAN
3 (June 1951): 17-24.

_____. "Who Designed Oliver Phelps' Ell?" CANTIQUARIAN 22 (June
1970): 13-15.

Elliott, Harrison. "Papermaking in Suffield." CANTIQUARIAN 2 (July
1950): 21-24.

Lewis, Thomas Reed, Jr. "From Suffield to Saybrook: An Historical Geography of the Connecticut River Valley in Connecticut Before 1800." Ph.D.
dissertation, Rutgers University, 1978. 225 p.

Sheldon, Hezekiah Spencer. DOCUMENTARY HISTORY OF SUFFIELD, IN
THE COLONY AND PROVINCE OF THE MASSACHUSETTS BAY IN NEW
ENGLAND 1660-1749. Springfield, Mass.: Clarke W. Bryan Co., 1879.
343 p.

Smith, Martin H. "Suffield: A Sketch." CQ 1 (1895): 165-72.

THOMASTON

LITCHFIELD COUNTY. Organized July 1875 from PLYMOUTH.

CEMETERY RECORDS AND CEMETERIES

NAME	ADDRESS	HALE NO.	CITATION
Hillside Cemetery	Marine Street	1	49:1-68
St. Thomas Cemetery	Opportunity Street	2	49:69-87

Index to Hale inscriptions: 49:88-113.

CHURCH RECORDS

CONGREGATIONAL CHURCH. Minutes, 1728-1921. Vital Records, 1730-1795. (CSL, LDS 2131).

HISTORICAL SOCIETY

Thomaston Historical Society, Town Hall, 158 Main Street, 06787. (203) 283-5072.

LIBRARY

Thomaston Public Library, 248 Main Street, 06787. (203) 283-5422.

NEWSPAPER

THOMASTON EXPRESS. Weekly. P.O. Box 250, 06787. (203) 283-4355.

The PRELIMINARY CHECKLIST lists one newspaper for THOMASTON.

PROBATE RECORDS

Thomaston Probate District, Town Hall, 158 Main Street, 06787. (203) 283-4141.

> The Thomaston Probate District was organized June 1882 from the Waterbury Probate District.

> ON FILE AT THE CSL: Estate Papers, 1882-1947. Indexes, 1882-1947. Inventory Control Book, 1882-1947.

TAX RECORDS

Hartford. CSL, Record Group 62. Abstracts, 1875-1936.

VITAL RECORDS

Town Clerk, Town Hall, 158 Main Street, 06787. (203) 283-4141.

> The town clerk's earliest birth record is 3 July 1875, marriage record is 23 November 1875 and death record is 15 August 1875.

PUBLISHED WORKS AND OTHER RECORDS

Gangloff, Rosa F. THOMASTON: ITS ORIGIN AND DEVELOPMENT. Waterbury, Conn.: Speed Offset Press, 1975. 374 p.

THOMPSON

WINDHAM COUNTY. Organized May 1785 from KILLINGLY. Towns organized from THOMPSON include PUTNAM.

CEMETERY RECORDS AND CEMETERIES

NAME	ADDRESS	HALE NO.	CITATION
New Boston Cemetery	New Boston	1	49:1-14
Wilsonville Cemetery	Wilsonville	2	49:15-28
Tourtellot Cemetery	1 1/4 miles east of Wilsonville	3	49:29-30
Bates Cemetery	Massachusetts State Line, near Little Pond	4	49:31-33
Carpenter Cemetery	Near Bates Cemetery	5	49:34
Joslin Cemetery	1 mile east of Little Pond	6	49:35-37
Porter Cemetery	1 mile south of Little Pond	7	49:38-41
Jacob Cemetery	1 mile south of Tourtellot Cemetery	8	49:42-43
Old East Thompson Cemetery	East part of town	9	49:44-63
New East Thompson Cemetery	East part of town	10	49:64-72
Dike Cemetery	Near Brandy Hill	11	49:73
Quaddick Cemetery	Near Quaddick Reservoir	12	49:74-76
Ross Cemetery	1 mile southwest of Quaddick Cemetery	13	49:77
West Thompson Cemetery	West Thompson	14	49:78-139
Whittemore Cemetery	North Grosvenor Dale	15	49:140

NAME	ADDRESS	HALE NO.	CITATION
Swedish Cemetery	Grosvenor Dale	16	49:141-44
Catholic Cemetery	North Grosvenor Dale	17	49:145-162
North Grosvenor Cemetery	North Grosvenor Dale	18	49:163-67
Cortiss Cemetery	1/2 mile north of North Grosvenor Dale	19	49:168-172
Winter Cemetery	3/4 mile west of North Grosvenor Dale	20	49:173
Aldrich Cemetery	1 1/2 miles west of North Grosvenor Dale	21	49:174-75

Index to Hale inscriptions: 49:176-222.

Clarke, Avis G. INSCRIPTIONS IN THE CEMETERY AT WILSONVILLE. Oxford, Mass.: Author, 1931. 136 p.

Tefft, Mrs. George Washington. "Epitaphs at Quadic, Connecticut." NEHGR 79 (1925): 333-35.

Mrs. Mary B. Bishop transcribed the records of several THOMPSON cemeteries. They are on file at the CSL.

CHURCH RECORDS

CONGREGATIONAL CHURCH. Records, 1730-1756. (NYGBS, LDS 2115). Baptisms, 1730-1795. Index. (CSL, LDS 1448, pt. 31).

NORTH SOCIETY OF KILLINGLY. Marriages, 1730-1795. BAILEY 2:50-65.

MANUAL OF THE CONGREGATIONAL CHURCH IN THOMPSON, CONNECTICUT, 1730-1901. Thompson: Congregational Church, 1901.

THOMPSON CHURCH RECORDS, 1730-1795. Putnam: Putnam Patriot, n.d.

HISTORICAL SOCIETY

Thompson Historical Society, Inc., P.O. Box 47, 06277.

LAND RECORDS

Land Records, 1785-1853. Index, 1785-1938. (LDS 2116 pt. 1-10).

LIBRARY

Thompson Library, Route 193 (P.O. Box 188), 06277. (203) 923-9779.

NEWSPAPERS

The PRELIMINARY CHECKLIST lists four newspapers for THOMPSON.

PROBATE RECORDS

Thompson, Probate District, Town Office Building, Route 12, P.O. Box 74, No. Grosvenor Dale, 06255. (203) 923-2203.

> The Thompson Probate District was organized 25 May 1832 from the Pomfret Probate District.

> Probate districts organized from the Thompson Probate District include the Putnam Probate District.

> ON FILE AT THE CSL: Estate Papers, 1832-1945. Indexes, 1832-1945. Inventory Control Book, 1832-1945. Court Record Books, 1832-1851.

Probate Records, 1832-1851. (LDS 2117).

VITAL RECORDS

Town Clerk, Town Office Building, Route 12, No. Grosvenor Dale, 06255. (203) 923-9900.

> The town clerk's earliest birth record dates from 1733, marriage record from 1746 and death record from 1760.

The BARBOUR INDEX covers the years 1785-1854. The births and marriages date to 31 December 1850 and the deaths date to 30 December 1854. It is based on the James N. Arnold copy of THOMPSON vital records made in 1909.

PUBLISHED WORKS AND OTHER RECORDS

Curtis, John Obed. "The Thompson, Connecticut Bank." OLD-TIME NEW ENGLAND 54 (1963): 106-11.

Stone, Frank Andrews. "Connecticut's Kilmarnock Scots." CHSB 44 (1979): 97-105.

TOLLAND

TOLLAND COUNTY. Organized May 1715.

CEMETERY RECORDS AND CEMETERIES

NAME	ADDRESS	HALE NO.	CITATION
North Cemetery	Crystal Lake Road	1	49:1-20
East Cemetery	Charter Road	2	49:21-39
South Cemetery	Cider Mill Road	3	49:40-80
Loomis Cemetery	1/2 mile southeast of Center	4	49:81
Grant Hill Cemetery	On Ursin 2 3/4 miles from Tolland Center	5	49:82
Northrup Cemetery	On land of Gardner Hall & Co.	6	49:83-84
Cemetery	Dimock Farm	7	(no citation)
2 Graves (Benton)	Old Chapin Farm	8	(no citation)

Index to Hale inscriptions: 49:85-108.

Eno, Joel Nelson. "Connecticut Cemetery Inscriptions. Tolland." NEHGR 72 (1918): 63-75, 114-31, 204-208; 73 (1919): 32-43.

CHURCH RECORDS

BAPTIST CHURCH. Minutes, 1847-1890. Vital Records, 1807-1904. (CSL, LDS 2125).

CONGREGATIONAL CHURCH. Minutes, 1806-1928. (CSL, LDS 2127).

METHODIST EPISCOPAL CHURCH. Vital Records, 1832-1912. (CSL, LDS 2126).

Hartford. CSL, Record Group 62. CERTIFICATES OF CHURCH MEMBERSHIP 1792-1810.

HISTORICAL SOCIETY

Tolland Historical Society, Benton Homestead, Metcalf Road, 06084. (203) 872-2787.

LAND RECORDS

Hartford. CSL, Record Group 62. Land Records and other records, 1741-1909.

Land Records, 1713-1850. Index, 1713-1932. (LDS 2123 pt. 1-11).

LIBRARY

Tolland Public Library, Tolland Street (P.O. Box 151), 06084. (203) 872-0138.

NEWSPAPERS

The PRELIMINARY CHECKLIST lists four newspapers for TOLLAND.

PROBATE RECORDS

Tolland Probate District, Town Hall, Tolland Green, P.O. Box 5, 06084. (203) 872-9985.

> The Tolland Probate District was organized 4 June 1830 from the Stafford Probate District.

> Tolland Probate District also includes the town of WILLINGTON.

> ON FILE AT THE CSL: Estate Papers, 1833-1960. Indexes, 1833-1948, (papers from 1925-1960 are arranged alphabetically, with a list). Inventory Control Book, 1833-1948. Court Record Book, 1830-1857.

Probate Records, 1830-1853. (LDS 2124 pt. 1-2).

SCHOOL RECORDS

Hartford. CSL, Record Group 62. Returns, 1827-1873. District Reports, Minutes, 1810-1878.

TAX RECORDS

HARTFORD. CSL, Record Group 62. Abstracts, 1733-1909 incomplete.

VITAL RECORDS

Town Clerk, Town Hall, 22 Tolland Green, 06084. (203) 875-7387.

> The town clerk's earliest birth record dates from 1665, marriage record from 1692 and death record from 1693.

The BARBOUR INDEX covers the years 1715-1850 and is based on the James N. Arnold copy of TOLLAND vital records made in 1913.

Hartford. CSL, Record Group 62. Vital Records, 1851-1900.

VOTER RECORDS

Hartford. CSL, Record Group 62. Lists, 1837-1916. Returns, 1788-1837. Certificates of Electors.

PUBLISHED WORKS AND OTHER RECORDS

Hartford. CSL, Record Group 62. Justice Court Records, 1789-1874. Oaths of Freemen 1802-1817. Town Meeting Records, 1798-1873.

Search, Robert M., and Search, Helen C. "Second Wife of Ichabod Hinckley of Tolland." CHSB 28 (1963): 30-32.

Waldo, Loren Pinckney. EARLY HISTORY OF TOLLAND. Hartford: Case, Lockwood and Co., 1861. 148 p.

Weigold, Harold. TOLLAND: THE HISTORY OF AN OLD CONNECTICUT POST ROAD TOWN. Chester: Pequot Press, 1971. 246 p.

TORRINGTON

LITCHFIELD COUNTY. Organized October 1740.

CEMETERY RECORDS AND CEMETERIES

NAME	ADDRESS	HALE NO.	CITATION
Center Cemetery	Rear of City Hall	1	50:1-68
Hillside Cemetery	46 Walnut Street (203) 482-8932	2	50:69-111
St. Francis Cemetery (Old)	Near Town Center office: 863 South Main Street (203) 482-4670	3	50:112-78
St. Francis Cemetery (New)	863 Main Street (203) 482-4670	4	50:179-201
West Torrington Cemetery	Goshen Road	5	50:202-18
Burrville Cemetery	Near Burrville Railroad Station	6	50:219-22
Jewish Cemetery	Winsted Road, 1 mile south of Burrville	7	50:223-24
Torringford Cemetery	Torringford	8	50:225-48
Newfield Cemetery	Newfield District	9	50:249-58
Fyler Cemetery	Newfield District	10	50:259
Bissell Cemetery	Hartford Road	11	50:260
Benedict Cemetery	Norfolk Road near Norfolk Town Line	12	50:261
Hinsdale Cemetery	Opposite Benedict Cemetery	13	50:262-63

Index to Hale inscriptions: 50:264-338.

CHURCH RECORDS

FIRST CONGREGATIONAL CHURCH. Minutes, 1826-1901. Vital Records, 1741-1775, 1787-1877. (CSL, LDS 2122). Index. (CSL, LDS 1448 pt. 31 32). Marriages, 1743-1801. BAILEY 7:68-71.

TORRINGFORD CONGREGATIONAL CHURCH. Records, 1757-1849. (CSL, LDS 2121).

Thomen, Ada Phelps. THE FIRST CHURCH TORRINGTON 1741-1841. PART I. BULLETIN NO. 4 OF THE TORRINGTON HISTORICAL SOCIETY. Torrington: Torrington Historical Society, 1951. 58 p.

HISTORICAL SOCIETY

Torrington Historical Society, Inc. (P.O. Box 353), 192 Main Street, 06790 (203) 482-8260.

LAND RECORDS

Land Records, 1733-1851. Index, 1732-1882. (LDS 2119 pt. 1-8).

LIBRARY

Torrington Library, 12 Daycocton Place, 06790. (203) 489-6684.

NEWSPAPERS

THE REGISTER. Daily. 190 Water Street, 06790. (203) 489-3121.

The PRELIMINARY CHECKLIST lists six newspapers for TORRINGTON.

PROBATE RECORDS

Torrington Probate District, 140 Main Street, 06790. (203) 489-2215.

Organized 16 June 1847 from the Litchfield Probate District.

The Torrington Probate District also includes GOSHEN.

ON FILE AT THE CSL: Estate Papers, 1847-1905. Indexes, 1847-1905. Inventory Control Book, 1847-1905. Court Probate Records, 1847-1857. (LDS 2120).

VITAL RECORDS

Town Clerk, Municipal Building, 140 Main Street, 06790. (203) 482-8521.

The BARBOUR INDEX covers the years 1740-1850 and is based on the James N. Arnold copy of TORRINGTON vital records made in 1961.

TORRINGTON: RECORD OF DEATHS IN TORRINGFORD 1777-1884. N.p., 1962. 25 p. (CSL).

VOTER RECORDS

Hartford. CSL, Record Group 62, Vault 11A. Map Case. List of Electors, 1904 (incomplete, A-Ga).

PUBLISHED WORKS AND OTHER RECORDS

Bailey, Bess, and Bailey, Merrill. THE FORMATIVE YEARS: TORRINGTON 1737-1852. Torrington: Torrington Historical Society, 1975. 104 p.

_____. THE GROWTH YEARS: TORRINGTON 1852-1923. Torrington: Torrington Historical Society, 1976. 148 p.

Eaton, Edward Bailey. "The Industrial History of Torrington." CM 9 (1905): 122-38.

Gaylord, Elizabeth. GLEANINGS FROM EARLY TORRINGTON HISTORY. Torrington Historical Society. Bulletin no. 1. Torrington: Torrington Historical Society, 1946. 31 p.

_____. TORRINGTON 1744-1944. Torrington: Torrington Printing Co., n.d. 77 p.

_____. TORRINGTON TOWN MEETINGS TRANSCRIBED FROM ORIGINAL RECORD BOOK. Torrington Historical Society. Bulletin no. 3. Torrington: Torrington Historical Society, 1948. 72 p.

Johnson, Charles H. MEMORIES OF WOLCOTTVILLE. Torrington Historical Society. Bulletin no. 2. Torrington: Torrington Historical Society, 1947. 84 p.

Orcutt, Samuel. HISTORY OF TORRINGTON, CONNECTICUT, FROM ITS FIRST SETTLEMENT IN 1737, WITH BIOGRAPHIES AND GENEALOGIES. Albany, N.Y.: J. Munsell, Printer, 1878. 817 p. (LDS 844,946).

TORRINGFORD: IN CONNECTION WITH THE CENTENNIAL OF THE SET-
TLEMENT OF THE FIRST PASTOR, REV. SAMUEL J. MILLS. Hartford: Case,
Lockwood, and Brainard Printers, 1870. 107 p.

Welch, Gideon H. "The Growth of Torrington." CM 9 (1905): 97-121.

Yarwood and Block, Inc. A MORE BEAUTIFUL TORRINGTON. Simsbury,
Conn.: Author, 1969. 90 p.

TRUMBULL

FAIRFIELD COUNTY. Organized October 1797 from STRATFORD.

CEMETERY RECORDS AND CEMETERIES

NAME	ADDRESS	HALE NO.	CITATION
Nichols Cemetery	215 Unity Road	1	50:1-18
Graveyard	Road to Nichols	2	50:19-22
Unity Cemetery	Unity Road	3	50:23-28
Brimsmade Cemetery	Trumbull Center	4	50:29-31
Riverside Cemetery	Trumbull Center	5	50:32-38
Booth or Daniels Cemetery	Daniels Farm	6	50:39-41
Tashua Cemetery	395 Tashua Road	7	50:42-55
Long Hill Cemetery	68 Middlebrooks Avenue	8	50:56-84
Northwest Cemetery	Northwest next to Railroad	9	50:85-86
Gate of Heaven Roman Catholic Cemetery	Daniels Farms Road (Office: (203) 378-0404)		(no citation)

Index to Hale inscriptions: 50:87-111.

Beach, E. Merrill. THEY FACE THE RISING SUN: A COMPREHENSIVE STORY WITH GENEALOGICAL MATERIAL AND COMPLETE CHARTING OF UNITY BURIAL GROUND--OLDEST CEMETERY IN TRUMBULL, CONNECTICUT 1730-1971. Chester: Pequot Press, 1971. 60 p.

UNITY CEMETERY TRUMBULL CONGREGATIONAL CHURCH, TRUMBULL, CONNECTICUT. Trumbull: First Congregational Church, 1962. 20 p.

CHURCH RECORDS

CHRIST CHURCH (EPISCOPAL). Vital Records, 1787-1923. (CSL, LDS 2129).

CHURCH OF CHRIST (CONGREGATIONAL). Records, 1730-1931. Index. (CSL).

CONGREGATIONAL CHURCH. Minutes, 1761-1849. Vital Records, 1783-1891. (CSL, LDS 2130).

UNITY CONGREGATIONAL CHURCH. Marriages, 1747-1774. BAILEY 7: 93-100.

Card, Lester. MARRIAGES AT THE TRUMBULL CONGREGATIONAL CHURCH. (LDS, 858,664).

HISTORICAL SOCIETY

Trumbull Historical Society, Inc., P.O. Box 321, 06611. (203) 268-0416.

Publishes THE GRISTMILL. 1964-- . 5/year.

LAND RECORDS

Land Records, 1798-1855. Index, 1798-1910. (LDS 2128 pt. 1-6).

LIBRARY

Trumbull Library, 33 Quality Street, 06611. (203) 261-6421.

NEWSPAPER

TRUMBULL TIMES. Weekly. White Plains Road, 06611. (203) 268-6234.

The PRELIMINARY CHECKLIST lists one newspaper for TRUMBULL.

PROBATE RECORDS

Trumbull Probate District, Town Hall, 5866 Main Street, 06611. (203) 261-3631.

> The Trumbull Probate District was organized 7 January 1959 from the Bridgeport Probate District.

> The Trumbull Probate District also includes the towns of EASTON and MONROE.

TAX RECORDS

Hartford. CSL, Record Group 62. Tax List, 1790.

VITAL RECORDS

Town Clerk, Town Hall, 5866 Main Street, 06611. (203) 261-3631 ext. 33.

The town clerk's earliest birth, marriage and death records date
from 1848.

PUBLISHED WORKS AND OTHER RECORDS

Backalenick, Irene. "Trumbull: A Town With Two Faces." FAIRFIELD
COUNTY 9 (March 1979): 12-19.

Bench, E. Merrill. TRUMBULL: CHURCH AND TOWN. A HISTORY OF
THE COLONIAL TOWN OF TRUMBULL AND OF ITS CHURCH WHICH WAS
THE CHURCH OF CHRIST IN UNITY, THE CHURCH OF CHRIST IN NORTH
STRATFORD, AND IS NOW THE CHURCH OF CHRIST IN TRUMBULL. 1730-
1955. Trumbull: Church of Christ in Trumbull, 1955. Reprint. Trumbull:
Trumbull Historical Society, 1972. 175 p.

UNION

TOLLAND COUNTY. Organized October 1734.

CEMETERY RECORDS AND CEMETERIES

NAME	ADDRESS	HALE NO.	CITATION
Union Center Cemetery	Union Center	1	50:1-12
East Cemetery	East part of Union	2	50:13-19
Armour Cemetery	Cleveland farm	3	50:20
Old Union Center	North of Union Center Cemetery	4	50:21-32
Lamius Daniel Cemetery	Across from Red School House	5	50:33-34

Index to Hale inscriptions: 50:35-44.

CHURCH RECORDS

CONGREGATIONAL CHURCH. Minutes, 1816-1922. Vital Records, 1759-1819. Indexed. (CSL, LDS 2133). Marriages, 1759-83. BAILEY 5:26-29.

Curtiss, George. HISTORY OF THE CONGREGATIONAL CHURCH OF UNION, CONNECTICUT. Danielson: Buroughs and Hopkins, 1914. 59 p. Index.

LAND RECORDS

Land Records, 1733-1858. Indexed. (LDS 2132 pt. 1-4).

LIBRARY

Union Free Public Library, 579 Buckley Highway, 06076. (203) 684-4913.

PROBATE RECORDS

UNION is in the Stafford Probate District.

SCHOOL RECORDS

Hartford. CSL, Record Group 62. School Records, 1796-1909.

VITAL RECORDS

Town Clerk, Route 171, 606 Buckley Highway, Stafford Springs, 06076. (203) 684-3770.

> The town clerk's earliest birth record is 20 November 1718, marriage record is 3 May 1736, and death record is 8 January 1731.

The BARBOUR INDEX covers the years 1734-1850 and is based on the James N. Arnold copy of UNION vital records made in 1911.

PUBLISHED WORKS AND OTHER RECORDS

"An Original Salt Box House Circa 1710." CANTIQUARIAN 15 (July 1963): 21-24.

Lawson, Harvey Merrill. HISTORY OF UNION, CONNECTICUT. New Haven: Price, Lee and Adkins Co., 1893. 509 p.

Wales, Solomon. UNION IN 1803. Hartford: Acorn Club of Conn., 1954. 12 p.

VERNON

TOLLAND COUNTY. Organized October 1808 from BOLTON.

CEMETERY RECORDS AND CEMETERIES

NAME	ADDRESS	HALE NO.	CITATION
Grove Hill Cemetery	Cemetery Avenue (203) 875-3158	1	50:1-139
Elmwood Cemetery	Bolton Road	2	50:140-72
Mt. Hope Cemetery	106 Main Street	3	50:173-85
Old Dobsonville Cemetery	Talcottville	4	51:186-93
Old North Bolton Cemetery	Bolton Road	5	51:194-205
St. Bernard Roman Catholic Cemetery	18 Tolland Avenue	6	51:206-56
St. Bernard Roman Catholic Cemetery	St. Bernard Church	7	51:257
Old Pioneer Cemetery	Barnforth Road		(no citation)
South West Cemetery	Talcottville Road		(no citation)

Index to Hale inscriptions: 51:258-334.

Barbour, Lucius Barnes. "Inscriptions from Gravestones at Vernon, Connecticut." NEHGR 83 (1929): 357-69, 496-504; 84 (1930): 84-93.

DOBSONVILLE, VERNON, CONNECTICUT. OLD WEST CEMETERY COPIED MAY 25, 1926. N.p.: Sabra Trumbull Chapter, DAR, 1926. 9 p.

Old Valley or Valley Falls Cemetery. N.p.: Sabra Trumbull Chapter, DAR, 1926. 15 p.

CHURCH RECORDS

FIRST BAPTIST CHURCH. Minutes, 1842-1939. Vital Records, 1882-1886. (CSL, LDS 2140).

FIRST CONGREGATIONAL CHURCH. Baptisms, 1747-1889. Marriages, 1763-1822. Deaths, 1774-1848. Rev. Allyn S. Kellogg, Comp. (CSL, LDS 2142). Members, 1824-1835. Comp. by Eva K. Thrall Smith (Mrs. Harry C.) (CSL, LDS 2142). Members, 1762-1873. Manuscript notes on the first 124 members. (CSL, LDS 2143). Vital Records, 1762-1940. (CSL, LDS 2139).

ROCKVILLE FIRST CONGREGATIONAL CHURCH. Minutes and Vital Records, 1837-1888. (CSL, LDS 2141 pt. 1).

ROCKVILLE METHODIST EPISCOPAL CHURCH. Vital Records, 1834-1937. (CSL, LDS 2144).

ST. JOHN EPISCOPAL CHURCH. Records: Minutes, 1888-1938. (CSL, LDS 2145). Vital Records, 1827-1879. (CSL, LDS 2144).

SECOND CONGREGATIONAL CHURCH. Minutes, 1848-1888. Vital Records, 1849-1888. (CSL, LDS 2141 pt. 2).

UNION CONGREGATIONAL CHURCH. Minutes, 1888-1934. Vital Records, 1888-1945. (CSL, LDS 2141 pt. 3-4).

INDEX RECORDS TO VERNON CHURCH RECORDS. (CSL, LDS 1448 pt. 35-36).

Johnson, Alvin D. HISTORY OF THE ROCKVILLE BAPTIST CHURCH, ROCKVILLE, CONNECTICUT 1842-1945. N.p., 1945. 102 p.

75TH ANNIVERSARY CELEBRATION 1888-1963 UNION CONGREGATIONAL CHURCH OF CHRIST. Rockville: Union Congregational Church of Christ, 1963. 40 p.

Talcott, Mary Kingsbury. "Records of the Church in Vernon, Connecticut 1762-1824." NEHGR 58 (1904): 193-98, 400-403; 59 (1905): 95-101, 208-14, 412-16; 60 (1906): 73-81, 199-205, 262-68.

HISTORICAL SOCIETY

Vernon Historical Society, (P.O. Box 537), 43 Hale Street. (203) 875-4631.

Publishes VERNON HISTORICAL SOCIETY NEWS.

LAND RECORDS

Land Records, 1808–1863. Index, 1808–1876. (LDS 2138 pt. 1–5).

LIBRARY

Rockville Public Library, 52 Union Street, 06066. (203) 875-5892.

MILITARY RECORDS

Sweeney, William V. WELCOME HOME DAY IN HONOR OF THE MEN AND WOMEN FROM ROCKVILLE AND VERNON WHO SERVED IN THE WORLD WAR 1914–1919. Rockville: n.p., 1919.

NEWSPAPERS

TRI-TOWN TRADER. Weekly. P.O. Box 210, 06066. (203) 872-8515.

The PRELIMINARY CHECKLIST lists eleven newspapers for VERNON.

PROBATE RECORDS

VERNON is in the Ellington Probate District.

TAX RECORDS

Hartford. CSL, Record Group 62. Tax Collector's Lists, 1880–1892.

VITAL RECORDS

Town Clerk, Memorial Building (P.O. Box 245), 14 Park Place, 06066. (203) 872-8591.

VITAL RECORDS OF BOLTON TO 1854 AND VERNON TO 1852. Vital Records of Connecticut Series I. Towns I. Hartford: CHS, 1909. 291 p.

VOTER RECORDS

Hartford. CSL, Record Group 62. Voter Lists, 1864, 1867, 1926.

PUBLISHED WORKS AND OTHER RECORDS

Brookes, George S. CASCADES AND COURAGE: THE HISTORY OF THE TOWN OF VERNON AND THE CITY OF ROCKVILLE, CONNECTICUT. Rockville: T.F. Rady and Co., 1955. 529 p.

Burr, B. Llewellyn. "The City of Rockville." CM 6 (1900): 60-74.

CENTENNIAL OF VERNON (ROCKVILLE), JUNE 28 TO JULY 4, INCLUSIVE, 1908. Rockville: T.F. Rady and Co., 1908. 120 p.

A CENTURY OF VERNON, CONNECTICUT 1808-1908. Rockville: T.F. Rady and Co., 1911. 159 p.

Cogswell, William T. HISTORY OF ROCKVILLE FROM 1823 TO 1871. IN-CLUDING ALSO A BRIEF SKETCH OF FACTS WHICH ANTEDATE THE INCOR-PORATION OF VERNON, AND BRING DATES UP TO THE TIME WHEN THE HISTORY BEGINS. N.p., 1872.

Smith, Harry Conklin. "The Centennial of Vernon." CM 12 (1908): 162-207.

VOLUNTOWN

NEW LONDON COUNTY. Organized May 1721. Towns organized from VOLUNTOWN include STERLING.

CEMETERY RECORDS AND CEMETERIES

NAME	ADDRESS	HALE NO.	CITATION
Gallup Cemetery	Pendleton Hill Road 3 miles south of Church	1	51:1-2
Robbins Cemetery	1/2 mile east of Church	2	51:2-16
Kennedy Cemetery	2 miles northeast of Church	3	51:17-30
Kinne Cemetery	1 mile south of Church, near Griswold town line	4	51:31-32
Gallup Cemetery	South part of town	5	51:32-33
Palmer-Newton Cemetery	Southeast part of town	6	51:33
Palmer Cemetery	South part of town	7	51:34
Brown Cemetery	North part of town	8	51:34-35
Potter Cemetery	Near Beach Pond	9	51:35
Lewis Cemetery	Near Beach Pond	10	51:35-36
Phillips Cemetery	North of Beach Pond	11	51:36
Bly Cemetery	North of Phillips Cemetery	12	51:37
Bitgood Cemetery	Northeast part of town	13	51:37-38
Bitgood Cemetery	(Not located)	14	51:38
Douglass Cemetery	(Not located)	15	51:38-38A
Tennant Cemetery	(Not located)	16	51:38A-38B
Reynolds Cemetery #1	(Not located)	17	51:38B
Reynolds Cemetery #2	(Not located)	18	51:38B

Soldiers Burials 51:40-43. Index 51:56-57.

Index to Hale inscriptions: 51:44-45.

CHURCH RECORDS

CONGREGATIONAL CHURCH. Marriages, 1729-1800. BAILEY 3:124-32.

FIRST CONGREGATIONAL CHURCH. Vital Records, 1723-1826. Mrs. J.L. Raymond, comp. (CSL, LDS 1700).

FIRST PRESBYTERIAN CHURCH. Records, 1723-1764 (Hist. Soc. of Penn., LDS 441,390).

VOLUNTOWN AND STERLING CONGREGATIONAL CHURCH. Records, 1723-1905. Index. (CSL, LDS 1448, pt. 8, 33). Minutes, 1727-1889. Vital Records, 1723-1914. (CSL, LDS 2137, pt. 1-2). Records 1779-1910, copied by Emma Finney Welch. (Hist. Soc. of Penn., LDS 441,390).

"List of Original Members or Signers of the Live Church of Voluntown and Sterling, Connecticut . . . as of 1723." NYGBR 65 (1934): 301.

"List of Original Members or Signers of the Live Church of Voluntown and Sterling, Connecticut . . . as of 1723." ANCESTRAL NOTES FROM CHEDWATO 13 (1966): 4-7.

"Voluntown Live Church . . . 1745-6 . . . Membership." ANCESTRAL NOTES FROM CHEDWATO 13 (1966): 94-96.

HISTORICAL SOCIETY

Voluntown Historical Society, Wylie School, Route 49, 06384. (203) 376-9761.

LAND RECORDS

Land Records, 1696-1851. Index, 1696-1920. (LDS 2135 pt. 1-7).

LIBRARY

Voluntown Public Library, 06384. (203) 376-0485.

PROBATE RECORDS

Voluntown Probate District was in existence from 4 June 1830 to 3 April 1889, when it became part of the Norwich Probate District.

VOLUNTOWN is part of the Plainfield Probate District.

ON FILE AT THE CSL: Estate Papers, 1831-1876 (papers after 1876 are under the Norwich Probate District). Indexes, 1831-1876. Inventory Control Book, 1831-1876. Court Record Books, 1831-1851.

Probate Records, 1830-1851. (LDS 2134).

SCHOOL RECORDS

Hartford. CSL, Record Group 62. Minutes of School Society and Town Meetings, 1798-1863.

TAX RECORDS

Hartford. CSL, Record Group 62. Military Tax Accounts, 1851-1854.

VITAL RECORDS

Town Clerk, Town Hall, Main Street, 06834. (203) 376-4089.

The BARBOUR INDEX covers the years 1708-1867 and is based on the James N. Arnold copy of VOLUNTOWN vital records made in 1910. The earliest birth date is 31 December 1850, marriage is 31 December 1850 and the death is 5 December 1867.

Robinson, Mr. Burr A., and Robinson, Mrs. Burr A. "Voluntown, Connecticut, Records. Marriage Records, 1751-1776. Court Records, 1751-1773. Kinney Family Records. An Original Manuscript." NYGBR 65 (1934): 301-8.

WALLINGFORD

NEW HAVEN COUNTY. Organized May 1670. Towns organized from WAL-
LINGFORD include CHESHIRE and MERIDEN.

CEMETERY RECORDS AND CEMETERIES

NAME	ADDRESS	HALE NO.	CITATION
Center Street Cemetery	Center Street	1	51:1-128
Holy Trinity Roman Catholic Church Cemetery	346 North Colony Street office: 250 Gypsy Lane, Meriden, 06450 (203) 237-3226	2	51:129-57
St. John Roman Catholic Cemetery	150 East Christian Street office: 250 Gypsy Lane, Meriden, 06450 (203) 237-3226	3	51:157-76
Wallingford Jewish Cemetery	223 Dudley Avenue	4	51:177
In Memoriam Cemetery	586 North Main Street	5	51:178-222
St. Casimir Cemetery	Doolittle's Crossing	6	51:223-24
Masonic Cemetery	549 Hall Avenue	7	51:225-28
Gaylord Cemetery	Gaylord Sanitorium	8	51:229-30
St. Peter and St. Paul Cemetery	1007 Durham Road		(no citation)

Index to Hale inscriptions: 51:231-93.

Benton, Mrs. Frederick P., ed. "Centre Cemetery." In CEMETERY RECORDS,
pp. 42-87. (LDS 850,401).

"Connecticut Headstone Inscriptions Before 1800-Wallingford." CN 10 (1978): 595-97; 11 (1978): 26-31, 220-25.

CENSUS RECORDS

Jacobus, Donald Lines. "Error in the Census of 1790 (Conn.)." NEHGR 77 (1923): 81.

CHURCH RECORDS

FIRST BAPTIST CHURCH. Minutes, 1817-1920. Vital Records, 1790-1920. (CSL, LDS 2181 pt. 1-3).

FIRST CONGREGATIONAL CHURCH. Vital Records, 1758-1894. (CSL, LDS 2179). Index. (CSL, LDS 1448). Marriages, 1759-1799. BAILEY 4:58-68, 5:122.

METHODIST CHURCH. Vital Records, 1895-1932. (CSL, LDS 2180).

ST. PAUL EPISCOPAL CHURCH. Vital Records, 1832-1900. (CSL, LDS 2182).

SECOND BAPTIST CHURCH. Minutes, 1790-1822. (CSL, LDS 2181 pt. 1).

"Items from Wallingford (Conn.) Church Records." TAG 16 (1940): 188-89.

HISTORICAL SOCIETY

Wallingford Historical Society, 180 South Main Street, 06492. (203) 269-2054.

LAND RECORDS

Land Records, 1670-1854. Index, 1670-1874. (LDS 2176 pt. 1-27).

LIBRARY

Wallingford Public Library, 60 North Main Street, 06492. (203) 265-6754.

MILITARY RECORDS

Jacobus, Donald Lines. "Wallingford Soldiers." NEW HAVEN GENEALOGICAL MAGAZINE 1 (1923): 241-48.

NEWSPAPERS

WALLINGFORD POST. Weekly. P.O. Box 9, 06492. (203) 269-1464.

The PRELIMINARY CHECKLIST lists seven newspapers for WALLINGFORD.

PROBATE RECORDS

Wallingford Probate District, Municipal Building, 350 Center Street, 06492. (203) 265-2081.

The Wallingford Probate District was organized May 1776 from Guilford and New Haven Probate Districts.

Probate districts formed from the Wallingford Probate District include the Cheshire, Meriden and North Branford Probate Districts.

ON FILE AT THE CSL: Estate Papers, 1776-1909. Indexes, 1776-1909. Inventory Control Book, 1776-1909. Court Record Books, 1776-1855.

Probate Records 1776-1855. (LDS).

VITAL RECORDS

Town Clerk, Municipal Building, 350 Center Street (P.O. Box 427) 06492. (203) 265-0911.

The BARBOUR INDEX covers the years 1670-1850 and is based on a copy of the original records made by Miss Ethel L. Scofield in 1914.

Vital Records, 6 April 1917-1920 clipped from the Norwalk HOUR. 141 p. (LDS).

VITAL RECORDS 1671-1818. (NYGB, LDS 2178).

Jacobus, Donald Lines. "Wallingford Vital Records, 1671-1706. In Land Records, Volume I." TAG 14 (1937): 22-33, 109-17.

PUBLISHED WORKS AND OTHER RECORDS

Curtis, George Munson. "Meriden and Wallingford in Colonial and Revolutionary Days." NHCHS PAPERS 7 (1908): 298-327.

Davis, Charles Henry Stanley. HISTORY OF WALLINGFORD, CONNECTICUT FROM ITS PRESENT SETTLEMENT IN 1670 TO THE PRESENT TIME, INCLUDING MERIDEN, WHICH WAS ONE OF ITS PARISHES UNTIL 1806, AND CHESHIRE, WHICH WAS INCORPORATED IN 1780. Meriden: Author, 1870. 956 p.

Gillespie, C.B. SOUVENIR HISTORY OF WALLINGFORD, CONNECTICUT, 1895. Meriden: Journal Publishing Co., 1895. 50 p.

Hale, Clarence E. TALES OF OLD WALLINGFORD. Chester, Conn.: Pequot Press, 1971. 154 p.

Kendrick, John B. HISTORY OF THE WALLINGFORD DISASTER. Hartford: Case, Lockwood and Brainard Co., 1878. 76 p.

Royce, Lucy A. "The Nehemiah Royce or Washington Elm House, Wallingford, Connecticut." OLD TIME NEW ENGLAND 25 (October 1934): 41-49.

Stanley, George Washington. WALLINGFORD IN 1811-12. Hartford: Acorn Club of Connecticut, 1961. 25 p.

Tucker, Robert L. "Addenda to 'Early Families of Wallingford.'" CN 2 (1969): 30-31.

_____. "Additional Genealogical Lineage for the 'Early Families of Wallingford, Connecticut.'" CN 13 (1980): 213-14.

WARREN

LITCHFIELD COUNTY. Organized May 1786 from KENT.

CEMETERY RECORDS AND CEMETERIES

NAME	ADDRESS	HALE NO.	CITATION
Old Cemetery	North of Center	1	51:1-30
New Cemetery	East of Center	2	51:31-32
Averill Cemetery	W.H. Hopkins farm, south part of town	3	51:33-34

Index to Hale inscriptions: 51:35-44.

Carter, Howard W., and Carter, N.R.C. INSCRIPTIONS IN CEMETERY AT WARREN, CONNECTICUT 1916. N.p.: Authors, 1916. 196 p.

CHURCH RECORDS

CONGREGATIONAL CHURCH. Vital Records, 1757-1931. (CSL, LDS 2154).

Curtis, Lucy Sackett. CONGREGATIONAL CHURCH, WARREN, CONNECTI-CUT 1756-1956. Warren: Brewer-Borg Corp., 1956. 136 p.

HISTORICAL SOCIETY

Warren Historical Society, R.F.D. Cornwall Bridge, 06754. (203) 868-7737.

LAND RECORDS

Land Records, 1786-1879. Index, 1786-1917. (LDS 2153 pt. 1-5).

LIBRARY

Warren Public Library, Sackett Hill, 06754. (203) 868-2195.

PROBATE RECORDS

WARREN is in the Litchfield Probate District.

TAX RECORDS

Hartford. CSL, Record Group 62. Abstracts, 1787-1851.

VITAL RECORDS

Town Clerk, Town Hall (P.O. Box 25), 06754. (203) 868-0090.

The BARBOUR INDEX covers the years 1786 to 1850 and is based on the James N. Arnold copy of WARREN vital records made in 1916.

WASHINGTON

LITCHFIELD COUNTY. Organized January 1779 from KENT, LITCHFIELD, NEW MILFORD and WOODBURY.

CEMETERY RECORDS AND CEMETERIES

NAME	ADDRESS	HALE NO.	CITATION
New Cemetery	Washington Green	1	51:1-41
Old Cemetery	1 mile southeast from Washington Center	2	51:42-57
New Preston Cemetery	Christian Street	3	51:58-81
Baldwin Cemetery	Baldwin Hill 2 1/2 miles from Washington Depot	4	51:82-83
Davies Cemetery	Private at Romford	5	51:84-85
Hartshorn Cemetery	Not located	6	51:84-85
Averill Cemetery	Kinney Hill Road		(no citation)
Davis Hollow Burying Grounds	Sabbaday Lane		(no citation)
Judea Cemetery	Judea Cemetery Road		(no citation)
Washington Green Cemetery	Parsonage Lane		(no citation)

Index to Hale inscriptions: 51:86-110.

Hemmingson, Marion Wilson. INSCRIPTIONS ON ALL STONES STILL STANDING IN EXISTING CEMETERIES IN THE TOWN OF WASHINGTON, CONNECTICUT, COPIED BY MRS. HELEN SHORE BOYD IN 1910. N.p.: Judea Chapter, DAR, n.d. 10 p.

CHURCH RECORDS

FIRST CONGREGATIONAL CHURCH. Minutes, 1741-1919. Vital Records, 1757-1845. (CSL, LDS 2196, and 2197). Marriages, 1749-1797. BAILEY 1:95-101. Marriages, 1770-1799. BAILEY 5:71-77.

ST. ANDREW EPISCOPAL CHURCH. Minutes, 1784-1939. Vital Records. (CSL, LDS 2198).

"Washington, Litchfield Co., Connecticut. Marriages (Rev. Daniel Brinsmade, Congregational Church in Washington)." NGSQ 23 (1935): 60.

HISTORICAL SOCIETY

Gunn Memorial Library, Historical Museum, Wykeham Road, 06793. (203) 868-7756.

LAND RECORDS

Land Records, 1779-1855. Index, 1779-1849. (LDS 2194, pt. 1-8).

LIBRARY

Gunn Memorial Library, Wykeham Road, 06793. (203) 868-7586.

NEWSPAPERS

The PRELIMINARY CHECKLIST lists three newspapers for WASHINGTON.

PROBATE RECORDS

Washington Probate District, Town Hall, Washington Depot, 06794. (203) 868-7974.

> The Washington Probate District was organized 22 May 1832 from the Litchfield and Woodbury Probate Districts.

> ON FILE AT THE CSL: Court Record Books, 1832-1855. Probate Records, 1832-1855. (LDS 2195).

SCHOOL RECORDS

Hartford. CSL, Record Group 62. Northeast School District Records, 1858-1882. Seventh School District Records, 1846-1847.

VITAL RECORDS

Town Clerk, Town Hall, Washington Depot, 06794. (203) 838-2786.

The BARBOUR INDEX covers the years 1779 to 1854 and is based on a photostat copy of volume one and the manuscript copy of volume two made by James N. Arnold. Both copies are in the State Library.

HISTORY OF ANCIENT WOODBURY by William Cothren (see below) includes a section of WASHINGTON vital records, pp. 312-426.

VOTER RECORDS

Hartford. CSL, Record Group 62. Elector lists, 1871, 1872, 1880.

PUBLISHED WORKS AND OTHER RECORDS

Cothren, William. HISTORY OF ANCIENT WOODBURY, CONNECTICUT, FROM THE FIRST INDIAN DEED IN 1659 TO 1854 INCLUDING THE PRESENT TOWNS OF WASHINGTON, SOUTHBURY, BETHLEHEM, ROXBURY, AND A PART OF OXFORD AND MIDDLEBURY. Waterbury: Bronson Press, 1854. 841 p. (LDS 2205).

Kilbourne, Dwight C. "Washington." CQ 4 (1898): 236-56.

Miller, Ogden. "Aspects of Washington History." CANTIQUARIAN 13 (July 1961): 15-18.

Seeley, Polly L. TWO HUNDRED YEARS OF WASHINGTON: A PICTURE BOOK. Washington, Conn.: Historical Museum of Gunn Memorial Library, 1975. 52 p.

Van Sinderen, Adrian. OUR HOME IN THE COUNTRYSIDE. New York: Author, 1957. 135 p.

WATERBURY

NEW HAVEN COUNTY. Organized May 1686. Towns organized from WA-
TERBURY include MIDDLEBURY, NAUGATUCK, PROSPECT, WATERTOWN and
WOLCOTT.

CEMETERY RECORDS AND CEMETERIES

NAME	ADDRESS	HALE NO.	CITATION
Calvary Cemetery	Office: 2324 East Main Street (203) 754-9105	1	52:1-134
St. Joseph Cemetery (New)	Hamilton Avenue Office: 2324 East Main Street (203) 754-9105	2	52:135-231
St. Joseph Cemetery (Old)	Hamilton Avenue Office: 2324 East Main Street (203) 754-9105	3	52:232-348
Riverside Cemetery	496 Riverside Street (203) 754-1902	4	52:349-587
Pine Grove Cemetery	390 Meriden Road (203) 753-0776	5	52:588-636
St. Mary Russian Orthodox Cemetery	Stillson Road	6	53:637-87
Lithuanian Association Cemetery	100 Plank Road	7	53:693-95
Brockett Hill Cemetery	Southern part of town	8	53:696-700
Waterville Cemetery	Waterville	9	53:701-6
Star Lodge (Benevolent Association) Cemetery	300 Stillson Road	10	53:707-8
Waterbury Hebrew Benefit Association Cemetery	Stillson Road	11	53:709-15

NAME	ADDRESS	HALE NO.	CITATION
Brass City Lodge Cemetery	Northeast part of city	12	53:716-22
Workman Circle Cemetery	290 Stillson Road	13	53:723
Melchizedek Cemetery	76 Plank Road	14	53:724-26
Buck's Hill Cemetery	Cemetery Road	15	53:727-36
New Pine Grove Cemetery	924 Meriden Road	16	53:737-49
East Farms Cemetery	3148 East Main Street	17	53:750-55
City Cemetery	Moved to Riverside Cemetery	18	53:756
Congregation Israel Sharis Cemetery	Woodtick Road	19	53:757-59
Payne Cemetery	Near Reservoir	20	53:760
Duggan Cemetery	St. Patrick Church	21	53:761
Old Cemetery	Site of Library Park	22	53:762-63
Grand Street Cemetery	Corner of Grand and Meadow Streets	23	53:764-92
All Saints Cemetery	203 Spring Lake Road (203) 755-2257		(no citation)

Index to Hale inscriptions: 53:793-1017.

"Headstones -- Waterbury, Connecticut." CN 12:226-29.

Prichard, Katherine Adelaid. ANCIENT BURYING GROUNDS OF THE TOWN OF WATERBURY, CONNECTICUT TOGETHER WITH OTHER RECORDS OF CHURCH AND TOWN. Publications of the Mattatuck Historical Society, vol. 2. Waterbury: Mattatuck Historical Society, 1917. 338 p.

CENSUS RECORDS

Jacobus, Donald Lines. "Errors in the Census of 1790 (Conn.)." NEHGR 77 (1923): 81.

Judd, Sturges M. 1876 CENSUS OF WATERBURY. N.p., n.d.

CHURCH RECORDS

FIRST CHURCH OF CHRIST (CONGREGATIONAL). Minutes, 1806-1875. Vital Records, 1795-1895. (CSL, LDS 2202).

ST. JOHN EPISCOPAL CHURCH. Minutes, 1761-1880. Vital Records, 1830-1927. (CSL, LDS 2201 pt. 1-2).

Anderson, Joseph. CHURCHES OF MATTATUCK. New Haven: Price, Lee and Adkins, 1892. 279 p.

A CENTURY OF HISTORY IN THE FIRST BAPTIST CHURCH IN WATERBURY, CONNECTICUT. Hartford: Case, Lockwood and Brainard Co., 1904. 206 p.

Kingsbury, Frederick John. A NARRATIVE AND DOCUMENTARY HISTORY OF ST. JOHN'S PROTESTANT EPISCOPAL CHURCH (FORMERLY ST. JAMES) OF WATERBURY, CONNECTICUT WITH SOME NOTICE OF ST. PAUL'S CHURCH, PLYMOUTH, CHRIST CHURCH, WATERTOWN, ST. MICHAEL'S CHURCH, NAUGATUCK, A CHURCH IN MIDDLEBURY, ALL SAINTS CHURCH, WOLCOTT, ST. PAUL'S CHURCH, WATERVILLE, TRINITY CHURCH, WATERBURY (ALL COLONIES OF ST. JOHN'S). New Haven: Price, Lee and Adkins, 1907. 181 p. Index.

HISTORICAL SOCIETY

Mattatuck Historical Society, 119 West Main Street, 06702. (203) 754-5500.

Publishes OCCASIONAL PAPERS, 1943-- . Irregular.

LAND RECORDS

Land Records, 1672-1850. Index, 1672-1855. (LDS 2199 pt. 1-30).

Prichard, Katherine A. PROPRIETORS RECORDS OF THE TOWN OF WATERBURY, CONNECTICUT 1677-1761. Publications of the Mattatuck Historical Society, vol. 1. Waterbury: Mattatuck Historical Society, 1911. 260 p.

LIBRARY

Silas Bronson Library, 267 Grand Street, 06702. (203) 755-2218.

MILITARY RECORDS

Anderson, Joseph. HISTORY OF THE SOLDIER'S MONUMENT IN WATERBURY, CONNECTICUT. Hartford: Case, Lockwood and Brainard Co., 1886. 170 p.

Burpee, Charles Winslow. MILITARY HISTORY OF WATERBURY, FROM THE

FOUNDING OF THE SETTLEMENT IN 1678 TO 1891, TOGETHER WITH A
LIST OF COMMISSIONED OFFICERS AND THE RECORDS OF THE WARS;
CONTAINING ALSO AN OUTLINE OF THE CHANGES IN THE MILITARY
ORGANIZATION OF THE STATE. New Haven: Price, Lee and Adkins Co.,
1891. 98 p.

Hartford. CSL, Record Group 29. State Military Census, 1917. Census.
List of compilers.

NEWSPAPERS

WATERBURY AMERICAN/WATERBURY REPUBLICAN. Daily. P.O. Box 2090,
06720. (203) 754-0141.

The WATERBURY AMERICAN/WATERBURY REPUBLICAN is indexed by the newspaper since 1940 and by the Bronson Library since 1976.

WATERBURY INQUIRER. Weekly. P.O. Box 1937, 06720. (203) 574-4477.

Wolkovich-Valkavicius, William. "The Impact of a Catholic Newspaper on
an Ethnic Community: the Lituanian Weekly Rytas, 1896-98, Waterbury, Connecticut." LITUANUS 24 (1978): 42-53.

The HALE NEWSPAPER INDEX to deaths and marriages includes the WATER-
BURY AMERICAN 14 December 1844-27 December 1867.

The PRELIMINARY CHECKLIST lists twenty-seven newspapers for WATERBURY.

PROBATE RECORDS

Waterbury Probate District, City Hall Annex, Chase Building, 236 Grand Street,
06702. (203) 755-1127.

> The Waterbury Probate District was organized May 1779 from the
> Woodbury Probate District.

> The Waterbury Probate District also includes MIDDLEBURY and
> WOLCOTT.

> Probate districts organized from the Waterbury Probate District in-
> clude the Naugatuck, Plymouth, Thomaston and Watertown Probate
> Districts.

> ON FILE AT THE CSL: Estate Papers, 1779-1945. Indexes, 1779-
> 1945. Inventory Control Book, 1779-1945. Court Record Books,
> 1779-1851.

Probate Records, 1779-1851. (LDS 2200 pt. 1-6).

VITAL RECORDS

Town Clerk, City Hall, 235 Grand Street, 06702. (203) 756-9494, ext. 262.

> The town clerk's earliest birth record is 16 December 1672, marriage record 28 December 1682 and death record 7 February 1702/3.

The BARBOUR INDEX covers the years 1686 to 1853 and is based on the James N. Arnold copy of WATERBURY vital records made in 1915.

PUBLISHED WORKS AND OTHER RECORDS

Anderson, Joseph. TOWN AND CITY OF WATERBURY, CONNECTICUT, FROM THE ABORIGINAL PERIOD TO THE YEAR EIGHTEEN HUNDRED AND NINETY-FIVE. 3 vols. New Haven: Price and Lee Co., 1896.

Bronson, Henry. HISTORY OF WATERBURY, CONNECTICUT. THE ORIGINAL TOWNSHIP EMBRACING PRESENT WATERTOWN, AND PLYMOUTH, AND PARTS OF OXFORD, WOLCOTT, MIDDLEBURY, PROSPECT AND NAUGATUCK WITH AN APPENDIX OF BIOGRAPHY, GENEALOGY AND STATISTICS. Waterbury: Bronson Brothers, 1858. 583 p. Index.

Brush, J.E.C. "Mattatuck of Yore -- Waterbury of Today." AMERICANA 32 (1937): 7-48.

Church, U.G. "The Reconstruction of Waterbury." CM 8 (1904): 625-29.

_____. "Sketch of Early Waterbury." CM 7 (1901): 118-32.

Joy, Patricia. THE HISTORICAL HERITAGE OF THE CITY OF WATERBURY; A BIBLIOGRAPHY OF LOCAL HISTORY MATERIALS IN THE SILAS BRONSON LIBRARY, WATERBURY, CONNECTICUT. Waterbury, Conn.: Silas Bronson Library, 1974. 7 p.

Kingsbury, Alice Eliza. IN OLD WATERBURY: THE MEMOIRS OF ALICE E. KINGSBURY. Waterbury, Conn.: Mattatuck Historical Society, 1942. 55 p.

Mattatuck Historical Society. JOHN W. HILL AND THE WATERBURY CANCELLATIONS: A CHECKLIST. Waterbury, Conn.: 1938. 47 p.

_____. WATERBURY, 1674-1974: A PICTORIAL HISTORY. Chester, Conn.: Pequot Press, 1974. 228 p.

Pape, William Jamieson. HISTORY OF WATERBURY AND THE NAUGATUCK VALLEY CONNECTICUT. 3 vols. Chicago: S.J. Clarke Publishing Co., 1918.

"Science of Modern Building." CM 8 (1904): 630-39.

Silas Bronson Library. Reference Department. A BRIEF HISTORY OF WATERBURY. Waterbury, Conn.: 1974. 6 p.

West, Florence. "Waterbury: Its Prominent Interests and People." CM 7 (1901): 133-45.

WATERFORD

NEW LONDON COUNTY. Organized October 1801 from NEW LONDON. Towns organized from WATERFORD include EAST LYME.

CEMETERY RECORDS AND CEMETERIES

NAME	ADDRESS	HALE NO.	CITATION
Mullen Hill or Howard Cemetery	78 Mullen Hill Road	1	53:1-12
Durfey Hill Cemetery	Niantic Road	2	53:13-14
Pepper Box Hill Cemetery	Great Neck Section	3	53:15
Harkness Estate Cemetery	Great Neck Section	4	53:16
Jordan Cemetery	240 Boston Post Road (203) 442-3893	5	53:17-120A
St. Mary Roman Catholic Cemetery	New London line near Hartford and New London Road	6	53:121-235
West Neck Cemetery	202 Great Neck Road	7	53:236-43
Old Rogers Cemetery	2 Shore Road	8	53:244-45
East Neck Cemetery	143 Niles Hill Road	9	53:246-59
Ames Cemetery	Near Montville line 1/8 mile opposite old school	10	53:260
Gorton Cemetery	On farm of Frank Steward	11	53:261
Morgan Cemetery	On farm of George Peabody	12	53:262
Old Quaker Hill Cemetery	Norwich and New London Road	13	53:263-66
New Quaker Hill Cemetery	Norwich and New London Road	14	53:267-83
Lakes Pond Cemetery	1140 Hartford Turnpike	15	54:284-86

NAME	ADDRESS	HALE NO.	CITATION
Caulkins Cemetery	Next to Old Church near Lakes Pond Cemetery	16	54:287
Sandpit Cemetery	Hartford and New London Highway	17	54:288
King Cemetery	On farm of Willis Minor, opposite Jordan Cemetery	18	54:289
Beckwith Cemetery	On Horace Landphear Estate Great Neck Section	19	54:290
Brown Cemetery	On property of Harry Gardiner Millstone, near Jordan Cove	20	54:291
Jewish Cemetery	Near Jordan Cemetery, Main Road New Haven and New London	21	54:292-302
Crane Cemetery	Crane's Woods on Fog Plain Road	22	54:303
Slaves Cemetery	On Eva Beebe property next to Cemetery #10	23	54:304
Unmarked graveyard	Northwest of #5	24	54:305
Scholfield Cemetery	On property of F. Schofield Quaker Hill	25	54:306
Raymond Cemetery	On the George R. Darrow estate at Oswegatchie	26	54:307
Darrow Cemetery	On Henry Hedden farm, at Great Neck	27	54:308
Brown Cemetery	At Jordan Cove (not located)	28	54:308A
Richards Cemetery	Old Colchester Road, on Richards estate	29	54:308B
Wheeler Cemetery		30	54:308B-9

Index to Hale inscriptions: 54:310-90.

Barbour, Lucius Barnes. "Connecticut Cemetery Inscriptions." NEHGR 98 (1944): 287-88.

Gates, Benjamin F. "Graveyard Inscriptions at East Neck, Waterford, Conn." NEHGR 57 (1903): 383.

Holman, Winifred Lovering. "Raymond Cemetery, Waterford, Connecticut." NEHGR 94 (1940): 394.

CHURCH RECORDS

CHRIST CHURCH (EPISCOPAL). Vital Records, 1850-1913. (LDS 2170).

FIRST BAPTIST CHURCH. Vital Records, 1786-1841. Mrs. L. Raymond, comp. (CSL, LDS 1700). Vital Records, 1786-1878. (CSL, LDS 2169 pt. 1).

SECOND BAPTIST CHURCH. Vital Records, 1835-1916. (CSL. LDS 2169 pt. 2).

HISTORICAL SOCIETY

Waterford Historical Society, 06835.

LAND RECORDS

Land Records, 1801-1856. Index, 1801-1855. (LDS 2168 pt. 1-6).

LIBRARY

Waterford Public Library, 49 Rope Ferry Road, 06385. (203) 443-0224.

NEWSPAPER

The PRELIMINARY CHECKLIST lists one newspaper for WATERFORD.

PROBATE RECORDS

WATERFORD is in the New London Probate District.

VITAL RECORDS

Town Clerk, Hall of Records, 200 Boston Post Road, 06385. (203) 442-0331.

The town clerk's earliest birth, marriage and death records date from 1801.

The BARBOUR INDEX covers from 1801-1851 and is based on the James N. Arnold copy of WATERFORD vital records made in 1911 and includes a list of freemen from 1802-1844.

PUBLISHED WORKS AND OTHER RECORDS

Bachman, Robert L. AN ILLUSTRATED HISTORY OF THE TOWN OF WATER-
FORD. Waterford, Conn.: Morningside Press, 1967. 114 p. Index.

_____. WATERFORD AND INDEPENDENCE, 1776–1976: OBSERVING THE
TWO HUNDREDTH ANNIVERSARY OF THE BIRTH OF THE UNITED STATES
AND THE ONE HUNDRED AND SEVENTY FIFTH ANNIVERSARY OF THE IN-
CORPORATION OF THE TOWN OF WATERFORD, CONNECTICUT. Water-
ford, Conn.: American Revolution Bicentennial Committee, Waterford, 1975.
43 p. Index.

WATERTOWN

LITCHFIELD COUNTY. Organized May 1780 from WATERBURY. Towns organized from WATERTOWN include PLYMOUTH.

CEMETERY RECORDS AND CEMETERIES

NAME	ADDRESS	HALE NO.	CITATION
Evergreen Cemetery	165 North Street (203) 274-4151	1	54:1-46
Old Cemetery	851 Main Street	2	54:47-85
Mt. St. James Cemetery	97 Porter Street	3	54:86-91
New Evergreen Cemetery	165 North Street	4	54:92-110
Hopkins Cemetery	East Boundary, Connecticut State Park	5	54:111-12
Mt. Olivet Cemetery	Platt Road (203) 274-4641		(no citation)

Index to Hale inscriptions: 54:113-47.

A CHRONOLOGICAL LIST OF PERSONS INTERRED IN THE OLD CEMETERY AT WATERTOWN, CONNECTICUT INCLUDING DATE OF DEATH, AGE AND FAMILY RELATION. N.p., 1884. 21 p.

THE OLD BURYING GROUND OF ANCIENT WESTBURY AND PRESENT WATERTOWN. Watertown: Sarah Whitman Trumbull Chapter, DAR, 1938. 145 p.

Prichard, Katherine Adelaid. ANCIENT BURYING GROUNDS OF THE TOWN OF WATERBURY CONNECTICUT TOGETHER WITH OTHER RECORDS OF CHURCH AND TOWN. Publications of the Mattatuck Historical Society, vol. 2. Waterbury: Mattatuck Historical Society, 1917. 338 p.

CHURCH RECORDS

CHRIST (EPISCOPAL) CHURCH. Minutes, 1784–1913. Vital Records, 1829–1850. (CSL, LDS 2192).

FIRST CONGREGATIONAL CHURCH. Minutes, 1799–1864. Vital Records, 1785–1887. Index. (CSL, LDS 2190).

METHODIST CHURCH. Vital Records, 1853–1941. (CSL, LDS 2193).

METHODIST EPISCOPAL CHURCH. Records, 1820–1826. (CSL, LDS 2191).

A NARRATIVE AND DOCUMENTARY HISTORY OF ST. JOHN'S PROTESTANT EPISCOPAL CHURCH (FORMERLY ST. JAMES) OF WATERBURY, CONNECTICUT, WITH SOME NOTICE OF ST. PAUL'S CHURCH, PLYMOUTH, CHRIST CHURCH, WATERTOWN, ST. MICHAEL'S CHURCH, NAUGATUCK, A CHURCH IN MID-DLEBURY, ALL SAINTS CHURCH, WOLCOTT, ST. PAUL'S CHURCH, WATER-VILLE, TRINITY CHURCH, WATERBURY (ALL COLONIES OF ST. JOHN'S). New Haven: Price, Lee and Adkins Co., 1907. 181 p.

HISTORICAL SOCIETY

Watertown Historical Society, 22 DeForest Street, 06795. (203) 274-2941.

LAND RECORDS

Land Records, 1780–1858. Index, 1780–1899. (LDS 2188 pt. 1-12).

LIBRARY

Watertown Library Association, 470 Main Street, 06795. (203) 274-6729.

NEWSPAPERS

TOWN TIMES. Weekly. P.O. Box 1, 06795. (203) 274-6721.

The PRELIMINARY CHECKLIST lists eight newspapers for WATERTOWN.

PROBATE RECORDS

Watertown Probate District, Town Hall, 37 DeForest Street, P.O. Box 7, 06795. (203) 274-5411.

> The Watertown Probate District was organized 3 June 1834 from the Waterbury Probate District.

Probate Records, 1834–1860. (CSL, LDS 2189 pt. 1–2).

TAX RECORDS

Hartford. CSL, Record Group 62. Tax lists, 1847–1848, 1851.

VITAL RECORDS

Town Clerk, Town Hall, 37 DeForest Street, 06795. (203) 274–5411.

> The town clerk's earliest birth record is 1759, marriage record is 1756 and death record is 1772.

The BARBOUR INDEX covers the years 1780–1850 and is based on the James N. Arnold copy of WATERTOWN vital records made in 1916.

RECORD OF MORTALITY OF THE TOWN OF WATERTOWN, CONNECTICUT FROM THE SETTLEMENT OF THE TOWN TO THE PRESENT TIME. Watertown: Perlee W. Abbott, 1889. 72 p.

PUBLISHED WORKS AND OTHER RECORDS

Dayton, Frederick. THIRD SERIES OF THE HISTORICAL SKETCH OF WATERTOWN, WITH THE RECORD OF ITS MORTALITY FROM 1858 TO 1871. Waterbury: Press of Cooke, Mattoon and Robbins, 1871. 29 p.

HISTORY OF ANCIENT WESTBURY AND PRESENT WATERTOWN FROM ITS SETTLEMENT TO 1907. Watertown: Sarah Whitman Trumbull Chapter, DAR, n.d. 114 p.

Klamkin, Marian. WATERTOWN THEN AND NOW. Derby: Bacon Printing Co., 1976. 144 p.

Richardson, N.S., and Dayton, Frederick. HISTORICAL SKETCH OF WATERTOWN FROM ITS ORIGINAL SETTLEMENT, WITH THE RECORD OF ITS MORTALITY, FROM MARCH 1741 TO JANUARY 1845 AND TO MAY, 1858. Waterbury: E.B. Cooke, 1858. 72 p.

WESTBROOK

MIDDLESEX COUNTY.   Organized May 1840 from DEEP RIVER.

CEMETERY RECORDS AND CEMETERIES

NAME	ADDRESS	HALE NO.	CITATION
Old Cemetery	Center	1	54:1-13
Lower Cemetery	South Main Street	2	54:14-32
Upper Cemetery	Old Clinton Road	3	54:33-57
New Upper Cemetery	North of Old Upper Cemetery	4	54:58-59
Small Pox Cemetery	Toby Mill Road, Farm of Paul Orsina	5	54:60
Ben Wright Cemetery	On Boylan Farm	6	54:61
David Wright Cemetery	Grove Beach, near Post Office	7	54:62
Cyrus Cemetery	Essex Road		(no citation)
Resurrection Cemetery	Horse Hill Road		(no citation)

Index to Hale inscriptions: 54:63-80.

CEMETERY INSCRIPTIONS.   Typescript.   67 p.   Index.   (NYGB, LDS 2155).

CHURCH RECORDS

CONGREGATIONAL CHURCH.   Vital Records, 1724-1838.   (CSL, LDS 2157).
SECOND CONGREGATIONAL CHURCH.   Marriages, 1726/7-1799.   BAILEY 2:113-20.   Marriages, 1758-1799.   BAILEY 7:57-61.

METHODIST-EPISCOPAL CHURCH RECORDS, WESTBROOK, CONNECTICUT (NEW HAVEN DISTRICT): BIRTHS, MARRIAGES, DEATHS, 1838-40, 1870-85, 1909-39. N.p.: n.d. 10 p.

Rumsey, Jean. FIRST CONGREGATIONAL CHURCH OF WESTBROOK, CONNECTICUT 1725-1899: BAPTISMS, MARRIAGES, DEATHS AND MEMBERSHIPS SUPPLEMENTED BY GRAVESTONE INSCRIPTIONS FROM WESTBROOK CEMETERIES. Oak Park, Ill.: Author, 1979. 220 p. Index.

HISTORICAL SOCIETY

Westbrook Historical Society, Boston Post Road, 06498. (203) 399-7473.

LAND RECORDS

LAND RECORDS 1840-1885. (LDS 2156).

LIBRARY

Westbrook Public Library, Boston Post Road, 06498. (203) 399-6422.

MILITARY RECORDS

Rumsey, Jean. FIRST CONGREGATIONAL CHURCH OF WESTBROOK, CONNECTICUT, 1725-1899: BAPTISMS, MARRIAGES, DEATHS AND MEMBERSHIPS SUPPLEMENTED BY GRAVESTONE INSCRIPTIONS FROM WESTBROOK CEMETERIES. Oak Park, Ill.: Author, 1979. 220 p. Includes an index to military service.

PROBATE RECORDS

Westbrook Probate District, Town Hall, Boston Post Road, 06498. (203) 399-6236.

   The Westbrook Probate District was organized 4 July 1854 from the Old Saybrook Probate District.

   ON FILE AT THE CSL: Estate Papers, 1854-1930. Indexes, 1854-1940. Inventory Control Book, 1854-1930.

SCHOOL RECORDS

Hartford. CSL, Record Group 62. School Report, 1883.

VITAL RECORDS

Town Clerk, Hall of Records, Boston Post Road, 06498. (203) 399-9723.

The BARBOUR INDEX covers the years 1840-1851 and is based on a photostatic copy of the original records.

Jacobus, Donald Lines. "Early Westbrook, Connecticut, Birth and Deaths."
TAG 24 (1948): 61-62.

WEST HARTFORD

HARTFORD COUNTY. Organized May 1854 from HARTFORD.

CEMETERY RECORDS AND CEMETERIES

NAME	ADDRESS	HALE NO.	CITATION
North or Old Center Cemetery	66 North Main Street	1	54:1-8
Old North Cemetery	30 North Main Street	2	54:9-61
Fairview Cemetery	64 Pleasant Street	3	54:62-88
Quaker Cemetery	148 Quaker Lane South	4	54:89-90
French Camp Grounds Cemetery	On Albany Avenue, near Reservoir	5	54:91
Skinner Cemetery	On Farm in Elmwood, where school is located	6	54:92
St. Mary Roman Catholic Cemetery	Near St. Agnes Home	7	54:93-102
Convent Mary Immaculate Roman Catholic Cemetery	Corner Park Road and Prospect Avenue	8	54:103-105
Jewish Cemetery	41 Meriline Avenue	9	54:106-10
Charter Oak Park Cemetery	Charter Oak Park	10	54:111-12

Index to Hale inscriptions: 54:113-43.

INSCRIPTIONS OF OLD NORTH MAIN STREET CEMETERY COPIED MAY 15, 1928. N.p.: Sarah Whitman Hooker Chapter, DAR, 1928. 18 p.

CHURCH RECORDS

FIRST BAPTIST CHURCH. Minutes, 1858–1940. (CSL, LDS 2231).

FIRST CONGREGATIONAL CHURCH. Minutes, 1736–1933. Vital Records, 1713–1933. (CSL, LDS 2227 pt. 1–3).

ST. JAMES (EPISCOPAL CHURCH). Vital Records, 1875–1940. (CSL, LDS 2229).

SOCIETY OF FRIENDS. Minutes, 1800–1823. (CSL, LDS 2230). Records, 1769–1898. (LDS 017,306–017,311).

THIRD CONGREGATIONAL CHURCH. Marriages, 1727–1799. BAILEY 2: 72–85.

Burr, Nelson Rollin. FROM COLONIAL PARRISH TO MODERN SUBURB: A BRIEF APPRECIATION OF WEST HARTFORD. West Hartford, Conn.: Author, 1976. 83 p. Index.

_____. THE STORY OF SAINT JAMES' EPISCOPAL CHURCH, WEST HART-FORD. Hartford: Church Missions Publishing Co., 1943. 28 p.

Spinks, Matthew. A HISTORY OF THE FIRST CHURCH OF CHRIST CONGRE-GATIONAL, WEST HARTFORD, CONNECTICUT. N.p., n.d. 174 p.

HISTORICAL SOCIETY

Noah Webster House and Historical Society of West Hartford, 227 South Main Street (P.O. Box 1758), 06107. (203) 521–5362.

Publishes: SPECTATOR. 1971-- . Quarterly.

Bennett, Gordon, and Meyer, Freeman W. "The Noah Webster House Restoration." CANTIQUARIAN 19 (June 1967): 6–9.

Jewish Historical Society of Greater Hartford, 335 Bloomfield Avenue, 06117. (203) 236–4751, ext. 35.

LIBRARY

West Hartford Public Library, 20 South Main Street, 06107. (203) 236–4561.

NEWSPAPERS

WEST HARTFORD NEWS. Weekly. 20 Isham Road, 06107. (203) 236-5884. Indexed by the West Hartford Public Library since 1973.

The PRELIMINARY CHECKLIST lists four newspapers for WEST HARTFORD.

PROBATE RECORDS

WEST HARTFORD is in the Hartford Probate District.

VITAL RECORDS

Town Clerk, Town Hall, 28 South Main Street, 06107. (203) 236-3231.

The town clerk's earliest birth, marriage and death records date from 1854.

PUBLISHED WORKS AND OTHER RECORDS

Hall, William H. WEST HARTFORD. Hartford: Jane A. Reid Press, 1930. 267 p.

Porter, William Smith. HISTORICAL NOTICES OF CONNECTICUT. 2 vols. in 1. Hartford: E. Geer Press, 1842.

Shepard, James. "Reservoir Park, West Hartford." CQ 2 (1896): 43-48.

WEST HAVEN

NEW HAVEN COUNTY. Organized 24 June 1921 from ORANGE.

CEMETERY RECORDS AND CEMETERIES

NAME	ADDRESS	HALE NO.	CITATION
Oak Grove Cemetery	871 Campbell Avenue (203) 933-8081	1	54:1-82
St. Lawrence Cemetery	280 Derby Avenue (203) 624-3980	2	54:83-186
Gong Keser Israel Cemetery	Farwell Avenue	3 & 8	55:187-512 55:513,540-41
Old West Haven Green	Town Center	4	55:514-23
Episcopal Church Cemetery	Campbell Avenue	5	55:524-33
Congregation Sharoa Taroah Cemetery	Farwell Avenue	6	55:534-35
Workmen's Circle Cemetery	Farwell Avenue	7	55:536-39

Index to Hale inscriptions: 55:542-683.

CHURCH RECORDS

CHRIST (EPISCOPAL) CHURCH. Vital Records, 1851-1879. (CSL, LDS 2234).

FIRST CONGREGATIONAL CHURCH. Minutes, 1724-1916. Vital Records, 1774-1852, 1863-1918. Index. (CSL, LDS 2233).

Jacobus, Donald Lines. "Churchmen of 1738 under Rev. Jonathan Arnold of West Haven, Connecticut." TAG 34 (1958): 246-51.

HISTORICAL SOCIETY

West Haven Historical Society, 06516.

LIBRARY

West Haven Public Library, 300 Elm Street, 06516. (203) 932-2221.

NEWSPAPERS

WEST HAVEN CITY NEWS. Weekly. P.O. Box 423, 06516. (203) 933-1000.

The PRELIMINARY CHECKLIST lists seven newspapers for WEST HAVEN.

PROBATE RECORDS

West Haven Probate District, City Hall, 355 Main Street, P.O. Box 127, 06516.
(203) 934-3421.
> The West Haven Probate District was organized 24 June 1941 from
> the New Haven Probate District.

VITAL RECORDS

Town Clerk, City Hall, 355 Main Street, 06516. (203) 934-3421.
> The town clerk's earliest birth record dates from 13 August 1804,
> marriage record from 23 June 1822 and death record from 21 No-
> vember 1810.

PUBLISHED WORKS AND OTHER RECORDS

Hartford. CSL, Record Group 33, Boxes 170-76. Materials for the HISTORY
OF WEST HAVEN. Notes, etc.

WPA Writer's Program. HISTORY OF WEST HAVEN. West Haven: Church
Press, 1940. 93 p.

WESTON

FAIRFIELD COUNTY. Organized October 1787 from FAIRFIELD. Towns organized from WESTON include EASTON and WESTPORT.

CEMETERY RECORDS AND CEMETERIES

NAME	ADDRESS	HALE NO.	CITATION
Norfield Cemetery	South part of town near Westport Town line	1	55:1-31
Lyons Plain Cemetery	Rear of Lyons Plain Church	2	55:32-41
Osborn Cemetery	Near Charles R. Morehouse property	3	55:42-43
Rollins Cemetery	East of Valley Forge	4	55:44
Tharp Cemetery	East of Lyons Plain	5	55:45
Devils Den Cemetery	Northeast part of town	5	55:46-47

Index to Hale inscriptions: 55:48-61.

KETTLE CREEK, NOW NORFIELD CEMETERY. TOMBSTONE RECORDS, 1767-1919. N.p.: n.d. 22 p.

CHURCH RECORDS

EMMANUEL (EPISCOPAL) CHURCH. Minutes, 1845-1942. (CSL, LDS 2220).

NORFIELD CONGREGATIONAL CHURCH. Minutes, 1771-1827, 1858-1941. Vital Records, 1757-1935. (CSL, LDS 2219). Marriages, 1757-1799. BAILEY 5:63-70.

HISTORICAL SOCIETY

Weston Historical Society, Coley Barn Museum, Weston Road (P.O. Box 1092), 06883.

LAND RECORDS

Land Records, 1787-1879. Index, 1787-1949. (LDS 2218 pt. 1-13).

LIBRARY

Weston Public Library, 56 Norfield Road (P.O. Box 1146), 06880. (203) 227-7679.

NEWSPAPER

WESTON FORUM. Weekly. P.O. Box 1186,06883. (203) 227-6398.

The PRELIMINARY CHECKLIST lists one newspaper for WESTON.

PROBATE RECORDS

WESTON is in the Westport Probate District.

> From 22 May 1832 to 1875 there was a Weston Probate District. The district also included EASTON and WESTPORT. Its records are at the Easton Probate Court. After 1875 Weston was merged with the Westport Probate District.

Probate Records, 1832-1858. (LDS 2217 pt. 1-2).

TAX RECORDS

Fairfield. Fairfield Historical Society. Tax list 1798.

VITAL RECORDS

Town Clerk, Town Hall, 56 Norfield Road (P.O. Box 1007), 06880. (203) 227-2090.

> The town clerk's earliest birth record is 23 March 1927, marriage record is 4 November 1756 and death record is 28 February 1794.

The BARBOUR INDEX covers the years 1787 to 1850 and is based on the James N. Arnold copy of WESTON vital records made in 1915.

PUBLISHED WORKS AND OTHER RECORDS

Farnham, Thomas J. WESTON: THE FORGING OF A CONNECTICUT TOWN. Canaan, N.H.: Phoenix Publishing, 1979. 266 p. Index.

WPA Historical Records Survey. INVENTORY OF THE TOWN AND CITY ARCHIVES OF CONNECTICUT. No. 1, Fairfield County, vol. 21, Weston. New Haven: Connecticut Historical Records Survey Project, 1940. (LDS 908, 156 Item 6).

WESTPORT

FAIRFIELD COUNTY. Organized 28 May 1835 from FAIRFIELD, NORWALK and WESTON.

CEMETERY RECORDS AND CEMETERIES

NAME	ADDRESS	HALE NO.	CITATION
Willow Brook Cemetery	400 Main Street	1	56:1-46
Upper Greens Farms Cemetery	77 Hillandale Road	2	56:47-71
Lower Greens Farms Cemetery	Shore Road	3	56:72-90
Christ Church Cemetery	Town Center	4	56:91-130
Assumption Roman Catholic Cemetery	King's Highway (203) 378-0404	5	56:91-130
Evergreen Cemetery	34 Evergreen Street	6	56:131-36
Post Road Cemetery	West Saugatuck	7	56:137-39
King's Highway Cemetery	King's Highway and Wilton Road	8	56:140-44
Taylor Cemetery	285 Wilton Road	9	56:145-50
Compo Colonial Cemetery	180 Green's Farms Road	10	56:151-52
St. Mary Roman Catholic Church Cemetery	21 Green's Farms Road	11	(no citation)
Platt Cemetery	385 Post Road		(no citation)

Index to Hale inscriptions: 56:153-96.

TOMBSTONE INSCRIPTIONS. DAR Genealogical Records 12 p. (CSL, LDS 1481).

Wakeman, R.R. "Names and Dates from the Old Burying Ground, Green's Farms, Conn., from the earliest date to 1897." FAIRFIELD COUNTY HISTORICAL SOCIETY ANNUAL REPORT, 1897, pp. 79-104.

CHURCH RECORDS

GREEN'S FARM CONGREGATIONAL. Marriages, 1742-1799. BAILEY 3: 151-67.

SAUGATUCK CONGREGATIONAL CHURCH. Minutes 1830-1885. Vital Records 1832-1926. (CSL, LDS 2225).

Eardeley, William Applebie. AMERICAN CHURCH RECORDS. Vol. 16-17, Records of the Congregational Church at Green's Farms in the Town of Weston, Fairfield County, Connecticut, Part I. Baptisms. Brooklyn, N.Y.: Author, n.d.

HISTORICAL SOCIETY

Westport Historical Society, 79 Myrtle Avenue, 06880. (203) 226-7656.

Publishes: NEWS NOTES. 1962-- . Quarterly.

LAND RECORDS

Land Records, 1835-1877. (LDS 2224).

LIBRARY

Westport Public Library, 19 East State Street, 06880. (203) 227-8411.

NEWSPAPERS

FAIRPRESS. Weekly. P.O. Box 5108, 06880. (203) 226-1275.

WESTPORT NEWS. Weekly. 136 Main Street, 06880. (203) 226-6311.

The PRELIMINARY CHECKLIST lists ten newspapers for WESTPORT.

PROBATE RECORDS

Westport Probate District, Town Hall, 110 Myrtle Street, 06880. (203) 226-8311.

The Westport Probate District was organized May 1835 from the

Fairfield, Norwalk and Weston Probate Districts. The district also includes WESTON and WESTPORT.

Probate Records, 1835-1854. (CSL, LDS 2223).

VITAL RECORDS

Town Clerk, Town Hall, 90 East State Street, (P.O. Box 549), 06880. (203) 227-3756.

The BARBOUR INDEX covers the years 1835-1850 and is based on the James N. Arnold copy of WESTPORT vital records made in 1914.

"Marriage Records of Westport 1830-1875." In MARRIAGE RECORDS OF NORWALK AND VICINITY, pp. 34-60. (LDS 1894).

PUBLISHED WORKS AND OTHER RECORDS

D'Amico, Anthony J. ITALIANS IN WESTPORT: A PERSONAL ACCOUNT FOR AN ETHNOHISTORY OF THE WESTPORT-NORWALK AREA FROM 1900 TO TODAY. New Haven: Connecticut Humanities Council, 1979. 16 p.

HISTORIC DWELLINGS IN WESTPORT, CONNECTICUT, 1730-1884. Westport, Conn.: Westport Historical Society, 1977. 22 p.

Hunt, Malcolm P. NAMES AND PLACES OF OLD NORWALK; WITH POR-TIONS OF WILTON, WESTPORT AND NEW CANAAN. Norwalk, Conn.: Friends of Lockwood House, 1976. 98 p.

Mahar, John L. HISTORY OF IMMIGRANT GROUPS FOR AN ETHNOHISTORY OF THE WESTPORT-NORWALK AREA FROM 1900 TO TODAY. New Haven: Connecticut Humanities Council, 1979. 19 p.

McCune, Mike. "Westport." FAIRFIELD COUNTY 9 (June 1979): 16-24.

Malm, Dorothea, and Robidoux, Joan. BIBLIOGRAPHY FOR HISTORIC SITE SURVEY OF WESTPORT. Westport, Conn.: Westport Historical Society, 1975. 15 p.

Slauehter, William. WESTPORT ARTISTS OF THE PAST: A BICENTENNIAL EXHIBITION, 1976; WESTPORT PUBLIC LIBRARY, WESTPORT, CONNECTICUT, JUNE 12-JUNE 30, 1976. Westport, Conn.: Westport Bicentennial Arts Committee, 1976. 32 p.

TRANSCRIPTS OF ORAL HISTORIES FOR AN ETHNOHISTORY OF THE WEST-PORT-NORWALK AREA FROM 1900 TO TODAY. New Haven: Connecticut Humanities Council, 1979.

WETHERSFIELD

HARTFORD COUNTY. Organized 1634. Towns organized from WETHERSFIELD include BERLIN, GLASTONBURY, NEWINGTON and ROCKY HILL.

CEMETERY RECORDS AND CEMETERIES

NAME	ADDRESS	HALE NO.	CITATION
Village Cemetery	35 March Street	1	56:1-116
Emmanuel Cemetery	1363 Berlin Turnpike	2	56:117-21
Cedar Hill Cemetery	Cedar Hill	3	56:122
State Prison Cemetery	Rear of the State Prison	4	56:123
Piaterer Verein, Inc. Cemetery	Back of Emmanuel Cemetery	5	56:124-25

Index to Hale inscriptions: 56:126-59.

Cemetery Records, 1887-1947. (CSL, LDS 2172).

Hartford. CSL, Record Group 62. First School Society. Cemetery Plot Owners, 1863-1903.

Tillotson, Edward Sweetser. WETHERSFIELD INSCRIPTIONS; A COMPLETE RECORD OF THE INSCRIPTIONS IN THE FIVE BURIAL PLACES IN THE AN-CIENT TOWN OF WETHERSFIELD, INCLUDING THE TOWNS OF ROCKY HILL, NEWINGTON AND BECKLEY QUARTER (IN BERLIN), ALSO A POR-TION OF THE INSCRIPTIONS IN THE OLDEST CEMETERY IN GLASTONBURY. Hartford: William F.J. Boardman, 1899. 372 p.

CHURCH RECORDS

BAPTIST CHURCH. Minutes, 1816-1919. (CSL, LDS 2175).

FIRST CONGREGATIONAL CHURCH. Minutes, 1734-1846. (CSL, LDS 2173). Minutes, 1706-1733. Vital Records, 1694-1908. (CSL, LDS 2174). Marriages, 1739-1799. BAILEY 3:7-29.

Shepard, James. HISTORY OF ST. MARK'S CHURCH, NEW BRITAIN, CONNECTICUT AND OF ITS PREDECESSOR, CHRIST CHURCH, WETHERSFIELD AND BERLIN FROM THE FIRST CHURCH OF ENGLAND SERVICE IN AMERICA TO 1907. New Britain: Tuttle, Morehouse and Taylor, 1907. 707 p.

Smith, Chard Powers. "Church and State in Wethersfield 1636-1639." NEQ 29 (1956): 82-87.

HISTORICAL SOCIETIES

Buttolph-Williams House, Broad and Marsh Streets, 06109. (203) 529-0460.

Historic Wethersfield Foundation, 400 Hartford Avenue, P.O. Box 3197, 06103. (203) 523-8106.

Webb-Deane-Stevens Museum, 203-215 Main Street, 06109. (203) 529-0612.

Wethersfield Historical Society, 150 Main Street, 06109. (203) 529-7656.

LAND RECORDS

Hartford. CSL, Record Group 62. Land Records, 1807-1913.

Land Records, 1635-1859. Index, 1640-1916. (LDS 2171 pt. 1-23).

LIBRARY

Wethersfield Public Library, 515 Silas Deane Highway, 06109. (203) 529-2618.

MILITARY RECORDS

"Alphabetical List of Soldiers and Patriots Wethersfield, Connecticut." MISCELLANEOUS RECORDS, CONNECTICUT DAR, 1975-1976, pp. 46-54.

Reynolds, Ronna L. 1775: WETHERSFIELD ENTERS THE REVOLUTION. Wethersfield: Wethersfield Historical Society, 1975. 48 p.

_____. 1776-1783: WETHERSFIELD IN THE REVOLUTION. Wethersfield: Wethersfield Historical Society, 1976. 57 p.

NEWSPAPERS

THE WETHERSFIELD POST. Weekly. 227 Main Street, 06109. (203) 529-7771.

The PRELIMINARY CHECKLIST lists five newspapers for WETHERSFIELD.

PROBATE RECORDS

WETHERSFIELD is in the Newington Probate District.

SCHOOL RECORDS

Hartford. CSL, Record Group 62. First School Society Treasurer's Book, 1863-1909.

TAX RECORDS

Hartford. CHS. Rate Book of Samuel Galpin, Tax Collector, First Society, 1812.

Hartford. CSL, Record Group 62. Rate Books, 1826-1931. Lists, 1800-1805, 1920-1921. Abstracts, Grand lists, etc.

VITAL RECORDS

Town Clerk, Town Hall, 505 Silas Deane Highway, 06109. (203) 529-8611.

The BARBOUR INDEX covers the years 1634-1868 and is based on the James N. Arnold copy of WETHERSFIELD vital records made in 1917.

Hartford. CSL, Record Group 62. Vital Record Abstracts, 1854-1891 (incomplete).

"Wethersfield Vital Records." TAG 9 (1932-33): 27-51; 10 (1933-34): 104-9.

WETHERSFIELD VITAL RECORDS 1830-1904 FROM THE FILES OF THE TOWN CLERK'S OFFICE. Typescript. 1973. (CSL).

VOTER RECORDS

Hartford. CSL, Record Group 62. VOTER LISTS, 1798–1891. Returns and Records, 1802–1840.

PUBLISHED WORKS AND OTHER RECORDS

Adams, Sherman Wolcott. "Diary of the Rev. Stephen Mix of Wethersfield." CM 6 (1900): 100–105; 7 (1901): 189–93, 400–402; 8 (1903–1904): 156–61.

Alves, C. Douglass, Jr. "Foote-Prints at the Buttolph-Williams House." CANTIQUARIAN 31 (December 1979): 13–17.

Andrews, Charles McLean. THE RIVER TOWNS OF CONNECTICUT: A STUDY OF WETHERSFIELD, HARTFORD AND WINDSOR. 1889. Reprint. New York: Johnson Reprint Corp., 1973. 126 p.

_____. THE MARITIME HISTORY OF WETHERSFIELD. Wethersfield, Conn.: Wethersfield Historical Society, 1977. 44 p.

Briscoe, Lilly Palmer. "The Colonial Dames' Wethersfield Houses." CANTI-QUARIAN 20 (June 1968): 6–13.

Clark, Delphina L.H. "The Buttolph-Williams House and Its Restoration." CANTIQUARIAN 8 (July 1956): 5–26.

Ely, Harriet W. "Window on Wethersfield." CANTIQUARIAN 13 (July 1961): 6–14.

Fox, Frances Wells. WETHERSFIELD AND HER DAUGHTERS GLASTONBURY, ROCKY HILL, NEWINGTON FROM 1634 TO 1934. Hartford: Case, Lockwood and Brainard, 1934. 123 p.

Friedland, Edward, and Pinney, Sidney D., Jr. "Historic Preservation in Action; The Ezra Webb House, Wethersfield." CANTIQUARIAN 26 (July 1974): 20–21.

Garrett, Wendell. "Antiques." ANTIQUES 109 (March 1976): 514–15.

Hartford. CSL, Record Group 62. Town Records.

Hicks, Lewis Wilder. "The First Civil Settlement in Connecticut." CM 7 (1902): 213–32.

Hinman, Royal Ralph. "Records of Wethersfield, Connecticut." NEHGR 15 (1861): 241-46, 295-98; 16 (1862): 17-22, 135-42, 263-68; 17 (1863): 261-64, 355-58; 18 (1864): 53-59, 179-81, 225-26; 19 (1865): 241-43, 317-20; 20 (1866): 13-20, 124-33, 204-10, 318-22.

HOMES AND DOORWAYS OF OLD WETHERSFIELD. Wethersfield: Wethersfield Women's Association, 1927. 53 p.

Kane, Patricia Ellen. "Joiners of Wethersfield." CHSB 35 (1970): 73-77.

Kuckro, Anne Crofoot. CAPT. JAMES FRANCES MASTER BUILDER BRICK ARCHITECTURE IN WETHERSFIELD BEFORE 1840. Wethersfield: Wethersfield Historical Society, 1974. 52 p. Index.

_____. "Early Brick Architecture of Wethersfield." ANTIQUES 109 (March 1976): 545-49.

_____. "Living with Antiques in Wethersfield." ANTIQUES 109 (March 1976): 560-67.

_____. "A Wethersfield Family Collection." ANTIQUES 109 (March 1976): 556-59.

Langdon, Carolyn S. "A Complaint Against Katherine Harrison, 1669." CHSB 34 (1969): 18-25.

"Lieutenant John Buttolph's Will and Inventory." CANTIQUARIAN 3 (November 1951): 17-21.

"List of Families in Wethersfield with Quantity of Grain in Possession of Each." CHS COLLECTIONS 21 (1924): 197-99.

Palmer, Frederic. "The Captain Thomas Newson House, Wethersfield, Connecticut." CANTIQUARIAN 16 (December 1964): 17-27.

Parsons, Myra Louise. "Webb House in Wethersfield." CANTIQUARIAN 3 (June 1951): 6-9.

Reynolds, Ronna L. "Wethersfield People and their Portraits." ANTIQUES 109 (March 1976): 528-33.

Stiles, Henry Reed. HISTORY OF ANCIENT WETHERSFIELD, CONNECTICUT. New York: Grafton Press, 1904. Reprint. Somersworth, N.J.: New Hampshire Publishing Co., 1974-75. (LDS 599,258).

Watkins, Susan Finlay. "Connecticut Needlework in the Webb-Deane-Stevens Museum." ANTIQUES 109 (March 1976): 542-44.

_____. "The Webb-Deane-Stevens Museum." ANTIQUES 109 (March 1976): 534-41.

Wieder, Lois M. "Historic Preservation in Wethersfield." ANTIQUES 109 (March 1976): 550-55.

_____. THE WETHERSFIELD STORY. Stonington, Conn.: Pequot Press, 1966. 57 p.

_____. "Wethersfield 'The Most Ancient Town' in Connecticut." ANTIQUES 109 (March 1976): 516-17.

WETHERSFIELD: A TOUR OF HOUSES AND HISTORY 1980. Wethersfield, Conn.: Wethersfield Historical Society, 1980. 31 p.

Willard, John C. "History in Towns: Wethersfield, Connecticut 1634-1964--the Architecture." ANTIQUES 86 (October 1964): 452-56.

_____. WILLARD'S WETHERSFIELD. West Hartford: West Hartford Publishing Co., 1975. 99 p.

Wyllis Papers. GOVERNOR GEORGE WYLLYS OF CONNECTICUT 1590-1796. Hartford: Hartford Historical Society, 1924. 567 p. Index. (List of Wethersfield families, pp. 361-72).

WILLINGTON

TOLLAND COUNTY. Organized May 1727.

CEMETERY RECORDS AND CEMETERIES

NAME	ADDRESS	HALE NO.	CITATION
Old Willington Hill Cemetery	Willington Hill	1	56:1-32
New Willington Hill Cemetery	Willington Hill	2	56:33-48
Morse Meadow Cemetery	Northeast part of town, miles from Center	3	56:49-55
Village Hill Cemetery	North part of town, 4 miles from Center	4	56:56-60
Stanton Cemetery	East part of town on Stafford Springs Road	5	56:61
Wheeler Cemetery	1 mile south of East Willington, on Wheeler Farm	6	56:62
Small-pox Cemetery	Near Button Shop, on land of Parisek	7	56:63
Hull Cemetery	East of Mill Pond, Picnic Grounds	8	56:64
Rock Garden Cemetery	In yard, 2d house from Church in South Willington	9	56:65
Old Buck More Cemetery (they have been moved)	Near Tolland Station	10	56:66
Several Graves (they have been moved)	Pinney Farm	11	56:66
Royce, stones moved to no. 13	Rounds Homestead	12	56:66

NAME	ADDRESS	HALE NO.	CITATION
(Unnamed Cemetery)		13	56:66
Marcy Cemetery	Benjamin Arnold Property	14	56:66
Single Grave	Old Lamb Homestead	15	56:66
Field stones	Poor farm, now Smekal Property	16	56:66
Single grave	Rounds Homestead	17	56:66
Sparks Cemetery	Joseph Kribance property	18	56:66
Maine Cemetery (one within wall and three outside)	On Old Maine Homestead now owned by Scuzzel	19	56:66

Index to Hale inscriptions: 56:67-84.

Eno, Joel Nelson. "Connecticut Cemetery Inscriptions-Willington." NEHGR 67 (1913): 63-65, 290-95, 376-79; 68 (1914): 198-200, 334-38; 69 (1915): 82-86, 182-87, 274-76, 334-42; 70 (1916): 242-44.

CHURCH RECORDS

BAPTIST CHURCH RECORDS. American Historical Society. (LDS 2165).

FIRST CONGREGATIONAL CHURCH. Minutes, 1803-1839. Vital Records, 1759-1911. (LDS 2167).

"Rev. Elisha Cushman's Record (First Baptist Church in Hartford 1813 to 1825, Philadelphia, Pennsylvania 1825-1829, Fairfield, Connecticut September 1829-1830, New Haven 1830-1833, Plymouth, Massachusetts 1834-1847, 1840-1863 by Son Rev. Elisha Cushman and contains marriages from Willington, Hartford, New Britain and Deep River until 1863). CHSB 7 (1942): 30-32; 8 (1943): 2-8, 12-13.

Southwick, G.O. HISTORY OF THE CONGREGATIONAL CHURCH, AND SABBATH SCHOOL, WILLINGTON, CONNECTICUT; 1728-1875. Stafford Springs, Conn.: A.H. Simonds, 1875. 22 p.

Sundt, Edwin E. A HISTORY OF THE BAPTIST CHURCH OF WILLINGTON, CONNECTICUT 1828-1928. New York: Schulte Press, 1932. 95 p. Index.

Talcott, Mary Kingsbury. "Records of the Church at Willington, Connecticut." NEHGR 67 (1913): 115-23, 215-22.

HISTORICAL SOCIETY

The Willington Historical Society, 06279.

Publishes THE HOURGLASS.

LAND RECORDS

Land Records, 1727-1855. Index, 1727-1902. (CSL, LDS 2166 pt. 1-8).

LIBRARY

Willington Public Library, Hall Memorial School, Route 32, 06265. (203) 429-3854.

NEWSPAPER

The PRELIMINARY CHECKLIST lists one newspaper for WILLINGTON.

PROBATE RECORDS

WILLINGTON is in the Tolland Probate District.

SCHOOL RECORDS

Hartford. CSL, Record Group 62. School District No. 8 1858 Assessment List.

TAX RECORDS

Hartford. CSL, Record Group 62. Abstracts 1823, 1826-1829.

VITAL RECORDS

Town Clerk, P.O. Box 94, 06279. (203) 429-9965.

> The town clerk's earliest birth record is 1718, marriage record is 1730 and death record is 1728.

The BARBOUR INDEX covers the years 1727-1851 and is based on the James N. Arnold copy of WILLINGTON vital records.

PUBLISHED WORKS AND OTHER RECORDS

CHRONOLOGY OF WILLINGTON, CONNECTICUT 1727-1927: THE FIRST TWO HUNDRED YEARS. Willington: History Committee of the Willington Historical Society, 1977. 120 p.

White, Harry H. "The Willington Glass Company." ANTIQUES 40 (August 1941): 98-101.

WILTON

FAIRFIELD COUNTY. Organized May 1802 from NORWALK.

CEMETERY RECORDS AND CEMETERIES

NAME	ADDRESS	HALE NO.	CITATION
Sharp Hill Cemetery	4 Sharp Hill Road	1	56:1-6
Joe's Hill Cemetery	Wilton-Ridgefield Road	2	56:7-12
Old Cemetery	Route 7	3	56:13-14
Comstock Cemetery	Wilton-Ridgefield Road	4	56:15-16
St. Matthew Episcopal Church Cemetery	244 Danbury Road	5	56:17-37
Hillside Cemetery	149 Ridgefield Road	6	56:38-75
Morgan-Davis Cemetery	Wilton-Ridgefield Road	7	56:76
Zion Hill Cemetery	470 Danbury Road	8	56:77-86
Ruscoe Cemetery	Spring Valley District	9	56:87
DeForest Cemetery	109 DeForest Road	10	56:88
Beers Cemetery	Nod Hill Road	11	56:89-90
Bald Hill Cemetery	827 Ridgefield Road		(no citation)

Index to Hale inscriptions: 56:91-117.

CENSUS RECORDS

Card, Lester. "Census of Wilton Parish in Norwalk, Connecticut, 1733."
NYGBR 70 (1939): 151-53.

CHURCH RECORDS

CONGREGATIONAL CHURCH. Marriages, 1726-1799. BAILEY 3:62-73.

ST. MATTHEWS EPISCOPAL. Minutes, 1802, 1847. Vital Records, 1834-1892. (CSL, LDS 2222).

AN HISTORICAL ACCOUNT OF THE CELEBRATION OF THE ONE HUNDRED AND SEVENTY-FIFTH ANNIVERSARY OF THE FOUNDING OF THE CONGREGATIONAL CHURCH, WILTON, CONNECTICUT JUNE THE TWELFTH, A.D. NINETEEN HUNDRED ONE. New Haven: Tuttle, Morehouse and Taylor Co., 1902. 62 p.

Hubbard, G. Evans. "Record of Marriages as copied from the Wilton Congregational Church Records." NEW CANAAN HISTORICAL SOCIETY ANNUAL, 1955, pp. 36.

Moore, Dorothy Lefferts. ST. MATTHEW'S PARISH WILTON 1802-1952. Wilton: St. Matthew's Episcopal Church, n.d. 48 p.

HISTORICAL SOCIETY

Wilton Historical Society, 249 Danbury Road, 06897. (203) 762-7257.

LAND RECORDS

Land Records, 1802-1851. Index, 1802-1919. (CSL, LDS 2221 pt. 1-9).

LIBRARY

Wilton Library Association, 38 Old Ridgefield Road, 06897. (203) 762-3950.

NEWSPAPERS

WILTON BULLETIN. Weekly. P.O. Box 367, 06897. (203) 762-3456.

The PRELIMINARY CHECKLIST lists two newspapers for WILTON.

PROBATE RECORDS

WILTON is in the Norwalk Probate District.

VITAL RECORDS

Town Clerk, Town Hall, 238 Danbury Road, 06897. (203) 762-5578.

> The town clerk's earliest birth record is 21 June 1819, marriage record is 16 August 1820 and death record is 28 January 1815.

The BARBOUR INDEX covers the years 1802-1850 and is based on the James N. Arnold copy of WILTON vital records made in 1915.

"Marriage Records 1808-1875." In MARRIAGE RECORDS OF NORWALK AND VICINITY, pp. 185-218. (LDS 1894).

PUBLISHED WORKS AND OTHER RECORDS

Bassett, Preston R. "The Towns in the Ridges: The Story of Wilton and Ridgefield." CANTIQUARIAN 17 (July 1965): 6-10.

Callahan, Jim. "Wilton Neither Village nor Town, Fortress nor Sanctuary, 'just home.'" FAIRFIELD COUNTY 9 (July 1979): 28-30, 32-35.

Davenport, John Gaylord. "Moses Stuart--The Man Who Unfettered Religious Thought in America." CM 11 (1907): 111-24.

Edson, Wesley. "Wilton, The Impossible Dream." FAIRFIELD COUNTY 3 (July 1973): 16-27.

EIGHTEENTH CENTURY DWELLINGS IN WILTON. Wilton: Wilton Historical Society, 1976. 48 p.

Hubbard, G. Evans. WILTON VILLAGE: A HISTORY. Annals of Wilton, vol. 3. Wilton: Wilton Historical Society, 1971. 64 p.

Hunt, Malcolm P. NAMES AND PLACES OF OLD NORWALK; WITH PORTIONS OF WILTON, WESTPORT AND NEW CANAAN. Norwalk, Conn.: Friends of Lockwood House, 1976. 98.

Junior League of Stamford--Norwalk, Inc. WILTON: ARCHITECTURALLY SPEAKING. Stamford, Conn.: Junior League of Stamford--Norwalk, Inc., 1980. 24 p.

Olmstead, Marian. WILTON PARISH 1726-1800. Wilton: Author, 1900. 44 p.

WINCHESTER

LITCHFIELD COUNTY. Organized May 1771.

CEMETERY RECORDS AND CEMETERIES

NAME	ADDRESS	HALE NO.	CITATION
Forest View Cemetery	Winsted	1	56:1–118
Winchester Center Cemetery	Winchester Center	2	56:119–40
Central Cemetery	Winsted	3	57:141–83
St. Joseph Cemetery (old)	Winsted	4	57:184–238
Hemlock Cemetery	Robertsville in Colebrook	5	57:239
Wallins Hill Cemetery	Winsted	6	57:240
Danbury Quarter Cemetery	Near Martin Tuttle, Winsted	7	57:241–43
Hurlbut Cemetery	Winchester Center	8	57:244
St. Joseph Cemetery (new)	East Winsted	9	57:245–49
New Winchester Center Cemetery	Winchester Center	10	57:250–51

Index to Hale inscriptions: 57:252–324.

CHURCH RECORDS

FIRST CONGREGATIONAL CHURCH. Minutes, 1784-1926. Vital Records, 1800-1927. (CSL, LDS 2185 pt. 1). Vital Records, 1778-1869. Typescript, Mrs. William Allen. (CSL, LDS 2226).

ST. JAMES EPISCOPAL CHURCH. Minutes, 1848-1918, 1928-1915. Vital Records, 1848-1951. (CSL, LDS 2187, pt. 1-3).

SECOND CONGREGATIONAL CHURCH. Minutes, 1853-1952. Vital Records, 1853-1951. (CSL, LDS 2185 pt. 2).

WINSTED UNITED METHODIST CHURCH RECORDS. Typescript. Winsted: Green Woods Chapter DAR, n.d. 15 p. Index.

HISTORICAL SOCIETY

Winchester Historical Society, 06098.

LAND RECORDS

Land Records, 1744-1857. Index, 1744-1866. (CSL, LDS 2183 pt. 1-9).

LIBRARIES

Beardsley Library, Munro Place, 06098. (203) 379-6043.

CATALOGUE OF THE BEARDSLEY LIBRARY AT WEST WINSTED, CONNECTI-CUT. Waterbury, Conn.: American Printing Co., 1875. 125 p.

Northwestern Connecticut Community College Library, 100 South Main Street, 06098. (203) 379-8543.

NEWSPAPERS

WINSTED EVENING CITIZEN. Daily. P.O. Box 499, 06098. (203) 379-3333.

The PRELIMINARY CHECKLIST lists nine newspapers for WINCHESTER.

The HALE NEWSPAPER INDEX for deaths and marriages includes the WINSTED HERALD for 14 May 1833-27 December 1867.

PROBATE RECORDS

Winchester Probate District, Town Hall, 338 Main Street, 06098. (203) 379-5576.

The Winchester Probate District was organized 31 May 1838 from the Norfolk Probate District.

The Winchester Probate District also includes the town of COLE-BROOK.

ON FILE AT THE CSL: Estate Papers, 1838-1912. Indexes, 1838-1912. Inventory Control Book, 1838-1912. Court Record Books, 1838-1851.

Probate Records, 1838-1851. (CSL, LDS 2184).

VITAL RECORDS

Town Clerk, Town Hall, 338 Main Street, 06098. (203) 379-4646.

The town clerk's earliest birth record is 12 November 1761, marriage record is 3 January 1760 and death record is 13 March 1770.

The BARBOUR INDEX covers the years 1771-1858 and is based on James N. Arnold's copy of the two-volume record kept by the Rev. Frederick Marsh made in 1916.

PUBLISHED WORKS AND OTHER RECORDS

Boyd, John. ANNALS AND FAMILY RECORDS OF WINCHESTER, CONNECTICUT. Hartford: Case, Lockwood and Brainard, 1873. 632 p.

Bronson, Elliott B. A NEW ENGLAND VILLAGE GREEN. Winsted, Conn.: Author, 1913. 23 p.

Eaton, Edward Bailey. "The Financial and Industrial History of Winsted." CM 8 (1904): 595-624.

Hulbert, Robert S. "Winsted--The Development of an Ideal Town." CM 8 (1904): 566-95.

Steel, David Warren. "Sacred Music in Early Winchester." CHSB 45:33-44.

_____. "Truman S. Wetmore of Winchester and his 'Republican Harmony.'" CHSB 45 (1980): 75-89.

Vail, Joseph H. "Sketch of Augustus H. Fenn." CQ 4 (1898): 197-200.

WINDHAM

WINDHAM COUNTY. Organized May 1692 from CHAPLIN, HAMPTON, MANSFIELD and SCOTLAND.

CEMETERY RECORDS AND CEMETERIES

NAME	ADDRESS	HALE NO.	CITATION
Ancient Cemetery	South Coventry Road	1	57:1
Old Cemetery	979 Main Street	2	57:2-133
New Cemetery	South Coventry Road	3	57:134-44
St. Joseph Roman Catholic Cemetery	Catholic Cemetery Road	4	57:145-226
North Windham Cemetery	Lakeside Road	5	57:227-740
Windham Cemetery	South Road (Office: 979 Main Street)	6	57:241-317
Greek Cemetery	North Windham Road	7	57:318
Barber-Brooks Cemetery	South part of town	8	57:319-20
Russian Austrian Cemetery	North Windham Road		(no citation)

Index to Hale inscriptions: 57:321-414.

Eno, Joel Nelson. "Connecticut Cemetery Inscriptions." NEHGR 71 (1917): 176-87, 300-310, 337-38.

Waterman, Edgar Francis. "Windham (Conn.) Cemetery Inscriptions: Additions." NEHGR 72 (1918): 78.

CHURCH RECORDS

FIRST CONGREGATIONAL CHURCH. Deaths, 1751-1814. (CSL, LDS 441, 390). Minutes, 1806-1924. Vital Records, 1700-1852. (CSL, LDS 2151).

ST. PAUL EPISCOPAL CHURCH. Minutes, 1832-1923, Vital Records 1832-1925. (CSL, LDS 2150).

SECOND CONGREGATIONAL CHURCH. Marriages. 1794-1799. BAILEY 7:75-76.

THIRD CONGREGATIONAL CHURCH. Marriages. 1735/6-1800. BAILEY 3:43-51.

Mattoon, Lillian G. PARISH RECORDS, ST. PAUL'S CHURCH, WINDHAM, CONNECTICUT (1835-1967). Windham: Author, 1967. 34 p. Index. (LDS 824,075).

Mattoon, Lillian G., and Mattoon, Donald P. CHRONICLE OF ST. PAUL'S CHURCH WINDHAM, CONNECTICUT, 1832-1964. Windham: Author, 1964. 85 p. Index. (LDS 824,075).

RECORDS OF THE CONGREGATIONAL CHURCH IN WINDHAM, CONNECT-ICUT (EXCEPT CHURCH VOTES) 1700-1851. Vital Records of Connecticut Series II: Churches. Vol. 8; Town 6. Hartford: CHS and the Society of Mayflower Descendants in the State of Connecticut, 1943. 153 p.

Willingham, William Floyd. "Religious Conversion in the Second Society of Windham, Connecticut, 1723-1743: a Case Study." SOCIETAS 6 (1976): 109-19.

HISTORICAL SOCIETY

Center for Connecticut Studies of Eastern Connecticut State College, Eastern Road, 06226. (203) 423-4581.

Windham Historical Society, 06226.

LAND RECORDS

Land Records, 1686-1854. Index, 1706-1875. (LDS 2147 pt. 1-19).

LIBRARIES

Eastern Connecticut State College Library, Eastern Road, 06226. (203) 456-2231 ext. 374.

Guilford Smith Memorial Library, 06226. (203) 423-5159.

Willimantic Public Library, 905 Main Street, 06226. (203) 423-6182.

NEWSPAPERS

THE CHRONICLE. Daily. Chronicle Road, 06226. (203) 423-8466.

The HALE NEWSPAPER INDEX to deaths and marriages includes:

> WILLIMANTIC JOURNAL, deaths and marriages 4 June 1861-27 December 1866.

> WINDHAM ADVERTISER, deaths and marriages 7 May 1818-4 March 1819.

> WINDHAM HERALD, deaths 10 December 1791-19 September 1816; marriages 10 September 1796-29 August 1816.

PROBATE RECORDS

Windham Probate District, Town Building, P.O. Box 34, 06226. (203) 423-3191.

> The Windham Probate District was organized October 1719 from the Hartford and New London Probate Districts. It also includes the town of SCOTLAND.

> Probate districts organized from the Windham Probate District include the Chaplin, Hampton, Hebron, Lebanon, Mansfield, Plainfield and Pomfret Probate Districts.

> ON FILE AT THE CSL: Estate Papers, 1719-1917. Indexes, 1719-1880. Inventory Control Book, 1719-1880. Court Record Book, 1719-1858. Special probate records, 1734-1867. (LDS 2148 pt. 105).

Records, 1719-1858. Indexed. (LDS 2149 pt. 1-11).

Hayward, Kendall Payne. "Windham (Conn.) Probate Records." TAG 23 (1947): 228-29.

SCHOOL RECORDS

Hartford. CSL, Record Group 62. Sixth District Register, 1875-1876.

TAX RECORDS

Hartford. CSL, Record Group 62. Abstracts, 1820–1868. Incomplete. Rate Book, 1805–1830.

VITAL RECORDS

Town Clerk, Town Building, P.O. Box 94, 06226. (203) 423–1691.

> The town clerk's earliest birth record is January 1667, marriage record is 28 November 1682 and death record is 1 April 1693.

The BARBOUR INDEX is based on the James N. Arnold copy of WINDHAM vital records made in 1911 and includes all births and marriages from 1691 to 31 December 1850 and deaths from 1691 to 7 September 1860.

PUBLISHED WORKS AND OTHER RECORDS

Larned, Ellen D. "A Revolutionary Boycott (July 16, 1774)." CQ 1 (1895): 153–54.

Thompson, Edmund Burke. HAWTHORNE HOUSE: A RECORD OF THE FIRST FIVE YEARS. Windham, Conn.: Hawthorn House, 1938. 8 p.

Weaver, William Lawton. HISTORY OF ANCIENT WINDHAM, CONNECTICUT, GENEALOGY CONTAINING A GENEALOGICAL RECORD OF ALL THE EARLY FAMILY OF ANCIENT WINDHAM, EMBRACING THE PRESENT TOWNS OF WINDHAM, MANSFIELD, HAMPTON, CHAPLIN AND SCOTLAND. Part I, A–Bil. Willimantic: Weaver and Curtiss, 1864. 112 p. Index. (LDS 2146.

Willingham, William Floyd. "Windham, Connecticut: Profile of a Revolutionary Community, 1755–1818." Ph.D. dissertation, Northwestern University, 1972. 369 p.

Windham Bicentennial Committee. A MEMORIAL VOLUME OF THE BI-CEN-TENNIAL CELEBRATION OF THE TOWN WINDHAM, CONNECTICUT. Hartford: New England Home Printing Co., 1893. 166 p.

WINDSOR

HARTFORD COUNTY. Organized 26 September 1633. Towns organized from WINDSOR include BLOOMFIELD, EAST WINDSOR and WINDSOR LOCKS.

CEMETERY RECORDS AND CEMETERIES

NAME	ADDRESS	HALE NO.	CITATION
Palisado Cemetery	97 Palisado Avenue	1	58:1-84
Riverside Cemetery	Pleasant Street	2	58:85-89
Elm Grove Cemetery	1340 Poquonock Avenue	3	58:90-125
Old Poquonock Cemetery	Marshall Phelps Road	4	58:126-27
St. Joseph Roman Catholic Cemetery	2135 Poquonock Avenue	5	58:128-36
Northwood Cemetery	Matianuck Avenue	6	58:137-40
Archer Cemetery	On road from Hayden Station to the west	7	58:141
Ellsworth Cemetery (single stone)	Kennedy Street	8	58:142
Town Plot	Next to Riverside Cemetery	9	58:143-44

Index to Hale inscriptions: 58:145-85.

Abigail Wolcott Ellsworth Chapter, DAR. CEMETERY INSCRIPTIONS IN WINDSOR, CONNECTICUT. Windsor: 1929. 178 p.

"Connecticut Headstone Inscriptions: Town of Windsor." CN 1 (1969-70): 72-74; 2 (1970-71): 17-18, 120-21, 190-92, 267-68.

CHURCH RECORDS

FIRST CONGREGATIONAL CHURCH. Minutes, 1685-1916. Vital Records, 1639-1932. (CSL, LDS 2211).

Hartford. CSL, Record Group 62. First Society Rate Book, 1782-1806.

NORTH WINDSOR CONGREGATIONAL CHURCH. Vital Records, 1761-1794. (CSL, LDS 2212). Marriages 1738-1800. BAILEY 4: 113-22.

SECOND CONGREGATIONAL CHURCH. Vital Records, 1771-1782. (CSL, LDS 2212).

TRINITY METHODIST EPISCOPAL CHURCH. Vital Records, 1840-1912. (CSL, LDS 2212).

Uriochio, William J. "Ecclesiastical Crisis in Colonial Windsor." CHSB 40 (1975): 19-30.

HISTORICAL SOCIETY

Ellsworth Memorial Association, 778 Palisado Avenue, 06095. (203) 688-9444.

Windsor Historical Society, 96 Palisado Avenue, 06095. (203) 688-3813.

LAND RECORDS

Land Records, 1640-1857. Index, 1640-1874. (LDS 2210 pt. 1-22).

Proprietors Records, 1650-1787. (LDS 2209).

LIBRARY

Windsor Public Library, 323 Broad Street, 06095. (203) 688-6433.

NEWSPAPERS

WINDSOR JOURNAL. Weekly. 176 Broad Street, 06095. (203) 688-4984.

The PRELIMINARY CHECKLIST lists seven newspapers for WINDSOR.

PROBATE RECORDS

Windsor Probate District, Town Hall, 275 Broad Street, 06095. (203) 688-3675.

The Windsor Probate District was organized 4 July 1855 from the Hartford Probate District.

VITAL RECORDS

Town Clerk, Town Hall, 275 Broad Street (P.O. Box 472), 06095. (203) 688-3675.

The BARBOUR INDEX covers the years 1637-1850 and is based on a copy of these records made by Matthew Grant and published in 1858 by Edwin Stanley Welles as BIRTHS, MARRIAGES AND DEATHS (below).

Parsons, Samuel H. "Record of Marriages and Births." NEHGR 5 (1851): 63-66, 225-30, 359-66, 457-64.

Welles, Edwin Stanley. BIRTHS, MARRIAGES AND DEATHS RETURNED FROM HARTFORD, WINDSOR AND FAIRFIELD AND ENTERED IN THE EARLY LAND RECORDS OF THE COLONY OF CONNECTICUT. Vol.1 and 2 of LAND RECORDS AND NO. D OF COLONIAL DEEDS. Hartford: Author, 1898. 73 p. (LDS 823,816).

PUBLISHED WORKS AND OTHER RECORDS

Andrews, Charles McLean. THE RIVER TOWNS OF CONNECTICUT: A STUDY OF WETHERSFIELD, HARTFORD AND WINDSOR. 1889. Reprint. New York: Johnson Reprint Corp., 1973. 126 p.

Auwers, Linda. "Fathers, Sons, and Walth in Colonial Windsor, Connecticut." JOURNAL OF FAMILY HISTORY 3 (Summer 1978): 136-49.

_____. "Reading the Marks of the Past: Exploring Female Literacy in Colonial Windsor, Connecticut." HISTORICAL METHODS 13 (1980): 204-14.

Bissell, Linda Auwers. "Family, Friends and Neighbors: Social Interaction in Seventeenth-Century Windsor, Connecticut." Ph.D. dissertation, Brandeis University, 1973. 253 p.

_____. "From One Generation to Another: Mobility in Seventeenth Century Windsor, Connecticut." WILLIAM AND MARY QUARTERLY 31 (1974): 79-110.

Fowles, Lloyd W. THE FOWLES HISTORY OF WINDSOR CONNECTICUT, 1633-1900. Windsor, Conn.: Loomis Institute, 1976. 102 p. Index.

Howard, Daniel. GLIMPSES OF ANCIENT WINDSOR FROM 1633 TO 1933. Windsor: Herald Press, 1933. 104 p.

_____. A NEW HISTORY OF OLD WINDSOR, CONNECTICUT. Windsor Locks: Journal Press, 1935. 428 p.

Kane, Patricia Ellen. "Joiners of Windsor." CHSB 35 (1970): 78-81.

"List of Families in Windsor with Quantity of Grain in Possession of Each." CHS COLLECTIONS 21 (1924): 190-95.

"List of Freemen of Windsor, Connecticut." NEHGR 5 (1851): 247-48.

McManus, James. "First Dental College in the World." CM 11 (1907): 429-38.

Olin, Charles Francis. "The Historic Old Town of Windsor." CM 8 (1903): 18-32.

_____. "Old Windsor. Retrospective and Photographic." CM 6 (1900): 456-74.

Olmsted, Fannie L. "Elmwood--The Home of a Distinguished American." CM 8 (1903): 313-23.

SOME EARLY RECORDS AND DOCUMENTS OF AND RELATING TO THE TOWN OF WINDSOR, CONNECTICUT 1639-1703. Hartford: CHS, 1930. 227 p. (LDS 496,840).

Stiles, Henry Reed. THE HISTORY AND GENEALOGIES OF ANCIENT WINDSOR, SOUTH WINDSOR, BLOOMFIELD, WINDSOR LOCKS AND ELLINGTON 1635-1891. 2 vols. Hartford: Case, Lockwood and Brainard, 1891. (LDS 417,935).

_____. A SUPPLEMENT TO THE HISTORY AND GENEALOGIES OF ANCIENT WINDSOR, CONTAINING ADDITIONS AND CORRECTIONS. Albany, N.Y.: J. Munsel, 1863. 134 p.

Stoughton, John Alden. WINDSOR FARMS, A GLIMPSE OF AN OLD PARISH. Hartford: Clark and Smith, 1883. 150 p.

Tudor, Mary S. "Miss Ruth Thompson Sperry, Local Historian and Genealogist." CM 6 (1900): 164-66.

Windsor, Harold F. "The Roads of Windsor." GEOGRAPHICAL REVIEW 21 (1931): 379-97.

WINDSOR LOCKS

HARTFORD COUNTY. Organized May 1854 from WINDSOR. Towns organized from WINDSOR LOCKS include EAST GRANBY.

CEMETERY RECORDS AND CEMETERIES

NAME	ADDRESS	HALE NO.	CITATION
Grove Cemetery	21 South Main Street	1	58:1-35
St. Mary Roman Catholic Cemetery	Spring Street	2	58:36-99
Denslow Cemetery	1 stone side of road south part of town	3	58:100
Old Catholic Cemetery	Rear of Leach's Coal Yard	4	58:101
Smyth Cemetery	St. Mary Church Cemetery on Spring Street	5	58:102

Index to Hale inscriptions: 58:145-85.

CHURCH RECORDS

YEAR BOOK AND CHURCH DIRECTORY OF GRACE METHODIST EPISCOPAL CHURCH, WINDSOR LOCKS, CONNECTICUT. Windsor Locks, Conn.: Grace Methodist Episcopal Church, 1931. 20 p.

HISTORICAL SOCIETY

Windsor Locks Historical Society, Noden-Reed Park, 58 West Street, 06096.

LAND RECORDS

Hartford. CSL, Record Group 62. Index to Land Records.

LIBRARY

Windsor Locks Public Library, 28 Main Street, 06096.   (203) 623-6170.

MILITARY RECORDS

A TRIBUTE (WORLD WAR I AND II).   Windsor Locks: Journal Press, 1953.

NEWSPAPER

WINDSOR LOCKS JOURNAL.   Weekly.   176 Broad Street, 06095.   (203) 688-4984.

The PRELIMINARY CHECKLIST lists one newspaper for WINDSOR LOCKS.

PROBATE RECORDS

Windsor Locks Probate District, Town Hall, Church Street, 06096.   (203) 623-2503.

> The Windsor Locks Probate District was organized 4 January 1961 from the Hartford Probate District.

SCHOOL RECORDS

Hartford.   CSL, Record Group 62.   Grammar School Register, 1866.

TAX RECORDS

Hartford.   CSL, Record Group 62.   Tax Records, lists, abstracts, ledgers, 1854-1881.

VITAL RECORDS

Town Clerk, Town Hall, Church Street, 06096.   (203) 623-4056.

> The town clerk's earliest birth record is 12 January 1873, marriage record is 13 January 1890 and death record is 1 January 1874.

VOTER RECORDS

Hartford.   CSL, Record Group 62.   Lists, 1957-1886.

PUBLISHED WORKS AND OTHER RECORDS

Hartford. CSL, Record Group 62. Court Records: Justice Court, 1860–1874.

Hartford. CSL, Record Group 62. Town Records.

Hayden, Jabez H. HISTORICAL SKETCHES. Windsor Locks: Windsor Locks Journal, 1900. 141 p.

Stiles, Henry Reed. HISTORY AND GENEALOGIES OF ANCIENT WINDSOR CONNECTICUT INCLUDING EAST WINDSOR, SOUTH WINDSOR, BLOOM-FIELD, WINDSOR LOCKS AND ELLINGTON 1635–1891. 2 vols. Hartford: Case, Lockwood and Brainard, 1891. (LDS 417,935).

THE STORY OF WINDSOR LOCKS. Windsor Locks: Windsor Locks Bicentennial Committee, 1976. 75 p.

THE STORY OF WINDSOR LOCKS 1663–1954. Windsor Locks: Windsor Locks Centennial Committee, n.d.

WOLCOTT

NEW HAVEN COUNTY. Organized May 1796 from SOUTHINGTON and WATERBURY.

CEMETERY RECORDS AND CEMETERIES

NAME	ADDRESS	HALE NO.	CITATION
Center Cemetery	Center of town	1	58:1-17, 33-34
Woodtick Cemetery	Woodtick Road	2	58:17-25,34
Northeast Cemetery	1 1/2 miles northeast of Center	3	58:25-29,35
South Cemetery	Near Southington Reservoir Dam	4	58:29-30, 35-36
Old Pike's Hill Cemetery	3/8 mile northwest of Cemetery #13	5	58:31-32

Index to Hale inscriptions: 58:37-47.

"Gravestone Inscriptions, Wolcott, Connecticut." TAG 12 (1935): 50-51.

Upson, Mrs. James W., and Sanford, Mrs. Burritt B. WOLCOTT CENTER CEMETERY. N.p.: Hannah Woodruff Chapter, DAR, 1928. 17 p.

CHURCH RECORDS

CONGREGATIONAL CHURCH. Minutes, 1826-1915. Vital Records, 1773-1922. (CSL, LDS 2215).

ALL SAINTS CHURCH. Minutes, 1811-1861. Vital Records, 1840-1869. (CSL, LDS 2214).

Jacobus, Donald Lines. "Farmingbury (Wolcott), Connecticut, Church Records." TAG 31 (1955): 112-14.

A NARRATIVE AND DOCUMENTARY HISTORY OF ST. JOHN'S PROTESTANT EPISCOPAL CHURCH (FORMERLY ST. JAMES) OF WATERBURY, CONNECTI-CUT; WITH SOME NOTICE OF ST. PAUL'S CHURCH, PLYMOUTH, CHRIST CHURCH, WATERTOWN, ST. MICHAEL'S CHURCH, NAUGATUCK, A CHURCH IN MIDDLEBURY, ALL SAINTS CHURCH, WOLCOTT, ST. PAUL'S CHURCH, WATERVILLE, TRINITY CHURCH, WATERBURY (ALL COLONIES OF ST. JOHN'S). New Haven: Price, Lee and Adkins, 1907. 181 p.

THE WOLCOTT CONGREGATIONAL CHURCH CENTER STREET ON THE GREEN, WOLCOTT, CONNECTICUT 1773-1973. Wolcott: Wolcott Congregational Church, 1973. 52 p.

HISTORICAL SOCIETY

Wolcott Historical Society, Inc., 06716.

LAND RECORDS

Hartford. CSL, Record Group 62. Land Records, 1814-1901. Grand Lists, 1854-1900.

Land Records, 1796-1860. Index, 1796-1914. (LDS 2213 pt. 105).

LIBRARY

Wolcott Public Library, 469 Bound Line Road, 06716. (203) 879-3663.

MILITARY RECORDS

Miller, Charles. WOLCOTT MEN WHO SERVED IN THE WAR BETWEEN THE STATES, 1861 TO 1865. Waterbury: Author, 1940. 11 p.

NEWSPAPER

The PRELIMINARY CHECKLIST lists one newspaper for WOLCOTT.

PROBATE RECORDS

WOLCOTT is in the Waterbury Probate District.

SCHOOL RECORDS

Hartford. CSL, Record Group 62. School Register, 1874-1875. Returns and miscellaneous records, 1851-1856.

TAX RECORDS

Hartford. CSL, Tax Abstracts, lists, receipts, 1797-1918.

VITAL RECORDS

Town Clerk, Town Hall, 10 Kenea Avenue, 06716. (203) 879-1098.

The BARBOUR INDEX covers the years 1796-1854 and is based on a copy of the vital records made in 1912. The earliest birth record at the town clerk's office is 1771, marriage record 1783, death record 1798.

Hartford. CSL, Record Group 62. Abstracts of Vital Records, 1842-1897.

VOTER RECORDS

Hartford. CSL, Record Group 62. Voting Returns, 1833-1906.

PUBLISHED WORKS AND OTHER RECORDS

Hartford. CSL, Record Group 62. Town Records.

Lions Club. WOLCOTT, CONNECTICUT 175TH ANNIVERSARY 1796-1971. Wolcott: Speed Offset Printing, 1971. 112 p.

Norton, Milo Leon. "The Wolcott Plateau." CQ 3 (1897): 199-205.

Orcutt, Samuel. HISTORY OF THE TOWN OF WOLCOTT (CONNECTICUT) FROM 1731 TO 1874, WITH AN ACCOUNT OF THE CENTENARY MEETING SEPTEMBER 10TH AND 11TH, 1873; AND WITH THE GENEALOGIES OF THE FAMILIES OF THE TOWN. Waterbury: American Printing Co., 1874. 608 p.

Pape, William Jamieson. HISTORY OF WATERBURY AND THE NAUGATUCK VALLEY, CONNECTICUT. 3 vols. Chicago: S.J. Clarke Publishing Co., 1918.

WOODBRIDGE

NEW HAVEN COUNTY. Organized January 1784 from MILFORD and NEW HAVEN. Towns organized from WOODBRIDGE include BETHANY.

CEMETERY RECORDS AND CEMETERIES

NAME	ADDRESS	HALE NO.	CITATION
East Side Cemetery	Pease Road	1	58:1-31
Milford Side Cemetery	Race Brook Road	2	58:32-43
North West Cemetery	Seymour Avenue	3	58:44-55

Index to Hale inscriptions: 58:56-71.

CENSUS RECORDS

Jacobus, Donald Lines. "Errors in the Census of 1790 (Connecticut): Woodbridge." NEHGR 77 (1923): 81.

"Woodbridge Inhabitants of Amity and Bethany, 1780." TAG 11 (1935): 192.

CHURCH RECORDS

AMITY CHURCH RECORDS. Index. (CSL, LDS 1448 pt. 8).

CONGREGATIONAL CHURCH IN AMITY. Marriages, 1742-1792. BAILEY 7:47-57.

Tracy, Louise. "Church Records of the Parish of Amity, (now Woodbridge), Connecticut." CM 10 (1906): 724-34; 11 (1907): 329-37; 12 (1908): 157-58, 313-16.

HISTORICAL SOCIETY

Amity and Woodbridge Historical Society, 5 Oak Hill Lane, 06525. (203) 387-2355.

LAND RECORDS

Land Records, 1784-1924. Index, 1784-1904. (LDS 2216 pt. 1-11).

LIBRARY

Woodbridge Town Library, 10 Newton Road, 06525. (203) 387-8681.

NEWSPAPER

The PRELIMINARY CHECKLIST lists one newspaper for WOODBRIDGE.

PROBATE RECORDS

WOODBRIDGE is in the New Haven Probate District.

TAX RECORDS

Hartford. CSL, Record Group 62. Tax Rate Book, 1789-1790.

VITAL RECORDS

Town Clerk, Town Hall, 11 Meetinghouse Lane, 06525. (203) 389-1517.

The town clerk's earliest birth and marriage records are 1746 and earliest death record is 1786.

The BARBOUR INDEX covers the years 1784-1832 and is based on the 1915 copy of the WOODBRIDGE vital records made by Miss Ethel L. Scofield.

PUBLISHED WORKS AND OTHER RECORDS

Marvin, Sylvanus P. "Early Woodbridge." NHCHS PAPERS 6 (1900): 101-32.

Woodbridge. Amity and Woodbridge Historical Society. Minutes, Selectmen, 1784-- .

WOODBURY

LITCHFIELD COUNTY. Organized May 1673. Towns organized from WOOD-
BURY include BETHLEHEM, MIDDLEBURY, ROXBURY, SOUTHBURY and WASH-
INGTON.

CEMETERY RECORDS AND CEMETERIES

NAME	ADDRESS	HALE NO.	CITATION
South Cemetery	U.S. 55, near Episcopal Church	1	58:1-32
North Cemetery	Church Street	2	58:33-93
New North Cemetery	Washington Avenue	3	58:94-113
Hartshorn Cemetery	South of the Episcopal Church	4	58:114
Indian Cemetery	On Monument opposite Orenang Avenue	5	58:115-16
Catholic Cemetery	Washington Avenue	6	58:94-113
St. Paul Cemetery	Main Street		(no citation)

Index to Hale inscriptions: 58:117-51.

"Connecticut Headstones, Woodbury--before 1800 Hale." CN 11 (1978):
225, 398-400.

CENSUS RECORDS

WOODBURY'S CENSUS CONTAINING A COMPLETE LIST OF THE NAMES
OF THE INHABITANTS OF WOODBURY, (ALPHABETICALLY ARRANGED), AS
TAKEN FROM THE CENSUS RETURNS OF JUNE, 1880. Woodbury: A.E.
Knox Publisher, 1880. 21 p.

CHURCH RECORDS

FIRST CONGREGATIONAL CHURCH. Minutes, 1838-1920. Vital Records, 1670-1909. (CSL, LDS 2206).

ST. PAUL EPISCOPAL CHURCH. Minutes, 1784-1856, 1838-1936. Vital Records, 1765-1923, 1898-1941. (CSL, LDS 2207 and 2208).

Jacobus, Donald Lines. "Woodbury (Conn.) Church Records, 1702-1718." TAG 21 (1945): 222-24, 265-68; 22 (1946): 56-58.

Walsh, James. "The Great Awakening in the First Congregational Church of Woodbury, Connecticut." WILLIAM AND MARY QUARTERLY 28 (1971): 543-62.

"Woodbury Church Records, 1670-1700." TAG 9 (1932): 17-26.

HISTORICAL SOCIETY

Glebe House, Hollow Road, 06798. (203) 263-2855.

Old Woodbury Historical Society, Main Street, P.O. Box 407, 06798.

Marshall, Helen Willard. "The Old Glebe House in Woodbury." CANTI-QUARIAN 4 (June 1952): 6-15.

LAND RECORDS

Land Records, 1659-1863. Index, 1659-1883. (LDS 2203 pt. 1-24).

Cothren, William. "Ancient Deeds in Woodbury, Connecticut (Copied from Town Records, Book I)." NEHGR 3 (1849): 69-70.

Hartford. CSL, Record Group 62. Land Records.

Jacobus, Donald Lines. "Items from Woodbury (Conn.) Land Records." TAG 17 (1941): 172-74.

LIBRARY

Woodbury Library, Main Street, 06798. (203) 263-3502.

MILITARY RECORDS

AMERICAN REVOLUTION BICENTENNIAL 1776 WOODBURY 1976, OLD WOODBURY IN THE REVOLUTION; THE FIVE PARISHES AND THEIR SOLDIERS. Woodbury: Woodbury Bicentennial Committee, 1976.

Boyd, Edward S. "First Records of the 1st Co. 13th Reg't Light Infantry Connecticut Militia, organized at Woodbury in 1795." CQ 4 (1898): 107-8.

NEWSPAPER

The PRELIMINARY CHECKLIST lists one newspaper for WOODBURY.

PROBATE RECORDS

Woodbury Probate District, Town Hall, 281 Main Street, 06798. (203) 263-2417.

> The Woodbury Probate District was organized in October 1719 from the Fairfield, Hartford and New Haven Probate Districts.

> The Woodbury Probate District also includes the town of BETHLEHEM.

> Probate Districts organized from the Woodbury Probate District include the Litchfield, New Milford, Roxbury, Southbury, Washington and Waterbury Probate Districts.

> ON FILE AT THE CSL: Estate Papers, 1720-1949. Indexes, 1720-1943 (papers from 1913-1949 are arranged alphabetically). Inventory Control Book, 1720-1943. Court Record Books, 1719-1850.

Probate Records, 1719-1850. (LDS 2204 pt. 1-10).

SCHOOL RECORDS

Hartford. CSL, Record Group 62. School register for District 8. Undated.

TAX RECORDS

Hartford. CSL, Record Group 62. Tax Abatements, Abstracts, lists, 1841-1908.

VITAL RECORDS

Town Clerk, Town Hall, 281 Main Street, P.O. Box 369, 06798. (203) 263-2144.

The town clerk's earliest birth, marriage and death record dates from 1670.

The BARBOUR INDEX covers the years 1674-1850 and is based on the James N. Arnold copy of WOODBURY vital records made in 1916.

Barnes, Leon M. BARNES' MORTALITY RECORD OF THE TOWN OF WOODBURY, FROM THE SETTLEMENT OF THE TOWN OF WOODBURY IN 1672 TO THE PRESENT DAY. Woodbury: Author, 1898. 213 p. Index.

Hartford. CHS. Town Clerk's record of deaths, 1818-1835.

VOTER RECORDS

Hartford. CSL, Record Group 62. Voter Records.

PUBLISHED WORKS AND OTHER RECORDS

Cothren, William. HISTORY OF ANCIENT WOODBURY, CONNECTICUT, FROM THE FIRST INDIAN DEED IN 1659 TO 1854 INCLUDING THE PRESENT TOWNS OF WASHINGTON, SOUTHBURY, BETHLEHEM, ROXBURY, AND A PART OF OXFORD AND MIDDLEBURY. Waterbury: Bronson Press, 1854. 841 p. (LDS 2205).

Hartford. CSL, Record Group 62. Town Records, Miscellaneous, 1820-1896.

Old Woodbury Historical Society. HOMES OF OLD WOODBURY. Waterbury: Hemingway Press, 1959. 263 p.

Stiles, Dan. TOWN OF WOODBURY, CONNECTICUT. Concord, N.H.: Sugar Ball Press, 1959. 112 p.

Strong, Julia Minor. THE TOWN AND PEOPLE, A CHRONOLOGICAL COMPILATION OF CONTRIBUTED WRITINGS FROM PRESENT AND PAST RESIDENTS OF THE TOWN OF WOODBURY, CONNECTICUT. Woodbury: Mattatuck Press, 1901. 359 p.

WOODBURY AND THE COLONIAL HOMES. N.p., n.d. 71 p.

Woodbury Bicentennial Committee. OLD WOODBURY IN THE REVOLUTION. Woodbury, Conn.: Author, 1976. 100 p.

Wrenn, Tony P. WOODBURY, CONNECTICUT. A NEW ENGLAND TOWNSCAPE. Washington, D.C.: Preservation Press, National Trust for Historic Preservation, 1975. 60 p.

WOODSTOCK

WINDHAM COUNTY. Organized 1686. Name was originally New Roxbury; name changed in 1690.

CEMETERY RECORDS AND CEMETERIES

NAME	ADDRESS	HALE NO.	CITATION
East Woodstock Cemetery	East Woodstock	1	59:1-26
North Woodstock Cemetery	North Woodstock	2	59:27-43
Bradford Marcy Cemetery	In west part of town	3	59:44-55
Bungay Cemetery	In west part of town	4	59:56-71A
Barlow Cemetery	In west part of town	5	59:72-84
Center Cemetery	Near center part of town on U.S. 53	6	59:85-95
Allton Cemetery	Southwest part of town, near Harris L. Sanger property	7	59:96
Hammond Cemetery	Southwest part of town	8	59:97
Swedish Cemetery	U.S. 45	9	59:98-99
Indian Cemetery	Northwest part of town	10	59:100
Indian Cemetery	Northwest part of town	11	59:101
Indian Cemetery	Northwest part of town	12	59:102
Indian Cemetery	Northwest part of town	13	59:103
Indian Cemetery	West part of town	14	59:104
Indian Cemetery	Southwest part of town	15	59:105
Indian Cemetery	Near Barlow Cemetery	16	59:106
Quasset Cemetery	U.S. 55 north of Wappaquasset Lake	17	59:107-19

NAME	ADDRESS	HALE NO.	CITATION
Woodstock Hill Cemetery	1-162	18	59:120-65
Brunn Cemetery	Single grave, 1 mile south of South Woodstock	19	59:166
Private Cemetery	North of Woodstock Valley, near Lake Keachis	20	59:167
Tomb	Road from North Woodstock to West Woodstock	21	59:168
Bolls Cemetery	Near Quasset Cemetery	22	59:169-70

Index to Hale inscriptions: 59:171-213.

"Cemetery Records." In CENSUS RECORDS . . . OF NEW YORK. Royal Paine, pp. 235-245, 250-60, 291-92, 305-11, 314.

"Chandler Inscriptions." NEHGR 15 (1861): 339-344.

Mrs. Mary B. Bishop and Mrs. Ellen D. Larned have transcribed numerous WOODSTOCK cemetery lists that are on file at the CSL.

CHURCH RECORDS

BAPTISMAL RECORDS. 1727-1799. (NYGB, LDS 2158).

FIRST CONGREGATIONAL CHURCH. Minutes, 1743-1926. Vital Records, 1756-1901. Records, 1727-1805. (CSL, LDS 2161 pt. 1-2). Index. (CSL, LDS 1448 pt. 34). Marriages, 1690-1780. BAILEY 1:104-14.

METHODIST CHURCH. Vital Records, 1827-1920. (CSL, LDS 2162).

NORTH WOODSTOCK CONGREGATIONAL CHURCH. Minutes, 1769-1838. Vital Records, 1727-1900. (CSL, LDS 1792).

WEST WOODSTOCK CONGREGATIONAL CHURCH. Minutes, 1743-1937. Vital Records, 1842-1884. (CSL, LDS 2163).

HISTORICAL SOCIETY

Quasset School. Woodstock Elementary School, Frog Pond Road, 06281. (203) 928-4630.

Woodstock Historical Society, P.O. Box 65, 06281.

LAND RECORDS

Hartford. CSL, Record Group 62. Land Records.

Land Records, 1749-1855. Index, 1749-1867. (CDS 2159 pt. 1-11).

LIBRARY

Howard Bracken Memorial Library, 06281. (203) 928-0046.

MAPS

Leter, John S. MAP OF WOODSTOCK, CONNECTICUT. 1883. 1886.

MILITARY RECORDS

Bishop, Mary B. LIST OF WOODSTOCK REVOLUTIONARY SOLDIERS. Woodstock: Author, 1932. 3 p.

Hartford. CSL, Record Group 62. Military Rolls, 1861-1901.

NEWSPAPER

The PRELIMINARY CHECKLIST lists one newspaper for WOODSTOCK.

PROBATE RECORDS

Woodstock Probate Records, Town Hall, Route 169, Box 123, 06281. (203) 928-6595.

> The Woodstock Probate District was organized May 1831 from the Pomfret Probate District.
>
> ON FILE AT THE CSL: Estate Papers, 1831-1929. Indexes, 1831-1929. Inventory Control Book, 1831-1929. Court Record Books, 1831-1853.

Probate Records, 1831-1853. (CSL, LDS 2160 pt. 1-2).

SCHOOL RECORDS

Hartford. CSL, Record Group 62. School Records, 1859-1899.

TAX RECORDS

Hartford. CSL, Record Group 62. Tax Records, 1878-1901. Assessor's Books, 1843 and 1853.

VITAL RECORDS

Town Clerk, Town Hall, Route 169, P.O. Box 123, 06281. (203) 928-6595.

> The town clerk's earliest birth record is 18 April 1689, marriage record 9 April 1690 and death record 13 November 1689.

The BARBOUR INDEX covers birth and marriage records up to 31 December 1850 and deaths to 27 December 1866 and is based on the James N. Arnold copy of WOODSTOCK vital records made in 1908. If the vital record was published in the VITAL RECORDS OF WOODSTOCK (below), ommitted from the BARBOUR INDEX.

BROWN DIARY, 1777-1900. (William C. Brown, Vital Records and Index.) (CSL, LDS 2164).

Hartford. CSL, Record Group 62. VITAL RECORDS, 1886-1897.

VITAL RECORDS OF WOODSTOCK, 1686-1854. Vital Records of Connecticut Series I. Towns III. Hartford: Case, Lockwood and Brainard C., 1914. 622 p. (LDS 496,830).

WEST WOODSTOCK MARRIAGE RECORDS, 1747-1788. 22 p. (LDS 1735).

VOTER RECORDS

Hartford. CSL, Record Group 62. Voter Lists, returns, 1885-1900.

PUBLISHED WORKS AND OTHER RECORDS

Bowen, Clarence Winthrop. HISTORY OF WOODSTOCK, CONNECTICUT. 8 vols. 1926-43. Woodstock, Conn.: Woodstock Public Libraries, 1973. 691 p.

Darbee, Herbert C. "The Woodstock Theft Detecting Society." CANTIQUAR-IAN 26 (July 1974): 5-11.

Duncan, Marie-Louise. "From Woodstock to Potomac: Acculturation then and now." SWEDISH PIONEER HISTORICAL QUARTERLY 28 (1977): 45-46.

Hartford. CSL, Record Group 62. Town Meeting Records, 1861-1891. Miscellaneous records, 1854-1903.

Lawson, Harvey M. "'My Country is Wrong'--Tragedy of Colonel Joshua Chandler." CM 10 (1906): 287-92.

McClellan, Jessy Trumbull. "A Long Journey on Horse-Back in 1788." CM 9 (1905): 185-89.

Morse, Abner. "Origin of Woodstock, Connecticut and Names of First Planters." NEHGR 18 (1864): 227-28.

Rabinowitz, Polly. "Woodstock, Connecticut: 'New Sweden?'" CHSB 39 (1974): 33-46.